10.66

THE
LOGIC OF
WORLD POWER

FRANZ SCHURMANN

THE
LOGIC OF
WORLD POWER

*An Inquiry into the
Origins, Currents, and
Contradictions of World Politics*

PANTHEON BOOKS

A DIVISION OF RANDOM HOUSE, NEW YORK

Library of Congress Cataloging in Publication Data

Schurmann, Herbert Franz.
The Logic of World Power.
Bibliography: pp. 568–73
1. World politics—1945–   I. Title.
D843.S336   327   73–18732
ISBN 0–394–48481–9

Manufactured in the United States of America

FIRST EDITION

Acknowledgments

Grateful acknowledgment is made to the following for permission to reprint previously published material:

Aviation Week & Space Technology, for excerpts from the March 23, 1964, April 6, 1964, and June 15, 1964, issues of *Aviation Week & Space Technology*, published by McGraw-Hill, Inc.

Le Monde, for a graph, "The Russian-American Arms Race," which was included in the article entitled "*Le second cycle des SALT: comment limiter durablement les armements strategiques offensifs*," from *Le Monde*, November, 1972.

The New York Times, for an excerpt from an article by Joseph Alsop from the March 11, 1973, Magazine (page 31). Copyright © 1973 by The New York Times Company. Also for excerpts from articles from the October 24, 1969, August 15, 1966, May 21, 1964, July 20, 1966, April 13, 1966, and the May 23, 1970, issues of *The New York Times*. Copyright © 1964, 1966, 1969, 1970 by The New York Times Company.

Random House: for the map from the frontispiece of *Notes of a Witness: Laos and the Second Indochina War* by Marek Thee. Copyright © 1973 by Marek Thee.

U.S. News & World Report, for the chart "How U. S. Power Dominates Most of the World," which appeared in the May 11, 1964, issue of *U.S. News & World Report*. Copyright © 1964, U.S. News and World Report, Inc.

The Washington Post, for an excerpt from the November 21, 1966, *Washington Post*. Copyright © 1966 *The Washington Post*.

Excerpts from the copyrighted article "A Captain's Last Letters from Vietnam," by Captain E. G. Shank, Jr., printed in *U.S. News & World Report* of May 4, 1964.

To My Friends

Contents

PART I

ARCANA OF EMPIRE

PART II

RUSSIA, CHINA, AND AMERICA

PART III

VIETNAM

1. Ideological and Bureaucratic Sources of the Vietnam War

FOREWORD

The making of this book began on February 7, 1965, when American planes began the continuous bombing of North Vietnam. The experiences that have shaped it came from the antiwar movement. The knowledge came from countless discussions with people who sought to know why America chose the path of barbarism in Indochina.

I owe much to periodic visits I made to the Institute for Policy Studies in Washington. While actively involved in the struggle against the war, at considerable risk to its survival, the Institute was also virtually alone among educational institutions in the 1960s in carrying out critical and systematic analysis of the war and its roots. My debts, personal and intellectual, to Richard J. Barnet are particularly great. Stimulated and supported by IPS, I became a participant in setting up a comparable though much more modest institute in San Francisco, the Bay Area Institute. Few experiences have taught me so much as working with an organization that started from seed. That it has had to survive independently without the succor of university or bureaucratic support made it clear what an organization really is—a group of people who believe in certain goals or causes working together with some degree of effectiveness and efficiency. The cause was opposition to the war and, in a much broader sense, to imperialism. Without the continuing if often erratic thought and action that went on in the Institute, I would not have wanted to write this book. My gratitude goes to Elaine Elinson, Tom Engelhardt, Martin Gellen, Steve Hart, Joan Holden, Alan Miller, Orville Schell, Nancy Strohl, Ruth Tebbets, Barry Weisberg, and others. Jon Livingston was always willing to discuss Asian and particularly Japanese matters. Some of my greatest pleasure and learning came from the never-ending seminar that Jim Peck, Dave Milton, Nancy Milton, and I kept going for so long. Starting from a common focus on China, it usually roamed over the whole world ending somewhere in America's politics. Not long after February 1965 I came to work with Peter Dale Scott and Reginald Zelnik on writing a small "citizens' white paper," *The

Politics of Escalation. Peter and I have continued talking for these years about broader issues of politics as well as more careful dissections of America's ruling institutions. The long talks with Stanley Sheinbaum, less frequent because he lived farther away, were equally rewarding. He was one of the first academics, in the late 1950s, to see what was emerging in Vietnam. I owe particular gratitude to my friend Daniel Lev, who knew vast amounts about Southeast Asia as well as other matters and who, at risk to himself, was active in early opposition to the war. Noam Chomsky was an inspiration and became a friend early in the antiwar period.

Though he would not wish me to say so, working the book into finished form with Jim Peck, now an editor at Pantheon, was a pleasurable experience of smooth, efficient, though long-distance collaboration.

Let me also mention some others whom I particularly valued: Jacques Decornoy (Paris), Peggy Duff (London), Estelle Holt (Vientiane, London), Tran Van Hué (PRG), Peter Limqueco (Stockholm), Paul Lin (Montreal), Oda Makoto (Osaka), Seymour Melman (New York), Marcus Raskin (Washington), Leonard Rodberg (Washington), Carl Riskin (New York), Leon Wofsy (Berkeley).

In this book, I almost always use "America" for the United States and "Russia" for the Soviet Union. I do so because the national character of each is characteristic enough to warrant the more national term. I tender apologies to Latin Americans who take offense.

Writing this last paragraph of the Foreword, which is the very last writing of the book, gives me a sense of transition, that what the book is about and what I participated in over the last years is moving from one chapter of history to another. Not that what was has ended but that it is assuming new forms, so that the response to the new challenges too will have to assume new forms.

F.S.

San Francisco
December 14, 1973

PROLOGUE

Since the end of World War II, the prime mover on the world scene has been the United States of America. It was America that tried to unify the war-shattered world in 1945 under a Pax Americana like the Pax Romana of Ancient Rome. Failing to include Russia in the new world order, America turned its efforts toward creating a free world anchored in the advanced industrial countries of Western Europe and eventually Japan. Brandishing its monopoly of armed might to keep Russia contained, America constructed its Imperium Americanum, envisaging it as a three-tiered structure—at the top, America with its vast political, economic, and military power, in the middle, the advanced industrial countries, and at the bottom, the poor nations which would gradually rise through aid, trade, and investment under the protection of the American eagle. In the mid-1960s America became emmeshed in a barbarous war in Vietnam to which any utilitarian calculation would have assigned small importance in the scheme of empire. As America stubbornly persisted in its craving to get something out of that war, turbulences of all kinds erupted which threatened the world order it had been constructing since the end of World War II. Social rebellions in various countries alienated large segments of the population from the established system. Domestic and international economies became shakier as America's obsession in Vietnam eroded its economic leadership. For all its massive fire power, American conventional military power was stalemated in Vietnam, and its strategic power matched by the Russians. Above all, the fulcrum on which the entire world order moved, the American government, was threatened by internal power struggles that seem to produce operational paralysis.

When world-spanning networks of power, wealth, and influence begin to crumble, a new historical stage is in the offing. The period that began around 1945 inaugurated a distinct historical stage. It began with revolutionary changes and now in the early 1970s is entering a period of transition.

The most revolutionary act at the end of World War I was the rise
of a socialist society in Russia; at the end of World War II it was the
creation of the American Empire. For the first time in the modern era
it seemed as if man's age-old dream of world unity would be fulfilled.
Other historical processes had their roots in the near or distant past
before the war, but the American Empire was a sudden, unexpected,
and new apparition. If before the war America's economy was one among
other great economies, after the war it became the central economy
in a rapidly developing world economy. If before the war America's
military had only sporadic significance in the world's conflicts, after
the war its nuclear umbrella backed by high-technology conventional
forces terrorized one part of the world and gave security to the other.
Above all, the once loosely jointed federal government of the United
States became a powerful, wealthy, and stable state, the axis on
which much of the world's politics, including those of America's enemies,
revolved.

The rise of the American Empire generated a series of changes
throughout the world which came to determine the course of history
in the quarter-century after 1945. America was the major factor that
gave rise to the extraordinary resurgence of industrial capitalism that
took hold in Western Europe, Japan, and several other countries and
enclaves. Contrary to the pessimism about capitalism's future that was
common in the late 1930s, the revival of capitalism in the postwar
period produced economic growth and affluence on a scale no socialist
society could match. Though capitalism has widened the gap between
the rich and poor nations, it has nevertheless done more to create a true
world economy than the entire economic history of mankind prior to
1945.

It was America that launched the process whereby subject territories
of European empires in Asia and Africa were granted independence.
Under the Monroe Doctrine, reinvigorated by Roosevelt, America created a regional bloc of the two Americas made up of sovereign states but
led by America. Under the postwar Pax Americana, America sought a
similar arrangement for the colonies in Asia and Africa. Yet the entry of
the Third World—Asia, Africa, and Latin America—onto the world
political scene was the great historical process that finally dethroned the
West as the sole active agent in the political affairs of the world.

It was the American monopoly of atomic weaponry that propelled the
terrified Russians to embark on a crash program of their own to produce
an atomic bomb, thereby creating the world's second greatest military
power. While other nations have shown themselves to be militarily
strong, since 1945 only America and Russia have maintained an overwhelming preponderance in advanced strategic weaponry.

It was America's counterrevolutionary fury that radicalized several revolutionary processes throughout the world that had been going on for some time. As America came to side with reactionary forces, notably in China, Vietnam, and Cuba, the revolutionaries again and again discovered how powerful a political-military weapon revolution among the oppressed masses was. American counterrevolution also ejected countries from the world system and so spurred on the appearance of a Second World, that of the socialist countries.

As is now apparent, the Second World is no world, but a number of independent countries with national economies whose solidarity, which once seemed based on the Sino-Soviet alliance, turned out to be transitory. But for all their economic weaknesses, the socialist societies modeled on the Soviet Union and radicalized by American counterrevolution have made social advances unmatched in the capitalist world. The Third World also is little more than a number of independent countries with national economies and polities linked to international capitalism for the most part, but not to each other.

Within the globe there still is only one world: that vast and intricate nexus of relations of power, wealth, and influence in which America occupies the central position. The great capitalisms of Western Europe and Japan have generated only moderate military and not much more political power. Russia has immense military power, but half a century of socialism has created a malfunctioning economy that produces vast quantities of technologically sophisticated wares, yet has difficulty satisfying elementary consumer needs. China has relatively little economic and military power, but wields influence because of its size, position, and revolutionary effect on other countries. But America alone has central military, economic, and political power, the combination of which is the foundation of the American Empire.

What began to wane in the late 1960s, clearly in relation to the Vietnam war, was this American Empire. That American conventional military power could not win in Vietnam meant that it might not win elsewhere. The fact that Russia seemed able to match every American military-technological thrust with its own turned a comfortable monopoly into an uneasy duopoly. The international quality of the dollar, perhaps more than anything else, reflects this waning centrality. While the dollar is still the key medium of exchange, reserve, and liquidity in the world economy, neither the American government nor the American economy are its sole source of strength, and both have become major sources of its weakness. The waning of American political power on the world scene may yet be reckoned the most fateful historical phenomenon a quarter-century after the end of World War II. The great alliance system which formed the three-tiered structure of the American Empire has been disintegrating. Western Europe with Britain as its newest member is going its own way, as are Japan and some of the smaller advanced countries like Australia, New Zealand, and Canada. Unlike the socialist camp, which had no inherent social and economic bonds other than Russian power holding it together, the American Empire is too interwoven a structure to disappear so easily. That the Pax Americana has weakened, however, is undeniable and irreversible.

Ironically, in 1973 concern for the survival of the American Empire came from its erstwhile mortal enemies, Russia and China, now mortal enemies of each other. In the 1950s, both the Russians and the Chinese believed that they were building a Second World which would eventually surpass the First World of capitalism and imperialism. By 1973 both had given up that notion and sought to enter the world economy centered on America. While there is fierce weaponry competition between America and Russia and rivalry for influence in many regions, the history of Russian foreign policy suggests that far from seeking America's destruction, the Russians want to maintain their equality in a duopoly, which they regard as the only viable basis for their own national security. They have little hope of ever gaining a weaponry preponderance that would make them invulnerable to American strategic attack. China, not in the competitive military race, denounces it, yet sees American military power as a possible deterrent to a Russian attack on China. Both Russia and China, for their own different reasons, want accommodation with the American Empire.

Russia and China also need America in other ways. That their poorer economies need the great American economy is clear from their purchases of food and technology, and the growing realization that perhaps only America—or the other advanced economies of Western Europe and Japan—can give the Russian and Chinese economies certain developmental thrusts that both have difficulty in generating themselves. Russia, despite its huge industrial plant, needs the world economy to pull it out of the consumer poverty that still prevails a half-century after the revolution. China, despite a steadily improving agriculture and light industry, needs the world economy for the development of its lagging heavy industry.

Western Europe and Japan, while pulling away from servile adherence to American policies, also realize that if the American Empire crumbles, they too will crumble. For years they bailed America out of its adventures in Indochina by supporting the dollar, though they would not send troops to fight. But as Washington threatens to withdraw ground troops from Europe, even France, America's coldest European friend, alarmedly demands that they remain. For the Third World, despite diminished capacity, supply, and will, America is still the major granary in time of famine, a major source of public aid and private investment, and a source of arms.

Looking at the history of mankind, it is not surprising that there are so many unexpected sources of support for the American Empire. Empires by and large have been seen as of great benefit, and their passing is regretted. The Roman Empire finally crumbled but the empire lived on in Western Europe as the Holy Roman Empire, which only Napoleon finally ended. In the East it lived on as Byzantium and then as the Ottoman Empire, which only ended after World War I. The Chinese Empire of two millennia created, maintained, and spread one of the greatest of the world's civilizations, which even its enemies on the peripheries have always admired. Even the much more short-lived British Empire lives on in the shadow form of the Commonwealth. The dream of world unity is present in every great civilization and religion. Western Christianity and Islam aspire to convert the whole world. Marx, while ridiculing religion, nevertheless believed that a material process, industrial capitalism, would unify the entire world, therefore seeing British imperialism as a progressive force. It was that material process which allowed Marx to envisage a smashing of all political institutions and the emergence of new revolutionary and democratic political forms without destroying the unity created by the economy. Today the world's two great Marxist powers are not convinced that that would be the case. History shows that darkness and war follow the collapse of empires. In 1973 a whole array of nations, once intent on restraining America's violent adventurism, came to fear what could happen if the world order, for which America was the core, collapsed.

Historically every empire has rested on a tripod of strength: an economy that spanned and in some way united its domains; a monopoly of military power absolute within its domains and adequate for security at its borders; and a political force that emanated from its state, particularly the central executive. The Roman Empire was fueled by intricate trading networks that linked all the key Mediterranean lands; its legions were paramount throughout the Western world; and the imperial institution, if not always the emperor, was able to exercise its will and authority in key matters of power. While economies in China were local and trade regional, the combination of a tax-collecting bureaucracy, a military that maintained law and order, and a policy-making central imperial institution sustained the Chinese Empire institutionally for two thousand years. Those same three elements are visible in the American Empire. As the consumer of half the world's manufactured products, America plays the key role in sustaining and expanding the remarkable world market system which was spawned in England and which, paired with industrially revolutionized production, created the world economy. All advanced capitalist nations are dependent on exports to the central

American market. All are dependent to one degree or another on the still central technology of America. And all are enmeshed in one form or another in the multinational and transnational forms of corporate organization that are preponderately American.

The Imperium Bellicum Americanum, the American war machine, is as complex as the economy. America's legions are stationed in parts of the world as far-flung as the British Empire; its Navy now controls the seas, aside from a rising Soviet naval competition; the weapons of the Air Force, planes and missiles, span the globe. But weaponry aside, America has created a network of Pentagons, the military forces of numerous allies and clients linked to the central Pentagon in Washington through arms procurement, personnel exchange and training, and, above all, common consultation and planning for possible wars. America is even more central for the world war machine than for the world economy, in that its technology and industry create the key weapons the network needs.

Most central, most mysterious, and, in 1973, most controversial is America's imperial institution, in the words of Arthur Schlesinger, Jr., its "imperial presidency." It was not the City of Rome that created Caesar but the legions in Gaul and Africa backed by the City's rising middle classes in opposition to the patrician Senate. It is what Americans modestly call "foreign policy" that created the imperial presidency and so it is not surprising that they do not understand it. It has always been difficult for political historians to explain the function of emperors, but Ezra Pound coined a term in a translation of a Chinese classic which indicates what the imperial institution must be above all else: the unwobbling pivot.

For a quarter-century after World War II, America was the unwobbling pivot, the constant factor, around which the world moved. America with its rich economy and powerful weaponry was vital not only for the rising capitalist nations but also, as a hostile yet not reckless enemy, for the socialist countries. It is only the history of the last quarter-century which shows that the main force for unity in the socialist part of the world has been the American threat. Russia and China, as this book seeks to show, became allies when threatened by America, and became estranged when America sought peace with one and kept up hostility toward the other. The receding of the American threat has given rise to hatreds, rivalries, and, above all, nationalisms among the socialist countries. Whatever unity there is in what is left of the socialist camp, mainly in Eastern Europe, is due to Russian power. There is no great international economy that links the socialist countries together. Socialism, in fact, has shown a marked tendency toward economic and political nationalism. It has also revealed a precariousness of political power at the top in contrast to the great solidity of the institutions it has created in society. Marxism-Leninism has brought about great revolutions in various parts of the world but without creating larger transnational unities and without resolving the problem of stable executive power. Yet the socialist nations show a defensive power unmatched anywhere in the world. Like the French revolutionaries at Valmy in 1792, revolutions are at their best when in defense against aggression by oppressors.

The demise of the socialist camp does not mean that the great revolutionary process that began with the French Revolution has ended. De Tocqueville saw that process as the inexorable march toward sovereignty by the people. Marx saw it as the succession of class upon class to power over the political economy until classless society prevailed throughout the world. The quarter-century since World War II has been revolutionary and the remainder of the twentieth century promises to be equally so, when the specters of wars and depressions rise again. But the scope of revolution has been much broader than just those heroic struggles that brought people's armies to power. It has also encompassed the full entry of working-class parties and unions into the politics of the advanced countries, usually in reformist and sometimes in reactionary ways. It has seen the rise of the Third World poor within America and the appearance in Western Europe of a new proletariat of foreign workers. It has seen the erosion of feudal oligarchies even in countries ruled by military and fascist regimes. While at times antidemocratic bureaucratization seems to be an irrepressible force, again and again democratic forces erupt from below as the bureaucracies begin to turn on each other. Every tyranny, even the most bureaucratically benevolent, eventually suffers revolt from below. All class domination, even by "middle classes" only recently emerged from poverty, is challenged by the rise of poorer classes.

But revolution, contrary to the nightmares of the ultraright, has led to the creation of state powers essentially national in orientation. When not facing a ferocious enemy, revolutionary internationalism has degenerated into periodic fraternal meetings not much different from those of the Second International. That revolution as well as counterrevolution strengthens national power partly accounts for the strange phenomenon in the early 1970s of the numerous rapprochements between leftist and rightist countries on bases of reciprocal national interest. This should not delude people into thinking that there is little difference between the two kinds of regimes. Rightist regimes—fascist or military dictatorships—suppress all politics within society to create a state power dependent on no other force than their own organized instruments of rule. Leftist regimes, notably in the early stages of revolutionary power or in countries with political practices of ongoing revolution, do just the opposite. They accentuate contradictions in society so that class conflict again and again

shakes up the entire society, fueling a political process which, while dictatorial, brings about comprehensive progress, sometimes erratic and confused, but always innovative and encompassing the entire society, not just
a few privileged enclaves. Nevertheless, that progress remains national, and
even where socialist countries have extended foreign aid, it has not led
to any solid new international system. In fact, the greatest instance of
socialist foreign aid was that extended by Russia to China in the 1950s,
which played a major role in China's industrial development but also in
bringing about the Sino-Russian split.

Writing in 1973, the prospects for world unity that seemed so bright
in 1945 are dimmer than ever. People are fearful that the collapse of
international systems, economic and political, as occurred in the early
1930s, could be repeated with catastrophic consequences. The nationalist
trend everywhere is rising as various interests clamor for protection against
foreign competition and threats. Labor unions in America want to shut
out foreign products to save American jobs. Communist labor unions in
Europe are foes of the Common Market, invoking the nationalist argument to get support from the working masses. What has made the
nationalist appeal popular is that the two main internationalist foes are
international capitalism and American imperialism, one a force for exploitation, the other for oppression and war. The multinational corporations, which have become international capitalism's chief organizational
instrument, consider profit not social need their top priority, an attitude
typical of modern capitalism since its inception that has become apparent
again with the energy crisis. American imperialism has become increasingly a militarized instrument of domination, using weapons to make up
for waning economic and political power. So hated are these two international forces that even fiercely counterrevolutionary Latin American
military regimes have experienced dissension in their ranks when they
became too involved with either or both of them. Yet these two forces
are all that still holds the world together.

Most leftists consider American imperialism the instrument of its
international capitalist master. Actually, it is the growing rift between
them that more than anything else is threatening the world's international systems. Ironically, this contradiction, on both sides of which
America stands, has also become the greatest threat to the American
Empire. The chief thrust of American imperialism, as this book argues,
is control. The chief thrust of international capitalism is and has to be
profit.

America could also go nationalist, through protectionism for example. If
so, the international economy will collapse with incalculable upheavals oc-
curring in Europe and Japan. If America recommits itself to the primacy
of international capitalism, it faces two consequences: a gradual reduc-

tion in military outlays as détente takes hold and growing worker protest arising out of the inevitable economic stagnatiin that takes place in the American economy without the impetus of defense spending. If a popular leftist notion of America as a gigantic corporation with the president meekly taking orders from a supreme board of directors were true, the American Empire, world capitalism, and, ironically, the socialist countries as well would be safer and more secure. In fact, a complex struggle between government and business has made for much of the political history of the United States of America. In that struggle, the government has become more and more powerful, and business has reached farther and farther into the world. It is the international economy that poses a counterweight to the might of the American state much more than national American business which, as the defense industries have learned, can easily be manipulated by the Pentagon. While government and business coexist well through accommodations and trade-offs, struggle arises when crises force the issue of who ultimately is master.

The struggle between internationalism and nationalism could be affected by the appearance of a massive enemy from outside the free world, a role for which Russia is the only candidate. Russia as common enemy was the chief factor that made it possible to build up the American Empire. The alarms of a new Russian imperialism are being sounded not only in America and certain European circles, but most of all in China. If Russia is indeed a "rising" imperialism, as the Chinese say, then that phenomenon could once again help a "waning" American imperialism revert to a waxing phase. As in the late 1940s, the strongest evidence for such a Russian imperialism is its growing military power, which it has shown inclination to export to distant parts of the world. Different currents of ideology and interest battle each other in Russia as they do in America, and it is quite possible that the Russians have also learned to export their contradictions in order to find unity at home. But Russia as the common enemy once again would allow America to rediscover that unity in crisis first learned in World War II then applied during the cold war period.

This Prologue has served to introduce a book, but also a historical stage which follows the one the book deals with, namely the 1970s and beyond. The struggles among the political currents that produced the Vietnam war are changing, but the currents remain. America can move in a nationalist or an internationalist direction or toward a new imperialism, but not without arousing opposition from the currents that lose out. But in whatever way America moves, that will be the decisive fact on the world political scene during this new stage of history.

PART I

ARCANA OF EMPIRE

Arcana, a hidden thing (*Oxford English Dictionary*). *Arcana Imperii*, from Tacitus, used in European political thought of the sixteenth and seventeenth centuries to designate the real motives and techniques of rule of the state, in contrast to those presented to the public.

CHAPTER 1

American Imperialism

Since World War II, relations among states have taken on a unique quality. A series of events occurred in and around the year 1945 which for the first time in human history gave the world an operational unity. The founding of the United Nations gave rise to hope for an eventual world government. And the new world monetary system created by the Bretton Woods Conference in 1944 promised a restoration of world trade. But most dramatic was the development and use of the atomic bomb. Its awesome destructive power made people believe that "one world" was not just a pious wish but a reality with consequences.

In 1945, America alone remained powerful, rich, and unscathed among the great powers. Victors and vanquished were in ruins or exhausted. The thirst for vengeance was not so great as after the first war, but the cries for help were greater. Even before the end of the war, postwar planning began in Washington. More important than the actual plans was the spirit of a new American role in the world which began to inspire Americans. A new world order had to be created so that the horror of a third world war could never erupt. And clearly there was only one country able in terms of power and wealth, and willing in its moral strength to bring such an order into being—the United States of America.

America, inspired by its great visionary President Franklin D. Roosevelt, attempted something which neither of its enemies, Germany and Japan, had aimed at, and which its allies, Britain and Russia, were unsympathetic to or did not comprehend. Nazi Germany and Imperial Japan were both expansionist powers whose "New Order" and "Greater East Asia Co-prosperity Sphere," respectively, could not disguise their main purpose: the exploitation of subject territories in the interests of the master race. Britain had an empire which Churchill was determined to defend against all attackers, including his allies. The British Empire was the precursor of the American empire. It was a vast aggregate of possessions acquired by English expansion and based on a world market sys-

3

tem centered on the British economy. It was held together by the only world-spanning weaponry of the time, the British Navy. But it never became a world order like the American empire, capable of integrating ever more elements into its system. As English expansionism slackened, the British economy lost its centrality, the British Navy declined, and the empire vanished. Thus, in the summit talks during the war, Churchill could only think defensively in classical balance of power terms of Britain, America, and Russia acting as coequals to keep the peace. Stalin's Russia had the narrowest vision of all. Once Stalin had destroyed his revolutionary and counterrevolutionary enemies, he could think of little else beyond giving Mother Russia an impermeable security cordon around her borders, which, of course, involved taking some territory in Europe and Asia.

The American empire did not come into being gradually like the British, but arose within the short space of a few years during World War II. The elements of that empire—America's political, economic, and military power—have been thoroughly analyzed, admiringly and critically, but the notion of a Pax Americana to span the entire world, bringing peace and prosperity, was the product of an ideological vision. No one more symbolized or expressed that vision than Franklin Roosevelt. In 1944, Roosevelt made the United Nations the main issue in his unprecedented fourth term campaign. He knew that Wilson's idealism had shattered against the wall of nationalist American interests, but was convinced that popular forces aroused by depression and war would bring him and his vision victory. And so it did, except that he was forced to abandon his visionary Vice President Henry Wallace for the hardheaded, more nationalist Truman. The visionary element in American politics has always baffled—and exasperated—rationalist political scholars of leftist and centrist political persuasions. But it has always been taken seriously by the right, who have sensed a revolutionary force in just that idealism.

What Roosevelt wanted was to remake the entire world in the American image, and particularly to repeat for the world what the Americans had done for themselves a century and a half before—to create one out of many, as the official American motto goes. Arrogance it was, but of a sort only revolutionaries are capable of. Roosevelt was one of the smartest, wiliest, and most chameleonlike politicians in American history, but he also had the extraordinary capacity, as all great leaders do, to listen to social forces, give them a voice, and, most important of all, to articulate hope. The collapse of capitalism and the rise of fascism convinced people that the systems of peace and progress that had been growing ever since the beginning of the nineteenth century finally were doomed. There was hunger for experimentation with new social and world orders even at the highest levels of interests, where the pessimism was even greater than at the bottom. Roosevelt, like other great leaders, was fascinated by history. He knew about the Pax Romana, based on law, united by legions, and thriving from great enterprising cities, which had ruled over the entire civilized Western world of the time. He knew how at the end of the eighteenth century, thirteen territorial fragments managed to make a new unity which electrified the world. He learned, evident from his four terms in the Presidency, that his inspirational messages had an amazing way of bringing in votes. He also witnessed the spectacle of democratic American armies fighting and liberating peoples virtually everywhere in the world. What Roosevelt sensed and gave visionary expression to was that the world was ripe for one of the most radical experiments in history: the unification of the entire world under a dominion centered on America.

Roosevelt's grand vision began to crumble as soon as he died and Truman, the practical politician from Missouri, substituted hardnosed policy. Yet it would be wrong to say that the vision died with him. It spawned policies that eventually led to the formation of the "free world," a collection of nations big and small led and dominated by America, which in the years following 1945 were to be tied together by growing military, economic, and political bonds. What died with Roosevelt was the hope that Russia could be woven into the new order, and, eventually, what came into being was a containment policy directed against Russia. But the kinds of policies that containment dictated for the free world were essentially those already sketched out in Roosevelt's vision: American military power strategically placed throughout the world, a new monetary system based on the dollar, economic assistance to the destroyed countries, political linkages realized through the United Nations and other international agencies. By the end of the 1940s, a new American world order had clearly emerged. America "lost" Russia in 1945 and China in 1949, but it gained the remainder of the world, which it proceeded to energize, organize, and dominate in a most active way.

A new imperialism was born in 1945 and Franklin D. Roosevelt was its visionary prophet. Imperialism has been imputed to America by its enemies ever since the end of World War II, implying that it was pursuing a conscious policy of empire building just as Britain had done or Japan, France, Spain, and Germany had tried to do. In the 1960s, as opposition to the Vietnam war grew, American radicals and even some liberals began to accuse America of "imperialism." While the teachings of Hobson and Lenin saw imperialism as a political fact arising out of the nature of capitalist economies, strictly speaking, the word "imperialism," through the suffix "ism," connotes a conscious policy, a doctrine whereby one nation seeks to transform itself into an empire. Whatever its material basis, imperialism is a conscious ideology, a set of ideas designed to implement actions. Furthermore, it relates to empire, the domination and organization of large expanses of territory constituting a considerable part of the globe. Roosevelt's vision, while advocating independence for colonies and recognizing the might of the other two superpowers, Russia and Britain, did indeed involve efforts by America to reorganize the world and to spread its instruments of military, political, and economic domination. Although Roosevelt's vision was never fully articulated, it achieved popular resonance in the notion of "one world" which his 1940 opponent Wendell Willkie assiduously propagated. With the founding of the United Nations at San Francisco and its establishment in New York, the new "one world" would have its capital in the United States. Although the "one world" notion disappeared rapidly after Roosevelt's death, it surfaced again in the notion of the "free world." By the early 1950s, the conception of the world as divided into two parts, one free and the other enslaved, one led by democratic America and the other dominated by totalitarian Russia, achieved wide credence within America and other countries. The doctrine of "one world" and its transmutation into the doctrine of the "free world" was a conscious ideology for dominating and organizing large expanses of territory constituting a considerable part of the globe.

Radical historians see the roots of post–World War II American imperialism in an expansionism which has characterized America since the early nineteenth century, and more particularly in the lunge beyond its continental boundaries at the time of the Spanish-American War. Few deny that America's dynamic capitalism, in its never-ending search for more capital, land, and labor, was and remains expansionist. Yet there is an important qualitative difference between expansionism and imperialism. Expansionism takes place incrementally. It is the adding on of pieces of territory, productive plants, land, and military bases. Older empires grew incrementally, and so has America. Since the end of World War II, America has continued to expand incrementally through spreading investment abroad, a network of client states and allies, and military bases located on every continent. But imperialism as a vision and a doctrine has a total, world-wide quality. It envisages the organization of large parts of the world from the top down, in contrast to expansionism, which is accretion from the bottom up. What Bretton Woods and Dumbarton Oaks conceived in 1944 was not the expansion of the particular interests of America and its allies, but the creation of world-spanning systems to be imposed by the highest executive organs of the governments of the countries concerned.

The main political conflict about foreign affairs in the period preceding Pearl Harbor is generally described as one between "interventionists" and "isolationists." The interventionists wanted to involve America as rapidly as possible on the Allied side, while the isolationists were prepared to see Britain fall before Hitler's onslaughts. But the bulk of the isolationists came from the American right and from populist constituencies, political currents that were traditionally expansionist. The right loudly approved acquisition of foreign territory and the populists favored inflationary programs, "free silver," for example. What the isolationists feared was that the Eastern Establishment in cahoots with perfidious Albion were using the pretext of a war against fascism to set up a world dominion ruled by the banks. Anti-Semitism, hatred of England, and often admiration of virile fascism formed a consistent world view among the isolationists in the 1930s. Roosevelt, the British, and the Jews wanted to make the British Empire into a world-wide empire ruled by the most powerful and wealthy. Hitler was expansionist but anti-imperialist, for he was willing to take on the mightiest empire in world history. If Hitler finally smashed Britain, the young, virile nations, America and Germany, could expand in their respective spheres of influence, the former in the Western Hemisphere, the latter in Europe and Africa. The isolationists, with their strong streak of racism, had more ambivalent feelings about Japan; many who adamantly opposed war against Germany were ready to fight Japan.

Roosevelt's vision of a new world order was not entirely different from the isolationists' caricature. Bretton Woods, which laid out the economic sinews of the new American world order, was a bankers' conference. And the Americans who led the way in proposing the United Nations at Dumbarton Oaks were predominantly men of the Eastern Establishment. What bothered the constituencies of the isolationists about this new American imperialism was that it would be set up at the expense of the most dynamic expansionist segment of American society, business. The isolationists were, by and large, probusiness (even the anti–Eastern Establishment populists); what is good for business is good for expansion. They feared that the new imperialism would soak business in the interests of a vast government-dominated world network. Moreover, they regarded banks as naturally conservative and cautious, likely to discourage expansion for the sake of monetary stability. That would leave government as the chief expansionist agent of society, a condition most businessmen at that time saw as dictatorship.

The struggle between "interventionists" and "isolationists" in the pre–World War II period can be reinterpreted as one between imperialists and expansionists. It simmered down during the war, but erupted with sudden ferocity afterward. The neo-isolationists lashed out against foreign aid, the Marshall Plan, the United Nations, and, above all, a policy that favored Europe, where there were few American economic interests at the time, over Asia, which was a natural area for American expansionism, as Admiral Alfred Mahan had lectured a half-century before.

VISION AND EXECUTIVE POWER: TOWARD A THEORY OF IDEOLOGY AND INTERESTS

If Roosevelt's vision of "one world" was an emerging doctrine of American imperialism, then one obvious and central fact about it has to be noted: it was conceived, formulated, and implemented at the highest levels of governmental power, by the President himself. Moreover, if one takes seriously the conflict between isolationists and interventionists, that vision was put forth against the opposition of a major part of the American business class, who constitute the great bulk of America's particular interests and were traditionally the most expansionist segment of American society. This points to something that people raised in or influenced by the Marxist tradition are prone to reject: the autonomous, innovative, and powerful role of the state. But one must go even further and see what was obvious at the time: that it was not from the state as a whole, the aggregate of executive, bureaucratic, and legislative agencies, but from the very pinnacle of the state that the vision originated.

Although I have begun with some historical observations, my real intent is theoretical, to sketch out a theory of relations between states in the last quarter-century. A theory is an explanatory device, neither true nor false in itself, which demonstrates its worth by generating a continuous chain of derivative explanations of phenomena that are not in conflict with conventional wisdom or certain testable hypotheses. In other words, a good theory is a satisfyingly productive one. People feel the need to construct theories when they are persistently faced with anomalies in important problems which existing theories cannot explain away. When such anomalies exist in the realm of human affairs, it is usually the historians who take command. They gather the salient facts, sort out the patterns, and construct generalizations. The process of generalization works from the bottom up, that is, from generally accepted facts. Theory construction, on the other hand, works from the top down, from the logical mind. Both, however, demonstrate their productivity by generating hypotheses that can be tested against generally accepted canons of evidence. The most exciting situation for learning occurs when theory, hypotheses, and generalization constitute a thriving, interacting trinity in which all grow.

The important problem that has produced anomalies during the quarter-century of the nuclear age is the nature of state-to-state relations. If one accepts the notion that America has been the prime mover in this new network of relations, then the important problem becomes the nature of American foreign policy since 1945, when the nuclear age began. Mounds of popular and scholarly material have been written on this subject. All the points of view, which implicitly are kinds of theories, agree that the world since 1945 has become a political whole: even minor events in a distant part of the world affect the global skein of relations. But, since the points of view are usually ideologically inspired, they naturally differ in their basic assumptions. The most popular point of view in America has been the notion that communism has been the prime aggressive force in the world, seeking to undermine and destroy the free world. The opposite point of view, initially held in the socialist countries and by the international left wing but increasingly prevalent among "revisionist" scholars, is that America has been the prime aggressive force in the world, seeking to undermine the socialist camp and destroy revolutionary movements. A third point of view, much more esoteric, is held largely by trained experts in the field of international systems. It sees global politics as a game in which the key actors are the great powers (primarily America and Russia), the key pieces are elements of power (notably nuclear), and the other pieces are a changing variety of political actors. While the first two points of view have produced the bulk of the literature, they have not been particularly theoretical. There has been little theoretical thinking in American popular anticommunist approaches. There appears to be a great deal in the Russian and Chinese approaches, particularly as expressed in their polemics during the early 1960s, but theory, dogma, and politics were too intertwined there to allow the theory to appear in simple and elegant form. "Revisionist" writers on the left in the West have only begun the process of theory construction, much of which tends to follow Marxist lines. The game theorists revel in what seem to be theories, but the penchant for mathematical model-building gives the illusion of productivity to games of infinite variation. Like mathematical economists, the game theorists make some simple assumptions about politics so that they can get on with the pleasurable task of constructing their models. But politics is what political theory has to be about, and if the game theories are not satisfyingly productive about the central problems of politics, then their value as theory evaporates. Still, as we shall see later, game theorizing has social-political significance, since the people who do it tend to cluster around one of the major currents determining American foreign policy.

When people do a lot of writing about a particular subject, it always means that they are bothered by it. One hardly has to press the argument that state-to-state relations since 1945, particularly with the ever-present threat of nuclear destruction, deeply bother people throughout the world. The phenomenon of nuclear power has produced the major anomaly demanding satisfying explanation in the contemporary world—not only is this power, which can virtually burn up the planet, the product of stupefyingly sophisticated technology, but the power to use it is so centralized that, at least in the United States, one person alone can make the final decision. This is symbolized by the little black box always in the presence of the President of the United States, which contains the signals to activate, deploy, and fire the nuclear weapons. This concentration of political power of enormous scope in the hands of the chief executive, only barely modified by fail-safe devices, seems to contradict all notions of politics. Politics is the realm of power, and power can be simply defined as the command over men and resources for the achievement of goals. The notion of goals is basic to politics. Men achieve power in political structures to advance or protect their own interests or those of constituencies with whom they identify. The President of the United States is presumed to wield power in the interests of all Americans, his constituency, although it is generally believed that he does so primarily for some and less so for others. In any case, politics presumes that he acts to achieve someone's interests, even if his overriding interest is entirely personal, such as assuring his re-election. Radical and liberal views of politics in America may differ on whose interests are being advocated by the President, but they agree that his power serves interests. Whether the President is the instrument of certain constituencies or their leader does not affect that argument.

The notion of politics as serving interests runs into a dilemma when one enters the nuclear field. That the President of the United States (and presumably also the chief executives of Russia and China) exercises nuclear power is obvious—he wields command over men and resources (nuclear strike forces) to achieve goals (the destruction of an enemy). But what and whose interests are served by nuclear war? Conventional (non-nuclear) wars serve real interests: that one side capture from or deny to the other side territory, populations, resources, prestige, or time. Even a war so murky as the Vietnam war can be explained in terms of interests. Nuclear war, however, does not envisage the capture or denial of anything to an adversary. It is theoretically designed to assure maximum destruction of an adversary with maximum survival for one's own side. Since it is in the "interest" of all living beings to survive, the concept of interest loses any theoretical force, for it has meaning only where interests can be differentiated into various kinds. At first, nuclear weapons were seen as just another kind of weapon with which to punish or threaten an aggressor. Then it was realized that no nation would pursue a deliberately suicidal course in order to get something it wanted, such as a chunk of another nation's territory. Notions of deterrence then became popular, implying that massive nuclear power could in effect deter a nation from trying for illegitimate gains. As the two superpowers, America and Russia, achieved overwhelming arsenals of nuclear weapons, deterrence lost its credibility, because each side simultaneously paralyzed the other with its power, thus presumably allowing the more normal politics of gain to go on. If power cannot be used, it can serve no interests. Under such circumstances, common sense and ulititarian assumptions indicate that the power should wither away to be replaced by more useful forms. Obviously nuclear power is not only not withering away, but achieving greater dimensions than ever before. If nuclear power only deters an adversary from using his own nuclear power, then we are forced to the conclusion that it exists in and for itself. Even this notion, however, can be explained in some sort of interest terms: there are productive facilities that make the weapons and thereby gain profit, research is stimulated which benefits other sectors of the economy, bureaucratic and corporate bodies get a share of the power deriving from involvement in nuclear programs. But this is true of all weapons procured by a government. The argument about a "military-industrial complex" implies that the real purpose for the vast accumulation of arms of all kinds is to service private corporate and public bureaucratic interests. It explains the baffling problem of why the government acquires weaponry far beyond the dictates of utility in terms of conventional political wisdom, which assumes that politics always serves interests. While there is some truth to this argument, closer examination quickly shows that too much is left unexplained and too much just is not so. It does not explain the quality, nature, and purpose of the strategic weapons the government decides it needs, and overlooks the fact that much military production is not particularly profitable for the corporations concerned. To say that the government acquires immense stockpiles of nuclear weapons just to fatten the profits of corporations and expand the power of certain bureaucracies strains the public imagination, which rightly senses something anomalous about the realm of nuclear weaponry.

The most common explanation given by the government for its nuclear power is that it enhances the nation's sense of security. All people "on our side" feel better if the country has adequate defenses based on nuclear weaponry. While interest theories of politics are offended by a notion so intangible as a "feeling of security," politicians know that it is a powerful argument. People want to be able to go about their daily business without fear of attack against themselves or their property. Security does not come from being surrounded by a Maginot Line of ramparts but from the knowledge that someone in society is competently dealing with public safety. In the community, police are supposed to provide this sense of security; in the nation, the military. But the military have no power to make decisions about the use of nuclear weapons. In the case of nuclear power, the sense of security comes from the President.

If people generally accepted the utilitarian "overkill" arguments about

given levels of nuclear weaponry, there would be little support for further stockpiling. For all the utilitarian arguments made by the Defense
Department bureaucracy to justify "parity," "sufficiency," or "superiority" in strategic weapons, the real deciding factor in the situation is the
public's sense of security. If the public feels secure, it will not support
extravagance in defense. If it feels insecure (or is made to feel insecure),
it will support virtually any level of expenditure to get back its sense of
security. The man in the most decisive position to influence the public's
sense of security is the President. If the man who alone has his finger on
the nuclear trigger tells the country it is safe or it is threatened, the mood
of the country will be correspondingly affected. No other politicians,
even those closest to the President, can have the same impact. Therefore,
just as the President naturally exercises the most extreme caution in
regard to the destructive power at his fingertips, so he is also extremely
careful in what he says or does about nuclear problems.

Nuclear power is obviously a realm of politics, for if politics is the
game of power, and power involves command over men and resources to
achieve goals, then the immense organizational and technical systems
that nuclear power has generated are political. But it is a realm of
politics in which interests do not play the decisive role. Governments
create nuclear systems not to benefit this or that particular interest but to
give security to all the people or to the free world or even to the world as
a whole. Security is intangible and unquantifiable, a mood which skilled
politicians sense and can take advantage of. But public moods are clearly
a reality, and for centuries organizations have existed to create and
service them. The Catholic Church, for example, is a gigantic organization whose basic purpose is to cultivate the faith of its adherents. It also
does many more practical things, such as teaching Christian ethics, min-
istering to the poor and the sick, solving problems in its communities.
But faith remains the living core of its entire corporate existence. It is no
coincidence that the largest organized religious body in the world is
headed by one man, the Pope. A sense of security is somewhat like
religious faith in its belief that there is a higher being with the power,
knowledge, and presence to protect people in a threatening world constantly in turmoil. Similarly, the essence of the faith from which a sense
of security derives is that there is a supreme being at the apex of the
political system who is the fountainhead of that faith. Nuclear power
therefore has created the need for a god. This notion should not be
surprising. Most civilized societies have gone through periods when kings
and emperors assumed some kind of divine form. Europe had its "divine
right of kings" and China had its "celestial emperors." Much of the
modern political process has resulted in the erosion of supreme and
autonomous executive power—absolute monarchies have turned into

constitutional monarchies and democracies have turned rulers into chief executives, periodically chosen leaders who are supposed to be little more than chairmen of the board. It is obvious that supreme executive power has made its reappearance in socialist societies (Stalin and Mao Tse-tung, for example), and now the nuclear phenomenon has also generated it in America. Never in American history has executive power been so centralized, far-reaching, and autonomous as at the present time. America is making a transition comparable to that of ancient Rome from republic to empire.

The anomaly people feel when trying to explain nuclear politics in terms of an interest theory begins to dissipate if we accept the notion that there is not just one but two realms of politics: the realm of interests and the realm of ideology. Nuclear systems belong in the realm of ideology; conventional weapons in the realm of interests. There is a qualitative gap of great importance between these two kinds of weapons systems and the power and politics they represent. This, however, reflects a much more basic gap between presidential power (the White House) and all other bureaucracies of government, including the Cabinet. The theme of qualitatively different presidential and bureaucratic politics is one of the main arguments in this book.

Understanding the realm of ideology requires an analysis of the Presidency. The analysis need not just flow outward from the personality and position of the President, but can flow inward from the context of power, issues, and conflicts in which he operates. The office makes the man as much as the man makes the office. Thus, one can learn as much about presidential power from understanding nuclear politics as from analyzing a specific decision or his decision-making powers. The President is the leader of a big political world which influences him as he influences it. He also is the only one who deals with the chief executives of other countries in an international game which has generated certain rules. Understanding that game, particularly the relations among the great powers, tells us much about presidential power. But to analyze it in terms of interest quickly leads to a dead end. It has to do with intents and intentions, actual and projected capabilities, all of which must be conceived of in a systematic sense, which I call ideological. More theoretical exposition is necessary, however, before the notion of a presidential realm of ideology can become productively useful.

ROOSEVELT'S VISION

Roosevelt's vision involved a new world order based on the principles laid out in the Bretton Woods and Dumbarton Oaks conferences. In retrospect, one can also say that nuclear power, which today has the most powerful global force of all, had its roots in another of Roosevelt's visions. Roosevelt probably never anticipated that this new weapon, which had not even been successfully tested at the time of his death, would be one of the great determining factors of world politics for the latter half of the twentieth century. Nevertheless, the immensely costly program to develop an atomic bomb never would have been undertaken in the United States were it not for his inspiration. It can be argued that had Truman, a man steeped in interest politics, become President a few years earlier (had he been Vice President then), the atomic bomb would not have been developed. Similarly, as most historians concede, it is doubtful that the United Nations would have been formed without Roosevelt's driving force. It is also questionable whether a new monetary system and something like the World Bank would have come into being even before the war had ended without the combination of Franklin Roosevelt and Henry Morgenthau.

Roosevelt is remembered outside the United States as a visionary, a man who would have brought world peace had he lived. Within the United States, those old enough remember him either as a man devoted to peace and justice or a dictator willing to destroy the free enterprise system to feed his dreams of world grandeur. Roosevelt started out as a master politician whom even conservatives supported as a smart and forceful leader. But as he moved to resolve the crisis of depression, he evolved dreams of a new America, and as he entered the crisis of war, he began to evolve his visions of a new world. Roosevelt's long-standing interest in the Navy, in faraway places, his early global travels, gave him a world consciousness, but whatever visions he had in his earlier years went little beyond those of most stamp collectors. The conclusion that Roosevelt's global visions grew as America became involved in World War II is inescapable. War and vision were closely interrelated in Roosevelt's mind.

One of the dictionary definitions of "vision" is "the act or power of anticipating that which will or may come to be." Great religious leaders who preach some divinely inspired message about the world and man are usually considered visionaries. The word "charisma" has had considerable vogue in recent political writing, but it has either not been very useful in operational terms or has been emasculated by imputing "new values" to the alleged charismatic leader. Moreover, much political writing assumes that because someone has charisma, he therefore becomes the leader of a political group. In fact, it is usually the reverse. Because an individual, for certain particular reasons, becomes the leader at the apex of a political structure, he develops "charismatic" qualities. Thinking of this "charismatic" leadership quality in terms of vision makes more common sense and is also more productive theoretically and practically. A vision is a form of prediction. If the prediction is absurd, quixotic, or mystical, few people will pay attention and even fewer will follow it politically. If the prediction strikes certain widely held chords of common sense, political wisdom or interest, or scientific evidence, however, it will be taken seriously. Scientific prediction is, of course, the most widely believed form, because experiments can be constructed to test it. Political prediction is more hazardous because the elements of the experiment cannot be controlled. But, as even opinion polling has shown, fairly valid political predictions can be made. Scientific prediction is only a highly specialized case of a common human activity— anticipation. All people anticipate what might come so that they can order their daily lives and make plans for tomorrow. The more disorderly the environment, the more people try to anticipate because no one can survive in a chaos. A political vision is a grandiose form of prediction of what the power relations among certain groups of people will be. A political vision that encompasses the globe is a prediction of what the relations among whole nations will be in years to come.

Scientific prediction cannot be divorced from the power of the scientist to create the conditions that will prove his prediction, the ability to set up experiments. The same is true of political prediction. Opinion polls are taken seriously because research agencies have the means to produce and sustain a process of empirical verification. Power is, thus, a socially necessary element if prediction is to be taken seriously. In the case of a political vision of global dimensions, no one would take it seriously unless it was made by someone who held power of global dimensions. Churchmen often talk about the unity of mankind, but few take them seriously because by design most churchmen lack power. But when the President of the United States talks of "one world," all listen because he has the power to attempt to bring it about. If the President of the United States were to tell the people that the world will be blown up in a nuclear holocaust in a few years unless something drastic is done, then a political process of great scope would immediately be unleashed. Anyone else who said so might achieve the distinction of a George Orwell but little more. The point is that the President of the United States has the power to create the conditions that verify his visionary prediction.

Thus, Roosevelt's vision of atomic power, a United Nations, and a postwar monetary system was not just passive prediction that all this would come about anyway. As with scientific prediction, the President of the United States could, by virtue of his vast political power, create the conditions that would bring these new military, political, and economic systems into being. Also like scientific prediction, Roosevelt's vision was based on elements of hard realities: on a considerable array of scientific, technical, and human resource facts which convinced him—and many others—that it could be done. Many of the bricks used to build the United Nations had been available since the pre–World War I period, before the League of Nations had been formed. The most active period for the formation of international agencies dated from the turn of the century. The bricks for the new monetary system were contained in the world-wide sterling system, which survived the abandonment of the gold standard in the early 1930s and only weakened because Britain was so badly hurt during World War II. Like so many Arab mosques in Spain, which were built with older Christian masonry, Roosevelt's vision was made up of elements already in existence. What was new was the whole structure, the product of a series of flashes of insight.

Roosevelt's vision of the postwar world was, thus, a prediction of what would be, made by the only man in the world at that time who had the power to bring it about or to set up the conditions that would show that the predictions were wrong. If atomic power had fizzled, if the United Nations had quickly collapsed, and if the dollar had not been able to sustain the international monetary system, Roosevelt's visionary experiment would have been reckoned a total failure. Only America and, in America, only Roosevelt had the power to generate a global vision. Indeed, the great international structures and systems of the postwar world were American creations: nuclear power, the United Nations, and the international monetary system. Russia, which symbolically abdicated from its own internationalism during the war by dissolving the Comintern and ordering the dissolution of the American Communist party, eventually reverted to it, but only *after* the cold war had begun.

SOME PROPOSITIONS AND OBSERVATIONS

Nations (or even cities and tribes) have turned into empires in the past, and, in spite of the vast historical differences, all these transformations have something in common. I shall make some general propositions on the subject, though they relate particularly to America of the postwar period.

A nation turns into an empire not simply by direct or indirect conquest, but by creating, developing, and maintaining a larger political system to govern its new dominions, clients, and dependents.

When a nation becomes an empire, a new political realm comes into being which I call the realm of ideology. This realm centers on the chief executive, and the military and political agencies he creates or assumes power over to carry out his global policies. In empires, the dominant ideology is imperial.

A nation is primarily concerned with national interests. Empires, in addition to pursuing their own interests as nations, also pursue goals deriving from the imperial ideology, which are frequently incomprehensible in terms of national interest.

The sources of imperial ideology are popular, but it is the great leader or executive projecting a vision who succeeds in transforming ideological beliefs into structures of organizational power.

Powerful realms of ideology turn outward to impose their will abroad, that being a mark of empire, except in the case of revolutionary countries, which project their power inward to revolutionize society.

I shall also make some practical observations on the basis of the theory developed so far. America became an empire in the closing days of World War II. For reasons that have yet to be explored, America made a qualitative leap from its traditional expansionism to a new global role whereby it tried to create and implement a world order. In this it succeeded, not in the form of Roosevelt's "one world," which would have included Russia, but in the form of the later "free world," which excluded Russia. America's assumption of an imperial role was obviously in part a response to the political vacuum brought about by World War II. But the theory also points to the enormous expansion of governmental power, particularly of the executive branch, as an element in this process. This expansion began in the crisis environment of the Depression but was greatly accelerated by the war. America's transition from nation to empire cannot be understood except in terms of the political visions of Franklin D. Roosevelt, which he had already gone far to implement before his death.

What I propose, in effect, is that when any nation has a political realm of ideology concretely visible in the form of a powerful chief executive, military and political structures with global concerns, and deep ideological currents purporting to bring about peace, progress, and justice in the world, it is on the way to becoming an empire.

POLICY

Roosevelt's visions for a postwar world order were dramatic. Yet one must not believe that they were unique and qualitatively different from those of following Presidents. If we regard vision as prediction, albeit of a grandiose sort, then it falls within the scope of a more commonly accepted form of executive activity, policy-making. Dictionaries define policy as a "course of action" which public and private organizations adopt for themselves. While one can speak lightly of an individual's policies, it is generally assumed that only organizations, and in particular large-scale organizations, adopt policies of any meaningful sort. The setting of policy is one of the main functions of the biggest organization in any society, the government. It is further assumed that policies, whatever their roots, are set only at the apex of the organization. The executive, not its bureaucracies, sets policy. Policy as a course of action can be defined as the setting of goals, the laying out of the directions to be taken in the pursuit of those goals, and the specification of means to be used. The notion of organizational policy is a modern one, so modern that even now French, German, and Russian do not have a separate word for it. For example, *"la politique des États-Unis"* translates either as "the politics of the United States" or "the policy of the United States." The same is true for German and Russian. The reason for this apparent lack of specificity is that the word "politics" has a more ideological connotation in these European languages than in American English. When we speak of politics, we tend to think in terms of the game of interests played out in legislatures or bureaucracies. Europeans see politics pretty much as I have defined policy. For them, politics is the game of policies pursued by the heads of governments, political parties, armies, and other bureaucracies. In terms of the theory of politics I am sketching out, European politics tends to be as much in the realm of ideology as in the realm of interests, and often primarily so. Europeans assume that politics is ideological, whereas Americans have generally not made that assumption.

Interestingly, the Chinese language as it has evolved through Chinese communism has a general word for "politics" (*cheng-chih*), but also three words for "policy." The general word *cheng-chih* means political power or, in a slightly older sense, the modalities of governmental rule. Thus, there is no connotation of goals, directions, or means in this word, just a sense of power. The three words for "policy," in a descending order of generality, are *lu-hsien*, which may be translated as "line," *fang-chen*, which may be translated as "strategy" and whose two elements denote "direction" and "pointing toward," and *cheng-ts'e*, which may be translated as "tactics" and whose elements mean "political strategems." *Lu-hsien* lays out the ultimate long-range goals, *fang-chen* specifies the directions to be taken to achieve those goals, and *cheng-ts'e* indicates the specific concrete actions to be taken. Put into a military context, the three words could be rendered as "war," "campaign," and "battle." War implies some ultimate goals which a nation has decided to pursue with force. A campaign is a line of action, for example, action undertaken to seize a certain city, occupy territory, or destroy enemy forces. Battles are the myriads of actions fought on a daily basis, the building blocks of campaigns and wars.

While this Chinese conception of policy will be useful in the construction of the theory, let me remain with the notion of policy as such without differentiation. Only executives in organizations can set policies, although, obviously, the roots of policy are to be found elsewhere in the society. In governments, only the chief executive can set policy. Even if a chief executive merely rubber-stamps an "option" presented to him by his officials, a potential policy becomes a real policy only when this is done. It is generally accepted, for example, that the National Security Council (NSC) under Eisenhower was never the real source of national policy, yet, as the Pentagon Papers show, ratification of a policy by the National Security Council was essential to its implementation. Roosevelt's visions were policies of innovative, far-reaching, and ambitious scope. But the important fact is that, unlike dreams, they were courses of action that led to the elaboration of strategies and structures that determined the fate of the entire world for the ensuing decades. Roosevelt made full use of his position as the most powerful chief executive until then in America's history and the ruler of the most powerful nation in the world to elaborate policies of commensurate scope and grandeur.

The essence of policy is anticipation. A policy, when it is first set, is a qualitatively different leap into the future. It sets certain goals which were not being pursued before. War is the most extreme form of new policy. It announces the intention of a country to seek the defeat and destruction of an enemy which earlier peace had precluded. General staffs may play around with contingency plans and games about potential enemies, but only war or warlike policy enables the military to make the transition from planning to action. What the setting of a policy says is that the projected new goals cannot be achieved by intensification of existing forms of political action, or that old goals cannot be achieved by persevering in given directions, or that existing means are inadequate. Whether ambitious or modest, radically or slightly different from the ongoing, all policies project something *new*. Since they are policies, not just wishes, they also suggest ways in which the goals can be achieved. They anticipate that if such-and-such is done, one can get what one wants. Thus, setting a policy is much like scientific prediction—the policy offers the means by which the "experiment" can be carried out. If it works, the "hypotheses" have been proven with the result that the government's power and control are expanded, just as successful scientific experimentation broadens man's power and control over nature.

Why do organizations make policies? If an organization is new, it presumably has to set policies so that it can go about achieving the goals for which it was set up. But the more significant question is why long-established organizations, like governments, decide to set forth policies, why they decide to do something new or different. The simplest answer is that there is something so wrong that just doing more of the same will get them nowhere. Take, for example, an event which occurred in late

March 1972; the assumption by the British government of direct rule
over Northern Ireland. The British government perceived that there was
something so basically wrong in Northern Ireland that continuing existing lines of action (pressuring Stormont to make concessions to the
Catholics, trying to enforce equitable law and order through the British
army, and interning Catholic dissidents) would just create more killing
and chaos. It was an anomalous situation which finally forced the British
to change the rules of the game. All organizations have a tendency
toward inertia; they tend to keep on doing what they have been
doing, a bit more or a bit less but always in the same way. This inherent
inertial tendency of organizations can collide with reality to produce
irresolvable contradictions, or different parts of the organization can
collide with each other to produce similar contradictions. The contradictions produce escalating dangers. They may be so intense that the goals
cannot be achieved, or different parts of the organizations (or different
organizations involved in the over-all situation) move too far in different
directions, or conventional means of getting things done become exhausted. Policies are sometimes adopted in order to seize an opportunity
to do something new, but more often they are adopted from a sense of
threat to what exists. The ideal policy is one which is inspired by a sense
of threat but which also displays such marvelous imagination in projecting opportunities that the old can be saved while gaining something
entirely new. A new policy does not necessarily change old ones, but it
always adds some new goals, directions, and means to the existing situation.

EXECUTIVES

Why is it that only executives can set policy? This question requires us to
look at the nature of organization. All organizations are made up of
executive, staff, and line sections, though the boundaries between them
are not always clear. The executive is the governing body at the pinnacle
of the organization—all large-scale organizations have executives. Staff
and line sections are bureaucracies, each of which is more or less specialized. Staff sections generate knowledge which the organization needs.
Line sections carry out its operations. If the organization's consumption
of knowledge is vast and its operations extensive, it will employ many
people as workers. Society enters organization through its workers. The
workers of an organization are almost always insulated from the executive by the bureaucracies. The bureaucracies are suborganizations which
in the case of government or large corporations are immense and exhibit
many of the characteristics of the over-all organization. Although the

bureaucracies can often be innovative and enterprising, particularly in corporations, by and large they tend toward routinization of existing policies and operations. One of the most important causes for bureaucratic routinization is the nature of budgets, which tend to remain more or less constant. Organizations dependent on budgets are subject to zero sum laws: if some spectacular change in policies occurs, some may gain but others will necessarily lose. Corporate suborganizations are not subject to budgetary constraints in the same way because the purpose of the corporation is to make more money and, thus, increase the size of the fiscal pie. Governmental bureaucracies, on the other hand, are generally under severe budgetary constraint because of the government's fiscal inelasticities. Thus, the natural tendency of an organization's staff and line bureaucracies is to do more of the same. The executive, on the other hand, is supposed to have an over-all view of everything that is going on in the organization, of the general environment in which it functions, and the sharpest sense and knowledge of the organization's purposes and goals. Even if the executive enjoys relatively little power over operations, he must at least have a broader consciousness than any other part of the organization. The executive is supposed to know what the situation is even if he cannot do much about it. His monopoly of consciousness is a key factor when it comes to making policy.

If and when contradictions become acute, demands begin to flow into the executive that "something be done." Within the organization, the various bureaucracies never work things out among themselves (although they do make alliances), but rather try to get the executive to do something, naturally of a sort that accords with their own interests. Outside of the organization, people look to the executive as the chief, not to some lower echelon bureaucracy, to resolve the problem. If something new is to be done, it will affect the organization as a whole, not to mention large numbers of people outside. This invariably means budgetary rearrangements, new kinds of operations, new goals and opportunities. Only if the new policy is made through the executive will it have binding force on the organization as a whole. Thus, the executive "legitimates" the new policy, not just for the obvious reason that he gave the order, but because his broad consciousness becomes a unique source of power during periods of crisis. The executive is presumed to have all the facts, to be supplied with the best available intelligence of all kinds, and to be the only real arbiter among the many well-thought-out options presented by his various bureaucratic advisers.

This suggests another proposition: that crisis acts to increase power at the executive levels of organization. A crisis (and in the course of this book we shall consider many) is an anomalous situation that poses a major threat. Since war is a succession of crises, it is not surprising that war always tends to increase executive power. When routine breaks down because of contradictions, only the executive can effectively set forth new policies to resolve the situation.

Related to this proposition on crises is the question that has often baffled people: How is it that so pivotal an office as that of the executive seems at times to consist of one man and a couple of advisers? How could an institution that seems so often to be dominated by one man be the lynch pin for an entire world order? While this book explores these questions in various ways, a simple answer can be given at this point. The greater the contradictions within the ruling structure of a country, the more this leads to the displacement of power upward until it fills the last and highest receptacle, the chief executive.

Policy is anticipation, and thus an act of faith. Since executives are presumed to have the best knowledge of the entire situation, people will naturally tend to have faith in them. If that knowledge is disputed, they will lose faith in their leaders.

What I have called vision is a particular form of policy. It is grand, innovative, and, in the modern world, global. It also sees the connection between various individual policies, weaving them together into a whole. Vision is like what the Chinese call "line" (*lu-hsien*). What they called "the general line of socialist construction" in the early 1950s was a set of major policies designed to modernize China. From it flowed several strategies and numerous tactics. The general line of socialist construction was a dream which the top leaders of China felt they had the knowledge and means to implement. Roosevelt's vision of "one world" was analogous, and, even after his death, influenced much of America's foreign policy for decades. Both were products of ideology. Both arose out of crisis situations (internal weakness and external threat facing China after the Liberation, and the wreckage of World War II, which Roosevelt saw as a threat to America). Both were propagated by men who enjoyed supreme executive power.

American imperialism is the product of Roosevelt's vision, his own ideological politics. I have already suggested that there is a link between war, empire, and executive power. The same kind of link can be seen between crisis, global policy, and presidential power for the decades following World War II. Each fed into the other. Crises led to new American global policies which in turn increased presidential power and centralization. But other variants of the equation work as well. As presidential power increased, new global policies were enunciated which in turn invariably produced crises. Each was and is both cause and effect of the others. America's decision to play a world imperial role made inevitable an environment of endless crises, more involvement in distant parts of the world, and an unprecedented concentration of power in the White House.

ORGANIZATIONAL FUNCTION
OF THE PRESIDENCY

The picture drawn of Roosevelt so far suggests an image of American Presidents as visionaries, policy makers, ideological leaders. While that is so more than most people suspect, there is a conventional conception of the role of the President which still is valid. Statutorily, the President is both chief executive and commander-in-chief. As chief executive, he presides over a Cabinet made up of other executives who sit at the apex of the vast organizations of government. Like the "chairmen" of socialist countries, his function as chief executive is to coordinate the manifold activities that go on in government. As commander-in-chief, however, he is the man who gives orders, the general who commands the generals.

By the design of the Founding Fathers who framed the Constitution, the President was supposed to be no less but no more than the chief executive and the commander-in-chief. The notion that he might become an ideological leader was abhorrent to them. America, unlike England, was to have no state church, which meant that the President could never become the spokesman for a particular set of values as opposed to others. The only values that were held binding on the country as a whole were those embodied in the Constitution, which decreed that America was subject to the rule of law guaranteeing all men certain inalienable rights. In domestic affairs, the President was regarded as the executor of Congress's will expressed through legislation. In foreign affairs, he enjoyed greater autonomy as the official solely responsible for the defense of the country. Nevertheless, while he held the power of supreme command in the area of defense and war, he could not initiate war or make treaties without the consent of Congress.

As the government got larger and bureaucracies began to cluster around the executive branch, the bureaucracies became the real executors of the legislation passed by Congress. While presidential power was obviously a vital factor in the legislative process, within the executive branch the role of the President became increasingly that of coordinator. The President held ultimate responsibility for drawing up the budget, and the chief aim of most Presidents as budget makers has been to maintain bureaucratic balance. Bureaucratic politics, like much of legislative politics, concerns interests. Governmental agencies by now are immense structures, employing thousands and occasionally millions of people, with contractual relations that go far and deep into the society. Since all bureaucracies dread shrinkage and are at least committed to the status quo, they each lay a heavy hand on the budget. If certain bureaucracies grow rapidly, this not only puts even greater pressure on the budget, but may threaten others with severe cutbacks. The President is the final arbiter of these conflicts and the general desire of most Presidents is to provide for new priorities without provoking mortal battles within the bureaucracy. The President's natural role is, therefore, as coordinator, a role not in conflict with his constitutionally prescribed prerogatives.

While the Constitution sought to curb the President's powers, it also granted him certain powers. The President is the boss of the executive branch, and, subject to limitations imposed by the Constitution and subsequent congressional legislation, he can hire and fire people at will. His Cabinet, for example, are his personal appointees and remain in office only so long as he wishes. Moreover, he has the right to issue executive orders to his civil and military bureaucracies which they must obey. In theory, these orders are subject to the same judicial scrutiny as congressional legislation; the Constitution as interpreted by the courts is the ultimate constraint on presidential power. In recent years, the issue of constitutional constraints has become particularly acute in the field of foreign affairs, which is mainly a sign of how enormous presidential power has become. This issue has become difficult in a technical sense because when the Constitution was framed, relations among countries were contractual, based on treaties in times of peace and, if war became necessary, on duly declared war. Particularly since 1945, the relations between America and other countries have become increasingly noncontractual, making a constitutional test difficult. For example, America and Communist China had no contractual relations of any sort between 1949 and the Nixon visit of 1972, yet a relationship of great ideological and practical importance existed between the two countries. Presidential power authorized flights over China to gather intelligence, which further envenomed the relationship. But how could an aggrieved party in China possibly bring a suit before an American court to test the constitutionality of the executive order authorizing overflights? Legally Communist China did not exist, and the government of the Republic of China was the sole government for all of China. If such a suit had actually been brought and tried before the courts, Washington could probably have easily demonstrated that the overflights were requested by Taipei and were well within the United States–Taipei Defense Treaty of 1954. What this simply illustrates is that presidential power has become so tightly wound up with national security that judicial or congressional review does little more than point out the anomalies in the situation. Rather than restrain presidential power, this just serves to expand it even further. Anomalous situations are fertile grounds not just for generating new policies but for increasing power.

Although Americans pride themselves on the unique character of their government, which enjoys one of the longest unbroken continuities in the world, the attributes of leadership which it has evolved over the years are not very different from those of other great powers. One of the main functions of the American Presidency is to formulate policy, which Roosevelt did on a grand scale. As chief executive, the President is also the board chairman of a vast bureaucratic empire, whose main task is the preservation of bureaucratic balance, at least through budgetary coordination. And it is clear that increasingly the President exercises direct power by commanding men and resources to achieve certain goals which he sets or accepts. The President thus has three main functions of leadership: *policy, command* and *coordination.*

There are some important differences among these functions in their political effects. Policy is initially and sometimes primarily in the realm of ideology. The President may enunciate a new policy as a statement of future goals or intentions, but so long as he does nothing (or little) concrete to implement it, it will have no (or little) effect on the skein of particular interests over which he presides. Thus, the President can proclaim that America henceforth is unswervingly committed to a policy of reducing air pollution, but unless some power is committed to policy, there will be little reverberation within the bureaucratic or corporate interests affected. If he actually commands that something be done and furnishes the men and resources to do it, then wheels will start to move. But once some wheels move, cries of anguish come from other quarters which regard the new power play as a threat to their own interests. In order to prevent even greater trouble from developing within his bureaucracies and within the broader skeins of interest outside in society, the President then is forced to seek a new harmony, to find a new consensus. He must recoordinate what was unhinged by his decision to implement policy by command.

CONTRADICTIONS BETWEEN POLICY, COMMAND, AND COORDINATION

Ideally, Presidents make policies, then look for ways to implement them, and finally reconcile all affected one way or another by the new policy. In political reality, all kinds of variants occur in the game of policy, command, and coordination. The President may loudly proclaim new policy but fail to back it up with command, which leaves the skein of interests undisturbed. Or he may decide to make some concrete moves in a new direction while piously proclaiming his adherence to the old. This ultimately produces confusion both in the realm of ideology and in the realm of interests, a situation holders of power often find to their advantage when they want to try something new. Or conversely, if a President makes some new moves of policy and command, the disturbances in the realm of interests may generate such forceful counterpressures that both policy and command are effectively negated. In order to be a good President (or, for that matter, a good leader in any dynamic organization), he has to be able to make policies to meet challenges (what I call anomalies), to commit the power to implement those policies, and to have the political wisdom to reconcile all his officials and external interests as well, so as to keep the system operating. Unfortunately, policy, command, and coordination contradict each other. The moment new policy is announced, it creates ripples of anticipatory excitement within the interests that will benefit and anxious dread among those that will lose out. Since the old goals will be replaced and, naturally, existing budgets threatened, the losers fight back. They may attack the new policy directly, or indirectly by creating intraorganizational struggles. If the President is determined to implement his policies, he may subject the dissidents to so much power that they finally accept defeat. Or he may try more devious methods. He may invent another new policy for the dissidents. He may try to increase the over-all budget so that while the dissidents may have to accept the loss of old goals, their resources will not be diminished or acceptable substitutes will be found. What also occurs frequently is that the President may discover that his power to coerce is limited and the pressure of bureaucratic balance too great, that he allows the new policy to remain at the rhetorical level awaiting a better moment for implementation.

The contradictions between policy on the one hand and command and coordination on the other arise out of a fundamental difference between the realm of ideology and that of interests. Since a situation of general anomaly generates the realm of ideology, its main characteristic is constant change. This can be easily seen in the role of the President during the last decades. He lives in an environment of constant challenges, opportunities, crises, which he alone is expected to handle. He develops new policies precisely to cope with that constant change and keep the ship of state afloat and moving on to its various destinations. By contrast, the basic characteristic of the realm of interests is stability, routine, and predictable and incremental change. Modern corporations, for example, search for the most secure possible environment so that they can plan for future growth with assured expectations. The same is true for bureaucracies. Contemporary sociology has correctly identified "routinization" as one of the basic effects of bureaucratization. Corporations and bureaucracies both want to function in a stable world. Yet their officials are fully aware of the waves of change constantly swirling around them. Thus, they look to their leaders to make policies that will abate the threats while at the same time maintaining harmony. The difficulty is that the leader, having greater consciousness of the magnitude of change and threat, will try to generate simple, grand policies which will eventually satisfy just about everyone, but which may adversely affect their short-term interests. The realm of interests would prefer that the chief executive just generate a series of discrete policies to meet the particular threat and safeguard the interests concerned. But the resulting chaos of policies acting against each other would either create even greater dangers or lock the chief executive into a state of paralysis.

This contradiction is exemplified by the conflicts that Roosevelt's new vision of a postwar order aroused in America even before the end of World War II. Roosevelt's vision saw a new Pax Americana which would give America military security, prevent the reoccurrence of a new depression, and spark new economic opportunities throughout the world, which would be (and, in fact, were) of enormous tangible benefit to American capitalist interests. In addition to his idealism, Roosevelt's practical sense as a leader convinced him that piecemeal policies designed primarily to service America's major interests would just lead to a repetition of what happened after World War I. America decided not to join the League of Nations out of self-interest. The victorious Allied powers eagerly grabbed for what they felt was due them, and thereby so stymied each other that they only guaranteed more trouble for themselves. Germany was defeated, but neither of the only two clearcut policies that could have been carried out against it was followed. It was neither effectively disarmed and put under international supervision nor was it welcomed back into the concert of nations (at least not in 1919). Roosevelt was convinced that only a new world order based on international systems could avert a third world conflagration. Yet, as happened after World War I, the same elements in America, which traditionally had been expansionist and were found mainly in the Republican party, lashed out against him. True, Roosevelt had won over some like Wendell Willkie, but others, like Robert Taft, kept up the drumfire of opposition even after his death. The expansionists opposed the new imperialism because they believed that the interests they represented would have to pay for the new schemes. Business had contributed mightily to the war effort, but on the understanding that when the war was over, the government would quickly revert to peacetime rules of the game, specifically, vastly reduced federal budgets. But imperialism would cost a lot of money, and business was expected to provide a large share of it. Why should a business sacrifice present earnings earmarked for its own corporate expansion to a federal budget which would give them to foreign governments to generate economic recovery abroad, which would benefit America generally but not necessarily the particular business that had poured its huge corporate taxes into the government?

The contradiction between imperialism and expansionism was temporarily resolved in the early 1950s, but not without bitter struggles the most violent of which were those between the "Europe-firsters," the imperialists, and the "Asia-firsters," the expansionists. Roosevelt's new policies collided with the realm of interests. One must give great credit for forging the resolution of the contradictions to Harry Truman, a man of no vision, but a fine machine politician. If Henry Wallace the visionary had remained vice president, his political ineptness probably would not have allowed that resolution to take place.

While command and coordination are in the realm of interests, they too are contradictory. Exercising command means exercising power—men are galvanized into action and monies provided to get some job done. In war, everybody gets into the act, which makes it a good situation for political leaders. But in peacetime (or what passes for peacetime), this is never the case. A leader who wants to get a job done selects his troops and in so doing bypasses others. In the late 1940s, for example, bitter controversy erupted in Washington between the Air Force and the Navy over the issue of B-52s or supercarriers. No one questioned the global policies which the planes and the ships were to service, but since the budgetary pie was limited and Truman feared inflation, choices had to be made. Every time the President or his advisers made a move toward one weapons system, a howl went up from the other side. Congressional allies were alerted and a storm of controversy descended around the President's head. Truman's budgetary options during peacetime were much more limited than Roosevelt's during the war. He thus faced the terrible dilemma that whenever he tried to exercise presidential command to move in a particular military direction, he tore up the already flimsy skein of military-bureaucratic harmony and produced political controversy, which played into the hands of his electoral enemies.

LEADERS

The contradictions of policy, command, and coordination point up one of the main paradoxes of leadership. A good leader, whether president or chairman of a great country, corporation executive or military general, chief of a political party or labor union or liberation movement, must be able to think out new policies, order often reluctant subordinates to get things done, and smooth over the controversies that always erupt among the top officials of the organization. The problem is that few are the human beings who combine all these qualities. Policy makers must be able to dream, to have flights of imagination, to be inventive and innovative. The crazy scientists of popular fiction are such people, but they are also so wrapped up in themselves that they are unaware of what goes on around them. Politicians can be good generals or ward bosses, constantly ordering people to get the job done, but they soon discover that they step on too many toes and often take the dictatorial way out of their problems. Such politicians are also so wrapped up in the hard, cold world of reality that they become contemptuous of dreamers. Increasingly common in the American world of leadership is the "fine administrator," the person who can pull everything together without suggesting anything new, upsetting the applecart, or exercising personal will and power.

People with a materialist approach to politics might object to what seems to be a "great man" theory. They might prefer to speak about the structural requisites of leadership or might consider the emphasis on leadership as pointless until the interest basis of politics is made clear. Whether leadership finds the person or certain people create the leadership is ultimately unanswerable. It is beyond doubt that the realm of interests is a powerful compelling reality. The material reality of a corporation will pretty much dictate what the individual who leads it does. Moreover, since corporation presidents are selected by boards of directors, usually in consultation with management, the realm of interests chooses someone who is known to serve it. The longer the realm of interests exists, the more it tends to develop intricate and binding rules of the game designed to ensure the preservation of those interests. But in the contemporary world, the rules of the game have been subjected to repeated onslaught, by war, revolution, and crisis (economic, political, social, cultural, or military). When that occurs, the system, inherently addicted to routinization, demands policy, and if the wreckage be severe enough, may go so far out of character as to seek some vision for salvation. In a crisis, power tends to move upward from middle-level realms of interest to the top leaders. Those who suggest the policies, or on rare occasions offer the visions, are accepted as leaders only if their message strikes chords of anticipation broadly shared by people of the constituency that has elected to follow them. The great leader is one who senses what is going on in that constituency, composes the requisite music, and directs its execution by an orchestra. The challenge for a creative synthesis is there and someone among the multitude of human beings will respond in a way that produces a broad following. What is involved here is the simple fact that all human beings not only act but also think and dream. Thinking and dreaming go on all the time in an organization, even while the members do the work they are supposed to do. Executives are generally quite aware of this and sum it up as "morale." In highly routinized organizations, morale may be a matter of indifference so long as the day-to-day job gets done. But in exceedingly unroutinized organizations, such as a combat squad on patrol, morale is obviously a factor of utmost importance.

SOCIAL CURRENTS AS THE BASIS OF POLICY

A leader is always the leader of a particular constituency which may range from the entire citizenry to a much smaller group of people. A leader might even decide that his constituency consists just of the other members of the board of directors over which he presides. When challenged to make innovative policy, the leader senses certain currents of thought, feeling, and aspiration which are commonly held by most or all of the members of the constituency. Using these currents as inspiration and adding a scheme made up of real capabilities of the organization, the leader comes up with a new policy which will gain him support from his constituency on both ideological and practical grounds.

Everyone knows that there are currents of thought, feeling, and aspiration commonly shared by large numbers of people in a society or in some smaller entity thereof. Thinkers in every human society, primitive and civilized, have for over two millenniums offered theories to explain what the fundamental nature of these broadly shared spiritual understandings are. Religions by and large believe that aspiration for a better world, a better life, and personal salvation form a major part of such currents. Marx, a nineteenth-century rationalist, believed that true consciousness would not only subsume aspiration and feeling to thought, but would show that the socially significant currents were expressions of material self-interest shared throughout a class. The French anthropologist Emile Durkheim believed that societies, like the bodies of living things, were organic wholes; the socially significant currents were, therefore, society's consciousness of what was important about itself. Whatever the ultimate explanation of this social spirituality, it obviously exists, and great organizations have been developed to feed from and into it: mass media, churches, schools and universities, cultural associations, and the institutions that pour music, books, and art into the public.

It is true and can be empirically shown that in contemporary complex societies certain classes of people cluster around certain cultural forms. Even a cursory examination of television and radio in America shows that certain kinds of programs with their corresponding commercials are aimed at certain constituencies. There are programs for the over-all population, conceived to be white and middle-class, and others for special ethnic, age group, and sectional constituencies. There are high-brow programs ("educational TV"), average, ordinary programs, and programs aimed primarily at the working class. Voluntary cultural associations which self-select their members naturally constitute constituencies which can be defined in terms of class or race. There are, thus, many cultures around providing a fertile and profitable field for industries that produce culture.

While the socially significant groupings in society are obviously the repositories of certain kinds of cultures, it is also true that organizations tend to produce certain common cultural characteristics among their members. Extreme forms of this tendency are, for example, the FBI and IBM, whose employees are trained to behave in a culturally uniform manner. Professional training in universities also tends to produce cultural uniformity in students which later professional associations reinforce. For example, even when trained social scientists hold divergent political views, they argue with each other in terms of agreed upon categories and a vocabulary of thought that they learned in school. Military officers are supposed to adhere to standard codes of behavior and are punished for acts of deviance which the society as a whole would simply disregard. Certain kinds of craft unions are so committed to cultural uniformity that they exclude racial minorities on the grounds that they would bring in discordance. That organizations tend to produce cultural uniformity should not be surprising. People in an organization relate to each other not only as workers but also as human beings, and the more they have in common as human beings, the more easily they can interact with each other.

The leader of a culturally uniform organization has a powerful weapon at his disposal when it comes to making new policy to meet crisis, challenge, or opportunity. If a general knows that his soldiers are patriotic, he can use that sentiment to get them to undertake hazardous missions which self-interest would tell them could only bring personal injury or death. If they are not patriotic, the general can either coerce them or try to demonstrate that what he orders them to do is not substantially different from what they have been doing. The clever general knows the shared sentiments of his soldiers and can use them to implement a new course of action. If his soldiers are not patriotic, the general may sense that they have powerful bonds of comradeship with each other and secondarily with other soldiers of their army. In the Vietnam war, generals ordered countless missions "to save American lives," knowing that when one soldier moved out, others would follow until the desired action had been carried out. The general's staff may be more exacting in their wish to know whether the new course of action will really work, but if they disagree, the general can also play on their shared understandings. Thus, if the action turns out well, it will enhance every staff officer's chance for promotion. This shared sentiment will get them to go along with the action.

The President of the United States has the most agonizing task of all when it comes to making new policy. He knows the new policy will affect the interests of certain constituencies in society and of some segments of the vast governmental organization over which he presides. Those whose interests will be benefited need not be appealed to in any special terms since gifts are never rejected. But those whose interests are endangered pose a special problem, as well as those constituencies which become anxious that somehow in the future the new policy could affect them adversely. To bring as many of them around as possible, the President has to look for shared sentiments powerful enough to make people forget their interests to some extent and support the new policy. Like a general in war, the President has to try to get many people to do things they would ordinarily be reluctant to do.

The great leader, then, is the person who knows how to become the political vehicle for certain currents of thought, feeling, and aspiration widely held by the constituencies he leads. Mavericks do not become great leaders. Great leaders may be mad, but those who support them believe they will be their vehicle, to fight for their interests or express their beliefs or both. During World War II and long after, there was heated argument within the Allied nations about the guilt of the German people for Hitler. Roosevelt appears to have believed that all Germans were responsible because there was something psychopathologically wrong with Germans. Stalin took a Marxist position, which saw Hitler as the instrument of Germany's ruling classes and absolved the German people of guilt. Stalin was a notorious believer in the primacy of interests over ideology (except for his own people's faith in him as leader), and considered Germany a practical, not an ideological problem. Roosevelt, in keeping with his visionary character, took a more ideological approach to the German problem. Since he regarded himself as the voice of the good American people, he saw Hitler as the voice of the bad German people. At a distance of a quarter-century, it appears that both Roosevelt and Stalin were partially correct. Major organized segments of German society put Hitler in power and, despite considerable unhappiness, supported him to the end. On the other hand, Hitler skillfully managed to identify himself with major currents in German society. Racism against Jews and Slavs was rampant. So was a populist hatred of big capitalists, big bosses, and arrogant intellectuals, for which bourgeois Jews furnished a convenient catchall target. Dark, brooding feelings arising from the horrors of World War I and the injustices of the postwar settlements afflicted a large part of the German people. Where Roosevelt was naïve and cruel was in not seeing that these spiritual currents were to a considerable extent the product of particular historical circumstances which an endemic German "authoritarian personality" exacerbated but did not create. He also failed to see that German Nazism was part of a general European fascist current which had powerful adherents all over the continent, especially France. Stalin's primitive Marxist explanation for Hitler was also partially wrong in that he could not conceive that major segments of Germany's ruling classes had turned against Hitler because they saw his madness as threatening their vital interests. Hitler and his gang managed to stay in power by sometimes crushing the people with the interests, but at other times, bludgeoning those interests with the threat of arousing the people's wrath against them. It is often forgotten that the little paperhanger was not the product of a rarefied German university, but a man with diverse and deeply felt experience in different popular circumstances. That experience gave him an uncanny sense of people's moods, which he used to whip them up to follow his policies. Two "material" elements are essential to understanding Hitler: the interests of the organizations that gave him his power and the faith of the constituencies of society that followed him wherever he went.

POLITICALLY SIGNIFICANT CURRENTS

The political leader stands both within and at the apex of the realms of ideology and of interests. But the source of the ideology comes from below; only his policies come from the top. We now come to the question of what currents of thought, feeling, and aspiration within society and within organizations are politically significant for the leader. First, it has to be regarded as axiomatic that there are no currents in any organizational constituency that cannot be found somewhere in the society of the nation in question. There are alien military occupations where this is not the case, but they are transient phenomena. A powerful corporate or bureaucratic organization may embody currents no longer widespread in society, but their source can always be found in the society past or present. I propose that the politically significant currents in society relate to three basic matters: the material interests of people (particularly work and jobs); their sense of order, security, and justice; and the social and physical quality of their life and that of the people with and among whom they live. These matters are politically significant because no person can gain anything in regard to them except through some larger power. Jobs are overwhelmingly provided by an economy which now has reached immense dimensions. Order is provided by police, security by armies, and justice by courts, which the government sets up and maintains. The social services like schooling, health, utilities, and sundry others, which give quality to life, are provided by large-scale administrative and corporate bodies. That these are indeed issues of prime concern to people can be seen in the 1972 election: people are concerned about unemployment and inflation; the Vietnam war, crime in the streets, the role of courts, corrections, and police; and "busing," welfare, and medical care.

Each of these matters of concern relates to certain large-scale organizations of society. Jobs are provided by corporations, government, and small-scale enterprises. The core of the productive economy is the corporation. The government skims off a portion of the wealth the corporation creates to provide for income-generating jobs, which helps, in theory anyway, to assure the full employment stimulus to the economy that the corporations need to produce even more. Corporation and government, as well as the economy as a whole, sustain a broad range of smaller income-generating enterprises (stores and restaurants, for example), which round out the full employment picture (again, in theory). The corporate enterprise, however, remains the key structure of the economy, and so takes the burden of blame for less than full employment. But reflecting the vastly growing role of the government in the economy, people now also blame governmental policy for unemployment. In its broadest sense, this area of concern can be said to relate to the economy, and in its most personal sense to work.

While the dynamic structures of the economy are increasingly integrated, the more rigid structures for external and internal protection are still formally separate. The segregation of the American armed forces from civil society is a reflection of the separation of foreign and domestic affairs in the politics of the American government. The FBI and the CIA are also jurisdictionally distinct agencies of government, the former concerned with internal protection, the latter serving the external defense interests of the United States. Moreover, the court and police systems remain formally separate. Even if there is increasing evidence for the formation of a *de facto* national police system centering around the FBI, the Supreme Court is still the apex of the judicial system, exercising autonomy vis-à-vis the executive branch of government. Nevertheless, armies, police, and courts together with their ancillary agencies all constitute organizations for the protection of the citizenry. People develop politically significant attitudes toward these three agencies of protection, and the ideological currents that have arisen in regard to them tend to follow similar lines. In budgetary terms, by far the greatest role in the domain of protection is played by the military. The American empire and the American military have grown hand-in-hand. Just as the corporation is the key to the economy, so the Department of Defense is the key organization in the domain of protection.

The social services are predominately provided by federal, state, and local bureaucracies. Large private corporations provide most of the utilities—telephone, gas and electricity, and some transportation (airlines). Far more than other producing corporations, however, they are so bound up with governmental regulatory and administrative agencies that where public ends and private begins is hard to delineate. The school systems are, in effect, parts of city and county bureaucracies. Health service is both private and public with the public sector rapidly growing. Welfare is entirely bureaucratic. Other services like water and waste disposal have been bureaucratic for a long time. Highway and road construction are entirely bureaucratic, by now largely financed by the federal government.

While most citizens in society hold political opinions about the economy, the state of their security, and the social quality of their lives, these opinions are periodically molded into fixed sets of ideas, which persist for a long while, often beyond their political usefulness. They are like the currents in an ocean always available for a ship captain to sail on. Good politicians have a keen sense of those currents and know how to play with them. The more clearcut and explicit they become, the more they take on certain qualities of doctrine and so become ideology. The *Random House Dictionary* defines ideology as "the body of doctrine, myth, symbol, etc., of a social movement, institution, class, or large group." That is a good working definition which avoids the clouds of verbiage political scientists have emitted on the subject. For example, "integration" is a word that symbolizes a major ideological current during the last few decades in America. Integration arose as a set of ideas opposed to segregation which held that the quality of social life was best served by keeping different races, particularly black and white, separate in all social situations (schools, restaurants, hospitals etc.). Integration holds the opposite. It became an ideological current when political leaders helped to organize the ideas into more systematic form and began to use them for purposes of political power. The word "integration" is sloganistic shorthand for this ideological current. Mention "integration" and a host of derivative ideas are immediately generated. Originally, the idea of integration was linked primarily to a particular organization, the NAACP, which proselytized largely among whites to gain acceptance for the idea and to discredit segregation. Gradually, liberal political leaders, mainly in the Democratic party, turned it into a major political current in the country. With the 1954 Supreme Court school desegregation decision, that current became woven into the law of the land. The combination of political idea, political organization, and political constituency turned the idea of integration into an ideological current. Political, of course, means something that relates to power. Integration as an ideological current relates primarily neither to the economy nor to the state of security but to the social quality of life. The proponents of integration have sought to use political power, mainly that of the federal government, to gain racial mixture in education, housing, employment, recreational facilities, cultural media.

Much of the murkiness that has arisen in learned discussions about ideology comes from the fact that many theorists do not take political talk at face value but look for something underneath it. Or they assume that there is or should be a single over-all ideology, which expresses the interests and intents of an entire social class—"bourgeois ideology," "working-class ideology," and so on. In this book I make the basic assumption that people are by and large politically conscious. People know what their own interests and aspirations are, and most of them have at least a rudimentary knowledge of how given political processes which affect those interests and aspirations operate. The American political system drastically limits the choices people can make in the political arena, but when they do choose, they generally do so wisely. This is not to say that people cannot be taken in by political public relations, but the most effective PR campaigns are those that appeal to real interests and aspirations. Interests change and aspirations can be aroused, so that people's political behavior also changes. But acceptance of the fact that the people are conscious of their own interests and aspirations is the basis of effective political action. So also with ideology. The words ideology uses may be esoteric, but the content must express the interests and aspirations of the constituency to which it is directed. If an organization propounds an ideology and large numbers of people support it in the political arena, then there must be no doubt that that organization and ideology have managed to tap the people's political consciousness. Those who bewail the false consciousness or political immaturity of the people, often in the most learned of words, are only expressing their own impotence and isolation.

I speak of ideological currents because the first impression one has of the politics of a complex society is of myriads of political ideas. But the political ideas that are relevant on a large scale and for a long period of time are much more limited in number. Major ideological currents are always recognizable by certain short, concise slogans, often only one word, which are repeated again and again, often like incantations. Some word slogans are: "integration," "anticommunism," "law-and-order," "busing," "containment," "black power," "power-to-the-people," "efficiency," "equal opportunity," "full employment," "saving American lives." These are all political catchwords familiar to anyone who has known the American political scene over the last decades. It is not difficult to conjure up the image of a political leader using them in innumerable speeches. What is common to all of these divergent catchwords is that each symbolizes a larger and more complex political outlook, is propounded by one or more political organizations that seek power through it, and is aimed at one or more constituencies. The louder, longer, and oftener one hears a catchword, the more certain one can be that it indicates the workings of a significant ideological current.

In 1971, the word "busing" sprang into prominence on the American political scene; by 1972, it had become a major political issue. As soon as the courts issued orders for busing schoolchildren, antibusing political organizations began to appear throughout the country. While most were local, the most national was the Wallace campaign organization. The chief constituencies of these antibusing organizations were white middle- and working-class people. The interests affected were obvious: these people did not want their children to be bused to schools in ghetto districts where the children were primarily poor and black. Their aspirations were also obvious: they wanted their children to get "quality education" (another ideological catchword), which meant an education in a non-poor, non-black school through which the children, it was hoped, could climb the ladder of success by an eventual college education. "Busing," which connotes antibusing, is now an ideological catchword going beyond the specific issue of busing schoolchildren. It points to a major world view of working- and middle-class people who live near ghettos. They believe that the good life consists of a decent job, housing, and family; that is what they want for their children. And they believe that education is the way to get it. They fear the proximity of poverty as mortally endangering their dreams for their children.

What distinguishes an ideological current from other political issues (taxes or municipal bonds, for example) is the strong element of aspiration in the ideas propounded. Ideological currents appeal both to people's interests and to their hopes and fears about the world around them and their place in it. All people hold to one or another kind of world view, which is a practical everyday sociology about how the society around them operates. When people say "money makes the world go 'round," they are expressing in capsule form a world view about the nature of the capitalist society in which they live. On the other hand, people also have hopes and fears about their present and future place in that society. The world view is an operational tool which enables them to set practical guidelines for themselves to move ahead. Thus, if money makes the world go 'round, in order to get ahead in the world, the obvious course is to set one's sights on making money. World views are not capricious but real reflections of real society. However, since the contemporary world is exceedingly complex, most people get their world view drummed into their minds over a long period of time, generally by school but increasingly by television, where the commercials far more than the actual programs are major vehicles for nurturing world view. World view on the one hand and people's hopes and fears on the other are the essential ingredients of ideologies. World views are closely involved in the busing controversy. Whites who oppose busing believe that stable suburban-type communities where people are generally homogeneous are the natural basis of society and anything that threatens that type of society is alien and subversive. Liberal advocates of busing have a much broader view of a society in deep conflict, the resolution of which is the only basis on which settled society in any form can be preserved. Conservative and liberal world views clash over the busing issue, as do conservative and liberal hopes and fears.

Those who enjoy power, wealth, and prestige in the realm of interests would prefer that ideology disappear altogether from the political scene. Daniel Bell heralded the "end of ideology" as a sign that America's major problems had been resolved and that the game of practical interests would take care of rough edges like poverty, war, and alienation. But however much the pragmatic elites and their counselors may deplore demagoguery, its obvious existence indicates that there is something basically wrong about the state of society. Even if political leaders fabricate the ideology, its elements come from the people. If the ideological appeal generates political success, this is eloquent testimony to the fact that these same pragmatic elites with all the power of their interests were not able to resolve the problems. Revolutionaries, of course, make use of ideology to arouse the masses against governments, since they have no entry into the realm of interests. Their success is directly related to the weakness and failure of the elites. But it is equally a sign of the weakness and failure of elites when supreme political leaders resort to ideological appeals. They do this when their technicians have failed. The realm of interests always regards it as dangerous when a leader begins to play with the realm of ideology, even if expressly in their own ultimate interests. This is because every time "the people" are brought into politics, the smooth workings of the skein of interests are disturbed.

Indeed, the prevalence of ideology in contemporary societies is a manifestation of the powerful democratic current that has been growing throughout the world ever since the revolutions at the end of the eighteenth century, as Alexis de Tocqueville noted. Ruling classes would love to tend their interests and take care of the people in the kind of closed-off environment characteristic of bank boardrooms. Bankers loathe democracy because they regard the interests of money policy as so complex that only trained professionals motivated by the highest concerns should deal with them. Democratic interference, such as, for example, a President decreeing protectionist measures to satisfy discontent in some domestic industry, appalls these bankers with their grave responsibilities. Every ideological current, however repulsive, has a mass basis in some segment of the population. Interest politics are always elitist—corporate and bureaucratic officials always like to do their jobs quietly without outside interference. Ideological politics, whether of the left, right, or center, are always democratic in that they necessarily involve major segments of the general population.

Ideology is the door through which the people enter the closed rooms of the realm of interests. That such periodic entry has more often than not ultimately resulted in just further serving the realm of interests should not be surprising. Challenged by such democratic invasions of their privacy, interests counterattack and emerge stronger than before. Or they finally come to realize that the leader who invoked the power of the people to ride roughshod over them actually did so out of a stronger commitment to them than to his constituencies. Nevertheless, while the end result may be satisfying to the interests, the exercise of democracy always disturbs them because next time they might not come off so well. All interests surround themselves with mystification so as to preclude external democratic interference. The kind of mystification bankers always used to ensure their privacy is also used by specialists in material or organizational technology. "Complex" is one of their favorite words. While things are certainly very complex in contemporary society, the constant invocation of that word is also designed to seal them off from scrutiny.

Elites, the people at the managerial level of organizations, always try to turn all politics into matters of interests. Executives by and large would prefer to have it this way too, but trouble periodically forces them to make new policies. Once this occurs, they are forced to become ideological and, thus, democratic. Visionary leaders are the most ideological and democratic of all, and it is they who most offend their elites. Mao Tse-tung did so in the Cultural Revolution when he called on the students and the soldiers, through ideological appeals, to help him to remove from power an entire skein of interests he felt was injurious to the Chinese Revolution. Roosevelt never went so far as Mao, but his visions offended the elites of America while appealing to widespread sections of the population. After Roosevelt's death, the elites quickly mounted a counterattack.

SECURITY AND THE DEMOCRATIC ORIGINS OF IMPERIALISM

The ideological currents in America that relate to its foreign policy from the end of World War II to the present do not relate directly either to the material interests of people or to the social quality of life. They relate to matters of order, security, and justice. When the United States became an empire at the close of World War II, foreign affairs assumed a very large place in the political minds of Americans. The ideologies propounded to justify the empire did not promise the people booty from foreign exploitation, nor did they suggest that the quality of neighborhood life would be improved by foreign aid to Nepal. Ideological appeals

were put entirely in terms of the dire consequences for America of world
chaos, the threats from foreign aggressors, and the chance to implement
American ideals in the benighted parts of the world. These appeals,
beginning with Rooseveltian interventionism and going down to Nixon's
new China policy, all found resonance among substantial segments of the
American population. In fact, if Roosevelt had not gone to "the people"
with his foreign policy ideals, it is doubtful that they could have been
implemented, since so many powerful officials were dubious about them.
Roosevelt was a master politician and well knew the various American
political constituencies. His power to command and coordinate his bureaucracies often weakened, but never his popularity with the electorate.

Roosevelt's vision of the new world order was an extension of his New
Deal philosophy. The core of that philosophy was that only big, benign,
and professional government could assure the people order, security, and
justice. Since he was not primarily oriented toward pushing business
growth, he incurred the wrath of the business community. He was not
concerned about such social quality-of-life issues as civil rights, which
allowed him to coexist serenely with Southern racists whose support he
needed in Congress. The Depression had rent the social fabric of order,
and fascism was threatening America's security. Roosevelt believed that
only a Pax Americana could give America the domestic security without
which the society could neither grow nor live adequately. While the in-
securities created by the Depression helped to give Roosevelt support for
his larger foreign schemes, the decisive factor was the war itself.

The events that led up to both world wars dramatically revealed to the
American people that their security, once believed to be assured by
continental isolation, was mortally threatened. In World War I, Germany's campaign of unrestricted submarine warfare threatened to give it
naval supremacy in the Atlantic. Americans did not want to get involved
in the war until the Kaiser appeared intent on threatening their continental security, not just with submarines but through plots in Mexico. World
War II had a much more dramatic beginning for America—Pearl Harbor. Again it was a powerful foreign navy that struck at the United
States. Even if Hitler had not declared war against America, America
would soon have joined the European part of the war. Nazi submarines
were seeking dominance in the Atlantic, just as the Kaiser's submarines
had tried to do. Pearl Harbor wrecked isolationist ideology overnight, although isolationist interests remained to reassert themselves after the end
of the war. What the isolationists did not realize was that their position
depended on the assumption that American security was inviolable. Between the outbreak of the European war and Pearl Harbor, Roosevelt
undoubtedly prayed for some dramatic demonstration that this was not
so, and his prayers were answered. It is a common phenomenon that

when one nation attacks another, the people of the attacked nation are instantly galvanized into action for defense. Elite planners, who always underestimate the power of ideology, usually fail to understand this. Lyndon Johnson never conceived that United States air attacks against North Vietnam, in his view a "raggedy-ass third-rate country," would provoke the most heroic and sustained resistance against American imperialism in modern history. Japanese and German blitzkrieg planners thought that by the time lumbering America got effectively into the act, they would have consolidated their gains and could, with expectations of success, offer the Americans a deal. True, France in 1939 did not so respond, unlike France in 1914. But the popular sentiment was there. What was missing was the ideological leadership to ignite the spark of resistance. Many French military leaders secretly sympathized with Hitler, and the politicians were too deep in their own realm of interest politics to act as leaders. Roosevelt was no Daladier, and while the fires at Pearl Harbor were still smoldering, he took command.

The defense of the French Revolution at Valmy should have demonstrated once and for all that foreign aggression against the territory of a democratic country will provoke democratic resistance. A democratic state is one in which ideological policies that purport to act by, for, and through the people prevail. France in 1792 was a democratic state, but the other European countries, which Napoleon's French arms easily conquered, were so feudal that even the elitist Prussians later decided to introduce popular reforms to produce greater national solidarity. Soviet Russia, for all of Stalin's brutalities, was a state with popular support, and its people defended it with the greatest popular heroism of the Second World War. America was a democratic state by tradition, and its democracy was further enhanced by the democratic politics of Roosevelt. The attack by the fascists in 1941 was a case of dictatorship attacking democracy.

Perhaps this widely held sense of national security in danger is a manifestation of nationalism—*"la patrie en danger,"* as the French have said for almost two hundred years. When a foreigner attacks the native soil, people generally see themselves in national terms and offer resistance. Pearl Harbor produced a nationalistic reaction in America. Once nationalism was aroused, so was consciousness of national security as a problem and of foreign affairs in general. Roosevelt made astute use of the ideological sentiments of nationalism aroused by Pearl Harbor to elaborate an ideology of imperialism through which he promised Americans order, security, and justice. Napoleon did the same with French nationalism, turning it into a grand imperial design to create a French Empire rivaling or supplanting that of Britain.

Roosevelt made imperialism into a powerful ideological current. He grafted his vision of "one world" onto his New Dealism, so that, by and large, the constituencies that supported his domestic New Deal programs also supported his schemes for a new world order. It should not be surprising that my theoretical argumentation has led to a notion of the democratic origins of imperialism. Ordinary people throughout America wanted, above all, a secure world, and the idea of one world forever without war had appeal for them. Just as the New Deal brought "social security" to America, so "one world" would bring political security to the entire world. No one then, not even communists, called it imperialism. In most people's minds, imperialism meant the building of colonial empires or, for those in the Marxist tradition, the export of capital by industrialized countries to backward ones for purposes of exploitation. Roosevelt was anticolonial and showed little expansionist interest in improving America's business opportunities abroad. Yet soon after his death, "one world" turned into the "free world," which communists regarded as the capitalist camp headed by America to seek world domination, and its advocates saw as free countries organizing themselves under American leadership for defense against Russian communist expansion and subversion. While Roosevelt was still alive, labor unions, which had been in the forefront of democratic militancy during the 1930s, were enthusiastic supporters of his world order. The split with Russia also split labor, and anticommunist labor became one of the chief bulwarks of Washington's free world policies.

People in the Hobson-Lenin tradition see imperialism as a political extension of expansionism. But if the political process that led to the creation of an American-dominated free world was American imperialism, then expansionism cannot be considered its prime cause. The prime cause for American imperialism was an immensely powerful American government motivated by New Deal ideology, which in its domestic and international forms spoke to the interests and aspirations for security of the American people, particularly its working classes. Imperialism meant big government, eventually big armies, and taxing the corporations to pay for it all, programs that appealed to the working classes. Particularly after the break with Russia, expansionist business realized that imperialism, far from interfering with the realm of private interests, actually served those interests by doing what they could not do themselves: once again rallying to the capitalist system people who had fallen away from it because of the Depression. Anticommunism was the indispensable ingredient for bridging the chasm between the realm of ideology and the realm of interests. From the capitalist point of view, imperialism was initially attractive not because it offered new avenues for expansion but because it offered security. The security Roosevelt's "one world"-ism offered was harder for the capitalists to accept because it promised to rally people to the system without providing any clearcut defense against the system's enemies. Anticommunism took care of that, and when a large part of American labor began to trumpet the anticommunist cause, business was finally convinced that imperialism could become a very good thing indeed.

These observations on the democratic origins of imperialism suggest further theoretical propositions. The realm of interests is marked by the tendency toward stability and routine, whereas the realm of ideology is marked by constant change arising from crisis, challenge, and opportunity. Lord Keynes noted that the basic tendency of all modern capitalist economies is toward stagnation. When economic stagnation leads to less than full employment, the government as the holder of supreme power must give the economic system the necessary stimulus to rekindle growth. Technically, it does this by deficit spending, which increases aggregate demand, which in turn stimulates business, a process that eventually redresses the fiscal imbalance produced by deficit spending. If the natural tendency of economic interests is to stagnate, this is even more true of political interests. The purpose of deficit spending is to get people once again to participate in the economy by spending through households. The huge public debt that results from deficit spending lashes people so tightly to the system that they have to participate whether they want to or not. In many peasant societies, areas of high tenant debt to landlords have often been the least revolutionary, for the bonds between peasant and landlord are so tight and intricate that the peasant sees revolution as meaning frightful sacrifice. Revolutions are made by those who have nothing left to lose. One of the main purposes of deficit spending and public indebtedness is to reattach alienated classes to the economic system. That this will also stimulate economic growth was Keynes's unique insight. In the more purely political arena, the purpose of any new policy is not just to get things moving again toward the achievement of goals, but to do so by rallying people to put forth a new kind of effort, which the ordinary workings of the realm of interests cannot do, not least because of their inherent tendency toward stagnation. I propose that the imperialism envisioned by Roosevelt and his presidential successors was to forge bonds between the realm of interests and vast classes of people throughout America and the world who, by becoming alienated from those interests, were beginning to tread the path of revolution. The Depression had shown that the realm of interests no longer was able to satisfy working people's aspirations for a decent material life. The Second World War had shown that existing interests were unable to safeguard their security, and that chaos had become so widespread that the interests themselves were endangered. Imperialism spoke eloquently to the demand for security on the part of both the people and the interests, but in doing so, demonstrated to the interests that the people could once again be rallied. They, of course, were already impressed by how remarkably the war itself had rallied the rebellious working classes. Once imperialism had rallied the discontented, selling the interests the New Deal's economic policies was less difficult. Business was willing to pay to stop revolution, but became eager to do so when further convinced that their spending would also eventually mean greater profits.

This leads to a further proposition: that imperialism is the child of revolution. Revolution is the world-wide process whereby whole classes of working people become alienated from the existing interests, generate new ideologies and organizations aimed at them, and seek power through their destruction, transformation, or replacement. Like revolution, democracy is not a static state but a process, the growing power of the people. While war has again and again been used by ruling interests to deflect revolutionary pressures, it has also proven to be a powerful stimulus to the revolutionary process. Economic crisis has had the same effect. Without the Depression, the New Deal would never have come into being. Without World War II, American imperialism would never have arisen. The American government of the 1930s and 1940s, symbolized by Roosevelt himself, was dominated by men from the higher social classes, who were obsessed by problems of order, security, and justice. They believed that unless those problems were resolved, the people at home and abroad would rise in revolutionary wrath. By 1945, many of them had come to believe that a new world order was the only guarantee against chaos followed by revolution. Wilson thought so too in 1919, as did Napoleon, a product of the stability-seeking Thermidorians, who fought for empire as a way out of the troubles within France. But not Mao Tse-tung of China, who as a true revolutionary wanted the revolution to go on and on and on *within* China itself, and always vetoed any export of it. Already in the 1930s, Roosevelt was prepared to make far-reaching concessions to revolutionary demands, particularly from the militant labor unions, in the larger hope of re-establishing order and security. In 1945, he was equally prepared to make such concessions to international revolutionary forces, notably Russia, for similar reasons. The concessions to Russia were too much for America's ruling interests to swallow, but their spirit of corporate liberalism made them finally realize that unless they could rally those classes lost through revolutionary alienation, they might lose everything. It was not Roosevelt's vision that they repudiated, just his policy toward Russia.

The "material" basis for the realm of ideology rests in the popular social forces that seek power at the expense of interests. Whether rebellious, radical, or revolutionary, all popular social forces hostile to interests form a source of power. Ideology, whether just a set of political slogans or a systematically worked out set of ideas, is the instrument whereby these social forces are mobilized for political action. That America's rulers since Roosevelt have used the realm of ideology to reconcile the popular forces of democracy and revolution to the interests shows the ideology to have been much more than an opiate for the people. That ideology and the popular force behind it was used to generate an American empire which the interests alone could never have achieved. Nor is it correct to say that revolution was deflected into imperialist directions. The fact is that the people supported the new imperialism for essentially the same reasons that the people of France supported Napoleon's conquests in Europe—partly out of nationalism but more out of a sense of revolutionary mission.

I speak of the realm of ideology because it also is a real "material" entity. Marxists might call it the state or the superstructure, but that notion has led to some erroneous conclusions, namely, that bureaucracies are superstructural whereas corporations are substructural. In fact, both bureaucracies and corporations (in addition to many other organizations in society) constitute interests. In socialist countries, the realm of ideology is the party (though many parties have turned into bodies of interests). In America, the realm of ideology is within the government and centers on its apex. Ideology generates organizations, which then join the realm of interests, a transition generally recognizable in quantum budget increases. Like all the old interests, these newer ones oppose the pressure for change that constantly emanates from the realm of ideology. The idea of a realm of ideology that physically includes little more than the White House may seem absurd, but, as this book seeks to show, immense power of a unique non-interest sort resides there.

Once a realm of ideology has arisen within the state, it persists even when the ideology that gave birth to it has turned into ritual dogma no longer fed by social forces. Or often it generates new ideologies which have relevance only within the state. This has happened in both America and Russia where a power-oriented geopolitics has become the dominant foreign policy ideology within the state, used by those in the bureaucracy but little understood beyond the ramparts of government. Institutions have an amazing persistence even when their original reason for existing has vanished. This also applies to the realm of ideology, which is ideology institutionalized.

However, this book maintains that all ideology ultimately springs from popular social forces—a notion directly at variance with Marx. For Marx, ideology was the belief system rulers used to delude the ruled into acquiescing in their domination. Revolutionaries were to provide the ruled with theory, the scientific exposition of the truth of their real condition. But Marx wrote at a time when religion and science were two giant protagonists, and science seemed inevitably on the side of revolution. Since then religion has declined, science has become the tool of interests capable of using it, and revolution the chief generator of spiritual belief systems. While Marx, were he alive, would be mortified to see that Marxism has become a kind of revolutionary religion, it is that phenomenon which explains why, in general usage, ideology has come to designate all kinds of belief systems deriving from social forces put to political use.

General usage considers fascism and nationalism ideologies as well as socialism and Marxism. Fascism and nationalism both meet the criteria set forth in this book for ideologies: they spring from popular social forces and have shown extraordinary capacity for generating power at executive levels of the state, unlike internationalism, whose social roots are weak and whose capacity to capture executive power is not much stronger. While all fascisms are nationalist, not all nationalisms are fascist, the difference depending on whether nationalism is prepared to collaborate with revolutionary forces for the acquisition of power. Fascism generally is fiercely counterrevolutionary. But both differ from socialist and Marxist ideologies in their inferior capacity to generate political organizations. Though there have been fascist and nationalist parties, by and large, these have been unstable and ineffective compared to the combat party of the communist type or the bureaucratic party of the social democratic type. Fascist and nationalist ideologies often have much broader appeal than leftist ideologies—appealing to the sentiments of middle and lower middle classes angry at their condition of life and fearful of external and internal enemies. It is that ability to tap a broad mass base that allows them to move directly into executive power. They soon discover, however, that their inferior organizational capabilities leave them with little more than a *führerprinzip*, the doctrine that social forces are directly expressed through some extraordinary leader. That socialist and democratic societies are not immune from such tendencies is quite apparent by now, though in the former the party remains and in the latter the interests. That prevents the kind of crises through which fascist and many nationalist regimes gyrate as they try to escape from incessant internal contradictions. Leftist ideologies of the socialist or Marxist type have a systematic quality which is expressed in some form of organization, a quality that interests naturally share as institutions.

INTERESTS AGAINST IDEOLOGY

By giving Roosevelt his fourth term in 1944, the American electorate did more than signify acceptance of the United Nations. It reaffirmed a progressive New Deal philosophy widely regarded as crypto-revolutionary by many conservatives. In 1944 it was already clear that the war would soon end and that New Dealism would be the dominant ideology of the postwar period. The New Deal probably saved American capitalism by preventing the labor-business struggles of the Depression from turning into class war. But it did so with an ideology which, in the eyes of people of the time, was more leftist than centrist. In retrospect, one can say that in 1944 the American electorate voted for imperialism. In subsequent years they would do this again and again, not because they were hoodwinked by labor fakers or reactionaries in liberal clothing, but because they perceived American imperialism as a progressive force, which would bring benefit to themselves and to the world as a whole. Both during the Depression and during the war, the American people had an overriding desire for security—security of employment and income and security from external attack. They wanted security to overcome the miasma of fear that had come over the country after the euphoria of the 1920s. They looked to government guided by the progressive values of social welfare to provide this security, and they looked equally to government to provide such military power that never again would a Hitler or a Tojo threaten world peace. Because of the Depression and the war, the American electorate swung to the left. Thus, when Roosevelt went to them to secure a mandate for his postwar plans, his vision had a populist and progressive aura to it. Like Wilson, the progressive quality of his vision assured him world-wide support and acclaim, regardless of what the interests thought of it.

Whatever the end result of American imperialism, its origins were democratic. But what was to become the real imperialism in the postwar years was not a simple expansion of Roosevelt's vision, but the product of a struggle with two other major ideological currents springing from the realm of interests. These two currents, which I call internationalism and nationalism, have roots deep in American history and persist to the present time. They are also rooted in basic American interests, particularly economic. Prior to 1945, as universalism and isolationism, they sought to restrain Roosevelt's flights of vision and channel presidential policy into more conventional directions. But once the war was over, they fought to replace Roosevelt's vision with policies of their own.

At the beginning of Part I, I noted three great events at the end of World War II which shaped the postwar world: the founding of the United Nations, the re-establishment of an international monetary system and world bank, and the development of atomic weapons. While not so intended, each of these events addressed itself to the key concern of one of the three currents. For the current that was to flow out of Roosevelt's vision, the establishment of the United Nations promised a new world of peace, security, and progress, a New Deal on a world-wide scale. The structures emerging from Bretton Woods addressed themselves to the key concern of the universalist current: free trade fueled by sound money. And the atomic bomb eventually became a symbol of the nationalist and isolationist obsession with military power. Actually, Roosevelt himself expressed all three currents. He was not a starry-eyed internationalist willing to disarm America, but a hardheaded military thinker devoted to the notion of American military power serving American interests—he was always interested in military bases. Although not adept at handling intricate economic problems, his Eastern patrician heritage made him sympathetic to the world trade concerns of Wall Street. And his growing stature as the leader of the free and the friend of the poor did as much as anything to make the United Nations into something above and beyond the League of Nations. Roosevelt was full of contradictions, which made him a superb politician. They sprang not so much from his pliant personality as from the facts of American political life.

UNIVERSALISM OR INTERNATIONALISM

The universalist current ran strong in the State Department, the agency of American government traditionally close to international business. It was the obvious agency to concern itself with postwar planning, and, as a bureaucracy with a long history, it did so from the perspective of its own interests. The main business of the State Department was, in fact, business. The main duties of its vast diplomatic network, particularly its consular corps, were to aid American businessmen in their dealings with foreign governments. Since the time of John Hay, the predominant ideological current governing the State Department was an "open door" policy, a commitment to free trade and protection of American property and businessmen in foreign countries. The State Department feared that postwar economic chaos could lead to a repetition of what happened after World War I: revolution·followed by fascism and war. Cordell Hull, as Secretary of State, regarded the United Nations as a political instrument which, by universality of membership, could compel members to adopt the principles of free trade and respect for property. Free trade, fueled by loans from the prosperous United States, could revive the devastated economies and thereby provide the firmest guarantee against new troubles. Peace would be the product of universally accepted free trade. The hope was entertained that even Bolshevik Russia might depart from its rigid hostility to free trade practices and thereby gradually rejoin the world community.

Free trade versus protectionism was an old issue in American politics, and the State Department traditionally stood on the side of free trade. The State Department has always been the most elitist governmental agency (its foreign service officers were recruited largely from graduates of Ivy League schools), and it is not surprising that it took its cues from the most elitist segment of American business, the Eastern Establishment. It was also the most internationally minded bureaucracy in the government. Only the State Department felt that it really understood how much America was intertwined with larger world systems, and within America only the Eastern Establishment with its far-flung business interests abroad was directly involved in the world scene.

The primary concern of the Eastern business establishment was making and keeping money on a grand scale through investments and trade that covered the world. Built into this basic commitment to money were a series of attitudes arising out of two centuries of practical experience. The Eastern Establishment loathed war and revolution. War destroyed property and increased the power of governments. Revolution was a mortal threat to property. The State Department traditionally reflected both of these attitudes. In its postwar planning, the assurance of peace was, next to free trade, its major concern. On the other hand, the State Department also held some of the most ferocious anticommunist views in government, reflected by many of its ambassadors. The coincidence of these two attitudes was manifested in State Department policies toward the Vichy government and in the person of the United States Ambassador to Vichy, William Leahy. The State Department maintained friendly ties with Vichy partly to prevent the war from spreading over the rest of France and the French Empire and partly out of instinctive support for a conservative, anticommunist regime determined to prevent Bolshevism from arising in France. It opposed de Gaulle because he wanted to drag the French Empire back into the war and create the kind of chaos that would permit the Communists to resurrect themselves.

The State Department was intellectually the heir of the Hamiltonian tradition that regarded government, particularly foreign policy, as too intricate a matter to be entrusted to the ignorant masses. How could the people be relied on to make judicious judgments about something so complex as international monetary policy? The State Department's elitism did not arise from a reactionary fear of the masses but from the comfortable conviction of men who, like bankers and financiers, held a monopoly of knowledge about the ethereal world of international relations. Its universalism was the reflection of a basic reality, that of the world market system. For two centuries, capitalism, spearheaded by Great Britain, had woven a nexus of economic and political interests spanning the entire world, on which all nations were dependent to one degree or another. The energizing force of this world market system was world trade, which, of course, was monopolized by the advanced and civilized nations. Trade brought profits to national enterprises and the raw materials which an expanding capitalism needed. While America did not approve wholeheartedly of the British Empire as the political expression of the world market system, it was regarded as irreplaceable for the preservation of that system. The pound sterling was the symbol both of the world market system as the leading reserve currency and of the British Empire by virtue of its Englishness. The British Empire was the closest thing to a world order since the Roman Empire. If World War II weakened Great Britain's ability to maintain that empire, this did not mean and should not mean that the world order too should disappear. Universalism was a further elaboration of the world order which the British Empire did most to bring about in the modern world and for the maintenance and further development of which America was to assume the guiding role in the post-1945 world.

Cordell Hull's universalism was an expression of the realm of interests. The interests were the international economy which for two centuries had been under the control of Englishmen and Americans. The internationalists saw both world wars as attempts by ferocious nationalisms to destroy the international economy. Conversely, they regarded the destruction of the international economy as the main cause for the rise of fascism, Bolshevism, and other barbaric political forms. The Bolsheviks took people's property away and the Nazis threatened to undo the world market system. While the Anglo-American elites exhibited natural tendencies to seek accommodations with both in order to avoid war, the Bolshevik and the Fascist/Nazi dangers had to be resisted when they came too close to the core of the international economic system. Hullian universalism was quite different from the American imperialism of the postwar period. It was politically and economically conservative. It wanted to restore what was and do as little new as possible. What had to be restored above all else was the world market system. If this was done, the Anglo-American business elite would have its power reaffirmed and, as the best custodian of a peaceful world order, could then do what was necessary to improve mankind's lot and prevent new barbarisms from arising. The State Department believed that if the world could be brought back to where it was before the turn of the century, before an ambitious Kaiser Wilhelm threatened its peace and security, the greatest good for the greatest number would be vouchsafed.

The insulated atmosphere of the State Department, like that of the great international banking offices, made it easy for them to think in terms of the logic of international relations and difficult for them to understand the popular furor which produced wars and revolutions. But visionary ideologies and innovative policies do not arise out of the realm of interests. Conservatism in the modern world means nothing more than a commitment to certain existing interests. Attempts to portray it as a moral or visionary force have failed for the simple reason that it can never conjure up hope and anticipation in people's minds. Hullian universalism would have liked to see a postwar world where governments came back into the hands of responsible conservatives (as eventually happened in the former enemy nations with Adenauer, Yoshida, and De Gasperi), where outlaw nations like Russia assumed international responsibilities by recognizing the obligations of participation in the world market system, and where the small and poor nations took the sensible path of slow, deliberate efforts toward improving their lot.

Universalism was, in essence, a benign, conservative internationalism. It flourished during World War II through close Anglo-American cooperation for the preservation of the existing world order. It was not nationalistic, and was willing to make major sacrifices in the area of national sovereignty. That this was possible without sacrificing national identity was due to the overriding fact that in the eyes of the universalists the English-speaking world was the world itself. No language was more widely spoken than English. Through the British Empire and America's far-flung private activities (businessmen, missionaries, educators), Anglo-American culture had become the predominant world culture, just as Roman culture had covered the known Western world two thousand years before. Above all, nowhere in the world could one find cultivated men with as deep a sense of moral responsibility as in London and the eastern seaboard of the United States. Moreover, these men had access to the greatest power in the world, the command over wealth. It seemed natural that the American and British worlds should eventually coalesce in an English-speaking union in which both would surrender archaic notions of sovereignty to the interests of a peaceful new world order.

The universalists, like all conservatives, were hostile to huge governmental power and above all to militarism. Like the Marxists, they believed that capitalism knew no boundaries. They thought that power was best invested in a class of wealthy, educated, and propertied men who had been taught responsibility in the finest schools. Government was to be their instrument, in which they served often at cost to themselves. Huge bureaucracies and huge armies would only produce the barbaric monstrosities of Nazi Germany and Bolshevik Russia. The universalist conservatives mistrusted the state as an irrational force. From it sprang lust for power and, above all, the drive toward war, which of all policies in government the conservatives most opposed. They tried to stem the drive toward war until it was inevitable, and during the war they tried to plan for postwar structures that would make a new war impossible. The universalist conservatives instinctively sympathized with Chamberlain's efforts to avoid war by appeasing Hitler. Roosevelt, as a sometime universalist, actively supported his efforts to settle the Czech crisis in 1938. The basic concern of the universalist conservatives was stability, and nothing was more conducive to stability than peace. The conservatives abhorred revolution, but they also abhorred war. Therefore, *both* Nazi Germany and Bolshevik Russia were abominations in their eyes. Yet if Germany ceased making war against other nations and Russia refrained from exporting revolution, there was no reason one could not coexist with them. It was regrettable that the German and Russian peoples allowed themselves to be governed by barbarians, but if they would just leave other people alone, there was no reason to make war against them.

This theoretical proposition suggests that conservative universalism, inclined toward a world order dominated by Anglo-American capital, was also committed to peace and to peaceful coexistence. Free, unfettered trade fueled by a stable international monetary system was the indispensable basis for any kind of rational world order. War as much as revolution was the deadly enemy of trade. Peace assured stability and stability was the necessary prerequisite for the accumulation and preservation of wealth. Peace was to be preserved at all costs except where the threat became mortal.

The universalist current, as the world view of international business, retained its power during the postwar years. It fueled postwar economic reconstruction of Europe, foreign aid to poor nations, and participation in United Nations activities, and argued for peaceful coexistence with Russia. It was not accidental that the breakthrough to peacful coexistence with Russia came under the conservative Eisenhower and that the breakthrough to China came under Nixon. Once Russia and China opened their iron and bamboo curtains respectively, the conservatives were more ready than others to espouse peaceful coexistence. While the right-wing military opposed it and the ideological liberals (like organized labor) shrank back, the conservatives made the move. In both Eisenhower's approach to Russia and Nixon's approach to China and Russia, trade played a major role. Peaceful coexistence could be meaningful only if Russia and China agreed to join the world market system. If they did, the conservatives foresaw that conservatizing forces would set in in both countries. The more these militantly revolutionary countries were involved in world trade, the more their barbaric regimes would be civilized under the weight of international responsibility. It would be too much to hope that they would once again accept the principle of private property, but accepting foreign investment was a step in the right direction.

Universalism was a World War II expression of capitalist conservatism. As the cold war made "one world" meaningless, universalism took on more modest postures. It advocated greater unity within the "free world," fought against trade barriers, supported internationalist programs. The conservatives eagerly joined the anticommunist crusade and needed little convincing that the Russians were intent on expanding Russian national power, as well as revolutionary communism, throughout the world. But they never lost their conviction that peace was best for profits, and it mattered little from which side of the Iron Curtain profits came. When the Russian threat was proclaimed contained, they were the first to initiate steps toward peaceful and profitable coexistence.

It was Joseph Schumpeter who, just prior to World War I, made a fundamental distinction between expansionism and imperialism. He argued for the peaceful nature of expansionist capitalism but warned of the warlike nature of imperialism, which emanated from the state. He regarded the state as the irrational principle par excellence, a relic from bygone days, a vestige of man's barbaric nature.

It was also during the first decade of the twentieth century that orthodox Marxists (like Lenin) argued with revisionist Marxists (like the Austrian Social-Democrat Rudolf Hilferding) about the role of "finance capital." Hilferding argued that the realm of money (banks, for example) constituted a unique power of its own. Lenin vehemently attacked this notion as undermining Marxism itself. Marxism taught that power sprang from production, and that money stood in relation to production as the state stood in relation to the ruling class—it was production's instrument wielded in its interests. Yet however much Marxists have tried to defend the labor theory of value (a theory of political economy which asserts that power derives from production, bourgeois economics has gone merrily and productively along developing structures of thought showing that the economy has a life and substance of its own fueled by production but not determined by it. Whatever the theoretical merits of the arguments on either side, they had important implications for political action. Finance capital theories tended to make the world of the economy a sealed entity which generated contradictions but seemed impervious to political action. Orthodox Marxism, which insisted on the primacy of labor and production as a source of power, opened the way for political action. Thus, if the industrial workers could be organized by a revolutionary party, they could pose a threat to the economy. Finance capital arguments, on the other hand, in line with classical economic thinking, presumed that movements within the economy depended on factors involving the society and even the world as a whole.

It is not accidental that the earlier debate on finance capital and the present smaller debate among radicals came about when the issues of free trade versus protection were being fought over in Europe and America. Around the turn of the century, a hundred years of movement toward free world trade was threatened by nationalism using governmental policy to favor domestic industry. Until 1914, international organizations made astounding progress. Yet at the same time a powerful countercurrent materialized, particularly in Germany and America, which sought tariff protections for rapidly developing but still fragile domestic industries. The world market system was gravely weakened by World War I, but with American help, re-emerged in the 1920s. It collapsed with the Great Depression, but Bretton Woods began the process of restoring it. From 1945 until the recent present, trade barriers were falling and international business, particularly in the form of multinational corporations, was making great strides. Less powerful nations like Japan and Britain put up protectionist walls, but the United States, the central economy of the world capitalist system, adhered to free trade principles. Now as the world monetary system is crumbling, the United States is moving toward more protectionist practices. If the protectionist wave should now reach global proportions, the world market system would disintegrate, and world trade could undergo severe convulsions, as it did in the 1930s. The system of multinational corporations is already threatened by seizures in Third World countries, but if the key countries themselves turn protectionist, then a Ford or General Motors plant in Germany or Britain would be multinational in name only. The world market system would, thus, revert to a network of national capitalisms relating to each other like sovereign nations.

The conservative universalist current has been primarily the expression of the Anglo-American view of the world market system. The orthodox Marxist view denies that there is any fundamental contradiction between productive and finance capital. Gigantic manufacturing corporations show the same tendency toward internationalism (multinational affiliations) as great banking houses, Marxists would argue. Yet the drive for protectionism obviously emanates from major sectors of the economy. In some instances, it can be explained as the effort by the government to protect marginal enterprises, such as textiles, from more efficient foreign competition. Yet in Japan, virtually the entire business class has supported the protectionist stance of the government. The purpose of protectionism is to allow Japanese manufacturing to develop rapidly from a low base without being swept aside or incorporated by more advanced Western enterprises. That gigantic American manufacturing enterprises are internationally minded is evident. But that does not preclude them from switching to a protectionist stance if they believe themselves threatened by external competition, as is now happening in the American steel industry, for example. Naturally, the more involved a corporation is in the international system, the more difficult it is for it to switch from internationalism to nationalism. This is most true for America's great financial institutions. The United States has long served as a capital market for the world, and the domino effect of a global protectionist wave could mean catastrophe. Government can always bail out manufacturing concerns like Lockheed, but it can do little to sustain the major financial institutions if they are threatened with disaster.

There is a spectrum of capitalist economic institutions ranging from local to national to global. In the advanced capitalist countries, small business has ceased to be a major factor in the economy. Thus, in effect, the spectrum ranges from national to international. Defense industries are eminently national, and as captive to the government are not affected greatly by changes in the world market system. In America, the oil companies have far-flung international interests, but the corporations by and large remain nationalistically American. The auto companies have been turning multinational, but their biggest market is still within the United States. The great New York brokerage firms are probably the most internationally involved and international in character of American economic institutions. American business, since the end of World War II, has acquired a powerful stake in the world market system, through direct investments and export and import of products, as a capital market and source of technology. If banks, as Fitch and Oppenheimer argue,[1] have acquired vast new powers over corporations turning into conglomerates, this may or may not mean a new primacy of finance capital. What it does mean is that the banks have become even more deeply involved in the international economic system by virtue of the fact that banks have traditionally been the chief participants in that system.

The universalist current emanating from the State Department during World War II initially reflected the concerns of the Eastern business establishment, although it had roots in the free trade political tradition. In many ways, universalism anticipated the great internationalization of the American economy following the end of the war.

If universalism expressed the world view of international business, then a proposition follows from the above argumentation: that United States business, as it moved further toward international involvement, became more committed to stability, peace, and coexistence.

While universalism grew out of a conservatism that abhorred war, chaos, and upheaval, the State Department also reflected the much better known hostility of all business, national or international, toward attacks on private property. Business was and remains anticommunist. For decades, the State Department favored conservative regimes which guaranteed property and free trade. Whether the London Poles, the Vichy regime, Trujillo in the Dominican Republic, the South African apartheid

[1] Robert Fitch and Mary Oppenheimer, "Who Rules the Corporations?"

regimes, or Franco, the State Department's rationale for its support has been simple: however deplorable their internal policies, they all maintain their international obligations, particularly toward United States business. But, as we shall see, traditional business anticommunism was different from the ideological anticommunism of the American right. Business and State Department anticommunism was practical. If revolutionaries threatened property, they should be opposed with whatever means were available, unless the means were disproportionate to the gains or unless violence would ensue that could threaten far more than originally was threatened. Thus, it was proper to try to remove Fidel from power in Cuba, but not if it threatened a war with Russia. This variety of anticommunism helped to bring business in line with the cold war but was not the most important source of cold war anticommunism.

ISOLATIONISM OR NATIONALISM

The isolationist current was opposed to universalism. On the surface, it seemed to imply doctrines that the United States should not get involved in the wars of other nations unless directly attacked. Historically, it appeared to derive from one of George Washington's basic principles of foreign policy, that the new United States must avoid "entangling alliances." In fact, isolationism was a form of American nationalism clearly expressed in its favorite slogan: America first.

Much has been written on the diverse interests and attitudes isolationism represented. Yet, as James MacGregor Burns wrote, what was common to all isolationists was the view "defense, yes; aid to the Allies, perhaps; but foreign wars—never."[2] The isolationists, except for their transient left-wing fringe, believed in American military power. Their congressional representatives voted eagerly for defense build-ups and displayed a typically nationalist admiration for the flag propped up by guns. They believed fervently that America should defend its interests by military force where threatened. Since those interests were obvious in Asia and Latin America, they were more prepared to challenge Japanese expansionism than that of Germany in Europe, and Mexico's nationalization of United States-owned oil companies aroused an angry furor. What they could support in Roosevelt was his espousal of a strong navy, but they distrusted the uses to which he was going to put American military power. The key issue of debate was the European war.

The isolationists were anti-imperialist, which, in the 1930s and 1940s, meant being against the *only* world imperialism of the time, the British Empire. They regarded it as a global conspiracy on the part of vast finan-

[2] James MacGregor Burns, *Roosevelt: The Soldier of Freedom*, p. 42.

cial interests centered in London abetted by similar interests in New York to dominate the world economy. The ultimate aim of Britain, they believed, was to create a world economic and political monopoly which would stifle the natural expansionist desires of late-comer powers, such as America. The isolationists were indeed expansionists, the true heirs of "manifest destiny." They saw a glorious future for America beyond its borders, but not particularly in Europe or Africa or Western Asia. They looked westward to East Asia and southward to Latin America. They believed in laissez-faire capitalism and were hostile to big government, whose only result could be to suppress freedom, the natural right of every individual to deploy his enterprise in the pursuit of his own interests. They believed in the individual, particularly the individual who decided to rise above the masses by acquiring wealth. They had a classical commitment to freedom, to a society subject only to minimal governance. Above all, they saw themselves as Americans, a definite, distinct, and proud nationality with a mission in the world. American, in the understanding of the day, meant white, Protestant, and male.

One can get a sense of the social nature of the isolationists by looking at the Americans who expanded into the Pacific during the late nineteenth century and on into the twentieth. There were three types: merchants, soldiers, and missionaries. Nowhere else in the world, save in Central America, could one find comparable numbers of such Americans. American traders found lucrative new enterprise in Hawaii, the Philippines, China, and in the interstices left open by other empires. Since the Spanish-American Wars, America had acquired major military bases throughout the Pacific. Missionaries were everywhere in the region preaching more by example than by word the superior nature of American man. Free enterprise in Hawaii showed what honest enterprise could achieve. By the end of the nineteenth century, a few American families, largely of missionary origin, had developed vast sugar and pineapple plantations, recruited Asians to work them, and made immense fortunes. All this occurred under conditions of "freedom" granted to them by the Hawaiian monarchy and then further assured by a beneficent American takeover. Through the Navy, the American military began to develop imperial qualities in the Pacific, most evident in the Philippines, which was run pretty much as a military domain. The effort of the missionaries was ideological, the preaching of Protestant Christianity. Nowhere else in the world did America assume such an ideological role. Europe was regarded as hopelessly corrupt, Latin America as lost to the Catholic Church, and Africa of little interest. Only Asia with its billion heathen seemed within the reach of conversion to Christianity. China, in particular, was the most ardently pursued target for full conversion.

The dreams and visions that the Pacific engendered were not greatly appreciated in the pro-European parts of the American east coast. The westward expansion of the United States was taken for granted, and, of course, America should pursue its interests in the Pacific. But the highly educated men of the Eastern Establishment could not understand the passion which motivated these dreams and visions, and hatreds which arose when they were thwarted. The Pacific symbolized a general American expansionism which in the 1920s appeared to have scored fantastic successes. In 1919, America rejected internationalism, returned to pursue its own narrow interests, and enjoyed an unprecedented boom. By 1930, the boom had collapsed. The expansionists saw the crash of the stock market and the subsequent breakdown of the international monetary system as conspiracies aimed at destroying them. When unions began to organize with the active support of the patrician Roosevelt, the expansionists saw an even greater conspiracy between the mighty of the Eastern Establishment and the communist-inspired labor unions to crush them in the middle. They saw themselves as the real driving force in America, the people who created enterprise and made the wealth which others, bankers and organized labor, then usurped. Expansionism and nationalism were identical in the minds of those who took the isolationist stance prior to 1941; the history of America in the Pacific had forged that identity.

If the nationalists saw expansionism and nationalism as identical, they pretended to see a similar identity between internationalism, communism, and imperialism. The big bankers of Wall Street were internationalist—so were the communists with their Marxist doctrines, and so were the British with their empire. Moreover, the growing alliance between the Roosevelt-led administration and the unions seemed to indicate a real alliance between the forces of international capital and their ostensible enemies, the revolutionary proletarians. All this could only be aimed at capitalism, as the nationalists saw it. The expansionist image of capitalism was that of the National Association of Manufacturers, which saw the corporation, producing and marketing things, and not the banks as the core of free enterprise capitalism. Socialism to them meant monopoly domination of the economy whether by immense finance capital, big government, or communist revolutionaries. When Hitler began to preach that an international conspiracy of capitalists, Jews, and Bolsheviks was trying to crush the expansionist drive of the German nation, many in the United States understood and sympathized. By the late 1930s, the Roosevelt–labor union alliance had expanded to include an emerging British-American alliance to oppose Germany. And after June 22, 1941, the archenemy of mankind, Bolshevik Russia, had joined. The conspiracy became horrifyingly real both domestically and internationally. At home, an Eastern Establishment–dominated administration was colluding with labor unions and Red-sympathizing intellectuals to establish an American socialism. Abroad, an alliance between America, imperial Britain, and Bolshevik Russia was developing against Germany, a country that was nationalist, expansionist, and capitalist in the best sense of the word. A climax was reached in the great lend-lease debates when Roosevelt was ready to turn over a significant number of American warships to Britain, which the isolationists construed as a weakening of American military power, an infringement on American sovereignty, and involvement in a war whose only favorable outcome could be a victory for British international bankers and Russian Bolsheviks.

American nationalism remained isolationist until December 7, 1941. When Japan attacked America, militant nationalism immediately joined the fray. Japan was a welcome enemy for the nationalists. It was a non-white power threatening American interests in the Pacific. It was already at war with America's special responsibility in the Far East, China. It was not at war with Bolshevik Russia, thus precluding Russian-American collaboration in the Far East, and, above all, the Japanese had the effrontery to attack their most admired symbol of American military power, the Navy. Hitler's declaration of war against America completed the picture of an attack on two fronts, and war against both Germany and Japan was accepted by all American nationalists.

Prior to December 7, 1941, the interventionists wanted war in Europe and the isolationists opposed it. War against Japan, however, was acceptable to both. It can be argued that the multifaceted Roosevelt was a nationalist and expansionist in the Far East but an internationalist and imperialist in Europe. Roosevelt was a Navy man, and believed in America's pre-eminent role in East Asia. The war in the Pacific was run along nationalist lines on the American side. Unlike the European theater where America and Britain had to conduct a joint war, the war in the Far East, except for Burma, was a strictly American affair. The Americans carried out their special relationship with China without benefit of British advice, and where, as in Burma, British and American actions came into contact, the relationships were bad, such as those between Stilwell and Mountbatten. Roosevelt easily assumed that British power had been shattered in the Far East and only America was able to oppose Japan. The nationalism of the war against Japan was evident, for example, in the racism that accompanied it. While there was deep ideological revulsion against the Germans, there was little anti-German feeling in a racial sense, as in World War I. But the Japanese were hated as an upstart race. Japanese, but not Germans and Italians, were interned in concentration camps in the United States. Japanese captives in the Pacific were much more cruelly treated than German captives.

Whereas the core belief of the internationalist current was the need for international systems, particularly economic, that of the nationalist current was the need for pre-eminent American military power. In a dangerous world, this was the only guarantee for American safety, for the defense of America's interests, and, in particular, for the assurance of the ever-continuing outward expansion of American enterprise. America must have a powerful navy and develop new technologies, such as air power, to the hilt. It must have a powerful army, although the nationalists were always suspicious of universal military service. Above all, the nationals there, notably missionaries, engaged in their own form of activ-the world, particularly in the Pacific. The Philippines and Cuba were seen as models for America to follow. While independence should be granted to the Philippines as it was to Cuba after the Spanish-American War, American power was to remain in the form of naval bases like Subic Bay and Guantánamo. The American military presence would assure an "open door" policy for American business to invest and do as it pleased in those countries. It would also assure the safety of American nationals there, notably missionaries, engaged in their own form of activity. The nationalists regarded military power as the main force supporting expansionism. It was, therefore, legitimate and necessary to destroy the military power of countries threatening America, such as Japan and Germany, and to do everything possible to prevent new military powers from arising which could threaten America, such as Russia.

CONTRADICTIONS BETWEEN INTERNATIONALISM AND NATIONALISM

The debate over America's role in the postwar world found both internationalists and nationalists making expected arguments. The internationalists wanted international systems which would guarantee a world market based on free trade, monetary stability, and political responsibility. The nationalists cared for little else beyond the assurance of American power, particularly military, in the postwar world. In 1919, these two currents had clashed and nationalism won out, although internationalism resurfaced with the Dawes and Young plans. During World War II, they clashed again. This time the outcome was not a synthesis or a compromise but something new—an American imperialism, which neither internationalists nor nationalists had envisaged.

The practical internationalists still thought in pre-1914 terms of a world led by the key powers, America and Britain, working closely together, with Russia's role to be worked out in a manner satisfactory to the world market system. The nationalists believed neither in "one world" nor in the Anglo-American partnership, and felt that America would only get into trouble if it departed from the sound utilitarian principle of self-interest first. Roosevelt's vision of a Pax Americana was in many ways a reincarnation of Wilson's earlier vision, but, unlike Wilson, Roosevelt had the good fortune to appear as a nationalist (in the Pacific), an internationalist (in Europe), and, above all, a popular leader spreading revolutionary ideas to the downtrodden masses of the world.

Both internationalism and nationalism, when stimulated or attacked, generated ideologies of their own, as we shall see. In the postwar period, they became prominent on the left and right of the American political scene. But they were not creative ideologies, and in themselves launched no new vision or policies. Internationalism was too elitist to elicit much popular response except where it coincided with left-wing internationalism. And left-wing internationalism had too little support within the American people to constitute a powerful popular ideology. The popular weakness of both forms of internationalism made them easy targets for nationalism, particularly when it assumed virulent anticommunist forms. Nationalism achieved its own greatest popular success during the McCarthy period, but as an ideology it collapsed when McCarthy began hitting too close to the Establishment. While internationalist and nationalist sentiments are deeply grounded in the American people, the ideologies they generated have remained confined to the left and right extremes of the political spectrum. Since Roosevelt's time, the dominant ideology in America has been one or another form of liberalism, and Roosevelt's role during the 1930s and during World War II was crucial in its fashioning.

A question widely discussed among historians is, Why did the cold war begin? A more appropriate question, in the light of my discussion, is, Why did American imperialism arise? Even Establishment journals such as *Fortune*, musing over the great changes coming over the world in the 1970s, speak of a Pax Americana that governed the world in the post–World War II period. It is my contention that the cold war erupted as a result of America's decision to create an empire, not the reverse. Inspired by Roosevelt's vision, America began to plan a postwar order in which it would be the dominant, guiding force and the source of morality. Russia did not or could not or appeared not to go along with this new order, and, *therefore*, the cold war began. Assuming the burdens of empire is a task not to be taken lightly, and virtually nothing in America's tradition, not even its expansionism, prepared it to assume responsibility for the entire world. Roosevelt did not propose that America join a new League of Nations, but that instead a United Nations be conceived and located on American soil and other nations be invited to join. The United Nations was an American creation which other nations joined largely out of the simple power-political realization that World War II had made America the mightiest nation on the globe. What, then, impelled Roosevelt and his closest advisers to undertake such a novel task? The simplest answer is fear—fear that the world would again degenerate into bloody conflicts, fear that civil wars would erupt, fear that economic and political systems would disintegrate not only from revolutionary pressures but perhaps even more from bitter conflicts within ruling classes themselves. Roosevelt's most profound experience from the American Depression was the vision of America's ruling classes turning against each other with a violence reflected in the bitter struggles waged in and around Congress during the 1930s.

There has been a current in revisionist scholarship that sees the determination of the United States to suppress revolution as the key moving force behind the development of the cold war. While there is much truth to this notion, it overlooks some of the basic fears weighing upon the men who ruled America during the 1940s. If the phenomenon of Bolshevik Russia was loathsome to them, equally if not more loathsome and frightening was the phenomenon of Germany. How could a country in the forefront of civilization and eminently successful in capitalist enterprise have turned into a barbaric monstrosity which showed little hesitation at plunging the world once again into a war? The internationalists were convinced that virulent nationalism was as deadly an enemy of capitalism as Bolshevik Russia. Twice within the century that had not yet reached its halfway point, German nationalism had attacked the world market system, turning what could have been a viable international order for keeping the peace, assuring economic stability, growth, and profits, and allowing the international elites to resolve their countries' problems, into a cauldron for unbelievably destructive war. How to prevent a new Germany, either Germany itself or some other nation, from arising was the central problem for the internationalists during the post–World War II period.

The conflict between the internationalist and nationalist currents in America during and after World War II was a reflection of one of the fundamental contradictions in world capitalism. This arises out of the conflicting tendencies of capitalism on the one hand to become a global system knowing no national boundaries and on the other to assume national forms. Karl Polanyi has advanced the notion that the world market system was the true innovative creation of the Industrial Revolution, and the most important force for peace in the nineteenth century. But toward the end of that century, national capitalisms, notably Germany, began to erode the internationalism of the world market system. Competiton, which had earlier occurred between economic units, now became competition between national units. Since armies are national, the recourse to armed conflict to advance national competition was a natural step. Prior to World War I, an extraordinary number of international institutions arose, at the same time as nationalist forces were waxing in the leading capitalist countries. As soon as World War I ended, the internationalist strain re-emerged, most notably in the form of the League of Nations. But internationalism was dealt a severe blow by the collapse of the gold standard and the rise of German fascist autarky. Polanyi saw both world wars as the inevitable consequence of the collapse of the world market system.

Polanyi points to another major factor that impelled the shift from internationalism to nationalism: the rise of the working classes. As the poor began to make increasing demands for a share of the wealth, the ruling classes saw themselves faced with the dread specter of revolution. To deny wealth to the poor would make revolution inevitable, but to grant it could lead to an escalation of demands which ultimately could destroy the economic basis of the reigning interests. The only solution that encompassed both was to create conditions in which the available wealth would expand at a rapid enough rate to meet the demands of the poor without infringing on the voracious appetites of the interests for new capital and profits. While the world market system offered ever-safer avenues for world-wide investment, marketing, and profits, it did not generate a rapid enough expansion of the national wealth to meet the rising demands of the poor. Only a consciously national policy pursued by the state could create the necessary wealth and avoid the terrible business cycles which laissez-faire capitalism could not. Germany, a late-comer on the industrial scene, took the lead in the shift toward national capitalism, but all other capitalist countries, including America, followed in one way or another.

The contradiction between international and national capitalism arises out of a phenomenon inherent in the capitalist system—uneven development. As capitalism leaps forward in certain sectors, it generates expectations in others. Those disadvantaged in the competition look to the state for remedy which will allow them to compete successfully or to make good losses incurred by inability to compete. And following on the heels of those desirous but incapable of competing are the poor, who demand a share of the surplus regardless of where it comes from. The paradox is that highly successful capital easily transcends the limits of sovereignty and views the state as an instrument for fostering internationalism, whereas less successful capital and the poor, in different ways, of course, view the state as a necessary instrument for satisfying their demands. The demands of the poor were revolutionary, for they wanted an ever-increasing share of the surplus, regardless of its size—they wanted a redistribution of the wealth even if it was static. But the demands of lesser national capital on the surplus were equally disturbing to the internationalists. They wanted high tariffs on foreign goods to allow their enterprises to prosper. They wanted no redistribution of wealth, which they saw as only coming out of their own pockets and whetting the appetites of the poor for more. And they wanted such substantial monies as the state spent to go for military power, which would guarantee their interests. The internationalists saw this process as a mortal threat to the world market system. Protection would dry up the flow of capital across national boundaries and stifle world-wide growth and profits. To deny everything to the poor would just lead to more trouble. To pour money into guns could only lead to more and bigger wars, as it did in the 1930s. The internationalists early foresaw the development of huge multinational corporations. They believed that these were the best guarantee for the peaceful and profitable growth of the entire world. In short, the surplus should be available to big international business, and if that disadvantaged the smaller entrepreneurs, it was the price of growth.

The internationalists in 1945 saw "Germany" and "Russia" as key problems. "Germany" meant war, which had to be forever banished. "Russia" meant revolution, which had to be contained. The solution to "Germany" was demilitarization of the world. The solution to "Russia" was transfer of some of the surplus to the poor. The nationalists saw themselves excluded from such a world. Like beaten-down Germany, they would be destroyed to pay off "Russia," the symbol of the revolutionary poor, and "Britain," the symbol of international capitalism.

That internationalism and nationalism were contradictory currents in America is evident from the great conflicts that rent the country between 1945 and 1950. The most general form this conflict took was "Europe-first" versus "Asia-first." The word "first" implied a conflict not just of priorities but of different world views. By and large, the pre-1941 interventionists emerged as Europe-firsters and the isolationists as Asia-firsters. The Europe-firsters believed that a healthy Western Europe was the major prerequisite for American security, and demanded that considerable monies be spent to bring this about. The Asia-firsters, who were mainly in the Republican opposition, saw the vast spending that such a program entailed as another New Deal measure to soak business for obscure international purposes whose end result would be only to create an even more powerful and dictatorial federal government. Meanwhile, legitimate American interests were being threatened by communism in Asia, chiefly China. To the Asia-firsters, the Democratic administration's tolerance of communism in Asia was an ominous replay of the worst features of the Roosevelt Administration. Here again, the American people were called on to bail out "Britain" in the West while in the East "Russia's" tentacles, in the form of Chinese communism, were painted as "agrarian reformers," movements of the poor for justice, to be accepted as legitimate forces. In the period 1945–1950, "Asia," especially "China," became the symbol of American nationalism. Senator William Knowland's advocacy of Chiang Kai-shek, so intense that he was nicknamed the Senator from Formosa, would seem ludicrous in retrospect except for the fact that Chiang Kai-shek had become much more than the symbol of determined anticommunism. Methodist by religion and married to an American-educated woman, a leader viewed by them as determinedly loyal to America, he was more American than most Americans. Like General Douglas MacArthur, America's most shining examplar of militant nationalism, Chiang was a beleaguered fighter struggling against an international communist conspiracy directed against him not only by Moscow and its Chinese tools but by Washington, New York, and Harvard as well. In that great conflict, the nationalists felt on the defensive, finding themselves threatened by a range of powerful forces intent on doing away with American nationality and sovereignty. The backlash of McCarthyism indicates how violent the conflict had become.

The bitter conflict for which McCarthyism was more symbol than substance eventually ebbed away in the 1950s for one major reason—"bipartisanship in foreign policy." Spearheaded by Senator Arthur Vandenberg's wartime rallying to Roosevelt's conception of a United Nations, the "liberal" wing of the Republican party accepted the premise that consensus must prevail over the basic issues of foreign policy. That they were able to force bipartisanship on the party against the opposition of conservatives like Robert Taft was manifest in their candidates in 1948 and 1952: the New York liberal Thomas Dewey and the wartime commander of Allied forces in Europe, Dwight Eisenhower. If bipartisanship had not been achieved in the postwar years, it is likely that the Republican party as the chief political vehicle of American nationalism would have mounted an even greater attack on the Democratic internationalist liberals, which could only have resulted in a foreign policy much different from the Pax Americana, which the United States succeeded in constructing.

A new ideology, different from both internationalism and nationalism, forged the basis on which bipartisanship could be created. The key word and concept in that new ideology was *security*.

SECURITY AS AN OPERATIONAL IDEA

No word better characterizes the New Deal of the 1930s than security, just as no word better characterizes the climate of that Depression period than fear. The institution of Social Security for the aged by Roosevelt's Administration typified the New Deal's ideology: unless people had assurance that they would not remain destitute victims of unpredictable business cycles, society would disintegrate into chaos. Only one institution in society, the government, could provide that assurance. If wealth had to be redistributed so that security could be achieved, the more affluent had to pay the price, lest by not doing so they lose everything. An important corollary to these Social Security policies was that injecting money into the economy to "prime the pump" would stimulate a business upturn. What appeared to be waste in order to calm people's fears was essentially similar to private investment, spending in order eventually to produce more income. It would be wrong, however, to see Social Security, loans and payments to farmers, relief measures, small business loans, and so on as simply devices to get corporate capital functioning again. There were twenty-five million unemployed in the 1930s, and class war in the form of militant industrial union organizing threatened to tear the country asunder. The crash providing of even a small degree of economic security was viewed as essential to prevent matters from getting worse. This ideology of security, deeply implanted in the administration, gave rise to an entire range of social legislation, most notably the Wagner Labor Relations Act, which gave unions unprecedented protection of the law. Unions were perceived as a form through which security could be achieved for the most dangerous element of the population, the blue-collar workers. The union meant protection.

The fear that gripped America in the 1930s was domestic. By the 1940s, it had become external as well. In 1941, American soil was attacked by a foreign power for the first time since the War of 1812. Moreover, German and Japanese armies were threatening to take over the entire Eastern Hemisphere, leaving America alone and isolated in the Western Hemisphere. Later as postwar planning proceeded in Washington, the concern for security became the dominant theme, uniting the universalists in the State Department, the ex-isolationist nationalists in the Republican party, and, of course, the key Rooseveltian liberals in the Treasury Department. Whatever form the postwar order took, above all, it had to provide security for the United States against another threat arising such as had provoked World War II. While the talk of security still roused the hackles of conservatives, who saw in it just another cloak for New Deal big government, the great majority of the people responded to it. They finally realized that the world was fundamentally chaotic, something few people had accepted in the nineteenth century. War and depression were endemic to people's existence unless active measures were taken to curb them. If "struggle" is the word most characteristic of Maoism and symbolic of its world view, then security and fear were symbolic of the major world view that governed the United

States at the end of World War II—chaos produced fear which could only be combatted with security.

It has been said many times that Roosevelt's vision of the postwar world was an extension of his New Deal to the world as a whole. The United Nations was to become the nucleus of a world government which the United States would dominate much as the Democrats dominated the American Congress. The essence of the New Deal was the notion that big government must spend liberally in order to achieve security and progress. Thus, postwar security would require liberal outlays by the United States in order to overcome the chaos created by the war. It is not accidental that the most ambitious New Dealish schemes for the postwar period came out of the Treasury Department, which was more Rooseveltian in ideology than any other governmental bureaucracy. But even when its plans assumed absurd forms, as in turning the Germans into a nation of farmer/herders, the Treasury most closely expressed Roosevelt's own ideas. It proposed the destruction for all time of the world's most virulent nationalism, that of Germany. If German and to a lesser extent Japanese nationalism were destroyed, the world would never again have to fear that an advanced capitalist nation would threaten the international system. Aid to Rusisa and other poor nations would have the same effect as social welfare programs within the United States— it would give them the security to overcome chaos and prevent them from turning into violent revolutionaries. Meanwhile, they would be drawn inextricably into the revived world market system. By being brought into the general system, they would become responsible, just as American unions had during the war. Helping Britain and the remainder of Western Europe would rekindle economic growth, which would stimulate transatlantic trade and, thus, help the American economy in the long run. America had spent enormous sums running up huge deficits in order to sustain the war effort. The result had been astounding and unexpected economic growth. Postwar spending would produce the same effect on a world-wide scale. By destroying Germany and paying off Russia, America and the world would achieve security from their two greatest fears—nationalist aggression and violent revolution.

By portraying America as an aggressively imperialist nation since the end of World War II (if not before), revisionist scholarship has washed away one of the most important factors that made American imperialism possible—the tremendous ideological appeal of New Deal doctrines of security. Wilson's Fourteen Points aroused widespread response from peoples throughout the world seeking national self-determination, much to the chagrin of the Versailles peacemakers. But Roosevelt's appeal was of a different order. America was the liberator with the power and money this time to prevent war from recurring. While American anti-colonialism was to have a great impact on the Third World countries, the biggest impact on Europe was the American ideology personified by Roosevelt and his New Deal. Virtually the entire communist movement from America to Russia to the European and Asian parties believed that America was coterminous with Roosevelt and the New Deal. Ho Chi Minh was so taken with America that he made the American Declaration of Independence the model for Vietnam's own declaration of independence from France. At the end of World War II, the dominant sentiment in the advanced countries was a yearning for peace and security, not for revolution. Nor was it different in a poor country like China. The Chinese Communists looked to America for some support in their efforts to secure a coalition government with Chiang Kai-shek so that they could cease at last the wars that they had been fighting since 1927. They wanted security from Kuomintang attack, which, when it came in 1946, impelled them back onto the path of revolution. America in 1945 held a virtual ideological monopoly in the world. "Communism" as a global ideology had withered as the result of defeats in Spain, the Nazi-Soviet pact, the disbanding of the Comintern and the American Communist party, the growing awareness of Stalin's purges of Russian and foreign Communists, and the obvious national character of the Russian resistance to the Germans during the war. At the end of World War II, people did not yearn for class struggle but for an end to struggle. War was so horrible an evil that nothing could be worse. No other nation seemed so dedicated to and capable of providing the security that the world wanted than America. The ideological power that this gave America was one of the most important weapons it wielded in the postwar period, and was decisive in enabling it to construct the Pax Americana, its own imperialism.

The internationalist current within the American foreign policy establishment sought to create international systems, particularly economic ones, which would so bind nations that a major war could never again occur. The nationalist current pushed for the maintenance and expansion of American power, particularly military power, so that America would be "safe" from all threats. But it was Roosevelt who began to advance schemes promising *security*, a security that would protect mankind not only from major wars but also from economic collapse. The genius of the American ideological approach was that security for the world had to be based on American power exercised through international systems. But for such a scheme to have a broad ideological appeal to the suffering peoples of the world, it had to emanate from an institution less esoteric than an international monetary system and less crude than a set of military alliances or bases. The institution Roosevelt chose was the United Nations, the matter to which he gave greatest attention during the last months of his life and the chief issue of the 1944 elections.

THE UNITED NATIONS

The United Nations was a creative synthesis of the three major elements of Roosevelt's political personality. It was an international system intertwined with the emerging international economic systems. It assured the primacy of American power, symbolically by its location within the United States and concretely by being an outgrowth of the alliances of the nations that had fought Germany, Japan, and Italy, the overwhelming majority of which were bound to the United States. The ideological appeal of the United Nations, going far beyond that of the League of Nations, was almost revolutionary in its promise to help the poor nations of the world toward independence, progress, and eventual equality with the powerful nations. Above all, the United Nations appealed to the universal longing for peace.

What Roosevelt feared most as he constructed his synthesis was the kind of nationalist reaction that had defeated Wilson. Unlike Wilson, who lost the League of Nations chiefly because of the opposition of Henry Cabot Lodge, Roosevelt managed to win over an equally potent isolationist opponent, Arthur Vandenberg. The substance of Vandenberg's acquiescence to the United Nations plan is indicated in a statement in his diary: "The striking thing about it . . . is that it is so *conservative* from a nationalist standpoint. . . . This is anything but a wild-eyed internationalist dream of a world State."[3] Somewhat less threatening but equally vexing was resistance from the internationalists, chiefly the State Department, whose position was based on the assumption of joint Anglo-American cooperation in the postwar world. Similar resistance came from a Britain suspicious of American infringement on its interests. Above all, Roosevelt banked on support for the United Nations from the American people, which he got in the 1944 elections. But each of the predominant currents within the American foreign policy realm eventually was satisfied by the emerging structure of the United Nations. The nationalists were satisfied that American power was safeguarded. The internationalists were satisfied that the United Nations would help to advance and consolidate other international systems, such as those established at Bretton Woods. And the liberals in the Democratic party who had come to power through the New Deal were inspired by the progressive ideological aura surrounding the United Nations.

What was the United Nations? It was a General Assembly which brought together all nations on an equal footing (one vote for each nation regardless of size), giving it the appearance of the American House of Representatives, an institution eminently democratic in con-

[3] Gabriel Kolko, *The Politics of War*, p. 270.

ception. It was also a Security Council which reflected the realities of
power rather than population and, like presidential power in the United
States, could veto action undertaken by the General Assembly. The task
of the Security Council was, above all, to keep the peace by preventing
aggression or punishing it when it occurred. The five great powers who
were its permanent members were to be responsible for the security of
the world. The General Assembly symbolized the liberal, revolutionary
appeal to the poor and the weak. The Security Council, depending on
what form it took, symbolized the predominant concerns of both nationalists and internationalists. Through the veto, each great power's national interests were forever safeguarded from encroachment by the
others. But as a council, it was also an arena of multinational cooperation, the ideal of the internationalists.

The role of China, interestingly and forebodingly, brought all three of
these currents together, particularly when it was made a permanent
member of the Security Council. No one insisted more strongly on
China's inclusion than Roosevelt, to the extreme annoyance of both the
British and the Russians. But since Britain and Russia had graver things
to think about, they were willing to accede to Roosevelt's quaint demand. China, the poorest of the poor, symbolized the little people of the
world who had been so cruelly wronged by war, imperialism, and economic backwardness. Bringing it into the Security Council dramatized
the New Deal doctrine that the poor too must have access to power.
Thus, China, always a great issue for the liberals, meant a further ideological triumph of the liberal ideal. At the same time, the inclusion of
China satisfied the Pacific-oriented American nationalists. China was
America's little brother, unswervingly loyal friend and ally and, above
all, was irremediably bound to America by its abject economic and
military dependence. China's being on the Security Council meant, in
effect, another American vote. Even the internationalists, who must have
smiled at China's great power pretensions, were willing to go along,
mainly because the man besides Chiang Kai-shek guiding China's destiny
was the American-educated banker T. V. Soong, who impressed all in
Washington as fully understanding the need for economic reforms. China
at least could be counted on not to obstruct the emerging international
economic systems, and because of its adherence to "open door" policies,
was actually heartily in favor of free trade, which was so dear to the
hearts of the internationalists.

The United Nations was Roosevelt's vision. It was the only new
revolutionary idea to emerge out of World War II. It was an ideological
creation and, by and large, remains so now. With its limited and shrink-
ing powers, the United Nations has never really linked up with the realm
of interests, except in the early days when, as during the Korean War, it

was used by the United States to advance American interests on the Korean peninsula. And even then, the Korean intervention was made by the Security Council, the less ideological of the United Nations' two bodies, and occurred because of the fortuitous absence of the Russians.

What was revolutionary about the United Nations? For the first time in world history, there was a concrete institutionalization of the idea of world government. Whereas the League of Nations was guided by an essentially nineteenth-century spirit of a congress of nations, the United Nations was openly guided by American political ideas, specifically those that led the Founding Fathers to form the United States in the eighteenth century. The revolutionary fact was that the United Nations began to act like a parliament or a national assembly or, more exactly, like the American Congress. And in the instances where its actions had operational consequences, it did indeed act very much like a national representative body, bringing force to implement its decisions. The United States fought for its interests in Korea under the United Nations flag. There was nothing revolutionary about the kind of world system Britain created through its empire. There was something revolutionary about the world market system that flowed out of Britain in the eighteenth century and created international capitalism. As a political system, the British Empire was just bigger and better maintained than that of the French or the Dutch. Britain's true imperial greatness was economic, not political. The United Nations, however, was and remains a political idea. The American Revolution had proven that nations could be constructed through the conscious and deliberate actions of men. Until then, it was assumed that they only grew naturally over long periods of time (it is not coincidental that the word "nation" derives philologically from the Latin verb "to be born"). Since the American Revolution, many new nations have been created. Czechoslovakia, created after World War I, became a model for many that followed. What Roosevelt had the audacity to conceive and implement was the extension of this process of government-building to the world as a whole. The power of that vision must not be underestimated, even as one looks at the shoddy reality that began to emerge even before the San Francisco Conference.

How revolutionary the idea of the United Nations as a world government was may become apparent again in the coming years. The inclusion of China to replace America's little brother Chiang Kai-shek in 1971 came at a time when the real fortunes of the United Nations were at a low ebb, but also at a time when the pressure for some kind of world governmental action to meet truly universal problems was rising, particularly in the area of the environment. In 1945, world government was deemed essential by many to keep the peace and provide security against war. Now many see world government as the only instrument that can regulate man's relationship to the environment so as not to deplete and destroy it. The essence of revolutionary ideas is that, once born, they go on and on, despite ebbs and flows, and, to the everlasting chagrin of conservatives, counterrevolutionaries, and reactionaries, emerge again and again, often at the most unexpected moments. The inclusion of China in the United Nations marked the end of one chapter of its history and the beginning of a new one. In the chapter now ended, the United Nations was practically coterminous with American imperialism.

The ruling interests of the United States finally accepted the United Nations because they correctly saw that it would establish a new imperial power for America. Many detested the rhetoric surrounding it, but were aware of its popular appeal. Churchill would have preferred a resurrection of the League of Nations dominated by a solid Anglo-American partnership, and feared that the liberal, anticolonial proclivities of the Americans could cost Britain her empire. Most baffled of all was Stalin, the heir to the great internationalist revolutionary Lenin. Preoccupied by Russian national interests, he was even willing to sacrifice revolutionary rhetoric in order to gain safety from any recurrence of external attack. Stalin feared that Roosevelt's vision and Churchill's maneuvers were capitalist tricks designed to outwit the Russians and get them to let down their guard. When Stalin won out over Trotsky, he was prepared to abandon revolutionary internationalism completely, but revolutionaries *outside of Russia* would not allow that to happen. Thus, while Stalin turned the Comintern into his own appendage and committed the most heinous of nationalist crimes, foreign Communists continued to believe in Russia because they believed that revolutionary internationalism was essential for world revolution.

AMERICA'S PROGRESSIVE APPEAL
AND THE LEFT

The dilemma the Communists of the world faced in 1945 was that the one great revolutionary vision came not from socialist Russia but from capitalist America. If fascism was the highest and last stage of capitalism in irresolvable contradictions, then America's leadership role in the fight against fascism coupled with the curiously socialistic aspects of the New Deal could mean that America, in its own peculiar way, was making the transition from capitalism to socialism. Earl Browder thought so and acquiesced in the dismantling of the American Communist party. This ideological dilemma of the Communists must not be underestimated as one looks at the reluctance of the West European Communists to seize power. The conventional explanation that Stalin dissuaded them from doing so is probably correct, but is not an explanation. After all, Communists in China, Yugoslavia, Albania, Greece, Malaya, and elsewhere were ready to disregard Stalin's avuncular counsels when they felt they had to. Until the cold war erupted and even thereafter, the Communists believed in America. They thought that Roosevelt was America, even though capitalist and fascist interests were struggling against his vision. Suppose Communist partisans had tried to seize power and set up a Red republic in Italy in 1945. It is almost certain that American occupation forces would have intervened just as the British did in Greece. The Americans were enormously popular in Italy, as elsewhere in Western Europe. They were liberators not just in a military sense but in an ideological sense. There is little likelihood that a Communist seizure of power would have gained much popular following *if* the Americans intervened, and those parties would have risked destruction at the hands of their enemies among Socialists, Republicans, and Liberals. It is a fallacy to assume, then, that the power was there for the taking by Communists in Western Europe and that only American power, wealth, and intrigue plus Stalin's cowardly duplicity stood in their way. A revolt against the British in Greece was one thing, but armed struggle with the Americans was another. Large and decisive numbers of people would have seen it as a fight of the ultraleft against the left. America in the immediate postwar period had a leftish aura about it. This aroused the fury of nationalists and reactionaries within the United States, but proved immensely helpful in the implementation of the liberation of France and Italy and in the occupation of Germany and Japan.

In the 1930s, Americans understood the power of ideology, and no one made cleverer use of that understanding than Franklin Roosevelt. As the cold war progressed, America lost the ideological struggle, and with the Vietnam war, lost even the capacity to understand ideology. Yet the obvious reminder of how potent ideology remains as a force is there for all to see. There is no explanation for the heroism, tenacity, and ingeniousness of the liberation forces of Vietnam (as contrasted to their Saigon enemies) except the moral beliefs that impel them. In 1945, however, America had won the ideological struggle, not just with the Fascists, whose appeal was limited, but more importantly with the Communists. When Stalin disbanded the Comintern during World War II, many communist parties throughout the world ceased looking to Moscow for guidance. It was from Washington rather that great progressive impulses were coming: for world government, for food relief and economic reconstruction, for the liberation of colonies, for reforms in Germany and Japan, for coalition governments including Communists. The Marshall mission to China in late 1945 came at a time when Rooseveltian policies were still in force and the cold war, announced by Church-

ill the following spring at Fulton, Missouri, had not yet erupted. That
mission signified to the world, and particularly to Communists, America's desires (at least in the realm of ideology) to see Communists take a
place in the governance of their countries. To Communists, reactionary
and capitalist forces, while not identical, were closely allied. America
had shown itself to be antireactionary and in some small ways even at
times apparently anticapitalist (had it not disbanded the German cartels
and the Japanese zaibatsu?). If America could, therefore, be counted on
to support the entry of Communists into governments, or at least not
oppose it, then there would be no need for the bloodshed and horror that
comes from every violent seizure of power. No less an advocate of armed
struggle than Mao Tse-tung shared this belief with many other Communists throughout the world, and, under American auspices, went to see
his archenemy Chiang Kai-shek to help to arrange a coalition government. When Chiang Kai-shek launched the civil war in July 1946, the
cold war had already erupted.

Roosevelt was to score his greatest victory after the war when the left
failed in all the advanced capitalist countries (Western Europe and
Japan) and even in some less advanced countries, and power passed
serenely back into the hands of the conservatives. In this he was aided,
of course, by Stalin, not through anything so crude as advice to Communists not to seize power, but through the example the Soviet Union set
in its march into the liberated countries. While Russia was surprisingly
willing to make concessions on the governmental make-up of these countries, its armies carried out depredations, looting, stealing, raping, as-
saulting on a scale that horrified the world. The same tales that were told
in the West about Russian misbehavior were heard in Korea and Japan.
While such actions were understandable in Germany, they were incomprehensible in Czechoslovakia, Manchuria, Korea, Poland, and Yugoslavia. By startling contrast, the behavior of the occupying Americans
was exemplary. Moreover, while the Russians dismantled machinery
and factories wherever they found them, the Americans were implementing new social policies in Germany and Japan. And again it
was the Americans who insisted on the Nuremberg and Tokyo trials to
try war criminals under newly emerging standards of international law,
rather than try and shoot them summarily, as was Russian practice.

World War I was followed by riot, rebellion, and revolution throughout Europe, particularly Germany. In Germany, revolution failed because the left was disarmed by the left. By contrast, Western Europe and
Japan remained remarkably stable in the period following World War II.
Revolution erupted in countries governed by outright reactionaries determined to destroy the left. Would the civil war have broken out in
Greece if the Americans, not the British, had occupied it? Would the

civil war in China have erupted again if Chiang Kai-shek had not attacked the Communists with the connivance of reactionary Americans?
If Thomas Dewey had been elected President in 1944, would the history
of Western Europe have been different? The theoretical argument advanced here suggests that there would have been a difference. Would the
European, Japanese, and Chinese lefts have trusted a new Republican
President as much as they trusted Roosevelt? Obviously not. But what
would this have signified? Even before Roosevelt died, there were powerful pressures within the American government to adopt stronger anticommunist policies. A Republican President would have given the green
light to conservative, reactionary, and counterrevolutionary forces
throughout the world to move fast against their leftist enemies to prevent
a repetition of what happened after World War I. De Gaulle, for example, insisted on his own liberation of Paris not just for prestige but to
prevent the Communist-led Resistance from seizing power. The Badoglio
regime in Italy was deeply worried about the rapid growth of the Partisan movement in the north. And, of course, Chiang Kai-shek was ever
ready to move against the Communists. In Greece, the British showed no
reluctance to use force against the left and provoked a civil war. There
are grounds for believing that if Dewey had become President, the swing
against communism which eventually came in 1946 and 1947 would
have begun even before the end of the war. It is not unlikely that this
would have provoked civil war in Western Europe as it did in Greece.
Would postwar Japan have been as tranquil under a Dewey regime as it
was under a Truman regime that was still guided by Roosevelt's ideology?

The Pax Americana that came into being after 1945 provided much
more economic, military, and political security, particularly for the advanced countries, than people had imagined at the end of the war as they
saw the immense destruction it had wreaked. The political security
would never have occurred if the Western European countries and Japan
had been rent by the kind of left-right strife that many of them had
experienced after World War I (even Japan had class war in the 1920s).
The failure of the left was a crucial factor in bringing about stability.
What many people forget is that the left is traditionally a defensive force
which displays its full strength only *after* being attacked by enemies. The
left not only was not attacked in the days immediately following World
War II, but, in Western Europe and Japan, was invited into governance.
When the cold war finally became evident to all, conservative forces had
well entrenched themselves in positions of power. America's progressive
ideology and actions stimulated by the Rooseveltian vision played a
major role in preventing the kind of revolutionary strife that had rent
Europe after World War I. Paradoxically, this same progressive ideology

made it possible to create an American imperialism that neither the nationalists nor the internationalists dreamed of or even wanted.

TRUMAN AND THE BEGINNING
OF THE COLD WAR

The practical inputs that Washington added to the United Nations in order to satisfy the domestic nationalists and internationalists are well studied and well known. They already were apparent in the San Francisco Conference. By the opening day of the conference, April 26, 1945, Roosevelt had been dead some weeks and Truman had already had a bitter exchange with Molotov. Conflict between America and Russia, of course, marked the entire wartime relationship and intensified as the war was coming to an end. But it occurred around real interests which clashed, notably on Poland. Conflict is normal within and between realms of interests. What began, though, on the day that Truman assumed office, was the ideological conflict. Given this book's conception of the executive, one can say that the cold war began the day that Roosevelt died. Roosevelt was a practical politician keenly aware of America's interests, which he was no less determined to defend than any succeeding American President. There are no grounds for believing that he would have taken a different stance on Poland, for example, than Truman did. But Roosevelt was determined to create an ideological realm arising out of his vision of the United Nations which would encompass Russia. At Yalta, Roosevelt and Stalin were friendly. Only two months later, Truman lashed out at Molotov in Washington. That behavior on the part of the supreme leader of the United States gave the signal for a profound ideological change in the United States that was to determine the character of the following quarter-century. It is generally accepted that the death of Stalin in March 1953 led to major changes in Soviet foreign and domestic policies. The death of President Kennedy, as we shall see in later chapters, also brought about major policy changes leading directly to the Vietnam war. It can be argued that the death of John Foster Dulles in May 1959 made possible the policy changes that led to the Camp David meetings of September 1959. The major function of great national leaders is to personify certain ideologies from which policies flow. At the root of every operation, no matter how institutionalized and surrounded by long entrenched bureaucratic interests, is a policy flowing out of some ideology, a world view informed by basic class outlooks. This is eminently true in foreign policy. The more changing and less routine an environment, the more new policies are propounded. This fact, in turn, tends to enhance the power, prestige, and influence of the supreme leader. He becomes the never-ending source of new policies which cut deep into the realm of interests, creating new ones, displacing old ones, redirecting, expanding, reshaping what already is going on. When the great leader dies, the fountain ceases to give water and dries up. Advocates of interests that were submerged during his lifetime rise up and seize the opportunity to stridently advocate their own interests or, more significantly, to implant their ideologies, their world views, their currents into the mind of the successor leader and his advisers. When Roosevelt died, his vision did not die with him. It continued to exercise a powerful appeal in America and throughout the world well into the days of the cold war. What ended with Roosevelt were the ideological elements over and above his national and international commitments, especially his populist progressivism, which held that the poor of the entire world, including Russia, could be incorporated into the evolving Pax Americana with profit for its interests and with security for all.

There are some interesting similarities between Truman's succession of Roosevelt and Johnson's of Kennedy. There are even similarities in the socially significant personalities of the four men. Both Roosevelt and Kennedy were Eastern aristocrats. Truman and Johnson were common men who made good; Missouri and Texas are not very far apart in geography and spirit. In the last year of his life Kennedy, like Roosevelt, began to develop visions of global peace. Johnson, like Truman, was a master operator in the labyrinth of congressional politics. As soon as Roosevelt died, the ideological wind changed dramatically in Washington, marked by an unexpected hostility to Russia. As soon as Kennedy died, Johnson vowed to "win" in Vietnam. When Roosevelt died, he was succeeded by a Vice President who had been imposed on him to replace the wild-eyed liberal Henry Wallace and who was at home in the realm of interests. Truman was a practical politician, as was Johnson. The realm of interests resumed command from the realm of ideology when Roosevelt died, and quickly swept aside the cloud of idealistic rhetoric which had been so characteristic of Roosevelt's reign. So too did Johnson sweep away the rhetoric about world peace which Kennedy was spreading after his American University speech and the signing of the Test Ban Treaty and in the last days of his life. Harry Truman "gave them hell," and Johnson vowed to bring the "coonskin back from Vietnam." Both acted tough from the very day they assumed office.

With Truman's accession to the Presidency, the creative synthesis of nationalist and internationalist interests with the Rooseveltian vision was broken. Truman was temperamentally a nationalist. He hated Nazis and communists with equal venom and once openly said he hoped they would kill each other off. Like Johnson, he was assiduous in arranging for defense contracts to benefit his constituents. Like many Southern Democrats and unlike most Republicans, he believed in big government and heavy federal spending to solve social problems. But he also assumed a vigorous nationalist stance in regard to foreign matters, supporting intervention but only in American interests. He was put on the 1944 ballot obviously as a nationalist balance to the heavily internationalist complexion that Roosevelt's government had taken. What is important to note about Truman when he assumed office was his fear of his own inadequacy, particularly that he might not be able to contain the conflicts within the government that would surely erupt after having been so long smothered by Roosevelt's commanding presence. He therefore adopted a style consistent with his own personality, which assured him of the capacities to command and coordinate that he needed as President: he talked tough like a nationalist. That style permitted him to pursue virtually all the foreign policies that Roosevelt had inaugurated and at the same time to block certain nationalist pressures deemed too threatening to the emerging postwar order. Truman must be reckoned the architect of American imperialism, to which he finally gave explicit policy form with his Truman Doctrine on Greece and Turkey in 1947. He is the true father of containment, the policy of postwar American imperialism.

If one moves ahead a few years into the Truman Administration, it becomes clear that the great foreign policy conflict became one between Europe-firsters and Asia-firsters. As America's fiscal resources shrank in the postwar years, in comparison to its global tasks, the nationalist Asia-firsters demanded priority for "Asia" (a concept that involved far more than defense of interests geographically located in Asia) and the internationalist Europe-firsters demanded priority for "Europe." Were the seeds of this conflict already evident in the early months of Truman's Presidency? Truman faced two major practical foreign issues (aside from the completion of the war against Germany and the establishment of an occupation regime) and one essentially ideological issue. The two practical issues were the composition of the government to rule Poland and the prosecution of the war against Japan. The ideological issue was the question of the nature of the United Nations. This issue can be disposed of quickly, for at San Francisco the new ideological stance of the Truman regime was very much in evidence. The American delegation to the United Nations conference assumed a strongly nationalist position, to which Stalin acceded. Vandenberg wrote in jubilation, "America wins!"[4] Stalin probably acceded because he better understood Truman's haggling than Roosevelt's lofty rhetoric and figured that there was less chance of being cheated. Only much later did he understand the implications of America's ideological shift which became evident in late April 1945.

[4] Kolko, *Politics of War*, p. 477.

INTERNATIONALIST ATTITUDES
TOWARD RUSSIA

The quarrel over Poland is generally regarded as the first act in the emerging cold war between America and Russia. Both America and Britain were, in different ways, committed to the Polish government in London, while the Russians wanted to install their own "Lublin government" in order to make certain that some new version of the anti-Russian Pilsudski and Beck regimes could never again arise. Britain, which thought mainly in balance of power terms, was more ready to compromise with the Russians than Washington. The Polish issue was of greatest concern to the internationalists in Washington, although Vandenberg, with his Michigan Polish constituency, demanded a tough stand against the Russians. For the internationalists, the Polish issue symbolized their greatest concern about the postwar world, namely, whether free trade, respect for property, openness to foreign enterprise, freedom of speech and travel, and representative government would exist in Eastern Europe. The internationalists of the State Department and their friends in the Eastern Establishment, such as Averell Harriman, loathed Bolshevism as a plague equal to Nazism. If Russia appeared to be incurably Bolshevized, no other part of the world should be allowed to suffer the same fate. The internationalists were willing to grant that Russia had national security concerns which should be recognized. What should never be recognized was Russia's right to impose political, social, and economic forms of governance on other nations in the name of national security. The conflict was most acute over Poland because Russia's most sensitive frontier was the one with Poland facing Germany and the West in general, and some form of a Russian presence had to be accepted (after all, the Russians had already occupied all of Poland). Yet if Russia, with physical possession of Poland, were willing to allow a form of government to arise that would guarantee the basic "freedoms," then it would be willing to coexist with the international systems which would re-emerge after the war. There would then be hope that Russia could be brought into the international arena, not just through political participation in a United Nations or military cooperation in the administration of defeated Germany, but also economically. And who knew but that this might lead to a thawing of the Bolshevik dictatorship. The internationalists firmly believed that there would be no peace in the world until Russia was de-Bolshevized. This, of course, did not mean that the West should be so foolish as to join the remnant Nazis in a new war of liberation against Russia. It did mean that America must bring all its power to bear on Russia to keep the doors of Eastern Europe open.

The internationalist side of Roosevelt's political personality believed in free trade, but his New Deal side suggested an alternative way to approach Russia with the ultimate aim of ridding it of its Bolshevik malignancy. If large-scale credits and aid were made available to Russia, it would gradually assume a more responsible stance in the postwar world. Moreover, with its vast destruction and endemic backwardness, Russia needed American capital goods in order to recover and achieve some level of prosperity. Surely, as its dependence on America grew, it would have to open its doors and allow those freedoms the internationalists regarded as essential to a viable world. The internationalists were not opposed to granting credits to Russia but, heeding their own interests, demanded that the cart not be put before the horse: nothing should be granted until Russia showed its willingness to cooperate with the United States on matters that were regarded as fundamental in Washington. Whereas for Britain, the Polish issue became more and more one of power politics, which could be compromised, for Washington's internationalists it became an issue of principle. Needless to say, the raising of issues of principle always baffled Stalin, who had long since forgotten what principles were except for the defense of his own country. But the real battle the internationalists were fighting over Poland was not with Russia or Britain, but within Washington.

The State Department was locked in never-ending battles with the War and Treasury departments over many different issues, of which the postwar regime for Germany was the most important. The Morgenthau-White scheme for the de-industrialization of Germany and a vast, worldwide New Deal symbolized for the State Department internationalists the ultimate idiocy of Roosevelt's vision (or personal hatred against Germans). They had no yearning for a new American imperialism. As conservatives, they just wanted to re-establish a sane world based on free trade, respect for property, and freedom, principles which would automatically assure Anglo-American dominance. The internationalists did not fear Germany's inherent evil as much as Roosevelt and Morgenthau did. The quashing of Morgenthau's plan to dismantle German industry was easily accomplished; more difficult was the struggle with the War Department, which tended to view everything in purely military terms. Obviously, fighting the war was a military matter, but for the internationalists, once the war was over, the role of the military was to cease. The internationalists were strongly in favor of demilitarizing not just Germany but all nations. The thought that rearmament would begin only a few years after the end of World War II was repugnant to them. Arms diverted money from more important economic investments. Moreover, arms were the source of malevolent nationalisms which had always been the enemy of international systems. In Schumpetrian fashion, they regarded a peaceful world as one best for international capitalism.

Paradoxically, while the internationalists at this time were much more anti-Bolshevik than the nationalists, they were also antimilitarist. German and Japanese militarism were evils that had to be expunged from those societies. Yet they feared that military influences were also becoming too powerful in the United States. What horrified many of the internationalists was not that the military was getting ready for a war of liberation against Russia, which die-hard Nazis were calling for, but that it was beginning to act as master and not servant in determining the fate of postwar Germany and, therefore, of Europe. General Eisenhower was dealing directly with his Russian military counterparts in a way that was creating a *de facto* solution of the German problem before the larger relations with Russia could be worked out. The internationalists were convinced that if Russia could be opened up to Western influence, Bolshevism would disappear, but generals were not the men to accomplish this.

For the internationalists, therefore, Poland was an easier issue to handle than Germany. Neither the War nor the Treasury Department had any hand in it. There were no American troops there and the issue of credits to Poland was moot until the question of the government had been resolved. For the internationalists, the way the Polish issue was resolved would determine what happened in Germany. If Stalin could overcome his national security paranoia enough to allow Poland to be free (even if Russian troops were still stationed there), then it was certain that whatever government assumed power in Germany would follow the same principles, again even with Russian occupation troops. Moreover, concessions on Poland would demonstrate Russia's willingness to live in a demilitarized world. One must remember that the internationalists, as members of the Eastern capitalist establishment, deeply believed that a free world was the only natural world for man. Nations were unfree only because malevolent forces, generally of popular origin, had built up walls around them owing to unreasonable fears. Educated and cultivated men, even of different cultural origins like T. V. Soong, had stated that they too regarded freedom—and free trade and property rights and the rule of law and free speech and the right of travel and investment—as the most natural tendencies of man. The internationalists were America's version of China's Confucianists, elitist but humane, believers in harmony rather than struggle, hostile to the military but conservative, and supremely and arrogantly confident that their way of life was the only conceivable one which guaranteed men "happiness, wealth, and long life," as the old Chinese saying *("fu-lu-shou")* goes. The struggle over Poland had to be won because it was, on the American side, an ideological struggle between conflicting currents in America as well.

Truman was angered by the entire Polish issue, showing that he did not fully appreciate the ideological problems involved. The actual "solution" of the Polish problem proceeded pretty much as the situation dictated: the Russians installed their Polish government, compensated Poland for lost eastern territory with new western territory, and brought a few London Poles into the Lublin government as a concession to the British and Americans. Stalin probably figured that he got what he wanted while he left the British alone to do their own dirty business in Greece, and American concern over Poland was probably motivated by the Polish vote. Yet the Polish controversy must be seen as the source of an ideological anticommunism which, in different forms, was to play a major role in American cold war politics. The internationalist current in Washington felt threatened by Russian unwillingness to make concessions. It saw this both as Bolshevism's unwillingness to de-Bolshevize itself and, somewhat later, as an irrefutable sign of Russian expansionism. While Roosevelt was alive, he had intimated again and again that he could handle the Russians, that Stalin would be reasonable, that Russia was so badly in need of American aid and reparations that it would elect to become a responsible partner in the emerging international systems, as it elected to join the United Nations. The subsequent vicious attack on the Yalta Conference as submission to Russia made sense in ideological if not in practical terms. Like Nazi Germany, Bolshevik Russia represented a force hostile to the re-emerging world market system, and if allowed to grow further, it could pose as mortal a threat to that system as Germany did in the Second World War.

While it is valid to regard the controversy over Poland as the first act in the cold war, it contributed mainly to the "cold" rather than the "war" aspect. The stiffening American attitude on Poland signified a turning away from Rooseveltian liberalism in foreign policy (meaning mainly a pro-Russian stance) toward a greater ideological conservatism. This was even more appreciated in European conservative circles after the August elections in Britain, which ousted the Tories and brought in a socialist government. The internationalists were as intent as ever on building up a new world market system, which demanded the economic reconstruction of Western Europe. This required responsible governments in the key countries. The Socialist victory in Britain made it all the more imperative that such governments be in power in the Continental European countries. France ruled by de Gaulle seemed relatively safe, but neither Germany nor Italy could be allowed to slide into further chaos. Before long Konrad Adenauer and Alcide De Gasperi came to power, reflecting a conservative internationalist ideology which greatly pleased the American internationalists. Both were strong Europeanists, vigorously anti-communist, and completely committed to the United States. Though it is sometimes overlooked, both Adenauer and De Gasperi were anything but war-mongers. In fact, Adenauer was often suspected of being secretly pleased that Protestant East Germany had been detached, leaving the West German Catholics a small majority and, therefore, presumably facilitating the creation of a Catholic union with France and Italy.

The internationalists' fondest dreams were finally fulfilled when Western Europe revived economically and began taking the steps that eventually led to the European Common Market. The Common Market was no socialistic creation but solidly based on free enterprise principles, for which the Germans became the staunchest advocates. While the American internationalist tradition grew out of Anglo-American cooperation during the preceding decades, in the late 1940s and 1950s, American internationalism became more and more oriented to Continental Europe. Britain was becoming a less desirable partner in the reconstruction of a world market system based on free enterprise than France, Germany, and Italy. The increasingly close ties between America and Western Europe naturally facilitated the great expansion of American multinational and transnational corporations into the European market. The re-emergence of American conservatism over the Polish issue must, thus, be seen as the first clearcut triumph for internationalist conservative laissez-faire capitalism. Western Europe could henceforth be reconstructed along such lines without the encumbrance of quasi-socialistic policies which Rooseveltian cooperation with Russia seemed to threaten. If there was to be no compromise with Russia over issues of free trade and freedom generally, then there was no way to establish in Germany a unified government that was socialistic. The Polish issue cleared the way for the eventual creation of a separate West Germany under uncontested conservative rule.

THE NATIONALISTS AND THE ATOMIC BOMB

If the "cold" aspect of the cold war arose out of the Polish issue, the "war" aspect came from the atomic bomb. Whereas the Polish issue was of major concern to the Europe-oriented internationalists, the issue of the atomic bomb was of major concern to the Asia-oriented nationalists. The internationalists had their Bretton Woods and Roosevelt the liberal visionary got his United Nations, but the nationalists, who knew nothing about the bomb's development, quickly laid claim to it as America's most prized possession.

During the summer of 1945, America massed a huge force to invade the home islands of Japan sometime toward the end of that year. The bloody ground combat, culminating in the invasion of Okinawa, promised an even greater bloodletting when American troops made their D-day landings on Japanese shores. On August 6 and 9, America dropped two atomic bombs on Japan, and within a few days the war was over and tens of thousands of American lives had been spared. In the minds of American nationalists, one fact seemed crystal clear: the dropping of the atomic bomb on Hiroshima and Nagasaki had forced Japan to surrender. The development of the atomic bomb gave the nationalists a vision of hitherto unsuspected American power. With a science and technology far in advance of the rest of the world, America was able to produce weapons of such destructiveness that it could force any and all enemies to knuckle under.

From a purely nationalist viewpoint, there is no mystery about Truman's decision to drop the bomb and America's subsequent monopoly of the occupation of Japan. The Pacific was an American ocean. When the Japanese destroyed the British Pacific fleet during the early days of the Pacific war, Britain was effectively excluded from the Pacific. Japan was America's major foe in the Pacific and had to be so completely destroyed that it could never challenge America again. "Frying her cities," as Curtis LeMay put it, was fit punishment, and dropping the atomic bomb on two of them just rounded it out. The beauty of the bomb was that it gave a clincher to the rapidly emerging doctrine of "victory through air power." That doctrine had been powerfully advanced by Japan itself through its air force's destruction of the British fleet, and further advanced by the great American air raids against the Japanese homeland. The bitter island battles, however, seemed again to give weight to the old argument that ground troops still had to go in and occupy territory. But when two little bombs were able to do with no loss of American lives what American ground troops could only have accomplished at fearful cost, the "victory through air power" doctrine seemed to be completely vindicated. The object of war is victory and victory is signified by the enemy's surrender. Japan had surrendered because it was threatened with total destruction through air-delivered fire power. That America only had two bombs to deliver at the time undoubtedly gave the air-oriented military some concern. But then, who can quarrel with success?

The nationalists had always been promilitary, but World War II was not a good example of the identity of nationalism and militarism. The immense conscript armies that fought largely in Europe were no basis for a continuing military tradition. Moreover, there were too many conflicts between outstanding nationalists like George Patton and generals like Omar Bradley and Dwight Eisenhower, who had more democratic and bureaucratic orientations. The nationalists never liked the draft, and the Southerners among them remembered being beaten by a draft army during the Civil War, an army which alarmingly spurred on Northern radicalism. The war in the Pacific was much more satisfying from a nationalist point of view. First, its most spectacular commander was a clearly nationalist figure who had worked his way through the Pacific theater. By contrast, Eisenhower was an upstart whom Roosevelt had advanced over forty-two other officers to command an essentially international and political coalition of forces. MacArthur fought an American war, whereas Eisenhower had too many proclivities to cooperate with the British and the Russians. Secondly, the Pacific war was not fought with masses of draftees but with crack naval, air, and ground units. The Marine, not the mud-slogging infantryman of European campaigns, was the hero in the Pacific. Thirdly, the objectives of the war in the Pacific were much more clearcut than in Europe—Japan was to be conquered, occupied, and then ruled, much as America had ruled the Philippines. In all this there was also a racist relish of seeing a white power chastise a non-white nation that had the temerity to become uppity. MacArthur himself reflected that racism when he ascribed to the Japanese the mental level of adolescents.

Prior to the post–World War II period, there was no real nationalist-military alliance. The United States Army was held in low repute by the people as a whole, and the Navy officer corps was an aristocratic institution which discouraged the ordinary man from joining. But in the 1930s, a new military current was developing, symbolized by Billy Mitchell. He preached the coming supremacy of air power and was dismissed from the service by military conservatives. Mitchell was a "zealot," in Anthony Downs's terms. But he was also an "advocate"—he wanted the Air Force to be staffed with new ambitious young men. He was a military radical. From Mitchell there developed a current of Air Force radical nationalism which was to lead to the creation of an independent Air Force and to make it the most dynamic and powerful arm of the military in the postwar years. While air power increasingly excited the nationalists, the dropping of the atomic bomb electrified them. All America needed was to develop a crack air-oriented military and it could rule the entire world, or at least assure itself of perfect safety from all threats. Above all, an air-oriented military force would be cheap, as contrasted with the costliness of an army of draftees. A nationalist expansionist capitalism could not be better served than by such a military force.

Russia entered the war two days after Hiroshima, three months to the day after the termination of the European war, as promised by Stalin at Yalta. Although there was concern in Washington about the prospects of Russian occupation of Manchuria and Korea, by and large, the nationalists welcomed Russian entry. MacArthur supported it from a purely military standpoint. Obviously, if American ground forces had to land on the main islands, a Russian attack on the Kwantung army would be most helpful. Curiously, during the war, nationalist hatred of Russia diminished as internationalist suspicion of it rose. The Russians were admired as stalwart fighters, and Stalin's gestures to dismantle the apparatus of international communism were appreciated. If Russia was finally shedding the idiocy of revolutionary trappings and becoming decently nationalist, this was to be welcomed, so long as Russia did not threaten American interests. The nationalists were not globalists and, thus, were quite willing to let Russia have its share of the pie in areas of the world, such as the Eurasian heartland, that were of no interest to America. When Japan surrendered, the nationalists felt triumphant. All of the Pacific was now under American control. Japan was under American occupation with only token Russian and British participation. China was ruled by a man loyal to America. The Philippines were once again American. And areas like Malaya and the Indies had reverted to a colonial rule with which America could well coexist.

V-J Day was a day of great euphoria for the nationalists, but within a few weeks a process started which was to arouse one of the bitterest conflicts in American history. The atomic bomb generated apocalyptic fears that within a short time contending nations might blow up the entire planet. World War II, fought to expunge the fear of war forever from the minds of men, now seemed to have launched an even greater fear, that of atomic annihilation. For the nationalists, the awesome power of the bomb posed no real foreign policy problems. It was an American monopoly and should obviously remain so. No nation would henceforth be able to challenge America, and since America was not an aggressive power, what better guarantee for world peace could there be than to preserve its atomic monopoly? The military, through the Joint Chiefs of Staff, took the same approach: they opposed any sharing of the bomb's secrets and demanded that America retain a monopoly over atomic power. This common position on the bomb was a major factor in developing the nationalist-military alliance which was to become so important during the cold war. But the monopoly was challenged, initially not from outside America but from within. Within weeks after Hiroshima voices were raised, notably that of Secretary of War Henry Stimson, calling for some form of internationalization of atomic energy. To the utter bafflement and outrage of the nationalists, they wanted an exchange of atomic knowledge with Russia as well as with Britain and Canada. Nationalist dislike of Russia may have abated during the war, but no nationalist ever conceived of Russia as an ally that could be trusted. Moreover, by August and September 1945 it had already become clear in Central and Eastern Europe that American-Russian relations were going to have rough sledding. For anyone, therefore, to make a proposal that the secrets of America's supreme weapon be shared with the Russians seemed puzzling at least and at most darkly conspiratorial. For the nationalists, the call for internationalization of atomic knowledge implied the emasculation of America just when it had achieved the greatest victory in its history. Furthermore, it would be a blow to the power of the military. The inevitable demobilization threatened to return the military to its prewar status of a relatively minor instrument of American power. In contrast to the military after World War I, which (except for the Navy) allowed itself to be dismantled, the post–World War II military, especially the rapidly emerging Air Force, was not prepared to suffer that fate. Manpower for all the services was soon to be decimated by the precipitate demobilization, which was anticipated. If now the atomic bomb, too, was to be demobilized, then United States military power would inexorably join the descending spiral. Thus, when Secretary Stimson in late September 1945 in a crucial Cabinet session proposed sharing atomic secrets with the Russians, the Joint Chiefs of Staff vigorously opposed it.[5]

The pressure for internationalization of the atomic bomb did not come initially from the internationalists, who thought primarily in economic terms. The bomb was a totally new phenomenon which fitted into none of the bureaucratic categories in Washington. The pressure came from the highest levels of the executive branch of government, far above the normal bureaucratic labyrinth. Only those in the most intimate circle of the White House knew enough about the atomic bomb to deal with it politically. Why did the campaign to share atomic secrets suddenly emerge? Truman, deep down a nationalist, had no enthusiasm for sharing, and Stimson's record does not explain why he should have become a leading advocate for internationalization. The real source of pressure was the political sociology of the process through which the atomic bomb was made in the first place. The array of brilliant scientists who had developed it were by national origins and temperament an international group. Nuclear physics originated in Europe, not in America, and despite war and fascism, retained its international character. There were still nuclear physicists in Germany, not to mention hundreds of other scientists whom the United States made intensive efforts to capture and enlist in its military-scientific programs. During the war, the military, personified by General Leslie Groves, had assumed tight control over the Manhattan Project. The scientists were to handle the science and technology while the military, as government's instrument, monopolized the politics. But the scientists refused to be apolitical, and even before the atomic bomb was dropped on Japan, began to agitate politically. First they lobbied for not dropping the bomb, and when it was dropped, they

[5] D. F. Fleming, *The Cold War and Its Origins*, vol. 1, p. 320.

continued their agitation for some form of international control over atomic energy. The military was furious at men like Oppenheimer and Szilard whose political arrogance was so different from the docility of the captured German scientists who did what they were told to do and did not meddle in politics. What the scientists were telling the White House was that it was only a matter of time before other nations, including Russia, would develop the atomic bomb. British scientists already had all the know-how even if American nuclear engineering secrets were denied them. The scientists concluded that unless the bomb was internationalized immediately an arms race of terrible proportions could result, pitting against each other not just hostile conventional forces, whose abilities to do mutual damage were still limited, but atomic weapons, which could destroy entire human societies, if not the planet itself. Two world wars had amply demonstrated man's basic irrationality, and unless extreme measures were taken to control this terrible force, there would be a biblical Armageddon.

Until August 6, 1945, the internationalism of science was commendable, but from the point of view of power politics not terribly important. After that date, the scientists (particularly nuclear physicists) became factors of power politics, and by virtue of the nature of science and the multinational character of scientists, were inherently internationalist. They were not really "American" as nationalists defined it. Moreover, they insisted on acting like internationalists by using their new-found power to demand the internationalization of the atomic bomb. Prior to Pearl Harbor, the nationalists, particularly the isolationists among them, feared the internationalists of Anglo-American finance capital as men hostile to American free enterprise capitalism. In the postwar period, that fear and hatred revived in the form of violent opposition to the Marshall Plan, to foreign aid, to Britain. But suddenly and unexpectedly a new and potent kind of internationalism surfaced with the explosion of the atomic bomb. If Anglo-American finance and banking capital threatened old-fashioned hard-working American enterprise by manipulation of the money supply, the new scientific internationalism threatened ultimately to disarm America altogether. If the atomic bomb was internationalized, it would be only a matter of time before the rest of America's military power was put under international control, an agency for which already existed in the form of the United Nations. The flag had always been the symbol of nationalism, and the military, for all its shortcomings in the eyes of the nationalists, was the most reliable and sacrosanct instrument of that symbol. The nationalists draped the atomic bomb with the American flag, and were horrified that the internationalist scientists wanted to strip it off. As the war came toward its atomic climax, the struggle between scientist Oppenheimer and General Groves intensified. Groves felt that, as an engineer and an organizer, he had supplied the practical know-how without which the bomb could never have made the transition from scientific idea to military reality. He was resentful that as success approached, the scientists tried to rob him and the military of the power they held over the bomb. The bitter conflict which was to develop in subsequent years between nationalist politicians and internationalist scientists was a direct outgrowth of the power struggle between Oppenheimer and Groves.

THE BOMB AND THE DRIVE FOR CONTROL

The issue of the atomic bomb was the most explosive controversy facing the executive branch of the American government in the months following the end of the war. Unlike the conflicts over the United Nations, Poland and Eastern Europe, and sundry other international and domestic problems, the question of the bomb was urgent. Its mere existence created a permanent crisis for the world. The nightmare that haunted American leaders was that Russia might gain access to nuclear know-how, proceed rapidly to develop its own bomb, and thereby create the distinct possibility that both sides would be impelled, not by their desire for war but by that terrible irrationality that seemed to govern even the greatest nations, to bring about the destruction of the planet by folly, accident, or maliciousness rather than by conscious design. The crisis politics crucial to understanding the cold war were born in the fall of 1945 in this controversy about the bomb. Washington knew that Russia too was scouring Germany for scientists and already had outstanding nuclear physicists like Peter Kapitza, and that the single-minded totalitarianism of the Russian government would make it possible for them, despite the ravages of war, to mount a crash program for the development of the bomb, as America had done with the Manhattan Project. That this is precisely what the Russians did is evident from the fact that barely four years later they exploded their first atomic bomb.

The controversy over the atomic bomb gave rise to one of the central drives of American imperialism—*control*. Virtually everyone agreed that the destructive power of the bomb was so vast that it had to be subjected to the tightest controls. The easygoing laissez-faire internationalism of the scientists could no longer be tolerated. A casual conversation between Oppenheimer and Kapitza could easily produce disaster; equally dangerous was a conversation between Oppenheimer and a British scientist. Free competition might prove beneficial economically by stimulating growth and was essential to the world of ideas and even of ordinary politics, but in the realm of nuclear physics it posed great dangers. The controversy that erupted in the weeks and months following Hiroshima was not over whether the bomb should be controlled or not, but over who should control it.

The nationalists never had any doubts as to who should control the bomb. Control should not only remain in purely American hands, but be vested in the military, specifically the Joint Chiefs of Staff who, unlike the White House, were entirely above politics. Nationalists regard the Joint Chiefs of Staff much like the Supreme Court, men who are professionally and not politically dedicated to a higher calling, the Supreme Court to the preservation of the Constitution and the Joint Chiefs of Staff to the defense of America. They were certain that if Russia and not America had the bomb, the Soviets would seek to extend their domination over the entire globe. At the same time, if the wrong people in the United States controlled the bomb, they could use that power to transform the country in their own image. The only situation the nationalists could conceive of where control of the bomb would play no role other than the military defense of the United States was if it was solidly vested within the military.

The internationalists were impressed by the fact that nuclear science was so international already that nothing could prevent Russia, Britain, and a host of other nations from ultimately developing their own bombs. The only conceivable way to stop that from happening was preventive war, which some of the nationalist military began to advocate. The internationalists, for all their anticommunism, were appalled by this prospect; a preventive war might produce horrors even greater than the atomic competition it was designed to prevent. Revolutionary pressures would arise out of the chaos of such a war and destroy international capitalism. In spite of their distrust of the Russians, the internationalists believed that there was no alternative but to involve them in the international control of nuclear energy. Since the United Nations was the only international institution available to exercise such control, various schemes like the Acheson-Lilienthal and Baruch plans aimed at turning it into a control commission for nuclear energy. The essence of the internationalist American plans was that a treaty for the regulation of atomic power and weaponry would be buttressed by the toughest prescriptions for sanctions in case of violations. The Baruch Plan sought to satisfy nationalist objections by denying the Russians veto power in the Security Council on the question of treaty violations. Thus, presumably, if Russia violated the treaty, the United Nations as a body could attack with military force to make it comply or to punish it as a naked aggressor.

The real victors in this controversy were neither the nationalists nor the internationalists but a new breed of political men now called the national security bureaucracy. Atomic energy was not internationalized, nor was its power allowed to remain in the hands of the military. Full control was eventually assumed by the highest levels of the United States government, symbolized by the creation of an Atomic Energy Commission (AEC) whose chain of command went directly to the White House. The nationalists fought hard to create a military advisory committee for the AEC, but when the final version of the McMahon Bill was adopted, this provision was rejected. The internationalists fought hard to provide for some cooperation with Britain and Canada on atomic matters, but this too was rejected. Atomic and subsequently nuclear energy were to be managed by the President of the United States as a monopoly with operations in the hands of a committee, the Atomic Energy Commission, which had no ties to any other bureaucracy of the government. Above all, only the President of the United States had the authority to determine how, when, where, and if an atomic weapon should be used in a conflict with a foreign power.

CONTAINMENT

By the summer of 1947 a new current in American foreign policy became evident, symbolized by the word "containment." This doctrine ostensibly derives from George Kennan, who, from his post as ambassador to Russia, wired home dire cables about the inexorable character of Russian expansionism. Russia might be communist in ideology, he noted, but the real force for its expansionism was nationalist and went far back into Russian history. Unless the free nations put up powerful walls to contain this expansionism, Russian power would ooze out over Western Europe and Asia, and before long America and its allies would be faced with a threat as great as that from Nazi Germany. Kennan's "cable from Moscow" came a little less than a year after former Prime Minister Churchill had given his famous Iron Curtain speech at Fulton, Missouri, in March 1946. Throughout 1946 there was no lack of voices within America speaking of the growing danger emanating from Russia. That a case could be made for Russian expansionism is obvious. Stalin had concluded that great power cooperation was no longer feasible and he might as well fasten his hold on Eastern Europe, as well as on the Soviet zone of Germany. The great atomic test at Bikini on July 1, 1946, was a bad sign, indicating that America was pushing the development of new atomic bombs to the hilt with the ever-present threat that they might be used against Russia. Negotiations for a coalition government in China had broken down, making civil war a certainty. Everywhere Russian-American relations were getting worse. In the euphoric days after Yalta, Stalin had been in the mood for concessions to the British and Ameri-

cans, but as the months of the Truman Administration passed, he realized that concessions were always followed by more demands.
Undoubtedly remembering his experiences with Hitler, Stalin decided
that the only language the capitalists understood was power, and moved
to consolidate Russia's control over its front entrance in Eastern Europe.

Whether Russia was or was not expansionist is not vital to understanding why the new foreign policy current of containment arose. The
facts marshaled by such eminent experts as George Kennan served an
already existing ideological need in Washington. The allegedly electrify-
ing impact of his cable of February 1947, and later his "Mr. X" article
in *Foreign Affairs*, was hardly due to their analytical brilliance. The
rising national security bureaucracy clustered around the White House
needed a view of the world that would fit the policies they were
beginning to develop.

Kennan's cables and articles, while meant for the bureaucracy rather
than the public, had the same ideological impact as *Mein Kampf* had
earlier in showing a nation bent on eating up the entire world. Kennan's
portrayal of Russia in terms reminiscent of Germany was more welcome to Washington than the rising theme of an international communist
conspiracy. Then in the forefront of an effort to uplift, liberate, and
reform the world, Washington had no stomach for an anticommunist
crusade which would line it up with the international right wing. But an
expansionist Russia could allow for the same kind of global united front
that was mounted to resist German and Japanese expansion.

The Democrats who ruled Washington in the postwar years were
committed to the notion that the American government had the key role
in bringing security, peace, and progress to the world. But they did not
yet have an operational ideology for America's new role in the world
comparable to New Deal ideology on the home front. The nationalists
and the internationalists already had world views that envisaged a definite external role for America. For the nationalists, what mattered was
dealing with other nations on an *ad hoc* basis for one purpose: serving
American interests. To make sure that those interests were respected,
America had to remain strong, and what better way to remain supreme
than to keep and enforce its own atomic monopoly. The internationalists
wanted an economic world based on trade and free enterprise with
threats and opportunities handled in utilitarian terms. What Kennan's
contributions made possible was the elaboration of a world view that
gave the government—not the military or the corporations—the leading
role in the new adventures abroad.

The origin of these imperialist policies cannot be dissociated from the
Anglo-American alliance which developed at this time and proved to be
closer and more harmonious than it was during the war. Laborite Britain,

which had aroused feelings of horror among American free enterprisers, turned out to be America's staunchest ally in the development of its imperialist policies. During the war, America and Britain collaborated mainly in the campaign against Germany. Elsewhere in the world, the two nations went their separate ways. In fact, to Churchill's fury, Roosevelt even showed inclinations to break up the British colonial empire. But after the war, America and Britain became close collaborators not just in Western Europe but throughout the world. Britain was in a precarious position when the war ended. It was heavily in debt not only to the United States but to many of its colonies as well, notably India. Moreover, with the Laborite victory in August 1945, Britain launched the welfare state, which imposed a new drain on its limited resources. Most significant of all, the tide toward independence from colonial rule seemed irresistible. The Laborites were more prepared ideologically than the Tories to grant political independence to the colonies, but they were still faced with the heavy burden of maintaining military forces in faraway places. Where "responsible governments" (mainly British-trained elites) would assume political leadership, London was usually glad to grant independence, since this did not involve jeopardy to British economic interests and political influence (after all, the newly independent countries elected to remain within the Commonwealth). But in too many parts of the world either there were no such responsible governments or real threats demanded the continued presence of British military force, at great cost.

In the five years following 1945, Britain had to keep a powerful military presence in Greece, Malaya, the Suez Canal, Jordan, and Iraq, and had to maintain far-flung naval and air units to preserve its credibility as a world military power. In addition, it had to maintain occupation forces in Germany and other parts of Western Europe. In Greece and Malaya, Britain fought Communist revolutionary movements which threatened to bring into power governments that could not be counted on to cooperate with Britain. In the Middle East (which included Greece), nationalist unrest and Arab-Jewish conflict threatened to spill over into regions from which most of the world's oil came. Iran was turbulent because of a left-wing government in Azerbaijan. Rebellious Kurds threatened the Mosul oil fields. King Farouk's rule in Egypt was unstable. Southeast Asia had the same kind of turbulence. Indonesian nationalists were threatening Dutch rule and Vietnamese insurgents would not let the French back into Indochina.

The British feared that the chaos that had beset Europe after the First World War would this time erupt in Asia and the Middle East. Almost everywhere in Asia, civil wars were threatening: between Hindus and Muslims in India, between Jews and Arabs in Palestine, between pro-

communist Turks and proroyalist Persians in Iran, and between pro-
colonialist and anticolonialist elements in Indochina, Malaya, Indonesia,
and Burma; in Greece, the struggle was between Communists and anti-
Communists. The Laborites did not share the Tories' confident assumptions that a few staunch British soldiers could easily restore law and
order. In fact, they suspected old empire loyalists in India and Palestine
of causing more trouble than was necessary. The Laborites shared one
attitude with the Tories: they were deeply anticommunist. Like Walt W.
Rostow two decades later, they believed that the communists were trouble exploiters who misused natural class and racial conflicts to obtain
power. They regarded them as a naked organizational force blindly loyal
to Moscow, from whom they expected moral and material support. Like
their American labor counterparts, the British Laborites had had considerable experience fighting communists in the labor movement. Bevin
criticized Churchill's easygoing friendliness with Stalin and himself preferred to spit in Molotov's face. In Greece, the Communists were receiv-
ing weapons from Tito, Moscow's loyal ally in the Balkans. In Iran, the
communist Tudeh movement was headed by an out-and-out Soviet
agent, Pishavari. In Malaya, Chin Peng was a Moscow-oriented Communist. Thank God that the Communists were still weak in India, where
responsible socialists like Jawaharlal Nehru or Islamic nationalists like
Muhammad Ali Jinnah could assume power from the British. And while
the Glubb Pashas favored the Arabs in Palestine, London knew that Ben-
Gurion was a socialist Zionist who could be expected to keep the communist virus out if a Jewish state came into being.

The postwar Anglo-American alliance had several facets. One was the
cooperation that flowed naturally out of Bretton Woods where, despite
strong disagreements about the postwar monetary system, America and
Britain assumed joint responsibility for maintaining the dollar and sterling as key world currencies. Anglo-American cooperation was vital for
the resolution of the German question and the eventual creation of a
separate Western zone ("Bizonia") out of which the German Federal
Republic emerged. Anglo-American cooperation was further necessitated by the fact that the British, even without American know-how,
were developing an atomic bomb. These and the many other strands of
the alliance naturally facilitated cooperation on the most difficult problem facing Britain: how to extricate itself from its outmoded empire
without going bankrupt, while assuring an orderly transition of power to
"responsible" governments. The Laborites were opposed to empire but
committed to the Commonwealth. With the enormous economic burdens
weighing on Britain, London could not afford to lose its share from
participation in a world market system that it enjoyed by virtue of far-
flung foreign investments, from its central role as a capital market and
banking center, and from access to markets in the sterling area.

While Britain felt it could still mount the military power to protect the emerging Commonwealth, it lacked the economic means to do so. If the Commonwealth, comparable formations like the "French Union," and sundry new nations were to be kept afloat, vast sums of money would have to be spent. The only source of such monies was the United States. With a combination of British (and French) military power and American money, the West would be able to maintain control over the emerging countries even while granting them political independence. For over a year after the war, Britain tried to struggle along with monetary infusions from the United States and Canada, but by early 1947 it was facing economic collapse. The British informed Washington then that Greece was on the verge of being taken over by the Communists, which, if it happened, would inevitably produce a domino effect in the fall of Turkey. Truman rose to the challenge and proclaimed his Truman Doctrine for Greece and Turkey. This was the first and most important policy action expressing the new doctrine of containment. It drew a line along the Greek and Turkish borders with Russia and its allies in Eastern Europe. In subsequent years, containment would pursue its line-drawing policies over the entire globe, each time proclaiming the line of demarcation an inviolable frontier. With the proclamation of the Truman Doctrine on March 12, 1947, the United States formally became an imperial power by assuming the mantle of empire from faltering Britain.

Assuming that mantle required, above all, an American commitment to provide the military means necessary to prevent threatened parts of the empire from falling into hostile hands. Defending the empire demanded military means of a particular nature: *conventional* forces (troops, ships, and planes) which could establish bases in threatened regions, engage in ground combat where necessary, or be introduced in sufficient numbers to prop up threatened regimes. As America found out during the Second World War and as it was to rediscover during the Korean and Vietnam wars, conventional forces are exceedingly costly. In contrast to strategic weapons whose initial heavy costs for research and development subsequently decline, conventional weapons, particularly troops, require constant or increasing outlays. By demobilizing its vast armies just after World War II, Washington was able to effect drastic cuts in its budgets. Aside from occupation forces in Germany and Japan, it no longer needed to maintain large standing forces. Britain, on the other hand, was unable to make a similar cutback in its budgets. Along with the increased burden of welfare spending, it was faced with the crushing costs of maintaining occupation armies in Europe and fighting forces in Malaya, the Middle East, and Greece, as well as vast naval installations throughout the world. To make things even worse, Britain also was committed to developing its own atomic capability. In March 1947, Britain formally requested America to take over this burden and

Truman responded with alacrity. The Truman Doctrine on Greece and Turkey aroused vigorous opposition within the United States, from both nationalists and internationalists. But when Truman invoked the specter of Russian expansionism, the voices were silenced and "bipartisan" support was given to America's new global imperial role.

Without the Russian threat, neither the nationalists nor the internationalists would have so meekly accepted the new American imperialism. The nationalists were horrified by the vast new spending which these commitments brought with them. They wanted to concentrate on strategic weapons, to maintain the American atomic monopoly, and to enforce that monopoly by a preventive strike against Russia if necessary. When the issue of universal military training was raised, the nationalists opposed it bitterly. They saw it as a device for creating a federal dictatorship which would bankrupt corporate enterprise and usher in a *de facto* socialism, while involving America in a whole range of conflicts where basic American interests were not threatened. America had no real interests in Greece worth defending, and money spent there was designed only to pull Britain's chestnuts out of the fire—*except* that the Greek Communists were Moscow's instrument. The extension of Russian power anywhere in the world was viewed by the nationalists as a threat, and so grudgingly they accepted the Truman Doctrine. But the Truman Doctrine involved more than providing American military protection to Greece and Turkey. Truman announced a vast program of economic and military assistance (foreign aid) to both countries, which set a precedent for the entire range of foreign aid programs which soon followed. Foreign aid to India and Pakistan could then easily be justified as preventive actions designed to avoid the creation of Greek-type insurgencies which would require even more costly military intervention (an analogy originally applied to Turkey).

The internationalists were primarily interested in Western Europe's economic recovery and wanted large-scale infusions of money into the European countries. Though inflation-conscious and not Keynesians, they did not regard these monetary infusions as waste. Economic recovery in Europe would lead to American loans being repaid, a stimulation of world trade which could only benefit America, and a climate of general economic stability which would incur new enterprise. They were as conscious of the Russian threat as the nationalists, but in a different way. The three countries of the emerging "Catholic Union" (France, Germany, and Italy) contained large, powerful Communist and Socialist movements. Italy voted to become a republic by ousting the monarchy which the American conservative internationalists regarded as a stabilizing force (like the Japanese Emperor). Communists and left-wing Socialists were growing so fast in Italy that a left-wing electoral triumph was a distinct possibility. In Germany, Adenauer's Christian Democrats were not threatened so much by Communists as by Social Democrats. True, Kurt Schumacher and Erich Ollenhauer were anticommunist and anti-Russian, but a Socialist assumption of power in West Germany was very disturbing. Socialist programs in Germany could wreck the emerging revival of free enterprise capitalism with damaging effects on the international market system. So also in France, where the Communist and Socialist threats were great and could oust de Gaulle from power. Socialism of any variety in the three great Western European countries would forever smash the dreams of a European economic union, since socialist governments would be forced to follow nationalist economic policies in order to pay for the vast social welfare schemes they wanted to introduce. The best European spokesman for this conservative internationalist current was Konrad Adenauer, who loathed Marxism, socialism, and Russia as essentially the same phenomena. Adenauer was not a "revanchist," the Russian term applied to post-Hitlerian Germans who wanted to retake lost eastern territories. He wanted to keep Russia or Russian influence out of Western Europe. If the Truman Doctrine on Greece and Turkey resulted in the United States committing itself more solidly to conservative Europe through money and troops, it was to be loudly welcomed.

Russian expansionism was the key to the acceptance within the United States of the Anglo-American program for the transfer of empire onto America's shoulders, the launching of the Marshall Plan to revive Western Europe, the institution of world-wide foreign aid, American rearmament, and especially the American government's new policy of peacetime fiscal expansionism. If Russia was expanding, that constituted a threat. A preventive nuclear strike, which the nationalists advocated, was too risky, because in the long run it would create even more chaos in the world and provide favorable conditions for anticapitalist movements. The threat could also be ignored or attempts be made to negotiate arrangements with the Russians to minimize it by mutual accord. But negotiation with the Russians was believed to be futile, inasmuch as they would not budge on opening the doors of their country to on-site inspection and control. So long as Russia was unwilling to join the international community on American terms, there was no way to convince the nationalists or the internationalists that it was becoming "responsible." The only solution was *containment*, the spirit of which is best captured in the French rendering of the word, *"endiguement." Endiguement* means building a network of dikes to hold in onrushing flood waters. Dike systems are costly, widespread, and must be hermetically sealed at even the most remote point. They not only protect populations from floods, but allow the working of fields so that wealth can be produced. Containment would not only protect the free world but allow the new world order based on the Pax Americana to flourish. It was the best possible doctrine to allow the formation of a peculiarly American type of empire.

All this suggests that whether or not Russia was expansionist is not crucial to understanding how the new foreign policy current of containment came into being. Whether Russia actually wanted to annex new territories directly, as in the case of eastern Poland, or indirectly, as through the Communist assumption of power in Czechoslovakia, was not the question. There was, however, a real and important form of Russian expansionism that had great effect on the formation of containment policies. Russia had decided to develop an atomic bomb and, faced with preventive war fulminations from American nationalists and militarists, also decided to keep large-scale standing ground forces. Those forces did pose a threat, for it was generally assumed that if Russia were attacked with atomic weapons, it would retaliate by occupying Western Europe. The Americans subsequently claimed that their nuclear power deterred the Russians from attacking Western Europe, while the Russians likewise believed that their massive conventional forces deterred the Americans from striking at them with nuclear weapons. Regardless of who struck first, however, war between America and Russia would lead to a Russian occupation of Western Europe and perhaps the British Isles as well. When Churchill and other British leaders spoke of the threat of Russian armies sweeping to the English Channel, they did not mean that Stalin was harboring some insidious scheme for world conquest for which he was just awaiting the opportune moment, but rather that if for some reason a Russo-American war should occur, this is just what would happen. The implication of these alarms was that under no circumstances must war be allowed to break out. The men who ruled Western Europe at this time had lived through two world wars and were fully aware of the unpredictable ways in which minor incidents could lead to great conflagrations. They also were aware that weak leadership bore major responsibility for the outbreak of those wars, for the inability to avoid it in 1914 and the inability to prevent it in 1939. The British in particular understood that the unexpected eruption of atomic power on the world political scene posed unprecedented dangers. Any minor incident—a border conflict, a sudden upsurge of irrationality in either Moscow or Washington, the collapse of a political regime in a sensitive intermediate area—could lead to a chain reaction of stroke and counterstroke until the inevitable climax was reached: American atomic weapons flying toward Russia followed by Russian military occupation of Western Europe (or the reverse). The British, with their greater socialist proclivities for control, were even more convinced than the Americans that the Anglo-American combine had supreme responsibility to exercise controls over the political-military elements of the world scene so that such a chain reaction could never occur.

American leaders, especially Harry Truman and Dean Acheson, came to the same conclusion. Their greatest fear, shared with millions throughout the world, was a third world war leading to the destruction of the planet itself. They did not believe that Russia wished to launch such a war. They feared rather that it would break out by accident, by the cumulative effects of political and military tensions that needed only some minor spark to erupt. While they publicly harped on the Russian threat, they were fully aware of other pressures toward war. A resurgent American military, particularly the Air Force, was pressing for action to prevent Russia from developing atomic weapons. Conservative regimes throughout the world were ready to manufacture incidents to get America involved. And, of course, American leaders suspected a profound irrationality within Russia itself which might lead Stalin to carry out some horrendously provocative action, such as he was presumed to have done in Czechoslovakia or by blockading Berlin. Atomic power necessitated drastic controls, and the evolving world tensions convinced them that these had to be extended farther and deeper through the world so as to make impossible, at least from the American side, an incident that could set off the chain reaction.

The authors of United States containment policy saw three great sources of danger. First, they were convinced that Russian development of atomic weapons and build-up of conventional forces posed a supreme danger. If the balance of power tilted away from the United States, pressures would rise from American nationalist circles and from countries contiguous to the Russian-controlled parts of the world to redress the balance, by anything ranging from a first strike against Russia to vast new military deployments or political and economic commitments. Secondly, they were convinced that any trouble in areas where Russian and American interests collided could have a Serbian effect leading from minor incidents, in domino fashion, to full-scale war. And thirdly, "chaos" in the free world could lead to changes in the geographical balance of power between Russia and America which, again, would bring pressures from within the United States and the threatened countries to redress the balance by forceful military action.

Their response to these three dangers constituted the core and essence of containment policy. First, failing any chance of achieving enforceable accords with the Russians on nuclear weapons, the United States had to undertake a crash program to develop weapons of such scope and quantity and so speedily that no matter what the Russians did, they would never be able to catch up. Furthermore, control over nuclear weapons and energy had to be removed from the military and placed in the White

House. Secondly, to eliminate any doubts from the minds of the Russians as to what areas America considered part of its empire and what areas it conceded to Russia, it undertook to draw demarcation lines which eventually encircled the Soviet Union from northern Norway to the 38th parallel in Korea. And thirdly, to prevent chaos, America undertook a vast program of foreign aid to promote economic development, first in Europe, and then in a whole array of poor countries, particularly those "threatened by communism."

Russia, of course, was the common denominator of each of these fears and the responses to them. It was the only power capable of matching the United States militarily. The world's major trouble spots—Berlin, Greece, Iran, and Korea—were in areas where Russia collided with the newly emerging American empire. And the most threatening form of "chaos" came from communist revolutionary movements in such countries as Greece, Azerbaijan, the Philippines, Malaya, Korea, Indochina, and, of course, China. Cultivated gentlemen like Acheson and Kennan, machine politicians like Truman, tough lawyers like Forrestal and Dulles, all shared an overwhelming fear born of two world wars and a great depression. The only way to banish that fear was to have total security or, as James Forrestal said in December 1947: "We are dealing with a deadly force and nothing less than 100 percent security will do."[6] Russian paranoia was easily matched by American paranoia, and both countries opted for the same solution: control, control, and more control.

THE WORLD VIEW OF CONTAINMENT

Although the popular sentiments of fear and yearning for security served to energize new policies, those policies were already in the making when the war ended. The war's end had launched a natural process of dismantling the political, military, and economic powers that government had acquired during the war. If that process were allowed to run its course, America and the rest of the world could face undreamt of chaos. The awesome new bomb alone demanded political and military controls of the highest order. And on the home front, a return to pre-1933 laissez-faire capitalism could lead, sooner or later, to a new crash. The solution to the challenge could not be just domestic, as in 1919. America had inherited the leadership and responsibility of the world. Thus, if controls were to be instituted to banish fear and assure security, it would have to be done by government and on a world-wide scale. But without some

[6] Fleming, *The Cold War and Its Origins*, vol. 1, p. 487.

way to exert force on the interests and make them accept the new policies, often at cost to themselves, it would not have been possible to carry out these policies. What containment needed was a credible view of the world, an ideology so compelling that it would create a new type of power to halt the dismantling process and build up the government in Washington for its new global and domestic roles.

The world view of containment quickly came to be a powerful new adjunct to general liberal ideology widely accepted both at home and abroad. Americans are generally unaccustomed to the idea that they are governed by ideologies, preferring to believe that ideologies are what foreigners have. It is accepted that ideas govern policies, but the conventional American view is that either these ideas are correct and true and action naturally flows from them or they are rhetorical lies designed to cover up sinister machinations. Correct ideas are usually supplied by trained experts or "intelligence agencies" created for the purpose of providing ideas, analyses, and facts.

In *Ideology and Organization in Communist China,* I defined ideology as a systematic set of ideas with action consequences for the purpose of creating and using organization. The socialist countries have created all kinds of new organizations out of their ideological currents. What is not yet realized in America is that the containment world view along with the general liberal ideology was the matrix out of which arose the vast apparatus of government dealing with national security matters. As the cold war progressed, mounds of writing—academic, popular, and officialese—appeared on the subject of "Soviet totalitarianism," which became a slogan for containment's view of Russia. The word "totalitarian," originally applied to Nazi Germany, was eagerly transferred to Russia. Yet for all the elaboration on this theme, George Kennan had already stated the core of containment's view of Russia in his famous "cable from Moscow":

> At bottom of Kremlin's neurotic view of world affairs is traditional and instinctive Russian sense of insecurity—And they have learned to seek security only in patient but deadly struggle for total destruction of rival power, never in compacts or compromises with it. . . .
>
> In summary, we have here a political force committed fanatically to the belief that with US there can be no permanent modus vivendi, that it is desirable and necessary that the internal harmony of our society be broken, if Soviet power is to be secure. This political force has complete power of disposition over energies of one of the world's greatest peoples and resources of world's richest national territory, and is borne along by deep and powerful currents of Russian nationalism. In addition, it has an elaborate and far flung apparatus for exertion of its influence in other countries, an apparatus

of amazing flexibility and versatility, managed by people whose experience and skill in underground methods are presumably without parallel in history. Finally, it is seemingly inaccessible to considerations of reality in its basic reactions. For it, the vast fund of objective fact about human society is not, as with us, the measure against which outlook is constantly being tested and re-formed, but a grab bag from which individual items are selected arbitrarily and tendenciously to bolster an outlook already preconceived.[7]

Noteworthy in Kennan's writings, and in much subsequent writing on Soviet totalitarianism by containment supporters, are the constant repetition of a "Russian" theme and the relatively little stress put on "communism." For Kennan, international communism is an instrument of Russian nationalism. It seems natural that a man versed in Russian affairs should take such an approach. But the echo that his views evoked so rapidly from Washington shows that they were just what it was looking for. While Kennan and other writers on totalitarianism did not crudely equate Communist Russia with Nazi Germany, essentially they saw the two countries as similar. Both were driven by intense nationalisms, Germany's arising from a deep-seated racism and a hunger for conquest, Russia's from an equally deep-rooted sense of inferiority and insecurity. Nevertheless, like Nazi Germany, Communist Russia was driven to expand beyond its borders, ever ready to pounce politically and militarily if it perceived some weakness in its opponents. Russia was driven, above all, by the desire to control, which gave it a totalitarian character. Communists everywhere sought to seize power so that they could establish police states in the image of Russia, detach countries from the West and swing them into the Soviet orbit. This was nothing more than naked Russian expansionism, little different from Hitler's. And like Hitler's expansionism, it constituted a permanent danger of war unless the West could put up such powerful dikes around the Russian flood that it could not gush out over its natural borders. Appeasement of Hitler led to World War II, and appeasement of Russia could only lead to World War III.

With the "one world" notions popularized during World War II and subsequently with the world-unifying effects of strategic air power, people had come to think in global terms. To this global consciousness (fully shared by the Russians and later the Chinese), the containment view added certain particular dimensions. There were two and only two great powers in the world, America and Russia. They were great by virtue of the immense land mass they possessed, their economic strength and potential, and their unmatched military power. Containment saw the

[7] Barton J. Bernstein and Allen J. Matusow, eds., *The Truman Administration*, pp. 202, 209.

free world headed by America as one in which yearnings for peace, security, and progress were the dominant force and were to be satisfied by democratic, not coercive, means. On the other hand, the communist world, headed by Russia was ever intent on threatening peace, security, and progress for the sake of deepening and extending Russian control. The world was locked in a struggle between two great powers, America with its allies and Russia with its satellites. Containment conceived of a dialectical relationship between the two countries in the sense that everything Russia did or did not do had a direct effect on America. Thus, the rise or fall of Russian industrial or agricultural output was not merely an internal Russian matter but would affect American military budgets. If Soviet or Czech arms were sent to some tiny Latin American country, the precarious balance of power between the two giants was immediately endangered. Similarly, what America did or did not do directly affected Russia. As American military advantage went up or down, Russian expansion was correspondingly either discouraged or encouraged. If an ally of America faltered, this could create a vacuum inviting the Russians to step in. The logical conclusion of containment was that if the building blocks of the free world were secure and the structures erected with them solid everywhere along the perimeter where the free and communist worlds met, then world stability would ensue. Countries in the free world could then go about the business of seeking peace, security, and progress in their own ways without threatening the security of the world as a whole.

While it has become fashionable to ridicule this cold war Manichaeanism, it served purposes beyond enabling America to build up its empire or Russia to fashion its own "socialist camp." Containment ideology asserted a kind of global unity which neither the nationalist nor internationalist current was able to do or even wanted to do. American nationalists came to develop their own world view centered on the notion of an "International Communist Conspiracy," which envisioned an insidious force, communism, of which Russia was a tool. As David Sarnoff once put it, "World communism is not a tool in the hands of Russia—Russia is a tool in the hands of world communism."[8] This view of Russia was the exact reverse of Kennan's. Communism was a force which permeated the entire world right up to the highest levels of the American government. Where containment provided a view of the world which seemed logical and practical (lines could be drawn at precise points to dam Russian expansionism), anticommunism could not define "the enemy" with any precision. Because of its messiness, it never had the powerful operational consequences of the containment world view, although na-

[8] David Sarnoff, "A Political Offensive Against Communism," in Walter F. Hahn and John C. Neff, eds., *American Strategy for the Nuclear Age*, p. 428.

tionalism, out of which one form of anticommunism grew, had much
deeper popular roots than containment, which never shed its ethereal
academic character. The free trade doctrines of the internationalists
ranging from Henry Wallace to John Foster Dulles imputed a kind of
unity to the world, but one that necessarily excluded Russia.

Containment also gave rise to the socialist camp. It imputed a unity to
the international communist movement which it had not had since before
Stalin's emasculation of the Comintern in the 1930s. Without the cold
war, Stalin would probably not have done much to aid China after its
liberation. Washington would have recognized the new Chinese government in 1949, trade between China and the outside world would have
continued, and the Communists would have had to muddle through in
China without the great stimulus of American hostility.

Containment asserted a global unity in an even more important sense.
It made the nuclear competition between America and Russia the central
fact of world history in the eyes of their respective governments. Out of
that competition came the notion of a "nuclear umbrella," which America and Russia each extended over the territories presumed to belong
indisputably to its camp. Containment, therefore, viewed the world as
characterized mainly by two immense entities in conflict. Each of them,
the free world and the socialist camp, was headed by one nation, different from all others by virtue of its size and power. The two entities were
engaged in a never-ending conflict which, however, could be frozen bit
by bit. But the process of freezing had to proceed from the top down.
First, the two superpowers had to freeze their own relationship, mainly
through a balance of military power whereby neither could strike at the
other. On the American side, the notion of how such a balance was to be
achieved shifted over time from superiority to parity to sufficiency. But
since from the very beginning of the notion of containment avoidance of
war was considered a supreme goal, some conception of a freezing of
military power on both sides was implicit. If balance was achieved at the
top, then the two superpowers could gradually proceed to arrange the
other parts of the world so as to exclude forever the kind of conflict that
could mushroom into nuclear war. Freezing the rivers of demarcation
between the free world and the socialist camp was regarded as the necessary prerequisite for building any bridges across them.

The containment world view was a creative synthesis of the nationalist
and internationalist currents with elements that fitted the liberal drive
toward bigger government and greater spending. Kennan's imputation of
nationalism to Russia was matched with the primacy assigned to America as the leader of the free world. Containment was an American policy
designed to serve American interests, symbolized by America's determination to retain a nuclear monopoly in the free world (Britain's feeble

nuclear attempts were not deemed a threat to that monopoly, nor was de Gaulle's later *force de frappe*). Thus, nationalists like Vandenberg could be satisfied that containment never envisaged a sellout of American interests. At the same time, the internationalists could be satisfied in the knowledge that containment was committed to the prime need for a free enterprise capitalist economy within the bounds of the free world, that it supported the United Nations and all efforts at conservative international cooperation in Western Europe, that it favored the revival of capitalist economies in Germany and Japan, and that, while advocating foreign aid, it did not favor using it to support socialist practices (like state-owned industries) in recipient nations. While satisfying nationalist and internationalist concerns, containment also made indispensable the leading political role of the executive branch of the United States government as the holder of supreme power over nuclear matters, the fulcrum of world-wide alliances and organizations, and the great provider of economic assistance to the free world.

Last but by no means least important was the fact that the world view of containment was believable not just to conservatives but to many progressives in America and other lands, unlike Hitler's anti-Bolshevism which made sense only to the European right. For all the ideological commitment of the left to the Russian Revolution and for all the sympathy much of the world showed Russia during its heroic struggle with Nazi Germany, the specter of Stalinism was abhorrent to a large segment of the left which could not forget the purges, the Nazi-Soviet pact, and the police state character of the Soviet regime. A closed-off Russia dominated by archaic ideas, terrorized by the police, and oppressing whole nationalities was the antithesis of what an internationalist socialist country in the Marxist tradition was supposed to be. Perhaps Stalin was most responsible for the easy triumph the world view of containment won in the late 1940s.

The world view of containment made it possible to build up the realm of ideology. Concretely, that realm took the form of the enormously expanded executive branch of the United States government. Its material basis was the federal budget, in which the foreign affairs and national security component played an ever-increasing role until by the early 1960s, it constituted not only the bulk of the budget but one-tenth of the gross national product of the United States. The executive branch acquired a monopoly over "national security policy." Constitutionally, this seemed to derive from the President's role as commander-in-chief. In times of peace, foreign affairs were to be conducted with the advice and consent of the Senate, which had to approve by two-thirds vote any treaties the President entered into. But the world view of containment enshrined a new doctrine, that of the cold war. The cold war was war, and even if not formally declared by Congress, "bipartisanship" in foreign policy signified acceptance of that war. This meant that, as in times of war, foreign affairs were virtually equivalent to national security affairs. More particularly, those foreign affairs that were construed as relating to the conflict between America and Russia were considered to be within the realm of national security. The executive branch thereby acquired a monopoly over all policies relating to national security, which ensured the President a minimum of interference in his national security policies from both the nationalists and the internationalists. Nationalists were strongly represented in Congress and in the military; internationalists were also strongly represented in Congress, with the State Department as their chief bureaucratic vehicle in government.

Presidential monopoly over national security affairs, over time, produced a range of bureaucratic institutions which were direct emanations of presidential power, such as the Central Intelligence Agency (CIA), the National Security Agency, the Atomic Energy Commission, and the various agencies concerned with foreign aid and information. In addition, it led to the creation within existing bureaucracies of top-level policy-making bodies concerned with foreign policy and national security affairs. This was to become most apparent in the Defense Department under Kennedy, where the International Security Agency (ISA), ostensibly a body that advised the Secretary of Defense on foreign affairs aspects of national defense, became a virtual "State Department." The ISA, as the Pentagon Papers reveal, was closer to the White House than to the military services over which the Secretary of Defense presided. It was concerned with "policy," whereas the services, by statute, were supposed to be concerned solely with "operations," that is, implementing policy.

The presidential monopoly over national security policy was the most important achievement of the government during the postwar period—an achievement constantly in danger of assault from nationalist and internationalist currents, which were excluded from the monopoly. Policy, as I have pointed out, means goals, direction, and methods. It specifies what is to be achieved; and by what routes; and it lays down the kinds of "capabilities" (in ordinary language, political, economic, military, and other weapons) to be used. Or, in the words of Samuel P. Huntington, policy means strategy and structure. The world view of containment reserved to the supreme leadership of America a very special kind of policy-making function. Since the American-Russian relationship was the most critical matter in America's foreign relations, since nuclear weaponry had created a *de facto* global unity, and since even minor actions in faraway places (Laos, for example) could have a direct bearing on the American-Russian relationship, only that body of the

American political structure which had total and comprehensive knowledge of the entire global picture could make national security policy. Congress or old established bureaucracies like the military services or the State Department, which represented particular interests, could not make national security policy because they were moved primarily by those interests and not by a disinterested awareness of the entire picture. Obviously, only the President and his national security bureaucracy could make national security policy for, by virtue of the great new intelligence agencies which surrounded them, only they had all the knowledge, all the facts, all the necessary wisdom.

Containment ideology envisioned an active role for America. The President was to be not just an arbiter who would decide from among various "options" presented to him by interest groups within the bureaucracy, a phenomenon of presidential decision-making power that was to become apparent (or seemingly so) under the Johnson and Nixon administrations. The duty of the President was to assure America's security and that of the free world primarily by creating conditions that would make it impossible for World War III to break out while preserving the interests of America and its free world clients and allies. Whether or not others shared that commitment either abroad or within the United States did not matter. The supreme criterion for judging the success of a national security policy was the fact that World War III had not occurred. If anyone argued that the fear of nuclear war was excessive and paranoiac (as Mao Tse-tung was alleged to have done), then the facts of nuclear destructive power could be presented to show that the madness was really on the side of the doubter. If a person feels threatened by an impending catastrophe of uncertain source, he will feel justified in fortifying his house and his grounds, stockpiling supplies, and keeping his family in a constant state of readiness. If the catastrophe should not occur, he can point to all the power, wealth, and internal discipline that this effort brought about. It was in this way, through the fears that nuclear weaponry generated, that the American empire came about. Abroad, the empire resulted in a degree of global organization that never before existed. At home, it created a vast American governmental power whose role is crucial to the maintenance of the economy and all other major social and political institutions in the country.

NUCLEAR WEAPONS AS IDEOLOGY

On August 6, 1945, America acquired a terrible new weapon which revolutionized all existing principles of warfare. As Japan's surrender showed, it was a weapon with which America could force enemies to

submit. Then, in the 1950s, nuclear weapons became a deterrent force
with immense retaliatory power. No nation could commit aggression
against America without fearing instant destruction of its entire population and territory. In the 1960s, the conviction began to surface that
nuclear weapons were not weapons at all because they could not be used.
If they were still to be regarded as weapons, then "overkill" capabilities
were pure waste, the point of marginal return having long since been
passed. If they were still to be regarded as deterrents, then merely a
demonstrable second-strike capability would be "sufficient" to give Russia or China pause before considering a strike against the United States.
Yet the accumulation of nuclear weaponry by America and Russia continues at so fast a pace that it is almost impossible to determine which
one has a first-strike capability. As one nuclear weapons system is developed and countered by the other side, another is dreamed up, as in an
endless chess game where move always produces countermove, and a
match ending in defeat, victory, or draw, is quickly followed by another.
One might think that although the unending accumulation of nuclear
weapons has lost much of its military significance, it is the kind of defense
spending that stimulates the economy. Even that is not certain. Nuclear
missile production provides few jobs and relatively small fiscal outlays
are needed to produce them (compared to bombers or carriers or submarines). However, while missiles are cheap, delivery systems, like Tri-
dent, cost astronomical sums. One might also assume that nuclear
weapons production creates inviting new fields of research and development with valuable spin-offs for other defense or civilian industries. Yet
even that does not seem to be true, since nuclear research and development has become so rarefied and specialized that direct application to
peaceful uses of nuclear energy are not apparent.

Now when Defense Department spokesmen appear before Congress to
ask for new funds for nuclear weapons and their delivery systems, incredulity is widespread. The inevitable argument they make is that the
Russians are devloping such-and-such a system and America has to
respond, or that America must develop such-and-such a system to force
the Russians, from a position of strength, into concluding arms control
agreements. And if the questioning gets too intense, the officials come up
with the clincher argument that not to vote the outlays requested will
"endanger national security," which usually suffices to collapse the opposition.

Nevertheless, there is a vast literature both within and outside the
bureaucracies that makes very convincing cases for whatever weapons
system is being advocated. Much of it is couched in abstruse terms, and
some even involves complex mathematical formulas, expressing the balance of power relationship between America and Russia. In fact, the

nuclear relationship between America and Russia is regarded as a game. At first, there was no game and only two pieces—the two atomic bombs dropped over Japan. But over time, a game developed with many pieces (new ones being added all the time) and a developing body of rules. Some of these rules were forced on the players by the nature of the weapons. Others were worked out in deliberative sessions, like the Geneva arms control talks and the more recent Strategic Arms Limitation Talks (SALT). Since the game has become so complex, ordinary mortals no longer understand it and are left with only the knowledge that, unlike chess, each piece of the game contains nuclear explosive material which could destroy everything.

The key fact about the nuclear game between America and Russia is just that—it involves (or is supposed to involve) *only* America and Russia. America and Russia are the world's two superpowers, that is, the only countries with incomparably advanced nuclear weaponry. As long as they continue to play the game, the basic security of the world is assured, for the game excludes the possibility of World War III. But the game is also a fact central to the containment world view. If the world is divided into two camps—the free world and the "Sino-Soviet bloc" (as it used to be called by containment's intellectuals)—then the successful playing of the game assures the perpetuation of that divided world. Playing the game signifies that the two superpowers accept each other's basic premises. On the American side, that means that the Russians agree not to make trouble in areas considered vital to the American camp, like Western Europe, and the Americans agree not to make trouble in similar regions of the Russian camp, namely Eastern Europe. Berlin in the 1940s, 1950s, and up until 1961 was the most important playing ground, in fact, was more important than arms control discussions. When the East Germans built the Berlin Wall, the containment lines in Europe appeared to have been completely drawn. Berlin ceased being a playing ground, and thereupon followed "arms control talks," the game being transferred from a geographical site to a negotiating table.

Just as in a chess game, a key question the two superpowers always ask is, What is the enemy's intention? Thus, when either America or Russia begins to develop a new weapons system, the other one feels it imperative to understand what its enemy has in mind. So long as it is a clearcut weapons development, the rules of the game do not appear to be violated, for the other side can make a matching response. Needless to say, these moves baffle ordinary people, including many in Congress, who persist in seeing the nuclear game as a military one involving "defense." It is hard for them to understand that multiplying "overkill" capabilities is essential for the game to continue. But gauging the enemy's intent involves much more than the weapons involved. It involves judging what he might want to do in real geographical parts of the world, particularly where the two worlds meet in sensitive confrontation. Thus, a quantum leap forward by the Russians in regard to some nuclear weapons system could mean that, while enjoying a temporary advantage, they might seek to advance their positions in the Middle East, for example. The containment demarcation lines are not clearcut as they are in Europe, so that the Russians might try to move a pawn forward there in preparation for a time when the lines might actually be drawn. A Russian move forward would have to elicit a countermove by the United States, which could take a variety of forms, each inherently dangerous (the least dangerous being the development of a new nuclear weapons system). Nevertheless, if move and countermove do not lead to crisis, then this has added one more rule to the game and thereby developed one more bond between the players.

Although the historical origins of the containment world view did not envisage the evolution of such an American-Russian nuclear game, the nationalist and internationalist elements that went into it facilitated bringing this about. The nationalists always held that America must be supremely powerful. The internationalists always held that some kind of global system must be created, whether through a world market system or the United Nations or in some other way. Containment made America supremely powerful and at the same time sought ways of bringing about a global unity which could assure peace without sacrificing American or free world interests. If the nuclear game was to be the instrument for bringing these conditions about, it was contingent on Russia's accepting the rules of the game. Thus, Russia had to become a kind of mirror image of America. And indeed, that is what happened. From Stalin's nationalist, closed-off Russia there arose a powerful USSR, which, as Mao Tse-tung could still say in November 1957, was "the leader of the socialist camp." The existence of a free world and a socialist camp was vital to the game. Moreover, it was vital that these two camps fill out gray areas, notably in the Third World, which escaped their control. America tried to do its bit by drawing lines, and there was no more avid line drawer than John Foster Dulles. Europe was divided by the Iron Curtain. Truman had already made the Greek-Turkish frontier with Russia and its clients a demarcation line. CENTO (Central Treaty Organization) included Iran and Pakistan. SEATO (Southeast Asia Treaty Organization) brought in Thailand. The 38th parallel became the demarcation line in Korea. The Taiwan Straits became a demarcation line on June 27, 1950. The 17th parallel became a demarcation line with the Geneva Accords of 1954. For the game to be played, it was necessary that move and countermove in the nuclear field be carried out in some systematic manner. But it was equally necessary that America and Russia maintain control over the areas assigned to each camp. No move that was not made by either America or Russia was to be allowed, except in areas of no mutual concern.

The study of the enemy's ideology was essential to both sides, for its ideology was construed as a sign of its intentions. Beginning in the late 1940s, reams of writing appeared in America on the subject of Russia. Every one of Stalin's and then Malenkov's and Khrushchev's speeches was minutely analyzed for clues to the thinking of Russia's leaders. Some defense intellectuals believed that there was an "operational code" that governed Soviet actions. Myriads of former Marxists and communists flocked to government agencies and their academic spin-offs to contribute their talents and experience in analyzing Russian documents. At a more rarefied level, other defense intellectuals with backgrounds in weaponry studies analyzed Russian "capabilities." Whether intent was deduced from speeches or capabilities or, as the more crude-minded military was wont to do, from real Russian actions or deployments, it all amounted to an effort to fathom their thought processes. After all, even behind the most naked military action there is a thinking mind with some sense of the ends and means involved. By the late 1950s, something called "convergence theory" began to emerge on the American side (and later was eagerly reciprocated by the Russians). Convergence theory, advocated by sociologists, economists, and political scientists, held that, for all their historical and ideological differences, Russia and America were becoming more alike as commonly industrialized societies. However true that may be in terms of simple indicators (the structure of industry, population patterns, occupational distribution, and so on), convergence theory also mirrored a phenomenon symbolized by the arms control talks between the two superpowers—they were beginning to understand each other's language and were allowing their thinking to be influenced by each other in ever more systematic ways.

The language of the nuclear relationship was the easiest to share because technical and scientific terms are international. But the common nuclear language provided the building blocks for comparable common political languages, which allowed any problem to be analyzed in terms of mutually understandable components and, therefore, more easily solved than if each message or signal was seen simply as an expression of will or sentiment. Summit conferences led to direct talks between American and Russian leaders. At the core of this pyramid, which gradually extended downward from its apex to its foundation, was the consciousness that any breakdown in the process could spiral upward and endanger the apex, the nuclear relationship. That could but must not occur, for the nuclear game was, above all other things, sacrosanct.

The ideological character of the American-Russian nuclear relationship can be seen in three words that Washington has been using during the past years to indicate its strategic posture: parity, superiority, sufficiency. As with all ideologies, words take on a transcendent importance. Certain words become symbolically important, and when they are changed, a signal goes out that policy has changed in some way or another. Anyone familiar with the course of the Paris negotiations on Vietnam is aware of the delicate semantics involved. So with the words parity, superiority, and sufficiency. Under the McNamara regime, the official stance was that America sought parity of weaponry with Russia. This signaled an intent to try to achieve a stand-off between the two superpowers. What was not realized at the time was that stand-off demanded that the Vietnam war be settled in such a way that containment's demarcation line, the 17th parallel, was restored. But when Clark Clifford became Defense Secretary, he began, ominously, to use the word "superiority" in regard to America's strategic posture vis-à-vis Russia. This was an aggressive move which signaled America's intention to move away from the notion of a stand-off. A potential new Russian-American arms race made the demarcation lines less sacrosanct. When Melvin Laird became Defense Secretary, he at first also spoke of superiority, but then Nixon revived an old 1956 Eisenhower term, "sufficiency." When the Nixon Administration backed off to a stance halfway between superiority and parity, it signaled an intent to the Russians of returning to a friendly policy but not quite so friendly as during the Kennedy and Johnson years. While the three words, parity, superiority, and sufficiency, have direct implications in budgetary terms for those involved, they mainly signify a general policy direction the administration has determined to pursue vis-à-vis Russia.

The nationalist view of nuclear weapons was nonideological. As Curtis LeMay once said, they are "just another weapon." The nationalists were suspicious about the growing bureaucratic rhetoric surrounding nuclear weapons, believing that the liberals were using it, always backed up by the horrifying prospect of total nuclear war, as a means of putting through policies anathema to the nationalists, such as arms control. The internationalist view of nuclear weapons was also nonideological. During the early postwar debates on atomic weapons, internationalists, such as Henry Stimson had shown himself to be on this issue, wanted to do away with them entirely, not just because they were too dangerous to mankind, but because they would muddy the emerging postwar politics. Subsequently, internationalist demands for the total destruction of nuclear weapons were modified in the direction of seeking arms control agreements. If arms control agreements were concluded that would put a permanent freeze on all types of nuclear and strategic weaponry, the power flowing out of the American-Russian nuclear relationship would cease, and the net effect, assuming no violation of the treaties, would be the same as doing away with them. Both nationalists and internationalists, therefore, took essentially practical approaches to the problem, each reflecting their own interest orientations. The ideological thrust relating to nuclear weaponry has come mainly from the containment liberals, the men of the national security bureaucracy who fashioned basic American foreign policy in the early postwar years and their successors. It is interesting that today the only voice with power behind it that demands complete destruction of nuclear weapons is China. The Chinese, as part of their basic foreign policy opposing "the two superpowers," naturally want to end the Russian-American nuclear relationship, which they regard as one of the great evils in the world. In practice, however, the Chinese follow a nationalist policy and are developing their own nuclear capabilities (as is France), believing (like France also) that a multipolar nuclear world is safer than a bipolar one.

Nuclear policy was the weapon with which America built its empire, for no other policy so clearly stated America's global intentions with ramifications for everything else. Nuclear policy was pure policy in that its operational consequences were nil or limited to building and deploying nuclear weapons which, of course, could not be used. The operational ramifications came in other areas—military, political, economic, and even cultural. But at the same time, by ultimately asserting a dialectical relationship to Russian nuclear power, nuclear policy helped to develop a universalism which nothing else could have achieved. The atomic bombs that destroyed Hiroshima and Nagasaki have turned out to be the first real steps toward the practical unification of the world.

CHAPTER 2

The Counterattack by Nationalism and Internationalism

American imperialism was not the natural extension of an expansionism which began with the very origins of America itself. Nor was it the natural outgrowth of a capitalist world market system which America helped to revive after 1945. American imperialism, whereby America undertook to dominate, organize, and direct the free world, was the product of Rooseveltian New Dealism. Two key convictions of New Dealism were that the free enterprise capitalist system was no longer capable of assuring full employment, the indispensable condition for social stability, through its own natural workings, and that the rising demands of the poor and oppressed could produce revolutionary chaos unless they were granted in one degree or another. From these two convictions arose a third with operational consequences: only a powerful national government could rescue free enterprise capitalism from its own contradictions (first term New Deal) and give economic security and hope to the militant masses (second term New Deal).

World War II proved to the Rooseveltian liberals that the New Deal could produce miracles if allowed to operate as its philosophy dictated. It also appeared to show, however, that those miracles happened only when people sensed themselves threatened by external enemies of an ideologically reprehensible sort. Fascism in all its varied forms was clearly an ideological enemy of radical New Dealism. When World War II ended, the euphoria of victory which characterized the post–World War I period was brief. Instead, a new fear of awesome proportions swept the world—the fear of atomic annihilation. No other exigency of postwar politics so justified the retention of immense governmental power exercised by a strong chief executive as the need to control atomic energy and its weapons. Nothing so fostered the growing power of that government as the universal demand for security from the dread possibility of atomic annihilation. Thus, instead of facing degeneration of government, as under Warren Harding, the American government after August 6, 1945, had a clear mandate for continuing its power. With that power, its New Deal liberal leaders felt that they could then begin to implement their other two convictions, not just for America but for the entire world. Just as they felt in the 1930s that the economy had to be treated as a whole, not just patched up in parts as Hoover tried to do, they felt after 1945 that the world had to be ordered as a whole, not piecemeal. They also believed that unless "the revolution of rising expectations," to use Adlai Stevenson's expression from the 1950s, could be met, chaos would encompass the world.

The theory I have been developing suggests a certain artificiality in American imperialism, that it was consciously contrived rather than naturally evolved. American imperialism was the product of the realm of ideology, not the realm of interests. The broad spectrum of American business, which constituted the chief interests of American society and whose political voice was the Republican party, was in a generally passive state at the end of the war. Big business was attracted by Hullian universalism's projection of a great new global market system which would spur free trade, and even by the possibility of doing business with Russia. All of American business wanted to end the irksome and dangerous wartime controls over prices as rapidly as possible, and, in particular, to lower tax rates so that more profits could be plowed back into new investments. While Wendell Willkie's "one world" philosophy found considerable resonance in business circles, their chief concerns at war's end were domestic. Unions had made alarming gains during the war and their power had to be cut back, which it was in succeeding years. Business welcomed reconversion because it saw great pent-up consumer demand fueled by vast wartime savings as providing a good market for consumer goods. Investment prospects abroad were not very inviting, and while there were promising foreign markets for American goods, the domestic American market seemed to be the most exciting arena for new profits. In short, there is little evidence that, at the end of the war, American business was straining at the leash to globally organize a war-destroyed external world.

The American military certainly had become an important arena of interests during World War II and was in no mood to shrink back to its prewar posture. Yet there also is no evidence that the military was either nationalistically expansionist or internationally imperialistic. The Army was virtually dismantled by the breakneck demobilization after V-J Day, and in the years after 1945 showed no great drive to reconstitute itself as a big force. "Mobilization" doctrines still prevailed, as Samuel P. Huntington has pointed out, meaning that peacetime ground forces should remain small with capabilities of launching a massive mobilization in case of war, pretty much as happened in the early 1940s. The Air

Force was caught in a struggle to establish itself as an independent service and was preoccupied with building up a Strategic Air Command to monopolize nuclear delivery systems. The Navy was traditionally expansionistic and intent on acquiring bases, particularly in the Pacific. Yet, in the spirit of classic national American expansionism, the Navy saw its role as mainly in the Pacific and was not thinking in global terms. MacArthur was busy democratizing Japan. Virtually all the top military leaders were economy-minded until the outbreak of the Korean War.

But as the new containment policy began to take shape, reaching a clear expression with Truman's March 1947 doctrine on Greece and Turkey, the attacks on the Truman Administration began to multiply. Henry Wallace's independent presidential campaign of 1948 was "left" internationalism's attack against containment. The "left" internationalists saw in the mounting cold war a threat to peace and, thus, to the workings of international capitalism. They feared a reversion to the 1930s, when nationalistic and autarkic blocs brought down the international economic system and produced World War II. Peace, they argued, was the only condition under which classic laissez-faire capitalism could prosper. The pacifist and communist left was naturally drawn to Wallace, producing an early version of that curious alliance between popular antiwar forces and certain Wall Street businessmen which would appear in the campaign against the Vietnam war. It is ironic that Wallace, who for all his social idealism deeply believed in world-wide free trade, was to be tainted with the brush of procommunism. There also was an attack by "right" internationalism against containment, symbolized by John Foster Dulles's blast, during the 1952 presidential campaign, against "the evil doctrine of containment."

The nationalist attack on the Truman Administration also assumed a variety of forms. Its racist subcurrents led to the 1948 Dixiecrat presidential campaign of Strom Thurmond, supported not only by Southern racists but by jingoists, nationalists, and militarists. Its antirevolutionary subcurrents led to a bitter campaign against labor unions in Congress, and to the campaign against "Communists in government" which produced McCarthyism. Its militarist subcurrents took the form of bitter opposition to the unification of the armed services in the newly created Department of Defense. The nationalists regarded this shackling of the military as a subversion of all the American principles of freedom and individualism and a direct road to governmental dictatorship.

While internationalist and nationalist attacks on the Truman Administration took various forms in the political arena, two overriding issues came to symbolize them: the Marshall Plan and China.

THE MARSHALL PLAN

The Marshall Plan was hailed by all the internationalists as one of the great expressions of American idealism and generosity, and the offer to include Russia seemed a genuine attempt to put a leash on the evolving cold war. Yet the essence of the Marshall Plan was to revive free enterprise capitalist economies in Western Europe and to prevent the formation of nationalistic and socialistic economies which might turn to autarky. West Germany not only became its most important beneficiary but turned into the most ardent advocate of classic free enterprise capitalism in the capitalist world. It is significant that the Marshall Plan, presented by Secretary of State George C. Marshall in his famous Harvard speech of June 5, 1947, came after the proclamation of the Truman Doctrine in March. It is even more significant that it was advanced at a time when the containment liberals were taking giant steps toward creating the centralized governing apparatus they felt was necessary to carry out their policies. In July 1947, Congress passed the National Security Act, which paved the way for the creation of the Defense Department and set up the National Security Council as a supreme cold war command headquarters. The bitter interservice battles that erupted as a result of these steps toward unification of the armed services were reflected in comparable battles within Congress. Congressional concern naturally was oriented toward the budget, for the new cold war programs inevitably entailed vast new expenditures. In early 1948, Walter Lippmann warned that America could not at the same time finance a global air force, a navy commanding all oceans, universal military service, heavy military research, the Marshall Plan, the states around the Soviet perimeter, and the good neighbor policy.[1] All of these were in the works before June 1947, save the program that was to lead to the Marshall Plan. The atomic energy program already was consuming huge federal funds. The growing controversy between the Navy and the Air Force over supercarriers and B-36 bombers was threatening to take bigger cuts out of the federal budget. The Truman Doctrine called for new funds to support Greece and Turkey, but at the same time a Korean aid bill was being argued about in Congress and pressure was mounting to give more aid to Chiang Kai-shek. While the internationalists, in one degree or another, accepted the need for better national defense, the area of greatest concern to them was Europe. In 1947, the entire Bretton Woods program was being threatened by Europe's inability to recover from the shambles of war. If capitalism failed in Europe, the drift toward forms of national

[1] Quoted in D. F. Fleming, *The Cold War and Its Origins*, vol. 1, p. 488.

socialism was inevitable. And if that happened, the part of American capitalism that was oriented to the world market system would disintegrate in Europe's wake.

The State Department was America's traditional repository of internationalist doctrines, and the agency of government most concerned about the worsening situation in Europe. Its Europe-oriented officials were hostile to communism and committed to conservative regimes which would preserve a free enterprise way of life. In the Far East, particularly China, a new breed of foreign service officer began to develop—idealistic, sympathetic with the new social movements that were arising there. But the Far East was of less concern to the State Department than other regions, so that it allowed aberrations to develop there, such as "China experts," which would not have been tolerated elsewhere. The State Department had been evolving views on postwar Europe since postwar planning began under Cordell Hull. Central to that planning was the notion that an economically resuscitated Germany was vital to the peace and security of Europe as well as America. But while the more extreme aspects of Morgenthau's proposals to de-industrialize Germany were easily disposed of, State Department views on Germany did not prevail in the immediate postwar years. In the interregnum between the resignation of Cordell Hull in November 1944 and the appointment of George Marshall in January 1947, the State Department lost considerable influence, manifest in the many secretaries of state that succeeded each other in that short period of time. Germany had been cut up into four zones, and the wrangling among the powers did not permit any unified policy to develop. Thus, the German economy continued to stagnate and alarming signs of a postwar inflation, comparable to Germany's post–World War I experience, began to reappear. If Germany was flat on its back, the economic situations of Britain, France, and Italy were not much better. European economic recovery could not be approached on a piecemeal, country-by-country basis. Only a unified plan could have hopes of bringing about recovery, and the full inclusion of Germany was vital.

In Secretary Marshall's Harvard speech, he stated:

> Any government that is willing to assist in the task of recovery will find full co-operation, I am sure, on the part of the United States Government. Any government which maneuvers to block the recovery of other countries cannot expect help from us. Furthermore, governments, political parties or groups which seek to perpetuate human misery in order to profit therefrom politically or otherwise will encounter the opposition of the United States.[2]

---

[2] Barton J. Bernstein and Allen J. Matusow, eds., *The Truman Administration*, p. 259.

The first sentence was an invitation to Russia to join the new plan for European recovery. Marshall himself noted the growing momentum of the cold war: "For the past 10 years conditions have been highly abnormal. The feverish preparation for war and the more feverish maintenance of the war effort engulfed all aspects of national economies."[3] This was the peace gesture advocated by the "Russian" position. But then Marshall went on to set a price for the inclusion of Russia: it must accept the recovery of Germany, the only country in Europe whose recovery was an issue of contention between Russia and America. Interestingly, Britain took the lead in calling for a go-ahead without Russian participation. Already on June 19, tough-talking British Foreign Minister Ernest Bevin made it crystal clear that Britain would proceed with Marshall planning with or without Russia.[4] As zealots in containment's cause, the British Laborites wanted no part of an economic arrangement that threatened their social democracy from a communist left or an international capitalist right. The last sentence in the above quote was standardly anticommunist, an early version of Rostow's definition of communists as "scavengers of the modernization process." It was just what John Foster Dulles and his right internationalists wanted to hear.

The three positions on the Marshall Plan revealed what might be called three basic subcurrents of the over-all internationalist current. The "Russian" position put strong emphasis on the need for peaceful coexistence and the avoidance of war. It argued that if concessions were made to Russia now, if trade links were opened to a Russia which desperately needed American goods, Moscow would be brought out of its isolation and eventually capitalism could penetrate the Russian world. The key focus of this subcurrent was trade. The "British" position placed major emphasis on the need for the resurrection of the world market system. As Marshall said in his June 5 speech:

> Long-standing commercial ties, private institutions, banks, insurance companies and shipping companies disappeared through loss of capital, absorption through nationalization or by simple destruction. In many countries, confidence in the local currency has been severely shaken. The breakdown of the business structure of Europe during the war was complete.[5]

The "British" position reflected the spirit of Bretton Woods and stressed the need for stable international monetary systems and growing liquidity capabilities. Partly because of its "British" character, but mainly because of its conception of a global market system, which could include Russia

[3] *Ibid.*, p. 257.
[4] Fleming, *Cold War and Its Origins*, vol. 1, p. 479.
[5] Bernstein and Matusow, eds., *Truman Administration*, p. 259.

or not, the "British" position was most compatible with the emerging containment doctrines. It was also helpful in inhibiting Britain's socialist government from sliding into economic nationalism and keeping alive its sense of responsibility for the "sterling bloc." The "German" position, exemplified by John Foster Dulles, was anticommunist, and while having a basic economic character was perhaps the most political of the three. It believed strongly in economic integration, particularly of Western Europe, which was seen to be impossible if European nations were ruled by socialist governments or were subject to strong labor pressure from the communists. Only governments committed to laissez-faire capitalism were considered capable of taking transnational steps toward larger economic integration. Naturally, European integration was impossible without Germany, and if all of Germany could not be included, then at least its most civilized and economically powerful western part had to be. It is no accident that Konrad Adenauer and John Foster Dulles were highly sympathetic to each other. Adenauer was an anticommunist Catholic Europeanist who, along with his disciple Ludwig Erhard, believed devoutly in classic free enterprise capitalism.

These three subcurrents of the internationalist current constituted the basic ideological views of the most powerful (and therefore internationally involved) segment of the American ruling class. Unlike containment ideology, which was manufactured in order to create a governmental structure capable of extending a new American imperialism throughout the world, the ideology of the internationalist current came directly from the American capitalist class. And as a class ideology, it reflected real interests. The "Russian," "British," and "German" positions were reflections of the interests of varying segments of the American capitalist class during those early postwar years and of their thinking about the future development and expansion of those interests. The "Russian" position arose out of the sector of the American capitalist economy that depended heavily on international trade. Thus, it is not accidental that it was espoused by the successful Midwestern farmer Henry Wallace. American farm output had soared during World War II, in contrast to the "dust bowl" years of the Depression. Since the American market was saturated, the only hope for new markets was expansion into food deficit areas. Western Europe, of course, was an attractive market, but its agriculture was basically intact. Food shortages in European cities were not entirely due to wartime destruction but to farmers' reluctance to sell food for soft currencies whose purchasing power was limited by the inability of Europe's economies to resume production. Western Europe was caught in a classic "scissors crisis." Russia with its population of two hundred million, suffering from vast destruction of its farm areas, was a natural market for American farm goods. There was money to be made by "selling to Russia," and a surprising number of American corporations were waiting in line to "do business with Ivan."

The "British" position reflected the interests of Wall Street and was, therefore, adequately reflected in the publications of the Council on Foreign Relations. Wall Street, as America's banking and brokerage center, was both a capital market and a custodian of currency. When the Full Employment Act of 1946 was passed, Wall Street business argued that some ten billion dollars in annual exports would be necessary to maintain full employment. The orientation toward foreign trade brought with it a corollary conviction: if currencies were not stabilized, then world trade would be endangered and, with that, the danger to a fragile postwar American economy would mount. The International Monetary Fund (IMF) and the World Bank created at Bretton Woods were the first steps toward implementing a program for trade and currency stabilization that was further developed by the Marshall Plan. With foreign currencies pegged to the dollar, which was anchored in America's virtual monopoly over gold, their values could now be stabilized. Accompanied by American insistence on free trade and "open door" policies and stimulated by World Bank and Marshall Plan loans and grants, the conditions were created for a rapid revival of international commerce.

The "German" position must be reckoned a forerunner of the great development and expansion of American multinational and transnational corporations into Western Europe in the 1950s and 1960s. The fact that, as a lawyer, Dulles represented German firms in the prewar period made him a natural exponent of integrationist free enterprise ideas. De-cartelization weakened the traditional German business structure, already weakened earlier by Hitler's *Gleichschaltung* and Hermann Goering's wartime state capitalist empire. German economic revival offered exciting opportunities for American foreign investment unencumbered by British socialist or French nationalist restrictions. Moreover, an open door to German industry would put pressure on the British and French to make things less difficult for the entry of private American capital.

For all the progressive rhetoric that accompanied the Marshall Plan, interests, not ideology, lay at its base. The internationalist segment of the American capitalist class was alarmed by the prospects of economic chaos in Western Europe which eventually would threaten big business in America. The internationalists well remembered that although the world depression of the 1930s was symbolized by the stock market crash of 1929 in America, its real cause was the collapse of the European economies. They were convinced that another depression in America would produce something far worse than a New Deal—a socialist dictatorship over the economy. But that socialist dictatorship could come even before a depression. There was nothing reassuring to the international capitalists in the Truman Administration. Spurred by the war, the atomic bomb, and by Truman's new commitments in the Middle East, the power of government was already growing alarmingly. An economic downturn could only accelerate the tendency toward big centralized government. The American way of life was based on a free economy, which was inextricably linked to a healthy West European economy.

In 1947, the "Russian," "British," and "German" subcurrents were politically incompatible. To offer Marshall Plan aid to Russia at the same time as General Lucius Clay in Germany was pushing for the rapid revival of German industry seemed to the Russians like hypocrisy at best or evil scheming at worst. The British likewise were alarmed by the supranational integrationist tendencies of the "German" position advanced by Dulles and his hostility to all forms of "socialism." Once the germ of the Marshall Plan idea had been launched publicly by Dean Acheson a month before Marshall's speech, the advocates of the "Russian" and "German" positions began to exert pressure on Marshall and Truman to have their own positions represented. Rather than try to straighten out these incompatibilities, Marshall threw them together, proposed them to the world, and then looked to see what would happen. Russian rejection of the offer made it possible to slough off the "Russian" pressure. British acceptance of a merger of the two German occupation zones into "Bizonia" in January facilitated an eventual compromise between the "British" and "German" subcurrents.

While the three internationalist positions, whatever their differences, agreed on the basic postulate of the Marshall Plan, that the United States government had to make available to Europe vast sums of money from the federal budget in order to finance economic recovery, the nationalists strongly disagreed. They regarded the fifty-billion-dollar Lend-Lease Program as a waste and the fifteen billion dollars advanced to foreign governments since the end of the war as an even greater waste. They feared that the impact of heavy taxation on America's businessmen would drive them to bankruptcy, thus facilitating the concentration of corporate wealth in a few monopolistic hands, which they regarded as a short step away from socialism. Moreover, they saw no way in which Marshall Plan aid would benefit their business constituencies. European nations might buy some American merchandise, but the nationalists never regarded foreign trade as a major source of profits. They believed that money was to be made at home and wanted nothing to dampen corporate initiative oriented toward the domestic market. Obviously, the "Russian" position infuriated them most of all. Close behind came the "British" position, which they saw as a plan to bail Britain out of its socialist misadventures. They were less opposed to the "German" position, and its advocacy by Dulles, a Republican, is not surprising. But

Germany was still too sensitive an issue, and no "German" debate ensued like the China one. Nevertheless, the clearcut anticommunism of the "German" position appealed to the nationalists and made the Marshall Plan more palatable. A "Russian" position would never have got past Congress, and a straightforward "British" position would have revived the pre–Pearl Harbor isolationist-interventionist debates, something that did happen to a degree.

CONFLICTS OF IDEOLOGIES AND INTERESTS

Both internationalists and nationalists alleged that the policies of the Truman Administration did not sufficiently take into account true American interests. They threatened to become a revival of the New Deal, which would take the form of vast new governmental powers and greatly increased spending. Aside from the atomic program, which increased both governmental power and budgets, Truman had made it clear as early as September 1945 that he was prepared to continue the welfare state policies of the New Deal. In the twenty-one-point message he sent to Congress that month, Truman proposed minimum wage, full employment, farm aid, housing, slum clearance, small business support, and public works legislation. If this legislation was passed by Congress, as intended, the federal budget would most likely soar. Both internationalists and nationalists feared that Truman's Fair Deal could produce a British type of welfare state, which would bankrupt business, give the government control over the economy, and do little to help revive the world market system. The internationalists demanded that a substantial share of the federal budget be devoted to reviving the European economies, which they saw as a *sine qua non* for the long-term health of the American economy. The nationalists opposed even that expenditure on the grounds that American business would be asked to pay for the rescue of non-American business and, even worse, to prop up socialist governments like that of Britain.

When Truman proposed his twenty-one-point message to Congress in September 1945, he was aware of the smashing Labour party victory in Britain and of the possibility that the American economy might revert to a depression, with a resulting popular clamor for governmental rescue. Under Roosevelt, the Democratic party, including some of its benighted Southern adherents, had learned to think macro-societally and macro-economically. Operationally that meant a strong federal government armed with sufficient political and fiscal power to take the responsibility for guiding the country onto the paths of security and growth. This typically Democratic concern for the "public interest" often violated specific interests. The Republican party, as the vehicle of the specific interests in America, reacted time and again by attacking Democratic policies. When the Republicans went along with Democratic policies, as in the case of the postwar bipartisanship on foreign affairs, it meant that they considered the policy line to be in general harmony with the interests they represented. When opposition mounted, as, for example, on the Marshall Plan and on China policy, it meant that there was a serious conflict between general policy and specific interests. The two key policies of the early postwar years that demanded considerable commitment of federal funds were atomic energy and its attendant military programs (like a strategic air capability) and the domestic welfare policies Truman proposed to implement reconversion and prevent the social turbulence of the Depression.

Increases in federal spending always aroused congressional opposition, particularly from Republican circles. While there was general agreement that the atomic energy program had to be funded, violent controversies broke out a few years after the end of the war over military programs. These controversies, as we shall see, played an important role in the nationalist counterattack against the emerging containment policies. Similarly, the impetus toward greater social welfare spending aroused predictable opposition, which took the form of direct opposition to the new welfare policies as well as conservative advocacy of antilabor legislation. The simple fiscal reality of the early postwar policies of the Truman Administration is that the atomic and welfare programs were threatening to take a greater tax bite out of corporate profits without any discernible return to the corporations. American monopoly over atomic weaponry would, of course, provide security, but this was in no way measurable in profits. Similarly, welfare legislation might help to prevent the kind of social turbulence of the 1930s, but such results likewise were not measurable in profit terms. The difficulty with the "public interest" policies of Roosevelt and Truman was that while the men of the realm of interests could be convinced in their minds that such general interest policies were vital for the preservation of the American system, they had trouble defending them in corporate boardrooms, which faced immediate problems of investment, sales, and profits.

While the propaganda surrounding the Marshall Plan made it sound like another New Deal program designed to help the poor, starving millions of the world, in fact, it promised clearcut returns to the American economy. It could not benefit specific interests as directly as cuts in corporate taxation, but it nevertheless laid out policies through which American exports would rise, American loans be paid back, and worldwide monetary stability be achieved, thereby combatting inflation. The

Marshall Plan was a general interest policy in the strictest sense, in the same way that anti-inflationary policies are general interest policies: ultimately the specific interests would benefit concretely from it. But many New Deal policies cannot really be considered general interest policies. Rather, as ideological policies, they were a kind of national insurance against disaster; they were national security policies designed to prevent both international and national disasters. As the Marshall Plan was succeeded by various European security policies culminating in NATO, its interest aspects, which promised tangible returns to the American economy, began to give way to its insurance aspects, the need to build up deterrents against anticipated disasters. But when the Marshall Plan was conceived in early 1947, the predominant thinking behind it was *economic*.

We can now proceed to some theoretical conclusions from the above argumentation. The predominant concern of the internationalist current was the *international economy*. Regardless of their differences over specific foreign policies, they agreed that a viable world market system based on monetary stability and fueled by a growing volume of international trade was vital to the preservation of American capitalism. During the 1930s, the international economy no longer existed as a consequence of the collapse of the gold standard. The Bretton Woods agreements began the process of rebuilding it. But until the Marshall Plan, the United States government was not yet operationally committed to fully implementing the Bretton Woods accords. The Marshall Plan made the preservation and development of the international economy a prime commitment of the United States government. Thus, the internationalist current was built into the bureaucratic politics of the government. This meant not only that America was to take the lead in fostering European recovery, assuring monetary stability, and helping to remove the tariff barriers to free trade, but that the state of the international economy was to become a major interest in the bureaucratic politics of Washington.

However, by making internationalism a policy commitment, the Truman Administration took sides in one of the most enduring and profound conflicts within the American realm of interests. In the classic struggle between free trade and protectionism, the Truman Administration sided with the free traders. The adoption of the Marshall Plan meant that Washington regarded the preservation of the international economy as a higher priority than exclusively serving the specific interests of the American national economy. The conflict between nationalists and internationalists had raged up until Pearl Harbor in the form of the isolationist versus interventionist controversy. It was silenced by the war. The immediate postwar policies of the Truman Administration did not revive it, but the development of Marshall Plan policies did and was to produce, in the following years, one of the bitterest struggles in the history of the United States.

Did the Truman Administration have to adopt the Marshall Plan? Could not Truman have just continued a policy of making more and more loans and grants to the European countries that needed them? The same funds expended under the Marshall Plan could presumably eventually have been allocated through *ad hoc* foreign aid or foreign loan practices. The Dawes and Young plans were proposed and implemented in the 1920s with nothing even remotely comparable to the bitter controversy that the Marshall Plan aroused. But those post–World War I plans were the creation of Republican administrations. The Republican party had always been made up of nationalist and internationalist elements, and while they were in conflict, nevertheless, they had always managed to achieve compromises. The postwar Harding, Coolidge, and Hoover administrations were essentially probusiness and dealt with problems on an *ad hoc* basis. Since the Truman Administration, as a Democratic administration, was more ideological, the Marshall Plan was more than a program to give money to Europe. It was an ideological commitment, and as such assumed far greater and longer enduring force than a simple, straightforward program of loans and grants. The Marshall Plan was a commitment to Western Europe, and, in the words of the controversy that quickly erupted, was a "Europe-first" policy.

The Dawes and Young plans were purely economic in nature. They aimed at stimulating German economic recovery so that Germany could pay reparations to Britain and France, who then could repay their wartime loans to America. The Marshall Plan could not remain solely economic. With the proclamation of the Truman Doctrine in March 1947, America had made a giant step in its containment policy, which was primarily political and military. The evolving policy posed real and agonizing problems concerning Russia, Britain, and Germany. If lines were drawn marking the permissible limits of Russian expansionism, as the British were pressing for (Churchill's Iron Curtain notions), then both Russia and Germany would be directly affected. The creation of Bizonia in January 1947 foreshadowed the partition of Germany and fed Russian fears that America and Britain were planning a revival of German power. After World War I, political and military problems receded into the background until they were brought to the fore again by Hitler's seizure of power. Europe's problems in the 1920s were primarily economic. In 1947, there was no way political and military questions could be separated from the economics proposed by the Marshall Plan. Secretary Marshall, in proferring somewhat naïvely the "British," "Russian," and "German" subcurrents, suggested an ideal economic arrangement for Europe where currencies would be stabilized, trade would flow from the Atlantic to the Urals, and Germany would restore its industries. While that was feasible from an economic point of view, it was impossible politically and militarily. The Marshall Plan did not fit containment to the requirements of the international economy but rather fit the international economy to the requirements of containment. In a manner characteristic of Democratic administrations since Roosevelt, it sought to use the forces of the economy to build structures of power rather than the reverse. The ultimate purpose of the Marshall Plan was to restore Western Europe's political and military power.

DISQUISITION ON A THEORY OF THE STATE

I shall digress here for several pages from the subject of the Marshall Plan to a discussion of the nature and function of the state. Without some theoretical conception of the state, it is impossible to explain the growth of American imperialism after 1945, the key manifestation of which was the elaboration of vast new state power. The reader should now be familiar with some of my ideas on the subject of the state.

Although Marx himself never developed a rigorous theory of the state (nor of classes), the conventional Marxist view of the state as the instrument of the ruling classes provides a materialistically satisfying explanation for its place in society. In Marx's time, this served to counter the idealist notions of the state, popularized by Hegel, which saw it as an emanation of divine will located in but not really of society. It also counters the eighteenth-century rationalist conception of the state as an artifice created by men to mediate the conflicts inherent in society and to impose discipline where individual men, even acting together, would not. The Marxist view also counters the romantic conception of the state as an emanation of the "general will," a structure that somehow expresses the inclinations of the entire society. Engels made a concession to the obvious fact that the state could not always be seen as the instrument of the classes that owned and controlled the means of production in his assertion that, although the state arises out of society, daily it becomes more distant from it. In the late nineteenth century, right-wing German political theorists, who tended also to be proponents of German military might, were enamored of theories of *raison d'état*, notions that the state had purposes explainable solely in terms of its own nature. Engels, who delighted in writing on military matters, conceded that there might be something to the notion of *raison d'état*. The military aspects of the state are, indeed, partly what make the Marxist conception difficult to accept as an operational explanation.

The conservative Austrian economist Joseph Schumpeter saw the state as intimately linked to war, and imperialism as an emanation of the state's inherent drive toward war. He regarded the state as a relic from feudalism which the perfect workings of capitalism, if they could ever occur, would do away with. Schumpeter, thus, propounded a theory of the "withering away of the state" under conditions of the full triumph of market capitalism throughout the world. Schumpeter's ideas are quite compatible with those of Marx except that each saw different forces preventing the full triumph of capitalism. For Marx, the existence of classes was its Achilles' heel. Since the ruling classes existed because of property, the abolition of private property would mean their destruction. But the existence of property increasingly created rigidities and inelasticities in the economy which froze the dynamism of the market which capitalism needed to grow and expand. Thus, a revolution that destroyed property and thereby destroyed classes would liberate man from the shackles that inhibited him from displaying the creative energies necessary for an economy to grow and so satisfy the needs of humanity. In a way, one can say that the Marxist theory of revolution envisaged the final triumph of capitalism, for communism would be the community of free men no longer governed by a state as under socialism. Communism is the ideal state of the economy as viewed by the classical economists minus the element of property. For Schumpeter, the enemy opposing the full triumph of capitalism was the state, which continuously introduced noneconomic drives into society, thereby building up structures of power that increasingly subverted the free forces of the economy. So discouraged was Schumpeter by the universal growth toward greater state power in the late 1930s that he despaired of capitalism as a viable system. Karl Polanyi essentially accepted Schumpeter's notion of the state as a force hostile to capitalism, but added another element: the growing power of the rising working classes. This power threatened revolutionary chaos if its increasing demands on society for a redistribution of income were not granted. Even governments committed to capital, property, and class rule were forced to grant some income redistribution for the sake of overall societal stability. Thus, the welfare state came into being.

It is a mark of the German tradition of political thought to see state and society as two separate entities, exemplified in the sociology of Max Weber. It is a mark of the Anglo-American tradition of political thought to see the state as an artifact made by men in order to meet certain collective needs. Therefore, the state, or government as the British and Americans prefer to call it, constantly changes and adapts as impulses strike it from society. For Schumpeter and Polanyi, the state is not inherently related to the economy, while the British and Americans see it as an institution deeply imbedded in society and, therefore, ever subject to society's demands. Marx stood somewhere in-between the German and Anglo-American views. His revolutionary humanism made it impossible to view the state as something so dichotomous to society (which to Marx meant the economy) that human action could not affect it in fundamental ways. On the other hand, he could not see it as a neutral mechanism for the arbitration of society's conflicts. For Marx, the crucial intervening variable was class. The real dichotomy in society was between ruling and ruled classes, and cut directly through the economy. But both ruling and ruled classes were inextricably bound to the economy. Therefore, the dichotomy was not absolute but was produced by particular historical conditions which human action (revolution) could overcome. While the state may daily grow more distant from society, as the instrument of the ruling classes, at least in its origins, it remains part of society. If revolution destroys a ruling class, the state falls; if revolution destroys the state, the ruling class falls.

The real difficulty in the Marxist view of the state as the instrument of the ruling class is that while state power *always* is national, the capitalist ruling class, according to the Marxist view, has to be international. Property may be national (or local) in a legal sense, but it is international under the laws of capitalism. For Marxism, law is a manifestation of the superstructure and, therefore, subject to the requisites of the substructure. Thus, the predominant tendency in a capitalist world should be for property to become increasingly international and internationalized. Capitalists will invest wherever they can make profits and their collective power will erode whatever legal and political barriers there may be to such transnational investments. While there is no doubt that many developments in contemporary economies, such as the proliferation of multinational and transnational corporations, show that there is force behind this Marxist view, throughout the world the national character of state powers is increasing. And the one place in the world where state power has become less national is Western Europe, just where free enterprise capitalism has been strongest. The Marxists must explain how, in terms of Marxist theory, a ruling class, which necessarily tends toward internationalism, produces state power, which historically tends toward nationalism.

The simplest way out of this dilemma, even in Marxist terms, is to discard the notion of the state as the instrument of the ruling classes and accept as a basic notion that state powers are national in character and that nations are as much basic units of mankind as classes, which in Marxist terms arise out of property. A nation is an expanse of territory defined by all-enclosing boundaries, which are drawn by governments through mutual agreement. It is a unit of defense, of common identity, and of commitment to common goals. These functions are made obvious to every international traveler by border police and military outposts, passports, and customs officers who levy tariffs on goods coming through. Historically, nations arose in Europe when kings imposed their rule over territories through powerful armies supported by rising urban bourgeoisies in opposition to entrenched rural aristocracies, whose commitments were local and international but not generally national. Nations were the product of revolutionary forces which sought to overthrow the rule of aristocratic feudalism. The pattern of nation-building in Europe, best exemplified in France, was a strong government headed by a centralizing king, a national and professional army subject only to the king's will, and a revolutionary class rising from below against an entrenched class. This pattern, which began in Western Europe, has repeated itself countless times throughout the world, particularly in socialist countries. There is a logic to it. If a revolutionary class seeks to destroy a ruling class, it must ultimately gain access to state power. Revolution succeeds only if the class enemy is struck from above and from below. But the logic goes further. If a ruler, such as a king, seeks to destroy his enemies, such as the aristocrats, he needs allies in society, and the most available allies are those classes that already thirst for the overthrow of the class to which the king is opposed. And if a nation is caught in bitter internal strife, it needs powerful armies to protect it from the voracious incursions of foreign enemies. History suggests a recurring pattern of a trinity of state power, a revolutionary class, and the army as factors producing nations. Nations are the result of powerful forces for change and come into being against the opposition of equally powerful conservative classes. Significantly, the most conservative force in Europe, the Catholic Church, was also the most international institution in European history. As nations arose, the Church and its aristocratic class allies declined.

To be effective, state power must be clearly defined. It, therefore, generates bureaucracies and laws which provide such definition. It also generates boundaries. The more defined it is, the easier the task of increasing and centralizing its power. Thus, from a Marxist perspective a paradox arises: as a revolutionary class rises against an entrenched class and reaches out for the instruments of state power, it becomes increasingly national in character. A Marxist would say that the class interests of the revolutionary bourgeoisie in Europe were local and international in the early stages of the struggle. The urban bourgeoisie strove to assert its power in the cities, where it arose against the landed aristocracy, and at the same time sought avenues of international trade which since Marco Polo's time had already spread beyond Europe. But as urban bourgeoisies sought larger political power in league with centralizing kings, they began to take on increasingly national character. This was particularly true of the French bourgeoisie even before the French Revolution. After the French Revolution, France became one of the most national of European capitalisms. The great world market system flowed out of England, not France. The constitutional histories of England and France reveal one major difference—while state power grew bigger, more extensive, and more centralized in France, in England the power of the kings constantly diminished in favor of Parliament. Parliament, the body representing the various interests of English society, became the battleground for protracted class struggle which continues to this day. The bourgeoisie never sought to *seize power* in England, as in France, thereby preserving its archaic features of strong commitment to local interests along with strong and growing commitment to the most far-flung international interests. Again, unlike France, England never became a nation. To this day, the British Isles contain discordant elements, like Ireland, Scotland, and even Wales, none of which has been fully integrated into a larger "British nation."

What happened in France with the revolutionary bourgeoisie has been repeated in virtually all socialist countries with the revolutionary proletariats. Revolution in Russia, China, Vietnam, Cuba, and other socialist countries has enhanced, not weakened, their national character. The more the revolution relied on state power, the more national it became. And it seems historically incontrovertible that these revolutions had no choice but to rely on state power. From their beginnings, they were mortally threatened by hostile intervention from abroad, which necessitated the formation of powerful armed forces under the aegis of the state.

The Marxist paradox can be resolved in Marxist terms if one accepts the notion that it is class war, not class, that produces the state. What is war? War is a struggle between two contenders for the achievement of a materially defined objective, such as territory. Territory is property, and the essence of property is its delimitations sanctioned by the laws of the state. For a Marxist, socially significant property is that which encloses the society's key means of production. However, property achieves its true social functions only if it generates exchange value, produces products that can be exchanged. The more exchange there is in society, the greater the division of labor and, therefore, the greater the affluence of the society. Taken to its ideal extreme, this should produce great fluidity and flexibility in property relations, where the physical property itself changes and shifts hands constantly in obedience to the requirements of the process of production. However, all property has another side to it. It constitutes a use value to its owner and, barring a favorable exchange situation, the owner will strive to preserve it at all cost. The more property becomes use value, as it did in feudal times in Europe, the more injurious its existence is to the larger social division of labor. Moreover, as property becomes more fixed under the conditions of scarcity that have traditionally prevailed in societies, the disparities between the haves and the have-nots become clearer. War, therefore, comes to supplant exchange as a means whereby property is transferred from an old to a new owner. But the more this happens, the more stubbornly the old owners cling to their property and increasingly resort to armed force themselves in order to protect it. Since war is harmful to both people and property, law intervenes to lay down rules with sanctions behind them to delineate property lines, establish contractual procedures for the possession and transfer of property, and define the rights of individuals and corporate bodies vis-à-vis each other. It is no accident that early European feudalism was a period of great legal creativity and that the law that arose at that time was closely related to property and contract. While, on the one hand, law strengthens the use value aspects of property by establishing property rights, on the other, it serves to reverse the tendency of property to become simply use value by establishing contractual procedures for its exchange. War creates, intensifies, and consolidates distinctions between human entities, like nations. Exchange has the opposite effect—it constantly breaks down distinctions and creates larger and ever more encompassing systems. Law stands between the two.

While there have always been generalized rules of behavior existing between different people, "customary law," by and large law has been sanctioned by some power over and above the contending parties. Since ancient times, law giving has been a function of the state. There have been significant exceptions. For example, in the Islamic world law derives from the Qur'ān, a situation unfavorable to the development of state power in Islamic regions except where mosque and state were united, as in the dual Caliphate-Sultanate of the Ottoman Empire. In Europe and in China, law giving and the nation-state have always been intimately related. While law served to turn the people within the nation away from war and back to exchange, it had the opposite effect externally. Property rights vis-à-vis other nations became increasingly defined, which produced more and more war. Even internally, law could have opposite tendencies, affirming property rights in some respects and loosening them in others. This had the cumulative effect of making domestic war more systematic, since law is by its nature systematic. Law systematized property rights and thereby produced classes of property and privilege and status. At the same time, it allowed war against property to evolve from simple robbery to a much broader and more political war of class against class.

Nothing so enhances the power of the state, actually and potentially, as wars against other nations abroad and wars among social classes at home. But war of any kind, external or internal, rigidifies property and at the same time arouses forces of violence determined to smash and seize that property. External wars produce armies and internal wars produce police forces. The existence of both large armies and police forces in themselves attests to a situation where have-nots seek avenues of war, not exchange, in order to seize property. When a government develops a large police force, this signifies a tight merger of state and ruling class interests. The interests of all ruling classes are the preservation of property (which can mean land, factories, money, privilege, budgets, status, fame, academic tenure, or anything considered a scarce commodity sought for the enhancement of power, prestige, or wealth). The main function of police forces is to protect persons and property against those who seek to aggress against them. When a nation develops a large army, this signifies either a desire to protect its national property or a desire to acquire other nations' property by force of arms.

But it is theoretically and practically wrong to believe that the sole function of the state is the preservation of property as use value to those who own it. Like the law which it spawns, the state is also committed to developing exchange, from which the wealth of the nation derives. Only where the state "produces everything," as in Russia, can it dispense with exchange, and the dismal history of the Russian economy over the last half-century shows the price that government has had to pay for its neglect of exchange. The more dynamic an economy, the more far-reaching will be the avenues of exchange. That means an ever-growing body of the citizenry must be involved in the process of exchange. In advanced capitalist countries, this has come to be known as the doctrine of full employment. But to foster exchange, property must be made more flexible and fluid, and doing this will require that its use value to certain people be sacrificed for the sake of its exchange value. Any infringement on property—taxation, for example—benefits people other than its owners. If the state is committed in a broad way to maximally accelerating exchange (as through full employment), then it will act in ways to injure property owners in favor of those who do not own property. The state may do this just to foster broader exchange on general principles or in order to appease revolutionary classes who are demanding a redistribution of property or to stimulate property-owning classes to become investors rather than *rentiers*.

One can say, in Marxist terms, that the state arises out of the irresolvable contradiction within ruling classes between property as use value and property as exchange value. A ruling class, as contrasted to an isolated landlord who just expropriates his tenants' surplus, must exchange as well as produce in order to gain surplus. That surplus is turned into property, which is either reinvested (creating more exchange) or saved (creating more use). What is saved but not reinvested provides

security but is withdrawn from exchange. What is reinvested generates
new wealth but reduces security. Investors always seek to deprive savers
of their savings, like banks which use people's savings to make profitable
investments. Savers willingly lend their savings if they feel they will get a
return. If they see the economy in turmoil around them, like the French
peasant, they will hoard gold below the floorboards. On a larger scale,
corporations always tend toward monopoly in order to have absolute
control over the factors of production, but governments, competitors,
and angry citizens smash the monopolies as a threat to free commerce.
Schumpeter and other conservative economists were wrong in believing
that the full triumph of capitalism would lead to a withering away of the
state under conditions of a global market system. The dynamic capitalist
creators of wealth always will turn wealth into property, creating gaps of
wealth between the haves and the have-nots and thereby creating classes.
As that property accumulates, a new generation of dynamic capitalists
will try to unfreeze it in the interests of growth, but at the same time
revolutionary pressure from the proletariats, those who do not have
property, will mount against them from below.

There is a further theoretical proposition I wish to make, which goes
beyond Marxism but can be stated in Marxist terms. The state is a set of
institutions which arises in order to resolve the contradictions within
society. Foremost among these are basic and irresolvable contradictions
within the ruling class itself. A ruling class can never escape the following dilemma: if it turns into a propertied class, it sacrifices the exchange
economy it needs in order to gain wealth, but if it chooses everlasting
enterprise, it sacrifices property and loses its character as a class. The
notions of the Polish economist Oscar Lange about "market socialism"
have indeed envisaged a perfect market arising under conditions where
socialism has done away with property and, therefore, classes. Let us
assume for the moment that a classless market system is possible. This
means that exchange eventually reaches the entire population of a country or of the world. In other words, the maximization of exchange and
the elimination of property will bring the propertyless into the exchange
system. Capitalist consumer economies have, in fact, done that to a
considerable extent. Driven by the need to raise "aggregate demand,"
they have brought ever greater segments of the population into the consumer economy. However, all capitalist economies, since their inception,
have been aided in this process by the state, which has acted to broaden
the avenues of exchange. The highest form this has taken in capitalist
societies has been the practice of Keynesian doctrines. Now, if the broad-
ening of exchange demands that the propertyless be brought into the
system of exchange and the role of the state is crucial in preventing a
ruling class from relapsing into a rigid property-owning, surplus-consum-

ing class, then one of the essential roles of the state is to bring the propertyless classes into the system.

While historically states have often arisen through external conquest, more common in recent times is the rise of new state power through revolutionary pressure from below. At first, the function of the state is the integration of the propertyless people of society into the society as a whole, something it does, because of its nature, along national lines. The state normally arises in opposition to ruling classes and ruling interests. Riding on the strength of popular movements, the new state has an ideological character (nationalist, socialist, fascist, democratic, even religious). However, once in power, it seeks accommodation with the ruling classes and interests, and, conversely, those interests seek to capture the state. The state arises as the realm of ideology but almost immediately is subject to infiltration from the realm of interests, the interests of the classes of property. Thus, the normal course of the formation of state power, a process which occurs very frequently in the life of a nation, is the creation of ideological, political, and military power, which results in a broad class of the dispossessed being integrated into the national entity, followed by a rapid merging with the dominant interests, essentially economic, within the society.

The word "normal" does not apply to revolutions like the Russian Revolution and its successors. The seizure of power by the proletariat in Russia was followed by the complete destruction of the dominant ruling classes, both feudal and bourgeois, and the total abolition of property. Revolutionary seizure of power in the Marxist tradition means destruction of ruling classes. There was nothing historically inevitable in the nature of the October Russian Revolution except the ideology of the Bolsheviks. The February Revolution was a more "normal" seizure of power in that the resultant regime sought accommodation with the realm of interests, a major mistake as it turned out. Marx's teachings of class struggle within the larger context of a unified world historical process were the core of the Marxist ideology that has spread to the farthest corners of the globe. Revolutionary Bolshevism believed that for Russia to be liberated, it had to be liberated from its own Russianness. That could only be accomplished if the revolution extirpated the entire realm of interests of Old Russia, its feudal and capitalist classes. The industrial proletariat has no fatherland, so believed all Marxists despite the shameful treachery of the Social Democrats in 1914. The economic system that capitalism had created was in its essence a world market system, and if capitalism had not yet become truly international, the forces of world history pushed it in that direction. And if the capitalist class could not fully accomplish that internationalization, then the revolutionary proletariat would. Thus, when the Bolsheviks used state power to smash the ruling classes, they believed that the systemic essence of the revolutionary proletariat would make the new Soviet state the instrument of a class inherently internationalist in tendency. And even if the Russian working classes were not yet fully conscious of the historical role of their class, vanguard ideology guided them into the historically correct directions. What the Bolsheviks misunderstood, because of Marxism's incomplete theories of the state and of classes, was the inherently and powerfully national character of all state power. They also underestimated the power of the state over classes—that it could remake the classes over which it ruled in its own image rather than the reverse.

Even if there was nothing inevitable in the October Revolution, the nature of Russian society created extremely favorable conditions for total revolution, that is, the destruction of entire ruling classes. Unlike in the more dynamic capitalist societies of Western Europe, property in Russia, whether land, factories, bureaucracies, or titles and privileges, had rigidified into patterns of use values. Even where capitalist energy had begun to break them up, as with the new industrial enterprises of Western Russia or kulak farming in the rural areas, the rigid hand of property clamped down again and again. In the years following 1917, Russia did not escape the effects of property, for the new Soviet state became the monopoly proprietor of all power, wealth, and privilege in the country, developing rigidities far beyond those of the Tsarist period. It may be argued that this would not have happened if revolutionary proletariats had seized power in Western Europe or if there had not been vicious intervention by the capitalist powers to destroy the revolution or, later, the ever-threatening capitalist encirclement of Russia. The threat of international capitalism forced the creation of a vast new army, which was to become one of the most powerful nationalist forces in the new Soviet Union. Nevertheless, Bolshevik ideology must bear a considerable burden of the blame for what happened. While Lenin unswervingly saw the need for the seizure of supreme state power in order to implement, sustain, and develop the revolution, and correctly perceived the enormous attraction the prospect of wielding state power aroused among the proletariats, he shared with virtually all Marxists an inability to see that the nature of the state was not determined by the nature of the class that spawned it but arose out of all the contradictions within society. Russia in 1917 was rent by class war and international war, and the October Revolution produced only more war, including what raged between the new ideological currents and practical interests which the victorious Bolsheviks had spawned. War produced not the dictatorship of the proletariat but the dictatorship of the state as supreme owner and master of property.

The state is made and remade constantly, in that new ideologies, new executives, and new bureaucracies constantly keep changing it. In America it is remade every four years. The remaking is "normal" in the sense that accommodation is immediately sought with the realm of interests. In Russia, that remaking also occurred, despite the appearance of "Soviet totalitarianism." But what followed remaking was not accommodation with the realm of interests but rather the repeated destruction of that realm. Stalin's purges destroyed the interests that had reclustered and reaggregated themselves within the Soviet state. But Stalin only did more brutally and more bloodily what Lenin had initiated with his smashing of the SRs and the Kronstadt Rebellion. What Lenin did reflected the fact that class war had become the predominant feature of the Russian Revolution. In class war, the revolution seeks to destroy, appropriate, and remake the property of the ruling classes. Property is interest—defined space buttressed by power, wealth, and prestige. In the later 1920s and 1930s, various groups developed bureaucratic interests within the Soviet state, which were the new property. Stalin smashed these interests, and physically liquidated the new proprietors. Much the same, though fortunately without the physical brutality of Stalin, occurred in China during the Cultural Revolution. The "capitalist-roaders" were the elements within the Chinese state that had developed new bureaucratic and political interests, new property, and in that sense had become "capitalists." Riding on an even more powerful and democratic tradition of class war than in Russia, Mao again and again led the revolutionary masses in the struggle to destroy the new property. The difference between the periodic remaking of the state in a capitalist country like the United States and in socialist countries like Russia and China is that in America the remaking occurs with a "respect for property" (that is, accommodation with the existing realm of interests), while in Russia and China it occurs through continuing destruction of such property. In Russia's case, if one accepts the Chinese accusations of revisionism, one can say that the form of remaking state power has become more "normal," in that vested interests are no longer destroyed but accommodated.

But what constitutes the remaking of the state? The impetus toward remaking certainly does not come from interests either within or outside the state. Interests already have their political channels and seek to gain advantage for themselves through the manipulation of those channels or through the interplay of various channels. If a corporation wants a tax break, it will not be so foolish as to lobby for a new federal agency, but will put pressure on existing agencies. If a bureaucratic interest feels disadvantaged, it may go outside of government to Congress and the people to lobby for itself, but it too is simply seeking more support for itself, not the creation of a new bureaucracy, which will just make an already complex bureaucratic arena even more so. The remaking occurs when a new ideology or a new ideological variant enters the state, which it can do only by passing through the supreme leadership of the state, its chief executive.

The key character of ideologies is that they come from below, from some segment of those who are disadvantaged in society. All, even the mildest, have some kind of revolutionary character. All reflect a revolutionary process which continues even while it may not produce spectacular outbursts. Operationally, ideology enters the social fabric through the state, and specifically, is funneled through the pinnacle of state power, the chief executive. It becomes institutionalized in its minimal and most mundane form through the creation of new bureaucratic structures, which consume a share of the state budget. In other words, a small-scale redistribution of income takes place which is designed to satisfy the demands of the new ideology. In its maximal form, ideology enters the social fabric by taking over the state entirely, destroying class and bureaucratic interests and creating an entirely new state power. In either case, a remaking of state power has taken place. Since conservatives have no desire to remake the state (they own property and interests and merely wish to retain and expand them) and since bureaucracies only tend to expand their own interests rather than create new ones, the only source of bureaucratic change is ideology. And the predominant ideologies of the world are those calling for change, most importantly that the exploited, the oppressed, the poor, those with little or no property, be given a greater share of the scarce property of society.

My proposition on the making and remaking of the state, thus, is the Marxist view of the state turned upside down. The state is not made as the instrument of the ruling class, but is made by, for, or through a revolutionary class which seeks a share of society's scarce resources held by the ruling classes as property. The periodic remaking of the state occurs in exactly the same way. However, once made, the ruling classes seek to capture state power and turn it into their instrument. The state is made and remade as the realm of an ideology that reflects the aspirations of revolutionary classes. But once made, it immediately generates new forms of property, bureaucracies. Like all property, these bureaucracies appropriate wealth, using the particular form of appropriation characteristic of the state, taxation. In this manner the state, which began as the realm of ideology, gradually turns into the realm of interests. As interests, it both competes and colludes with the other interests of society, a process eventually leading in inexorable fashion to accommodation with those interests. Yet the more the state turns into the realm of interests, the more distant it becomes from the revolutionary class that created it and, of course, from newer revolutionary classes which arise. This continuing pressure from below is the reason for the periodic remaking of the state. The more normal this making and remaking of the state, the more every remaking is accompanied by accommodation to existing interests. When the state encounters difficulties in reaching an accommodation, it seeks in whatever way it can to enlarge the available surplus so as to satisfy all interests, existing as well as emerging ones.

In capitalist countries, democracy is the predominant form of government. In a democracy, people freely elect chief executives at national, regional, and local levels, as well as parliamentary officials. The capitalist class cannot rule directly or through its chosen instruments because it is caught in an irresolvable contradiction, pulling it in opposite directions. As a system of free enterprise seeking ever broader avenues for expansion, it strives constantly to break down existing forms of property. It must destroy savings and turn them into investment. As conservative and classical economists have long recognized, the inherent tendency of capitalism is to break down interests wherever they exist, particularly in the state, which create ever more rigid and inelastic forms of property and interest. Thus, the triumph of capitalism would, theoretically speaking, lead to a withering away of the state. On the other hand, as a ruling class, the capitalist class strives with all its might to preserve its property, to make its savings inviolable, to build walls around its ownings to protect them against all aggressors. Thus, while one tendency of the capitalist class is to create ever more freedom by eroding structures of interests, the other, equally inherent, is to create more unfreedom by generating structures of monopoly power, prestige, and wealth. The contradiction arises that if the tendency toward freedom becomes predominant, it inflicts injury on owners of property, who see no prospect of turning savings into investment and cling even more tenaciously to the property they have. The *rentiers* thus make war on the investors. But if the reverse occurs, then the capitalist class turns into a rigid property-owning class which increasingly stifles the dynamism of the economy and finds itself in a position where it can rule only through naked power of the police and the military, whose sole purpose is the defense of power, wealth, and privilege.

While the capitalist class is, thus, forever engaged in a civil war within itself, the revolutionary process goes on in the form of the propertyless classes making ever more shrill demands on the system for a redistribution of wealth. And as the revolutionary classes have learned, such redistribution can only occur, in even a minimal form, if they gain access to state power. In stagnant feudal societies, the property-owning classes clamp a rigid hold on state power and use every device of repression to keep the revolutionary classes out of power. As the inevitable stagnation increases, so does the repression. But capitalist societies cannot afford such stagnation, which endangers the very existence of capitalism itself.

Unlike feudal societies, they must grow constantly, which requires conditions of freedom. Thus, in capitalist societies a segment of the capitalist class realizes that property must be unfrozen for the sake of growth. It accepts, for example, the need for some redistribution of income (new forms of taxation) in order to keep aggregate demand high and permit economic growth to continue. This puts that segment, momentarily, on the same side as the revolutionary classes who demand the same thing but for different reasons. On the other hand, the same segment of the capitalist class that clamors for more freedom can rapidly turn in the opposite direction when it sees the infringement of property assume excessive forms endangering the very existence of its own class.

If a segment of the capitalist class sides with the revolutionary classes, this arouses fierce opposition from others whose property is endangered. But if the capitalist class adopts a solid front against all revolutionary demands, this not only arouses the fury of the revolutionary classes but can easily produce economic stagnation. And in those cases, as in Nazi Germany, where the lesser property owners united temporarily with segments of the revolutionary classes (German workers) against the big international capitalists, the free enterprise system is mortally endangered. From the point of view of a capitalist class which contains both these warring elements, there is no alternative but to create a democratic state which somehow expresses the interests of freedom and of property, but also the aspirations of the revolutionary classes. Through that state and its "regulative" functions, the capitalist class seeks "compromises," which must be made day after day to keep the entire system functioning. Those "compromises" must satisfy the requisites of full employment, law and order, and economic growth.

In a capitalist society, only a democratic state can satisfy these requisites, but, as we have already seen, only at the cost of imperialism. A democratic state means the popular mandate, which provides the revolutionary classes with the chance of electing their own chief executives and parliamentary officials. On the other hand, the state means power, and power creates its own form of interests and property which can be brought to mesh with the interests of private capital. The state is an unavoidable necessity for the capitalist class, but it is danger and opportunity at the same time. The capitalist class has no choice but to play the democratic game lest it court its own destruction.

In America, the Republican party has been the party of the ruling class. It is the party of interests, and has not been ideological since the days of Lincoln. It also contains in itself the two warring segments of the capitalist class, reflected in its "liberal" and "conservative" wings. The "liberal" wing has been predominately Eastern and international big business, strongly oriented toward economic growth and expansion abroad, committed to free enterprise but also cognizant of the need for federal spending to stimulate aggregate demand and produce full employment, generally supportive of basic democratic freedoms, concerned about war and social ills. In its present "conglomerate" form, liberal big business has realized its cherished dynamism of making and remaking property with one major aim in mind: to make ever greater profits through ever newer forms of enterprise. The "conservative" wing of the Republican party has been smaller business, Western and Southwestern, strongly opposed to heavy taxation, violently anti-welfare, hostile to all infringements on property rights, militantly committed to military and police power in order to protect power, wealth, and privilege. It has also been most fiercely opposed to the forms of state power that seek to bring about some kind of income redistribution in order to accommodate the demands of the revolutionary classes.

The Democratic party, since the days of Wilson and Roosevelt, if not before, has been the party of the people, and it is still the party of the disadvantaged. It has been the party of urban ethnic groups fighting against the dominant Anglos, of Southern racists who lost out in the Civil War, of the labor unions. Recently it has once again become the party where newer revolutionary forces (non-white peoples, youth, women, and others) inject their demands into the system, taking the habitual road of seeking state power to achieve them. The one common denominator of all these disparate elements has been and remains their hunger for state power in order to redirect income toward themselves. Southerners have remained loyal to the Democratic party because they needed federal spending to develop the South, and, indeed, the defense-induced boom in the South since the war has paid off handsomely. Labor unions have gained prolabor legislation giving them greater power in their struggles with management. The more recent poor have gained a whole array of welfare measures. And the city machines have gained patronage, jobs to distribute to their political adherents in the cities. The ethnics, the working class, the non-white poor, and now the socially alienated women and youth are all revolutionary classes—all have made ideological demands for a basic redistribution of income in ways that have threatened the workings of the capitalist system, even though again and again they have been paid off with a larger share of the surplus without impairing the system. Nevertheless, the system has but to falter, the expanding pie has but to contract, and those revolutionary demands will immediately resurface. The Southerners in the Democratic party could hardly be considered revolutionary, yet their affiliation with the Democratic party is much like that of the German petite bourgeoisie with Hitler's National Socialist German Workers' party. They represent lesser property interests as much endangered by free enterprise capitalism as by revolutionary socialism. Their political proclivities are fascist, shown in their adherence to the Democratic party, whereas those of non-Southern *rentiers* have remained conservative Republican, like the Goldwaterites.

The Democratic party has usually come to power in America either when the workings of the capitalist economy broke down or when revolutionary classes became powerful political factors. Wilson came to power on a wave of socialism and progressivism arising out of the rapid development of an industrial proletariat fed by immigration. Roosevelt rode to power on the waves created by the crash of 1929. However, when capitalism has worked well and the revolutionary classes have been dormant, Republicans tend to come to power. They have also come to power when Democratic ideology has produced excesses, such as wars abroad, which frighten the internationalists, or infringements on property at home, which frighten the nationalists. Wilson became too much a prisoner of his own ideology and fell from power. During the 1920s, the realm of interests took back power from the realm of ideology, and the government in Washington at that time could indeed be considered an instrument of the ruling classes. As Coolidge said, "The business of government is business." The excesses of the Wilson Administration—war and ever deeper involvement in Europe's troubles and working-class violence symbolized by the IWW—aroused a reaction in the country. Wilsonianism as an international and domestic ideology was crushed, and the working classes remained dormant until the Depression. With the specters of war and revolution seemingly banished, the Republicans could present to the electorate the vision of an ever-expanding capitalist economy which brought more and more people into the consumer economy while at the same time protecting property rights. The collapse of that vision inevitably brought the Democrats back into power in 1932.

JAPAN AS IDEAL CASE OF CAPITALIST CLASS EXERCISING STATE POWER

In Japan, since the end of the war, there is a remarkable contemporary example of the kind of regime that governed America in the 1920s. Japan has been ruled by one party, now called the Liberal Democratic party (LDP). As in Coolidge's America of the 1920s, the business of the LDP-dominated government of Japan is business. For two decades, it has pursued policies oriented toward "high growth rates." *Kōdo seichō*, the slogan for LDP policies, entered the popular language much as *Wirtschaftswunder* became popular during Adenauer's and Erhard's Germany. Until the late 1960s, the Japanese government refrained from any substantial rearmament, citing their constitution's prohibition and justifying it by the American "nuclear umbrella." Freed from the burden of defense spending, Japanese governments have funneled all their resources and energies into an economic expansionism that has brought affluence to Japan and taken its business to the farthest reaches of the globe. War has been an issue only in that the people and the conservative government have resisted involvement in foreign wars like Korea and Vietnam. Making what concessions were necessary under the Security Treaty with the Americans, the government has sought only involvement that would bring economic profit to Japanese enterprise. Even now in the early 1970s, the much feared pace of rearmament is slow. At the same time, despite the rapid growth of unions after the war and the appearance of socialist parties and a small but influential Communist party, the ruling classes of Japan have not had to fear seriously the rising of the masses. In fact, with wage rises averaging 15 percent per year during much of the 1960s, potential discontent has been replaced by the search for affluence. With the conservatives keeping war out of Japan and creating general affluence, war and revolution have waned as social issues on which leftist political movements could build. The socialists, as elsewhere in advanced capitalist countries, have split and fragmented. The once vociferous unions have become docile in the face of rising affluence. The most spectacular protest has come from the students, again much as in other capitalist countries. But that protest has been largely moral and ideological, designed to halt any further drift of Japan toward involvement in America's imperialistic wars and alliances. I regard students as in the realm of ideology in contrast to workers, who are in the realm of interests, which may help to explain the frequent antipathy between them. Many Japanese conservatives, deep down, were not unhappy over the protest since any new military involvement could damage their spectacularly successful international capitalism. Because of the absence of war and revolution, the conservatives control Japan to such a degree that state and ruling class are virtually indistinguishable. As a result, Japan today is one of the great expansionist powers in the world. But, as is evident to anyone who follows Japanese politics, the ruling class is averse to returning to the policies of imperialism, knowing from experience that imperialism is bought at the price of expansionism and the risk of war.

The extraordinary triumph of capitalism in Japan (as in West Germany) could not have occurred without its defeat in World War II and the American occupation, which dealt a fatal blow to Japanese nationalism, militarism, and imperialism. From its inception in 1870, Japanese capitalism had always been closely linked to the state and fully appreciated the enormous benefits of military conquests. But before the war, just as afterward, the mood of the Japanese government was conservative in the literal sense. Old men, the ruling genro wanted to hold onto the great gains Japan had made and were fearful of losing them in some larger catastrophe. But in the frontier regions of Korea and Manchuria, new adventurous, militarist, imperialist, fascist zealots were arising who wanted to propel Japan onto the path of world conquest. Many were young army officers with plebeian origins. Increasingly hostile to the Tokyo government, they came to regard their leaders as vile, profit-hungry merchants. The new nationalism and militarism also had strong feudal elements deriving from a pre-1869 aristocracy, the samurai or *bushi,* who had lost much of their power with the Meiji Restoration. The samurai were a warrior aristocracy, which is what *bushi* literally means. The nationalists and militarists developed an anticapitalist bent, accusing the Japanese bourgeois of putting profits before national defense and the people's welfare. Unlike the German Nazis, who created a bureaucratic dictatorship that sought to put the German capitalist class under its control, they tried a combination of terror (assassination) and accommodation. The result was the rise to power in the mid-1930s of governments civilian in composition but committed to far-reaching external adventures to build up the empire. Talk about a Greater East Asia Co-prosperity Sphere became particularly common during the liberal Konoe government. The imperialist solution was a way out of the violent clashes between militarists and conservatives; it satisfied the former's insatiable appetite for more territory and the latter's fearful concern for economic gain and security. Without it, the Japanese government would have been torn to shreds, as it almost was by the wave of assassinations in 1936.

While Japanese imperialism collapsed the day Japan surrendered, it took the occupation to extirpate nationalism and militarism. The Japanese left, which praised many occupation measures, also later accused it of carrying out a sham purge of nationalists and militarists. But the fact remains that the occupation destroyed the Japanese armed forces. The present Japanese Self-Defense Forces, like the West German *Bundeswehr,* are an entirely new creation, though some old imperial officers helped to build it up. The MacArthur constitution prohibited Japanese rearmament. The educational reforms, which prohibited teaching nationalist doctrines, were actually followed. Nationalists and militarists were purged from office, although many, such as Prime Minister Nobusuke Kishi, later returned to power, prestige, and wealth. The American occupation destroyed the organizational structures of nationalism and militarism.

But even more importantly, unlikely as it may seem today, the occupation liberated the revolutionary classes of Japan—the peasants through a land reform which even the left acknowledges as successful, the workers through policies allowing and encouraging the formation of labor unions and left political parties, and the intellectuals through a far-reaching educational reform which generalized and democratized education. Even the Communists were encouraged in the very early days of the occupation. But at the same time the occupation encouraged Japan's bourgeoisie to revive a free enterprise economy and, as the cold war unfolded, to seize and hold state power. This class by and large welcomed the occupation reforms, even though now it has regrets about some of them.

The American occupation helped to complete the capitalist revolution in Japan which began with the Meiji Restoration of 1868 by crushing the right and liberating the left, thus ridding the bourgeoisie of its two main threats, war and revolution. The left was much less a threat to the Japanese bourgeoisie than the right, and in the 1930s had only been a threat through its incorporation into the right as a fascist force. The liberation of peasants, workers, and intellectuals permitted the development of a free market economy which formed the basis of the "high growth rate" successes of the 1950s and 1960s. The American occupation accomplished for Japan much what the Civil War did for America, according to Barrington Moore's arguments—it destroyed feudal vestiges, which froze property, and freed the country's capitalist energies for industrial expansion.

The American occupation made it possible for a state power to develop in Japan that was truly the instrument of the capitalist ruling class, as it never had been before. The destruction of the right and the liberation of the left were prerequisites for the new postwar political system, but the context which finally allowed it to achieve its full triumph was the restoration of the world economy by the United States. As peasants, workers, and intellectuals joined the labor force of a growing capitalist economy, the world market system provided the needed outlet for Japanese products and sparked the Japanese economic miracle. Thus, the liberation of the left, rather than producing mass political movements seeking to wrest state power away from the bourgeoisie, produced just the opposite, a huge consumer society forsaking politics for affluence. The progressive character of the American occupation was essential for the full triumph of capitalism in Japan. If America had moved into Japan in 1945, as it did into Vietnam in the 1950s, with policies aimed at upholding the status quo (landlord power in the countryside and neocolonialist military and police power in the cities—the nature of the Diemist regime), postwar Japan would most likely have returned to the condition of the 1920s when the nationalists, the bourgeoisie, and the revolutionaries were caught in increasingly bitter conflict.

The Japanese government today is one of the most practical, interest-oriented governments in the world. It is virtually devoid of ideology. While there are severe contradictions between nationalist and internationalist tendencies within the capitalist ruling class (exemplified in Tokyo's continuing policy of restricting foreign investment in Japan), they are less severe than in America because of Japan's need to export in order to survive. The flaw in this otherwise admirable picture of capitalist success is Japan's unavoidable dependence on the world market system and its need for peace and stability in the international environment. If depression and war should again seriously menace Japan from abroad, the right and the left would again become major political forces threatening the capitalists' monopoly over state power. Until recently, America appeared to have international commitments that squared precisely with these two basic needs of the Japanese ruling class. It was the cornerstone of the world market system and the nation most committed to its maintenance. And in spite of its aggressiveness in East Asia, America seemed committed, according to containment policy, to general stability in the region or at least to localizing wars. By the early 1970s, Japanese conservatives' confidence in America had eroded. It was no longer clear that America considered preservation of the world market system as a prime policy or, even if it did, whether it had the ability to implement it. Vietnam, and Nixon's new political-military doctrines upset the general pattern of East Asian stability, which had emerged under Eisenhower and which Kennedy appeared committed to furthering. The danger signals are already evident—increasing pressure for rearmament, gradual revival of nationalist ideas, the strength of a curious fascist-type party, the Kōmeitō or "Clean Government party," the growing strength of the Communist party, and, above all, the slow but persistent decline of the Liberal Democratic party's electoral majority.

The American occupation came close to smashing Japanese state power—it would have been smashed had the emperor system been destroyed, as there were pressures to do from both Japan and America after the war. It did away with all armed forces. It did away with the secret police and, in the early days, so democratized the Japanese police force that in the 1950s it was among the most timid in the world. It made the office of prefectual governor (*chiji*) elective rather than appointive (a democratic institution which soon eroded). It helped to reestablish a rule of law in Japan which put important constraints on the actions of the state. In short, the American occupation created a true bourgeois democracy in Japan by weakening rather than strengthening the state. Since 1868, state power in Japan had inexorably grown stronger, despite the bourgeoisie's attempts to slow it down by stressing the political role of the Diet. The American occupation reversed this process. What can be concluded from the case of Japan since 1945 is that the state became the instrument of the ruling class precisely because it was weakened. It was weakened to its right by the destruction of military power and to its left by a social emancipation that brought the revolutionary classes into the system.

SOME FINAL COMMENTS ON THE MARSHALL PLAN

As is evident, I do not regard the state as automatically the instrument of the ruling classes. In fact, to the contrary, I see it as the ever-renewed structure through which revolutionary forces in any society enter the body politic. I also regard it as normal for the state always to seek accommodation with the ruling interests, which is difficult if the interests of the ruling classes and of the state are equally powerful. The best of all possible worlds for a capitalist ruling class is where the state, in Schumpetrian fashion, is efficient enough but also weak enough to be the pliable tool of the ruling elites. Japan (and perhaps West Germany) is a splendid example of just such a situation in the modern world.

Theoretically, one can say that the Marshall Plan was the product of a counterattack by one of the most important segments of the realm of interests in America, the internationally oriented capitalist class, against the state, which even under the hardheaded Truman retained its character as the realm of ideology. The state arises out of war and revolution, and the Democratic party showed itself to be the prime vehicle for making and remaking it. The central concerns of the Truman Administration were war and revolution, and the modus operandi it chose to deal with them was to increase the scope and power of the state. In no comparable period of American history did the state undergo such an accretion of power as in those early postwar years (omitting the temporary inflations of state power during wartime). Domestically, the Truman Administration implemented defense programs which set the course for all succeeding American administrations and welfare programs which eventually led to the great social welfare programs of the Kennedy and Johnson administrations. Abroad, it initiated a containment policy that was intended to handle the problems of war and revolution on a global basis.

What would postwar America have been like if Dewey had been elected in 1944? The theory I have sketched out suggests that it would have been quite different. Under Dewey, the state as the realm of ideology would have contracted and the realm of interests would have reasserted its power. The Republicans would have tried to revert the government to what they considered its natural role, as the instrument of the ruling classes. They would have faced acute contradictions between their nationalist and internationalist wings, as well as violent assaults from the opposition Democrats. Dewey undoubtedly would have maintained the atomic monopoly as Truman did, and also would have initiated some form of American rearmament after postwar demobilization. But would he have moved toward the creation of a global American imperialism? The theory suggests that he would not.

Dewey was no isolationist, but being an internationalist is not the same as being an imperialist. What the world would have been like with Dewey as President is impossible to say, yet the theory suggests that it does make a difference who is President. It suggests further that imperialism is a conscious construct which not only was rapidly built but also could be rapidly dismantled. Lastly, it suggests that imperialism and the world market system are not identical. In the early 1970s, the two great protagonists of a capitalist world market system, Western Europe and Japan, are extricating themselves from American imperialism. It is not certain that they can do so without endangering world capitalism, but it is by no means certain that it is impossible. It is quite possible that capitalism can survive without American imperialism. De Gaulle believed this and made it the cornerstone of his foreign policy. Under Dewey, Washington's policies would have been more capitalistic and less imperialistic, and as such would have exacerbated the domestic class struggle (e.g., labor-management conflict) rather than calmed it, as generally occurred under the postwar Democratic administrations. But the key question is, What would have happened internationally? Would there have been a cold war?

Under a Dewey administration there would undoubtedly have been the same conflict between nationalists and internationalists as during the Truman Administration. What would Dewey have done when faced with pressures to back Chiang Kai-shek to the hilt or to execute a preventive atomic strike against Russia? How would he have responded to pressures to aid Britain, revive the German economy, and make the world once again safe for the world market system? Would he have shown the kind of caution that characterized the Eisenhower Administration and was in such marked contrast to Truman's adventurousness? The theory suggests that the realm of interests would have dictated a practical *ad hoc* approach to postwar problems rather than an ideological and systematic one. Practically speaking, from the point of view of American ruling class interests, America under a Dewey administration would have had to develop substantial military power, pump money into Western Europe, and would have been inclined to aid Chiang Kai-shek, perhaps even by dispatching American air power to intervene in the Chinese civil war. But all these measures do not add up to a cold war with two camps pitted against each other in a Manichaean struggle. In 1947, the Russians matched a growing American imperialism with a bloc of their own, inaugurated through the formation of the Cominform. But as a precursor of the socialist camp, the Cominform was threatened from its inception by internal discord. It was by no means clear that the Chinese Communists were prepared to join, and in 1948, Yugoslavia split with Russia. What made the socialist camp a reality was common opposition to American imperialism, which all saw as a world-wide force threatening them in an ideological and systematic way. In other words, it is quite possible that under a more pragmatic American President the socialist camp would never have arisen. Stalin would have been quite pleased to see the Americans bogged down in China and would have continued to haggle over Germany until Russia's security needs were met. He perhaps would have been even more pleased if Dewey had sent troops to Greece to crush the Communists without making a doctrinal pronunciamento, for the action would have been directed against Yugoslavia, whose leader Tito was a thorn in Stalin's side.

The real contradictions in the world would have been no different under Dewey than they were under Truman. But it is by no means certain that Washington would have chosen the path of empire to cope with them. It is likely that America would have been more expansionistic and less imperialistic, thus producing a multipolar rather than a bipolar world, something that is only now coming into being.

CHINA

The counterattack from the internationalists was followed by a far more vigorous and vicious counterattack from the nationalists. By the end of 1947, what was to be called the "China Lobby" had already begun its attacks against the Truman Administration for permitting China to fall to communism. While Europe (Britain, Germany, Russia) was the key concern of the internationalists, China became the focus and preoccupation of the nationalists.

A quarter-century later, the fury of that attack, which reached its most vicious form in the inquisitions led by Senator McCarthy, is still difficult to explain in rational terms. The real target of the right was not so much the left as the liberals of the Roosevelt and Truman administrations who had fashioned wartime and postwar policies. The right alleged a vast conspiracy, initiated at Yalta, designed to turn over much of the world to communism. McCarthy accused Roosevelt, Acheson, and Marshall as key figures in this conspiracy, and singled out China as the region of the world where it had had its greatest success. There the valiant Chiang Kai-shek, devoted and loyal friend of America, had his back against the wall as Communist hordes attacked him. While he was fighting for his life, men in the State Department were betraying him, thus assuring a Communist victory. These traitors were aided and abetted by known Communists and egged on by socialist Britain, whose sole concern was to make deals with the new Communist rulers of China for the sake of its own business interests. When John Foster Dulles spoke of the "evil doctrine of containment" in 1952, he was echoing the sentiments of the right. Communism was a vast international force which had already captured Russia, was fastening its hold on China, and was mortally threatening America from without and within. America had no choice but to wage all-out war with this "International Communist Conspiracy" and could not rest until victory was won.

So emotional was the nationalist attack and so ideological its language (anticommunism was its own international creed) that even now it is difficult to discern the real practical interests that were involved. There were no major American investments in China as there were in the Philippines. No American troops fought there, so that military defeat was not an issue. There were sentimental ties to China woven for over a century by missionaries, and it could be argued that part of the motivation of the right was the defense of America's manifest destiny to spread the gospel to the heathen, who were now threatened by a horrendous false gospel. But even fanatically Catholic Spain, when it built its empire, was motivated as much by the lust for gold and power as it was by the burning desire to spread the faith. The only phenomenon in recent American history comparable to the rising of the right in the late 1940s and early 1950s was the rising of the left in the late 1960s. What China was for the right, Vietnam was for the liberals. The two countries came to symbolize what were essentially intra-American struggles. In both instances, the vehemence of the attack directed against the government can only be explained politically by the fact that groups of people and social constituencies that backed them had once held power, lost it, and were fighting with all feasible means at their disposal to regain it. In the late 1960s and early 1970s, it was the left liberals, who had been shut out of power by Johnson. In the late 1940s, the right conservatives, nationalists par excellence, were fighting desperately to regain power in Washington after almost twenty years of liberal rule.

While the internationalists, including even such archconservatives as John Foster Dulles, had easy access to government, the nationalists felt powerless even within their own preferred Republican party. In 1940,

1944, 1948, and 1952, the liberal wing of the Republican party managed to nominate its own presidential candidates—in 1952 they picked Eisenhower, a man who not only was uncertain in his political affiliation but had been closely associated with policies of the Democratic administrations. True, in 1960 they picked a right-winger, but Nixon identified with Eisenhower. In 1964, when they finally got their man, a Republican victory seemed more improbable than ever, regardless of the candidate. The small-town provincial businessmen who made up the bulk of the Republican party's political structure had been losing out steadily since the beginning of the Depression, both to a vast federal government which was carrying out domestic policies anathema to their interests and to gigantic corporate forces which were concentrating ever more of the wealth in their own hands. To these men, Washington, New York, and Boston symbolized all the forces that were destroying the essence of America. Washington was big government; New York was international money; and Boston radiated a foreign-minded academia which in its very appearance was un-American. The essence of America was the small town with its white, middle-class population, its generally Protestant or decently Catholic religion, its values of individualism, private enterprise, and national pride.

Traditionally, the right conservatives had been isolationist, believing that America had no right to pursue any foreign policies other than those explicitly serving its interests. But in the late 1940s, they adopted alien China as the symbol of their struggle and appeared to advocate a worldwide war against communism using every means available including the atomic bomb. True, the isolationists in the pre–Pearl Harbor period were more eager to fight Japan than Germany. But there was no "Japan versus Germany" controversy then like the "Europe-first versus Asia-first" one in the late 1940s. A major variable entered the political picture in the post-1945 period which was not present in 1940, and that variable was military. The great China controversy of the late 1940s in America cannot be understood without understanding the controversies over military goals, strategies, and structures that were raging at the same time. Let us, therefore, look at these military controversies before the better known China issue. As is characteristic of military debates in American governmental circles, issues are *always* couched in technical terms in order to pay lip-service to the accepted doctrine that the military concerns itself only with means, never, God forbid, with ends. Yet running through all these military debates were views of the world that involved far more than dry competitiveness as to which weapon better served American defense needs.

AIR FORCE VERSUS NAVY

The most dramatic military controversy of the post-1945 period was between the Air Force and the Navy. It was fought out in the bureaucracy, in Congress, and, through the media, in the public in general. While it is usually described as a controversy of bombers versus carriers and naturally involved budgets, in fact, it was a doctrinal conflict over the kind of war America should prepare itself for in the future. It, therefore, involved an understanding of political tendencies throughout the world, on which estimations of America's national defense needs were based. As one can discern through the clouds of technical verbiage, the Navy and the Air Force (as well as the Army) had divergent understandings of the major tendencies of world politics. The ascendancy of one or another understanding had direct effects on the particular interests involved. It could mean that an entire service arm would be virtually dismantled so that the others, whose programs and weapons were deemed better suited to meet the potential threat, could be built up to optimal readiness. The demise or grave weakening of one service would have repercussions far beyond the service itself. It would mean fewer or no contracts for the industries producing weaponry for it. It would threaten the economies of regions traditionally associated with that service, and would affect a large range of other interests which had traditionally clustered around it.

In the period approaching 1950, the United States Navy came to feel that it was threatened with virtual destruction by a rapidly mushrooming new service arm, the Air Force, with no tradition or history of its own but with a new power that at times seemed to make it the one and only instrument of national defense. What made the Air Force a mortal enemy of the Navy was the combination of a traditional doctrine of warfare with the new power of the atomic bomb. The whole American military at that time accepted the doctrine of no war or all-out war, except for police actions or landings of Marines, which were not regarded as war. That doctrine held that America should try not to get involved in any war except under conditions of clear and present danger, but once involved should mobilize all its forces to achieve victory over the enemy. But the atomic bomb had radically changed the nature of war. A few atomic bombs delivered to the enemy's heartland could inflict so much human and material damage that it would be impossible for the enemy to pursue his aggression. The death of millions would deprive his armies of replacements and back-up support, and the destruction of his industries would quickly deprive him of supplies and weaponry. World War III would last at most only a few short weeks (unless, of course, the

enemy acquired his own atomic capability). The key to victory, therefore, was delivery of the atomic bomb to the enemy's heartland, which
meant possession of a long-range bomber fleet. The Air Force was the
logical delivery vehicle for atomic bombs, particularly in view of the
general understanding that Russia was America's principal enemy and its
vast heartland was vulnerable only to bomber attack.

If America was to persevere with its no war or all-out war doctrine
and atomic bombs signified an extremely short war, then the need for a
navy as a fighting arm became exceedingly questionable. Troops would
be necessary to occupy territory and ships would have to transport them
to distant shores, but battleships, aircraft carriers, cruisers, destroyers,
and patrol boats would be superfluous. Russia did not have a navy, and
even if it did, the key military action would be over the vast Eurasian
land mass, not in the oceans. A stout merchant marine would make
much more sense for such a war scenario than a costly navy. In the past,
America's enemies, particularly Japan, had depended on navies to advance their military and political aims. But Russia was a land power
with huge armies. Its great threat to the world was a ground invasion,
and the only major region so threatened was Western Europe. Russia
was able to survive industrially in World War II because its industries
were located beyond the Urals where the Germans could not reach them
and because America was a major supplier, neither of which would be
true in a Russo-American war. An army, yes, perhaps. But a navy just
did not make much sense in such a war.

Until the Korean War, even before the new commitments undertaken
in 1947, Washington was extremely economy-minded. The military
shared that philosophy even as it proposed its usual absurdly inflated
budgets. If United States defense needs required a high-speed program to
develop atomic weapons and concentration on a 70-group Air Force,
less budgetary resources would be available for the Navy and the
Army. Budgetary constraints would require a fine perusal of requests,
which would be rejected unless they accorded with the needs arising
from the general understanding of world politics.

It was under these conditions that the Navy began to argue strongly
for the building of new aircraft carriers. From a narrow interest point of
view, their demand for carriers was perfectly understandable. Battleships
were outmoded and the new capital ship was obviously going to be the
carrier. As a traditionally established interest, the Navy believed that it
was entitled to a new but comparable form of capital ship. But carriers
were incredibly expensive and their potential usefulness in the generally
accepted war scenario could not be convincingly demonstrated. At most,
carriers could launch fighters or small-size bombers from their decks in
the vicinity of the enemy's shores. But how could such aircraft reach the

distant inland industrial centers of Russia? Compared to the swift speed of B-29s or B-36s, the lumbering carriers would take at least a week to position themselves offshore, and then their potential damage-inflicting capability, even with atomic bombs, would be limited. No matter how hard the Navy tried in the years 1945–1950, it could not win the intellectual argument with the Air Force. In April 1949, the Navy suffered its worst defeat since Pearl Harbor when the new flush-deck carrier it so ardently wanted was rejected by Truman's much disliked economy-minded Secretary of Defense Louis Johnson. That resulted in the great "revolt of the admirals."

The defeat of the flush-deck carrier meant far more than the loss to the Navy of a particular weapons system. It meant a general downgrading of the Navy in the United States defense posture and even more a rejection of its world view, the philosophical basis for its very existence as it was then constituted. The United States Navy was essentially a Pacific Fleet, inasmuch as it granted the British Navy primacy in the Atlantic. Prior to Pearl Harbor, the United States Pacific Fleet shared power with two others, the British and the Japanese. When the Japanese destroyed the British Pacific Fleet in the first weeks of their war and then the Americans destroyed the Japanese fleet, the American Navy reigned supreme in the Pacific. If the entire Eurasian heartland was to be contained by a string of bases, obviously the major task in the Pacific would fall to the United States Navy. The British fleet might have Gibraltar and Suez and even Singapore, but the United States Navy had Pearl Harbor, Yokosuka, and Cavite Bay. No carriers meant no bases. And if the Navy was turned into a fleet of submarines and troop carriers, its "traditional role in diplomacy," as the conventional accounts so quaintly put it, would be finally extinguished. For all of his visionary internationalism, Roosevelt still was a strong partisan of the Navy and fought for the base notion. Truman, however, was a landlocked Midwesterner whose only military experience had been in the Army. Bases seemed obsolete to the men of his administration. They thought in terms of atomic bombs, long-range aircraft, and troops stationed in key regions of the world. Moreover, the Truman men were liberals who preferred the Army and the Air Force to the Navy, which was deeply conservative by tradition. In the spring of 1949, despite Communist victories in China, a war in Indochina, and the independence of Indonesia, nothing in the Pacific was as menacing as Russian power in Europe. The loss of scarce raw materials to hostile governments would be a serious matter, but choices had to be made in matters of defense because of the extreme sparsity of budgetary resources. Under the zero-sum budgetary terms which still prevailed in Washington before the Keynesianism of an ever-expanding pie was aroused by the Korean War, flush-deck carriers would do damage to more important defense efforts, in the areas of atomic and air power. The Navy defeat of April 1949 symbolized the general downgrading of the Pacific as a region of prime American military-political concern.

While the Navy could fight the usual bureaucratic battles to keep its budgets and programs, now it had to counterattack intellectually. In early October 1949, when the House Armed Services Committee was holding hearings on the carrier versus bomber controversy, Admiral Arthur Radford openly challenged the "atomic blitz" scenario which by that time was a doctrine firmly embedded in the government: "I do not believe that the threat of atomic blitz will be an effective deterrent to a war, or that it will win a war . . . there is no short cut, no cheap, no easy way to win a war."[6]

Radford's testimony came only two weeks after the first Russian atomic detonation, an event of capital importance to the Washington national security bureaucracy. Obviously, once America's atomic monopoly was broken, the atomic blitz scenario would begin to crumble and the way would be opened for alternative scenarios. That it did not crumble is evident from Washington's eventual decision to go for the H-bomb and its subsequent doctrine of "massive retaliation" (a variant of the atomic blitz doctrine). But the moment the Russians had "the bomb," World War III was no longer so simple as it appeared until September 1949.

In 1951, the Navy got its carriers and the Pacific Seventh Fleet, in particular, was well on the way to becoming one of the world's most powerful military forces. The Korean War is usually cited as the turning point in the reversal of American military policies, as indeed it was. While the war finally did away with bureaucratic and congressional resistance to vast new defense budgets, the shift in American political-military policies was already evident months before its outbreak. The well-known National Security Council Paper No.68 (NSC 68), adopted early in 1950, had begun to sketch out new policies, the most striking aspect of which was to sharply increase defense spending, something the Truman Administration had been reluctant until then to do. NSC 68 was sparked by the Russian atomic explosion and by the "loss of China," but philosophically it was entirely in the spirit of containment policy. Since it anticipated a loss of the American atomic monopoly (unless some spectacular breakthrough was made with the H-bomb), it advocated greater reliance on conventional forces to counter Russian expansionism, particularly in Europe. This led to the forces-in-being concept, the need for conventional forces based on ground troops to be stationed in threatened

---

[6] Paul Y. Hammond, "Super Carriers and B-36 Bombers: Appropriations, Strategy, and Politics," in Harold Stein, ed., *American Civil-Military Decisions*, p. 517.

parts of the world, which eventually led to NATO and other alliances. NSC 68 reaffirmed the primacy of Europe in American political-military thinking and can be seen as an attempt to reformulate containment policy under the changed circumstances of the lost monopoly of atomic weapons. But as the foundations of the atomic blitz theory were crumbling, other global views could come into prominence. Admiral Radford's testimony in early October 1949 sounded the opening note of those new views.

THE AMERICAN MILITARY AND TAIWAN

The Navy's most significant victory after the defeat of its flush-deck carrier proposals was over the issue of Taiwan. Up to early September 1949, the Joint Chiefs of Staff had recommended against "overt" American military action to defend Taiwan. However, in early December, as Tang Tsou notes, the Joint Chiefs "reversed their earlier position," and recommended sending a fact-finding mission there and granting increased military assistance to Chiang Kai-shek's Nationalists. By late December, Senator Robert Taft was recommending that the Navy be dispatched to Taiwan. And in early January, Senator Knowland released a letter from former President Herbert Hoover advocating that the United States give naval protection to the Nationalists in order to keep Taiwan, the Pescadores (Penghu archipelago), and possibly Hainan Island out of Communist hands.[7] That right-wing Republicans were the most ardent supporters of the defend-Taiwan campaign is well known. But more significant was the conversion of the Joint Chiefs of Staff to it.

The Joint Chiefs of Staff was far from the monolithic body it was to become in the early 1960s when it faced its mortal enemy, Robert McNamara. It was a typical bureaucratic committee which reflected all the rivalries and contradictions of the services its members represented. In addition, it had to face a Secretary of Defense (James Forrestal and then Louis Johnson) who represented White House policies, notably the constant call for economizing in defense. Although a Navy man, Admiral William Leahy, served as an informal chairman of the Joint Chiefs until March 1949, the dominating spirit came from the Army and the Air Force. The Air Force's source of power was the new military capabilities arising out of the atomic bomb. The Army's influence could be traced mainly to men like Dwight Eisenhower and Omar Bradley who had long and faithfully served the two Democratic administrations and were Europe-firsters by virtue of their World War II experience. The Chief of

[7] Tang Tsou, *America's Failure in China*, pp. 527–30.

Naval Operations, Admiral Louis Denfeld, was regarded as a conciliator and did not take on the role of advocate (in Anthony Downs's sense) until the carrier controversy reached a point of fever heat, whence he was removed. While the spirit of compromise again and again led the Joint Chiefs to make concessions to the Navy, on the vital issues inevitably the combination of White House, Army, and Air Force power decisively outweighed whatever influence the Navy could bring to bear. Thus, until early September 1949, the majority of the Joint Chiefs of Staff supported the White House in its policy of not promising Chiang Kai-shek military support to defend his new redoubt in Taiwan. Any defense of Taiwan would be almost exclusively a Navy matter, and furthermore could easily involve America in a distant war, which would adversely affect its defense capabilities in areas of more direct concern, like Western Europe, or its strategic bombing posture vis-à-vis Russia.

During the three months between early September 1949, when the Joint Chiefs of Staff recommended against holding Taiwan, and early December, when they reversed themselves, not only had the Russians exploded their first atomic bomb, but the Chinese Nationalists had removed their capital to Taiwan. In fact, as Tang Tsou relates it, it was the official removal to Taiwan on December 8 that led to the National Security Council meeting that brought forth what was the new, allegedly only "military" recommendation from the Joint Chiefs of Staff. It could not have been Mao's trip to Moscow (he arrived there on December 16) or the Sino-Soviet alliance (announced in February 1950) that prompted the Joint Chiefs' reversal on Taiwan. That there was strong Navy pressure to involve America in its defense is evident from the curious career of Admiral Charles Cooke, commander of the Seventh Fleet from December 1945 to February 1948. Despite congressional refusal in 1949 to authorize a formal aid mission to Chiang Kai-shek, Admiral Cooke, then retired, showed up in Taiwan as a representative of the "International News Service" and in 1950 became "coordinator" of a "private" outfit, Commerce International China, made up of retired military officers, whose purpose was to funnel aid to Chiang Kai-shek.[8] The Navy had a long history of amicable ties with Chiang Kai-shek through the American wartime naval adviser Admiral Milton Miles, and Cooke's mission to Chiang was but a continuation of it. While Chiang Kai-shek had long before December 1949 been transferring his gold and other resources to Taiwan, the official shift of the capital from Chungking to Taipei could only have been made if he had some assurance from America (or some Americans) that it would support him against any Communist attempt to take Taiwan. Since no such guarantee was forth-

---

[8] Tsou, *America's Failure in China*, p. 559 n. 24; Peter Dale Scott, *The War Conspiracy*, p. 210.

coming from the White House, or, until early December from the Joint Chiefs of Staff, it could only have come from the Navy. The China Lobby Republicans were vocal and influential, but they had not been particularly successful in getting Washington involved in the China conflict. The word of Admiral Cooke as ex-commander of the Seventh Fleet carried much more weight with Chiang Kai-shek, who thought almost exclusively in military terms, than the fulminations of William Knowland and Styles Bridges. But Cooke and his good friend Admiral Radford could not even suggest guarantees until they had more solid backing in Washington. Lacking much chance at the White House, they finally got support from the Joint Chiefs of Staff.

Without American support, Chiang probably never could have held on to Taiwan. Only two years before, his henchmen had committed horrible massacres in putting down a rebellion. Hatred against the Nationalists was extreme, and an underground Communist party was operating. Chiang's resignation from the presidency the previous January had led to a fracturing of the rickety coalition of warlords, bankers, and politicians that constituted the Kuomintang (KMT). Although he still commanded much of the party apparatus, held much gold, and wielded much power, Chiang's trump card for years had been his alleged ability to get foreign powers to pull his chestnuts out of the fire. He had received considerable American support during the war while conserving his forces and avoiding battle with the Japanese. He had a powerful lobby operating for him in Washington during the civil war, which, despite its failure to get America fully involved, managed to extort considerable monies from the Truman Administration. He and Madame Chiang were the only Chinese really popular among Americans. Who ever heard of the interim president Li Tsung-jen?

In the early months of 1950, a loud crescendo of demands went up from right-wing Republicans to commit the United States Navy to the defense of Taiwan. At the same time, they were voting down aid to South Korea. Republican Representative Donald Jackson of California put the Taiwan versus South Korea case in succinct terms worthy of the geopolitics of Admiral Mahan. Dismissing South Korea as a "dead-end street without an escape," he described Taiwan as "a point in the line of defenses which include Japan, the Philippines, and Okinawa, all essential and vital to the national defense of the United States."[9] In early December when Chiang Kai-shek resumed power in Taipei, he had already learned from his Navy friends of the momentous change in attitude of the American Joint Chiefs of Staff and knew that his chances to get United States military protection were good.

[9] Quoted in Tsou, *America's Failure in China*, p. 537, n. 219.

THE BUREAUCRATIC DISEQUILIBRIA PRODUCED BY THE RUSSIAN ATOMIC BLAST

The Russian detonation of its first atomic bomb in late September 1949 forced a turning point in American political-military thinking on a global scale. Admiral Radford's arguments of early October 1949 that the atomic blitz no longer was an effective deterrent now made sense. With its own atomic bombs, Russia now could risk a move forward without fearing immediate unilateral atomic retaliation from America. The White House's adamant opposition to any preventive strike to take out Russian atomic installations and Russia's own unexpected speed in developing the bomb would mean that in a few years' time America's atomic deterrent might be reduced to zero. Under these circumstances, more old-fashioned forms of deterrence would have to be sought. NSC 68 suggested increased troop levels in Europe and a generally expanded defense program. But the Navy was ready with its own program for containment: forge a ring of bases held together by naval power all around the land mass of hostile Eurasia. Only after the Russian atomic explosion did the Joint Chiefs of staff finally accept the Navy's world view, though without abandoning the official one, which was to be rescued shortly by NSC 68.

A theoretical point can be made here which will be important in explaining subsequent events, particularly the escalation of the Vietnam war in 1964. As is clear by now, I regard America's nuclear power as an essential, if not the essential, element in its imperialism. That imperialism was formed through a containment policy which led to the division of the world into a free world and a socialist camp. The free world came under American control and influence through a variety of devices but the "nuclear umbrella" was essential. America originally regarded its nuclear power as a deterrent force inhibiting any Russian move across the demarcation lines laid down by containment. At the same time, America presumed that it would not be the first to attack, that it would not really practice "rollback" against Russia. Subsequently, Russian development of nuclear weapons led to mutual deterrence, which simply reinforced the American intent not to attack first, given the threat of Russian retaliation. The chief instrument of American imperialism is its government, and the vanguard of the government is its executive branch. The natural tendency of all state power is to expand. Since nuclear power is an essential component of American state power, it likewise tends to expand. But all nuclear power is relative to the nuclear power of an enemy. Any sudden and drastic change in the nuclear balance of power with an enemy (Russia or China) will have direct effects on the extent of the power of the chief executive. Whenever America's nuclear power expanded in absolute and relative terms, so did the power of the chief executive within the bureaucracies of government. But when an enemy made a nuclear breakthrough, the power of the chief executive suddenly contracted, creating a dangerous period of power imbalance. The theoretical point behind this is that during a time of sudden contraction of executive power, "aggressors" will strike. While potential aggressors are usually depicted as external enemies waiting to pounce in Pearl Harbor style upon America, in fact, the true aggressors are within the government. During that period of executive weakness, the losers in the bureaucratic power struggles lunge forward with their own views, programs, and interests to try to recapture the power they have lost to the executive.

In terms of bureaucratic power, therefore, it is in the interest of the American chief executive to maintain nuclear power at stable levels. If nuclear power expands too rapidly, the enemy will be forced to respond with a counter-build-up of his own, which in turn will produce dangerous imbalances in internal bureaucratic power. If nuclear power contracts, then internal enemies of the executive will seize on that period of weakness to crash through with their own interests. A moderately increasing nuclear capability, regardless of absolute levels of nuclear weaponry or overkill waste, suits the executive best, provided that external enemies are not frightened into excessive response.

The explosion of the first Russian atomic bomb in September 1949 was the first serious blow to the steadily growing power of the American chief executive since 1945. The Russians obviously developed the bomb because they were unwilling to rely on American defensive intent for their security. But when the Russian bomb exploded, the internal enemies of the chief executive, particularly the Navy and the cluster of interests centering on the China Lobby, counterattacked and snatched victory of sorts from the jaws of a defeat that had been looming until then. There was a comparably dangerous period in late 1963 and in 1964 as the Chinese moved toward the explosion of their first atomic bomb, which came in October 1964.

Until September 1949, the Navy and the China Lobby were losing in the bureaucratic struggle to the steady advance of containment. Despite token concessions, the Navy saw its great Pacific role being whittled down more and more, and the China Lobby saw the prospect nearing that Washington would eventually recognize the new regime in China. But starting in late September 1949, the tide began to turn. The Navy vigorously pleaded for its carriers in the October hearings and the military came to accept the vital need for the defense of Taiwan. The violent attacks in Congress on the Truman Administration and the rise of Mc-

Carthyism in early 1950 were manifestations of this counterattack, which succeeded when the Korean War broke out in June 1950 and Truman committed the Seventh Fleet to the defense of Taiwan. The victory in 1950 of the losers in 1949 did not make their world view or their interests dominant in the government. Containment marched on even under the later Eisenhower Administration. But the losers became a powerful interest group which, particularly through the military and the intelligence agencies, could not be dislodged from the government. Their minority power, so to speak, was to grow from crisis to crisis, leading eventually to the Vietnam war. Vietnam became their bailiwick, and even as public disdain for the war grew in the late 1960s and early 1970s, these perennial losers were more determined than ever to hold on to what they had. The American chief executive, whether Democrat or Republican, remembering the crises, blackmail, and power struggles of a quarter-century, knew no other way to handle this cluster of minority interests than through a never-ending series of compromises.

THE RIGHT, ROLLBACK, AND COVERT WAR

We must now go back and examine the China Lobby side of this nationalist counterattack against the dominant policy of containment. The nationalists were by and large right-wing Republicans who represented the more traditional, nonurban parts of the country, particularly in the Middle West and the West. That they were extremely anticommunist need hardly be stressed. But they hated even more the entire Roosevelt tradition of big government, social welfare, and support of labor. Their antilabor sentiments were probably most directly related to their interests. Generally small provincial businessmen, they regarded unions as mortal threats to their very existence. Senator William Knowland, who ruled Oakland, California, like his own fiefdom, was horrified by the sudden mushrooming of labor's political power there during the immediate postwar years, and his organ, the *Oakland Tribune*, had no hesitation in labeling it a communist plot. The fact that Oakland was next to liberal, academic Berkeley made it easy for Knowland to see threads leading from the upstart labor challengers to his power to both Washington and Berkeley. The right-wing Republicans were conservatives who became reactionaries as they saw the new power of labor rising throughout the country. They counterattacked in Congress, succeeding finally in getting legislation passed (chiefly the Taft-Hartley Act) that began to put labor in its place. These right-wing Republicans saw themselves as losers not just to the Democrats and to labor, but even to the liberal wing of their own party. Western Republicans like Knowland were anti-Eastern, fearing Eastern big capital, which controlled the liberal wing of the

Republican party, almost as much as the government and the unions. Knowland is said to regard Oakland as a true bastion of the West as contrasted with cosmopolitan San Francisco, allegedly controlled by Eastern money. In 1948, the right-wingers again failed to nominate their man Taft, but at least they had hope of an electoral victory. When Truman won, the cause of right-wing Republicanism seemed more hopeless than ever.

What must be explained is not how these conservatives became reactionaries, but how they became international counterrevolutionaries committed to hot war against communism wherever it reared its ugly head. That this was not just rhetoric is indicated by the word "rollback," which they adopted as their leitmotiv. Rollback, whose very mention frightened socialist countries into believing that American forces were ready to invade them, was a deliberate policy of seeking to "liberate" captive nations from communism. Chiang Kai-shek took rollback so seriously that he believed that America might well join him in his crusade to regain Mainland China. Moreover, he and other counterrevolutionaries found it difficult to believe that the immense concentrations of American air and naval power, particularly in the Pacific regions, were intended just for containment or deterrence purposes. Chiang Kai-shek's program for rollback was the most concrete. He indicated that he would provide the ground forces (some 600,000 men) and America had only to provide air and naval support. When his forces landed on the China coast, uprisings would erupt throughout China and, as in his Northern Expedition of the mid-1920s, he would quickly sweep north to Peking. The obvious fallacy, other than misinterpretation of Communist domestic strength, was that such an invasion would probably have launched World War III or at least gravely risked it. Why, therefore, did these conservative Republicans, many of whom only a decade before had been isolationists, appear to be advocates of a third world war to free the world from communism? Fighting for domestic rollback of labor and big government is easily understandable, but practicing rollback against Russia and then China was a far more dangerous matter. What was the general interest of the nationalists who argued that America was lost unless China was saved? How would fighting communism abroad in China, Korea, Vietnam, or elsewhere serve that general interest? Wars mean quantum leaps in government spending, which may provide temporary windfalls for some but pose too many dangers for the future. These lesser capitalists generally believed that the best way to fuel business expansion was to shackle labor and cut taxes. Their hostility to war, expressed in their earlier isolationism, seemed to square best with their interests. In terms of the realm of interests, how did isolationism turn into rollback anticommunism?

The first step in the answer is to note that rollback notions were seriously entertained only for East Asia, not for Eastern Europe. Despite the agitation of Eastern European refugees, West German revanchists, and Europe-oriented anticommunist Americans, America never developed covert warfare (the operational form of rollback) there as it did against the socialist countries of Asia (chiefly China and North Vietnam). When the East German workers revolted in the summer of 1953, no move was made to help them. And when the Hungarian Rebellion erupted in October 1956, despite some flickers of encouragement from Radio Free Europe, America did not act, either overtly or covertly. In the immediate postwar years, anticommunist guerrillas were fighting in the Ukraine (the Bandera gangs), but no Vang Pao or Armée Clandestine aided and abetted by the CIA ever developed. Whether from fear of Russia or for other reasons, such as strict adherence to containment policies, America decided not to pursue covert war in Eastern Europe.

By contrast, since 1950, America has pursued a far-reaching covert war in East Asia reaching deep into Chinese and North Vietnamese territory. Overt rollback almost occurred when MacArthur crossed the 38th parallel and with the blessing of Truman and the United Nations proceeded to "unify" Korea. In association with Chiang Kai-shek's overt rollback policies, American governmental agencies since the early 1950s were involved in far-reaching programs of dropping arms to insurgents in China, landing commandos on the China coast, and sending sabotage teams deep into Chinese territory. One of the most important points of departure for that anti-China covert war was Laos, which became the theater par excellence for covert war. The most important reason for the secrecy with which Washington covered its operations in Laos was that they were being directed not only against North Vietnam but against China. That this covert warfare often went on in opposition to the dominant containment policies enunciated in Washington demonstrates the power of the entrenched interests committed to rollback policies. Since Washington's dominant policies eschewed rollback, something had to be given to minority bureaucratic interests to compensate them for their policy losses. Covert war in East Asia was the "compromise" form that rollback took.

Rollback as an open and avowed policy has been pursued by only three "countries": Taiwan, South Korea, and South Vietnam. During the 1950s, Chiang Kai-shek, Syngman Rhee, and Ngo Dinh Diem repeatedly called for military action to "liberate" their divided countries from Communist rule. In 1960, Syngman Rhee was ousted and replaced by Park Chung Hee, who was more willing to accept Washington's containment policies. Diem's successors, notably Khanh and Ky, still shouted for a "march north" (*bâc tien*), in 1964 and 1965, but Nguyen Van Thieu was willing to settle for control over South Vietnam alone. Only Chiang has consistently held to his "counterattack the Mainland" notions, but as he has aged into his mid-eighties, they have turned into crumbling slogans. While American liberals regarded the calls for rollback by America's Asian anticommunist clients as amusing rhetoric, in fact, their rise in volume directly paralleled the rise in American-directed covert war in East Asia. Naturally, Chiang, Rhee, and Diem always hoped it would turn into overt war so that they could realize their reunification dreams, but since containment barred that, they were willing to settle for covert war. Rollback always was regarded as a military notion, that is, armed reconquest of territory held by Communists. But the error so many observers have made was to equate it with overt war and, therefore, regard it as an anachronistic relic from the early days of the cold war. In fact, the real form rollback took was covert war—war waged with clandestine military forces often supported by the regular armed forces of the United States.

Rollback was the great right-wing Republican slogan of the late 1940s and early 1950s, and was vehemently espoused by John Foster Dulles to replace the "evil doctrine of containment." While Dulles did not practice rollback in Europe, following his Republican internationalist sentiments, he did so in East Asia, following the sentiments of his Republican nationalist side. Under his brother Allen Dulles, chief of the CIA, America developed a vast apparatus for covert war in East Asia aimed primarily against China but involving more directly Korea, Taiwan, Vietnam, Laos, Thailand, and even Burma. John Foster Dulles could not shake Chou En-lai's hand at the 1954 Geneva conference because his brother Allen was waging war against China, and the handshake would have been a symbolic policy act indicating Washington's attempts fully to apply containment policies in East Asia. The American covert war agencies and their East Asian allies would have taken it as a sign that Washington was again turning against them, as it had during the Truman Administration. By the 1950s, the rollback policies advocated by right-wing Republicans in the late 1940s had become bureaucratically entrenched as covert war in East Asia. During the 1950s, under the Eisenhower Administration, America did not practice any substantial covert war outside of East Asia, except perhaps the brief adventure in Guatemala and the beginnings of the Bay of Pigs invasion. The CIA was helpful in the overthrow of the Mossadegh government in Iran, but there is no evidence of large-scale covert war actions in the Middle East. Nor was there any in Eastern Europe. It was Kennedy who tried to transform covert war concentrated in East Asia into a global counterinsurgency in conjunction with Washington's new policies toward the Third World.

EXPANSIONISM IN THE PACIFIC

We now come back to our original and obvious question, Why did the right-wing nationalist Republicans so vehemently seize on the China issue during the late 1940s and advocate a rollback of Chinese communism, something they came close to getting as the Korean War threatened to spill across the Manchurian borders? In seeking an answer, recall a theoretical distinction made in the early part of this book between imperialism and expansionism. Whereas imperialism sought to organize large spaces of the world for purposes of control, expansionism directly reflected the most basic drives of nascent rather than mature capitalism —the search for new areas of investment, new markets, and raw materials under conditions of political safety and unencumbered by governmental regulation or union interference. The frontier hypothesis of Frederick Jackson Turner has been considered, and is, one of the truest explanations of America's growth. As business matured in the eastern United States, new enterprise developed in provinces farther west. But the advance of the frontier always went hand in hand with the extension of American political dominion, which invariably took military form. As American armies secured the West and the Southwest from the Indian and remnant Mexican menace, business moved in, ranging from the lonely homesteader to the railroad magnate. By the turn of the century, the frontier had leaped far into the Pacific, its most notable conquest being the Hawaiian Islands.

Three types of Americans have moved westward with the frontier since its opening early in the nineteenth century: the entrepreneur, the soldier, and the missionary. Farmers, miners, and merchants crowded into the West, soon followed by more elaborate business ventures. Armies were there from the beginning, and the missionaries followed. The missionaries took the farthest leap westward shortly after the Civil War as they began to pour into China. Enterprise quickly followed. Lastly came the armies, in the form of Admiral Dewey's fleet, which took the Philippines. That westward expansion, which Richard O'Connor describes in his *Pacific Destiny*, had an evangelical, mercenary, and martial character, and so aroused a predictable romanticism throughout America. Americans also expanded southward into Latin America, but on a more limited scale. When Admiral Mahan pinpointed the areas of American expansion as the Pacific and the Caribbean, he thereby excluded South America. Not until the 1920s, when America began to develop oil interests in Venezuela, did American business become seriously interested in the continent below the Panama Canal. No real romanticism ever developed around American expansion into the Caribbean. No large numbers of missionaries went to Cuba as they did to Hawaii and China. The lands of the Caribbean were there simply to be exploited.

No purer example of American expansionism exists than Hawaii, which can truly be regarded as a model of how the expansionists would have liked to transform all of East Asia. By the mid-nineteenth century, the missionaries had virtually conquered Hawaii. Even today, hardly any other place in the world has so many churches per square mile. As these missionary caterpillars transformed themselves into entrepreneurial butterflies, they became great land-owning plantation magnates. Even today, over 80 percent of the land is owned by a small number of whites or their "benevolent" trusts, many of whom, like the Dillinghams, are descendants of the early missionaries. By the turn of the century, Pearl Harbor, the great American naval base, had come into being, and today under the rule of CINCPAC (Commander-in-Chief, Pacific) is still the largest American military installation in the Pacific and the headquarters of all Pacific military action. Plantation agriculture, military installations, and tourism are the chief "industries" of Hawaii, providing just about its entire employment. A small minority of whites remains in control of the economy. From the mid-nineteenth century on, a great immigration of Orientals began. They have become Hawaii's middle class while others, Filipinos, Portuguese, and native Hawaiians, constitute the manual labor force. The white American entrepreneur, missionary, and soldier rule over a peaceable non-white population. Until statehood was granted, it seemed that the Hawaiian model could be repeated elsewhere in the Pacific. In fact, American conservatives opposed Hawaiian statehood, as many Americans in Hawaii had opposed its formal annexation at the turn of the century. From the conservative nationalist point of view, the ideal would have been a native government like the old Hawaiian monarchy controlled by an economy in American hands, held in check by an American military presence, and spiritually guided to correct values by Christian missionaries. Hawaiian statehood was espoused mainly by mainland American liberals and supported by the Hawaiian Oriental middle classes, who regarded it as a way out from under the crushing domination of their haole overlords.

The American conquest of Hawaii was not the terminal point in a mainland expansion that had stretched to the shores of the Pacific, but the starting point of a different kind of expansion. Mainland expansion had taken place in territory only thinly settled by Indians. Through massacres, the United States Army managed to clear the way for settlement. But the conquest of Hawaii did not involve settlement, and only recently have haoles moved there in great numbers. Hawaiian expansion was pure expansion by a small minority of soldiers, entrepreneurs, and missionaries who constituted themselves into the ruling elite over a "native" society. Until 1945, further Pacific expansion was blocked by Japan and to a lesser extent by Britain. But after 1945, the entire Pacific seemed to be open to this expansionist American trinity. American forces found themselves stationed throughout all of East Asia, including China. Missionaries began pouring back on the heels of American victory. And exciting new prospects for business and commerce were opened up by the defeat of earlier Japanese and British competitors.

The expansionist drive for soldier, missionary, and entrepreneur can be explained in greater detail. As already noted, for the American military the expansionist drive in the Pacific was overwhelmingly naval. The Navy was traditionally hungry for bases. After 1945, it began to develop new ones at a rapid rate—on the newly seized Pacific islands, in Japan (Yokosuka and Sasebo)—and rebuilt the bases in the Philippines. The fascination of Asia for American missionaries is well documented. Except in Latin America, American Protestant missionaries were nowhere so active. Africa, India, and the Middle East were largely the preserve of British and European missionaries. The conversion of China to Christianity seemed to have some strange theological significance to many of the Protestant missionaries. Sun Yat-sen's Christianity and, even more, Chiang Kai-shek's conversion to Methodism played a major role in the support mobilized for him in the 1930s and in the post-1945 period. Traditional American business interests in East Asia had been in plantation agriculture, mining and prospecting (notably for oil), and shipping. Raw materials shortages during World War II and stockpiling policies had generated an intensive new drive to acquire scarce metals, including many that came into demand because of technological advances. Moreover, the war had created a great new demand for oil, which unleashed an oil prospecting boom throughout the world. Traditional American shipping interests in the Pacific were joined by an exciting new interest— commercial aviation. Whereas Britain competed for European aviation, American aviation had a virtual monopoly over East Asia. As America rapidly demobilized after the end of the Pacific war, military transportation needs remained high. Civil aviation took over from military air transport. Moreover, the continuing warfare in East Asia increasingly required air power for transport and logistical purposes, which various civil American air interests were eager to satisfy. Claire Chennault got into the game early with his Flying Tigers, and after the war moved rapidly to organize one of the then biggest airlines in the world, Civil Air Transport (CAT). While the notorious Air America ultimately came to take on covert war operations, initially it was organized, like CAT, for profit as well as for war. During World War II, a new business interest opened up—construction. Construction companies, like Morrison-

Knudsen, had made great profits and quickly saw the prospects of more arising from the military base construction of the postwar and cold war periods.

What is unique about American expansion in the Pacific is that it was the only part of the world where the trinity of military, missionary, and business drives came together. American business has expanded into Latin America but not the military, except in the Caribbean. American missionary activity in Latin America has tended to focus on such remote areas as Ecuador, Peru, and Bolivia, which are of lesser interest to business (despite Bolivia's tin) or the military. The expansion of American multinational corporations into Europe was entirely different from that of the newer and rough-and-tumble enterprises like Kaiser Industries or Morrison-Knudsen or airlines like Pan Am. The biggest and oldest American corporations expanded into Western Europe not through pioneering enterprise but through financial dealings carried on in quiet bankers' offices.

The Pacific was the traditional area of American expansionism but not of the new postwar imperialism, which focused initially on Europe. It is not difficult to imagine the excitement that Japan's defeat in 1945 produced in the hearts of those who still dreamed of going westward. Europe in 1945 was in ashes and could only look forward to dreary occupation. But except for Japan, East Asia was alive and vibrant. Manila had been badly destroyed during the fighting, but tropical cities even in ruins looked better than gray Hamburg or Cologne. For the expansionists, the prospect opened up that all of the Pacific could be transformed into a kind of Hawaii. With American military power supreme in East Asia, entrepreneurs and missionaries finally had the political protection they had sought for a hundred years. Asian backwardness invited American capital without fear of competition from European or Japanese interests. And the white man's triumph over yellow Japan opened the minds and hearts of Asians to his gospel. Unless one understands the Asian optimism that gripped many Americans in 1945, one cannot understand their rage when Marx, not Jesus, assumed ascendancy in China.

Why was China so central to this expansionist vision of the Pacific that it produced the rage of McCarthyism? China meant different things to the admirals, the cowboy business venturers, and the fundamentalist missionaries. Aside from these feelings among citizens of civil society, China also meant different things to the actors in the game of Washington bureaucratic politics. We shall see later the explosive consequences when the civil and bureaucratic conceptions of China met. To the admirals schooled in the teachings of Admiral Mahan, China meant a great Eurasian land power. As long as it was weak, poor, and tied to America, it constituted no threat. But as Communist armies rolled over China, the admirals suddenly found a new hostile great power arising where, after the defeat of Japan, it had been presumed there was no longer any significant great power threat to America. Red Russia and Red China together appeared to bear out the direst of Admiral Mahan's predictions.

To the entrepreneur, China had various meanings. Of course, all Pacific entrepreneurs dreamed of the vast China market, which Carl Crow had described in his book *Four Hundred Million Customers*. But China was also over ten million Overseas Chinese located everywhere in the Pacific, where they played commanding roles in the economies of Pacific countries and territories. A unified Communist China could mean ten million Communist Overseas Chinese who could wreak havoc with expansionist business plans if they wanted to. With the Japanese, the British, and the French effectively excluded from the Pacific after 1945 and the absence of native bourgeoisies in the East Asian countries, the Overseas Chinese were the only economic power other than America in the Pacific. When Chiang Kai-shek set up his government on Taiwan, he did American business a favor by keeping them out of Communist control and influence. Overseas Chinese were and still are the indispensable middlemen in virtually all business ventures in East Asia and the Pacific. Despite persecution in the Philippines, Indonesia, and Malaya, they remain central to the economies of those countries.

To the missionaries, the Chinese posed a unique challenge. China was the great land of philosophy, whose Confucian teachings were not unlike those of Protestant Christianity. The cultures of Japan, Korea, and Vietnam all derived philosophically from China. The Pacific islands were animist, but early successes soon convinced the missionaries that they had little to fear from animism. Other countries were Buddhist or Islamic. The missionaries regarded Buddhism, with its ornate trappings, as somewhat like Catholicism and Islam in Malaya and Indonesia as a distant and weak intrusion from Arabia. China had been the central focus of American missionaries since the mid-nineteenth century, and by 1911 they could rejoice that their ideological foe Confucianism was vanquished. That Christianity would be China's next great creed was obvious to them, so that the unexpected appearance of the hideous and alien creed of Marxism seemed unnatural and temporary, soon to be swept aside by the liberating armies of Christianity.

THE AMERICAN RIGHT, THE AMERICAN MILITARY, AND CHIANG KAI-SHEK

None of these three interests in itself would have been enough to create the China Lobby, and all three together could not have turned rage into action without having secured an entry into government through the

military controversies of the late 1940s. The missionaries were the first
to raise the cause of China because of their access to the media. *Time*
and *Life*, published by Henry Luce who was born in China of missionary
parents, played a major role in bringing the China issue to national
attention. Another missionary, Representative Walter Judd of Min-
nesota, led the fight in Congress. The soldiers were quick to join the fray,
notably Claire Chennault and Admiral Charles M. Cooke. Entrepreneurs
like William Pawley, former head of Pan Am's subsidiary in China, and
Alfred Kohlberg, "importer-exporter," brought business interests into
the China Lobby. Former Ambassador William Bullitt published a major
article in *Life* in December 1947 urging a crash program to save Chiang
Kai-shek. Bullitt was regarded as vehemently pro-French and anti-
Russian in his days as the last American ambassador to France before
the fall of Paris, and his anticommunism appears to have been the major
factor in his conversion to the China Lobby. Pro-Navy sentiments were
probably partially responsible for the enthusiastic advocacy of China
Lobby causes by William Knowland, whose Oakland fiefdom depended
on income generated by the Port of Oakland, and Styles Bridges of New
Hampshire, with its big Portsmouth naval yard. The China Lobby was
made up of disparate elements, and its political clout derived originally
from the fact that its cause was adopted by the right wing of the Republican party. But it was America's Pacific destiny that provided the source
of the fanaticism that the China Lobby was to display, reaching its
extreme form in McCarthyism.

The right-wing Republicans, generally grouped around the Taft wing
of the party, nurtured deep hatred for the Truman Administration,
continuing from their sufferings during the Roosevelt period. But the
Marshall Plan served to transform that hatred into more systematic opposition. In a general atmosphere of inflation-consciousness, where even
the prospending Democrats saw the need for budgetary economizing, the
addition of Marshall Plan spending on top of rising defense costs promised considerable tax increases with little demonstrable benefit to the
constituencies served by the small town right-wing Republicans. Defense
spending concentrated increasingly on nuclear and air power programs,
and predictably these were approved by overwhelming majorities in
Congress. The nuclear program benefited largely those states like Mas-
sachusetts, California, Washington, New Mexico, and Tennessee where
nuclear testing and research installations were already operating, and air
power programs naturally benefited the states that had aircraft industries, notably California, Washington, Missouri, Connecticut, and Georgia. Both liberal and conservative congressmen were in a bullish mood
so far as defense was concerned. Except for those internationalists who
wanted peaceful coexistence with Russia, the mood of the country was

strongly prodefense. After all, who could quarrel with the need for security after the holocaust of World War II? Thus, the right-wing Republicans could not pretend that they were the chief guarantors of the
nation's military might. In 1947, their opposition to the Marshall Plan
was almost entirely grounded on fiscal conservatism—why should good
money be thrown down the "rat holes" of Europe?

By 1948, right-wing Republicans began to sound the Asia-first versus
Europe-first theme. The Berlin Airlift was the first major commitment
of American military force since 1945. It came at a time when the China
Lobby was calling not only for more money and matériel for Chiang Kai-
shek but for dispatching air power to support the Nationalists in their
battles with the Communists. Chennault in particular agitated for recruit-
ing a "private" air armada along the lines of his Flying Tigers. The Air
Force was not very enthusiastic about the Berlin Airlift because it was
purely a transport and logistical operation. The Air Force saw its prime
mission as bombing, with preference for strategic bombing but with no
less an eagerness for tactical bombing where the need arose. Nevertheless, there was no real opposition to the Berlin Airlift because the need
for the defense of Europe was universally accepted within the military
(even the Navy) and was shared by the greater part of Congress. Still,
the voices demanding that some form of air power be committed to help
Chiang became shriller. After China "fell," a theory widely held by
American military men was that Chiang's lack of air power had doomed
him to defeat.

China Lobby agitation subsided somewhat with the 1948 election
campaign but rose again in 1949, reaching a crescendo at the turn of the
decade. It was in early 1950 that Senator Joseph McCarthy made his
appearance with his famous Wheeling speech. While China Lobby agitation repeatedly provoked the administration into making token gestures
of aid to Chiang Kai-shek, by and large it was not deflected from its
course of seeking some form of accommodation with the new Communist regime. The publication of Dean Acheson's White Paper in July
1949 was a clear signal to the Chinese Communists, that if they showed
their independence from Russia, a relationship with America might be
possible. After all, just the previous year, the most radical communist
country in Europe, Yugoslavia, which had shot down American planes
and was sending weapons and money to the Greek guerrillas, had broken
with Russia and was seeking an accommodation with the West. Mao Tse-
tung, so long spurned by Stalin, seemed an even more likely prospect for
such a break. In the same summer of 1949, Mao published a series of
vitriolic pieces denouncing the United States and affirming the Chinese
Communists' support of Russia. Yet, as Seymour Topping has recently
brought to light, he also sent an emissary to Ambassador Leighton Stuart

suggesting that talks be held with Washington on the possibility of diplomatic ties. Britain quickly went ahead and recognized the new government, an act it would not have carried out, in view of the close Anglo-American ties, without some encouragement from Washington. While Acheson's rhetoric undoubtedly embarrassed Mao and Mao's rhetoric did not ease Acheson's tasks in the face of China Lobby opposition, the situation remained fluid until Mao Tse-tung went to Moscow on December 16, 1949, and after arduous negotiations concluded an alliance with Stalin.

There is no reason to doubt what Acheson tried to make clear in the White Paper: the Chiang Kai-shek regime was finished so far as the Truman Administration was concerned and the Chinese Communists had become the *de facto* rulers of China. There also is no reason to doubt that at least the policy-making parts of the Washington foreign policy bureaucracy had no interest in preserving a "free" Taiwan. Even interest in South Korea was not very great. Not only Acheson but Douglas MacArthur himself in March 1949 had excluded South Korea from America's Pacific defense perimeter.[10] Other things being equal, Washington probably would have eventually recognized the new Peking government. After all, the United States had maintained diplomatic ties with the Eastern European countries, and the accepted doctrine was that diplomatic recognition did not imply moral approval. But the situation changed radically after Mao Tse-tung's visit to Moscow and the appearance of what Washington was to call the "Sino-Soviet bloc." Under the terms of the Sino-Soviet treaty, Mao made some far-reaching concessions to Russia, notably in Manchuria and Sinkiang. Now Russian power again seemed to stand all along the Sino-Korean frontier, reversing the effect of Russian troop withdrawals. Even more serious, it now appeared to have an open door stretching as far south as Hainan Island and Indochina. The China Lobby charged that it was obvious all along that the Chinese Communists were just what they called themselves, communists in the service of Stalin, the master of international communism. Acheson found it harder and harder to respond to these accusations, and as the apostle of containment weakened, the attacks against him grew.

THE ORIGINS OF THE SINO-SOVIET ALLIANCE

Why did Mao Tse-tung go to Moscow and conclude an alliance that put China in a state of considerable subservience to Russia? Mao's secret of success till then had been based on the principle of revolutionary self-

[10] Tsou, *America's Failure in China*, p. 507.

reliance. But in the three months of negotiations from December 1949 to February 1950 he appeared to have so abandoned that principle that Dean Rusk contemptuously referred to the new China as a "Slavic Manchukuo." Did Mao believe that the Russian atomic explosion had so changed the world balance of forces that China should now cast its lot with Russia as the winning side? Hardly. As early as August 1946, in his interview with Anna Louise Strong, he had expressed skepticism about the capacity of atomic bombs to decide wars. The most obvious recent event prompting Mao's visit to Moscow must have been the removal of the Nationalist government to Taiwan on December 8, 1949. That this matter was not taken lightly in Washington either is evident from the fact that a special National Security Council meeting was immediately held to discuss it. Mao had already expressed his view on America's support of Chiang Kai-shek to Anna Louise Strong. When she asked him how long Chiang could hold out if American aid were cut off, he responded, "A bit over a year." In that same interview, Mao also expressed himself on the subject of the new American-Russian rivalry. While admitting the possibility of a war between the two countries, he felt that the main purpose of the rivalry was to allow American imperialism to bring other countries under its sway. Here he touched on the subject of bases: "True, these bases may be directed against Russia, but in actuality, the victims of American aggression are not Russia but those countries in which the bases are established." If Mao's thinking remained consistent from August 1946 to December 1949, then he must have been convinced that Chiang's unexpected decision to resume power on Taiwan was due to an American decision to hold it and protect him with military force.

Mao had had considerable experience, particularly during General Marshall's mission to China, with the phenomenon of what the Chinese call "two-handed policies." What American diplomats told him did not always square with what other Americans, particularly military and intelligence people, did. As a student of Chinese history, Mao was not so naïve as to take seriously American propaganda that in foreign policy all American officials spoke in unison. Different bureaucracies did different things, and what leaders said was more often than not the expression of policy intent rather than operational fact. How could Mao take seriously Acheson's assurances that America had no commitment to defend Taiwan when the former commander of the Seventh Fleet, Admiral Cooke, went there to "advise" Chiang Kai-shek? Chiang's arrival on Taiwan was followed by a naval blockade of the China coast and brutal air raids against Chinese coastal cities, including Shanghai. If America had, in fact, committed itself to keeping Chiang in power on Taiwan, then China faced the prospect of unending war. Its coastal cities depended on food imports to survive and the blockade created great suffering in those cities. Since the Communists had no air power of their own, Chiang's planes could bomb with impunity. Meanwhile, with American aid, Chiang could organize a new army from among the two million Mainlanders who fled to Taiwan. With chaos still reigning in many parts of China south of the Yangtze, what was to prevent Chiang, after a suitable time for regrouping, from attempting a landing on the China coast with the Seventh Fleet offshore ready to back him up? Mao believed that the period of Marshall mission negotiations was a cover-up permitting Washington to funnel enough "surplus" war matériel to Chiang so that he could resume the civil war. Why shouldn't Acheson's White Paper be regarded in the same way? While Peking and Washington were exchanging jibes, accusations, and feelers, Chiang and his American friends Cooke, Chennault, and Pawley would be feverishly preparing for a counterattack.

Stalin was no friend to the Chinese Communists, but neither was he an enemy. Mao believed that Russia was basically defensive, seeking peace to recover from war, whereas America with its new-found power was the major aggressive force in the world. He did not think it likely that America would attack Russia for the simple reason that Washington feared Russian power. Instead, it would move against weaker and softer areas of the world where it could commit aggression with impunity. Mao knew that the exceedingly cautious Stalin would not be easy to maneuver into giving China a guarantee against American attack, and, indeed, the 1950 Sino-Soviet alliance was formally directed against a new "Japanese" imperialism. It did not provide the absolute security of a Russian "nuclear umbrella." Stalin managed to haggle a large number of concessions from Mao for the equivocal guarantees he gave and the loan he made to the new government. There can be no explanation for Mao's extraordinary and untypical concessions other than his fear that Chiang Kai-shek, having found new and unexpected sources of American support, had decided to continue the civil war from his redoubt on Taiwan.

When Chiang Kai-shek quit the presidency in January 1949, Mao read that correctly as his acceptance of defeat in the civil war. But it was also his realization that, in spite of his China Lobby friends, American support was waning. The major defeat the United States Navy suffered in April, when the flush-deck carrier was vetoed, meant that the one American military force that could effectively intervene in support of Chiang was declining. As Marxists, the Chinese Communists always looked for the material bases of policies and actions, and the absence of the Seventh Fleet in the waters off the China coast portended well for American withdrawal. But as we have seen, from late September 1949, the tide changed and the Navy bounded back into the picture. In March 1950,

Chiang resumed the presidency, and in June, the Korean War broke out. Chiang was eventually to gain his most magnificent ally in Douglas MacArthur, who came out openly for the defense of Taiwan in defiance of Washington bureaucratic rules that interbureaucratic disagreements must be kept within closed walls. When Truman interposed the Seventh Fleet in the Taiwan Straits on June 27, 1950, he thereby not only "leashed" Chiang but the United States Navy as well. The Korean War diverted attention from the extremely sensitive area of Taiwan to the less crucial area of Korea. MacArthur, of course, saw it as the opening gun of a grand rollback of communism in Asia, and took steps on his own to cement a Tokyo-Taipei axis. When he visited Taiwan on July 31, 1950, with the prior approval of the Joint Chiefs of Staff but not of the State Department, he was making publicly clear what Chiang Kai-shek knew already, namely, that some significant segments of the United States military were prepared to make policy on their own. Tang Tsou notes that the State Department was concerned that "the United States appeared to be speaking with two voices."[11] Despite the failure of the Korean War to turn into true rollback, the ties between Chiang Kai-shek and the United States military, and later the CIA which had been purged of its original anti-Chiang bias, continued to grow.

THE NATIONALIST-MILITARY ALLIANCE

Let us now return to the important theoretical and practical question of how the right-wing Republicans, most of whom had come out of an isolationist tradition, turned into rabid anticommunist interventionists and made Chiang Kai-shek the symbol of their cause. All political parties are concerned with one thing: how to get and hold power. For the right-wing Republicans, as 1948 drew to a close, power was more elusive than ever. Except for some antilabor legislation, the most they got for their causes were crumbs here and there. Through the Marshall Plan, the Democrats had gained the support of big business. Even the most conservative of the internationalist Republicans, John Foster Dulles, was working for the Truman Administration. The bipartisanship in foreign policy that Vandenberg pushed appealed to the liberal wing of the Republican party but not to its conservatives. Their cherished beliefs in individualism, enterprise, God and Country, seemed forever incapable of getting their man into the Presidency in the face of the growing welfare-state sentiments of the people. But after their 1948 defeat, a new and exciting avenue for securing power opened up. As the bureaucratic con-

---

[11] Tsou, *America's Failure in China*, p. 567.

flicts and power struggles within the government became fiercer, the protagonists began to turn to Congress for support. But opposition congressmen seized the opportunity to intervene in those conflicts through hearings and a variety of other public displays of the "issues." The Republican right wing discovered that there was powerful bureaucratic opposition within the government to prevailing policies and moved fast to take advantage of the opportunity it presented. The most notorious figure in this game was Joseph McCarthy, who took on liberals in the State Department, the Morgenthau remnants in the Treasury Department, and finally the Army. But while the Republican right wing welcomed the purge McCarthy sought to bring about, basically they sought a more enduring relationship to segments of the bureaucratic power structure.

Until the great split between the Air Force and the Navy, the military services seemed pretty much under the control of the chief executive. Congress as a whole was prodefense and such caviling as there was on defense spending was due to general fiscal attitudes or specific pork-barrel interests. Originally, the Navy had no outspoken advocates in Congress comparable to Stuart Symington, the Air Force advocate, and appeals to Congress to help override adverse decisions were not particularly effective. But in late 1949, what had been a monolithic ideological posture on national security policy began to crack. The Russian atomic explosion and the "loss of China" began to raise alternative ideological and political perspectives with direct power implications. Until the Korean War made it possible to realize NSC 68's prescriptions for a leap forward in defense spending, zero-sum budgetary conditions still prevailed. If the Air Force was to be developed as planned or an H-bomb put together, this would mean fewer funds and programs for the Navy and the Army. Supporting one or another service was not just a pork-barrel matter, but involved the most fundamental world views out of which foreign policy arose. To be pro-Navy meant to follow an Asia-first view. A pro-Army policy was a Europe-first policy since the major forces-in-being were to be stationed in Europe. A pro–Air Force policy was basically Europe-first, though the Korean War opened up new Asian perspectives for the Air Force. If the right-wing Republicans were not Asia-firsters by tradition, they certainly were anti-Europe and anti-British. The Europe-first policies of the hated Democratic liberals and those of internationalist Republicans aroused the deepest opprobrium from the right-wingers. Thus, when these policies began to crack in the fall of 1949, the right-wingers quickly gravitated to the Asia-first protagonist in the bureaucratic struggles, the Navy. The right-wing alliance with the Navy was far from forced. The Navy was the most conservative of the armed services, evidenced by its last-ditch resistance to racial integration. The Korean War brought about an important conversion to the new Asia-first cause: Douglas MacArthur, the new shogun of Japan and one of the most conservative generals in the United States Army. In subsequent years, particularly during the Kennedy Administration, the right-wing-military alliance would spread to disgruntled members of the Air Force.

What the right-wingers discovered in the winter of 1949–1950 was that an alliance of electoral losers with like-minded bureaucratic losers was a major new source of power. Each camp, congressional and bureaucratic, could count on the other to mount campaigns for their special interests. Perhaps the most successful player in this game was old Mendel Rivers from South Carolina, who managed to cram his home district with all sorts of Navy and Air Force installations while rendering those services invaluable help in getting their programs through Congress and the White House's budget officers. While many of the alliances were temporary and *ad hoc*, there was one grand alliance that overshadowed them all: the right-wing–military alliance on Asia.

In any country, nationalists are generally promilitary. In the pre–World War II period, the isolationists, while prodefense and proflag, were not particularly identified with the military services. The Navy was Roosevelt's special preserve anyway. In the post-1945 period, the nationalist right wing was promilitary, but so was everyone else. But as the controversy over MacArthur showed, by the early 1950s it made an ideological difference which military service one supported. MacArthur became the great symbol of American nationalism, and his return from Japan after being fired by Truman was an event of national importance. The right-wingers wanted to run him for President, but the internationalist wing of the Republican party demurred and finally prevailed upon Eisenhower to run. Nationalist interests thus became identified with the right-wing Asia-first military, producing not just an ideological but a practical alliance with considerable benefits for the interests involved. The most immediate pay-off was the Navy's new carrier program.

The right-wing Republicans (as well as their Southern Democratic counterparts) were, of course, anticommunist. Anticommunism also became the dominant creed in the military. But it meant different things to different people. To the containment liberals of the Kennan variety, communism was an expression of Russian imperialism and anticommunism meant opposition to Russia. To the Lovestonites, communism was a conspiracy of power-hungry political intellectuals manipulating legitimate grievances of workingmen to create dictatorial governments and parties. To many ordinary property-owning Americans, communism was robbery by the lazy of the hard-earned gains of people who worked their way up from nothing. By the early 1950s, the anticommunist climate was so pervasive in America that the mildest form of anticommunism was disdain for those so duped coupled with pleas for tolerance on the grounds that they constituted no clear and present danger. But to the right-wingers and the military, being anticommunist meant being willing to go to war at the right time and place against any communist foe. To them, pacifism was little better than covert communism. They saw communism as an international conspiracy, an ever-expanding force seeping through every hole it could find in the ramparts of the free world. A willingness to fight or at least to be tough was considered the only true test of anticommunism. Truman already well understood this on June 25, 1950.

The right-wing tradition in America had not been particularly militant, and where it was, it tended to be directed against internal enemies. Militancy abroad was not part of the American conservative tradition. But as the grand alliance between the right wing and the military developed, militancy came naturally. Considering themselves losers in the face of aggressive liberalism and communism, they easily went over to a permanent counterattack both abroad and at home. It is not difficult to see why the figure of Chiang Kai-shek appealed to them, aside from the alliance's practical interests in holding onto Taiwan. Chiang was a spectacular loser, beaten on the battlefield by Communists and stabbed in the back by liberals. Yet he was determined to continue the fight in the face of world-wide propaganda that depicted him as a corrupt and cowardly dictator. He was a Christian and a soldier and, above all, had been America's constant friend. Ideologically he fitted the American nationalists' need for a symbol far better than Syngman Rhee or Ngo Dinh Diem. Rhee was just a politician and Diem was too blatantly Catholic to soothe the feelings of the generally WASP right-wingers.

Chiang Kai-shek made full use of the unexpected opportunities provided him in late 1949. For over two decades, his Nationalists played major and indispensable roles in United States–directed covert warfare throughout East Asia. Wherever the CIA went, there also went the Chinese Nationalists, making use of natural networks provided by the Overseas Chinese. The Nationalists supplied the CIA and other United States covert war agencies with saboteurs, commandos, agents, pilots, smugglers, spies, and "businessmen" to help out in the complex world of East Asian transactions. But Chiang also did not neglect his intellectual role as the world's leading anticommunist. By the 1960s, the Asian Peoples' Anti-Communist League (APACL) had become the world's most important anticommunist ideological organ. As late as 1964, it had the pleasure of being addressed by Richard Nixon. In an era in which Americans have written extensively on virtually every part of the world, there is an extreme shortage of books on Taiwan. But, then, that is perhaps not so surprising, for the real political history of Taiwan since

1949 would be virtually equivalent to a history of American covert war in East Asia. Chiang Kai-shek and Douglas MacArthur share the honor of being symbolic heroes for the American right wing with only one other person—J. Edgar Hoover, whose FBI was as secretive and conspiratorial as Chiang's Taiwan. One might conclude that the American right has a natural proclivity toward the kind of plots and conspiracies it has always alleged in others.

ACCOMMODATIONS AND TRADE-OFFS

By the outbreak of the Korean War, the realm of ideology had made those accommodations with the realm of interests that made it possible for successive administrations to carry out foreign policy with a workable consensus ("bipartisanship"). The accommodations led to the making of what Washington likes to call "commitments." The main difference between a commitment and a policy is that policies are (or should be) firm as to goals, but are flexible as to means and operations. Commitments are just the opposite. They are unclear as to goals but firm to the point of rigidity as to operations. All basic United States foreign policies flowed out of the containment current. These involved: 1) the maintenance of pre-eminent American nuclear power; 2) the drawing of demarcation lines between the free world and the socialist camp; and 3) the build-up and organization of free world countries, with priority to those located near the demarcation lines. The basic goal of containment policy was the creation of a Pax Americana, which would prevent a new world war from erupting, unify the free world under American aegis, and give the member countries economic growth and political stability.

Containment policy as such was not inflexible. What made it inflexible in certain parts of the world was that the United States government had to make specific commitments in its process of accommodation to the realm of interests. The most important of these arose out of controversies surrounding the Marshall Plan and China—Germany symbolized by Berlin and China symbolized by Taiwan became inflexible commitments. Berlin was the cause of Adenauer's Christian Democrats and of the Dulles wing of American internationalism. Free Berlin was a much better symbol for big business internationalism than semi-socialist Britain or annoyingly nationalist France. The commitment to Berlin was rigid but, from 1961 on, increasingly irrelevant. Free enterprise capitalism had scored so smashing a triumph in West Germany that it no longer needed Berlin as a defense against the Russians, or the British and French with their lesser enthusiasm for laissez-faire.

Much more difficult and explosive was the accommodation to the nationalists over the China issue. While the advocates of containment desired flexibility in their East Asian policies, nationalist pressure and the events of the Korean War drove Washington into making specific commitments. On June 27, 1950, Truman made a major commitment by including Taiwan in the American defense perimeter. As MacArthur's rollback began to get out of hand, Truman made another commitment by finally drawing a line in Korea, which the 1953 armistice ratified. Eisenhower made yet another commitment with the Geneva Accords of 1954, by acquiescing in the drawing of a line at the 17th parallel through Vietnam. These commitments were the products of "compromises" between nationalist "hawks," who wanted to push ahead as far as possible, and containment "doves," who feared that aggressive rollback might unleash World War III and, even if it didn't, would threaten the global skein of containment relationships which Washington was so laboriously building up.

The nationalist current has always posed the most dangerous challenge to presidential power. With control over key operational bastions of command, it has been able to exercise enormous pressure on the chief executive. Since nationalist concerns were strongly East Asian, that pressure has had grave consequences for American policy in that part of the world. As the pressure grew, so did Washington's commitments to various East Asian interests. And as the struggle between policy and operations intensified, those commitments hardened more and more.

In later chapters, I shall explore how that struggle led to the escalation of the Vietnam war. But here I am still concerned with working out the theory and laying forth the general patterns of American foreign policy. Although the struggle reached explosive levels in times of crisis, it also had a day-to-day aspect. The national security bureaucrats had, after all, to get along with the military in the normal routine of working out problems of national defense. I would like to suggest one important form the working relations between the masters of policy and the masters of operations assumed.

In his book *Kennedy Justice*, Victor Navasky details the bitter struggle between Attorney General Robert Kennedy and FBI director J. Edgar Hoover. Kennedy and Hoover finally managed to achieve an accommodation, which Navasky describes as follows:

> In the areas which Robert Kennedy cared about most—organized crime and civil rights—he made a Faustian bargain, trading policy for power. If the FBI would agree to join Kennedy's crusade against organized crime and his maneuvers for equal rights, then he would enlarge the Bureau's formal jurisdiction, increase its budget, and leave it alone.[12]

12 Victor Navasky, *Kennedy Justice*, p. 155.

I suggest that this *trade-off of policy for power* is characteristic of the entire relationship between the chief executive and the military. What organized crime and civil rights were for Robert Kennedy, nuclear policy was for his brother John Kennedy and other Presidents. Nuclear policy is not simply military policy but primarily the great power relationships among America, Russia, and China. Like J. Edgar Hoover on civil rights, America's military leaders have never been enthusiastic about any easing of the cold war for the simple and obvious reason that a thaw could lead to the dread specter of disarmament. But again like Hoover, the military chieftans generally accepted the new great power relationships if they got something in return. Naturally, higher budgetary allocations are a prime reassurance to a military bureaucracy fearful of cutbacks. An expansion of formal jurisdiction, for example, vis-à-vis the civilian officials of the Defense Department, is also a welcome assurance against hostile centralizers. But being left alone is perhaps most important. What it meant in Vietnam was that the military would be allowed to pursue its war until final victory unencumbered by the White House's desire for some negotiated end.

The most important trade-off of policy for power in Washington over the last quarter-century has been between the President and the military on nuclear policy. Nuclear power began as a presidential monopoly but, as we have seen, became involved in bitter controversy during the postwar years as the military sought to gain control over nuclear weapons. As the White House asserted its control over strategic nuclear weapons, the military sought control over tactical nuclear weapons. When Air Force General Curtis LeMay described nuclear weapons as "just another weapon," he was saying that the Air Force should have operational control over nuclear weapons just as it did over conventional weapons. What this meant concretely was that once the President had announced a policy of "war," the Air Force should then have sole jurisdiction over when, how, and where to drop nuclear weapons. Over the years, the White House has fought vigorously to remove any vestige of such powers from the hands of military commanders. It construed the question of using nuclear weapons in any manner whatsoever as a policy question involving America's relationships to other hostile nuclear powers, namely Russia and China. In time, this led to the policy understanding that all nuclear questions automatically involved great power relations. Thus, a nuclear bomb dropped on some rebellious tribesmen involved America's relations with Russia and China, whereas simply bombing them into oblivion by conventional weapons implied, at most, "limited war." "Limited wars," in fact, were wars that were non-nuclear. When Air Force and Navy chiefs bitterly attacked the concept of limited war, they were arguing against the notion that using nuclear weapons necessarily involved great power relationships. Since United States nuclear power presumably acted as a deterrent against both Russia and China, they could not understand how dropping some small nuclear weapons, say in Indochina, could provoke any significant hostile response from the great powers. Nevertheless, the White House appears to have succeeded in its quarter-century effort to make all nuclear questions policy matters under its exclusive control.

The linking of great power relationships with the nuclear question led to White House attempts to extend its control over operations in other than nuclear matters. Thus, for example, when President Johnson, allegedly, kept tight control over the bombing raids over North Vietnam, he was arguing that inasmuch as those raids affected American-Chinese relations they came under exclusive White House jurisdiction. The military could not bomb where and when it wanted in terms of pure military exigencies. Naturally the military resisted, seeing this as yet another presidential encroachment on its power. The recurrent result of that struggle between White House and Joint Chiefs of Staff was compromise. The military was allowed to bomb somewhat more than the President wanted but within strict limits, which he frantically tried to communicate to the other side. On October 31, 1968, President Johnson announced the most dramatic trade-off of policy for power in the war up to that time. He stopped the bombing of North Vietnam but allowed the military to transfer all its bombing operations to Laos. Peter Dale Scott begins his book *The War Conspiracy* with the observation that "in the two decades since 1950, the year of the Korean War and the China Lobby, there never has been a genuine U.S. de-escalation in Southeast Asia."[13] This is so because every de-escalation in policy has been followed by a trade-off somewhere else so that the established interests could continue their war.

Lyndon Johnson was once quoted as saying that all the power he had was nuclear power and he could not use it. As President, he did indeed hold full sway over nuclear policy and the concomitant sphere of great power relationships. But every time he asserted that power, for example, in vetoing bombing that could provoke Chinese intervention, he undercut his equally ardent desire to negotiate an end to the Vietnam war so that he could be re-elected in 1968. On July 15, 1971, Nixon announced that he had accepted China's invitation to visit Peking, thereby inaugurating an entirely new chapter in great power relationships. This was at a time of intense pressure to end the war in Vietnam, marked by the publication of the Pentagon Papers. Contrary to what appeared to have been an American drift away from Thieu, Washington reaffirmed its commitment

13 Peter Dale Scott, *The War Conspiracy*, p. xiii.

by supporting his fraudulent re-election, and then made good the commitment with the massive American escalation of the war in the spring of 1972. I shall have more to say about this trade-off of China policy for Vietnam power later. The theoretical and practical point to be made here is that the central concern of the chief executive has been a monopoly on nuclear power and great power relationships with the main goal, flowing directly out of containment doctrine, of avoiding a nuclear war or World War III. But to achieve this, all Presidents, regardless of their particular inclinations, have had to make concessions of power to nationalist and military interests, which have involved budgets, jurisdictions, weapons— and "limited war." When Johnson so often pleaded for people to understand that he was fighting in Vietnam to avoid World War III, he was telling the truth. He was struggling to contain the powerful pressure from the Joint Chiefs of Staff, who sought to gather into the "operational" sphere everything they could and to wage the war as they saw fit.

Thus, one can say that the predominant form the relationship between the chief executive and the nationalist-military alliance took was a trade-off of global policy for regional power. And the region that was most crucial in this relationship was East Asia. Containment could pursue its policies anywhere in the world without fearing an immediate backlash from the nationalists and the military. Even in the matter of Cuba, the backlash came mainly from the nationalists, not the military. East Asia, however, was sacred to both.

THEORY AGAIN

We are now approaching the end of Part I. I have advanced certain theoretical propositions and sketched out generalized patterns of American foreign policy for the postwar period. The following section summarizes the theory and patterns with some further elaboration on both and some anticipation of what will come in later chapters. What I lay forth here are the guiding analytical principles for parts II and III of this book, which becomes progressively more concrete until, lastly, I deal with specific decisions on the Vietnam war.

The core of those theoretical propositions is the recognition of the dual nature of the state—as a realm of ideology and a realm of interests. The realm of ideology centers on the chief executive of the state, and the realm of interests centers on the state's bureaucracies. The realm of interests tends to remain fairly stable over time, while the realm of ideology changes constantly, leading to what is one of the most striking features of state power—its repeated making and remaking. As the realm of ideology changes, it inflicts or tries to inflict those changes on the realm of interests, which naturally tends toward inertia. The agencies of change which the realm of ideology creates over time in turn transform themselves into interests and, thus, gradually join the realm of interests. This invariably happens as the agencies lose their qualities as direct emanations of executive power and develop power of their own.

It is this process that gives the state another important dual feature: while having a liberating effect on society as it impels change, it invariably contains the seeds of repression, as its agencies of change turn into agencies of interest.

The realm of interests within the state, whatever its particular origins, usually meshes with the realm of interests within society. In other words, bureaucracies eventually come to develop a mutually satisfactory accommodation with corporate and other interests, usually marked by the back-and-forth transfers of key personnel from bureaucracy to corporation and vice versa. The realm of ideology, on the other hand, arises out of the turbulence within and between societies, out of revolution and war. That realm generates agencies of the state that are instruments of power, the capacity to mobilize men and resources for the achievement of goals. Ideological power is directed toward change, whereas interest power is directed toward maintenance or incremental expansion. Thus, although a new ideologically motivated state agency will seek to change interests both within and outside the state, over time the process of accommodation will set in.

War is conflict between states and, therefore, necessarily national. State power always has a national character in that it has delimited geographical boundaries. War by its nature produces constant change. Only power at supreme executive levels can cope with these changes so as to wage war successfully. War creates a need for executive power, so that fertile ground exists for the elaboration of ideologies that enhance that power and at the same time for enabling the state to cope with the turbulence within society.

The revolutionary character of any society arises out of the systematic exploitation, oppression, and deprivation of rights and protection of certain classes of the population. These classes have essentially only one avenue of ameliorating their lot, which is through the acquisition of political power. But since power in the realm of interests is denied them, their only hope is to seize state power. Contrary to what many frustrated radicals believe, popular forces and elements have constantly entered the state, often as simple employees but equally often as direct wielders of power. Popular forces do enter the state at the supreme executive level and, once there, they undertake a certain remaking of the state. Revolution is an extreme form of the remaking of the state where an entirely new realm of ideology is created which then destroys or significantly rearranges the realm of interests of both the state and society. A more normal form of entrance into power by revolutionary classes is in league with the chief executive, even if he is a traditional king or president. The chief executive always seeks to expand his power vis-à-vis the interests, as, for example, in the centuries-long struggle between king and nobles in the countries of Europe. He needs ideological and organizational power to fight the interests. War and its variants automatically confer organizational power, namely, military. Alliance with one or more of the revolutionary classes of society, as, again for example, the alliance of the European kings with the revolutionary urban bourgeoisie against the landed magnates, provides ideological power. Any chief executive who fails to fight the interests soon finds himself at their mercy; he can then only manipulate not command them.

It is not accidental that revolution and war are related. Revolution in its extreme form is the entry of an entire class into the realm of state power, the total destruction of existing interests, and the elaboration of mighty new ideologies and organizations of change. War is the reverse. It begins with change, leads to mighty state power, grinds down existing interests, and opens the door to the entry of revolutionary forces—unless, as usually happens, the forces of counterrevolutionary reaction set in.

That revolution and war have been for two centuries forces bringing the powerless classes into the realm of power now seems evident to all except those left intellectuals who delight in painting pictures of crushing, unbeatable ruling class power. The power of Marx's vision was that capitalism, by smashing the inert forms of feudal production, had launched a dynamic process which would inevitably lead to the overthrow of all ruling classes and their instruments of power. Today Mao expresses the same vision when he speaks with confidence of the unbeatable wave of revolution that will sweep over the world. As conservative thinkers like Schumpeter, Polanyi, Ortega y Gasset, and, much over a century ago, Alexis de Tocqueville recognized, the entry of the forces of popular sovereignty into the political arena and their acquisition of power was inexorable. Conservatives believe that whatever the defects of governance by traditional interests, it is always more just and humane than the tyrannies imposed by the forces of revolution. Where so many conservatives, in effect, agree with Marx is in believing that what they fear, those "dictatorships of the proletariat," are inevitable. Marx saw that capitalism, in order to gain surplus and maintain domination, had to bring into the process of production the most revolutionary of classes, the emerging industrial proletariat. Unlike all previous modes of production, it had to invite revolution into its domain in order to develop. Even at ebb tide when all seems quiet and rulers can be benignly neglectful, the revolution keeps going on, not just because the powerless seek power, but because capitalism, with its inherent need for "full employment" and reliance on "aggregate demand," must invite the powerless into the system.

All modern capitalist societies are revolutionary in that capitalism requires some redistribution of income in order to remain dynamic. As some income is redistributed, expectations rise far beyond the level of redistribution, creating pressures for greater changes. Capitalism cannot survive without the aggregate demand that full employment provides, and, as Lord Keynes recognized, that condition can no longer be assured unless the state undertakes certain kinds of income redistribution in order to promote investment and demand. Naturally, if the state is the instrument of income redistribution, then the revolutionary classes will seek alliance with it in order to bring about an even greater redistribution. In precapitalist countries where property has frozen into rigid forms, redistribution has often not been possible without revolution. In capitalist countries, capitalism's basic need to maintain a certain liquidity and elasticity of property has created conditions more favorable for income redistribution. Thus, capitalist countries have tended to be democratic, thereby giving the revolutionary classes avenues of access to state power. But they also have immense realms of interest, which are hostile to income redistribution and are primarily concerned with preserving their own interests, their own properties. Thus, while the alliance of the chief executive with the revolutionary classes may bring about some income redistribution, the state's need to seek accommodation with the realm of interests puts sharp limits on its scope.

The crises of war and revolution enhance the power of the realm of ideology and weaken the realm of interests. That invariably leads to war between the two realms, as the realm of interests fights back hard to reassume control of the state. Thus, revolutionary advances that the state makes will invariably be checked by the counterattack of old and new interests, thereby turning the state once again into a repressive instrument. In socialist countries, revolutionary class war continues on after the seizure of power and gives the new state power (as the realm of revolutionary ideology) the means to destroy re-emerging interests again and again. The "dictatorship of the proletariat" is the realm of ideology unencumbered by the realm of interests. In capitalist countries, there is class conflict but not class war. Thus, a government that has come to power with the support of revolutionary classes naturally tends to seek accommodation with the interests.

Modern capitalism, unlike all other and earlier forms of social organization, has both a national and an international character. Its international character springs out of the world market system, whose essence is continued economic growth and rising levels of world trade within an overarching framework of global monetary unity. Capitalism's national character is less unique. As in all societies, including socialist ones where property still exists, wealth takes the form of property which in one way or another is territorially defined. It is obvious that any nation will strive to maximize the national wealth. Somewhat crudely one can say that production tends to be national whereas exchange tends to be international. Production must take place on property—land, labor, and capital together constitute a territorially defined unit of production. Exchange, however, is a never-ending process which always tends to break down the inelasticities of property. The national character of production is evident in socialist societies like Russia where production is fetishized and exchange devalued.

Thus, modern capitalism generates interests of both a national and an international character, producing two different capitalist world views. Since the economy is the key to all capitalist societies, these world views have an essentially economic character. The world view of the internationalists is of the primacy of a world market system ultimately covering the entire planet. The world view of the nationalists is of different national economies competing for scarce wealth, in which priority must of course go to one's own national economy. The internationalist view sees the sacrifice of national economy as essential to the generation of greater wealth, whereas the nationalist view sees national sovereignty as the indispensable prerequisite for the acquisition of wealth.

When these world views enter government through the state's realm of interests, they generate political currents. As bureaucratic outlooks with powerful interests in society behind them, these currents play a major role in the formation of all governmental policy, foreign and domestic. As a political and bureaucratic current, the internationalist current seeks broad international cooperation beyond the bounds of national sovereignty. The nationalist current, on the other hand, is preoccupied with national power and national interests. In American history, the conflict between these two currents has taken the form of a conflict between "free trade" and "protection."

The current that flows out of the capitalist state's realm of ideology is motivated by the natural tendency of all state power to expand. Its central concern is security. Since war and revolution have brought the realm of ideology into being, its main means for creating security are to impose systems of control over broad expanses of territory and people and at the same time to improve the conditions of the revolutionary classes. The realm of ideology thus acts simultaneously to bring about progress and impose control.

It is this drive for security, fueled by the immense power of the realm

of ideology, which gives rise to imperialism. Imperialism is the phenomenon of one very powerful country ("superpower," as the Chinese now
say) organizing large spaces of territory in the world for purposes of
security of a sort that will bring some progress to the poor but also
subject them to controls that will guarantee stability. Imperialism is
an emanation not of the realm of interests but of the realm of ideology.

Different from imperialism is expansionism, the natural tendency of
productive interests to go beyond national boundaries in search of new
accretions to their property. Expansionism is national in character, in
that foreign interests are simply subordinate units of a specific national
interest. Thus, a transnational corporation is a product of expansionism
because the company concerned is just a foreign arm of a domestic
company. The internationalist counterpart of nationalist expansionism is
universalism, whereby a domestic interest joins with foreign interests in
an entirely new supranational body. Multinational corporations are universalist, as is the European Common Market, which can hardly be
regarded as the expansionist creation of any of its constituent nations.
On the other hand, Volkswagen do Brasil and the Nissan Corporation of
America are instances of German and Japanese expansionism.

The government, as the Founding Fathers wisely realized, has three
main functions: 1) to redistribute income through taxation; 2) to defend
the country through military power; and 3) to ensure equity and legality
through the law. In the United States, these functions are divided among
the three great branches of government (legislative, executive, and judicial). From the beginnings of American constitutional history, the President alone has monopolized military power, which, since 1945, has been
the main avenue for the expansion of the power of the state. But the
atomic age brought in an entirely new kind of military power going far
beyond that of the navies and armies of the pre-1945 period. It was
already apparent on August 6, 1945, that atomic power would soon
reach a level at which it could destroy the entire planet. Whereas conventional military power had long been a part of the realm of interests of the
state, atomic power was something entirely new. The atomic bomb and
the subsequent development of nuclear bombs gave the realm of ideology
unprecedented power not only within America but over the entire world.
The vast power conferred by America's nuclear monopoly in the early
postwar years was the principal impetus turning America in an imperialist direction. Security for mankind could only be achieved if nuclear
power was tightly controlled at the pinnacle of state power and if the
world was so organized that no nation could ever provoke a war that
would bring about the use of nuclear weapons.

The second most important impetus to American imperialism was the
realization that chaos would only fan revolutionary flames, leading to a

general breakdown in political stability throughout the world. Thus, as America reached out to control the world in order to prevent a third world war, it also launched a vast campaign to improve the material conditions of people, symbolized by a long succession of foreign aid programs.

The American government's commitment to universalism and expansionism, symbolized by the Marshall Plan and China policy respectively, came as a result of accommodation between the realm of ideology and the realm of interests, which feared that the immense increase in the government's military and political power and the vast outlays destined for economic recovery and foreign aid might harm the interests of both international and national capital.

The natural thrust of the realm of ideology and the interaction between it and the realm of interests resulted in the formation of the three predominant currents of American foreign policy since 1945: containment, internationalism, and nationalism. Each of these has become deeply imbedded in the many bureaucracies of the government, and conflicts between them can often be found within the same bureaucracy. Broadly speaking, however, the containment current has been strongest at the level of presidential power and in agencies directly linked to the Presidency. The internationalist current has been strongest within the State Department, with its tradition of reflecting the interests of American business abroad. And the nationalist current has been strongest within the military.

All bureaucracies of the state depend on budgets for their wealth. The state earns no money on its own, except through interest-bearing trust funds and borrowing. Where the budget remains stationary over a period of time, a zero-sum situation exists in the political process—what one bureaucracy gains another loses. Since the realm of ideology must constantly cope with a changing world and, therefore, must initiate new programs, a stationary budget always produces bitter interbureaucratic conflict. Only a rapidly growing budget, an "expanding pie," can permit the realm of ideology to innovate without alienating the interests. The notion of the "expanding pie" need not be seen only in fiscal terms. It can involve policies and commitments as well.

The popularity of Keynesianism as an economic philosophy within United States governmental circles can be explained, of course, in terms of the vital role assigned to the state in the sitmulation of the economy. But it also is the one philosophy that allowed for an "expanding pie," which best served the cause of both innovation and accommodation. A rising budget sustained by a growing economy is the best of all possible worlds for the government.

The natural thrust of containment, the current producing American imperialism, leads toward the formation of a bipolar world. Unlike internationalism, which is truly universal in its aspirations, containment seeks to draw lines of demarcation between the "enemy and ourselves," to borrow a phrase from Mao Tse-tung. Containment generated not only the free world, that portion of the world subject to the Pax Americana, but, as a reaction, the socialist camp. The maintenance of a bipolar world required a nuclear duopoly of America and Russia. Each super-power asserted control over its respective half of the world by means of its "nuclear umbrella." The acceptance of nuclear nonproliferation be-yond the duopoly was crucial for the maintenance of both imperial camps. The development of other nuclear powers, therefore, constitutes a grave threat to imperialism.

It is a fundamental assumption of both American and Russian policy that nuclear weapons can never be used. That assumption can, of course, be easily violated, but only at grave cost to the parties involved and all of humankind. As long as the assumption is observed, the exclusive pur-pose of accumulating nuclear weaponry is ideological. Nuclear policy indicates the ideological thrust of the two superpowers. "Parity" implies a desire for stabilizing détente; "superiority" implies accelerating rivalry; and "sufficiency" implies something in-between. Practical arguments about the waste of "overkill" are irrelevant inasmuch as what counts is the relative balance of forces between America and Russia. The overkill arguments imply that nuclear weapons are weapons, whereas in fact, they are the material underpinnings of major foreign policy ideology.

There are three nuclear powers other than America and Russia: Brit-ain, France, and China. By the late 1960s, Britain had tacitly abdicated its nuclear role. France's nuclear program, the so-called *force de frappe*, was developed as a declaration of independence from American domina-tion. France is a major capitalist power with strong internationalist as well as nationalist-expansionist thrusts. It is a vital and cooperative member of the Common Market, but at the same time is a major expan-sionist power (notably in Africa). China's nuclear program, as we shall see, was its declaration of independence from Russian domination.

American imperialism grew out of war and revolution and has sought to banish both with imperialism's favorite weapon—control. For Amer-ica (and for Russia as well), nonproliferation of nuclear weaponry was the only basis on which world peace could be assured. While Britain's nuclear program eventually faded away and France's remained basically an annoyance, China's nuclear program was perceived as a mortal threat. If China had nuclear weapons that it refused to submit to con-trols, then dozens of smaller powers could get them with the clear and present danger of some "irresponsible dictator" unleashing World War III.

But China also was a revolutionary country committed to furthering world revolution, and nowhere else did that commitment constitute so grave a challenge to America as in Vietnam. American imperialism was confident that it alone could bring true progress to the backward countries, whereas the communists, in Rostow's phrase, were "scavengers of the modernization process," who used discontents to acquire political dominion.

The Vietnam war, which at the time of this writing in the spring of 1973 is still with us in the form of murderous American bombing in Cambodia, was indeed the supreme test for American imperialism, as I shall explain in Part III. From the beginning, that war had a dual purpose: to crush the Vietnamese revolutionaries and so demonstrate to the world that no insurgency could threaten American power or defy American will; and to force China into accepting the discipline imposed by the new bipolar world that America and Russia were constructing.

The Vietnam war was also a vital test for the American Presidency, for success not only would mean that America had demonstrated its capacity to control world events but also would give the Presidency the power it needed to carry out its policies of remaking the country and remaking the world.

PATTERNS OF AMERICAN FOREIGN POLICY

By the summer of 1951 when the armistice negotiations at Panmunjom began, the basic patterns of American foreign policy for the 1950s and 1960s had been set. America had developed commitments to both Western Europe and East Asia, which were expressed in inflexible demarcation lines. In Europe, the line ran from the Russian-Norwegian border in the Arctic down to the Russian-Turkish border in eastern Anatolia. But the key containment line was the one running down through Germany, which would not be completed until 1961 when the Berlin Wall was built—a victory for containment despite the crocodile tears. In East Asia, Truman drew the first line through the Taiwan Straits on June 27, 1950. He began to draw a second line when he sacked the rollback-minded MacArthur in April 1951 and paved the way for an eventual restoration of the 38th parallel with which the armistice line roughly coincides. In the summer of 1954, Eisenhower drew a further line at the 17th parallel in Vietnam.

In Europe, Washington's containment policy makers tried again and again to bring the Common Market under firmer American control by linking it with NATO. They pressed for British membership in the Common Market, manipulated Bonn against Paris, and devised international-appearing devices like the Multi-lateral Force (MLF).

In Asia, Washington was committed to the deployment of vast military power on its side of the demarcation line. At the same time, however, it accommodated to the rollback pressures of the nationalists by fostering a covert war whose main target was revolutionary China. As it was, Chiang Kai-shek was not allowed to land his armies on the China coast (if he ever was able to do so), but he was encouraged to land commandos and saboteurs and to provide numerous operatives for other covert wars in Southeast Asia.

The Korean War dramatized all the conflicts raging in Washington. The Europe-firsters feared that it would divert America's attention from Europe. The Asia-firsters hoped that it might yet lead to rollback and "liberation" of China. The containment liners were terrified lest the war escalate to conflict with Russia. What emerged from these conflicts were a series of hard-fought compromises which again and again broke down, creating a situation of permanent crisis in East Asia which has lasted down to the early 1970s.

The first compromise, as already indicated, was Truman's interposition of the Seventh Fleet in the Straits of Taiwan. This gave Taiwan to the United States Navy but forbade the Navy from supporting any rollback attempt by Chiang Kai-shek—"leashing" Chiang Kai-shek it was called. The second compromise came with the firing of MacArthur and the Panmunjom negotiations. This enjoined the United States Army from mounting a ground counteroffensive against the Chinese in order to push them out of North Korea, as MacArthur had tried to do late in 1950. The third compromise was the "Manchurian sanctuaries." Despite intense nationalist pressure to unleash the Air Force against Manchuria in order to bomb supply lines, Washington maintained the Yalu as a demarcation line for the Air Force. For two years these compromises locked Truman into paralysis: he would not escalate to war with China yet he was unable to end the war. The ostensible issue was Chinese and North Korean prisoners of war. It has been said that Eisenhower threatened to use the atom bomb against China and that this forced the Chinese and North Koreans to back down. It is a fact that the Air Force pounded North Korea with unprecedented savagery early in 1953, destroying much of its irrigation system. It is still unclear what kinds of compromises within the bureaucracy Eisenhower had to make to break the logjam.

The unexpected war along the 38th parallel plunged Washington into immediate crisis. Needless to say, had there not been bitter factional conflict in Washington, Truman would have been less likely to take the lightninglike action he did. The alleged North Korean invasion of South Korea was a spark threatening to ignite a conflagration. But the inflammable material was as much in Washington as in East Asia. As we shall see, other crises were to constitute important milestones in the evolution of the Vietnam war.

What eventually emerged out of the Korean War was a basic containment policy toward China. Washington accepted the "loss of China," and accepted as a reality the Sino-Soviet bloc in which China enjoyed the protection of the Russian nuclear umbrella. A rollback war against China would inevitably run the risk of a Russian-American nuclear war, so predominant containment thinking went. But unlike in Europe, where Washington kept up its diplomatic ties with Eastern European countries and did not strenuously try to discourage East-West trade, in East Asia it adopted a policy of nonrecognition and isolation of China. Washington not only prohibited all trade between America and China but took vigorous steps to discourage other countries from trading with China. The isolation of China was containment's concession to rollback, which took concrete form in a vast anti-China covert war. The covert war was openly propagated by Claire Chennault and backed by Admiral Radford, then chairman of the Joint Chiefs of Staff. Chennault wanted to organize a new Flying Tiger organization of flyers to carry out missions over Mainland China. Taiwan, South Korea, South Vietnam, Laos, and Thailand became the central focuses of operations for this covert war all around China's borders. Quemoy, the offshore island on the Fukien coast, became the testing ground for Chiang Kai-shek and his American supporters to judge how far Washington was willing to move along the scale from containment to rollback. The full extent of the covert war against China still is not known but it involved: harassment and patrolling by planes and ships of the Seventh Fleet; sending commando teams into China directly from Taiwan, or from Laos and Thailand; overflights and electronic surveillance; support of remnant Kuomintang forces in Burma, Thailand, and Loas; drops of weapons to insurgents in China, notably the Kham-bas in Tibet; and, above all, extensive support for any and all operations Taiwan was engaged in, short of outright invasion.

The end of the first Indochina war was marked by another compromise. What all parties had assumed to be a temporary zonal dividing line at the 17th parallel soon turned into another of containment's permanent demarcation lines. Washington rapidly proceeded to install a new regime in South Vietnam under Ngo Dinh Diem and to create a new nation. Diem, unlike Chiang Kai-shek and Syngman Rhee, was not really a rollbacker and concentrated his efforts on South Vietnam. Curiously, some American right-wingers attacked Diem as Washington's stooge in much the same terms as the left did later on. By the late 1950s, despite a festering insurgency, Washington came to regard South Vietnam as a model of nation building. But while South Vietnam became contain-

ment's bailiwick, the rollback-minded practitioners of covert war gained
a new country in which to unfold their operations—Laos.

If the full history of America's secret operations in Laos were ever
written, it would also be a history of the bureaucratic politics of American foreign policy. Unlike in South Vietnam, where containment had
managed to draw a clearcut line at the 17th parallel, there were no lines
in Laos. The government of Souvanna Phouma, which came to power in
1954 with the Geneva Accords, professed "neutralism." Despite Dulles's
fulminations about the "immorality of neutralism," it was tolerable in
countries like India where commitments were weak. But in East Asia,
where commitments were strong, neutralism was a nonexistent category
in terms of Washington's bureaucratic politics. The State Department,
which vigorously pursued the containment line in East Asia, strove to
turn Laos into a pro-Western bastion by building up Souvanna's army
with United States assistance. The CIA, which was the chief practitioner
of covert war in East Asia during the 1950s, preferred to use the right-
wing Thai-oriented forces in Laos as a peg on which to construct an
intricate network of covert war forces launching actions against both
China and North Vietnam. Naturally Taiwan was deeply involved in
these operations. When Souvanna fell from power in 1958 and the right-
wingers Phoui Sananikone and Phoumi Nosavan came to power, a process of accelerating crisis was created which by late 1960 seemed capable
of unleashing World War III.

During all the East Asian turbulence in which America was involved
since the beginning of the Korean War, the central focus was always
China. The world has forgotten the Quemoy crises of 1954 and 1958,
yet these are most symbolic of the struggle between the containment and
rollback lines which was being fought out in Washington. Quemoy and
its sister island Matsu are located just off the Fukien shoreline, opposite
the port of Amoy. They have virtually no military value since no invasion of the China coast could be launched from Quemoy and Communist
seizure of the islands would have brought them no closer to the seizure
of Taiwan. But Quemoy was a symbol of rollback and a dangerous chink
in the containment demarcation line Truman had drawn through the
Taiwan Straits. The containment policy makers constantly urged Chiang
to pull his forces out of Quemoy but he responded by building them up
even more. Chiang's plan for rollback called for unconditional support
by United States naval and air forces to assist him in a landing on the
China coast. Naturally such support would have involved extensive
bombing of China, as was later done over North Vietnam. As a cautious
man, Chiang had no illusions that this counterattack would succeed and
there are no indications that he ever made serious preparations for an
invasion of China. Nevertheless, each Quemoy crisis, big and small, was

a test of how far his friends in Washington were able to push America toward a rollback policy. The Quemoy crisis of late July and August 1958 was the most serious. The Seventh Fleet moved up to the three-mile limit of Chinese territorial waters in support of Chiang's massive pouring of troops and weapons into Quemoy. At exactly the same time, Souvanna Phouma fell from power in Laos and was replaced by the right-winger Phoui Sananikone. The simultaneity of these two events might appear coincidental except for the fact that in March 1958, the National Security Council had adopted a policy document on Vietnam (no. 5809) calling for its eventual reunification under "anti-Communist leadership." One of the authors of the Pentagon Papers notes the "roll-back over-tones" in this document.[14]

The late 1950s marked, as we shall see, a major transition in American foreign policy. At the same time that Eisenhower responded to his internationalist inclinations by moving toward peaceful coexistence with Russia, he also gave in to nationalist pressure and moved further toward rollback policies in East Asia, evident in the upsurge of covert warfare, particularly in Laos. Containment would again be put to the test, and never more dangerously than during the Vietnam war. That transition was bound up with major changes in global and nuclear policies. However, until the late 1950s, containment appeared to be winning its struggle against rollback in East Asia. In late 1954 and early 1955, when admirals like Radford and Carney were furiously arguing for war against China, Eisenhower stood up for containment and finally prevailed upon the Chinese Nationalists to evacuate the Tachen Islands, some two hundred miles north of Quemoy. The Sino-American ambassadorial talks launched in 1955 were a further victory for containment, even though Dulles was unable to get Peking to accept a permanent demarcation line through the Taiwan Straits. Covert war was as far as containment was willing to go in its concessions to rollback, and the overt use of military force against China was vetoed.

The key controversy between the two lines, containment and rollback, was over the question of Russian intervention. The rollbackers, like Admiral Carney, Chief of Naval Operations, argued in March 1955 that China's war potential should be destroyed with atomic weapons, and while Russia would provide China with arms, it would not "intervene directly."[15] The containment advocates disagreed, feeling that any direct attack against China would inevitably trigger Russian commitments under their nuclear umbrella. It was in the context of these arguments

[14] *The Pentagon Papers: The Defense Department History of United States Decision-making on Vietnam*, 5 vols., The Senator Gravel Edition (Boston: Beacon Press, 1971–1972), vol. 1, p. 267.

[15] D. F. Fleming, *The Cold War and Its Origins*, vol. 2, p. 716.

that the doctrines and controversies on "limited war" arose. Limited war was a containment concept, for it involved wars in which both sides accepted the limits of military action beyond which a general war would be triggered. The rollbackers bitterly ridiculed the notion and, like Air Force General Nathan Twining, argued that war once initiated had to be fought to total victory regardless of where it might lead. They further believed that American military power was so great that Russia would not intervene directly in any conflict because intervention would bring a nuclear holocaust over its land. The rollbackers would use the same arguments as the Vietnam war was building up, that neither the Russians nor the Chinese would intervene if the Americans bombed North Vietnam.

Containment wanted a two-Chinas policy much like what had been achieved in Germany. If Peking accepted Taiwan as a separate state, then the stage would be set for formalizing all the demarcation lines in East Asia. America could then proceed to organize the free Asian world much as it had organized or helped to organize Western Europe. Japan, with its booming economy, naturally would play a key role in the new East Asia Co-prosperity Sphere. South Korea, Taiwan, South Vietnam, and Thailand would become showcases of prosperity contrasted with the poverty of the communist-held portions of East Asia. SEATO was envisaged as an Asian counterpart of NATO, whose main purpose would be to provide forces-in-being for security against attack. Naturally, as SEATO became stronger, the more aggressive military forces in East Asia (in the client countries and within the United States military) would in turn be contained.

But unlike Russia, China was not prepared to accept containment. Chinese policy veered toward peaceful containment in 1955 (as did Russia's) and then toward advocacy of revolution later in the 1950s. By the early 1960s, China was regarded as the chief ideological instigator of national liberation movements throughout the world. Chinese policy hardened after November 1957 when Mao Tse-tung, in Moscow, made his famous statement that "the east wind prevails over the west wind." Yet in March 1958, China pulled its last troops out of North Korea. We shall go deeper into Chinese foreign policy in Part II, but in this context it is important to note that China *never* made a move to accept American containment policy in any form whatsoever. While Russia argued for the recognition of two Germanies, Peking (and Taipei) said flatly, without ever wavering, that there was only one China. Peking was willing to accept the kind of peaceful coexistence the internationalists had been advocating for Europe and was prepared to continue fighting the kinds of wars the nationalists were inflicting on it, but would not accept the compromise solution of containment. Peking has been consistently "extremist," opting for either war or peace, not the middle course of permanent cold war.

While it is clear what goals containment policy was pursuing vis-à-vis China and elsewhere in East Asia, the real goals of the minority rollbackers are not clear. Chiang Kai-shek has been pictured as a bloody warmonger thirsting eagerly for World War III so that he could return to power on the ashes of his country. Barry Goldwater is said to believe he lost the 1964 election so badly because people felt that, if elected, he would start a nuclear war. What is often overlooked by liberal and radical critics of the right is that the right-wingers really see communism as an expansionist force constantly pushing, slithering, or oozing forward unless checked. The notion of demarcation lines is ridiculous because communism will always find ways of circumventing obstacles. A subversive movement deep within friendly territory can be more effective in weakening Freedom's forces than a direct military onslaught. The right-wing rollbackers, both American and Asian, had in mind three directions along which America had to move to assure its safety against the communist threat: 1) build up strong anticommunist regimes along China's periphery whose rule would be guaranteed by powerful military and police forces; 2) maintain high levels of conventional American military power, particularly naval and air, all along China's borders; and 3) seize on every opportunity to inflict damage on China if it could be done without unacceptable losses. The rollbackers could not understand why the liberals refused to face the fact that Freedom was in a permanent *war* with Communism. The Chinese civil war, which continues to this day in the eyes of both Peking and Taipei, was but a variation of the larger war between Freedom and Communism. As expansionists, the American nationalists felt that they were facing up to a counterexpansionism which, unchecked, would one day march up San Francisco's Market Street, as former Senator George Murphy once warned.

In these terms, it is obvious that rollback policies made great strides in East Asia after the Korean War. Whereas the Asian containment policies anticipated by George Kennan, in his visit to Japan in 1948, called for Japan to be the anchor of America's East Asian policies, the rollbackers preferred the smaller countries of Taiwan, South Korea, South Vietnam, and Thailand, where authoritarian regimes created stable conditions for the American military presence. The price containment paid for these small-country victories of the rollbackers was Japan's hesitant aloofness from America's Asian policies. Unlike West Germany, which became Washington's active instrument in furthering its policies in Europe, Japan, while firmly committed to the relationship with America, was reluctant to get too deeply involved in American military and political adventures in East Asia.

Containment and rollback have both had thrusts of their own independent of what the Chinese or the Russians did. These two currents could not coexist harmoniously in East Asia because the war that rollback was waging against China went directly against the basic containment doctrine that war must not be waged against countries in the socialist camp, and only "limited wars" in response to communist "aggression" across the demarcation lines were acceptable. Washington's containment bureaucrats could live with covert war so long as everyone pretended it did not exist. Thus, long after it was evident how extensive United States–directed covert war had become in Laos, Washington continued to deny it piously. Washington was not being hypocritical, but showing extreme fear at the possibility of opening a Pandora's box which could create intense power struggles within the bureaucracies, not to mention the effect that such admissions could have on larger global policies.

The Chinese use the phrase "two-handed policies" to describe the policies of their enemies, meaning that what Washington and Moscow do in one respect may be entirely contradicted by something they do in another. Washington's two-handed policies in East Asia are not the result of duplicity, but of a fundamental struggle between two different foreign policy currents which from time to time accommodate to each other, but then again break loose to go their independent ways.

Both the theory and the generalizations lead to the conclusion that whereas American actions in Europe were an ever-changing mix of containment and peaceful coexistence, in East Asia they were a mix of containment and rollback. In the remainder of the world, where American commitments were less hardened, foreign policy generally has been pragmatic—at times serving American interests and at others serving American ideology.

In Part II, I shall analyze the relationships between America, Russia, and China, and in Part III, the genesis of the Vietnam war. Relationships between the great powers were the bailiwick of containment and, organizationally, of the chief executive. In fact, the chief executive derived ideological power from them, which he used in his conflicts with the interests. The Vietnam war was an inevitable consequence of American expansionism into the Pacific; but the predominant interests involved in that war have been military. During it, the great bulk of America's conventional forces were concentrated in East Asia. The American military became an Asian force and, naturally, developed interests rooted in the Asian scene.

In this book, I spell out one side of the great bifurcation in foreign policy between Western Europe and East Asia. While it had roots in earlier developments, this bifurcation was also shaped by the creation of global geopolitical symmetries in which the containment-minded strategists in Washington delighted. During the *Pueblo* crisis, W. W. Rostow was reported to have suggested that America seize a Soviet ship as a "symmetry of response."[16] While Rostow's proposal was dismissed as "outrageous," in fact, the entire Vietnam war and much of the cold war were waged by Washington's strategists in terms of such symmetries, which they themselves fashioned. And since they had the power of government behind them, the symmetries became real. America's enemies adapted to them and, especially the Vietnamese, turned them successfully against America.

In the early 1970s, a new dual symmetry appears to be emerging, one that grew out of the crude Europe-first or Asia-first controversy of the late 1940s. It involves, in one part, relationships between America, Russia, Western Europe, and the Middle East; and in the other, America, China, Japan, and Indochina. Later, I shall try to show how Middle Eastern crises played a role in the Indochina war, creating an either/or choice: either major efforts are made in the Middle East or they are made in Indochina. In more technical terms, it is the "one-and-one-half war" concept.

The Middle East connotes oil, and Indochina has come to connote weapons (the vast array of explosive instruments that America has unleashed there). Western Europe is the Common Market, internationalist, integrated, globally conscious. Japan is a national economy advancing and protecting its own interests while a part of the world market system. America, facing monetary crisis and trade and payments deficits, is still caught in the ancient contention between internationalist free traders and nationalist protectionists. Internationalism wants a stable monetary system and assurance of its interests, particularly oil. Nationalism wants to cut down Japanese economic incursions and to continue military and economic expansion into Asia.

As with all Presidencies since the end of World War II, the chief executive wishes to satisfy both currents but cannot do so. Under normal circumstances, a pluralism should reign, such as occurs in the market, so that *ad hoc* accommodations and arrangements could be made—a process of never-ending trade-offs. But these Presidencies are also prisoners of the symmetries they have created, which are far more binding than they were in the late 1940s. As is implied by the "one-and-one-half war" concept, those symmetries call for a priority choice between Western (Russia) and Eastern (China) theaters, not so much in terms of real war but in terms of commitments.

In the early 1970s, American imperialism, spearheaded as always by

[16] Reported by Trevor Armbrister, quoted in Peter Dale Scott, *The War Conspiracy*, p. 141.

executive and military power, is looking at new regions in which to practice its arts, notably the Middle East, whose oil constitutes the jugular of the world economy. The currents outlined in this book and their organizational expressions within the state remain, so that policies and operations of the future will be the product of much the same parameters that shaped the policies and actions of the period since 1945.

PART II

RUSSIA, CHINA, AND AMERICA

CHAPTER 1

China and Russia as Allies

When Mao Tse-tung journeyed to Moscow in December 1949 and concluded an alliance with Stalin, what Washington liked to call the monolithic Sino-Soviet bloc was born. Communist power stretched in an unbroken mass from Berlin through Russia and China to Pyongyang. When Mao Tse-tung took his second trip to Moscow in November 1957, he made a declaration that squared with all the notions then current in Washington: "The socialist camp must have a head, and that head is the Soviet Union. The Communist parties and workers' parties of all countries must have a head, and that head is the Soviet Communist party." Unlike the free world, which was held together by alliances, the communist bloc was seen as a totalitarian structure autocratically dominated by Moscow. Furthermore, its ramifications went deep into the free world in the form of communist parties which owed unswerving loyalty to Moscow. But only three years after Mao Tse-tung's 1957 reaffirmation of Russian leadership, signs of a split between Russia and China began to appear. Washington's defense intellectuals excitedly began to debate its nature, with liberals generally arguing that it was real and conservatives arguing that it was minor and ephemeral. As the decade of the sixties unfolded, the split became wider and wider until in the early months of 1969 it produced a small war between Chinese and Russian armies.

The perception by the Americans first of the alliance between Russia and China, then of the split, played a central role in the operational thinking of the major American political currents. The conservatives in Washington held doggedly to their conviction that the Sino-Soviet bloc was real until the evidence of hostility between China and Russia was no longer possible to deny. The military only finally accepted the reality of the split in early 1969 when millions of Chinese and Russian troops were facing each other in hostile confrontation. The liberals, on the other hand, had always suspected that such a split might occur. In late 1949, they argued that Mao Tse-tung had all the makings of a Tito. With Russia then conceived as America's principal enemy, a Titoist China would have well served Washington's containment policies. But in the early 1960s, the implications of the split were understood differently. Russia was now *"embourgeoisé,"* and China, as the fountainhead of world-wide insurgencies, was America's principal enemy. Although some internationalist-minded liberals and conservatives called for more trade with both communist countries, in the great debate in Washington over the nature of the Sino-Soviet split only the voices of the nationalist conservatives and the containment liberals really counted.

There was little disagreement between conservatives and liberals on the issue of China. China was seen as a rabid ultrarevolutionary power, willing to risk nuclear war so that communism could triumph on the ashes of destruction, and actively engaged in aiding and abetting subversive movements throughout the world. The disagreement related to Russia. While the liberals believed that Russia was "settling down," the conservatives felt that it was no less committed to the violent destruction of America than China. Russia and China might disagree over tactics, but their goals of world rule were identical. The liberals held out hope that China too might someday "settle down." If America remained tough with China as it was with Russia, time and economic development would see a new generation of "pragmatists" and "moderates" come to power there. Like Stalin, Mao would be succeeded by a Chinese Khrushchev, and containment could be made to work in Asia as it was working in Europe.

Such was the debate as it unfolded publicly. Conducted by outstanding intellectuals in America and other free world countries, it produced a deluge of literature. But its parameters were delineated by the categories admissible within the bureaucratic conference rooms in Washington. The debate was always over the "Sino-Soviet split." America's role in that split was never mentioned. Both liberals and conservatives assumed that America was a passive power which reacted only when provoked, and conversely, that Russia and China were aggressive and expansionist. There was occasionally some talk, more behind the closed doors of the bureaucracies than in public, as to what actions America might take to "influence" the split, but such discussion was generally out of bounds. The debate was carried on by experts, whose task was to inform the bureaucracies and the public of what was really going on in Russia and China. Unless they happened to be in the national security bureaucracy, they were to keep their fingers out of the policy-making pie.

However, as Part II of this book seeks to show, America was the active agent in generating the "Sino-Soviet bloc" in the first place and then also played the primary role in generating the great split between China and Russia.

GLOBAL POLITICS

By the late 1960s, it had become commonplace in foreign affairs circles to speak of a triangular relationship between America, Russia, and China. With President Nixon's Kansas City speech of July 1971, the triangular relationship with its primarily political-military focus was expanded to a pentagonal relationship with the addition of Western Europe and Japan, as economic giants, to the other three great powers. To speak of either triangular or pentagonal relationships implies that there is a unitary global politics of a sort that a move by one of the major players affects the positions of all the others. But the appearance of such notions in the late 1960s was also an implicit but real admission of America's active role in the Sino-Soviet split.

Until the outbreak of the Korean War, global politics meant European politics, as it had for centuries. American, Russian, and European leaders all assumed that if Europe could be stabilized, the basic peace and security of the world would be assured. The idea of a "Third World" lying outside of Europe and America that could affect the central politics of the West seemed ridiculous. Everywhere there were poor and backward countries to be helped and civilized. And there were all kinds of trouble in the non-European countries which made life difficult for the West. But it seemed inconceivable that conflicts outside of Europe could in themselves determine the fate of the world.

The Korean War was the watershed marking the end of a tradition of global politics centering on Europe and the beginning of a new period in which politics became truly global.

Even before 1950, it was clear that America, unlike Europe, had major Asian as well as European interests (except for France's stubbornness in Indochina, the only other countries with major East Asian interests, Britain and Holland, were in the process of slowly liquidating them). This did not mean that America's dual Asian and European role was part of a larger unitary political process. But in 1950, America proclaimed international communism as the real source of the aggression in Korea and sought to mobilize the entire United Nations to combat it. Three decades earlier, when the revolutionary process was checked in Western Europe, Lenin was reputed to have said that the road to Paris leads through Peking. If communism now struck at Korea, it obviously was designed to divert American men and resources from Western Europe, which was in the process of rearming. Washington's argument that Korea was a test of the free world's will to resist aggression was so convincing (backed, naturally, by America's immense power to persuade) that the Korean War became a war waged by the United Nations, the world's most prominent symbol of global unity.

If the Korean War was a watershed in world politics, what made it so was the alliance concluded only months before between the Soviet Union and the People's Republic of China. In America, the explanation for Sino-Soviet unity given by right-wing anticommunists was simple: both Russia and China were governed by an International Communist Conspiracy. The containment liberals, following George Kennan's thinking, saw Russia and China as separate national powers with common as well as conflicting interests, Russia's superiority and China's needs giving the former a commanding role. The explanation of the left for Sino-Soviet unity was basically the same as that of the anticommunists: both Russia and China were socialist countries in common opposition to American imperialism. Neither the left nor the right really accepted the split when it came, in contrast to the liberals who foresaw it as early as the spring of 1960.

Both the unity between China and Russia and then the split were based on elements of ideology and interest. As explained in Part I, ideology means in part an operational world view, here the way in which Russians and Chinese see the trends in world politics, particularly those hostile, friendly, or neutral to them. Interest means concrete matters that provide gain or loss for the parties concerned. Since interests are tangible, we will begin with an examination of the interests held by Russia and the Chinese Communists on the basis of which a relationship could have been constituted.

RUSSIA AND CHINA—INTERESTS

Prior to the 1950 alliance, Russia and China had no common interests save for Manchuria and Sinkiang. China was a vast backward country which had little to furnish Russia and little capacity or inclination to take much from Russia. Chiang Kai-shek welcomed Russian arms for his soldiers, but he had much more bountiful sources of weaponry among his American friends. The Russian Far East (*Dalnyi Vostok*) was a thinly populated region of scant importance to the Russian economy. The island of Sakhalin had oil deposits, and Russia's repossession of it in its entirety after the war had some economic importance. But even in 1945, Russia's most important sources of oil were in the Caucasus. Russian interest in Manchuria centered mainly on the Central Manchurian Railway, which provided more direct access to Vladivostok than the circuitous Trans-Siberian Railway. Manchuria had been industrialized by the Japanese, and is still today the heavy industrial heartland of China. But in 1945, the Russians showed their basic disinterest in it by dismantling its industry and removing it to Russian territory. When Russian troops evacuated Manchuria in 1946, they showed no overwhelming concern about the Central Manchurian Railway. As the civil war interrupted rail traffic, the Russians simply used the old route, which skirted Manchuria. The vast province of Sinkiang, with its suspected oil and mineral deposits, had potentially greater concrete interest for Russia. But Sinkiang was so undeveloped that lack of roads and railways would make eventual exploitation of its riches very difficult. Throughout the period of Nationalist rule, the Russians maintained amicable relations with the independent warlord of Sinkiang, which did not unduly trouble Chiang Kai-shek. After 1945, the world became dimly aware of a non-Chinese Communist movement operating in the Ili River region, the northernmost part of Sinkiang. The Ili Communists were closely linked to Russia, and Stalin probably saw them as an instrument for assuring control of Sinkiang if China fell into complete chaos. When the 1950 Sino-Soviet alliance was concluded, Stalin immediately allowed the movement to be absorbed into the Chinese Communist party. Sinkiang has always had a romantic aura about it, like Tibet, but in interest terms, it does not even begin to compare with Russian interests in Eastern Europe or the Caucasus.

The defeat of Japan removed the last major threat to Russian interests in the Far East. With Sakhalin and the Kurils incorporated into the Soviet Union, with an independent Korea (albeit in two parts), and with Manchuria part of chaotic China, the Russian presence in the Far East, such as it was, seemed secure. Whether China was hostile or friendly to Russia did not seem to matter very much, for China was so weak compared to Imperial Japan that it had little in the way of gain or loss to offer Russia.

Stalin said to Foreign Minister Matsuoka in 1940, "I too am an Asiatic." But these were empty words, for Stalin had little interest in Asia. When Roosevelt proposed China as a member of the Security Council of the United Nations and wanted to give it a voice in European affairs, Stalin was incredulous, seeing it simply (and correctly) as an American trick to gain a proxy vote. For all his crudities, Stalin was a Marxist and believed devoutly that where there was industrial production, there was power. Real power, therefore, existed in America, Western Europe, and Russia, with perhaps a little in Japan. Until the conclusion of the Sino-Soviet alliance and the Korean War, there is no indication that Stalin's major foreign policy concerns went anywhere but westward from his country. Manchuria and Sinkiang had some importance for Russia, but were far from being vital.

In the late seventeenth century, Russia was the first Western country to have concluded treaties with China. These delineated the boundaries between the two countries, which are now under contention. But the

4,000 miles of boundary went through wasteland thinly populated by nomads and hunters. A Russian religious mission was able to reside amicably in Peking until the revolution mainly because, despite their common boundaries, the two countries were very remote from each other. No culture or spiritual values linked them. The "Asian presence" in Russia was Muslim Turkic and Buddhist Mongol. Some Chinese immigration began late in the nineteenth century, but it never remotely achieved the scale of Chinese immigration to other parts of the world. Russians have an historical fear of Tatar hordes invading from the east and the Chinese have a long history of Tatar invasions from the north. But it has been only in the recent past that they have seen each other as the new Tatars. The Sino-Russian treaties of the late seventeenth and early eighteenth centuries actually served the purpose of ridding both countries once and for all of any new Tatar danger—the Tatars, Turkic and Mongol nomads were separated into Russian and Chinese tributaries. Separation, not proximity, was the basic aim of the Russian tsars and the Chinese emperors.

Both Tsarist Russia and Imperial China were expansionist powers— by the seventeenth century, Russian power had already reached the Pacific and China had conquered Sinkiang and Tibet. But neither country was able to fill out its expansion with settler populations or major economic investments. Siberia remains thinly populated to this day and, until very recently, Chinese did not emigrate to either Sinkiang or Tibet. The Russians went into Siberia much as the French penetrated so much of North America, as traders and adventurers, without leaving behind a material substructure. When the Chinese population did expand within its own borders, the initial rush was into Manchuria, overwhelmingly to the south and center. Northern Manchuria, where China borders with Russia, is still thinly populated.

Late in the nineteenth century, Tsarist Russia expanded into Manchuria and Korea, but it was soundly trounced by the Japanese early in the next century. If he had wanted to, Stalin could easily have alleged Russian interest in Manchuria and demanded some territorial or other form of compensation at the end of the war. In Europe, he annexed great expanses of territory on grounds of Russian national interest that still contain large numbers of non-Russian peoples. Moldavia may now be a Soviet republic and may use Cyrillic script, but its people and language are indistinguishable from those of Romania, to which it had been attached to form Bessarabia. In East Asia, Stalin contented himself with the annexation of southern Sakhalin and the Kurile Islands. While there would have been an outcry, as with Poland, if he had decided to slice off a part of Manchuria and incorporate it into the Soviet Union, the fact is that in 1945 he would have gotten away with it.

In the winter of 1949–1950, when Mao and Stalin were negotiating their alliance, there were no major historical or recent interests that either bound the two countries together or provoked major conflict between them. There were even fewer common interests between the Russian and the Chinese Communist parties. The Russian occupation of Manchuria in 1945 and the dramatic Chinese Communist sweep into Manchuria at the same time were dichotomous to each other. The Russians moved down the rail lines and occupied the cities, which they then dutifully turned over to the Nationalists. The Chinese Communists moved in from the southwest through the countryside, having little recorded contact with the Russian occupation forces. They acquired large stocks of Japanese weapons and supplies, and captured many technically qualified soldiers, some of whom served them during their offensives. If the Russians "allowed" these Japanese forces to surrender to the Communists in violation of SCAP directives that they were to surrender only to duly constituted United Nations forces, then that could be construed as a minor act of of generosity. But the Chinese Communists never received Soviet weapons, and any weapons of Soviet origin in China were held by the Nationalists, who acquired them in accordance with the provisions of the 1945 treaty between Russia and Chiang Kai-shek's China. During 1946–1949, the Russian press gave scant attention to the momentous civil war in China. In fact, there are grounds for suspecting some Russian hostility toward the Chinese Communists. In 1948, Anna Louise Strong, already then a close friend of Chairman Mao, was expelled from Russia as an "American spy."

It is inconceivable that Stalin concluded an alliance with the People's Republic of China, which was already then a subject of virulent debate in America, Russia's principal enemy, just to gain some advantages of interest in Manchuria and Sinkiang. Dean Rusk's characterization of the People's Republic as a "Slavic Manchukuo" in 1951 was a faithful reflection of Kennanist thinking, which interpreted all of Russia's actions in concrete interest terms. Just as Japan added Manchuria to its empire because it needed the space and the resources, so Russia for comparable reasons was adding all of China to its empire. Kennanist thinking, which formed much of the basis for containment ideology, held that since Russia's expansionist drive in Europe had been checked by 1949, it then sought new avenues for expansion in Asia.[1] The difficulty with this view is that it holds up only in a metaphysical sense, if one imputes to Russia some *Ur-drang* or primeval urge toward expansion coming out of the Russian lands. As a practical notion, expansionism presumes some concrete reasons of interest for expanding. Thus, one could allege Russian

[1] See Adam Ulam, *Expansion and Co-existence*, p. 514.

expansionism into northern Iran to protect the vital Baku oil fields or toward the Dardanelles to have an outlet into the Mediterranean or into Poland and Germany to protect Russia's western frontiers. Then the gains for such expansion have to be measured against the risks incurred. From 1945 to 1949, Russia took major risks to assure its control over Poland and eastern Germany, but it did not press aggressively its long-term interests in Turkey and Iran. The interests Russia had in China or even in Manchuria and Sinkiang were minor compared even to those in Turkey and Iran. The alliance with China was a great risk for so cautious a man as Stalin to undertake. It imposed great burdens on Russia. And when the Korean War erupted, it faced Russia with the possibility of World War III arising out of an area of minor interest to it. If Stalin wanted his own "Manchukuo," he could have gotten it with far less risk in 1945. The explanation of the Sino-Soviet alliance of 1950 is not to be found in interest terms. An ideological explanation is necessary.

RUSSIA AND CHINA—IDEOLOGY

In 1949, the Russian and Chinese Communists shared a common formal ideology—both were Marxist and both were Leninist. The Marxist component was a particular world view, which saw capitalism as the great force for world unity and growth, but held that there were irresolvable contradictions of such magnitude in capitalism that it would decay in stagnation or destroy itself in wars, and that class struggle was the revolutionary vehicle through which the productive potential of capitalism would be realized in the form of socialism. The Leninist component prescribed a particular form of political organization and action to achieve revolutionary victory and socialism, namely, a vanguard party functioning in military fashion to struggle unremittingly for the final goals of revolution and socialism. All communist parties that belonged to the Comintern in the 1920s and 1930s accepted the principles of Marxism and Leninism as their guidelines for theory and action. But adherence to the Comintern signified a further principled understanding—that the October Revolution was the vanguard revolution for all other revolutionary movements in the world and that the Soviet Union, as the world's first socialist country, was the model for all movements proceeding through revolution to the construction of socialism. Marxism, Leninism, and the vanguard role of the Soviet Union were, therefore, the basic formal principles of all communist parties.

When Stalin abolished the Comintern during World War II, grave damage was done to the simple but powerful structure of international communism. Despite the nationalistic aberration of fascism, Marxists of all political varieties still viewed capitalism as an organized international force which revolutionaries could hope to oppose only if they generated counterorganization. The Comintern seemed to be revolution's answer to capitalism. Ramifying through its member communist parties throughout the world, the Comintern was the general staff of the world revolution, whose commander-in-chief was the mighty Soviet Union. Revolution meant war against capitalism and imperialism, and wars can only be fought with armies, organized phalanxes of troops guided by goals, strategies, and tactics, which have to emanate from a central headquarters. Trotskyists did not quarrel with that conception of the international revolutionary struggle, but regarded Stalinism as unfit, incapable, and unwilling to make the Soviet Union the true leader. But Stalin's abolition of the Comintern was a logical outgrowth of his own contribution to communist ideology, the notion of "socialism in one country." Communist parties everywhere during the 1920s and 1930s were national, but Communists still held to the notion that the "proletariat has no fatherland," and the Comintern promised a political internationalism to come. Stalin, a non-Russian, Lenin's main adviser on nationality questions, and subsequently an ardent Great Russian patriot, reversed a century-old trend from nationalist to internationalist thinking. He made it clear in his words and actions that he believed that all proletariats have fatherlands, and that revolutions, therefore, must be seen in national terms. Even before World War II, Stalin's purges had decimated the Comintern, ridding it particularly of its most internationalist elements, who happened generally to be the most intellectual of the Communists.

When World War II ended, powerful communist parties had reappeared, largely as a result of their leadership roles in the antifascist struggle. In Europe, there were Yugoslav, Italian, French, Greek, and Albanian communist parties, which fought heroically against the Germans and the Italians. In Asia, aside from the Chinese Communists, communist parties or movements appeared in Indochina, the Philippines, Burma, and Korea, all of which had been occupied by the Japanese. The American Communist party had decided to dissolve itself. The communist and workers' parties that grew up in eastern Germany, Poland, Romania, Hungary, and Bulgaria cannot be disassociated from the presence of Russian troops in those countries. While these parties and movements had no formal organizational connections with the Communist party of the USSR, they fully shared its formal ideology, accepting the three basic tenets of the Comintern: a Marxist world view, a Leninist form of party organization, and the vanguard role of the Soviet Union as the world's first and leading socialist state.

All these communist parties abhorred Trotskyism, which they regarded as a mortal enemy of proletarian internationalism. Regardless of

Stalinism's shortcomings, which some of them conceded in private, communists throughout the world believed firmly that there could be no effective international movement without the Soviet Union as its anchor. World War II appeared as a complete vindication of communist views. Fascism, like imperialism, was seen as a necessary form of capitalism. When Hitler invaded Russia and made it his principal enemy, communists saw this as a continuation of capitalism's ardent desire to destroy the world's first socialist state, which had begun as soon as the October Revolution triumphed in Russia. Why, then, were capitalist countries like America and Britain allied with Russia against Germany? World War II, as communists saw it, began as a typical rivalry among imperialist powers, much as in 1914. However, popular and progressive forces were so strong in these capitalist countries that they were unable to extricate themselves from the war against Hitler so that the fascists and the communists could destroy each other. The struggle against fascism was arousing an even more profound struggle in the bourgeois countries against capitalism itself. The ruling classes were caught between two pressures, one coming from a rival imperialism and capitalism, the other from rising anti-imperialist and anticapitalist forces. Hitler's fanatical war of destruction against the Soviet Union convinced the communists that the Soviet Union was indeed capitalism's mortal enemy. When America, shortly after the end of World War II, went on an anticommunist offensive, the analysis seemed even more vindicated. The great rallying cry of the communists in the 1930s, "Defense of the Soviet Union," an issue on which Trotskyism floundered, seemed to be absolutely correct for national parties which saw themselves in the revolutionary vanguard of the struggle against capitalism, imperialism, and reaction in their own societies.

While anticommunists have regarded communism as some immense protean force ever waiting to pounce on poor and weak free countries, most communists saw themselves as small movements always threatened with total extinction by an array of hostile forces. To be a communist revolutionary meant dedicating oneself to a virtually unattainable goal: the transformation of an entire society along socialist lines in the face of the immense entrenched power of established interests. It was much easier to become a liberal reformist and to achieve something within the interstices of the system. The existence of the Soviet Union as a model and a power gave all communists the conviction that no matter how puny their movement might be, their real power and importance far exceeded their numbers. As communists, they had to be taken seriously by their enemies, as they were by the European and Asian fascists of the 1930s and as they would be again by the Americans and their allies after 1945. But if the communists needed the Soviet Union to give them domestic power beyond their numbers, they also had to reciprocate by adhering to the general guidelines of Soviet policy. To deviate could result in an attack on the party in *Pravda*, which mainly would damage its national power and influence. Thus, even without the formal discipline of the Comintern, communist parties had to remain closely bound to the Soviet Union.

All communists believed that their own revolutionary struggle was inextricably linked with the world-wide struggle between the forces of socialism and progressivism on the one hand and those of capitalism, imperialism, and reaction on the other. In 1945, they believed that the great victory against fascism had pushed the political spectrum throughout the world sharply toward the left. The right had been destroyed or gravely weakened, and the bourgeois democratic center faced a militant left which was not entirely communist or even preponderately so, but which was clearly progressive. During the war, a solid alliance seemed to have developed between the progressive forces of all political shadings and the communists. The only leftist group excluded from the alliance were the Trotskyists, who were seen as ultraleftists willing to sacrifice all chance of a rise to power for the sake of their "permanent revolution." Thus, in 1945, communists throughout the world were convinced that the governments in all countries would have to move farther to the left, and that in such governments communists would play leading roles.

Just before World War II erupted, all the great bourgeois democratic countries were still caught in the Great Depression. Every teaching of Marxism and every shred of common sense indicated that capitalism would again rapidly face dire economic difficulties in the immediate postwar years. Economic difficulties would mean a powerful and militant labor movement which this time could not be crushed by fascist measures. Lenin had taught the inevitability of a violent seizure of power by the revolutionaries, and if some communist parties secretly hoped that this could be avoided, they all remained wedded to the teaching in principle. However, as disciplined communists, they also believed that the time had to be ripe for such a seizure of power. It was ripe in Yugoslavia because fascism had destroyed all existing power and the communists just stepped into a vacuum. The situation was different, however, in Western Europe. The political institutions of Western European countries had remained largely intact, the progressive left forces were powerful and, by and large, reformist, and the communist parties themselves were still organizationally weak. All signs portended a new crisis in capitalism in which the chances for a rise to power by the left were better than they ever had been. The task of the communists was to use their new power and influence to organize themselves into the most effective political weapon on the left so that when the time came, supreme power would pass into their hands, with or without violence.

In 1945, most communists were in favor of coalition government and peaceful coexistence because they believed that world capitalism would shortly face a crisis so severe that mankind would have no salvation except revolution. The argument that Stalin discouraged the Western European communist parties from seizing power which was then for the taking is not the central point. Stalin may have pursued a very practical foreign policy designed to ensure Russian national security regardless of what happened in the larger world, but as a Marxist he shared the same view of the world as other Marxist communists. His chief political economist, Eugene Varga, periodically wrote essays predicting the imminent crisis of capitalist economies. Whether Stalin, Thorez, Togliatti, or Tito, all communists shared that belief, and continued to share it until the cold war convinced them that capitalism had found a new way to avert its own doom: massive rearmament, repression of the left, and a new holy war against the Soviet Union. That new awareness came within a few years after the end of World War II, but in 1945 it was hardly yet discernible.

In 1945, it was not the Comintern or Stalin or some other organized entity that gave unity to the international communist movement, but the forces of world history itself. From 1917 to 1927, the Russian Communist party actively directed revolutionary movements throughout the world, and its leadership was exuberantly but disputatiously accepted. That phase ended with the virtual destruction of the Communist party of China. With the implementation of "socialism in one country," Russia went from the offensive to the defensive, and the Comintern was regarded by Stalin and many foreign Communists as an instrument for the defense of the Soviet Union. But in 1945, there was no longer any need to defend the Soviet Union. It had won a smashing victory and seemed to be permanently out of danger. The world revolution could once again go on the offensive. But now no Comintern was needed to direct that revolution, for the destruction of capitalism from within would give Communists throughout the world a golden opportunity for the seizure of power, which, like an overripe apple, would not even have to be plucked from a tree but simply picked up off the ground. All that was necessary was caution and patience, two qualities Stalin had in abundance. A precipitate move to take power would only arouse unnecessary resistance from the bourgeoisie. The best course was to maintain the United Front, join coalition governments, and build the communist parties into powerful organizational weapons based on the working class and other productive classes.

The Chinese Communist party, while remote from the centers of world capitalism, held to the same estimation of the forces of world history in 1945 as did other communist parties. They believed that the world-wide victory against fascism was made possible by a revolutionary and progressive tide which was propelling the bourgeois countries farther and farther to the left. Chiang Kai-shek himself had been forced leftward in the mid-1930s by rising anti-Japanese sentiment within his own Kuomintang ranks. And while he was scheming day and night how to continue his bandit extermination campaigns against the Chinese Communists, they felt confident that they could enter into negotiations with him. America was, of course, playing two-handed policies in China—urging a coalition government between Communists and Nationalists with the one hand and supporting Chiang Kai-shek to the hilt in his frantic drive to reoccupy China with the other. Such perfidiousness made perfect sense because while progressive forces were strong in America, they still had to compete with reactionary forces, which would not willingly leave the stage of history. The communists' understanding of the forces of world history, their world view, taught them that the progressive forces in America would get stronger and stronger, undercutting more and more Chiang Kai-shek's obduracy.

The Chinese Communists' view of the Soviet Union was identical to that of communists and progressives throughout the world. As Mao Tse-tung told Anna Louise Strong in her interview with him in August 1946, "The Soviet Union is the guarantor of world peace. It is a powerful factor impeding reactionary forces in America from achieving world domination. As long as there is a Soviet Union, reactionary forces in America and in the world will never fundamentally be able to realize their ambitions." Peace was seen as being clearly in the interests of communists, for Marxist analysis taught that capitalism and reactionary rule could not long survive under conditions of world-wide peace. Peace in China would mean, for example, that America would cease pouring military supplies into Chiang Kai-shek's armies. Mao's reference to reactionary forces in America also reflected general communist thinking that all bourgeois countries had political forces of the left, center, and right. The left consisted of progressive forces, of which the communists were only one part, which desired world peace and, thus, peaceful coexistence with the Soviet Union. The right consisted of reactionary forces, fascist and imperialist in character, which persisted on the already trodden path of Hitler, Mussolini, and Tojo, seeking to avert inherent capitalist crisis by internal repression and foreign adventures. The center consisted of liberal forces which sought a middle path between these two extremes.

In July 1946, the civil war resumed in China after the collapse of the Marshall Mission. Mao attributes Chiang's resumption of the war directly to aid and encouragement from America. Yet even this unexpected resurgence of right-wing forces did not basically change Mao's world view nor that of communists elsewhere. Peace would be much more difficult to achieve than they had believed in the euphoria of victory, but a basic progressive tide remained strong in the bourgeois countries, including America. If the centrist forces that led to the dispatch of the Marshall Mission to China had to give ground to the reactionaries, a time would come again soon when they would have to veer back toward the progressives.

THE RISE OF REACTIONARY FORCES

The basic elements of this communist world view were to remain constant until the later stages of the Sino-Soviet split when the Chinese evolved the concept of "Soviet social imperialism." What began to change, however, in the late 1940s, was the communists' estimate of the relative strength of the progressive and reactionary forces in the world, particularly in America. The founding of the Cominform in September 1947 was an admission by the Russians that a new worldwide situation was arising. The violent hostility shown by the Russians toward the Truman Administration and their constant unfavorable comparisons of it with Roosevelt's reflected their growing conviction that they had overestimated the strength of the progressive forces and underestimated that of the reactionaries. The constant clamor for a "preventive war" against Russia from American right-wing and military circles was, for the Russians, a sign of growing reactionary power. Aggressive fascism had appeared only fifteen years after World War I, with Hitler's rise to power in Germany. This was capitalism's way of resolving economic crisis. Now bourgeois democratic America appeared to be jumping the gun by moving in a fascist direction even before an economic crisis. Like Hitler, Truman was beginning to persecute communists, saber-rattling against Russia, and launching America on the road to rearmament. The events of 1947 all boded ill for coexistence: Truman inserted American power into the eastern Mediterranean, wrecked four-power cooperation in Germany by the formation of Bizonia and the introduction of a West German currency, and launched a Marshall Plan which the Russians saw as mainly an instrument to further American domination in Europe. All hope of international cooperation on the control of atomic energy had collapsed by the end of 1947 and, with the National Security Act of 1947, America was launched on a campaign of rearmament stressing its technical military power.

Stalin saw no alternative but to revert to the thinking of the 1930s when the key issue for the international communist movement had been "defense of the Soviet Union." The Cominform was not a new Comintern, however, but an instrument for consolidating Russian power in Eastern Europe and binding Western European communist parties closer to Moscow. Stalin, like most Russians and most European communists, was convinced that Germany remained the touchstone of global reactionary power. Fascist forces were still powerful in West Germany, and nothing would be more natural than for reactionary forces in America to tap them in order to push America itself in a right-wing direction. Fascism elsewhere in the world, for example in China, was no valid criterion for the strength of reactionary forces in America, but fascism in Germany, whose western half was under American control (the Russians were not impressed by either the British or the French presence in the occupation forces), was a clearcut weathervane for the currents in America.

It was in 1947 that the first tentative speculation surfaced in United States Army circles about the possibility of eventual German rearmament.[2] While official American policy was still solidly opposed to it in any form, the Russians saw this as a sign of growing reactionary power in America. The formation of the Cominform accelerated the process of integrating Eastern Europe into the Soviet system. It obviously spurred on the Czech Communists to cease functioning as a compliant member of a bourgeois democratic coalition government and to seize power in March 1948. If a German menace was to reappear soon, the Czechs had particular reasons for concern. The Czech Communist party in the 1930s, while numerically strong, had been organizationally weak, and did not revive until the liberation of Czechoslovakia by the Russians. Seizure of power would give the Czech Communists a chance to build an organization so powerful that it could survive even under a new fascist occupation.

Tito reacted differently to the new system of control that Stalin was attempting to impose in Eastern Europe. Yugoslavia differed from all other Eastern European countries in that its unity was exceedingly precarious because of deep ethnic hatreds: Serbs and Croats had slaughtered each other during World War II; some Macedonians were arguing for unification with their close cousins, the Bulgars; discontented minorities identified with countries bordering Yugoslavia to the detriment of national unity. Tito was a devout communist but also a Yugoslav patriot. Convinced that acquiescence in the Soviets' plans for Yugoslavia could mean a break-up of the country, he resisted. His expulsion from the Comintern was probably intended to pressure him into line or to call for his overthrow by forces loyal to Moscow. When that gambit failed, Tito quickly abandoned his hitherto solid world view. Since, unlike his socialist neighbors to the north, Tito had no deep-seated fear of a revived Germany, he quickly achieved a rapprochement with the United States.

[2] Laurence W. Martin, "The American Decision to Rearm Germany," in Harold Stein, ed., *American Civil-Military Decisions*, p. 646.

But his basic foreign policy stance was neutralism, which he later attempted to promote into a neutralist camp to be a third world force
between the socialist and capitalist camps. Tito never abandoned his
belief that Russia was basically a force for world peace, but he also
realized that Russia was a threat to the national integrity of Yugoslavia.

The Chinese Communists, who in 1947 were fighting for their lives in
the civil war, had already experienced the upsurge of reactionary forces
in the form of an American-backed Chiang Kai-shek. But the formation
of the Cominform had little practical operational meaning for them.
They were not members of it, they were not anxious to join, and the
European Communists were not anxious to have them. The Chinese
Communists, perfectly logically, supported Moscow in its split with
Yugoslavia. Tito's defection from the socialist camp weakened the Soviet
Union, which was bad for world peace and for the cause of communism
everywhere. But until Mao Tse-tung went to Moscow in December 1949,
there was no indication that the Chinese Communists sought any relationship with the Soviet Union other than ideological. The Cominform
was a European body closely linked to Russian foreign policy interests.
Thus, there was no conceivable reason for Chinese Communist membership. Moreover, Stalin was still suspicious of the Chinese Communists,
having once derogatorily called them "red outside, white inside." That
they were revolutionaries was obvious, but whether they could be
counted on to subject themselves to international communist discipline
was highly dubious.

The one overriding issue that bound communists and progressives
together throughout the world was *peace*. As communists were excluded
from governments, progressives purged, and anticommunism became
shriller and shriller, the only effective counterforce was some form of
mass movement. Communists saw their principal role in mobilizing as
broad a spectrum of the left as possible to put pressure on the centrists in
government to deter them from new provocations against world peace.
Anticommunists naturally saw "peace" as a cryptocommunist trick to
prevent the free world from defending itself against communist attack
and subversion. No Comintern was necessary to direct such a movement,
for it flowed naturally out of the communist world view. All the little
people in the world wanted peace, but peace also was a deadly enemy of
capitalism. Peace now would sooner or later bring on the revolution.
Naturally, communists dreaded nothing so much as ultraleft extremists
("Trotskyists") preaching violent seizure of power and quoting Lenin to
that effect, thereby alienating the progressives. Armed revolution was
acceptable and noble in distant, backward countries like China, which
were ruled by feudal reactionaries. But in the capitalist West, ultraleftism
was bitterly denounced by communists.

The Chinese Communists were active participants in the world peace movement and were warmly welcomed by the Russians and all other communists. But in the peace movement, no hard-and-fast distinctions were made between communists and progressives, so that it never was clear into which category the Chinese Communists fitted. The civil war then raging in China was an internal matter for the Chinese themselves, irrelevant to the larger matter of world peace. Peace meant peace among the great powers, chiefly America and Russia.

In his interview with Anna Louise Strong, Mao Tse-tung expressed doubt that America would launch a direct attack against Russia. Rather, he saw a process by which "reactionary factions" in America would try to gain as much control as they could over peripheral lands: by setting up military bases, turning countries into American satellites, bringing Great Britain and Western Europe under their domination. He also saw the anti-Soviet campaign in America as a pretext for these reactionary forces to suppress the American working class and other democratic elements. But, Mao felt, the more the American reactionaries extended their sway, the more opposition would be aroused against America, making it less and less likely to be in a position to strike against Russia. Mao regarded American-occupied Japan and South Korea as in the same category as "Kuomintang-controlled China," but just as his basic optimism about the future of the revolution in China allowed him to envision a time when China would shake both Chiang's rule and American domination, so, Mao implied, the peoples of other American-occupied territories would rise up and throw off their shackles.

Already in the 1946 interview, one can see the elements of what later were to become basic Chinese policies for facing imperialist threat: resist and do not compromise. Resistance will lead to a situation where, as Mao said to Anna Louise Strong, "one day the American reactionaries will discover that the peoples of the entire world will be arrayed against them." If the Soviet Union, communists, progressives, and oppressed peoples throughout the world resist American encroachment, then the inherent contradictions within American capitalist society will intensify. As the reactionaries and imperialists shrink back, progressive and centrist forces will gain in strength, turning the pendulum once again toward peace. Mao's conviction that imperialism and all reactionaries are paper tigers was not very different from the general communist view that capitalism always stood on the brink of collapse which it sought to stave off through foreign imperialist ventures, external aggression, and internal repression of progressive forces.

AMERICA: THE NEW COMMON ENEMY

The fact that communists throughout the world shared the same world view did not in itself imply active formal relations between them. However, as that world view began to focus on America as an increasingly implacable foe of the Soviet Union and all communists, they came to have a common concrete enemy. All communist parties were organized on a national basis and their natural enemies were the capitalist, reactionary, and feudal forces within their own countries. Each revolutionary struggle was, therefore, particular and different from the others. Ever since 1927, Mao had fought the Comintern on this issue, and Stalin's final abolition of the Comintern elicited no cries of regret from the Chinese Communists. But the appearance of a common external enemy which interfered in the internal revolutionary struggle changed the character of that struggle. This was the case with Japanese aggression against China in the mid-1930s. But in World War II, Imperial Japan did not become an enemy of the Soviet Union until the very last days of the war. Therefore, there were no concrete grounds for envisaging practical relations between the Chinese and Russian Communists for a common war against Japan. But in the late 1940s, America began to emerge as the common enemy, threatening Russia with atomic attack, feverishly building up anti-Soviet power in Europe, and actively intervening in the Chinese civil war by supporting Chiang Kai-shek.

One has to be unaware of the entire history of Chinese communism to believe that Mao Tse-tung would have eagerly rushed into an alliance with the Soviet Union as soon as he became convinced that Chinese communism faced an external enemy, America, committed to its destruction. Mao had gone through years of bitter power struggle within the Chinese Communist party. The experience of the United Front with the Kuomintang, which, despite all its difficulties, the Communists regarded as the correct line, had taught Mao that collaboration with a political force external to the Communist party was difficult, tricky, and dangerous. He well knew the history of comparable power struggles within the Soviet Communist party, the Comintern, and the international movement in general. What made communists what they were was their belief in the larger forces of world history and of the peoples of their own society. Power struggles were painful, but they were epiphenomenal. Nevertheless, Mao's own experience had taught him that the best course for communist parties was to retain their autonomy and integrity so as to keep the lines of policy, command, and coordination as clean as possible.

By the summer of 1949, the fear of a Russian-American war, which had risen in 1947 and 1948, began to wane. The Berlin blockade ended in May 1949, thus removing the fuse from Europe's most dangerous powder keg. American and Russian troops had pulled completely out of Korea. Most important so far as China was concerned, America was making some signs of wanting to accommodate itself to the new power emerging in China. True, the NATO treaty had been formally signed in April, which the Russians denounced as another step in the search by the Anglo-American bloc for world domination. The communist world view did not shift back to its hopeful stance of the immediate postwar period, and the sense of an America being pushed more and more to the right by reactionary forces remained strong. But the urgency had gone out of the situation. Thus, there was no pressing need for the Chinese Communists to rush headlong into an alliance with Russia. Nor was there any pressing reason for Stalin to deviate from his practical foreign policy interests in Europe and to undertake an activist foreign policy in Asia.

I argued earlier that the explosion of the Russian atomic bomb announced by President Truman on September 23 created a chain reaction in the Western Pacific which led to Chiang Kai-shek's resumption of power on Taiwan. It also produced a chain reaction in Western Europe which, by the end of 1949, appeared to be leading directly to German rearmament. Regardless of how much the State Department denied any intent to rearm Germany, a rash of articles appeared in the Western press advocating rearmament or implying that it was coming anyway. Konrad Adenauer made statements that true German sovereignty was not conceivable without some participation in European defense. It was also in the fall of 1949 that the issue of American bases in fascist Spain first arose. To the embarrassment of the State Department, high-ranking officials of the United States Navy visited with Franco, while in America itself right-wing forces mounted a sizable press campaign to have Spain readmitted to the councils of free nations. Britain and France were opposed to any dealings with the Franco regime. Britain's socialist government, which tried to outdo America in its anticommunism and opposition to Russia, could not afford to be accused of moving toward the right. The Laborite position was that they were resolutely opposed to totalitarians of the left and the right, and that democratic socialism was the only true ideology combining progress, growth, and freedom. The French government, facing a strong left, both communist and socialist, was in the same predicament as London. The United States Navy, on the other hand, was interested in building a new Atlantic-Mediterranean role for itself independent of the British fleet. American naval forces were already independently based at Leghorn (Livorno) and Naples, but all other potential naval bases in the Mediterranean were held either by the British or the French. Spain not only had a long coast on the northern

Mediterranean, but held a strip on the southern Mediterranean in Spanish Morocco. With its conservative predispositions, the United States Navy naturally had no objections to dealing with Franco, the erstwhile friend of Hitler and Mussolini, just as it welcomed collaboration with Chiang Kai-shek in the Far East.

From a purely military point of view, the NATO decision to raise some forty-five to fifty divisions in Western Europe made sense in view of what many expected to be an eventual breaking of the American nuclear monopoly by the Russians. But predictions of when that breakthrough would occur ranged from early in 1951 to a more probable date of 1954.[3] Until then, America's atomic power was regarded as a stable deterrent against Russia's ground forces. But once the American atomic monopoly was broken, Western Europe would have to mount conventional forces comparable to Russia's. Logically, West Germany's population of fifty million offered a tempting source for a great part of the newly needed ground combat forces. Moreover, the Germans were a people of demonstrable military talents, unlike the French and Italians. Politically, of course, any thought of German rearmament was extremely difficult to sell to the nations of Western Europe, who only a short time before had experienced German aggression and oppression. The fact that America did not officially advocate this until after the outbreak of the Korean War did not prevent the Russians from seeing the current of pressures for German rearmament mushrooming upward among right-wing forces within the United States. The emerging Spanish-American rapprochement coming at exactly the same time as intensifying talk about German rearmament convinced them that, once again, the tide of reaction was running high in America.

Until the fall of 1949, Stalin's world view and his practical foreign affairs did not intersect. Even if, contrary to immediate postwar thinking, American reactionaries were much more powerful than he had thought, the practical implications of that phenomenon were not yet clear. Contradictions between, among, and within capitalist countries were something Stalin had always emphasized, and he was confident that they would continue to rage and erupt. If he remained flexible, there were always ways he could use these contradictions to Russia's advantage.

Even through the Berlin blockade, the German problem remained an American-Russian problem or, at most, a four-power problem. In Stalin's eyes, America was feverishly building its power in Western Europe. As a Marxist, Stalin was a realist who believed that countries made war for practical reasons and interests. The revival of Western Europe was vital for American and world capitalism, so that it was not surprising

[3] D. F. Fleming, *The Cold War and Its Origins*, vol. 1, p. 521.

that the Americans, under the guise of anticommunism, were pouring in men and resources in order to turn it into an American protectorate. The Americans wanted to control Western Europe for reasons comparable to Stalin's for wanting to control Eastern Europe, and while that portended unending friction, it did not necessarily mean war. There are good grounds for believing that Stalin genuinely wanted international control of atomic power, that he basically was not opposed to trade with the West and even credits, and that he desired perpetuation of four-power control over Germany. But when he saw that that was not in the cards, he proceeded to do exactly what the Americans did: develop his own atomic bombs, foster his own trading bloc in Eastern Europe and build up East Germany into a state similar to the emerging West German Federal Republic. If the Americans wanted to build a wall of containment around Russia, a line separating the two camps which neither would violate, Russia was quite prepared to accept the Iron Curtain. Stalin had no interest in revolutions external to the sphere of Russian interests. In any case, peace, not revolution, was the principal international progressive issue of the day.

The prospect of German rearmament in the fall of 1949 changed everything for Stalin. Theoretical world view and practical foreign policies now intersected. The world view made Stalin see these tentative proposals for German rearmament as the small beginning of a current that would eventually lead to a full fascist revival in the West. His dramatic turn toward Asia, evident in the conclusion of the alliance with China, cannot be disassociated from this. But during the 1930s, Stalin had faced two enemies, not one. While Germany was the greatest threat, Japan presented a considerable danger in the east. Every Russian remembers the shock to Russian society of Tsarist Russia's defeat at the hands of the Japanese in 1904–1905. If the Kwantung army had swept out of its Manchurian bases to occupy the Russian far east in the mid and late 1930s, Stalin's Russia would have been dealt a severe blow, which could have tempted Hitler to strike in the west or even aroused a revolt within Russia itself. Stalin's politics toward Japan are only dimly known. We know that in the spring of 1939, Russia and Japan fought a small-scale war on their common borders. As it happens, the Japanese were soundly trounced. A year before, Stalin had purged Russia's top military leaders, Tukhachevsky and Bluecer. Bluecher had been Soviet Far Eastern commander until his purge, and was responsible for defense against possible Japanese attack. No Russian military commander, remembering Tsarism's disdain of Japanese military prowess at the turn of the century, would have thought lightly of provoking the Japanese. It is possible that Bluecher was purged because he opposed such military adventurism against the Japanese, and that Stalin was determined to deal them a heavy blow so that he could then conclude a pact with Japan. If that was so, history showed Stalin to have been correct, because Japan did conclude a nonaggression pact with Russia which it respected.

While some American circles, by the fall of 1949, talked about Japanese rearmament, Article 9 of the "MacArthur Constitution" prohibited Japan from ever again building up a regular military force. Moreover, unlike West Germany, where the 1948 currency reform had rekindled the economy, Japan remained in economic paralysis, made worse by severe deflationary policies. Nevertheless, it was a nation of 100 million literate and skilled people who could someday again provide the manpower and resources for major military actions in East Asia. This long-range estimation of Japan's eventual military potential undoubtedly played some part in the Sino-Soviet alliance which was expressly aimed only against Japan. The conventional explanation for labeling Japan the target of the alliance is that Stalin did not want to commit himself too directly to the defense of China from an attack by America, then China's only conceivable major external enemy. While that explanation is partly correct, it overlooks the fact that both the Russian and the Chinese Communists could easily foresee a time when Japan would tread the same path that West Germany already appeared to be on. Stalin, like Mao Tse-tung, believed that his country could not risk facing enemies on two fronts. There is no reason not to believe that the Sino-Soviet alliance, among other things, was indeed directed against an eventually rearmed Japan. But Japan was not the major issue that prompted Stalin to enter into the alliance or what was uppermost in Mao Tse-tung's mind when he went to Moscow to conclude it.

CHINA: GOLDEN OPPORTUNITY FOR STALIN

The most plausible explanation for Stalin's turn eastward is that the victory of the Chinese Revolution presented an unexpected golden opportunity. The Russian ambassador followed Chiang Kai-shek to Canton, but Moscow quickly rectified that error by recognizing the new People's Republic of China two days after its official formation. The thinking that led Stalin to accord such rapid recognition to Peking may be revealed by another event of diplomatic recognition which occurred only a few months later. On January 18, 1950, Peking recognized the Democratic Republic of Vietnam, and on January 30, Moscow followed suit. With China in the socialist camp, Russian influence now extended deep into East Asia. It was probably not so much the purely Asian aspect of these new facts of power politics that interested Stalin, but that the Western imperialist and colonialist powers had major interests in East Asia which they were struggling to hold on to.

Britain held Hong Kong and Portugal (a member of the newly formed NATO) held Macao, colonies that certainly would be threatened by the new revolutionary China. The British were also then embroiled in a bloody counterrevolutionary war in Malaya against Communists whose leader Chin Peng (in Mandarin, Ch'en P'ing) and whose overwhelming membership were Chinese. Huks were still dangerously active in the Philippines. The Dutch, under intense American pressure, had sur-rendered Indonesia, but pro-Dutch and reactionary guerrillas (like the Dâr-ul-Islâm) were fighting the new republic. And, most important, the French were fighting a bitter colonial war against the Viet Minh, a political formation not so different, in Russian eyes, from the Chinese Communists.

Stalin, as Adam Ulam has pointed out, strongly believed in the possi-bilities of exploiting contradictions within the capitalist camp to Russia's advantage.[4] World War II proved to him that these contradictions were so intense that rather than getting together to destroy the socialist Soviet Union, the capitalist powers fought each other in a war of incredible ferocity. As American policy became increasingly anti-Soviet after World War II, Stalin believed that these contradictions could again be exploited. America might look with equanimity on German rearmament, but Britain, France, and other West European countries who had suf-fered terribly at German hands would be bitterly opposed. Britain, France, Holland, and Portugal also had important colonial interests in East Asia which were threatened on the left by revolutionary movements and on the right by an American takeover. How could a practical realist like Stalin explain American pressure on Holland to relinquish Indonesia other than by the notion that American monopoly capitalist interests sought to displace those of Holland? The Indonesian archipelago was rich in raw materials, particularly oil, which the Americans were avid to acquire for purposes of military stockpiling as well as economic exploita-tion. Washington only gave major support to France's struggle in Indo-china after the outbreak of the Korean War in June 1950. Before then, Franklin Roosevelt's suggestion that the French abandon Indochina still seemed to be official American policy. And was it not Roosevelt, also, who suggested to a furious Churchill that the British return Hong Kong to China?

Immediately after 1945, the greatest threat to European colonial rule had come from America. But the European powers, ravaged by war and abjectly dependent on America, had no other choice than to acquiesce and relinquish their colonies one after the other. Revolution from the left posed a new threat, while also creating new opportunities. Britain and France, in return for concessions from their anticolonial foes brought

---

[4] Adam Ulam, *Expansion and Co-existence*, p. 501.

about by the power and influence of the Soviet Union, might reciprocate by maintaining a hard stance against German rearmament in Europe. Before 1949, Russia had no power and little influence in East Asia, save in North Korea and possibly liberated Manchuria. But alliance with the new China would change that completely. China had a common border with Vietnam, and the Viet Minh had originated in China. Chinese were fighting in Malaya. Overseas Chinese interests gave China potential access to every corner of the vast territories and islands of Southeast Asia. And, of course, hostile relations of potentially major scope were arising between the new People's Republic and America.

Such Europe-for-Asia trade-offs were possibly already in Stalin's mind when he concluded the alliance with China. During the final phases of the Geneva negotiations on Indochina in 1954, French renunciation of the American-sponsored European Defense Community (EDC), in which a new German army would have played a major role, prompted Moscow (and Peking) to pressure Ho Chi Minh to accept the "provisional" demarcation line at the 17th parallel. Although the Americans quickly became the chief beneficiaries of this through Ngo Dinh Diem, in the summer of 1954 it appeared as if partition had left the French time to consolidate their not inconsiderable economic, cultural, and residual military presence in South Vietnam, Cambodia, and Laos. Vietnamese and Chinese retain bitter memories of the 1954 Geneva Accords. They paid in blood, sweat, and tears for Moscow's gains on the European front, while Moscow argued that the greater cause of world peace had been served.

Stalin's turn eastward suggests that alliance with China was a means to an end that he had pursued ever since the rise of Nazism in Germany —assuring Russia's national security against any repetition of a land invasion such as Napoleon had carried out, the Germans had done to some extent in World War I, and finally Hitler's, which came close to destroying the Soviet Union entirely. Neither Tsarist nor Soviet Russia had overriding national interests in the Far East that would have made alliance with China as natural as, for example, American alliance with Britain or the countries of Western Europe. Nor did Stalin's world view make such an alliance natural. That their common "communist" character automatically made Russian and Chinese Communists divisions of the grand army of international communism was ludicrous to Stalin.

There was much of practical value that Russia could gain from alliance with China, and there did not appear to be much danger for Russia in terms of great power relations. Washington could do nothing concrete about the new alliance except protest. If it reciprocated by intensifying its campaign to rearm Germany, Stalin could argue that the Americans had already decided to embark on this dangerous course and that Russia's main hope was that the other European capitalist powers, chiefly Britain and France, would throw a monkey wrench into the American plans. But there was a risk of another kind in the alliance, which was to shape the character of Sino-Soviet relations until after the death of Stalin. By the fall of 1949, Stalin realized that his attempt to topple Tito from within had failed. Many Westerners were already speculating about the Titoist possibilities in Chinese Communism, and Stalin's suspicious, cautious, and pessimistic character certainly must have recognized that these strange guerrillas who called themselves communist were under no Soviet control whatsoever. Relations with the Chinese Communists had been amicable because there were no relations. If Stalin allied himself with Mao Tse-tung, and some years later Mao decided to break with Russia as Tito had done, the blow to Russian prestige and influence could be devastating. The two months of arduous negotiations that Mao and Stalin carried on in Moscow between December 1949 and early February 1950 are evidence of the fact that neither side entered the alliance lightly.

As a result of the Sino-Soviet alliance and the Korean War, which erupted less than six months later, Russia acquired a degree of power, influence, and prestige in China that no one would have predicted in 1949—except some extreme anticommunists who saw it as a natural manifestation of the International Communist Conspiracy. Russian political, military, and economic advisers began to pour into China; all of the rapidly emerging new institutions of the People's Republic of China were borrowed virtually directly from the Soviet Union; Russia became the chief weapons supplier to the Chinese armed forces. While Stalin undertook a sizable effort to help China to industrialize, this focused almost exclusively on Manchuria, which the Chinese in early 1955 claimed had turned into an "independent kingdom" under the rule of the antiparty element Kao Kang. Western, chiefly American, China experts, who had earlier argued that the Chinese Communists were "agrarian reformers," were appalled by the mounting evidence that China was turning into a new Soviet Union. Yet one cannot fault them for not having predicted this train of development. Little in the Yenan experience of the Chinese Communists foretold the emergence of a Soviet China so soon after the Liberation. The Yenan period had been one of flexible methods, democratic spirit, and a cautious approach to problems. True, in his typical way, when Mao felt that the moment of crisis and opportunity had come, he gambled big. In 1946, when the civil war erupted again, he suddenly went back to radical agrarian revolution and once again helped to bring about the kind of upheaval on the land that occurred after 1927. But radical agrarian revolution had eventually shown itself to be a two-edged sword—it helped the new Communist forces to establish themselves in central China but was not conducive to building new and lasting organization. Obviously, the gamble was necessary in 1946, for Chiang Kai-shek felt confident that with American help he could finally achieve his decades-old dream of killing off every Communist in China. But even before the Communists had won the civil war, Mao urged an end to the revolutionary violence on the land, and by mid-1949, land reform was carried out in more orderly and less violent ways. While one could say that Mao Tse-tung understood agrarian China, neither he nor many other Chinese Communists could pretend to understand that vast extent of modern urban China centering on Manchuria and Shanghai. Why did the Chinese Communists not adopt a more cautious approach upon final liberation, feel their way into this new situation, and, when they had achieved the confidence of experience, launch some decisive new policies? Why did they, and Mao Tse-tung, make this seemingly rash decision to turn China into a new Soviet Union, and in the process allow it to fall under powerful Soviet influence?

WHY CHINA TURNED TOWARD RUSSIA

Mao Tse-tung, who never before had left China, traveled to Moscow by train, spent two months there, and returned by train. The widely publicized photographs of Stalin and Mao together fully expressed the depth and power of the new alliance that had been concluded. If the specter of German rearmament conjured up a sense of crisis for Stalin, the liberation of China was but an opportunity to be exploited. For Mao Tse-tung, alliance with Russia had to be motivated by something far more than opportunity. Mao shared Stalin's caution in exploiting opportunities, moving all his pieces carefully so that when the decisive moment came, he could act with near-certainty of success. In the entire history of his leadership of the Chinese Communist party, only a sense of crisis ever impelled him to make radical moves or take big risks. Defeat in 1927 impelled him to launch an agrarian revolution. Impending defeat in 1934 impelled him to gamble on the Long March. Fratricidal strife within the party during the Long March pushed him to abandon his natural conciliatory character and take supreme command, which he did at the mid-March party conferences of Mao-erh-kai and Tsun-i. Crisis in 1946 led Mao once again to resort to radical agrarian revolution. But what was the crisis in 1949, when liberated Chinese were dancing the joyous *yang-ko* in the streets?

From the summer of 1949, Kuomintang warships and planes began a blockade of the China coast. In September, Washington turned over more warships to Chiang's regime to serve only one purpose—blockading Mainland China. Kuomintang planes began to bomb coastal Chinese cities, causing large loss of life and damage to property. When Chiang resurrected his regime on Taiwan in early December 1949, the blockade and bombing of China appeared to be becoming permanent. For behind Chiang, whose power had been shattered, stood the United States, and particularly the Seventh Fleet then still commanded by Admiral Radford, a man of virulent hostility to Chinese communism. In the late 1940s, China was extremely vulnerable to the effects of blockade. Virtually all its great cities from southern Manchuria down to Kwangtung are on the coast. Western and Japanese colonial presence had led to a vast increase in trade and a huge increase in population. The surrounding agricultural lands, including the fertile Yangtze River valley, were incapable of feeding the entire population. Thus, the coastal cities came increasingly to rely on food imports from abroad. When trade broke down in the aftermath of World War II, the United Nations Relief and Rehabilitation Administration (UNRRA) rushed in with food aid, which, despite the corruption, helped to prevent starvation in those cities. The food situation worsened as the civil war intensified, but never became disastrous, for foreign trade continued to bring in food. The cities earned their foreign exchange partly by manufacturing the products that were exported but mainly as entrepôts for Inland China goods. This was the famous comprador economy so widely described in Chinese and foreign literature. The compradors were the middlemen between Inland China, whose farms and mines they well knew, and the distant foreign markets, whose agents resided in Shanghai and other cities. Thus, in a sense, all the coastal cities of China were comprador cities whose link to the larger world market was vital for their survival. To cut them off from foreign trade altogether and at the same time to subject them to aerial and naval bombardment was an act of war against a whole population.

Chiang Kai-shek already had experience in blockades against his Communist enemies. Despite a formal united front against the Japanese, he maintained a blockade against the liberated areas. But since these were all peasant regions, the blockade was mainly an inconvenience. Blockading the coastal cities was another matter. Chiang Kai-shek, whose greed for power was the dominant passion in his life, had no scruples about this. If the people of the cities were starving, then perhaps they would revolt and welcome him back, for with the Kuomintang, the foreign freighters would return. After World War I, Britain was bitterly denounced for continuing its blockade of Germany. The British, who were morally outraged by unrestricted German submarine war, were now showing themselves to be as cruel as the Germans. American pressure finally induced them to return to civilized conduct. In 1949, anticommunism was already so virulent in America that protests against the barbarism of Chiang's blockade were muted and the public never understood that its real purpose was to create mass starvation. The later American trade embargo against China (like the even later one against Cuba) had the same aim—if economic chaos could be produced in the cities, then the Communists could possibly be overthrown by revolts from within.

In his farewell letter to Leighton Stuart, the last American ambassador to China, Mao cried out: "Blockade! Let the blockade go on eight or ten years, and still all the problems of China will be resolved. The Chinese people do not fear death, so why should they fear difficulties? Lao Tzu once said: 'The people do not fear death, so why should death frighten them?' American imperialism and their running dogs the Chiang Kai-shek reactionaries are not only trying to 'frighten us with death,' but they are trying to make us die."[5]

Even at the time, the Communists' protestations that they truly wanted a coalition government in Nanking were ridiculed. Why should they want a coalition government when China was theirs for the taking? The reason was obvious. A coalition government would assure that China's lifeline to foreign markets and foreign countries remained open. The Chinese Communists had no experience whatsoever in administering cities. Mao had always argued that the "national bourgeoisie" had a major role to play in the Chinese Revolution. This was the entrepreneurial and business class of the coastal cities whose role was vital in the economic life of those cities. Imagine, for example, a Chinese Communist takeover of Hong Kong, a total blockade imposed on it, and revolutionary destruction of its business class. The result would be instantaneous economic paralysis with over three million mouths to feed from Inland China sources. In 1949, China's urban population was already not far from the hundred million mark. The problem of handling such a vast population under conditions of a complete cutoff of external trade was staggering, to put it most mildly. A coalition government in 1949 would have meant, practically, that the "liberals" would have continued to be a powerful administrative force in the cities. The Communists, of course, would have controlled the army and dominated the capital, Peking. If socialism, that is, nationalization of property, had been introduced, it would have been a long process, depending on how rapidly the Communists gained experience in handling the problems of the world's most populous country. Coalition government was a practical solution to the challenges facing the Chinese Communists, one that accorded with their own interests and ideology.

What were the Chinese Communists to make of the little hints Ache-

[5] Mao Tse-tung, "Farewell Leighton Stuart!" in *Selected Works of Mao Tse-tung*, 4 vols., Chinese edition, trans. Franz Schurmann (Peking, 1960), vol. 4, p. 1500.

son was throwing out about eventual recognition, compared to the real, concrete, and hostile fact of a Kuomintang blockade actively aided and abetted by a slew of "private" advisers around Chiang Kai-shek like Chennault and Admiral Cooke, whose links to American Air Force and Navy circles remained strong? Had not the Tokyo government in the 1930s constantly protested its desire for peaceful relations with China while its military men, both army and navy, were inflicting depredations? On June 30, 1949, Mao Tse-tung issued an article on the "People's Democratic Dictatorship" which, as Tang Tsou notes, had a "sobering effect" on official thinking in Washington, which was hoping for Chinese Titoism.[6] Mao stated flatly that China would lean to one side (the Soviet Union) and never to the other (imperialism), and that there was no sitting on the fence, no third road. But he also said that "we must trade," and to the question of aid from the British and American governments, he responded that "it was still too early to think about that." Mao repeatedly invoked the name of Sun Yat-sen and his contrasting experiences with Russia on the one hand and the imperialists on the other: "Sun Yat-sen had plenty of experience, and suffered for it, and was taken in. We should remember Sun's words and never again be taken in. Internationally, we belong to the anti-imperialist front headed by the Soviet Union. It is only there that we can seek truly friendly help, and not look to the imperialist front."

In the Washington White Paper, which was issued a short time later, Acheson appeared to be saying to the Chinese Communists: First break with Russia and then perhaps we can have relations. Even if there had been no Kuomintang blockade, the slightest consideration of such an offer would have seemed ludicrous, repulsive, and dangerous to the Chinese Communists. Even if Russia had not been much help during the revolution, it had never done them any harm compared to the imperialists. Moreover, the Communists' world view taught without reservation that Russia genuinely desired and sought peace, and that all the new troublemaking came from imperialists and reactionaries.

If there was absolutely no chance that the new government in China could be recruited for America's new containment schemes, there was also no hint in any of Mao's writings at the time of a hard-and-fast alliance with Russia. Mao was prepared to seek "foreign aid" first from Russia rather than from Britain and America, but he also wanted to continue trading with any and all foreign powers. His message to the British and the Americans was blunt: You have done us much harm over the past hundred years, but if you now show by your actions that you truly want good relations with us, then we are prepared to explore

[6] Tang Tsou, *America's Failure in China*, pp. 504–506.

avenues of friendship and cooperation. But under no circumstances could such friendship be based on an anti-Soviet Titoism.

On September 28, 1949, Congress passed a new military assistance bill with seventy-five million dollars for China, and some American warships were turned over to the Chinese Nationalists. On December 8, Chiang Kai-shek restored Kuomintang power on Taiwan. Washington's response, in Mao's eyes, was crystal clear—militarily it was pumping new weapons, particularly ships and planes, into Chiang's arsenal and politically it had surreptitiously encouraged him to establish a rump regime on Taiwan. Mao had always regarded America as the main prop behind Chiang, and he saw Chiang's quitting the presidency as a sign not only that his position in China was deteriorating but that American support was beginning to ebb, as was indeed the case. But the dramatic re-establishment of the Kuomintang regime on Taiwan meant only one thing: while Acheson was making vaguely friendly noises, the iron hand of American imperialism was recommitting itself to the Chinese civil war. China would never again be "taken in" by such duplicity.

Little is known about the internal debates within the Chinese Communist party at this time, and little new has been revealed by the documents coming out of the Cultural Revolution. It is possible that the military victory that united China for the first time since 1911 could easily have led to a new political pluralism in which a variety of independent communist kingdoms would have sprouted throughout China, albeit under some formal unity centered on Peking. Warlordism was too recent a memory for the Chinese to exclude that possibility. The Chinese Communist field armies were closely identified with certain commanders, giving them a powerful source of political influence at the highest reaches of the leadership. Twenty-two years of war from 1927 to 1949 had been a unifying factor, but would unity prevail under peacetime conditions? Moreover, the Chinese Communist party, for all its glorious heroism, was still not in a position, organizationally and ideologically, to govern a country so vast as China. Revolutionary excesses during the land reform had forced the leadership to crack down from above. In the urban areas, the party was a tightly knit underground structure, effective but not numerous. Liu Shao-ch'i, the theorist of Leninist organization, commanded the urban segment of the Chinese Communist party and gave it the elitist character for which he would be bitterly attacked during the Cultural Revolution of the mid-1960s. If one adds to all these elements making for potential disunity the sudden and unexpected victory, which brought the Communists a vast range of responsibilities for which they were virtually unprepared, then it is not difficult to see why in the fall of 1949 Chairman Mao Tse-tung saw the victory of Liberation as a situation of crisis.

From all his writings until 1949, it is clear that Mao had a clear conception of Chinese communism's assumption of power, for which a coalition government was essential. Mao, like most other Chinese intellectuals, both communist and progressive, regarded China as a kind of dual society—"half-feudal, half-colonial." Half of China, the great inland rural regions, was still caught in a backward premodern social system based on landlordism and attendant feudal relations. The other half, urban and coastal China, had already been refashioned into a modern social system under the impetus of imperialism and colonialism. Two decades of experience had shown the Communists that their power resided in Inland China, where the combination of peasants and soldiers had created an extraordinarily dynamic new social system. No coalition government could ever have induced Mao to compromise on those "base areas." But no conceivable coalition government was ever in a position to make such a demand. Yet even as the Kuomintang was sinking in the mire of defeat, Mao Tse-tung continued to press vigorously for a coalition government, and negotiations between the Communists and Li Tsung-jen, Chiang Kai-shek's interim successor as president, continued well into 1949. A coalition government would have best served Mao's political goals, both domestic and international. Domestically, the liberated areas of Inland China would have remained intact under the political leadership that had evolved since the days of the Long March. In the urban regions, the new Kuomintang, freed from Chiang's reactionary power, would have carried on administration in alliance with Mao's forces.

It is tempting to try to trace Liu Shao-ch'i's downfall during the Cultural Revolution to a longtime antagonism between him and Mao, as indeed was done at the time. Whether or not there was a fundamental conflict between the two leaders is difficult to say, but certainly the issues that each represented indicated conflicting options. Liu, as the leader of the underground Communist movement in the cities and the white regions, had a much more orthodox approach to organization than Mao. Obviously, the easygoing life style of the liberated territories, which so impressed foreign visitors, could not be practiced in the cities where Tai Li's Gestapo was ready to kill every Communist it found. In 1949 and even after final Liberation in 1950, there was widespread debate in China about whether the underground party should go public (*"kung-k'ai ch'i-lai"*). To go public was to assume leadership positions in the new organizations and institutions that were sprouting up after Liberation, which obviously an underground group could not do. The debate suggests a conflict within the leadership as to who should "seize power," to use a phrase from the Cultural Revolution. Not only did the underground party eventually go public, but the entire Chinese Communist party was transformed. It was construed to be the party of the working class, and the way was cleared for thousands of urban workers and intellectuals to enter it. Literacy was made a necessary criterion for party membership, which rapidly led to the expulsion of thousands of peasant liberation army cadres who had fought heroically during the wars but were deemed unfit for leadership during a period of socialist construction. The Communist party that "seized power" in the cities in 1949 and 1950 was more Liu's than Mao's.

But with the collapse of any hope for a coalition government, there was no meaningful alternative for the Communists but to take over all power in the cities. Chiang Kai-shek's flight to Taiwan and resumption of the civil war with "private" American backing quickly led to the emigration of two million people to Taiwan, most of whom were exactly the urban bourgeois elements that, under a coalition government, would have administered the country. Li Tsung-jen, despite his formal hold on the presidency of China, had shown himself completely powerless in the face of Chiang Kai-shek, who still controlled the armies and monies, and had the vital links to American support.

Thus, in the fall of 1949, liberated China faced a dual crisis: one coming from the blockade and air raids which threatened urban China with chaos and starvation, the other from dangerous conflict within the leadership arising from a fundamental failure of policy. By then, it was apparent that the general line for the liberation of China that Mao had pursued with such stunning success had failed in its final stages. The people's Liberation Army had achieved a victory that even the wildest optimists had not dared to predict in 1946. It is completely consistent with Mao Tse-tung's writings and actions before and after 1946 to believe that it was he who took the daring gamble in 1946 of radical land reform, retreat to the hills, and all-out military struggle against Chiang Kai-shek. During the Cultural Revolution, it was alleged that Liu Shao-ch'i had advised caution in 1946, when Mao's policies of "daring to rebel" were proved to be historically correct. Liu always was a more orthodox communist than Mao, and, like Stalin, may have counseled a steady build-up in preference to an all-out struggle with its risks of defeat. But whatever the case, Mao's policies prevailed. The other side of the coin of Mao's radical domestic policies, however, was his vision of a liberated China which would remain divided into two zones until the conditions for socialism were ripe in the cities. In theory, the question of a coalition government should have been independent of any external involvement. That, of course, meant America. If the Americans ceased supporting Chiang Kai-shek, then defeat would leave the Kuomintang no alternative for survival but some sort of compromise with the Communists serving Mao's interests as much as those of the remnant Kuomintang. That other aspect of Mao's vision, the formation of a coalition government to bring China into the transitional stage of a "New Democracy" or a "People's Democratic Dictatorship" based on an alliance of the working class, the peasantry, and the urban petite bourgeoisie, was wrecked by American imperialism's renewed interference, into China's internal affairs in 1949.

I have now laid out what I believe to have been the situation out of which the Sino-Soviet alliance of February 1950 grew. While Stalin began to sense growing crisis in Europe from the specter of German rearmament, China presented a golden opportunity to increase Russian power and influence in East Asia, where Western imperialism and colonialism had major interests. For Mao Tse-tung, Stalin's Russia was the only external hope he had to face the dual crisis of blockade and growing strife within the leadership. If China's trade lifelines abroad were to be cut, Russia was the only possible source of economic aid. If American military might, warships and planes, were to be committed to the "defense of Formosa," then China would face more war and blockade for years to come. Who else but Russia could provide some deterrent force against America? Perhaps above all, alliance with Russia could have a powerful unifying effect on the Chinese Communist party, which, whatever its internal differences, held to an ideological world view in which the Soviet Union played a central role.

Mao Tse-tung personally went to Moscow and brought back the alliance with Russia. He himself bargained with Stalin, one of the hardest bargainers in the world. Mao made some painful concessions to Stalin, but in view of China's precarious situation at the time, he also brought home major Soviet commitments. The concessions are well known. The Russians were granted the right to set up special "joint corporations" in Sinkiang, were allowed to continue operation of the Central Manchurian Railroad until the end of 1952, and were granted bases at Dairen (Talien) and Port Arthur. If there were further concessions on China's part, such as a "special relationship" to the quasi-autonomous regime of Kao Kang in Manchuria, they are not known. But, whatever the skepticism of the Western press, Mao got important and tangible commitments of Russian support. Stalin agreed to loan China three hundred million American dollars, not a great deal in comparison with American foreign aid and relief grants, but it was part of a general Russian commitment to aid the industrialization of China. Ports all along the China coast were opened to Russian and Eastern European ships, which could transport cargo bought in the noncommunist world.

It was one thing for the Kuomintang to stop free world shipping to China, much of which was done by countries allied to America. It was another to stop Russian or Eastern European ships, which could involve the Americans in a confrontation with the Russians. Whatever Stalin's ulterior motives about Manchuria might have been, Russian aid to China during the remainder of his life was generous. Not only did it pour economic and industrial aid into China, but after the outbreak of the Korean War, Russia became China's main supplier of weaponry. Stalin always exacted a price for his aid, but he delivered what he promised. As the term "nuclear umbrella" became more common, the alliance was interpreted to mean a Russian guarantee to intervene with nuclear power if China was directly attacked by America. By the fall of 1950, it was clear that the Americans feared Russian intervention in the Korean War if American forces carried it to Chinese territory. Since the commitment was never tested, no one can know what exactly its nature was. But there can be no doubt that the alliance acted as a deterrent against America during the Korean War. Lastly, Mao returned to China with a striking transformation in Russia's relationship to the Chinese Communists. Whereas earlier Russia had been indifferent and lukewarm to Chinese communism, afterward it became China's most ardent supporter on the international scene, particularly in the United Nations, where it led the struggle for Chinese membership.

THE SOVIETIZATION OF CHINA

There can be no doubt that the same circumstances that produced the Sino-Soviet alliance also brought about the Sovietization of all of China. Whether or not Mao approved of the rapidity with which China was Sovietized is impossible to say, but it is clear that it worked. With an institutional wasteland and socio-economic chaos facing them on the morrow of Liberation, the Chinese Communists adopted a simple expedient: imitate the Soviet Union for any and every situation. The central government was quickly set up from scratch as a replica of the Soviet government. Key economic institutions were directly borrowed from the Russians. For example, the Chinese Communists imposed on China the Soviet system of banking, which enabled them to set up a tightly centralized but far-flung and deep-penetrating (as the Chinese say) money and credit system. Within a short time, by a combination of administrative discipline and diverting most cash flows into the banking network, the Chinese Communists broke the back of an inflation that had wracked China for decades and reached catastrophic proportions in the last years of Kuomintang rule. The party itself was remodeled along Soviet lines, with urban worker and intellectual elements dominating its membership. Heavy industry was lionized and Manchuria became China's model region. Sovietization of the armed forces began and accelerated rapidly after the outbreak of the Korean War. The only comparable instance in world history of one nation so massively importing the institutions of another is Japan after the Meiji Restoration of 1868. Japan at that time, like China in 1950, feared imminent invasion by predatory imperialist powers and saw its only possible salvation in arming itself with the spiritual, organizational, and material weapons of its enemies.

As a process, Sovietization began well before the fall of 1949. Derk Bodde had already noted in his Peking diary the signs of Sovietization in liberated Peking the previous spring. Manchuria, of course, which was under a quasi-autonomous administration, was Sovietized from the time of its liberation. Since the Soviet Union had a positive and central place in the world view of the Chinese Communists, China would have experienced considerable transformation along Soviet lines even if no Sino-Soviet alliance had been concluded in February 1950. But so long as a coalition government was still possible, as it was well into the summer of 1949, there were limits to Sovietization. There were still extensive foreign economic interests in the coastal cities which could not be nationalized if a coalition government prevailed. Bureaucratic capitalist interests, wealthy businessmen like the Soongs and the Kungs, had their property confiscated, but the property rights of the "national bourgeoisie" were to be respected. Although Sovietization proceeded rapidly in Peking and Manchuria where there were few foreign interests (all Japanese interests in Manchuria had already been nationalized by the Kuomintang), it could not proceed in the same way in Shanghai, Tientsin, Canton, and other coastal or up-river cities. What China would have been like if a coalition government had indeed come to power, Chiang Kai-shek had disappeared into American exile, and Washington, like London, had recognized the new People's Republic is impossible to say. The total Sovietization of China, for all its drawbacks, turned out to be a great success, evident in major economic achievements and the effective political unity of the country.

THE KOREAN WAR: CONTAINMENT VERSUS ROLLBACK

The outbreak of the Korean War confirmed the worst Chinese fears about American hostile intentions. On June 27, 1950, two days after battles erupted between North and South Koreans, America intervened massively in Korea and, by the fall of that year, appeared ready to carry the war to China itself. Yet, in a strange way, Truman's actions on June 27 were partly intended to reassure the Chinese that America did not plan to invade China. By interposing the Seventh Fleet in the Taiwan Straits, Truman "leashed" Chiang Kai-shek, preventing him and his backers in the United States Navy from continuing their blockade. The blockade had produced the most hostile reaction from Britain, America's chief ally. Britain's recognition of the new Peking government was largely motivated by the desire to protect its extensive interests on the China coast. British merchant ships ran the blockade, and London made clear that it would send in the British Navy to protect them if they were threatened by Kuomintang gunboats. The British knew that the highest levels of the Truman Administration, notably Acheson, were against the blockade, and were confident that neither recognition nor running the blockade would arouse a hostile reaction in official Washington. Naturally, British recognition unleashed a torrent of anti-British reaction among the American nationalists. But although reactionary and nationalist elements in the United States military, chiefly the Navy, shared this feeling, the Joint Chiefs of Staff were still dominated by Europe-oriented military men like Bradley and, unofficially, Eisenhower, who considered British cooperation vital for the defense of Europe. The interposition of the Seventh Fleet on June 27 was a triumph for containment, not for rollback nationalism. That it was not a secure one was evident in the mounting right-wing agitation in the United States to "unleash Chiang Kai-shek" and, in particular, the machinations of Douglas MacArthur.

MacArthur's widely publicized visit to Chiang Kai-shek in August 1950 was an ominous sign that the "leashing" of Chiang could soon end. MacArthur wanted Kuomintang troops to participate in the Korean fighting. While it is questionable that Kuomintang troops would have constituted much of a military gain for the United States in Korea, their participation probably would have opened the door to war between America and China. The war in Korea was formally waged not by the United States but by the United Nations, where Chinese membership would be heatedly debated until November, when Chinese "people's volunteers" entered the Korean War. Even a few Kuomintang troops in Korea would have committed the United Nations to the Chiang regime well before Chinese intervention and would have facilitated a further commitment to Chiang Kai-shek's cause. Many member nations were uneasy about UN sponsorship of the war anyway, and to have been dragged into Chiang's campaign to "counterattack the Mainland" would probably have wrecked that body. The British, in particular, were violently opposed to any venture against China. Not until MacArthur's purge in April 1951 did the threat of a larger war against China diminish. Like what was to happen in Vietnam, the policy decision in Washington not to carry the war to China would not spare Korea from two more years of destructive war. But a larger war against China had been averted, which, unlike the war "limited" to Korea, would have produced a chain reaction involving far more than the danger of Russian intervention. Because of Britain's opposition, a war against China could have wrecked containment's political, military, and economic plans for Europe.

The circumstances leading to the outbreak of the Korean War on June 25, 1950, are still obscure, and only slightly less obscure are the circumstances that prompted Truman not only to intervene in Korea but to interpose the Seventh Fleet in the Taiwan Straits. The official Western version, on the basis of which Washington secured United Nations support for the war, was that North Korea attacked and tried to conquer South Korea, a case of blatant aggression. The official North Korean version, accepted by other socialist countries, was that South Korean forces invaded North Korea and were thrown back, leading to American intervention. More sophisticated Western explanations are that Stalin was trying to test American "will to resist" by attacking territory that America had not included in its defense perimeter or that he was hoping to embroil the Americans and Chinese in a war in order to ease American pressure on Europe. Aside from great power involvements in Korea, the reasons for the war are not difficult to understand. South Korea was in utter economic stagnation, guerrilla movements were active in several southern provinces, and the political structure, such as it was, was threatened with collapse just a few weeks before the war by Syngman Rhee's disastrous defeat at the polls. Conditions in North Korea were better but also difficult. Collectivization had aroused considerable peasant discontent, and Kim Il Sung's harsh rule produced much the same type of tensions as in Soviet-dominated countries of Eastern Europe. But both North and South Koreans shared one burning conviction: if they could only unite, Korea's problems could be resolved. North Korea had the industry, South Korea had the agriculture, and together they could embark on the road to economic development. The Korean peninsula has no national minorities and, despite some minor differences in dialectic, the same language is spoken everywhere and the same culture prevails. When Russian and American forces finally pulled out of Korea in 1949, the way seemed clear for the Koreans to resolve their own differences. Fighting went on constantly at the 38th parallel, and at the time of John Foster Dulles's famous visit to it just weeks before the war, tension was particularly great. Both sides were ready and eager for war.

There is no evidence to indicate that prior to June 25, 1950, Korea was a matter of particular concern to the new People's Republic of China. Nor was it much of an issue in the struggle between liberals and conservatives in America. Formosa, not Korea, was the center of heated dispute. In fact, congressional right-wingers voted against an aid-to-Korea bill on grounds that priority should go to Taiwan. The United States Navy had little interest in Korea, and the Air Force had even less.

Korea had been an Army responsibility, but with the final withdrawal of American troops in 1949, Army interest likewise ceased. MacArthur, as the new shogun of Japan, naturally was concerned with Korea, but he joined Acheson in refusing to bring it within the United States defense perimeter. Dulles's visit to Seoul just a few weeks before the war suggests that Syngman Rhee, a longtime resident of Washington and Honolulu, may have been attempting the kind of approach to the right-wing Republicans that Chiang Kai-shek had been practicing with such success. But since a "Korea Lobby" did not appear, no undue weight can be attached to the Dulles-Rhee contacts. Russia completed the triangle of great powers concerned with Korea. But here the picture is entirely obscure. Whether Stalin aided, supported, tolerated, commanded, or was entirely ignorant of Kim Il Sung's intent to grapple with South Korea probably will never be known. What seems certain, though, is that neither Stalin nor anyone else could have foreseen on June 25 the rapidity and massiveness of the American response two days later.

The nature of Truman's stroke, coming at a time when right-wing Republican attacks were mounting in fury on the Taiwan and China issues, suggests that more was involved than the simple desire to "repel communist aggression" and demonstrate America's "will to resist." The great danger, in the eyes of Truman and Acheson, was that the flare-up in Korea could link up with the Chinese civil war and drag the United States into a larger conflagration that would pose not only dangers of a confrontation with Russia but grave challenges to the Anglo-American alliance. The interposition of the fleet was a classic containment action, for it drew a line between potential combatants. Because of the growing warmth between the United States Navy and Chiang Kai-shek, Truman could never have "leashed" Chiang and the Pacific fleet at the same time if the urgency of Korea had not erupted. War on June 27 gave him power he did not have a few days before, and he used it with what one has to reckon as great genius.

The Chinese vehemently protested the interposition of the Seventh Fleet as a further indication of Washington's growing support of Chiang. Yet it also seems clear that Chinese fears of possible hostile American action arising out of the war abated somewhat. It is unlikely that they would have sent the high-ranking delegation led by Wu Hsiu-ch'üan to the United Nations to argue for membership in the fall of that year if they had believed imminent a war against them under United Nations auspices. China became alarmed only when MacArthur's troops were pushing deep into North Korea toward the sensitive Yalu River frontier. On June 27, 1950, Washington seemed to be sending what it likes to call "signals" to the Chinese, saying: Our intervention in Korea is not directed against China so long as Chinese Communist forces do not attempt to take Taiwan; in return, we will force Chiang to end the blockade and air raids against Chinese coastal cities. The Chinese "understood" those signals but were obviously "confused" when a different set began to emanate from MacArthur's actions in Korea and his autonomous politicking with Chiang Kai-shek. The facts of the Korean War are well known and need not be repeated in any detail. Chinese intervention removed the immediate military threat from the Yalu frontier and the purge of MacArthur in April 1951 signified Washington's abandonment of what appeared to be a growing rollback policy. By the summer of 1951, the Panmunjom talks had started, indicating that all three great powers involved (America, Russia, and China) had accepted the notion that the Korean War was a "limited" war. That the Korean people had to undergo two more years of suffering so that the great power understandings could be worked out was regarded by the geopoliticians as a necessary sacrifice to avoid World War III.

Whatever hesitations may still have existed in Peking over the Sino-Soviet alliance were washed away by the Korean War. America had shown itself to be a clear and present threat to China's national security, and the only source of help was Russia. Russian arms quickly poured into China, bringing about a Sovietization of the People's Liberation Army in organization as well as weaponry. P'eng Te-huai, who succeeded Lin Piao as commander of Chinese forces in Korea, fought a Russian-style war against the Americans, different from the kind the Communists had earlier fought against the Japanese and the Kuomintang. Instead of the mobile squad tactics they had used so successfully during the civil war, the Chinese used "human wave" assaults, which had been a major Russian tactic in both world wars. Russian advisers were placed at all echelons of the Chinese armed forces. Russian pilots, as the Russians now admit, flew many of the Migs which engaged the Americans in aerial combat. But most important of all, the Soviet Union became what the Chinese and the Vietnamese like to call a "great rear area." It supplied all the help it could without getting directly involved in the conflict.

But Russia had a much more important active role to play as protector. It served as a major deterrent force against America. American planes would have bombed the Manchurian "sanctuaries" had it not been for the threat of Russian intervention. John W. Spanier, in his book *The Truman-MacArthur Controversy and the Korean War*, implies that it was an "accidental" bombing of a Russian air base in Siberia on October 10, 1950, that sent Truman flying to Wake Island to confer with MacArthur.[7] Chinese reasoning was that Washington's reluctance to

[7] John W. Spanier, *The Truman-MacArthur Controversy and the Korean War*, pp. 110–11.

expand the war to China was due to fear of Russian intervention. And when MacArthur, like generals and admirals who would succeed him in the United States military establishment, ridiculed that notion as cowardly fear and plunged ahead, Washington cracked down in the interests of preserving world peace. There was no other way to explain American restraint. The Korean War, thus, became the first test of the Russian nuclear umbrella over China.

In all their vituperations against the Russians, the Chinese never have accused them of heinous behavior during the Korean War. They have noted bitterly that the Russians forced them to pay for all the weaponry they were sent, and with pride that they have repaid every ruble they borrowed. From the Chinese and North Korean point of view, the Russian role during the Korean War was correct and proper. The preservation of world peace was a particular responsibility for the nuclear powers, then only America and Russia. Neither during the Korean War nor afterward have the Chinese Communists ever advocated risking larger nuclear war as a way of gaining advantage in local or special wars (what Americans called "limited wars"). But in the early 1960s, Russians and Americans accused the Chinese of precisely that. The accusations formed an important part of the Sino-Soviet dispute, and will be examined later. There is no evidence from either the Chinese or the Russian side of any serious conflict between them during or after the war. Washington's geopolitical anticommunists naturally ascribed that to China's satellite status, but we need tarry no longer over that shopworn manner of explaining things.

SINO-RUSSIAN SOLIDARITY

The Korean War made the socialist camp an operational reality; it fused ideology and interests. The instrument of that fusion was American imperialism. Ideology identified capitalist, imperialist America as the enemy of the socialist Soviet Union. But interests also identified America as the common enemy threatening the vital interests of both Russia and China respectively, Germany and Taiwan. Moreover, nuclear weaponry made the ideological rivalry between capitalism and socialism a confrontation that could explode at any time into World War III. It was no longer possible for Mao or other Chinese Communists to argue that China's vital interests on Taiwan were not inextricably bound up with the larger global confrontation between capitalism and socialism, between America and Russia. American imperialism had unified the world as Marx one hundred years earlier had predicted capitalism would do. The Korean War demonstrated that unity.

The Korean War turned out to be a golden opportunity for the Chinese Communists to mobilize the entire country, implant the institutions they were borrowing from the Soviet Union, and lay the basis for what was to be a program of rapid economic development, the first five-year plan, beginning in 1953. As was so often the case in the history of Chinese communism, external threat in the form of war proved to be a powerful stimulus for internal mobilization and organization. Chinese and Korean losses were heavy, but the war could have been much worse without the support of Russia. In Chinese eyes, it was Russian power, not American restraint, that made the Korean War a "limited war."

The alliance with Russia was popular in China. Everywhere visiting Russians were feted and addressed as Soviet elder brother (*"Su-lien ko-ko"*). So also in Russia, where Chinese students and apprentice scientists were enthusiastically greeted. For much of the world, China was a heroic country which had just come victoriously out of one of the world's great revolutions. Although Korea was less well known, the example of a small country being bombed to bits by American planes aroused widespread sympathy and support. The once progressive image of America began to vanish, to be replaced by one of capitalist and imperialist ferocity.

Mao Tse-tung undoubtedly was unhappy with a state of the world where the particular interests of his revolution, movement, and country passed out of his control. Yet who could argue with a message transmitted by both ideology and interests? Ideology is more than rhetoric or inspirational theology. Where it is powerful, as in the case of Marxism-Leninism or American containment theories, it is a kind of systems analysis on a global scale believed and propagated by political formations, particularly governments, which themselves were largely the product of ideologies. Who could argue with the obvious fact that the relationship between America and Russia was central to all world politics? And that nuclear power was central to that relationship? Who could argue with the fact that America had singled out West Germany and Taiwan as regions of strategic interest to itself, precisely the areas that both Russia and China construed as threats to themselves? Who could argue with the fact that all of America's actions emanated from the same political body, like fingers from a hand? That body was American monopoly capitalism. The power of this logic was so great that it was able to achieve what the Comintern in all its machinations toward the Chinese Communists had never been able to achieve—to tie China into the international movement guided and dominated by the Soviet Union.

THE TRANSITION FROM STALIN
TO KHRUSHCHEV

The compelling logic could not obscure other phenomena which were becoming of increasing concern to Mao Tse-tung and other Chinese Communist leaders. Russia was beginning to acquire an alarming degree of control over the inner workings of China, most obviously in Manchuria. Already in 1948, Manchuria constituted an autonomous region of China. It had its own separate currency and the only newspaper in China, other than the Peking one, that called itself *People's Daily*. It even issued its own postage stamps marked "restricted for use to the Northeast" ("Northeast" being the Chinese word for Manchuria). Since postage stamps are a sign of national sovereignty, the use of separate Northeast stamps implied that Peking did not exercise full sovereignty over Manchuria. Manchuria was governed by Kao Kang, who was purged in the summer of 1954 (announced in February 1955) for having tried to set up an "independent kingdom." He was also the head of China's first central planning commission, which drafted the first five-year plan. Little is known about the circumstances leading to the purge except that he was in opposition to the Chinese leaders in Peking. What is suspected but cannot be verified is that Kao Kang had some sort of special relationship with Russia. Stalin, true to his promises, returned the Central Manchurian Railroad to China at the close of 1952, but who ran it, Peking or Mukden? In later years, as the Sino-Soviet conflict intensified, one of the most vehement and persistent allegations hurled by the Chinese against the Russians was that they constantly tried to interfere in internal Chinese affairs and get their sympathizers in positions of political power. In other words, the Russians were attempting to turn China into a satellite. From what is known of Stalin's behavior in Eastern Europe during the postwar period, it is quite likely that he tried to bring China into the same kind of operational control.

Old habits are hard to change, and one of Stalin's most ingrained habits was his obsession with centralized control. Stalin trusted nothing he could not control. He knew full well that the circumstance that created the Sino-Soviet alliance was the existence of clear and present danger from a common enemy, and that this could change. Once the Korean War was over, the American threat would recede and China would no longer have the same impetus to remain loyal to Moscow. Manchuria provided a tempting source of leverage against Peking which Moscow was in a good position to capture and manipulate. Manchuria was the center of virtually all China's heavy industry. Moreover, Soviet industrial aid to China went overwhelmingly to Manchuria. A crash program of industrialization and modernization was inconceivable for China unless it were based there, and Manchuria could not develop without massive Soviet aid. It was a recently settled region of China and, therefore, did not have the same village-based society as China proper. Modern farming methods, first developed by the Japanese, were widely used in Manchuria. A network of railroads assured easy communication throughout the region. The people were literate, industrious, and intelligent. The Japanese had had little difficulty in keeping Manchuria in their grip from 1931 to 1945, although they committed the error of formally detaching it from China. It is difficult to believe that Stalin would have overlooked the tempting opportunity of turning Manchuria into a Far Eastern Poland and thereby vastly expanding his power within the Chinese political system as a whole.

The death of Stalin is generally regarded as a major factor clearing the way for a settlement of the Korean War. Another generally held explanation is that the new American President, Dwight Eisenhower, threatened to drop an atomic bomb on China if the Chinese did not come to terms. Like the circumstances surrounding the outbreak of the war, those surrounding its conclusion in the summer of 1953 remain obscure. Syngman Rhee and Chiang Kai-shek, ardently committed to their rollback dreams, were opposed to a settlement and used the prisoner issue to block one. The official United States position was that prisoners should not be forced to return, while the Chinese and North Korean position was that all prisoners on both sides should be returned. A compromise appeared to have been reached through the appointment of a neutral body headed by an Indian general to interrogate the prisoners as to their desires. Even then, Rhee threw a monkey wrench into the process by unilaterally freeing thousands of North Korean prisoners to be absorbed into South Korean society. In the end, it was the Chinese and North Koreans who made the decisive concessions, for they must have known that the intensive organizing and indoctrinating by Nationalist Chinese, South Korean, and American agents made it unlikely that the bulk of the prisoners would or could voluntarily return to their homelands.

The inauguration of the Panmunjom talks in the summer of 1951 signified that all sides, save Rhee (and, in the background, Chiang Kai-shek and his supporters in the United States political-military structure), had agreed on the re-establishment of the 38th parallel (with which the battle lines essentially coincided) as a demarcation line. On the American side, the dragging on of negotiations and fighting had two positive results. It permitted the Air Force to engage in a massive bombing campaign of North Korea designed to prove the thesis of victory through bombing. And it permitted the growth of agitation within the United States, led by Navy admirals and China Lobby Republicans, to "unleash" Chiang Kai-shek. Eisenhower's victory did, indeed, lead to an "unleashing" of Chiang Kai-shek, but the operational effect was not an invasion of Mainland China but the launching of a massive covert war against China. Yet for all the right-wing pressure on Eisenhower to continue and intensify the Korean War, it is clear that the new general-President, with his orientation toward Europe, wanted to end it. Talk of unleashing Chiang alarmed the British, whose alienation could not be risked because of its indispensable role in the build-up of forces in Western Europe.

Conceivably, Stalin was not entirely displeased with the dragging on of the war. As long as the Panmunjom talks went on (and, at times, they were temporarily broken off), it was unlikely that America would expand the war to Chinese or Russian territory. The continuing war permitted Russia to expand and consolidate its power and influence in China, particularly in Manchuria. If the Chinese Communist leaders in Peking were worried about this extension of Russian power, there were no signs of it at the time. But as long as the war went on, there always was the threat that the Americans could suddenly decide to expand it. Pressure on the Truman Administration to allow the Air Force to bomb the Manchurian sanctuaries was intense, and the discovery in Manchuria of what the Chinese claimed were germ warfare bombs dropped on Chinese territory was a further confirmation of their worst fears that America might yet expand the war. Again the larger logic dictated that China had to accept dangerous infringements on its national sovereignty by the Russians in order to face an even greater clear and present danger, that of American attack.

Stalin's death appears to have signaled a dramatic change in the relationship between Russia and China. Chou En-lai rushed to Moscow and was the only non-Soviet communist invited to be a pallbearer of Stalin's coffin. While China clearly was Russia's most important ally in the world, this symbolic gesture was meant to have a larger meaning. It is obvious from the anti-Beria agitation which developed so quickly after Stalin's death that the Soviet leaders so long dependent on him were in a state of disarray. For all their disagreements, they must have felt that a foreign policy signal was absolutely essential to prevent some reckless gesture by America. Stalin died on March 5, 1953. Just one month earlier, Chou En-lai had proposed a resumption of the temporarily broken truce talks at Panmunjom. What was to prevent the Americans, who, on June 27, 1950, had already shown how fast they could move, from suddenly accepting Chou's offer, making peace in the Far East, and returning the full weight of their attention and resources to Europe? If there were growing subsurface frictions in the Sino-Soviet alliance, might China not begin to tread the Titoist path, as had been predicted only a few years before? The symbolism of Chou En-lai carrying Stalin's coffin could only mean that the Russians for the first time were showing that they needed China. Until then, it was the Chinese who needed the Russians. While Chou En-lai would have gone to Moscow anyway, he could easily have refused the offer to march at the head of the funeral procession, electing to march with other non-Soviet communist dignitaries. In what was clearly a moment of deepest crisis for the Soviet leadership without Stalin, the Chinese leaders, seemingly without hesitation, had elected to stand with them.

Chou En-lai's dramatic gesture of solidarity on the day of Stalin's funeral began the golden period of the Sino-Soviet relationship, which reached its highest point with Khrushchev's visit to Peking in September 1954. By then, both Mao Tse-tung and Khrushchev had resolved their most dangerous internal political challenges and emerged victorious. In the summer of 1954, Kao Kang had been toppled from his power in Manchuria, and with him much of the Northeast political machine he had set up. Manchuria came firmly under the control of Peking for the first time since the Liberation. Kao's most important ally was Jao Shu-shih, who had been building up a similar machine in the Shanghai region. Through control of much of the apparatus of economic planning, the Kao-Jao clique, as the Chinese call them, were in a position to usurp power from the leaders in Peking. In Russia, during that same summer of 1954, Khrushchev emerged triumphant in the struggle with the neo-Stalinist group centering on Malenkov, Molotov, and Kaganovich. Coincidentally or not, Kao Kang's fall from power in China and Malenkov's in Russia were announced almost simultaneously early the following year. But when Khrushchev and his sizable entourage arrived in Peking that September, it was made abundantly clear in the many photographs of a jolly Khrushchev with a merry Mao that these were the two supreme leaders of their respective countries. The agreements concluded at that time have to be construed as favorable to China. The Russians gave up their last extraterritorial rights in China and, while committing themselves to further substantial economic assistance to China, the terms of trade and assistance were genuinely bilateral, with the Chinese for the first time acting as fully equal partners with the Russians. There are even grounds for believing that Mao and Khrushchev may have taken a personal liking to each other. Both shared an earthy peasant personality which contrasted with the suspiciousness of Stalin and the coldness of Molotov. Betrayal by a friend is considered one of the worst crimes in the Chinese code of ethics, so that what they saw later as Khrushchev's betrayal of China must in part be understood in terms of the euphoria of 1954.

DÉTENTE

By September 1954, it seemed that the American threat had abated both in Europe and in East Asia. The Geneva Accords on Indochina, concluded on July 21, 1954, appeared to be a supreme affirmation of the correctness of the Sino-Soviet analytical understanding of world politics. France was badly torn because of the Indochina war and the defeat at Dienbienphu was a stunning victory for the liberation forces. France was also torn at home by the issue of German rearmament, symbolized by the European Defense Community (EDC). Washington was pressuring the French to ratify EDC and at the same time urging them to continue the conflict in Indochina. Yet at the decisive moments of the battle of Dienbienphu, despite the intense urgings of Radford and other American military leaders, Eisenhower vetoed American intervention (just as Truman finally had vetoed an extension of the Korean War to China). To both the Chinese and the Russians, it seemed that fear of a larger conflict with the socialist camp was the main deterrent against American aggressiveness. The European Defense Community was essential to the American plan for a rearmed Germany and the Russians considered its defeat the most vital matter for their national security interests. The Chinese considered removal of the American threat from their southern borders equally vital for their national security. The Geneva Conference, while technically concerned only with Indochina, was actually a conference on global politics. A trade-off was achieved. Mendès-France agreed to vote down EDC but was given a face-saving settlement in Indochina, partition at the 17th parallel, which would allow the French to salvage some of their interests while, eventually, the Viet Minh would assume political control over all of Vietnam (through elections). The settlement also partially satisfied the Americans who, while not signing the agreement, indicated that they would observe it. The Vietnamese were not happy with it, but, as communists, they could not argue with the larger logic that had brought it about, particularly since it had prevented the Americans, with their vast military power, from joining the war.

What the Geneva Accords meant was that both the Russians and the Chinese were prepared to accept the basic premises of America's containment policies. Until then, neither was yet fully convinced that the drawing of demarcation lines that had been going on in Europe and East Asia constituted a basic American policy. Containment did not fit any of the Marxist categories the Communists were accustomed to thinking with in their world view. Capitalism was aggressively expansionistic unless deterred by superior force or unless competition between rival capitalist powers deflected their energies away from the socialist camp. But the Americans seemed seriously interested in drawing and observing lines of demarcation. Propaganda aside, they did not take advantage of the workers' revolt in East Berlin in the summer of 1953, a time of acute quarreling within the Russian leadership, to push rollback policies. Neither the Russians nor the Chinese could ever conceive of the demarcation lines as permanent frontiers, if for no other reason than that nations that had historical reasons for being unified would eventually reunify. But the demarcation lines seemed to be a device for avoiding global war between the socialist camp and the free world, a cause to which all communists were committed. By its actions both in Europe and in East Asia, America had now shown that it too was not eager for a third world war.

If the years between Khrushchev's visit to Peking in September 1954 and the Twentieth Soviet Party Congress in February 1956 were the golden years of the Sino-Soviet relationship, they also marked the first real détente in international tensions since the end of World War II. In Europe, the Austrian State Treaty in May 1955 set the stage for the first great West-East summit conference at Geneva in July. The official Russian world view (fully shared by the Chinese and other communists) was that the world was divided into a socialist camp, a capitalist camp, and neutrals belonging to neither. Despite Dulles's fulminations against the "immorality" of neutralism, Washington formally accepted Austria's neutral status. The Austrian treaty seemed to provide a model for other parts of the world where both sides would accept neutrality as a status filling out the gaps between the demarcation lines.

Late in April 1954, the historic Bandung Conference was held. Though members of both great camps were present, most of the participants, like India, considered themselves neutral, and the conference must be reckoned a celebration of neutralism, of which Chou En-lai showed himself an eager supporter. In May, to everyone's surprise, Khrushchev visited Belgrade and buried the hatchet with Tito. He made no attempt to lure Tito back into the Russian fold, and instead Yugoslavia joined India and Egypt as a leading advocate of neutralism. Finally, out of the July summit conference there arose the Sino-American ambassadorial talks, marking the first official contact between the two countries since the Liberation in 1949. Adam Ulam remarks that "to many observers the year 1955 appeared the most hopeful of the post-war era insofar as the relaxation of international tensions and prospects for an East-West settlement were concerned."[8]

By the end of 1955, it appeared that Russian and Chinese fears about their national security over the issues of Germany and Taiwan respec-

[8] Adam Ulam, *Expansion and Co-existence*, p. 564.

tively had abated. The spirit of Geneva signified a new era of peaceful coexistence between America and Russia in Europe, and in East Asia the Quemoy crisis of the spring of 1955 also passed with Chiang Kai-shek being forced by the Americans to evacuate the Tachen Islands several hundred miles north of Quemoy. The larger communist world view which had identified a mushrooming American imperialism as a mortal threat to the socialist countries could now reassess that threat in terms of a world where the two great camps effectively deterred each other from launching a world war. In communist eyes, Eisenhower and Dulles, as Republicans, were the real representatives of the American ruling class, in contrast to the social-democratic or social-fascist figure of Truman, who had to show his anticommunist toughness in order to please his masters on Wall Street. While neither the Russians nor the Chinese were very keen on Dulles, Eisenhower seemed to be a practical, down-to-earth, business-minded general who had no need to bluster in order to flaunt his power. Revolution would and should go on elsewhere in the world, but not in a way that threatened the growing equilibrium between the socialist camp and the free world. Some years later, Khrushchev would develop his notion of peaceful competition between the two systems, whereby socialism's growing productive power would eventually "bury" capitalism's stagnating economies.

The new détente in the global confrontation of the two camps was followed by a turning inward on the part of Russia and China. Both countries faced major problems of development which could not be resolved while world tensions remained as high as they had been. Moreover, the peoples of both countries wished to escape from decades of war and privation and begin to build their own lives. Russian economic policy was finally able to shift from the concentration on heavy industry which Stalin had initiated in 1928. Khrushchev's line was that Russia should stress high technology industries which would enable it to compete with America in every area of science and technology, but at the same time should divert more resources to agriculture and consumer goods. This naturally meant cutbacks in the budgets of the Stalinist "steel-eaters," as Michel Tatu labels those who had justified their policies on the grounds that Russia had to maintain a high level of conventional military power to deter an attack from the West. Khrushchev's conflicts with military leaders like Zhukov were undoubtedly due to their apprehensions over his excessive eagerness to see coexistence as permanent and to cut down conventional forces.

The new line in economic planning demanded some basic changes in economic administration and management, particularly some modification of the excessive centralization on which Stalin had relied. But to decentralize also meant to lift a whole range of controls over Russian society. The lifting of the controls over spiritual life led to "the thaw." Khrushchev's speech at the Twentieth Party Congress in February 1956 marked the decisive break with the Stalinist line and led directly to the upheavals in Eastern Europe. When the Poles revolted in October, Khrushchev found himself forced to deal with Gomulka as an equal, the same way as he dealt with Mao. The Hungarian revolt was another matter. Not only had Nagy announced his intention of withdrawing from the Warsaw Pact, but the Hungarian crisis came at the same time as the Suez crisis. The East-West détente was crucial to Khrushchev's domestic programs, and the foreign policy principles on which it was being built would have been seriously endangered if Hungary's defection had led to an altering of the demarcation lines. The Chinese attitude toward the Hungarian revolt was entirely consistent with their acceptance of these principles. They backed the Nagy regime much as they had that of Gomulka, but within hours of Nagy's announcement that he was withdrawing from the Warsaw Pact, *Hsin-hua* broadcast a statement denouncing him. Like the circumstances surrounding the Russian invasion of Czechoslovakia in August 1968, those surrounding the Hungarian revolt are still obscure. Did Nagy's defection from the Warsaw Pact spark the invasion or did the entry of Russian troops spark Nagy's withdrawal? As in the case of Czechoslovakia, Russian statements just before the invasion were mild, making it seem like a bolt of lightning on a lightly clouded day. There can be no doubt that the larger foreign policy issues were the crucial factor in the Russian invasion of Hungary. (The invasion of Czechoslovakia, the Russians maintained, was to forestall a move from West Germany!)

The reverberations of the events in Eastern Europe and Khrushchev's new domestic line continued to pose challenges to his rule until early June 1957, when he finally won out over his opponents. Khrushchev's reign remained secure from then until his fall in October 1964. During that period, he began to carry out both the foreign and domestic policies he had been advocating since his rise to power. Those policies were, in sum, détente with America, expansion of Russian political and economic influence in the Third World, and a domestic program of all-out stress on high technology industries (for example, space and missile programs), rapid development of agriculture and consumer goods industries, and reform of the archaic Stalinist system of political rule, centralized administration, and repressive social control.

China's domestic problems were, of course, quite different from those of Russia. Stalin had at least begun to deal with Russian backwardness, but virtually nothing had been done in China with a backwardness far worse than Russia's ever was. The great event in China in 1955 was the collectivization of agriculture, and no elaborate economic or social analysis is necessary to understand why it occurred. Peace, stability, and industrial development had produced a burgeoning population which soon would exceed Chinese agriculture's limited capacities to feed it. Large-scale capital investment in agriculture was out of the question. Chinese export capabilities were too limited to allow for extensive food purchases abroad. The only hope was to rationalize the fragmented state of agriculture with its tiny family-owned plots by combining them into larger units which could be farmed more efficiently with existing methods. In contrast to Russia, collectivization was by and large a success in China, and by 1957 and 1958 the food situation had greatly improved. But while the Chinese followed Stalin's example in collectivizaton, they departed from it by launching a program of decentralization of economic controls and administration. Again unlike Stalin, they saw the need to stimulate consumer goods production for both consumption and export. The best way to do that was to stimulate the myriads of small-scale enterprises that had always existed in China by taking away the heavy hand of planning and allowing them to produce under some semblance of market conditions.

There was also a political and cultural thaw in China, called the "hundred flowers," coinciding with the thaw in Russia. After a short period of intense attack against bourgeois intellectuals in 1955 (the anti–Hu Feng campaign), the Chinese leadership reversed itself in early 1956, calling for greater freedom of speech and expression. "Let a hundred flowers bloom" meant that all varieties of different opinions should and could be expressed. Because of their Yenan experience, a major part of the Chinese leadership intuitively believed in decentralization, and, thus, welcomed such tendencies in Russia and in the socialist camp as a whole. The Chinese role in Eastern Europe in 1956 was in harmony with these beliefs. The Chinese influenced the Poles in their moves to seek autonomy from Russian control, notably when Eduard Ochab visited Peking in September. While these Sino-Polish contacts undoubtedly displeased Khrushchev, they were not a major factor in the subsequent deteriorating relations between Russia and China. China fully supported Russia in its intervention in Hungary, thereby showing its unflinching adherence to the principle of solidarity of the socialist camp. The Chinese believed that the socialist camp could function effectively only as a community of equals, which would require a decentralization from the monolithic structure Stalin had created. But decentralization could not reach the point of endangering the unity of the camp, a principle as sacred to the Chinese as the principle that each member nation of the camp should be the master of its own destiny.

Much has been made of Chinese dissatisfaction with Khrushchev's anti-Stalin speech at the Twentieth Party Congress, but recently revealed speeches by Mao from that period indicate that this was not a major factor in the Sino-Soviet dispute. Denunciation of Stalin seemed to the Chinese a dangerous break in the legitimacy of the political system and threw into doubt the role of leadership. They may also have been worried that if the revelations went too far, old specters from earlier periods of Chinese-Russian relations might be dredged up and prove to be embarrassing.

If the year 1955 saw the beginnings of the understandings that would lead to an East-West détente, 1956 witnessed a dangerous but successful testing of them. In November 1956 both East and West faced dangerous crises in their respective camps which could have wrecked the emerging configuration of the world. America could conceivably have intervened in the Hungarian revolt, as Cardinal Mindszenty urged. But despite Dulles's ideological espousal of rollback ideas, it elected not to do so. The Anglo-French invasion of Egypt was a dangerous violation of the principle that America was the leader of the free world, but when the British and the French submitted to American demands that they terminate the invasion, they signified their adherence to that principle. The communist and the containment world views not only coincided but worked out in practice. Both held that the two great world camps had to be headed ideologically and operationally by the two great powers, America and Russia. World peace depended on this bipolarity. China accepted this principle by ending its agitation in Eastern Europe as soon as Russia invaded Hungary, and Britain and France accepted it by knuckling under to Dulles over Suez. Suez was a traumatic experience for Britain, for it finally demonstrated that Britain could no longer act autonomously on the world scene. Thus, one can say that the "spirit of Geneva" emerged unimpaired from the turbulent events of 1956.

NEW TENSIONS

By the end of 1957, world tensions were increasing and in 1958 would produce dangerous crises both in the West (Berlin) and in the East (Quemoy). The turning point seemed to be Russia's successful launching of sputnik, the world's first orbiting satellite, in October. Only shortly before, in August, Russia had successfully test fired its first intercontinental ballistic missile (ICBM), thus demonstrating a delivery capability that could deposit nuclear payloads anywhere within the continental United States. America at this time was concentrating on intermediate range ballistic missiles (IRBMs), which it could launch against Russia from bases around the Sino-Soviet perimeter. The cries of "missile gap" which arose in America reflected the fact that something major had changed in the emerging bipolar balance of power. Mao Tse-tung apparently thought so too, for in November, in Moscow, he delivered the famous speech in which he asserted that "the east wind prevails over the west wind," implying that Russia had gone beyond parity with America to superiority. Unlike the tensions at the end of 1956, the tensions at the end of 1957 were open-ended, much like those in the fall of 1949. In both instances, the change was marked by a qualitative leap forward in Russian strategic power, but a leap forward that expressed much broader tendencies. Something important had happened to change the situation radically between the end of 1956 and the end of 1957.

The change was clearly and surprisingly evident in China. At the beginning of 1957, China was in a relaxed mood with a hundred flowers sprouting and even blooming in some instances. By the end of the year, it was in the grip of the biggest purge since the Liberation (the antirightist movement) and millions were working on great hydraulic projects in a campaign that led directly to the Great Leap Forward. If the signs of a clear and present crisis were not evident, those of a sense of dire urgency were. The mood at the end of the year obviously had something to do with Mao Tse-tung's second and last visit to Moscow, in November. He went there as the drumbeat of the antirightist movement was becoming louder and louder in China, as bureaucracies were being shaken up and their workers sent to the countryside, and as great armies of peasants and intellectuals were toiling in the bitter cold of winter to build waterworks in preparation for the planned leap forward in farm production. Was it crisis or opportunity that sent Mao to Moscow?

CHINA'S ECONOMIC, MILITARY, AND POLITICAL OPTIONS

From a surface view, it seemed that China's main problem in 1957 was to elaborate a second five-year plan. Collectivization had been a gamble, but it had worked, and while much remained to be done, the mood was for consolidation of the gains achieved. The general outlines of the new plan were clear. Agriculture was to have a far greater priority than it had under the first five-year plan, which would require greater state investment in the agricultural sector. Greater incentives were to be given to consumer goods production. A way of thinking about the economy, generally associated with the Minister of Commerce Ch'en Yün (who disappeared from the limelight during the Great Leap Forward but returned with the Cultural Revolution), began to emerge. If farm production increased, its products could be sold at low prices to light industry, which would manufacture them into consumer and export goods. These products would be sold at high prices on the domestic market and, of course, for foreign exchange on the export market. Taxation of light industry would constitute the major revenue base for the government, and export earnings would bring in foreign exchange with which needed capital goods could be acquired, mainly, of course, from the countries of the socialist camp. The state would continue to invest heavily in capital goods and defense industries.

The spirit of Ch'en Yün's thinking was that the Chinese economy would grow steadily but safely and in a more balanced and comprehensive manner than during the first five-year plan. All three major sectors of the economy—agriculture, light industry, and heavy industry—would grow in tandem rather than the lopsided leap forward in heavy industry which characterized the first five-year plan. What was not said openly, however, was that such a reallocation of the state's resources would necessitate sacrifices somewhere. The Chinese state budget was still in a zero-sum situation, so that stress on previously unstressed sectors would have to mean sacrifice from a sector that earlier had high priority. That sector, of course, was heavy industry, which included not only capital goods industries but defense industry. Since all Chinese economic planners indicated a commitment to continued development of capital goods industries, the cuts would have to come from defense. Because of the Korean War, China maintained an immense army with full capabilities for conventional war. As all nations, from the poorest to the mighty United States, have learned, conventional war capabilities are exceedingly costly with little return to society. Armies with large numbers of conventional weapons just eat up budgets, as Sukarno found to his dismay in Indonesia. Development of strategic industries at least produces technological innovations and research and development infrastructures which are economically useful. One must assume, therefore, that the second five-year plan as it was evolving early in 1957 called for cutbacks in defense spending.

Such cutbacks seemed eminently justified in the light of the détente then developing. China had launched large-scale demobilization in the fall of 1955 and pared down the People's Liberation Army to a few million men by 1956. With the settlement of the Indochina war, the threat of an American attack had receded. Khrushchev himself felt that the world-wide threat had abated and was proposing similar developmental programs in Russia, diverting resources from the "steel-eaters" to the hitherto neglected consumer and farm sectors. What China saved on defense could be put into agriculture. Collectivization had created the institutional conditions for a more rational farm production. With the tiny plots consolidated into large units, new technological and organizational methods could be more efficiently applied. In other words, collectivization had assured that investment in agriculture would not be wasted.

Yet there was one further factor in the picture of economic planning for the second five-year plan for which we have only scanty though compelling evidence. In April 1956, Mao Tse-tung gave an important speech, "The Ten Great Relationships," which, though never published in China, reached the West in the wake of the Cultural Revolution. In that speech, Mao made a seemingly paradoxical statement on the subject of atomic weapons: "Do you genuinely want atomic bombs? If you do, you must decrease the proportion of military expenditure and increase economic construction. Or do you only pretend to want them? In that case you will not decrease the proportion of military expenditure, but decrease economic construction."[9] This is not so paradoxical in light of Macmillan's defense policies in Britain after Suez or de Gaulle's *force de frappe* policies in France after the Algerian war. Nor is it paradoxical in light of the defense strategy that Senator George McGovern enunciated in the electoral campaign of 1972. What Mao was saying was that if a strategic (that is, nuclear) defense capability was substituted for a conventional one, then considerable savings could be realized, which could be pumped into economic construction. After Suez, Macmillan decided that Britain could no longer afford to maintain large-scale forces-in-being and decided to stress nuclear weapons instead. De Gaulle's *force de frappe* was a substitution for the still sizable French army, which he cut down after Algeria (almost getting assassinated in the process). While what Britain saved on its policy of retreat from east of Suez did not greatly help its economy, France's retreat from the Algerian war was followed by an economic boom. The seeming paradox comes from the memory of the vast outlays needed to produce atomic bombs in the 1940s and 1950s. In fact, costs for producing nuclear warheads for both advanced and follower nations have declined, whereas costs for conventional weapons have continued to remain high for all. Costs for nuclear weapons have risen dramatically where they have been paired with advanced offensive delivery systems, submarine launched missiles, for example.

"The Ten Great Relationships" was a major speech taken very seriously in China. Liu Shao-ch'i referred to it in some detail in May 1958, implying that it set basic guidelines for Chinese policy. The reason that it was not published could very well have been that Mao, perhaps for the first time, was suggesting that China should begin to develop its own nuclear weapons capability.

China and Russia concluded a nuclear-sharing pact in October 1957

[9] From Stuart Schram, ed., *Chairman Mao Talks to the People* (New York: Pantheon Books, forthcoming in 1974).

just before Mao's visit to Moscow. Exactly what the Russians committed themselves to share with China has been a matter of discussion among Western defense analysts. Walter Clemens notes that China's first public indication that it would produce its own atomic weapons came in May 1958, which may lend further significance to Liu's references to "The Ten Great Relationships" at that time.[10] But regardless of when and how the Chinese actually commenced making nuclear weapons, it must have been preceded by major political-military and economic decisions.

By early fall 1957, a new current on economic planning became evident in China which can be qualified as a fast but risky strategy as contrasted to the slow but sure one advocated by Ch'en Yün. The fast but risky strategy won out, leading to the Great Leap Forward of 1958, which was a crash program for the rapid development of agriculture and light industry. The popular slogan of the Great Leap Forward was *"to k'uai hao sheng"*—"Much! Fast! Quality! Economize!" In reality, it was the spirit of much and fast that prevailed, reminding people of Stalin's earlier *shturmóvshchina* ("storming") approaches to production. The new current could not have been predicted from the calm discussions on the second five-year plan which prevailed in the opening months of 1957. Something, therefore, must have happened to produce the extraordinary sense of urgency that built up in China in 1957.

The awkward official designation for the economic thinking underlying the Great Leap Forward is contained in the slogan "simultaneous development of industry and agriculture under conditions of preferential development of heavy industry." What this implied was that China's leaders were going to attempt what appeared virtually impossible in view of China's meager resources. They were going to make major new investments in agriculture and light industry while maintaining the previous policy of heavy investment in capital goods industries. The policy of the first five-year plan, preferential development of heavy capital goods industries, was possible because the Chinese followed Stalin's model of squeezing savings out of agriculture, keeping consumer goods production down, and pumping all available resources into heavy industry. Ch'en Yün had proposed a reversal of this policy but by the end of 1957, Chinese leaders were saying: Let's do both! The conventional understanding of what Mao tried to do in the Great Leap Forward is that he tried to use organized and motivated manpower as a substitute for capital. Thus, in the absence of investment resources for new steel plants, people were urged to make their own backyard steel furnaces using material at hand and relying mainly on manpower to turn out a few ingots of iron and steel. This view naturally suited the Western image of Mao as a "roman-

[10] Walter C. Clemens, Jr., *The Arms Race and Sino-Soviet Relations*, p. 18.

tic revolutionary" who disdained the constraints of economic reality and believed in the triumph of the will. Fortunately, in recent years, a new image of Mao has begun to surface in Western writings, more in keeping with the image current during the 1930s: a visionary, yes, but also a leader with great common sense and attuned to reality. But whether it was Mao the romantic revolutionary or Mao the visionary pragmatist who launched the Great Leap Forward, the fact remains that by the end of 1957, some deep sense of urgency, even of crisis, was pushing China at an ever-accelerating speed toward the Great Leap Forward.

Heavy industry in the Chinese and Russian parlance of the time meant industries that the government regarded as strategic, both those that produced capital goods for eventual investment in the general economy and defense industries. If the Chinese were contemplating making atomic weapons as early as 1956, then the approach of the beginning date of the second five-year plan, January 1, 1958, demanded that resource allocation and investment plans be drawn up for such a program. Making atomic bombs is a costly venture, as the United States discovered in World War II, and for a poor and backward country such as China, the cost is even greater (even with shortcuts made possible by following American and Russian approaches). If heavy industry was to be "preferentially" developed as it was during the period of the first five-year plan, with yet a new program of developing a nuclear weapons capability added to it, the burden on China would be truly staggering. If we presume that the Chinese did, in fact, build a nuclear program into their second five-year plan, then it took them just under seven years to produce their first atomic device, which they detonated in October 1964. Those were seven very difficult years for China.

When the Russians concluded the nuclear-sharing pact with China in October 1957, they must have known that the Chinese were contemplating the manufacture of nuclear weapons. To know whether the Chinese were serious about producing nuclear weapons, beyond mere rhetoric, all they needed were the broad outlines of the second five-year plan, and at that time, the Russians still had access to information on China's economic plans and policies. That they did not like the idea is clear from what was to happen only a few years hence. But they did strike a bargain with the Chinese, agreeing to furnish them some "know-how" (which may have involved a sample atomic bomb, as some Western writers have speculated). October 1957 was not a calm period in Russia either. While ordinary citizens were euphoric over sputnik's first orbital flight around the earth, Russian leaders were extremely concerned about the effects their successful test of an ICBM in August would have on their relationship to America. Even if they were as confident as their public words implied that the world balance of power was shifting in their favor, the Russian leaders were no fools. They knew from experience that America's reactions to the double fact of ICBM and sputnik would, at the least, be unpredictable. And that unpredictability would be heightened if the Americans learned that the Russians were planting atomic weapons in China and encouraging the Chinese to make their own— China being, of course, America's most hated enemy. Even assuming a supremely confident Khrushchev at the time, he must have known that he was taking a dangerous gamble in agreeing to support a developing nuclear program in China.

THE POLITICAL SCENE IN CHINA

In February 1957, Mao Tse-tung gave his famous speech "On Correctly Resolving Contradictions Among the People." It was originally circulated in China on magnetic tape, and was only published in an abridged (and perhaps revised) form on June 19. In China, the word "contradiction" is much more forceful than the word "relationship," which Mao had used the previous year. Colloquially, it can often be translated as "trouble." There is little doubt that Mao Tse-tung was appalled by the events in Hungary the previous November, as he would be by the events in Indonesia in October 1965. In both cases, the chief event was the sudden and total collapse of a communist party. Even granted that the Hungarian Communist party was foisted on the Hungarians by the Russians at the end of World War II, how could a party that was supposed to be a party of the people be so brittle that a few blows would shatter it? Obviously the Hungarian party had imposed an inept dictatorship on the people which allowed volcanic forces to build up until they exploded. Mao's prescription in the past for such situations had been "rectification," allowing criticisms to emerge freely so that the real discontents could be ascertained and corrective measures be taken. His speech was an analysis of the major contradictions within Chinese society, but nothing was said about foreign policy (at least, not in the published version). The operational result of the speech was a rectification movement that began, in a rather mild fashion, in the early spring of that year. As during the Cultural Revolution, wall posters went up throughout China (mainly in cities and usually in universities) criticizing wrongdoings of party cadres. But in May, rectification suddenly exploded into a torrent of attacks on the Communist party itself and on Russia. For the first time since the Liberation, leading intellectual and political figures were accusing the party and Russia of the most serious crimes. These denunciations were not only shouted from soapboxes which had been hurriedly set up on university campuses, but some of them were published in the newspapers, not the official *People's Daily* but remnant bourgeois news-papers like the *Kuang-ming Jih-pao* and the Shanghai-based *Wen-hui-pao*.

The explosive discontent with the party was alarming enough, but more alarming were the bitter attacks against Russia. What was unique about the May explosion was that major issues of foreign policy were suddenly and unexpectedly drawn into the public arena. For the first time since the Liberation, public voices, some with a certain degree of authority, were questioning the alliance with Russia. When the crack-down came on June 8 and the antirightist movement was launched, all criticism of Russia vanished. Shortly thereafter, Lu Ting-yi, then head of the propaganda department of the Central Committee, gave a speech in which he castigated the anti-Russian agitation of the rightists:

> Uniting with the Soviet Union not only is a demand of the Com-munist Party but was a demand put forth by Mr. Sun Yat-sen long ago. Mr. Sun's testament addressed to the Soviet Union still moves us deeply when we read it today. The line that divides revolution from counter-revolution is whether one unites with or opposes the Soviet Union. Sino-Soviet solidarity is the main bastion of world peace, and in the greatest interest of all mankind. Without the firm solidarity of China and the Soviet Union, there is no reliable guar-antee for world peace, and mankind could suffer the greatest of disasters. Therefore we demand unremitting support of this solidar-ity. But the rightists are different from us. They are using reaction-ary nationalist ideology to stir up the masses and sow discord between China and Russia. What they say is simply a translation of the tune spread by imperialism and Chiang Kai-shek. They want to make us believe the Soviet Union is a "red imperialism" and does not treat our people on an equal basis.[11]

It was the crackdown of June 8 that changed the mild atmosphere of the beginning of 1957 to the one of urgency and frenzy that marked the Great Leap Forward. More and more rightists were publicly denounced. Thousands of intellectuals who worked in offices and universities were sent to do manual labor in the countryside. That same summer, a social-ist education movement was launched in the countryside which sparked the "mobilization" atmosphere that was to reach a high point the follow-ing year with the commune movement. Many if not most of the rightists purged were bourgeois in social background and constituted that scarce talent which the Communists had so hurriedly recruited in the days following the Liberation. As in the Cultural Revolution later, Western observers naturally sympathized with their fellow professionals who were

---

[11] Speech of July 11, 1957, in *Jen-min Shou-ts'e 1958* (*People's Handbook*, 1958), p. 87, translated by the author.

being so brutally mishandled by radical revolutionaries. But the fact is that many of the rightists did have links to Taiwan, like Huang Ching (David Yui), who was the nephew of Yü Ta-wei, one of the leading military figures in Taiwan. Particularly harsh were the attacks against the minor parties, most of which functioned as a kind of liaison to Chinese outside of China, including Taiwan. The accusation of being anti-Soviet was one of the most severe leveled against the rightists, and in the background were further accusations that some of them actually had contact with Taiwan. One woman, active in the Taiwan liberation movement, was accused of having written a letter to Chiang Kai-shek.

One can say with assurance that foreign policy was a major issue in the explosion of May 1957. Considering the massiveness and extent of the purges, one can also say that the public criticisms were a mere surface reflection of currents running deep and wide within the Chinese political structure.

To unravel the picture further, one might consider another theme in the economic thinking of Ch'en Yün, the notion of *tzu-li keng-sheng*, ("self-reliance"), which made its appearance at this time. This term has a stronger flavor in Chinese than in English—"rebirth through one's own efforts." *"Tzu-li keng-sheng"* would become one of the most important economic slogans in China in the period after 1960 when economic relations with Russia were broken. Even at this time, self-reliance meant that China should not be so unilaterally dependent on external support for its program of economic development. This, of course, meant that it should develop import substitution programs and try to produce as much domestically as it could. But no Chinese leader even remotely conceived of the possibility that China could ever do without imports. Until the mid-1950s, China's trade, more out of necessity than choice, was almost exclusively oriented toward the socialist countries. As long as America retained its trade embargo against China and blackmailed other countries to follow suit, China's trade possibilities outside the socialist camp were limited. However, if trade restrictions should ease, then a new range of import and export markets would open up. This was particularly true in Southeast Asia, where a large Overseas Chinese population played a central role in commerce and would be of great help in marketing Chinese goods. The goods that China could export to Southeast Asia were all of the light industrial kind. Moreover, many of them were of a sort that appealed to the traditional tastes of Chinese and other Asian peoples. On the other hand, many Chinese food products were unnatural to the tastes of Eastern Europeans. For example, the Chinese consume a large array of shellfish, as do other Asian peoples. Eastern Europeans abhor shellfish. The Chinese and other Asians also consume a wide range of fruit and vegetable products, whereas Eastern European tastes are rather limited in this respect. Ch'en Yün's proposals for future economic development involved considerable development of light industry as a source of domestic revenue for the government as well as foreign exchange. From a purely rational point of view, an export-oriented light industry would make most sense if China could again have access to its traditional markets in Southeast Asia as well as other parts of the world. The Chinese did subsequently sell immense quantities of canned goods to Eastern Europe, again out of necessity not choice, and visitors to Warsaw and Moscow in 1960 could see them stacked in immense mounds on the shelves drawing few buyers.

But international trade had become a political question of the highest level because Washington had decided to make it so. The American trade embargo against China had never been airtight and ships called on Chinese ports after the blockade withered in 1950. Nevertheless, American power was so great that nations wishing to trade with China always risked incurring the wrath of Washington. Moreover, Kuomintang machinations among Overseas Chinese made it difficult for their businessmen to contemplate marketing Mainland China products. Obviously, if the American attitude toward China changed, then the possibilities of trade would improve dramatically.

Ch'en Yün was minister of commerce, and trade was one of his primary concerns. Trade was also an essential element in the economic program which he saw as a basis for the second five-year plan. Though he left the political stage when the Great Leap Forward was launched, trade remained a major element in the economic policies underlying it. During the years 1958–1960, Sino-Soviet trade soared, leaping 25 percent a year until the break in economic relations (and even then only declining rather slowly). The Sino-Soviet economic relationship during the Leap was on a trading basis. The Russians allowed the Chinese to place orders for capital goods and other items they needed and worked these orders into their own economic plans. The Chinese, in turn, fully paid for these goods in immense amounts of food, raw materials, and light industrial products. It was this massive outflow of farm products to Russia that in 1960 aroused rumors inside and outside of China that the leaders were sending food to Russia while Chinese people were suffering from dire food shortages. However, it obviously was not Ch'en Yün's notion that this greatly increased trade should flow to so unnatural a market as Russia. Even then, China was earning several hundreds of millions of dollars in foreign exchange through its trade with Hong Kong, which is justly regarded as the gateway to Southeast Asia. The most rational expansion of China's foreign trade was through this gateway.

To put it most bluntly, the newly evolving second five-year plan, in which Ch'en Yün's thinking seemed to be playing so important a role, required an easing of Sino-American hostility so that China's natural markets in Southeast Asia could be made accessible.

THE SUDDEN HARDENING OF AMERICAN POLICY

At the beginning of 1957, the prospects for an easing of Sino-American tensions were not altogether bad. While the ambassadorial talks at Geneva had not produced any spectacular results, the frequency of contact helped to create a *de facto* relationship between the two countries. From the summer of 1955 when they began until the end of 1957 when they were broken off, there had been over seventy official meetings. The chief issue of difference appeared to be an American demand that the Chinese renounce the use of force in the Taiwan Straits and Chinese refusal to acquiesce in anything that would legitimate a "two-China" situation. The Americans wanted official Chinese acceptance of containment's demarcation line in the Taiwan Straits. While the Chinese refused categorically to do so, they implied that they had no intention of trying to regain Taiwan by military means. Nevertheless, the very existence of the talks helped to create a milder atmosphere. A number of Americans traveled to China at this time, and the Chinese issued invitations to leading American journalists. Although the State Department still refused to allow them to go, Dulles's opposition appeared to be weakening. In late April, he indicated that he might be willing to allow a few correspondents to visit China. The least cold statement on China came from Eisenhower himself on June 5, when he indicated that trade with China could not be stopped anyway, and perhaps it was not so bad an idea. An increasing number of articles had been appearing in the American press advocating a resumption of trade. Agitation for the China trade was particularly active in San Francisco, which suffered from the embargo. The mounting pressure for trade with China prompted *U.S. News & World Report* to publish an article in its June 14 issue in which, as could be expected, it poured cold water on hopes of spectacular gains from such trade. But the appearance of the article indicated how significant the pressure for lifting the trade embargo had become.

Then, on June 28, Dulles journeyed to San Francisco, a favorite location for American officials to make major pronouncements on China, where he delivered one of the most ferocious attacks on China ever made by an American government official. Dulles's speech slammed the door tightly shut on an opening toward China that, slow as it was, had been widening ever since the summer of 1955. By coming to San

Francisco, the country's leading center of agitation for trade with China, Dulles completely erased the impact of Eisenhower's comments on trade only a few weeks before. The Sino-American relationship thereafter worsened, reaching a point of extreme crisis in the Quemoy near-war of August-September 1958.

A harbinger of this renewed worsening trend in Sino-American relations came from an unexpected source—Japan. In February 1957, Nobusuke Kishi, a World War II war criminal, had become prime minister of Japan, succeeding Tanzan Ishibashi who after a few weeks as prime minister resigned because of "illness." Kishi, at that time and ever since, has been among the most ardent advocates of Chiang Kai-shek's cause in Japanese official circles. In early June, he visited Chiang Kai-shek on Taiwan and told the generalissimo publicly that "if you could recover the Mainland, I think that would be very good."[12] For a Japanese prime minister to espouse Chiang's rollback policies was unprecedented and alarming. Japan had been forced to recognize the Chiang government on Taiwan as a condition for American signature of the peace treaty in 1951 (negotiated by Dulles). But cagey old Shigeru Yoshida had done his best to keep Japan out of the Sino-American imbroglio. The peace treaty and the United States–Japan Security Treaty had tightly lashed Japan to America, but this did not mean that Japan was Washington's catspaw. Yoshida was a business-minded conservative who considered Japan's involvement in World War II a disaster and wanted to take no chances that it would again be involved in a major war. To get enmeshed in the tangle of American political-military alliances in which Taiwan played a central role seemed to Yoshida and his successor Ichirō Hatoyama something to be avoided if at all possible. Kishi, by contrast, was not only a conservative but a reactionary. His support of Chiang in June 1957 was a reflection of reactionary sentiments from which he has never deviated.

It is generally assumed that changing economic conditions brought Kishi to power. By 1957, Japan's economic miracle was well under way and exports became a key concern. It was Kishi who negotiated various reparations agreements with countries in Southeast Asia, thus laying the groundwork for the massive Japanese economic presence there today. There was also rising agitation for trade with China. Kishi's foreign minister, Aiichirō Fujiyama, favored expansion of the China trade and supported the private agreements between China and Japanese firms that were worked out at the time. Fujiyama thereafter became one of the leading advocates of better Sino-Japanese relations. The team of Kishi and Fujiyama was one of those compromises between different factions

[12] *Asahi Shimbun*, June 4, 1957; referred to by Chou En-lai in an interview with Japanese journalists on July 25, 1972 (*see Jen-min Shou-ts'e 1958*, p. 425).

and currents of Japan's ruling party, the Liberal Democratic party (LDP), that seem to mark Japanese governments. Fujiyama's attitudes seemed to be closer to those of the previous prime minister Hatoyama than to Kishi. Until the advent of Prime Minister Tanaka in 1972, Japanese prime ministers have symbolized their country's relationship to America in keeping with their "low posture" stance. Kishi's reign (1957–1961) coincided not only with a period of extreme fidelity to America but with one of extremely bad relations between China and Japan. Kishi clearly was not interested in expanding Japan's trade toward China and, aside from the assured market in America, saw Southeast Asia as the most promising market for Japanese goods. Naturally, close ties with Taiwan could give the Japanese access to the Overseas Chinese business community. Conversely, any rapid expansion of Mainland China's trade into Southeast Asia could constitute dangerous competition for Japan, which otherwise had no major competitors to fear in that part of the world. It is quite likely that Kishi's "vision" for Japan was analagous to that of Adenauer in West Germany—in return for joining America's complex "defense" arrangements in East Asia, in which Taiwan played a central role, Japan could assure itself of undisputed access to lucrative new markets.

WEAPONRY CONFLICTS IN WASHINGTON

The first half of 1957, the beginning of Eisenhower's second term, was marked by considerable turmoil reflected in an important shift in defense policies from the "New Look," a strategy of massive retaliation to deter Russia from inciting wars, to the "New New Look," a strategy which envisioned the possibility of limited nuclear wars without risking central war with Russia. The turmoil produced not only intense interservice rivalry which in 1960 prompted Eisenhower to castigate the military-industrial complex but also two famous reports on the defense posture by the prestigious Gaither and Rockefeller committees. As a result, another reorganization of the Department of Defense was undertaken in 1958.

The turmoil was created by a policy commitment of Eisenhower's that came to dominate his entire second term: the fight against inflation to be waged by cutting government spending. Though not a businessman, Eisenhower came to share many of business's convictions. One was that communism would conquer America by bankrupting it. If the communists caused trouble all over the world and forced the budget up to astronomical heights, the resultant runaway inflation would destroy American business, which would mean the end of the American way of life. Perhaps just because he was a general with simple and direct ideas, Eisenhower fully accepted that argument. He was determined, in his second term, to follow deflationary policies even if this caused temporary business recessions—as it did. In early 1957, military spending rose alarmingly.[13] At the same time, pressures to increase nondefense spending were also rising. Eisenhower was convinced that unless the lid could be put on defense spending, the budget would spiral out of control.

The New Look or "massive retaliation" policies of the Eisenhower first term seemed designed to assure a stable or even declining budget. America would build up a massive strategic nuclear capability which would be directed against the Russians if they made trouble anywhere in the world. Since this should make the Russians timid about doing anything to antagonize Uncle Sam, a process of gradual stabilization of world tensions should ensue. It would then be possible for the United States to cut back on its sizable and extremely costly conventional forces (planes, ships, and men). By late 1956, this policy seemed to be working, and Eisenhower was re-elected on a peace platform. What constantly upset the budgetary picture, however, were the machinations of congressmen in league with disgruntled military men. Every time a budgetary reduction was proposed for one of the services, its agents would get Congress to reinstate the stricken item in the budget. The Democrats, as the opposition party, were more than eager to play the pork-barrel game to the intense anger of Eisenhower.

While it was possible to resist pork barrel pressures, distasteful as it was, new strategic arguments were being advanced that began to call in question the basis of massive retaliation policy. Not only had the Russians exploded a hydrogen bomb in 1954, but they were rapidly developing a manned bomber capability which could eventually match that of America. Moreover, Britain exploded its own hydrogen bomb in May 1957, which broke the American nuclear monopoly on the free world side. America obviously could not retaliate massively if it itself was threatened with massive retaliation. It followed logically, so to speak, that if the Russians were no longer deterred from troublemaking by massive retaliation, they would proceed to make trouble. America obviously had no choice but to meet a challenge where faced with one, but it could not do so by launching a central nuclear war. Thus, the notion of "limited war" became increasingly popular.

A limited war, like the Korean War, would be fought with non-nuclear weapons up to a point that never would threaten central nuclear war with the Russians. The doctrines of limited war were popular with both the Army and the Navy but strongly opposed by the Air Force, notably the Air Force Chief Nathan Twining, who chaired the Joint Chiefs of Staff (JCS) until Kennedy took office. The Air Force was obviously

13 Samuel P. Huntington, *The Common Defense*, p. 94.

afraid that limited war was an opening for its Army and Navy enemies to capture as much of the budget as they could under the conditions of painful scarcity that prevailed until Kennedy took office. The Army enthusiasm for limited war is well known through General Maxwell Taylor's book of 1959, *The Uncertain Trumpet* (which Mao Tse-tung read with considerable interest). With his forceful and cultivated advocacy for a capability to fight "brush-fire wars," Taylor was a leading candidate for a major role in a new administration, which he got as Kennedy's chairman of the Joint Chiefs of Staff. Less known but more important is the Navy's advocacy of limited war ideas.[14] The Navy's "traditional role in diplomacy" had always given it the chief role in fighting brush-fire wars, and the Marines were ever ready to be transported by ship to some distant trouble spot to make peace or inflict justice. Exactly as in 1949, the Navy now again argued that America must develop a greater capability to deal with brush-fire challenges throughout the world.

But a new weaponry element had entered the situation in the mid-1950s, what Samuel Huntington calls "meeting limited aggression with limited use of nuclear weapons."[15] The development of small nuclear warheads or "tactical" nuclear weapons suggested a qualitative distinction between strategic nuclear weapons, which would only be used in central war, and tactical nuclear weapons, which would and could be used in limited wars. "Tactical" presumably implied that such weapons were to be used only in battlefield situations, whereas strategic weapons would be dropped on an enemy's cities. Since the Air Force specialized in strategic bombing and delivery, it naturally was not overly enamored of tactical nuclear weapons. The Air Force considered the Strategic Air Command (SAC) the core of its service, where it reigned supreme in the field of strategic bombing. Its tactical functions, on the other hand, forced it into collaboration with other services more directly involved in battlefield situations. But like the Army, the Navy was a battlefield service, and assigned the highest importance to its tactical air arm. Since 1945, the Navy (and the Army as well) had sought entry into the exclusive nuclear club. The development of tactical nuclear weapons and, even more significantly, the evolution of the notion of "limited" use of nuclear weapons seemed to be a golden opportunity for the Navy to go nuclear. Coincidentally or not, *U.S. News & World Report*, in its May 17, 1957, issue, published a long article by a Navy man outlining why the Navy should have a tactical nuclear capability.

The most important result of this rethinking of massive retaliation was the growing stress on intermediate range ballistics missiles. Unlike the Russian crash program to develop an ICBM to counter America's

[14] Huntington, *The Common Defense*, p. 103.
[15] *Ibid.*, p. 106.

manned bomber capabilities, the Americans stressed the development of shorter-range missiles. The most widely publicized IRBMs of the mid-1950s were the Thor and the Jupiter and, predictably, a bitter battle erupted between the Air Force and the Army over who should have which missile. The Air Force regarded the missiles from a "strategic" viewpoint, in terms of their capabilities to reach key targets deep within Russia. The Army, on the other hand, was more concerned with repelling Russian aggression in Western Europe and, therefore, tended to see them in a tactical sense, as a supplement to artillery and tactical air power to be used to destroy enemy bases, supply lines, and troop concentration points. In any case, the shorter range (as compared to ICBMs) of IRBMs (1,000–2,000 miles) required that these missiles be installed outside the continental United States in countries on the periphery of the Sino-Soviet bloc. By the autumn of 1957, Washington was mounting public and private pressure on NATO countries to allow the installation of American IRBMs along the European periphery of Russia. The shrill cries of "missile gap" that followed sputnik masked the extreme anxiety arising in Europe at this time at the prospect that Russia and America might decide to slug it out, in limited fashion of course, on the soil of Western Europe. The deepest apprehension of the Russians was that IRBMs would be installed in West Germany and that the right-wing Adenauer government would gain some degree of control and influence over them. Coincidentally or not, in its May 3, 1957, issue, *U.S. News & World Report* published an interview with Konrad Adenauer in which he indicated that Germany should be given some access to nuclear weaponry.

In the spring of 1957, America's relations with Britain and France were still strained because of the Suez affair. Macmillan, to Washington's considerable displeasure, decided to cut back on Britain's costly conventional forces and stress its nuclear capability. In mid-May 1957, Britain exploded its first hydrogen bomb and became the third country in the world to have an H-bomb capability. While no one feared that Britain might suddenly decide to resurrect its empire through nuclear blackmail, its breakthrough in the nuclear field amounted to a kind of political-military declaration of independence from America. While containment liberals like Acheson feared that the Anglo-American alliance might be weakened, Dulles, who in Marshall Plan days had always taken a "German" position, favored closer political-military collaboration between America and West Germany. Adenauer was Dulles's model European, and a booming West Germany constituted the best guarantor in Europe for both free enterprise capitalism and a firm anticommunist stance. Thus, while America offered its IRBMs to all NATO countries, the issue became increasingly one of "A-bombs for Germany." The specter of a

Washington-Bonn axis frightened not only the Russians but the British and French as well, playing a major role in their decision to end the acrimony over Suez and return to the fold of the American alliance.

Putting IRBMs in Western Europe turned out to be a drama in Dullesian brinkmanship which actually worked in the long run. The Russians responded, on the one hand, by offers to negotiate some kind of settlement and, on the other, by tough moves, the most serious of which was the Berlin crisis of late 1958. Russian threats had the predictable effect of reuniting the NATO countries around America, and Russian offers kept the door open for agreement, which could lead to stability. The longed-for agreement finally came in 1959 and was capped by the momentous—and fateful—meeting of Eisenhower and Khrushchev at Camp David in September 1959.

THE POLITICAL EFFECTS OF THE IRBM PROGRAM

The American decision in May 1957 to put Matador guided missiles into Taiwan was part of a larger program to put IRBMs in various countries surrounding the Sino-Soviet bloc. Naturally, the country of utmost sensitivity to the Russians was Germany. It is not unlikely that the challenge to Khrushchev's leadership that erupted in May and was led by the Old Guard was motivated by this new situation. Since his 1955 summit meeting with Eisenhower, Khrushchev had been counting on peaceful coexistence with America as the basis for his program of diverting resources from defense to economic construction. The only justification for drastically cutting down Russia's conventional military capabilities was proof that no threat from Western Europe, particularly Germany, need be feared. The defeat of the European Defense Community in 1954 and the subsequent turn toward moderation in Washington's policies seemed to be convincing evidence that the threat had abated. But if it suddenly loomed again like a storm on a sunny day, the old Stalinists and Russia's ground force–minded military leaders could accuse Khrushchev of having been duped by the capitalists. Khrushchev was almost ejected from power at this time, and only his unprecedented appeal to the full Central Committee saved him—or so the outcome has been explained in Western sources.

The conventional American explanation for the sudden turn toward IRBMs is that Washington knew that the Russians, through their intensive missile and aircraft programs, would soon match American capabilities, and new means had to be found to counter the Russian threat. In 1949, the new means involved a turn from exclusive emphasis on atomic blitz to a build-up of conventional forces all around Russia (and China).

What Washington did not realize or considered unimportant were the *political* implications of its response. Conventional forces (planes, ships, troops) require bases outside the continental United States, which always act as an instrument of political leverage on the countries in which they are located. The containment liberals have always maintained that such bases have a restraining effect on unstable governments, such as South Korea was in the 1950s, as well as shoring up their defensive capabilities. The Russians and Chinese, understandably, took a different view of the matter. But regardless of what exact function such bases had, setting up a base in a foreign country always created a new political situation. It created uncertainty in a situation whose parameters were before then at least known and knowable, even if they were threatening. Washington's intellectual defense planners have always prided themselves on trying to create certainties in the world so that an enemy would always know what response to expect from America if it tried an aggressive act. But something new, particularly of a military nature, always creates dangerous uncertainties and impels the opponent once again to "prepare for the worst possible situation." No one can say what would have happened if America had responded to Russia's attempts to catch up by simply vastly extending its continental defense system and launching a crash ICBM program of its own or building up its missile-launching submarine force. That would not have changed any political realities, which implanting IRBMs on foreign soil did.

The IRBM program was primarily oriented toward Europe, and the Air Force and the Army, the two services that were arguing over Thor and Jupiter, were also primarily interested in Europe. NATO had given the United States Army a new role, allowing it to rise from the depths to which it had sunk in the post-1945 period, and anticipation of finally having some sophisticated hardware like a Jupiter filled it with joy. The Air Force, of course, saw missiles as just another weapon in its arsenal of strategic weapons aimed at Russia and China, but was determined to maintain absolute control over them. Again, as in the past, the Navy seemed to have the least role in this exciting new program. The Korean War had so soured the military on Asian wars that it came to form what Roger Hilsman called the "never again school"—never again fight a war on the Asian mainland (unless with nuclear weapons). That America would once again get involved in a Korea-type war in East Asia seemed inconceivable in the mid-1950s. Therefore, talk of "limited war" (as contrasted with Taylor's "brush-fire wars") referred mainly to Europe. Naturally, Europeans did not relish the notion of a limited war fought on their soil, but the thought was still prevalent that at a time of Western weakness, the Russians might lunge and occupy Western Europe. The Navy's Polaris capability did not become operational until the early

1960s, so that in the mid-1950s it still played only a minor role in European defense. If European defense was still top priority—as it had been since the late 1940s—then East Asia and the U.S. Navy would essentially be out of the running for the new programs and the new technology.

MATADORS, THE NAVY, AND TAIWAN

On May 6, 1957, Washington announced that it was sending to Taiwan an Air Force detachment of Matador guided missiles. The Matadors were actually not missiles but pilotless jet bombers electronically controlled by ground crews. They had a range of 600 miles and could carry atomic warheads.[16] The report passed virtually unnoticed in America, but in China it was noted with extreme alarm at a time when the intense agitation of the May explosion was building up. *U.S. News & World Report* explained the sending of the Matadors as a response to a "Red build-up in Asia," and lamented that the absence of nuclear weapons in South Korea gravely endangered America's defensive posture there. Late in June, the Chinese and North Korean members of the Korea Truce Commission officially protested that America was introducing "new-type weapons" into South Korea in violation of the armistice agreement. The protest was dismissed in Washington as so much communist propaganda. While America's Strategic Air Command always had the capability of dispatching nuclear bombs to China by manned planes, it was based in the continental United States and its command and control were centered on Washington. But Taiwan and South Korea were governed by fanatical rollback-minded regimes surrounded by equally fanatical anti-communist American military men. Missiles with a nuclear delivery capability stationed in Taiwan and South Korea were a matter far different from the known and accepted threat from the Strategic Air Command.

The Matador unit assigned to Taiwan was an Air Force unit but was commanded by a Navy captain. Navy control was further confirmed by the announcement some weeks later of the establishment of a unified theater command CINCPAC at Honolulu. While the Air Force later would develop Asian interests of its own, the Matadors have to be reckoned as Navy inputs into a part of the world it regarded as its own domain. Thus, if IRBMs with nuclear warheads were to be installed in Britain, France, and Germany, the Matadors meant an extension of the program to Taiwan, but under Navy auspices. And if "new-type weapons," presumably nuclear, which the Chinese alleged were being introduced into South Korea, served the same purpose as the Matadors, then

16 *New York Times*, May 7, 1957; *U.S. News & World Report*, May 17, 1957.

South Korea would join Taiwan and the Western European countries as part of a world-wide IRBM belt around the Sino-Soviet bloc. An IRBM belt based on Taiwan and South Korea was mainly in the Navy's interests compared to the predominately European and continental United States interests of the Air Force and the Army.

In mid-May 1957, some of the biggest bureaucratic changes in the history of the Eisenhower Administration took place. Both the Secretary of Defense Charles Wilson and the Secretary of the Treasury George Humphrey resigned. Shortly thereafter, Admiral Radford stepped down as chairman of the Joint Chiefs of Staff and was succeeded by Air Force General Twining. Resignations of top officials are not passing affairs of personal preference, as Americans should realize by now. They signify changes in policy. For three of the top officials of an administration to resign at the same time indicated that major policy shifts were in the wind. Of the top officials, only John Foster Dulles remained to provide continuity with the first Eisenhower Administration. For the Navy, the advent of an Air Force general as chairman of the Joint Chiefs of Staff was particularly alarming. Admiral Radford did not always get for the Navy what it wanted, but he symbolized Navy predominance in the highest military councils of the United States. The Air Force, unlike the Army, was aggressive, arrogant, and very popular in the public and congressional eye. In view of Eisenhower's overwhelming victory at the polls, his firm commitment to fight inflation, and the continuing concern with the Russian threat, the outlook for the Navy was not particularly good.

Nevertheless, at this time the Navy gained a political-military position as important as the chairmanship of the Joint Chiefs of Staff, which it lost to the Air Force. On June 30, 1957, it was announced that a new unified command for the entire Pacific region headed by Admiral Felix Stump had been set up. This command, generally called CINCPAC (pronounced sink-pack) from the title of the commander-in-chief, was to become, in succeeding years, one of the most important centers of political as well as military power in America. Since Stump's appointment, every CINCPAC has been an admiral—the list going from Stump, Felt, Sharp, McCain, to Gayler appointed in 1972. The CINCPAC command is the headquarters for all military operations in East Asia, though South Vietnam was removed from its command in 1964. But its political power (or "diplomatic role," as the writer Frederick Simpich calls it) is attested by the fact that a political adviser from the State Department was assigned to it from the beginning. Simpich notes that Admiral Radford earlier had with "tireless and brilliant energy, formed in effect a second foreign service in the Pacific."[17] That the announcement

---

[17] Frederick Simpich, Jr., *Anatomy of Hawaii*, pp. 225–26.

of the new unified command to be located in Honolulu and headed by Navy admirals known for their ferocious views on China was made two days after John Foster Dulles's San Francisco speech was hardly coincidental.[18] The establishment of the unified command also meant that the Air Force Matadors on Taiwan now came under full Navy control.

While all United States military leaders held hostile views about China, none matched in ferocity those of Navy admirals. Admiral Radford's views on China were well known, and Admiral Carney, chief of staff of the United States Navy, from time to time delivered equally ferocious blasts against the Chinese "menace." Leaving aside its anticommunist fervor, the least that can be said of the Navy's propaganda was its contention that China's threat was as great as that of Russia, if not greater. In other words, they were continuing the old Europe-first versus Asia-first argument. But the objective situation in the spring of 1957, both in East Asia and in Washington, was not very promising for Asia-first views. Despite *U.S. News & World Report*'s hints of a "Red build-up" in Asia, there was no evidence of it. China was in its "hundred flowers" period and in early May was emmeshed in its rectification program. Japan never appeared more closely linked to America and its Asian policies than at that time, under Kishi. There was no sign of a Chinese move to seize Taiwan. South Vietnam seemed to be entering a period of stability after Ngo Dinh Diem's crushing of dissident groups (like the Binh Xuyan), and his widely hailed state visit to Washington in early May. Not only was there no clear and present threat in East Asia (unlike Europe, where Washington argued that the Russians were rapidly developing missiles and aircraft), but China seemed more amicable than ever before. The China Lobby image of China was, for the first time, being publicly challenged in America, and voices began to be heard suggesting that perhaps the time had come to seek better relations with China.

One of the darker mysteries of this period surrounds Taiwan itself. In late May, a mob burst into and virtually wrecked the American Embassy in Taipei. The ostensible reason was the people's anger over an American who had killed a Chinese and been spirited out of the country by United States authorities. Yet a segment of the mob headed straight for the supersecret code room of the embassy and did away with some of its most important papers. Few observers accept the official explanation that the attack was a purely spontaneous affair. Yet there is no evidence of what kind of official Kuomintang connivance, if any, was involved. The internal power politics of the Kuomintang are among the murkiest in the world. But one general issue seems to have dominated them since

[18] *New York Times,* July 1, 1957.

December 1949: how much control America should be allowed to exercise over the Taipei government. Some factions apparently advocated close cooperation with the Americans and others a more independent posture. Some advocated collaboration with the United States military and others preferred to work with nonmilitary agencies like the CIA. Chiang Kai-shek himself had no reason to trust the Americans, for certain currents in Washington continued to agitate against him well into the 1950s. Yet so long as the Chinese Communists remained the common enemy of both the KMT and the Americans, these factional conflicts could be contained. The situation could change dangerously if that common enemy ceased to exist.

Ever since Chiang had been forced to evacuate the Tachen Islands in 1955, the growing signs of détente in East Asia constituted dangerous omens for his regime. If the unthinkable should happen and Peking and Washington somehow agreed to bury the hatchet, an explosion could erupt on Taiwan. The two million Mainlanders were anxious to return to China. If reconquest was out of the question, many of them would, in traditional Chinese fashion, begin to think of accommodation. Signals were already coming from Peking, transmitted through, among other channels, the "minor parties," like the Chinese Kuomintang Revolutionary Committee in Peking. Chiang's entire power position on Taiwan depended on the common enemy and his adroitness and ability to procure American support. He undoubtedly believed that China's "hundred flowers" mood and the Bandung spirit were typical Communist tricks to deceive the Americans and get them to abandon Taiwan. He knew that image had to be destroyed, and at some point, he decided he knew how to do it.

From some point in 1957 to the summer of 1958, Chiang dispatched an immense army equipped with the most advanced weapons to the islands of Quemoy and Matsu. His air force managed to obtain deadly Sidewinder air-to-air missiles from the Americans, which, as the Quemoy fighting in September 1958 was to show, gave him air superiority over the Communists. What he intended to do with that army is unclear, but one thing was certain: the Communists would have to deploy major forces on the Fukien coast in case he tried to land, which would create the possibility of an armed clash, in short, a crisis. Chiang by now knew quite well that crises had a way of propelling the Americans into aggressive actions. It almost worked during the Quemoy crisis of September 1958.

If there were warnings from Washington urging him not to undertake such a risky course of action, other voices, notably those of the American admirals, were supportive. Getting the Sidewinder missiles was proof that his charisma still worked in Washington, and that his allies within the American military-political bureaucracy could still deliver. What Chiang's role in the stationing of the Matadors on Taiwan was is not known, but it certainly did not displease him. The Matadors with their offensive capability, their range of 600 miles with atomic warheads, were a sign of American commitment to his cause, which was offensive roll-back. The United States Embassy was an arm of the State Department which, despite Dulles's tenancy of the office of Secretary of State, was anathema to Chiang. The State Department was viewed as still crawling with men who shared the ideas of the China experts whose purge Mc-Carthy had brought about. What better way to deliver a dramatic warning to those seeking to appease "Red China" than by wrecking the United States Embassy?

DRAMATIC SHIFTS IN CHINA

The stationing of the Matadors on Taiwan was a clear and persuasive signal to Peking that the mild Sino-American thaw that had begun in 1955 was freezing over again. Nineteen forty-nine appeared to be repeating itself. As soon as forces in Washington seeking some accommodation with the New China made headway, counterforces reacted and swung the United States government back into its old anti-China groove. As the summer and fall months passed, and the Chinese saw Chiang feverishly pouring military forces into Quemoy under the benevolent watch of the Seventh Fleet, their estimation of the change in Washington was vindicated. In any case, Dulles's speech of June 28 was a ringing statement that Washington was veering away from any policy of accommodation with China. With the appearance of a new Japanese anticommunist belligerence in the form of Prime Minister Kishi, the clouds were again darkening in East Asia. One immediate result of this new trend in events was to scuttle all the thinking that had up till then gone into the formulation of the second five-year plan. What was the purpose of developing an export industry when access to the outer world, particularly Southeast Asia, would be blocked and when China might again face blockade? Chiang's warships were still blockading a thousand-mile stretch of the coast up from Amoy and Foochow, and if tensions heightened, the entire coast could once again be shut off.

Although the Chinese (like the Russians and the Americans) wrote and talked about economic planning as if it had no relationship to foreign policy, the fact is that estimation of the external environment was the basis of all planning. Was the environment to be peaceful or hostile? —that was the key question. And if it was somewhere on a scale ranging from peace to war, what was the "mix" likely to be? Economic planning is not a rarefied exercise in technical management. It involves decisions that affect the lives of virtually everyone in society. Expectations are created not only within the bureaucracies but among the people as a whole. If the assumptions underlying that planning are suddenly shattered, the reverberations will be quickly felt throughout the government and throughout society. On May 6, 1957, when the Pentagon announced the stationing of Matadors on Taiwan, a fatal blow was dealt to the foreign policy assumptions that had gradually been gaining strength in China. If the environment along the China coast was once again to become hostile, how could one justify cutting defense spending in order to invest in agriculture and light industry? If trade was to be blocked, why build up an export industry? And if war was again threatening, how could one raise people's expectations about a better life?

I have talked to people who were in Peking during that explosive month of May and one of the impressions they relayed was that "the center was in a state of paralysis." That impression vanished on June 8, when the official *People's Daily* appeared on the newsstands with its editorial "Why Is This?" People knew immediately that a new line had been decided upon, and all criticism ended. But during the few weeks of the vacuum, when the leaders at the top were arguing over the new situation and deciding what was to be done, criticism had poured out. While criticisms of Russia were naturally noted eagerly by outside observers, the general tone was nationalistic. There were no attacks on Mao Tse-tung or any other top leaders of the country. In fact, virtually all the critics voiced confidence in China's socialism and satisfaction with the great achievements that had been made. Many called upon Mao to lead China onto a new socialist path that would be independent from Russia's. Since many of the critics were intellectuals of bourgeois background or non-Communists who had rallied to the new government after the Liberation, it was simple later to attack them as ideological followers of Imre Nagy who wanted to take China out of the socialist camp. Nevertheless, these bourgeois critics did reflect, in extreme form, a line of thinking that was current at the highest levels of the leadership. In the light of subsequent events, particularly the Cultural Revolution, one can begin to identify that line of thinking. Indeed, it is from around this time that one can detect ideological currents, analogous to those I have identified within America, that guided and dominated the thinking of various groups within the Chinese leadership. The current that these bourgeois critics reflected can, provisionally, be called the current of "self-reliance." During the Cultural Revolution, the Russians and others would call it blatant nationalism.

CONFLICTS OF CURRENTS IN CHINA

"Self-reliance" won out in the domestic field in January 1961, when the leadership radically altered internal policy in the wake of the break in economic relations with Russia in July–August 1960 (the abrupt withdrawal of Russian technicians), the unprecedented natural disasters, and the difficulties ensuing from the formation of people's communes. That policy involved priority for agriculture, followed by stress on light industry, and last, heavy industry. At that time, it also involved a return to some market-type conditions (which were severely criticized during the Cultural Revolution). But administratively, it was marked by a far-reaching true decentralization where peasants and firms were allowed to retain a considerable amount of resources and reinvest them as they saw fit without being subject to the full rigors of a command economy. Above all, in view of the disasters that struck China at the time, it meant a slowdown in the breakneck pace of development that characterized the Great Leap Forward. Self-reliance was "nationalistic" simply because it saw that China had no recourse other than to go it alone, to make do with its own resources.

The obverse of self-reliance in 1957 was economic dependence on Russia. This thinking held that China had no other choice for its economic development than to import massive amounts of capital goods from Russia and, in particular, to rely on Russian aid, support, and protection for its national security. At the beginning of 1961, China no longer had that choice. Khrushchev's withdrawal of technicians at a time when China was undergoing intense agony made any renewal of economic dependence on Russia virtually impossible—or possible only on terms of humiliation to the Chinese. But in 1957, the choice was not only still present but clearcut. The Chinese leadership chose dependence on Russia, and, as in the fall of 1949, this was symbolized by a visit by Mao Tse-tung to Moscow. Later in 1957, Sino-Russian relations were hailed as a shining example of internationalism and contrasted with the bourgeois nationalism propagated by the rightists.

In the latter months of 1957 and throughout 1958, Liu Shao-ch'i would play one of the most prominent roles on the public Chinese political scene. In December 1958, Mao Tse-tung resigned from the "presidency" of China and was replaced by Liu, an event that was generally and correctly interpreted as a loss of power for Mao. In late 1960, Liu himself was to suffer a loss of power, and his humiliation in Moscow in November 1960 revealed that he was unable to make Khrushchev change his policies toward China. He rallied again in the summer of 1962 and retained power until his fall in the summer of 1966. In his manner, thinking, and experience, Liu was an orthodox communist. As the leader of the underground party in the "white" regions, he headed a tightly knit apparatus which had to remain conspiratorial in order to survive. He, thus, missed much of the exhilarating democracy which reigned in Yenan. Whether he liked the Russians or not is immaterial. In the early 1960s, he attacked Yugoslav and Russian revisionism as intensely as any other leader in China, but always from the vantage point of the orthodox communist. He had played the major role in re-creating the Chinese Communist party after the Liberation as an essentially urban, working class–based, vanguard organization. He believed in organization and further believed that all organization had to have a clear-cut chain of command. Organization was his specialty, and ideology was construed as correct thought that would enable a communist to function effectively within organization. As an orthodox communist, he also fully accepted the premises and experiences of a half-century of Bolshevik rule in Russia. Those premises involved extreme sensitivity to external threat (understandable in a man who had fought in the underground) and a conviction that control had to be exercised constantly so that things did not get out of hand. Until his own humiliation in Moscow in November 1960, he considered the Soviet Union a resounding socialist success, a model for China, and China's natural friend and ally.

When the turning point came in China in early June 1957, it was not difficult for Liu to lead the campaign against the bourgeois nationalist rightists and to celebrate the grand alliance between Russia and China, which he did in a major speech at the time of the November celebration of the Russian October Revolution (when Mao was in Moscow). No man is more reviled in China today than Liu Shao-ch'i. Attacks on him initially centered on his domestic revisionist policies (a capitalist-roader). But later attacks increasingly implied that he was a tool of the Russians, a man willing to sell out China to Moscow's interests. While it is hard, but not impossible, to see that in the 1960s, there can be no doubt that in the latter half of 1957, Liu Shao-ch'i was the Chinese leader who most symbolized the unbreakable friendship between China and Russia.

In the early part of 1957, two currents were contending in China. One advocated self-reliance and the other dependence on Russia. Ch'en Yün headed or at least symbolized the first, and Liu Shao-ch'i clearly headed and guided the second.

While no one publicly charged Ch'en Yün with espousing a bourgeois rightist world view in 1957, his concern with trade indicates that he and those who thought like him had some definite notions as to the nature of the world situation. If imperialism was truly based on capitalism, this meant a long-range trend toward the one kind of global condition most lucrative to capitalism, a world market system linked together by ever-expanding trade. If American capitalism had fundamental system needs to trade with China (and with Russia), why could China not do so? With its socialist government and firmly led by a Communist party, there was no danger whatsoever that trade could once again become the opening wedge for imperialism to enter China. The official retention of the "national bourgeoisie" as one of China's revolutionary classes had only one practical significance: they were a link to the Overseas Chinese and to the broader world market system. They also had domestic significance as people with needed business talents, but these were replaceable. Their far-flung ties with the overseas world (chiefly Chinese), however, were not replaceable. With recessionary trends in America and in Japan, why would American capitalism not reach out to new markets such as those potentially available in China?

The self-reliance current in China considered the internationalist current in America, particularly its elements tending toward peaceful coexistence and more trade, as the most basic to American capitalism. Therefore, once the dangers of war had receded, that current would become predominant and provide new opportunities for China.

Liu Shao-ch'i's current, on the other hand, accepted the orthodox Russian view that the world was divided into two hostile camps and that China had no choice but to align itself unreservedly with the socialist camp. Even after he began to denounce Soviet revisionism in the early 1960s, Liu continued to hold to this view. It was Russia, he maintained, that was destroying the solidarity of the socialist camp. China's attacks against revisionism had only one aim: to force Russia back into a position that held the unity of the socialist camp to be the highest priority for all communists. Chinese attacks against Yugoslavia at this time stressed not only the degeneracy of that country's internal system, but the fact that, in the interests of self-gain, Yugoslavia had deserted the socialist camp and sold out to the imperialists. If the Russian line of a world divided into two camps most closely fit the containment current in America, then so did Liu's current. Like the Russians, Liu gave primacy to the building of the camp and, of course, to China's role in it. Like the Russians also, he was extremely suspicious of any accommodation with the West, particularly America, that was not anchored in hard and fast realities.

MAO'S ROLE AND MAO'S CURRENT

Where did Mao Tse-tung fit into this picture? Since the beginning of the Cultural Revolution, the Russians have portrayed him as a bourgeois nationalist with Napoleonic pretensions, and painted the political system of China as a "military-bureaucratic dictatorship." In other words, Mao in their eyes represents the bourgeois side of China that was never effaced after the Liberation. The emerging relationship between China and America which became evident in the spring of 1971 simply confirmed to them the truth of what they had all along suspected. But leaving aside biases of one sort or another, one must at least say that Mao Tse-tung represented the entire tradition associated with the long Yenan experience of Chinese communism. It was Mao who launched the rural revolution in 1927; it was Mao who emerged as the dominant leader during the Long March; and it was Mao who was hailed as the leader of Chinese communism during the Seventh Party Congress in 1945. Much has been written about the Yenan experience of Chinese communism, but its spirit and character can be summarized in one word: revolutionary.

Revolution meant "*fanshen*," turning all that was upside down so that something new and better could emerge. If the spirit of the Liu current was organizational and that of the Ch'en Yün current pragmatic, the spirit of Yenan was experimental. The Yenan communists took the word communism at face value—a future society where men would be free, equal, happy, productive, and imaginative, and where collectively they would be a benefit not a terror to mankind. Certainly there was a utopian quality to Yenan communism, as there also was a practical and a cunning side, and a sense of caution and a certain conservatism. Yenan communism may have been sparked by the radical values flowing out of the May 4th Movement and the Communist party of the early 1920s, but the human environment in which it grew up was set by the peasants of China. The Russians, predictably, with their loathing of everything that is peasant (in Marx's words, "village idiocy"), regard peasant revolution as a primitive form of rebellion that goes nowhere or leads in dangerous directions unless channeled by a vanguard Communist party. In the 1940s, Americans were far more favorably inclined toward Yenan communism than the Russians, but in the 1960s, the great new crop of policy-oriented social scientists and defense intellectuals turned into ardent admirers of Liu Shao-ch'i and reviled Mao as a crazy old man seeking to recapture an adolescence of rebellion.

The Mao Tse-tung current, as one can see from the Great Leap Forward and the Cultural Revolution, fitted into neither of the other two. It was utopian and not pragmatic, and it believed in spontaneity rather than careful organizational control and guidance. Mao was then and is now committed to the notion that only "uninterrupted revolution," constant change, will finally lift China out of its backwardness. He is one of the few great leaders today who preaches and practices the pioneer spirit. Mao has always been primarily concerned with the revolution in his own country, and that concern has made the People's Republic of China one of the most exciting, experimental, and extraordinary societies in a world increasingly made up of dullness or bloodiness.

While one can see the logical and necessary foreign policy components of the other two currents, what sort of foreign policy stance follows from the Mao Tse-tung current? There is a famous (if not the most famous) saying of Mao Tse-tung which gives a clue: "Power grows out of the barrel of a gun." The entire history of Chinese communism since the disaster of 1927 taught the Communists that without independent armed power, they were doomed to destruction. But while the Chinese Revolution came to rely on armed power, the Kiangsi and Yenan experience taught them other lessons. For one thing, it taught them that if their movement did not see itself in some larger national and global context, it would degenerate into just another of the many armed utopian peasant movements that had erupted in China in the course of millennia. The Japanese invasion of China gave the Chinese Communists opportunities that they would have missed had they blockheadedly continued with their ultraleft line of radical revolution. Marxism and Leninism and the intellectuals taught them something about the larger logic of world politics which turned out to be as useful, in some instances, as several divisions of soldiers. And the Kiangsi and Yenan experience taught the Chinese Communists that unless society was solidly behind them so that they could swim like fish in the ocean, then they were doomed to defeat.

If Marxism gave the Chinese a productive world view, Leninism gave them methods of organization. The Communist party of China had taken that vast country, whose people, the great writer Lu Hsün once wrote, were like grains of sand, and turned it into a mighty unified nation. Mao is a Marxist and a Leninist. He had no disagreement with Liu Shao-ch'i on those grounds. At the same time, Mao evolved certain notions of "new democracy" which sketched out an image of a progressive China with many bourgeois elements left in it. These notions made him amenable to a united front with Chiang Kai-shek and, later, on the eve of final victory, to a coalition government with the remnant forces of the Kuomintang. Extrapolating from Mao's Marxism-Leninism, on the one hand, and his notions of "new democracy," on the other, one can say that he was open to the possibilities of foreign policy provided by either or both of the other two currents. Collaboration with Russia made eminent sense, but so did openness to American capitalism, assuming it was not hostile. In the summer of 1949, Mao saw no contradiction between "leaning to one side" (that is, toward Russia) and at the same time making overtures to America.

When Mao Tse-tung brought Ch'en Yün back out of obscurity in the early days of the Cultural Revolution, he signified the initiation of a new foreign policy line that eventuated in Nixon's visit to Peking. But it would be an error to assume that Mao suddenly chose to identify himself with a current that in late 1957 had been denounced as bourgeois rightist. In 1966, as the Liu current was definitely expunged from Chinese politics, the Ch'en Yün current came back in—but as *a* not *the* current guiding Chinese foreign policy. It is probably safe to say that early in 1957, Mao Tse-tung was quite sympathetic to the Ch'en Yün current, without sacrificing any of his sympathy and support for the Liu current. If the international environment was settling down, why should China not explore new avenues of foreign trade? And why should this in any way endanger its close and friendly ties to Russia? Anyway, were not the Russians themselves beginning to tread the same path?

But in order to discover some unique Mao Tse-tung element in the area of foreign policy, we must again return to the saying, "Power grows out of the barrel of a gun." Translated into terms of power politics, this means that a movement or a government must have its own independent armed forces which rely on no outside force for weapons, men, and supplies. The Chinese Communists in 1927 were crushed because they did not have independent armed forces. And the tragedy of Indonesian communism in 1965 can be ascribed to the same condition. That immense political structure, the biggest Communist party in Asia except for that of China, vanished virtually overnight as murderous soldiers and fanatic Muslim villagers slaughtered a half-million Communists. In 1957, China's armed forces were still alarmingly dependent on Russia. Except for small arms, China produced little heavy weaponry and had to import everything from Russia or Eastern Europe. It was also dependent on Russia in another way. Because of the strange new power situation created by nuclear weapons, China found itself under a Russian nuclear umbrella that it did not itself hold. In August 1959, under the impact of the events that led to the Camp David meeting, Marshal P'eng Te-huai was purged from the Chinese leadership. P'eng had led the Russian-supplied and Russian-guided Chinese forces in Korea, and had remained a staunch advocate of continuing reliance on Russia. He had definite military notions of his own, namely, that China's armies had to be big and fully equipped with conventional weaponry so that they would always be prepared to meet another challenge like Korea. No matter how they were twisted, P'eng's military theories always required far-reaching reliance on Russia, which was a political even more than a military fact.

If China wished to achieve self-reliance in weaponry, it would have to build up its strategic industries, a program tantamount to giving China a network of heavy industry comparable to that of Japan or Britain. That, as the Chinese realized, would take time. Furthermore, if China's scarce resources were to be reoriented toward agriculture and light industry, this would delay the achievement of a heavy industry base even more. But there was another way China might achieve self-reliance and independence in the military sphere—by developing its own nuclear capability. During the Great Leap Forward, Westerners were amazed by the often repeated Chinese slogan of catching up with Britain in steel production. Even then, Britain's domestic economy was ailing, and either Japan or Germany seemed a much worthier capitalist model to emulate. But, unlike either Japan or Germany, Britain had atomic bombs, and in May 1957, it acquired a nuclear capability. Britain and America were linked culturally, as China and Russia were linked ideologically, but, in Marxist eyes, that alone could not explain the tightness of the Anglo-American alliance. Nor could the British economy, which showed too many signs of decay. What clearly explained it was that Britain was an independent military power, and the sign of that independence was its own nuclear program, which it pursued in the face of American disinterest at some times and opposition at others.

It is quite consistent with Mao's thinking and the current he represents (and the remarks he made in his 1956 speech, "The Ten Great Relationships") that it was Mao himself who conceived, advocated, and implemented China's program to develop an independent nuclear capability.

Prior to May 1957, there seemed to be no inconsistency among these three foreign policy currents. If conditions were favorable, why should China not expand its external trade? And why should China not continue on the path of harmonious cooperation with Russia, which Khrushchev himself advocated? And why should China not at the same time lay the foundations for an independent nuclear capability? A second five-year plan encompassing these three premises was not difficult to envisage. Some resources might have to be switched from heavy industry, which would make the military men unhappy and uneasy, but such problems could be worked out. In any case, some slowdown in the development of heavy industry could be matched by increased imports of capital goods from Russia. All leaders in China in 1956, when the generally harmonious Eighth Party Congress met, appeared to agree that some basic changes in economic development had to be made. Obviously, then, they would have to be ready for factional fights over who got what and how much.

CHINA TURNS AGAIN TOWARD RUSSIA

Mao's global thinking involves the notion of principal and secondary enemies and a basic strategic premise that at all times one must have only one principal enemy. In the summer of 1971, when the final struggle with Lin Piao was reaching a climax, a major article in the *People's*

Daily laid forth this notion (as is customary, using the allegory of "Japanese imperialism" of the 1930s for Russia):

> ... Even though Communists oppose all imperialisms, one had to make a distinction between Japanese imperialism which was aggressing against China and such other imperialisms of the time which were not carrying out such aggression. One had to make distinctions about imperialisms which under differing circumstances and at different times adopted different kinds of policies. Chairman Mao, using the revolutionary dialectical method of dividing one into two, has made scientific distinctions in regard to the enemy camp in which he clearly differentiates who is the principal enemy, who is the secondary enemy, and who is a temporary or an indirect ally. This concrete and exact distinction served the purpose of isolating to the highest degree possible the principal enemy of the Chinese people at that time, namely Japanese imperialism which was aggressing against China.[19]

There is no evidence whatsoever that Mao or any other top leader in China in 1957 saw Russia as an eventual enemy. Nevertheless, there were many Chinese leaders including Mao who were unhappy over the innate Russian drive to gain control over all its allies. Russia may not yet have been an enemy, but it also was not the perfect friend celebrated in official propaganda. If the American threat had continued to ebb, as it seemed to be doing early in 1957, China might eventually get some breathing space during which to put its independence on a more solid foundation, particularly an independent military capability. But with the Matadors on Taiwan, America once again revealed itself to be not only China's mortal enemy but, in Mao's thinking, the principal enemy.

The changing external situation gave victory to the Liu Shao-ch'i current and the victors decided to make it absolute by launching a purge of all political figures associated with the opposing current. Hundreds of rightists were publicly denounced, but no major figures were attacked, in contrast to the Cultural Revolution. It is reasonable to presume that Mao himself blocked any open purge of key leaders like Ch'en Yün, in the expectation that circumstances might once again change to make the policies of this current more appropriate. During the Cultural Revolution, Mao made the opposite decision—to go all-out and purge once and for all from the Chinese political scene all top leaders who had been associated with the pro-Russian current. The Ch'en Yün current did not lose out altogether because some of its economic notions, particularly the stress on agriculture and light industry, became guiding policies of the Great Leap Forward.

[19] *Jen-min jih-pao* (*People's Daily*), August 17, 1971, translated by author.

While Mao seems to have fully supported the Liu current's renewed adherence to the alliance with Russia, he most likely insisted that the terms of renewal must involve Russian help in giving China an independent nuclear capability. If Britain had an H-bomb as America's ally, why should not China, as Russia's closest ally, also have one? Negotiations were obviously under way in the summer and early fall between Russia and China on the subject of nuclear aid. They culminated in the secret Russian-Chinese nuclear sharing agreement of October 15, 1957. Only in 1963, when the Russians signed the Partial Test Ban Treaty with America, did the Chinese reveal the existence of that agreement and the fact that the Russians had broken it in the summer of 1959 as a "gift" to President Eisenhower.

Mao's second and last visit to Moscow came shortly after the agreement was concluded. But it also followed Russia's successful test of an ICBM in August and the spectacular launching of sputnik in October. The similarities between the events leading up to Mao's 1957 visit to Moscow and the 1949 situation are clear. Both in the first half of 1949 and in the first half of 1957, chances seemed good for at least less hostile relations with America. In both years, America suddenly reversed its policy trends and adopted a hostile stance toward China. In both years, the Russians scored major breakthroughs in the nuclear field. In fact, the first Russian atomic explosion in September 1949 and the double ICBM-sputnik breakthrough in the fall of 1957 had the greatest impact on American political-military thinking of all the technological breakthroughs the Russians achieved before and since (there was much less furor in Washington over Russia's H-bomb breakthrough in 1954). The events of 1949 were followed by the Korean War. Who could fault Mao or any other Chinese leader for believing that the similar events of 1957 would soon lead to the threat of another war in East Asia? They were certainly not wrong on that score, for the Quemoy crisis of 1958 came close to plunging America and China into war with each other.

If the events on the China coast aroused in China a deeper sense of urgency and crisis in the latter part of 1957, the same was true in Russia. In 1949, the Russians had become increasingly alarmed at the prospect of German rearmament. In 1957, they expressed alarm over the prospect of nuclear weapons stationed on German soil with Adenauer's government involved in their command and control. If America was embarking on a policy of ringing Russia and China with nuclear-tipped IRBMs, why not give China a nuclear capability? There must have been vehement arguments within the Russian leadership on this issue. Russian military leaders undoubtedly argued that the Chinese should be given no nuclear capability unless Moscow could exercise complete control over it. But if Mao insisted on Chinese command and control or at least a decisive voice in the program, then the Russians could not have the centralized dominance that they wanted. Nor could China be rebuffed, for it was Russia's most important ally. The May events had shown that there were anti-Russian currents in China, and who knew but that China might suddenly change its policies if America dropped its irrational hostility. The Chinese alliance put heavy burdens on the Russian economy, and the festering conflict in East Asia always threatened to involve Russia in an area of secondary national interest. And, of course, if America discovered, as it undoubtedly would, that Russia was aiding China to develop its own nuclear weapons, the hostility and threat to Russia would increase even more. Yet like Stalin in the winter months of 1949–1950, the Russians had no choice but to negotiate arduously with the Chinese and work out agreements not just on nuclear sharing but on trade and aid.

In Moscow, Mao addressed the Supreme Soviet and received thunderous applause. He also went to Moscow University and spoke to Chinese students there, most of whom were studying science and technology. Some of them must have been from Dubna, the great Russian center for nuclear research. Mao's speech to the students is best known for his remark that "today it is not the west wind which prevails over the east wind, but the east wind which prevails over the west wind." But he also said, "The socialist camp must have one head, and that head is the Soviet Union; communist and workers' parties of all countries must have one head, and that head is the Soviet Communist party."

Mao officially went to Moscow to attend the international congress of communist and workers' parties. Despite wrangling and differences, the congress issued a declaration reaffirming the fundamental principle of the unity of the socialist camp and united opposition against the imperialist camp headed by America. There is no reason to doubt that Mao fully meant what he said to the Chinese students at Moscow University. The Russians, by concluding the nuclear sharing pact, made a major gesture showing their willingness to treat China as an equal. In return, Mao accepted the premise of the unity of the socialist camp under Russian leadership.

With his country's national security assured as far as possible in the face of the looming threat in the Taiwan Straits, Mao returned home with one predominant concern on his mind: the need to revolutionize Chinese society by completing the revolutionary process in China's great rural regions. No one disagreed on the need to drastically transform Chinese agriculture, but how to do it was another matter. Ch'en Yün's program of slow but sure capital investment in agriculture was out of the question now that the foreign policy props (trade) had been knocked out from under it. Mao's prescriptions for the revolutionization of agriculture were communes, militias, and peasant initiative. His vision for the Great Leap Forward was inspired by the Yenan experience where a combination of cooperative approaches in farm work, peasant-soldier self-defense militias, and simple but innovative approaches to production (both agricultural and light industrial) had brought about miracles during the 1930s and 1940s. In the summer of 1958, as Mao Tse-tung (and Liu Shao-ch'i) toured China, the vision was rapidly coming into being. Communes began to sprout up with extraordinary rapidity; militias were organized and arms distributed to the peasants; and peasants began to make all kinds of products that they never before would have dreamed of. Despite the failures of the Great Leap Forward at that time, Mao held to his ideas, which have now been, by and large, realized in the rural areas. The fast but risky approach instituted in 1958 did not work, but the slow but sure approach that followed in early 1961 did—and by the beginning of the 1970s had resulted in ten years of bumper harvests.

There can be little doubt that Liu Shao-ch'i and others of his current were alarmed by the seemingly anarchic nature of the communization movement. All orthodox communists had been taught to abhor "spontaneity" and Liu was no exception. If the communes became too decentralized, grain deliveries could be endangered. Distributing arms to peasants seemed dangerous to many military leaders, notably P'eng Te-huai, who opposed the formation of militias. And the intense and chaotic manufacture of so many wierd things like backyard steel created immense waste which China could ill afford. By early 1959, the Great Leap Forward was proceeding in a much more orderly and organized fashion under the slogan, "All the country is a single chessboard," and by 1960 many of the communes had been transformed into military-type organizations where the people were led to work by party cadres as if to battle. The official explanation for the failures of the 1959–1960 period is unprecedented natural disasters. The Western explanation is mismanagement. But some of the failure must be ascribed to the clash of two very different approaches symbolized by Mao and Liu. Spontaneity and control do not mesh very well. In the Cultural Revolution, the two traditions of Chinese communism, the one coming out of Yenan and the other out of the underground movement in the cities, had their final confrontation. Yenan won out.

In March 1958, China finally withdrew all its troops from Korea, thereby signifying its disinclination to fight another war like the Korean War, unless forced to do so. China's stance thereafter was fundamentally defensive. The purge of P'eng Te-huai in the summer of 1959 decided the issue of dependence on Russia for conventional weaponry—henceforth there would be no dependence and China would have to manufacture its own arms. China's ground combat forces remained small throughout the 1960s, and, because of their domestic responsibilities, had little capability to pour over China's borders in some massive foreign invasion. It was a superb army, as the short border war of 1962 with India showed, but it was small. In the 1960s, as Washington began to sound the alarms of "Chinese expansionism," America's hawks could not convincingly allege that huge Chinese armies were poised to lunge across their borders. Rather, the line from Washington went, the Chinese were fomenting wars of liberation, egging on others like the Viet Cong or the Pathet Lao to make trouble for the free world. More darkly in the background was the specter of a billion Chinese armed with nuclear weapons ready to blow up the world in pursuit of their mad revolutionary ambitions. However distorted this image, there was considerable truth to it. Mao was and remains a revolutionary. He considers revolution a good thing for peoples, countries, and individuals. While he always maintained that his practical revolutionary concern was limited to his own country, he never hesitated to praise revolutionary tendencies wherever he saw them (Bangla Desh, perhaps, being a strategic exception). He has even argued that revolution is the only path toward world peace. On the other hand, for all his alleged deprecation of the destructiveness of nuclear weapons, Mao made China a nuclear country. It is not unrelated that Charles de Gaulle, one of the foreign leaders he truly admired, gave his country a nuclear capability and declared France's independence from American domination.

DOCTRINES OF "LIMITED WAR"

"Limited war," as the term indicates, means a war fought within limits, specifically a non-nuclear war. The limits are set by higher political authorities and translated into "rules of engagement," the operational limits of the fighting services. The higher political authorities could not be just the theater commander or even the Joint Chiefs of Staff because limits depend on an enemy understanding and accepting them. At the minimum, this requires some mutually understandable signaling between the highest political authorities on both sides and diplomatic contact. If one side declares war on the other in the traditional sense, such contact is unnecessary. Roosevelt's policy of unconditional surrender made all contact, except the most surreptitious, between the Allies and the Axis powers impossible. War, thus, became a slugging match between two opposing military forces and was ended by military men from the opposing sides agreeing to a ceasefire.

The Korean War was a limited war in every sense, with the most dramatic limit on the American side being the tolerance of Manchuria as a "sanctuary." The limited war notion implied a high degree of political control over military operations. For this reason and others, it was generally detested by military men. General Twining attacked the notion of limited war in the most scathing terms.[20] MacArthur loathed it and was purged because of his refusal to abide by the limits Truman set upon him. The often heard right-wing slogan, "There is no substitute for victory," is an attack on the limited war notion. One should be cautious about getting involved in wars, but once involved, the military should be given free rein (free from political control) to win in whatever way it considers professionally correct. Until the Vietnam war, the Korean War was the most unpopular among military men. American boys were fighting and dying, yet United States air power was prohibited from destroying enemy supply lines in Manchuria. The military found itself part of a larger chess game being played in Washington for reasons and objectives distant from the well-understood concept of victory. The "never again" mentality that dominated American military thinking after the Korean War held that America should never again allow itself to be dragged into an Asian land war unless it could go all-out for victory, using all available weapons (including nuclear weapons) and attacking all targets related to the war.

The most primitive explanation for the Army's enthusiasm about limited war is that since its role in modern warfare appeared to be declining, it had to find a new role and mission, and limited war fitted the need. The same argument was also made over a decade later when the Army developed an enthusiasm for the antiballistic missile (ABM). The Army's interests were always more precarious than those of the Air Force and the Navy and a limited war capability would give it a new share in the skein of military-budgetary interests. However, the Army's interest in limited war can also be explained in other terms. Army generals, unlike the chieftans of the other services, had a long tradition of high public service. Several Army generals had become Presidents, but never an admiral. General Marshall had been a distinguished Secretary of State and Secretary of Defense. General Eisenhower had been a university president and then became President of the country. General Taylor himself had a reputation in Europe of being one of the most civilized and intellectual American military leaders. The United States Army was clearly the most liberal and democratic of the services, in contrast to the hoary conservatism of the Navy and the peculiar elitism of the Air Force. It was not accidental, therefore, that in the latter half of the 1950s, a kind of alliance arose between the Army and the liberal Democrats in Congress. Symbolic of this was the growing friendship

[20] In *Neither Liberty Nor Safety: A Hard Look at U.S. Military Policy and Strategy.*

between Maxwell Taylor and John F. Kennedy, and it was not surprising that Kennedy named Taylor the chairman of the Joint Chiefs of Staff when he became President. The Army was less hostile than the other services to the notion of political ("civilian") control of the military, for it better understood the fact that all wars are basically political in the long run. Wars are fought for political power and the winning of battles is just part of the struggle, something Clausewitz recognized long before.

The notions of limited war rested on the conviction that the growing success of containment, the gradual elimination of the danger of nuclear war between the great powers, could actually make the world a much more turbulent place. Communism was still expansionistic, and pervasive instability at various key points of the world provided temptations for communists to move in and gain advantage for themselves. This could cause brush-fire wars which America, in its own interests, had to resist. But the old-fashioned notion that all one had to do was to send in some detachments of Marines to clean up the mess was no longer appropriate. These were no longer isolated local disturbances with no relevance beyond themselves, but part of a larger cold war between the two camps. Korea had demonstrated that. Thus, every move on the local scene had to be orchestrated in terms of a very broad strategy which only the highest political authorities could and should work out. Taylor's notions of limited war presented in *The Uncertain Trumpet* eventually led to Kennedy's grand schemes for dealing with insurgencies throughout the world ("counterinsurgency"). Both Kennedy and Taylor saw the program of counterinsurgency in its widest geopolitical sense as an integral part of a process whereby America sought to preserve world peace, assure stability in the free world, and help the poor nations to develop toward prosperity. In the eyes of these advocates of limited war, massive retaliation was a ludicrous policy. If Russia and America deterred each other from nuclear war, what about the rest of the world? If there was no plan, no comprehensive program, no rational application of power, then the chaos and anarchy of a brush-fire war could get out of control and produce central war even under conditions of mutual deterrence. The Korean War had come close to sparking World War III, and careful planning and management of America's defense system could avoid that.

Eisenhower was never enamored of all the talk about limited war. While he sympathized, as an Army general, with the notion of firmer political control over the military, he knew from experience how difficult that was to achieve. During his first term, he exercised control through a close personal relationship with Admiral Radford. And during his second term, despite the 1958 reorganization of the Defense Department, he adhered to established policies while pursuing his central concern:

fighting inflation by keeping the defense budget and other federal spending down. With the new prominence of the Air Force under the Joint Chiefs of Staff chairman Twining, the doctrines of massive retaliation continued to prevail—the Strategic Air Command remained the core of America's military system. Eisenhower's gift, as he demonstrated in World War II, was an ability to work with all kinds of discordant elements without creating controversies.

Limited war was a good liberal notion in the late 1950s, so that it is not surprising that a number of university social scientists, among them Henry Kissinger, wrote books on the subject. Defense intellectuals in the State Department, in the tradition of Paul Nitze, were also enthusiastic about the notion of limited war. The liberals were in favor of anything that would increase political control over the military. Kennedy's election marked a great triumph for the liberals, and during his administration they made the most ambitious attempt yet to shackle the military. This is the story of McNamara's administration of the Department of Defense.

The Army already started to move toward doctrines of limited war in 1955. The Air Force was always opposed. Initially, the Navy also evinced no interest in the notion. As Huntington notes, "Only after the retirement of Admiral Radford in 1957 and the shift in State Department thinking away from massive retaliation did naval leaders become outspoken advocates of greater limited war preparations."[21] Huntington expresses surprise that the Navy did not become interested earlier in limited war, since "traditional naval doctrine" as "the principal military instrument of diplomacy" should have made it naturally sympathetic to the notion. But the eruption of Navy "enthusiasm" about limited war in 1957 is understandable if one considers that during the first Eisenhower Administration the Navy had a powerful voice in the highest councils of political leadership through Admiral Radford and that in 1957 it lost that voice.

NAVY "ENTHUSIASM" FOR LIMITED WAR

The Navy did well in World War II, and Admiral Leahy's friendship with Roosevelt and Roosevelt's own advocacy of the Navy was reassuring. The Truman Administration, as we have seen, was a very bad period for the Navy. Things changed in 1953 with the appointment of Admiral Radford. Despite his ferocious views on China and communism and his obvious loyalty to the Navy, Radford seems to have functioned as a

[21] Samuel P. Huntington, *The Common Defense*, p. 347.

"statesman," not as a Navy hatchetman. The Navy was well taken care of budgetarily and did get its carriers, but it cannot be argued that defense policy took a naval line. The Air Force remained the chief service during Eisenhower's first administration. But the Navy well remembered the bitter years of the Truman Administration and could easily anticipate another Democratic administration in 1961. The Democrats were showing their habitual preference for the Air Force and the Army. Furthermore, their softness on China and orientation toward Europe once again boded ill for the Navy.

One of the traditional Navy doctrines that predisposed it toward limited war was central to its operational ideology. This was the notion that carrier-based air power could play a decisive role in ground combat. This could not be tested in Korea because the Air Force had land bases in Japan and the proximity of Russian ships always created a hazard for naval units. But the Indochina war of the early 1950s, particularly the battle of Dienbienphu, seemed to provide a God-given chance to test it. The Air Force had no bases anywhere nearby, and its long-range Strategic Air Command planes could not be used because they had to be on a state of constant alert in case of war with Russia. But the Navy had carriers which could move at virtually no risk into the Gulf of Tonkin and send waves of fighter-bombers over the battlefield of Dienbienphu. What had been an amorphous guerrilla war until then became a classic conventional battle. Vo Nguyen Giap was following classic doctrines already applied by the Chinese during their war with the Kuomintang. Just as at the right moment the Chinese Communists had forged all their mobile guerrillas together into a powerful army which took on the finest of the Kuomintang armies and then attacked the cities, Giap was moving from guerrilla to conventional war. Air power could now be applied for the first time with a promise of turning the tide. During the Chinese civil war, Chiang and his China Lobby friends argued that air power could have made a difference. That notion was spelled out in a book by the French general Lionel Chassin, who as commander of French air forces in Indochina naturally felt that with air power he could achieve in Indochina what Chiang, without air power, was not able to achieve in China. Admiral Radford put powerful pressure on Eisenhower to intervene in the battle of Dienbienphu, and Dulles seems to have supported him. Eisenhower vetoed the plan.

The Navy, of course, obeyed the commander-in-chief, but it pursued its obsession with tactical carrier-based air power with even greater vigor. The Navy's demand that field commanders be given tactical nuclear weapons grew out of this doctrine, for what could be more logical than that the same planes that dropped conventional bombs be permitted to drop nuclear bombs—tactical ones, of course, which would be used in battlefield situations. But the first Indochina war opened up another vision to the Navy: wars that would follow the model of the Chinese civil war rather than the Korean War. In Korea, two armies fought a war more European than Asian in appearance. But the Indochina war seemed like a carbon copy of the Chinese civil war in several respects. Communist guerrillas operated everywhere, whereas guerrillas had played only a minor role in Korea. The Communists fought not just militarily but politically and diplomatically, whereas in Korea Syngman Rhee and Kim Il Sung had firm control over their respective sides and the diplomacy was waged at the most rarefied levels of great power relationships. Revolutionaries agitated large segments of the population, whereas in Korea, the brief North Korean occupation of South Korea had created widespread hatred of the occupiers. Above all, the model that had worked in China and at the time of Dienbienphu seemed to be on the verge of a similar success in Indochina could easily be applied elsewhere in Southeast Asia. Next to Indochina was Thailand which had many of the same conditions as the countries of Indochina. Malaya was still combatting a major insurgency. The Philippines, America's great redoubt in Southeast Asia, was fighting a Communist insurgency. The Sino-Vietnamese model of revolutionary warfare taught that at some decisive point the guerrillas would have to go over to conventional war. At that point, air power would be decisive, and could be delivered only by the Navy.

The notions of limited war evolving at this time did not encompass guerrilla warfare. But the Navy men argued that the Indochina war was a true limited war, not simply a guerrilla war. The battle of Dienbienphu would have been impossible without the military supplies and artillery that poured in from China. China was the great rear area for the Viet Minh. Thus, if American air power intervened at Dienbienphu, it would have to be limited. Navy men did not particularly subscribe to the notion of the Air Force that there should be no limits to war. They had always fought limited wars and understood the political restrictions on war. But they also enthusiastically felt that war was possible under such limitations. One could bomb Viet Minh forces without bombing China. Or one could bomb supply depots just north of the border without bombing the rest of China. Or one could bomb China without bombing Russia. The Viet Minh might have started as guerrillas, but at the decisive point they could not fight without Chinese and Russian support. The limits should be set by the political leaders in Washington, but Dienbienphu offered a golden opportunity to test out a sacred Navy doctrine with good chance of demonstrable victory.

Nothing seemed more natural to the admirals reared in the thinking of Admiral Mahan than that the great hostile Eurasian land powers should

seek to break out of their landlocked isolation and seek access to the
oceans and the world's trading routes. Russia had the barrier of Western
Europe to overcome, but China with its long Pacific coastline already
had access to the Pacific. Communism gave China a new weapon with
which to press outward: organized revolutionary warfare using indige-
nous forces but backed by the full might of the hinterland powers. Indochina was the classic example of how Chinese expansionism was
proceeding.

In September 1954, the SEATO Treaty, which Dulles had labored
mightily to bring about, was signed in Manila; the signatories included
America, Britain, France, Australia, New Zealand, the Philippines, Thailand, and Pakistan. SEATO's formal zone of responsibility included
neither Taiwan nor Indochina (and also excluded Northeast Asia).
Nevertheless, by virtue of the responsibilities and commitments of the
signatory powers, these regions were, at least by implication, included.
Under the provisions of the Geneva Accords of 1954, France maintained
interests and responsibilities in all three countries of Indochina. Britain
possessed Hong Kong, Singapore, and had formal ties with Malaya.
America's commitments to Taiwan had been established by Truman's
interposition of the Seventh Fleet in the Taiwan Straits. Though the
tangle of commitments by the signatory powers was far worse than in the
case of the West European countries, Dulles clearly hoped that SEATO
would eventually turn into an East Asian NATO. It should become the
vehicle by which the signatory powers, whose commitments encompassed all the strategic regions of Southeast Asia, could in time evolve a
single common policy backed by unified military force.

In December 1954, however, America concluded a separate defense
treaty with Taiwan which deepened its ties to Chiang Kai-shek as Britain, the most important adherent to SEATO after America, was seeking
to improve its ties with the People's Republic of China. But the revelations of the Pentagon Papers now show that SEATO was a paper tiger
virtually from the outset. A few seemingly minor items in a chronology
published in the United States government version of the Pentagon Papers (not included in the Beacon edition) tell the story. On February 11,
1955, the Joint Chiefs of Staff advised the Secretary of Defense that
America should not enter into combined military planning for defense of
the SEATO area nor disclose its plans to SEATO members.[22] On June
7, 1956, Admiral Radford briefed the National Security Council on
strategy for the defense of South Vietnam, and on July 11, the Joint
Chiefs of Staff directed CINCPAC "to prepare a contingency plan based
on the quick response strategy as set forth by Admiral Radford in the
June 7, 1956 briefing to the NSC, for defense of South Vietnam." On

[22] U.S. Department of Defense, *United States-Vietnam Relations, 1945–67*, 12 vols.
(Washington, D.C.: Government Printing Office, March, 1969), IV.A.4., p. Y.

October 1, 1956, CINCPAC completed "OPLAN 46–56" for the defense of South Vietnam, and on March 19, 1957, OPLAN 45–56 was formally approved by the Joint Chiefs.[23] At that time, the French presence had been virtually eliminated from South Vietnam and replaced by a new American one. With unilateral American commitments to Taiwan and South Vietnam and with the refusal of the Joint Chiefs of Staff to share any of its defense plans for Southeast Asia with America's SEATO allies, there no longer was any hope of transforming SEATO into an East Asian NATO. Taiwan and South Vietnam were clearly the most dangerous regions of Southeast Asia, yet the SEATO signatory powers were asked to tie themselves to the American tail without any voice over where the front part of that creature might decide to go. Washington would eventually pay the price of its unwillingness to share power and responsibility with its allies. Thus, in 1964 when Rusk and McNamara traveled all over East Asia and Western Europe trying to drum up SEATO and NATO support for the venture in Indochina, only token forces were offered (and, in the case of the Thai and Philippine units, only after immense bribes in "aid" were paid).

Washington's inability to turn SEATO into a meaningful force is fully understandable in terms of the United States Navy's attitudes. The Navy, as we have already seen, was deeply fearful that all the machinations going on in Washington to "unify the services" would destroy its autonomy. The events of 1949 had already shown what unification and rationalization meant for the Navy. Admiral Radford's tenure as chairman of the Joint Chiefs of Staff was reassuring, but SEATO could be another threat of the same kind. Once CINCPAC's operations were entangled with those of other countries, operational autonomy would be lost. Moreover, the political attitudes of the two chief SEATO countries after America, Britain and France, were highly suspicious. Britain seemed forever intent on regaining its commercial interests in China, and France was a degenerate country willing to bargain with the communists just to keep some rubber plantations in Indochina. Moreover, entanglements with SEATO could shackle the Navy's freedom of action in regard to Taiwan. The Navy appreciated the defense treaty with Taiwan since it was a simple bilateral arrangement between the Republic of China and the United States of America. In fact, it was even more than that. Operationally, it became a Taipei-Honolulu axis in which Chiang's military men worked with officers from the CINCPAC's command for their common goals: resisting China. The evolution of an autonomous American defense plan for South Vietnam added it to CINCPAC's domain without the fear of bothersome interference from SEATO.

The Navy did not like the small thaw that seemed to be developing in

---

[23] *Ibid.*, pp. LL, MM.

the frozen relations between Peking and Washington. But there was nothing it could do, aside from resisting being drawn into dangerous entanglements like SEATO. As a conservative service, the Navy also had a tradition of respecting civilian authority, and while it might lobby for its point of view, did not believe in usurping power. But there was another stone wall against which the Navy felt it could not knock its head. The predominant military doctrine in Washington was still massive retaliation and Admiral Radford, for all his Pacific background, fully subscribed to it.[24] That doctrine called for cutbacks in conventional forces, and while the Navy fought tooth and nail against such cuts, it could not defy the logic under which they were ordered. So it also had been in the spring of 1949. The Navy was furious over its defeat on the carrier issue, but it could not controvert the "atomic blitz" doctrine—not until September. But in the spring of 1957, massive retaliation was coming apart at the seams. All intelligence reports indicated that the Russians were nearing new technological breakthroughs which then did come with ICBM and sputnik later in the year. The IRBM program was launched in anticipation of those breakthroughs. IRBMs installed in countries surrounding Russia were designed to reinforce not to replace massive retaliation. The Russians might be able to shoot down American long-range bombers and launch a missile or two against the continental United States, but IRBMs would threaten them with a holocaust of destruction in return. Nevertheless, the erosion of the massive retaliation doctrine provided a golden opportunity for the ideologically sensitive Navy.

If the threat of massive retaliation was receding in 1957 (as the threat of atomic blitz receded in 1949), then the Communists were sure to move forward again. There was no evidence of a "Red build-up," as U.S. News & World Report was trumpeting in the spring of 1957, but logic and world view dictated there would be. For the Navy, it seemed logical that the renewed communist aggression would come in East Asia. They considered the Bandung spirit a communist smokescreen—"sugar bullets," to borrow a phrase from the Vietnamese—to lull the free world into passivity. Chou En-lai in Indonesia was the advance patrol of an army that would surely follow. It was only a matter of time before another Korea, another Indochina would erupt. Although an Air Force general, General Twining, in his book *Neither Liberty nor Safety* described Navy sentiments about China in terms they would fully agree with. "The Johnson Administration," he noted acidly, "has thus far given no assurance that it will face up to the Red Chinese leadership at places and times which are most favorable to the destiny of free men."[25]

[24] Huntington, *The Common Defense*, p. 99.
[25] Twining, *Neither Liberty nor Safety*, p. 293.

By the mid-1960s, the Air Force had come around to the view that China had finally to be dealt with. The Navy had held that view since the early 1950s, and in 1957, when most people in the world were beginning to breathe easy after a decade of crisis and tension, it saw growing urgency, threat, and crisis. Needless to say, Chiang Kai-shek was delighted with the new awareness and proceeded to build up Quemoy at a breakneck pace.

Kennedy's beliefs on global politics held that only a stable relationship between the two nuclear superpowers, America and Russia, could guarantee world peace, and if it broke down because of a sudden change in the balance of power, then trouble would begin to erupt all over the world. The operational extension of that notion was that true stability could only be created by working downward from that relationship, assuming that it was finally solidified, and extinguishing potential trouble spots with a network of power. Kennedy, like all containment liberals, was committed to the cause of world peace, but his vision of how to assure and ensure it was an American imperialism that would organize the peace on its side of the demarcation lines while at the same time working out the nuclear balance of power.

The containment liberals failed to realize that there was a difference between a nuclear balance of power that involved only a nuclear arms race (dangerous as that was) and one that involved the territories of countries. A Strategic Air Command force aimed at Russia was bad enough, but at least its command and control structure was clean and linked directly to the White House. IRBMs in Germany or in Taiwan were another matter. It meant not just the bare fact that America had some weapons implanted closer to Russia and China, which theoretically were just designed to reinforce the emerging balance of power. It meant that American power was further emmeshed with German and Taiwanese politics whose leaders' aims were quite different from those of American leaders. Political influence can go both ways. Containment liberals implied that American forces stationed abroad would make the leaders of foreign countries more "responsible" and susceptible to American control. But did Matadors on Taiwan cool down Chiang's passion for reconquest of the Mainland or were they further signs of America's commitment to his cause? The Russians and Chinese were politically astute enough not to take the words of containment coming out of Washington at face value. American liberals have ridiculed the Russian and Chinese propensity to read avidly what *U.S. News & World Report* or other business and military journals say. They maintain that the right-wingers are not in control, that they do not make policy. Indeed, it has been the containment liberals who, by and large, have made policy in Washington. But policy and operations are not the same thing, and policy itself is not always what it appears to be. For the Russians and the Chinese, the American right wing was a political faction, and when Washington-Bonn or Washington-Taipei relations became too close, they were convinced that the pendulum in Washington was swinging rightward toward a more aggressive stance on the world scene.

GROWING AMERICAN OPERATIONAL INVOLVEMENTS IN EAST ASIA

The growing ideological concern with limited war in America was accompanied by a rapid expansion of operational involvements in East Asia. These took three main forms: military deployments, covert warfare, and military and economic assistance. Initially, the chief military deployment was the positioning of the Seventh Fleet at crucial points (the Taiwan Straits, the South China Sea, and the Gulf of Siam). Subsequently, this led to sending troops to Thailand and to South Vietnam (initially as "advisers"), and later to building air bases (first in Thailand, then in South Vietnam). Eventually, of course, it led to full-scale war. These deployments or "shows of force" only aroused concern in America at times of crisis (such as Quemoy in 1958 and Laos in 1960–1961), but they always aroused the greatest apprehension in China, North Vietnam, and North Korea. Through them the Navy demonstrated its power and interests in Southeast Asia.

Covert war was in the hands of the CIA. While during the Truman Administration the CIA reportedly had been hostile to Chiang, the Eisenhower Administration saw a complete change in attitude. Directed by John Foster Dulles's brother Allen, the CIA began to cooperate closely with Chiang's apparatus, and through it gained far-reaching access into all the countries of Southeast Asia. Chiang had made strenuous efforts to organize the Overseas Chinese in his own service, which, because of their dependence on commerce, was not difficult to accomplish. The CIA thus gained access to networks that would have been virtually impossible to construct by itself. Thailand became a key base of operations for the CIA, as it later was for the United States military. Remnant Kuomintang military forces roamed the hills along the Chinese borders with Burma and Laos and frequently made forays into Yunnan province. The CIA not only linked up with these forces but, following older French and British practices, began to ally itself with many mountain tribes that inhabited the entire stretch from the Burma-India border to the flatlands of the Red River delta in North Vietnam. These highland people were historically hostile to lowland peoples (like the Laotians, Thais, and

Vietnamese) and had regarded the colonial powers as a bulwark against their encroachment. In China, their enemy was, of course, the Chinese. The most famous of the CIA-Montagnard alliances was with a segment of the Meo tribes of Laos led by Vang Pao. What most interested the CIA were the raids of these tribes deep into Chinese and North Vietnamese territory. In Tibet, the CIA dropped arms to Kham-ba tribesmen who for decades had plagued Chinese and Tibetans alike as bandits. The arms drops and the increasingly threatening actions of the Kham-bas spurred the Chinese on to send large armies into the Lhasa region, sparking the Tibetan uprising of March 1959. But the CIA also began to play politics, the most notorious example being its support of the Laotian right wing headed by Phoumi Nosavan. As is well known by now, the CIA was actively engaged in the subversion of governments. From the extreme hostility of Allen Dulles and his successor John McCone toward China, it is not difficult to deduce that the CIA fully shared Chiang Kai-shek's ardent desires to roll back communism there. Its means were necessarily limited to harassment and sabotage, but its close association with the most reactionary forces in East and Southeast Asia assured that rollback had, in addition to the voice of the United States Navy and other military leaders, also that of the CIA in the highest policy councils of the United States.

Military and economic assistance was in the domain of the State Department and became a powerful weapon for buying governments. Recipient countries stretched from Korea through Taiwan to an array of countries in Southeast Asia. The State Department was soon to discover that its official control of aid monies did not mean operational control. Military Assistance and Advisory Groups (MAAGs), while formally under the jurisdiction of the United States ambassador, in time came to represent military rather than diplomatic interests. And the CIA operated with virtual independence from all ambassadors. The battles between different American bureaucracies in East Asia were almost as bitter as the wars themselves, although without the bloodshed. The end result was to deepen American involvement and commitment. Nevertheless, the State Department always represented a containment presence, serving as a counterweight to the more militant rollback proclivities of the Navy and the CIA.

ANOTHER ASIAN WAR INEVITABLE

The Chinese drew exactly the same conclusion from the situation in mid-1957 as the militant partisans of limited war doctrines in America: another Asian war was inevitable. China plunged into the Great Leap

Forward with both an evangelistic sense of moving from socialism to communism and another sense of desperate urgency to ready the country for a new international confrontation. Stalin had launched his own Great Leap Forward—collectivization and heavy industrialization—in 1928 and Fidel Castro—the Ten Million Tons of Sugar—in 1970 on the same grounds. Mao knew from his Yenan experience that revolution not only created a better society and spurred on production, but also readied the people for war and defense. Thus, while small-scale industry was being developed throughout rural China and communes were being formed, Mao also ordered the rapid development of village militias in the summer of 1958. Arms were distributed to villagers as a sign that the militias were intended as a real military force. The People's Liberation Army began its own military build-up in Fukien opposite Quemoy and readied itself for the eventual confrontation. By pulling their troops out of Korea, the Chinese indicated that they did not want to fight a war beyond their borders, but by amassing forces in Fukien they showed their determination to fight if China itself was attacked. The Quemoy crisis of August–September 1958 was the inevitable result.

During the Quemoy crisis, Chiang and his United States Navy backers wanted one thing above all else: the go-ahead signal from Washington to bomb Communist targets on the Mainland, especially airfields. The Nationalist Air Force, even by itself, had air superiority, and if United States carrier-based planes were added to it, it would have absolute invincibility in the air. Exactly what Chiang intended to do after bombing had begun is not clear. Perhaps he truly believed that uprisings would spring up all over China, and his armies could then return to be welcomed as liberators—virtually without bloodshed, as during his famous Northern March of the mid-1920s. But once the ice of American reticence to strike at China was broken, the bombing could go on and on, escalating with virtual impunity to the Americans and the Nationalists. For one thing, bombing could quickly lead to a full reimposition of the blockade against the China coast. The Seventh Fleet was already in position, and American warships were escorting Chiang's forces as they streamed into Quemoy and Matsu. There can be little doubt that what finally deterred the Americans from giving Chiang the go-ahead signal was fear of Russian intervention. China still enjoyed the protection of the Russian nuclear umbrella. On July 31, 1958, Khrushchev flew to Peking. It was revealed subsequently that he proposed to the Chinese setting up a joint Sino-Soviet naval command under Russian control which Mao angrily rejected. But at the time, Khrushchev's visit signified a reaffirmation of Russian commitment to China. As during the "Manchurian sanctuary" controversy of the Korean War, Washington was fearful that an attack against China could mushroom into a nuclear war with the Russians. And again, predictably, the right-wingers, particularly in the Navy, ridiculed the fear of Russian intervention, arguing furiously that the Russians would not move, other than to send more weapons to China.

Larger global concerns again prevailed in Washington, and Eisenhower restricted United States intervention to shepherding Nationalist ships up to China's three-mile coastal waters line. But Washington did more than that. As the terrible fear of nuclear war increased, the advocates of containment gained renewed strength and persuaded Dulles to resume the Sino-American ambassadorial talks broken off at the end of 1957. The talks were moved from neutral Geneva to Communist Warsaw, symbolically putting the issue of China within the broader framework of Russian-American relations.

While, no doubt, a certain rancor began to develop in Sino-Russian relations in 1958, the Russian nuclear umbrella had again shown itself to be a powerful deterrent against American adventurism in the Taiwan Straits. How close the Americans were to launching their own planes to bomb Fukien airfields or "allowing" Chiang's planes to do so will probably never be known. But, as at the time of Dienbienphu and the first Quemoy crisis of early 1955, Eisenhower imposed a flat veto over any such offensive action. Khrushchev's proposal for a joint Sino-Soviet naval command was obviously motivated by fear that the Chinese, like the North Koreans in 1950, might embroil Russia in a confrontation it did not want. Khrushchev also must have had serious misgivings about China's infant nuclear program. In an interview with American reporters, he made disparaging remarks about China's communes, which infuriated Mao. To make criticisms to the imperialists' media at a time when China was in the throes of its most ambitious revolutionary experiment seemed to be a heinous violation of the spirit of communist solidarity. Khrushchev was irritated that the Chinese were talking of a "transition to communism" before they had even a rudimentary industrial base. Russia under his leadership would make the true transition to communism. Irritants clearly were developing between China and Russia, but the basic principles on which the alliance rested were still unimpaired. Russia was still supplying China with all the capital goods it needed, was presumably fulfilling its part of the nuclear sharing agreement, and appeared to be fully taking China's side in the Quemoy controversy. If Khrushchev had private worries about Chinese militance in the Quemoy region and even if he had voiced them to the Americans, no change was yet apparent in the equation that flowed from the nuclear umbrella, that an overt American attack on China would bring a Russian response with nuclear content.

The following year, 1959, that equation would be badly wrenched; in

1960, it was cracked; and in 1963, with the signing of the Partial Nuclear Test Ban Treaty, it was finally destroyed. The Sino-Soviet split
began in the summer of 1959.

In the spring of 1959, the Chinese were caught in the turmoil of the
Great Leap Forward. The major material challenge they faced was to
raise agricultural output to a level so that they could pay for the vastly
expanded import of capital goods from Russia, invest in the rapidly
developing program of building small- and medium-scale industries, and
still have enough left over to feed the peasantry. The 1958 harvest had
been excellent, but disturbing meteorological signs warned that 1959
might be very different. If food production went down in 1959, China's
leaders would find themselves facing the same terrible choice Stalin had
to make in the early 1930s: Who should eat, the worker or the peasant?
As happened after collectivization in 1955, the leadership decided on a
slowdown in the pace of communization and began to push for greater
balance in the economy. Under these conditions, nothing would be more
disastrous than a drastic change in the external environment. China
needed Russia more than ever, for if there were shortfalls in farm output,
it might not be able to meet its export commitments to Russia. If another
Quemoy crisis occurred, Russia would again be needed to prevent full-scale
war from erupting. China's soldiers were heavily involved in domestic
public works projects, and mobilizing for defense would be detri-
mental to the fulfillment of economic targets. Mao had turned to Russia
at times of urgency and crisis (1949 and 1957), but the Russians had
also turned to China at critical times in their history (1953, when Stalin
died, and 1956 at the time of the Hungarian revolt and subsequently at the
threat to Khrushchev's rule in May 1957). Above all else, while China
had fought the Americans in Korea for its own national security reasons,
it also carried the ball for the entire socialist camp. The need for Sino-
Russian solidarity was never greater than in the spring of 1959.

THE BEGINNINGS OF THE SINO-SOVIET SPLIT

The great blow that sparked the split between China and Russia came in
June 1959. Khrushchev suddenly informed the Chinese that, as a condition of détente with America, he was unilaterally abrogating the nuclear
sharing agreement of October 1957. There had been no public knowledge of the agreement until August 1963 when, in response to unilateral
Russian signing of the Test Ban Treaty with America, the Chinese announced its existence. In an official government statement released on
August 15, 1963, the Chinese stated:

> As far back as June 20, 1959, when there was not yet the slightest
> sign of a treaty on stopping nuclear tests, the Soviet Government

unilaterally tore up the agreement on new technology for national defense concluded between China and the Soviet Union on October 15, 1957, and refused to provide China with a sample of an atomic bomb and technical data concerning its manufacture. This was done as a presentation gift at the time the Soviet leader went to the United States for talks with Eisenhower in September.[26]

A fortnight later, the top leaders of China met in a series of tumultuous meetings lasting through July well into August (known as the Lushan meetings), which culminated in the dismissal of China's leading military figure, Marshal P'eng Te-huai, commander-in-chief of Chinese forces in Korea and Minister of Defense since September 1954.

Like Liu Shao-ch'i in 1966, who had been touring abroad just before his downfall, P'eng Te-huai had returned to Peking only a week before June 20, the day the Russians broke the agreement. He had met with Khrushchev in Tirana, and then held talks with Russian military figures in Moscow. The tour had lasted almost two months. It began while the Berlin crisis was still acute and ended when the foreign ministers conference in Geneva had already made progress in settling it. The settlement of the Berlin crisis was one of the major preludes to Khrushchev's September visit to America. If there had been some deal between Moscow and Washington on nuclear weapons involving China, as the Chinese allege, then Khrushchev at least acquainted P'eng Te-huai with his May 28 thinking on the subject. P'eng Te-huai was an old-fashioned Chinese general who believed in the power of conventional forces. Armies had won the civil war, armies had stalemated the Americans in Korea, armies would make the difference in the future. But armies needed weapons to fight, and in the 1950s China had no other source of weapons than Russia. The Russians produced huge quantities of conventional weapons and were willing to export them, particularly the obsolescent ones, to other countries. China had little possibility of being able to manufacture sufficient conventional weapons in the near future. What made more sense than to keep China's armies strong, import weapons from Russia, and rely on the Russian nuclear umbrella?

This may have made sense to P'eng Te-huai and Khrushchev and to others in the Chinese leadership, but it spelled disaster to Mao. No principle of politics was more sacred to him than that "power grows out of the barrel of a gun." The Communists had always depended on external sources for weaponry and support, but they also always strove mightily to reduce that dependence and make themselves "self-sufficient." Until June 20, 1959, it seemed possible to trust and rely on the Russians, but afterward, who could trust them any longer? There was

[26] *People of the World Unite, for the Complete, Thorough, Total and Resolute Prohibition and Destruction of Nuclear Weapons*, pp. 28–29.

another facet to the disagreement between Mao and P'eng. The nuclear program was not only Mao's policy but a source of his own power within the leadership. Liu Shao-ch'i had already succeeded in "demoting" Mao the previous December, thereby demonstrating his grip on the party machinery. If the nuclear program were now to be scuttled and P'eng's views to prevail, then Mao would have lost whatever influence and power he had over the army as well. With Liu running the party and P'eng the army, what would be left for Mao except to become an "old Buddha" (as he himself put it)?

Following the purge of P'eng Te-huai, Lin Piao re-emerged on the political scene after a decade of obscurity. While, in 1971, Lin may have developed independent thoughts, until then he was a loyal follower of the Chairman. Through Lin, Mao managed to reassert his control over the army. Years before the Cultural Revolution began, the soldiers of the People's Liberation Army were reading the little red book. Mao would not finalize his control of the army until the fall of 1965 (with the purge of Lo Jui-ch'ing), but after Lushan, he began the process of resuming command. Mao sees himself as a great teacher, but he also is a great soldier. He took off the uniform in 1949, but ten years later put it on again.

Outside observers invariably tend to forget that these monumental power struggles involved important policy issues. It is rather amusing that Western analysts of China usually see only the power struggles and rarely the issues, but when, on rare occasions, they look at the controversies in Washington, they see only the issues and never, God forbid, the power struggles. In Peking, Washington, or elsewhere, power struggles and policy issues are inextricably interwoven. Western analysts did not see the basic issues involved in the power struggles in China of 1959 not only because the Chinese did not talk about them, but because of an ideological taboo on any issue that involved America. Nuclear subjects are taboo in America, Russia, and China because they affect the most sensitive areas of national security policy. But it takes little imagination to see that during the month and a half of struggle at Lushan, China's nuclear program was a central issue. Overt issues, such as opposition to the militia and to the communes on P'eng's part were also central issues, but they arose as part of a nexus in which the nuclear question played the pivotal role.

There were obviously widespread misgivings and opposition to the communes which, already by the summer of 1959, seemed headed straight for disaster. Obviously, many in China believed that it could not yet afford independence. And, because of the cautiousness endemic to many political leaders, even more felt that Mao's emerging course of defying Russia was pure adventurism. Were the communes really revolutionary or the utopian products of a mind blinded to reality? Was China's nuclear program not similarly utopian in view of the insurmountable lead America and Russia had in nuclear science, technology, and industrial capabilities? And was not risk-taking just like Dulles's famous brinkmanship, a product of arrogance and fanaticism?

The Lushan meetings brought three issues to a boiling point—revolution, independence, and risk. The specific revolutionary issue debated was the question of militias and more generally of communes. P'eng Tehuai opposed the militias, preferring a system of military reserves. Reserves could be mobilized in an emergency and quickly incorporated into the regular forces of the PLA, thus multiplying manyfold China's ground troop capabilities. But militias are essentially defensive units which do not function beyond a short radius of their village bases, as was the case during the Yenan and civil war periods. For P'eng, it was inconceivable that at a time when China was facing the threat of another Korean-type war that its ground forces should be reduced to a bare minimum, and that its national security should rely on a puny nuclear program and an amorphous network of militias made up of peasants whose main concern was their fields. This could only mean that Mao was putting revolution ahead of national security. It was even more true of the communes. It was inconceivable that there should be wrangling about whether people eat at home with the family or in communal mess halls when China faced potential disaster in agricultural output. Mao's constant talk about "spirit" (*ching-shen*) infuriated the hardheaded pragmatists within the military (and also, undoubtedly, within the party). Obviously, soldiers' morale was important, but what would that morale be like if their families were worked to the point of exhaustion and then had nothing to eat anyway? Mao's response to these arguments was always that what was done today served the cause of assuring the long-range transformation and stabilization of Chinese society. If China directed all its energies just to meeting the threats of its old and emerging enemies, it would be no different from so many of its past dynasties which were so dominated by the fear of foreign invasions that, though they were able to resist them for a while, they eventually fell before their onslaughts. Revolution was the only way China could assure its own survival.

No issue has more plagued the international communist movement since its inception than independence. The communists opted for dependence on Russia in the knowledge that they were thereby bending revolutionary principle. Much of the hatred communists have felt for the Trotskyist apostates was due to the fact that the latter hurled this back in their faces with all the glee and viciousness of which the left has always been capable. The Chinese communists had themselves fought through the struggle of independence or dependence on Russia, on the Comintern, on the international movement. Mao's position had been one of ideological and policy solidarity with Russia and the Comintern but accompanied by full operational freedom for the Chinese Communists to advance their own cause. The Sino-Soviet alliance had changed that, and the Korean War, which demonstrated how real global politics were, made it even more difficult to observe a dichotomy between common world view and differentiated practice. What made it difficult to argue for independence in 1959 was that dependence had brought major tangible benefits to China. So what if the Russians wanted China to end its nuclear program? If China was attacked with nuclear weapons in the coming years, only Russia had the means of responding in kind. And if the attack was conventional because Russian nuclear power deterred the Americans from using nuclear weapons, then armies, not a few primitive atomic devices, would make the difference between victory and defeat. Independence now might only spur the Americans to attack. Why incur the risk?

Mao knew in July and August that he was taking a big risk in purging P'eng Te-huai. And he knew that the Russians knew it. Both the Russians and the Chinese knew from their vast experience in politics that when a leading official was purged, it meant a change in policy. P'eng Te-huai had been close to the Russians since the Korean War, and his purge meant that a break was opening up between Russia and China. As soon as Khrushchev ended his visit with Eisenhower at Camp David, he flew directly to Peking, where he received an icy welcome from Mao and other dignitaries at the airport. He never returned to China. Nothing more dramatically symbolized the triangular relationship of America, Russia, and China than those two trips of Khrushchev; nothing more eloquently testified to the direct relationship between Russian-American issues and Khrushchev's breaking of the nuclear sharing agreement.

What must never be forgotten about the thought of Mao Tse-tung is that the question of political power (*cheng-ch'üan*) is always at its operational core. Marxism passes over the question of exercising political power and Leninism makes some simple but forceful prescriptions about how revolutionaries should organize themselves, but the entire Chinese philosophical tradition, basically one of political philosophy, alerted Mao to the complexities of the problem of power. Mao is no Confucianist, having sensed long ago that for all their homilies about humility, the old Confucian gentlemen always had a hidden lust for the power, influence, and trappings of office. Mao shares the Chinese peasant's distrust of all entrenched political power and his conviction that such power invariably becomes exploitative, repressive, and reactionary regardless of the high-sounding phrases with which it surrounds itself. For Mao, the sight of a powerful party machine with entrenched interests and an equally powerful army with a growing caste of career officers was a cause for deepest alarm. He had already voiced some of his worries about the party in his

February 1957 speech on contradictions among the people, but in the summer of 1959, the immediate area of worry was the army. Mao himself had not brought the issue to a head, his erstwhile friend Khrushchev had, by stabbing him in the back. That Mao had many enemies who wanted to consign him to the oblivion and impotence of apotheosis was obvious to him. But he was also convinced that behind him were broad social forces, particularly in the peasantry, which neither P'eng Te-huai nor Liu Shao-ch'i was able to tap. What Mao had learned in the past—and what is his great genius—was not just that revolution and independence were the best policies for China and its people in the long run, but that by taking risks to adhere to these principles against opposition inside his party and abroad he was able at the same time to break the ever-recurring power elites which he regarded as the bane of China from its imperial beginnings two thousand years before. If men lustful for power inside and outside China shed tears when the great men of the Chinese Revolution fell into the dust, Mao knew that the people of China, particularly its peasants, would shed no tears. For centuries, government had been the mortal enemy of the peasant. Government for the peasant was at its best when it was indifferent, just collecting its prescribed taxes. But whenever an emergency occurred, it was the peasant who was squeezed. In the summer of 1959, Mao struck over an issue of foreign policy of momentous concern to China, but at the same time he struck—successfully—at the expanding structure of entrenched power within China itself.

KHRUSHCHEV'S BREAKING OF THE NUCLEAR SHARING AGREEMENT WITH CHINA

Why did Khrushchev break the nuclear sharing agreement of October 15, 1957? From the statements that the Russians made at the time of the signing of the Test Ban Treaty in 1963, which the Chinese widely publicized, it is clear that both Russians and Chinese saw it as intimately linked to the question of West Germany gaining nuclear weapons from America. Thus, in its long official statement of August 3, 1963, the Soviet government stated:

> Were it not for the consistent and resolute struggle of the Soviet Union against the spreading of nuclear weapons, a struggle backed by its nuclear might, the militaristic forces in the West, and above-all the West German revenge-seekers who are making an all-out effort to get hold of nuclear weapons, would have been much closer to their goal than they actually are now. . . .
>
> . . . the nuclear arming of West Germany must not be allowed

in any form, because providing these weapons to a state whose foreign policy is based on revanchism, on a revision of existing national frontiers in Europe, would greatly increase the danger of a new world war.[27]

By the summer of 1963, the question of West Germany gaining nuclear weapons had largely disappeared as an issue (its final gasp being the plan for a Multi-lateral Force). The Test Ban Treaty that all countries were urged to sign became the precursor of a nuclear nonproliferation treaty which, as the name itself implies, was designed to make sure that newer nuclear powers would not develop. But in the spring of 1959, the issue of atomic bombs for West Germany was still acute. Adenauer, in the face of resistance within his own party, appeared to be pressing for nuclear weapons, and, surprisingly, even such architects of containment policy as Acheson and Kennan appeared to be in favor of giving them to him. Nuclear weapons were already in West Germany and elsewhere in Western Europe in the form of American IRBMs, but they were as yet exclusively under American command and control.

The main political event in America in the spring of 1959 was the resignation of John Foster Dulles on April 16, 1959, and his death a little over a month later. From the Russian and Chinese point of view, Dulles's departure was a "purge," brought about by an act of God but nonetheless a purge. When a major leader disappears from the political scene, major changes in policy occur. And so they did. With Christian Herter, the atmosphere in the State Department shifted dramatically toward a spirit of peaceful coexistence. While it is true that Mikoyan's visit to America in January presaged some new thaw in Russian-American relations, it is hard to imagine that Khrushchev could have come in September if Dulles was still alive and Secretary of State. Dulles and Adenauer were extremely close, a relationship the Russians viewed with the greatest alarm. Dulles had betrayed the French and the British over Suez, but he had never betrayed Adenauer. While IRBMs were being placed in Europe by the military, Dulles appeared to be the vehicle by which the Germans would get political access to them. When he resigned and was replaced by an entirely different political figure, the Russians concluded that a new turn in American policy was taking place.

Walter Clemens, in his study of Sino-Soviet relations over the arms issue, regards the Chinese reference to a "presentation gift" to Eisenhower as a distortion, citing, among other facts, that the invitation to Khrushchev was not made until July and that the nuclear issue between Russia and China was still not entirely settled in Khrushchev's post–Camp David visit to Peking.[28] Only the tiniest handful of people are still

[27] *People of the World Unite*, pp. 194–95.
[28] Walter C. Clemens, Jr., *The Arms Race and Sino-Soviet Relations*, pp. 19–20.

alive who know what secret communications transpired between Eisenhower and Khrushchev during the summer of 1959. Until the archives are opened, one can argue only from circumstantial evidence and the general logic and patterns of the situation. There can be no doubt that all Russian leaders viewed the prospect of nuclear weapons under West German command and control as the gravest threat to Russia's national security. The Russian preoccupation with West German "revanchism" indicated a fear that certain elements in West Germany might some day come to power which would seek a forcible reunion of Germany and a recovery of lost territory beyond the Oder-Neisse. If that occurred and West Germany had nuclear weapons, it would constitute a force pushing the entire NATO community farther and farther to the right. Germany was already the most powerful economy in Western Europe and had its own Bundeswehr, albeit under NATO. With nuclear weapons, it would become the dominant force in Western Europe, dwarfing Britain and France.

The logic and pattern of Russian behavior indicates that they have always been in favor of nuclear nonproliferation, except for the brief period of their nuclear sharing pact with China. It also indicates that they have always desired some form of great power arrangements to keep the world under control. Their constant insistence on maintaining vestigial fictions of four-power rule in Berlin (reaching its most absurd form in the continued incarceration of Rudolf Hess in Spandau prison) is symbolic of this commitment. The Russians, like many American Communists, believe that American monopoly capitalism is dominated by two different forces: one based on military industries seeking war and aggressive expansion abroad, the other based on nonmilitary industries seeking peace for the purposes of trade, profit, and peaceful expansion. When the bad, aggressive forces of American monopoly capitalism were in the forefront, Russia had no choice but to arm itself likewise and take a tough stance. But if the peace-minded capitalists came to the forefront, then Russia could relax its guard. Khrushchev had based his policies on the assumption that the peace-minded forces of capitalism would gain ascendancy over the war-minded forces. While the evidence was conflicting during the 1950s, the predominant trend was toward peace, so it appeared to Khrushchev and Mikoyan in 1959. Dulles's passing from the scene seemed like a dramatic transition from the old aggressive policy to a new one of peaceful coexistence.

If peace was in the air, to give the Chinese nuclear weapons, particularly at a time when they were undergoing some "wild pseudorevolutionary" experiments, would only be grist for the mills of American hawks. The hawks would then argue that if China got nuclear weapons, why should not the Germans get them? And if a militant China was to be

Russia's principal ally, why should not powerful Germany replace Britain as America's chief ally in Western Europe? The circumstantial evidence of Khrushchev's post–Camp David visit to Peking suggests that he did discuss China with Eisenhower and informed him, if the Americans did not know it before, that he had broken the nuclear sharing agreement with China. Camp David brought a dramatic improvement in Russian-American relations, which were temporarily frustrated by the U-2 incident the following year. No such improvement could have occurred unless the Russians felt that Washington had made concessions to them on the issue of Germany, for otherwise Khrushchev could never have justified his policies to his colleagues in the Politburo, many of whom were still suspicious of the thaw.

THE CHINESE BEGIN THE ATTACK
ON THE RUSSIANS

Whether or not there was an explicit understanding between Eisenhower and Khrushchev on the issue of nuclear weapons for China and Germany, soon after Camp David, Khrushchev found himself the target of attack from the Chinese. In the spring of 1960, articles began to appear in the Chinese press attacking "revisionism," particularly "Yugoslav revisionism." By the summer of that year, Chinese delegates to international socialist meetings were making these attacks the key theme of all their speeches. This first overt sign of a split between Russia and China was quickly perceived in America. Even before the dramatic withdrawal of Russian technicians in July 1960, American government agencies were convoking "academic conferences" in which the main theme, surprising at least to some of the participants, was: Is there a Sino-Soviet split? But the real question which hovered in the shadows of these "conferences" was whether the split was real enough to remove the Russian nuclear umbrella from China. There was no definitive answer at that time, and it would only come some years later when the Test Ban Treaty was signed. All the Chinese critiques were still made as loyal members of the socialist camp.

The Chinese use of Yugoslavia to make their differences with the Russians public served two purposes: first, it made it possible to attack the Russians without doing so explicitly, so that the door was kept open to a reconciliation, and second, it was a way for the Chinese to show their solidarity with tiny Albania, which at that same time was extricating itself from the Russian orbit. Yugoslavia was a safe, pure ideological symbol, for China had no interests whatsoever there. Yugoslavia had already gone a long way toward "restoring capitalism." Internally it had reintroduced a market economy and externally it had turned toward the

West. The Yugoslavs had carried out this double betrayal of socialism for the narrowest of selfish national and material interests. The Chinese saw the Russians treading the same path: embracing American imperialism, abandoning their commitments to the socialist camp, and feverishly pursuing the ideals of the affluent society.

Albania, as a symbol, served a different purpose. Here was a small, desperately poor country surrounded by old and new enemies which chose risky independence over safe but slavish subservience to the Russians. It was reported by Western and Yugoslav sources that the Russians were involved in an attempt to overthrow Enver Hoxha, the Albanian leader. When it failed and the alleged leaders were imprisoned and executed, the Albanians angrily turned against the Russians. They also accused the Yugoslavs of complicity. The Albanians are a proud people, showing that sense of independence characteristic of mountain people throughout the world. They are predominately Muslim and surrounded by Orthodox and Catholic Christians. Before their conversion to Islam, a Christian heresy known as Bogomilism flourished in the mountains of Albania, as it did in Bosnia and Herzegovina, most of whose people also subsequently converted to Islam. The Turks, who conquered them, wisely preferred to leave them alone. And when the Balkan peoples threw off Turkish rule, the Albanians were in the forefront of the resistance. The Albanian Communist party had been closely linked to the Yugoslav Communists during World War II, but sided with Russia at the time of the Stalin-Tito break in 1948, thus enabling them to shake off Yugoslav tutelage. Historically, the Russians had no interests in Albania, and economically, Albania was a drain on them. But it was the only socialist country with a Mediterranean coastline, and as Russian interests expanded in that part of the world after the Aswan agreement with Egypt in 1956, the Russians wanted to build naval bases there. Khrushchev's visit to Tirana in May 1959 signified a growing Russian interest in Albania, and it is not inconceivable that the Russians became irked with Hoxha's stubbornness and wished to replace him with someone more loyal to Moscow. By supporting Albania, the Chinese could express one of their own main grievances against the Russians: that they always sought to subordinate all countries and movements in the socialist camp to their own purposes.

KHRUSHCHEV'S REACTION

The most dramatic event that the first months of the Sino-Soviet split produced was the sudden withdrawal of all Russian technicians and advisers from China in July and August 1960. While Russian personnel no longer exercised the control they had in earlier years, they were busy throughout China helping to install machinery, build factories, and supervise areas where Russian aid was involved in China's industrialization. Without any forewarning, all Russians suddenly departed, taking their blueprints with them. Huge generators that they were installing in massive hydroelectric projects were left to rust, for without the blueprints and the technical advice, the Chinese were in no position to build them themselves. The Chinese were stunned, and in subsequent years have never failed to mention this as one of the supreme acts of Russian treachery. In some instances, friendly Russian advisers tried to help the Chinese to adjust, but in most, there was no time. They were told to pack their bags and their gear—everything—and get on the first train leaving China.

Khrushchev obviously did this in a fit of fury against the Chinese and probably hoped the blow would help to topple Mao from power. But it has been generally overlooked that the withdrawal of the technicians came only shortly after the failure of the Paris summit meeting of the Big Four late in May. The cause for the summit's failure was not the U-2 incident in itself, but rather Eisenhower's unwillingness to assure Khrushchev that it would not happen again and that he would punish those responsible. Khrushchev's policy line of peaceful coexistence had been predicated on his special relationship with Eisenhower, so clearly demonstrated at the Camp David meeting. That American "militarists" would launch U-2 overflights just when the summit was meeting in order to sabotage it came as no surprise to Khrushchev. That someone in Moscow should leak news of the shooting down may or may not have been what he desired. After all, the Russians have an extraordinary ability to keep virtually everything secret, so that it is not impossible that some of Khrushchev's enemies in the Russian power structure decided to leak the news for the same reasons that the CIA, or certain segments of that agency, decided to launch the overflights. But all could yet be salvaged if Eisenhower, the supreme leader on the other side, would exercise his vast power to make it crystal clear that nothing would be allowed to sabotage this vital summit meeting. The meeting was vital because all four great powers were meeting in Paris, without Germany, to settle the affairs of Europe. Never since the end of World War II had it seemed possible to resume the four-power relationship that had evolved during the war. With a working relationship between America, Russia, Britain, and France, Russian worries about Germany could forever be banished. A particular foreign policy of peaceful coexistence with America was a major (if not the major) source of power for Khrushchev. He alone could deliver the President of the United States, which was a powerful piece in the chess game of Politburo politics.

A few years before, Khrushchev could count on the Chinese to back him up in internal Politburo disputes, but now that support also was gone. It seemed inconceivable to Khrushchev that peaceful coexistence between America and Russia should not be the principal goal of all socialist countries and movements. To be attacked from American right-wingers and militarists was expected. To be undercut by a weak American President only made Khrushchev's position weaker. But to be attacked from the left as well seemed like a replay of the Trotskyism that the Russians had fought so long. Nothing more was to be gained from continuing the charade with Eisenhower, despite his pleadings that Khrushchev resume the summit. Khrushchev's power was again threatened from within his own country and the socialist camp as a whole. Until monolithic power had been restored, Khrushchev could not again afford to play the fool before the capitalists.

From the summer of 1960 to the Cuban missile crisis of October 1962, Khrushchev's public stance hardened. His anger and brusqueness at his 1961 Vienna meeting with Kennedy are well known, and another Berlin crisis—the last one—occurred that same year. In January 1961, the same month as Kennedy's inauguration, Khrushchev propounded doctrines about national liberation movements similar to those heard from Peking. These well served the Kennedyites who themselves were beginning to concoct doctrines of counterinsurgency. In November 1960, eighty-one delegations of the world's communist parties met again in Moscow, and while the Chinese were still dissatisfied with the final declaration, it nevertheless represented a basic reaffirmation of the militant declaration of 1957. Khrushchev's shift from the "right" back to a "left" position reflected Russian estimations that right-wing and militarist forces in America were stronger than they had thought. And, indeed, the events of 1960 seemed to bear that out. Trouble was rapidly brewing in Laos, and in the winter of 1960–1961 again threatened to unleash a nuclear war between America and Russia. There was little in the American presidential campaign that augured well for peaceful coexistence. Nixon was a right-winger, and for all his protestations that he intended to continue Eisenhower's peace policies, the Russians found it hard to believe him. Kennedy seemed even worse. With his constant reiteration of the theme of America's impaired national security, he seemed like a rerun of Truman, whom the Russians detested. Whoever was elected in November 1960, the pendulum seemed to be swinging rightward once again in America.

Khrushchev's swing "leftward," however, did not imply any desire to mollify the Chinese, which the Stalinist hard-liners had never advocated. Their prescription for Russian foreign policy was caution abroad but monolithic controls at home and within the socialist camp. Liu Shao-ch'i's attendance at the November 1960 meeting of eighty-one communist and workers' parties was a personal humiliation for him. Khrushchev and other Russians spread abusive and disdainful remarks about China, which was then in the throes of its worst economic crisis since the Liberation. But, above all, Khrushchev decided to flaunt his power by pushing the attack on the Albanians, which reached a high point at the Twenty-Second Soviet Party Congress in November 1961 where Khrushchev openly denounced them. The signals Khrushchev was sending to Mao via the Albanians was clear: The solidarity of the socialist camp, based on opposition to American imperialism anywhere and everywhere, demanded complete subordination of all its members to Moscow.

THE SINO-RUSSIAN POLEMICS

Khrushchev, however, was no Stalinist, and completed symbolic de-Stalinization by having Stalin's corpse removed from the mausoleum on Red Square. He had no illusions that Russia could once again hope to dominate its satellites as Stalin had been able to do. Yet he had to demand that China make one major concession to Russian supremacy (or leadership) in the camp, which was to abandon its nuclear program. Adam Ulam has argued that "the diplomatic maneuvers executed by Khrushchev in 1958–1959 were part of a grand design through which he hoped to effect at least a partial solution of the German problem as well as to prevent or considerably delay the Chinese acquisition of nuclear weapons."[29] With the failure of the Paris summit, whatever understanding there had been in the summer of 1959 between Washington and Moscow about nonproliferation of nuclear weapons to China and Germany was imperiled. But Khrushchev could not return to 1957 when he offered China nuclear know-how and more as a response to the American IRBM program. The Quemoy crisis had revealed how explosive the East Asian situation was, and the looming crisis in Laos furnished equally dangerous auguries for the future. If China had a nuclear capability and became involved in a war with America, this could inexorably draw in Russia. Another major difference between 1957 and 1960 was that the political friendship and alliance between Mao Tse-tung and Khrushchev, which had been helpful to each in his internal struggles, now was shattered. The only way now that China could show its willingness to remain a loyal member of the socialist camp was to abandon or curtail its nuclear program.

The early arguments of the Chinese in the split all had as their theme that the solidarity of the socialist camp in opposition to American imperialism and in support of the world revolution had to be the top

[29] Adam Ulam, *Expansion and Co-existence*, p. 628.

priority for all members, primarily Russia. The Russians did not disagree with that notion, but held that the avoidance of nuclear war had to be an equally top-ranking priority. The Chinese retorted that while they were not against peaceful coexistence as a specific tactic or policy, it could never be turned into a major foreign policy principle for the socialist camp. The Russians responded that peaceful coexistence had to be a principle of foreign policy because of the horrifying prospect of nuclear war, which would make revolution meaningless. Naturally, when the Chinese made statements about "a truly beautiful system"[30] which would arise on the ashes of a nuclear war unleashed by the imperialists, the Russians thought they were mad.

On the surface, it seemed that the Chinese were arguing that world revolution had to be the supreme goal of the socialist camp and of all communist parties, and that risks had to be taken, even the risk of nuclear war, to further that goal. The Russians seemed to be arguing that peace was the supreme goal and that risks, even the risk of cooperation with America, had to be taken to achieve it. It was not difficult for Russians and many other communists to see in this dispute a resurrection of the old dispute between Stalin and Trotsky. While Stalin increasingly emphasized the need to build socialism in one country and the concomitant need to preserve the larger peace, Trotsky had argued for the "permanent revolution." Naturally, Westerners, particularly liberals, sided with the Russians in the dispute. Russia's concern about nuclear war showed a rationality which derived from the enlightenment of *"embourgeoisement."* As the chances for an affluent society were improving in Russia, its leaders and peoples were more and more disinclined toward revolutionary adventures abroad and at home, and more aware of how much they had to lose in the event of World War III. China, on the other hand, was a primitive, backward country which had much less to lose in a nuclear war. It was ruled by fanatic revolutionaries who read Marx and Lenin dogmatically and literally and wanted only to drive their populations on toward ever new revolutionary ventures. In short, what the Chinese wanted was war and more war. That this reading of the dispute fitted the major ideological currents developing in America will be pointed out shortly.

The Sino-Soviet dispute was marked by an exchange of polemics written in abstruse yet powerful Marxist-Leninist language. Not since the 1920s had the left throughout the world seen such exciting debates. The eradication of Trotskyism from the international communist movement in the 1920s was followed by the dogmatic aridity of Stalinism. The recoil from intellectual polemics was justified on the practical grounds

---

[30] Quoted in Ulam, *Expansion and Co-existence*, p. 630.

that while intellectuals were arguing, real challenges, opportunities, and, above all else, dangers were overlooked. Another steel factory in Magnitogorsk was worth far more than all the words spewed out by the intellectuals. In the 1930s, that position seemed justified because the vociferous Trotskyites were, by and large, little more than roving bands of intellectual polemicists. But in the early 1960s, the polemics were being waged by the two great socialist powers themselves. What they said had to be taken seriously because behind their words was power. The Russians called the Chinese "dogmatists" and the Chinese called the Russians "revisionists." The main act of revisionism the Russians were guilty of was the propagation of the notion that nuclear weapons had changed the world in a decisive way that Marx, Engels, and Lenin could not have foreseen. Marx once hoped for an all-Europe war of liberation against Tsarist Russia, for this would give the proletariat a chance for revolution. Both Marx and Engels hailed the American Civil War as a war of liberation which would hasten the revolution. Lenin saw the First World War as a chance for a revolution that had been ebbing in the stagnant peace of the pre-1914 period. While World War I was extremely bloody, it was not yet a war of total destruction. World War II, on the other hand, had come close to being just that, particularly for Eastern Europe, but also for Germany and Japan. Nuclear weapons guaranteed that World War III would be even more—it could result in the annihilation of mankind. The Russians agreed that class struggle was still the main motor force of world history, as proclaimed in the *Communist Manifesto*. But the rise of socialist countries in the wake of the October Revolution had opened up new forms of class struggle unknown in the nineteenth century. The socialist countries could now construct powerful new economies which would soar ahead as those of the capitalist countries faltered from internal contradictions. Naturally, capitalism would turn to warlike imperialism to escape from the contradictions, and would even consider suicidal total war. But socialist power now acted as a deterrent force to stay the bloody mad hand of imperialism, leaving it to sink, eventually, in the morass of its own contradictions. Peaceful coexistence was really a new form of the international class struggle, the Russians argued, and in the process, capitalism would be "buried."

While the dispute reflected or masked practical differences between China and Russia, it obviously was a clash over world views. Every communist party always operated with a certain "systems analysis" of the trend of world politics. Understanding the world was a way of situating every small local action in the larger picture. It was a way of assessing the importance of the skirmish or the battle in the context of the larger war. If that "systems analysis" should be faulty or seriously questioned, then the nature of the entire war is put into question. Trotsky had challenged Stalin's world view, but Stalin came back with an incredibly simple yet powerful argument which leftists throughout the world accepted: since the Soviet Union was the world's first socialist country, the nature of the trend of world historical forces could be immediately determined by the attitudes, policies, and actions of socialism's class enemies, the capitalist and imperialist powers, toward the Soviet Union. No intricate theory was necessary to provide a world view, for history itself generated the proper one. The concrete historical fact of the Soviet Union was, therefore, the basis of all theory. Clearly, only Soviet leaders in the Soviet government knew all the facts about how hostile external forces related to the Soviet Union. Therefore, what they said and did had to be the basis for the world view of communists throughout the world.

The Russians had propelled themselves into a doctrinal trap. With the evolution from a single socialist country (the Soviet Union) to a socialist camp with many countries, the litmus test of world view could no longer be applied exclusively to the Soviet Union but had to be applied to the camp as a whole. Khrushchev had cultivated the notion of the camp to a high point in the mid-1950s, and the great party meetings of 1957 and 1960 were powerful expressions of its reality and its many arms extending throughout the world. The Soviet Union was granted primacy by virtue of its advanced economy and experience, but Khrushchev himself had subscribed to the notion of the basic equality and independence of all members. Thus, the proper analysis of the actual facts of the trend of world history demanded that the views of all members be heard, and, as within single communist parties, unanimity be achieved, albeit through arduous internal struggle. Soviet interpretation of how socialism's enemies related to the camp was important, but no longer, as under Stalin, the sole and immediate source of truth.

The Russians, like the Pope, had fallen into the habit of believing that whatever they said ex cathedra was infallible truth. Yet when they encouraged the "bishops" to convene periodically in "Rome" to discuss important matters, they found themselves listening to alternative notions of what really was happening and, in the case of the Chinese and the Albanians, being flatly told that they were wrong. The issue of nuclear weapons seemed so self-evident, so true to the Russians that they believed it was only Maoist perverseness that inhibited all communists and progressives from immediately sharing their view. The Chinese responded that the mere fact that the Russians said it did not make it true. Furthermore, in a situation where there were obviously differing and conflicting estimations of the trend of world history, the Russians were treading a dangerous path by departing from theoretical orthodoxy. The Chinese have never argued that theory should automatically determine practice, but theory is the most powerful link in the international movement. Mao Tse-tung never quarreled with Stalin over theory, but he exercised his own operational autonomy to do for his revolution what he and his co-leaders felt was right. Stalin had been discredited by Khrushchev. The Chinese disapproved but went along with it. In any case, de-Stalinization lessened the power of the "Pope" and made the "bishops" —all of them—participants in the deliberative process on questions of doctrine. Never was it more necessary than under these changed conditions for the international movement to adhere to commonly accepted doctrine until new doctrines had been collectively worked out.

THE DISPUTE ON NUCLEAR WEAPONS

The official (that is, practical and nonideological) Chinese position on nuclear weapons is given in the following statements of the Chinese government in August 1963:

> Should or should not China itself master the means of resisting U.S. nuclear blackmail?
> True, if the Soviet leaders really practiced proletarian internationalism, China might consider it unnecessary for it to manufacture its own nuclear weapons.
> But it is equally true that if Soviet leaders really practiced proletarian internationalism, they would have no reason whatsoever for obstructing China from manufacturing nuclear weapons.[31]

The Chinese were saying that if all fundamental decisions in the socialist camp were truly made collectively, then the entire array of ideological and practical questions concerning nuclear weapons would first be argued out by the members of the camp before any basic decision was made. Thus, before Khrushchev could go to Eisenhower and make an agreement on nonproliferation of nuclear weapons, he would have to convene all the members of the camp (or at least the key members) and argue it out. If all agreed that nonproliferation was the correct policy, then China would decide not to continue with its nuclear program. Similarly, in the absence of such collective discussion, the Russians would have no justification for unilaterally breaking their agreement to help the Chinese to manufacture a bomb. But such collective discussion and decision making would only be possible if all members were at least united by the same world view, the same "systems analysis" of the trend of world events. If the Russians were arguing that American imperialism was making an historic shift from war to peace and the Chinese were arguing that it was still as war-minded as ever, then serious differences in world view ex-

[31] People of the World Unite, p. 39.

isted. Under conditions of "proletarian internationalism," the Russians had no justification for taking a major step that deeply involved China without first seeking to iron out what was the true trend of world events. In the absence of any agreement on world view, the socialist camp had no choice but to stick to established doctrine that the highest form of class struggle in the world was that between imperialism and socialism. This would leave the Russians free to deal with America in terms of their *own* interests, but never in a way that would affect the interests of *others*.

In its crudest terms, the Chinese retort to the Russian argument about the horrors of nuclear war was that they were using the specter of total destruction to blackmail others, notably the Chinese themselves, to knuckle under to Russian control. In fact, the reiteration of the theme of "nuclear blackmail" (*hô ê-cha cheng-ts'e*) is one of the constants in Chinese attacks on both America and Russia. In 1954, Mao and Khrushchev had agreed that America was making an historic shift from war to peace policies, and both nations themselves shifted to policies of peaceful coexistence. But the "spirit of Geneva" and the "Bandung spirit" were not accompanied by any doctrinal revisionism. The theory remained the same and practice was flexible. But from the summer of 1959 on, Khrushchev embarked on his own ideological and practical paths without any consultation with the Chinese. He began talking about a "transition to communism" on his own and then ridiculed the Chinese for saying the same thing in 1958. He not only propounded the new doctrines of peaceful coexistence without consulting seriously with the Chinese (he informed them), but made deals with America, China's and the socialist camp's mortal enemy, that directly affected China's interests. The image of Khrushchev as an ideological and political adventurer began to grow in the minds of the Chinese, reaching a high point with the Cuban missile crisis.

One cannot understand the emotional depth of the Sino-Soviet dispute unless one sees the contempt in which the Chinese held Khrushchev—a contempt that even his successors shared when they accused him of harebrained schemes. Moscow was China's "Rome," the fountainhead of the world view of Marxism-Leninism. For all Stalin's errors, crudities, and cruelties, the Chinese always felt that he maintained the integrity of the doctrine, even though what he did in practice strictly followed his own and Russia's practical interests. But Khrushchev began to gyrate ever more wildly, both in theory and in practice. The Chinese might have overlooked the ludicrous scene of his wishing to visit Disneyland and then his pounding the desk with a shoe in the United Nations if it were not a reflection of his generally wild and adventuristic nature. Such a man had the audacity to speak of peaceful coexistence as a new principle, as a creative development of Marxist-Leninist theory! Granted the Russians were frightened of a nuclear war, having suffered terrible destruction in World War II. Granted the Chinese believed they still had to run risks, both those they incurred themselves and those that were forced upon them from the outside. These were valid, practical concerns which could be dealt with without tampering with theory. To the Chinese, and to Mao in particular, Khrushchev seemed to be using Russia's ideological and political power to make his own interests those of the socialist camp as a whole.

CLASHES OF WORLD VIEWS

There were essentially three major issues in the dispute: 1) the dangers facing the socialist camp and the international communist movement, chiefly those coming from America; 2) the prospects and problems for communist, revolutionary, and progressive forces throughout the world; and 3) the role of the socialist camp vis-à-vis imperialism and revolution. The most comprehensive exposition of both the Russian and Chinese views on these issues is contained in the Russian letter to the Chinese dated March 30, 1963, and the Chinese response dated June 14, 1963. William Griffith rightly put them at the head of the list of the documentary material that forms the latter half of his book *The Sino-Soviet Rift*. The Chinese held up their response for three months, and only issued it when intense talks were going on between Russia and China on the issue of the Test Ban Treaty which Moscow was preparing to sign with Washington. On the surface, there seemed to be little disagreement in substance on these three issues, although obvious disagreement in emphasis. Both Russians and Chinese agreed that American imperialism posed a mortal danger to the camp as a whole, to its member countries, and to revolutionary forces throughout the world. They both vowed full commitment to the world revolution. And both Russians and Chinese agreed that the unity and solidarity of the socialist camp was vital both for meeting the threats from imperialism and for furthering the world revolution. Yet as one reads the lengthy and tedious texts, major differences of world view become apparent.

First take the Russian letter, which says flatly:

> It is perfectly obvious that in our age the main content and the chief trends of the historical development of human society are no longer determined by imperialism but by the world socialist system, by all the progressive forces struggling against imperialism for the reorganization of society along socialist lines.

Moreover:

> Under present-day conditions it is the duty of all champions of peace and socialism to use to the utmost the existing favorable opportunities for the victory of socialism, and not to allow imperialism to unleash a world war.

> Thanks to the achievements of the Soviet Union and other fraternal countries the correlation of forces in the world changed substantially in favor of socialism and to the detriment of imperialism. An important part in this respect was played by the ending of America's monopoly of atomic and hydrogen weapons and by the creation of a mighty war potential by the Soviet Union.

> Our Party fully adheres to Leninist principles and to the principles expressed in the Statement [of 1957 and 1960], in saying that socialist revolution is not necessarily connected with war. If world wars bring about triumphant revolutions, revolutions are nevertheless quite possible without wars.

The letter then lists as the first two major issues to be discussed between the Russian and Chinese parties: 1) "Questions for the further strengthening of the might of the world socialist system . . . [and] how faster and better to secure a victory for the socialist countries in peaceful economic competition with capitalism"; and 2) "the need to pool the efforts of all peace-loving forces for the struggle to prevent a world thermonuclear war."[32]

These few phrases contain the essence of the Russian world view. The chief revolutionary fact in the contemporary world is the existence of a socialist camp headed by the Soviet Union. That camp has superseded imperialism and capitalism, notably America, as the prime actor and mover on the world scene. While imperialism is caught in a descending spiral of its own doom, it can yet unleash a world war. But because of Soviet nuclear power, the socialist camp need no longer fear the massive retaliation of American power, though strenuous efforts must yet be made fully and finally to exorcise the danger of a world war. In view of the still great dangers of a thermonuclear war, all revolutionary actions must be divided between those that would threaten a world war and those that would not. The first must be avoided, while the latter may be pursued. Therefore, the priority concerns of the Russian and Chinese parties, as the leading communist parties of the world, must be the strengthening of the camp under Soviet leadership, the pooling of com-

---

[32] "Letter from the Central Committee of the Communist Party of the Soviet Union to the Central Committee of the Communist Party of China, March 30, 1963," in William Griffith, *The Sino-Soviet Rift*, pp. 244, 245, 244, 255.

mon efforts for economic competition with imperialism, and an all-out struggle to make a nuclear war impossible.

Now the Chinese letter. After calling for a return to doctrinal orthodoxy—"the general line of the international communist movement must take as its guiding principle the Marxist-Leninist revolutionary theory concerning the historical mission of the proletariat and must not depart from it"—the Chinese letter itself says flatly:

> This general line proceeds from the actual world situation taken as a whole and from a class analysis of the fundamental contradictions in the contemporary world, and is directed against the counter-revolutionary global strategy of U.S. imperialism.

> U.S. imperialism is pressing its policies of aggression and war all over the world. . . .

> Certain persons now actually hold that it is possible to bring about "a world without weapons, without armed forces and without wars" through "general and complete disarmament" while the system of imperialism and of the exploitation of man by man still exists. This is sheer illusion.

> The people of the world universally demand the prevention of a new world war. And it is possible to prevent a new world war.

> The question then is, what is the way to secure world peace? According to the Leninist viewpoint, world peace can only be won by the struggles of the people in all countries and not by begging the imperialists for it.

But:

> It cannot, therefore, be said that with the emergence of nuclear weapons the possibility and the necessity of social and national revolution have disappeared, or the basic principles of Marxism-Leninism, and especially the theories of proletarian revolution and the dictatorship of the proletariat and of war and peace, have become outmoded and changed into stale "dogmas."

Furthermore:

> If . . . any socialist country unilaterally demands that other fraternal countries submit to its needs, . . . prevents other fraternal countries from applying the principle of relying mainly on their own efforts in their construction and from developing their economies on the basis of independence, . . . then these are pure manifestations of national egoism.[33]

[33] In Griffith, *The Sino-Soviet Rift*, pp. 260, 264, 273, 274, 275, 281.

These phrases likewise contain the essence of the Chinese world view. The key fact of the world scene is an aggressive American imperialism which still seeks to foment war and impose exploitation throughout the world. The prime mover and actor remains America, not the socialist camp. As throughout the history of communist movements, the main role of the camp is to defend itself against predatory imperialism. Compromise with America for the sake of peace is sheer illusion, for America simply will find other areas in which to foment wars. Not compromise but constant struggle is the only way to prevent a world war. Revolutions are a form of that struggle. Revolutionary struggle will make a thermonuclear war less rather than more likely. The unity and solidarity of the socialist camp is the main guarantee for world peace and success in revolutionary struggle. But that unity and solidarity can only exist if the inherent independence of each member country is fully recognized and accepted.

The Russians had a vision of a growing and thriving socialist camp facing an imperialist camp that was beginning to split and stagnate. Since, as Marx taught, economic strength was the source of all political power, naturally the Soviet Union held the principal position in the socialist camp, just as America did in the imperialist-capitalist camp. The inevitable economic contradictions within capitalism were beginning to appear, having been delayed by the massive military expenditures or the cold war. In the Third World, the forces of national liberation and social revolution were gaining strength, which hurt imperialism but benefited socialism. The only danger that socialism and revolution faced was thermonuclear war. Therefore, if the imperialists were willing to remove that danger, impelled, naturally, by Russian nuclear power, then the path would be opened to an eventual crumbling of imperialism and capitalism and the triumph of revolutions throughout the world.

The Chinese, painfully aware of the massive backwardness of their own country, did not have the same vision of a growing and thriving socialist camp. They saw dangers lurking everywhere, which they did not believe would disappear if there no longer were a threat of thermonuclear war. They shared with the Russians the belief that imperialism was caught in a process of decline (the "paper tiger" thesis), but they felt that its weakness made it more dangerous than ever. The only way to contain these dangers was to struggle against imperialism everywhere, not to make the illusory assumption that it would lose its fangs once the threat of nuclear war disappeared. All members of the socialist camp and all communists and revolutionaries were involved in a multifaceted and multifront struggle against imperialism. They must respect each other's independence to wage that struggle as they saw fit, and only on the basis of such respect could the true unity and solidarity of the camp be resurrected.

Scholars on China have written that one of the great value changes the Chinese Revolution brought about was to substitute the value of struggle for the older Confucian value of harmony. But it also substituted the value of equality for the older Confucian value of status and hierarchy. In the Sino-Soviet dispute, the Russians constantly called for harmony within the camp, but in the shadows was the pervasive assumption that there was a clearcut ranking among the members, and those ranked highest naturally were qualified to speak and act for those lower down. The Soviet Union, with the most advanced economy, the most powerful military, and a half-century of socialist experience, was, obviously, at the top of the hierarchy. The Chinese, on the other hand, true to their own revolutionary experience, constantly called for struggle—not just against imperialism but within the camp itself. No superficial declaration of common purpose could brush under the carpet the profound differences between the two great communist parties. Only through the trauma of struggle could a true unity of purpose once again be achieved. But while this struggle was going on, neither side had the right to take unilateral action that gravely affected the interests of the other. Whether China should persevere with its nuclear program was a matter that the Chinese never regarded as settled. They considered Russia's dealing with America about their nuclear program heinous and an arch-betrayal. The Russians, with a different tradition of struggle from the Chinese, considered the issue of nuclear nonproliferation so obvious and their own advanced consciousness so correct that they simply acted on their convictions and then, like an irked parent with an unruly adolescent, tried to bring the Chinese to their senses.

This titanic struggle between China and Russia would be reflected in the later 1960s in the conflict between the "New Left" and the "Old Left" which erupted in many different countries. The Chinese position in the Sino-Soviet dispute was essentially that taken by Mao Tse-tung within his own country in the 1950s—independence, revolution, and risk. Every socialist country, every communist party, every progressive and revolutionary movement had the right to decide on its own how to advance its own cause, the only constraint being the imperative not to thereby damage the interests of others in the movement. The revolutionary transformation of people, of nations, and of the world could never be abandoned, lest the revolution be simply an excuse for a new class of rulers to come into power. Lastly, the risk of struggle and more struggle must never be renounced for an illusory safety, for the enemy, at home and abroad, is ever ready to pounce. The Russian position flowed directly out of the Soviet Communist party's own experience. Not independence but the building up of a monolithic solidarity under vanguard control and direction was the only way the left could survive and grow.

Revolution was a dramatic word, but in the end what counted was power. The side whose power was greater than its enemy's would prevail. Nothing was worse than taking risks that could produce disaster. Caution and cautious build-up were the only sure paths to eventual victory.

Central to all Marxist-Leninist analysis of the trend of historical forces is the nature of the enemy. Marxism-Leninism is a combative philosophy, for it views class struggle as the central fact of all human existence. Peace is simply an illusion which masks real struggles. For all the Chinese charges of a Russian preoccupation with "peace," ideologically at least, the Russians have never abandoned the basic Marxist notion of class struggle. However, the Russians and Chinese differed fundamentally in their understanding of the nature of that struggle. The Russians have always taken a rather dogmatic approach to imperialism and capitalism, namely, that in the end economic factors are the dominant determinants of politics. Central to capitalism is the ownership and control of means of production, and the power flowing from that depends on profits. America is the world's leading capitalist power. Regardless of its irrationalities, its proclivity for war, aggression, and adventure, what it seeks in the long run is world economic power. And it seeks to achieve that power by accumulating countries, factories, land, allies, and clients, and by preventing socialism and revolution from achieving power on their own. If war becomes impossible, then America must still engage in vigorous competition to keep what it has against challengers and to expand into new areas of enterprise. For Khrushchev, the international class struggle had become a competition between a declining imperialist-capitalist system and a rising socialist system.

Mao Tse-tung, on the other hand, put more weight on the *Communist Manifesto* than on *Das Kapital*. The central fact of human history is class struggle, which arises because some men have power and oppress and exploit the many who do not. The nature of class struggle is manifold, differing from time to time, from people to people, from circumstance to circumstance. Competition, war, oppression, exploitation, and even peaceful coexistence are all forms of the class struggle. Imperialism is indeed the highest stage of capitalism, preceding its eventual decline and disappearance from the world. But all that means is that imperialism's death throes struggle is itself all the more multifaceted. To assert that there is a single overriding form that struggle takes, such as that all imperialism ultimately seeks is the power of more profits, is rank dogmatism and "economism." To assert a rank order in the hierarchy of world class struggles is a misuse of scientific analysis for advancing the particular interests of one socialist or revolutionary group. To assert that America's fundamental aims are to build a world economic empire and to enunciate binding policies on the basis of that is a fundamental denial of the principle that Marxist theory must be flexibly applied in terms of the concrete circumstances of each and every struggle. America is not a single-minded giant corporation but an octopus with many arms, each seeking in different ways to further its power and destroy revolution.

The historic bases for these differing world view assessments of America are obviously due to the fact that the America the Russians saw was the America they faced in Europe, whereas the America the Chinese saw was the America facing them in the Western Pacific. Where the Russians saw the forces of peaceful coexistence eating at the walls containment built in Europe, the Chinese saw the forces of a rabid anticommunist rollback ideology advancing beyond the demarcation lines laid down by the men of containment.

From the Russian habit of seeking to reduce all analysis of the trends of world history to one or two key elements naturally emerged the operational conclusion that all communists, progressives, and revolutionaries must pool their forces to deal with these elements. Since, so far as imperialism was concerned, those key elements were the threat of nuclear war and the political-economic competition of the two camps, naturally the Soviet Union should lead the struggle. Thus, no matter how fraternally polite relations might be between the Chinese and the Russians, in the end, the Chinese had to agree to subordinate their own goals to the higher priority of the goals flowing from the Russian analysis. Just as naturally the Chinese refused to accept this single main factor analysis and, in a spirit deriving from a long guerrilla tradition, argued that in a war waged by many on different fronts and in different ways against a common enemy, the key fact was the war itself, which would continue so long as imperialism existed. In that war, all had a part to play and each combatant must be trusted to play its part as it best saw fit. And if there were differences of opinion or even major clashes of interest between combatants, these must be painstakingly argued out until common agreement was achieved.

Obviously, it would be wrong to say that all these differences in world view were simply a way of disguising the one great practical issue dividing the Chinese and the Russians: nuclear weapons. But it would be equally wrong to say that without the nuclear issue these ideological differences and their ensuing political splits would have appeared anyway. The nuclear issue was the one overriding concrete issue of interest that lashed the Chinese and Russians together. Otherwise, there were almost as few common interests between the two countries as there had been in the period before the Liberation. Trade was vital to China, but, as it demonstrated, it could manage without capital goods from Russia. And Russia always regarded trade with China more as a burden than a gain. Common military interests developed during the Korean War but ceased thereafter. Khrushchev's efforts during the 1958 Quemoy crisis to create a common military front in East Asia failed. Not until the Vietnam war would Russia and China again develop a common military interest in East Asia. China never became a member of the Warsaw Pact, nor did it ever participate, except peripherally, in the joint economic planning and integration of Eastern Europe (COMECON). The purge of P'eng Te-huai ended Chinese military dependence on Russia. What remained was the Chinese nuclear program which the Russians from 1959 on (if not before) regarded as a growing threat to their interests. Clashing interests between the two countries brought the smoldering world view conflict into the open. In 1956, when Khrushchev denounced Stalin, the Chinese began to show their ideological disagreements with the Russians, but since interests were not involved, this remained a disagreement. But from the time of Camp David onward, interests were centrally involved in the dispute, which, thus, became a rift, then a chasm, and eventually led to an enmity where each seems to regard the other as its principal enemy.

CHAPTER 2

China and Russia as Enemies

If 1957 saw the beginning of the breakdown of the East-West thaw that had begun to emerge in the summer of 1955, 1960 saw a gathering of war clouds. While Berlin would again became a crisis issue in 1961, by and large the dangers of war in Europe appeared to have passed for good. The Cuban missile crisis of October 1962 brought the Western world to the brink of panic. In retrospect, one can say that the failure of the Paris summit in May 1960, the Berlin crisis of August 1961, and the Cuban missile crisis of October 1962 were but detours to a Russian-American détente which was finally—or so it seemed at the time—signed and sealed in July 1963 with the Test Ban Treaty. Even before then, Washington and Moscow began to cooperate or, as the Chinese would say, collude and compete in a new "Holy Alliance" to halt revolution throughout the world. But the war clouds were gathering in East Asia and assumed dramatic form in the Laos crisis of the winter of 1960–1961. In December 1960, the National Front for the Liberation of South Vietnam (NLF) was formed in Hanoi, which became a pretext for rapidly expanded American involvement in South Vietnam during the first months of the Kennedy Administration. American military deployments were building up rapidly, not just in South Vietnam, but in Thailand and in the waters of the South China Sea. In all the agonizing debates in America over the origins of the Vietnam war, one obvious fact has generally been overlooked: with the political and military build-ups on both sides and the escalation of tension that had been going on ever since 1957, a larger war was all but inevitable. The doctrines generated during the mid-1950s in Washington had a self-fulfilling prophecy built into them. They taught that limited war was bound to come and, therefore, free men must make preparations to meet it. But every one of those preparations was a form of intervention which invariably elicited a response from the other side.

Ideology did not create the Vietnam war, "crises" did. Even these would not have created it unless powerful and extensive American interests had grown up in East and Southeast Asia. Those interests have been almost entirely bureaucratic. The classic corporate economic interests were focused more on the Philippines, Malaya, and Indonesia. But bureaucratic interests are as powerful as corporate interests, and in many instances even more powerful. The Navy, the CIA, and the State Department had heavy bureaucratic investments in that part of the world by the end of the 1950s. In the 1960s, the Air Force would join them and develop its own investments. Last of all came the Army, which made the bloodiest and most disastrous investment in South Vietnam—a half-million soldiers. These interests colluded and competed, to borrow a phrase from the Chinese, and in the process spurred each other on to even greater efforts and investments. But all bureaucracies, no matter how ferocious, have a built-in timidity—they are always reluctant to undertake something new unless they are given the green light by leaders or unless some higher ideology gives them a sense of a grand design. The limited war doctrines of the late 1950s gave them the operational ideology they needed, and the crises that ensued moved the leaders at certain critical junctures to give the bureaucracies the green light to try something new.

CHINA'S INTERNAL CRISIS

In China, as the summer harvest figures began to come in, the leaders in Peking realized the enormous scale of the disasters afflicting China. The specter of famine which seemed to have been banished once and for all by the revolution again returned. Although the Chinese authorities mounted a massive food distribution campaign which prevented famine, peasants in many parts of the country had to eat bark and grass as they had in olden times. Food riots broke out in various areas, and the PLA had to impose martial law. Army morale itself was bound to be affected by the food shortages as soldiers received discouraging letters from home. Compounding this was the sheer exhaustion of the population. Throughout 1960, party cadres had been pushing the population toward greater efforts in the fields and the factories, but to little avail. As food shipments to the cities dropped, so did shipments of raw materials and industrial crops like cotton. Factories closed down everywhere creating a depression. Millions of workers were "laid off," and the lucky ones managed to rejoin relatives in the countryside. Officially, natural disasters and the Russian withdrawal of technicians were cited as the two main reasons for the drop in farm output. Yet, obviously, the Great Leap Forward had severely overtaxed the Chinese economy and the Chinese people.

In late 1960, Peking quietly arranged for the purchase of huge quantities of Canadian wheat. Canadian exports to China amounted to only 13 million dollars in 1960 but soared to 125 million dollars in 1961, and remained at about the same high level in subsequent years. No official announcement was ever made in Peking, but the news quickly got out. Vancouver became an immediate beneficiary. The rapid expansion of its port facilities, which made San Francisco green with envy, was made possible by the new China trade. Canadian prairie farmers had the same problem of farm surpluses as American Midwestern farmers, and the unexpected China outlet came as a great boon. Much prosperity was created in Manitoba from the few dollars the Chinese had available to make such purchases. The wheat was used to feed the city populations of China, thus re-establishing what had been an old trading pattern: the dependence of China's great coastal cities on overseas food supplies. China as yet had little to export to Canada in return, and had to pay in hard currency, which it earned from exports to Hong Kong, Ceylon, and a few other areas, as well as from remittances from Overseas Chinese which continued to come into China.

Taiwan was naturally elated over the catastrophes in China and had visions of an impending return to the Mainland. In America, Joseph Alsop electrified the world of national security strategists by a column which proclaimed a descending spiral of collapse in China. Chiang Kai-shek began gearing up his military machine once again for some sort of action against the Mainland. But the greatest threat came from the United States. As the Pentagon Papers reveal in their usual cursory discussions of the Laotian situation:

> The crisis in Laos was now at its peak [April 26, 1961]. At 10 p.m. that night the JCS sent out a "general advisory" to major commands around the world, and specifically alerted CINCPAC to be prepared to undertake airstrikes against North Vietnam, and possibly southern China.[1]

In view of the irrepressible urge to mount air strikes against Asian communists that CINCPAC had demonstrated during the 1958 Quemoy crisis, it was not difficult to see how the Laos "crisis" which had been building up throughout the latter part of 1960 could easily lead to an air war, not just against North Vietnam, but against China.

In the fall of 1960, Mao Tse-tung's ideological role in China was further enlarged by the publication of Volume IV of his *Selected Works*. The selections all dealt with the civil war period 1945–1949. But, curiously, the last five all dealt with America, and with the famous 1949 White Paper on China. Scholars on China and, needless to say, millions

[1] *The Pentagon Papers: The Defense Department History of United States Decision-making on Vietnam*, The Senator Gravel Edition, vol. 2, p. 42.

of Chinese are well familiar with the Chinese habit of discussing immediate problems couched allegorically in past history. Volume IV was
issued in September, and two months later Liu Shao-ch'i went to Moscow to try to heal the Russian-Chinese breach. The last item was dated
September 16, 1949, well before Mao's visit to Moscow in December
1949. As I have already argued, while the Chinese Communists had no
intention whatsoever in 1949 of joining any "Titoist" front aimed at
Russia, they still had an open mind on relations with America. In September 1949, the issue had not yet been settled. One could say, therefore, that Volume IV was trying to create allegorically the impression
that the Sino-American relationship in the fall of 1960 stood at the same
point as in the fall of 1949.

Certainly, in one respect, the similarity is close. In the fall of 1949,
the Chinese Communists wanted trade with the bourgeois countries to
avert famine and depression in the great coastal cities. Their decision to
purchase Canadian wheat showed that they had the same desire in the
fall of 1960. Circumstances were much the same during the two time
periods. Inland China was in a state of chaos (though obviously much
better organized in 1960), and urgently needed the trade to feed the
coastal cities. The selections in Volume IV dealing with America clearly
speak to this desire for trade.

The most striking difference between 1949 and 1960 is that whereas
America supported the Nationalist blockade of China and imposed its
own trade embargo in 1949, in 1960, it seemingly made no serious move
to prevent the Canadians from selling wheat to China. Canada was
vulnerable to American pressure concerning China, as Prime Minister
Diefenbaker discovered in the 1950s, and if Washington had put the
squeeze on the Canadians in late 1960, it is doubtful that they would
have been able to agree to the wheat deal. America, too, had enormous
farm supluses, and a starving China conjured up images of great fortunes
to be made by selling to it. Eisenhower himself, on June 5, 1957, had
indicated no great opposition to trade with China, but later that month
Dulles abruptly cut off all talk of it. But the story was different in
1960.

It is also curious that it was not until the spring of 1962 that Peking
became alarmed about the possibilities of a Nationalist invasion. At that
time, it reportedly demanded assurances, which it got, from the American ambassador in Warsaw that Washington would not support or condone such an invasion. Why did not Chiang Kai-shek decide to strike in
the winter of 1960–1961 when China was at its lowest and weakest
point since the Liberation? Obviously, he did not have the capabilities
for a real invasion, but he had always argued that American air and
naval support (bombing) was all that was needed, and that even a small
attack would provoke uprisings all over China.

WASHINGTON'S FIRST DISCREET
MOVE TOWARD CHINA

Clearly some circles in Washington were wondering whether the time had not come to deliver a knockout blow against China. Joseph Alsop's columns, which so often before and so often after would express Washington's tough-line thinking, showed that the notion of a "descending spiral of collapse" afflicting China was current in Washington. Yet for the first time, Washington made a discreet move toward China which went beyond containment toward peaceful coexistence: it did nothing to dissuade Canada, its closest neighbor and ally, from selling wheat to China in order to avert starvation. But, on the other hand, a crisis was brewing in Laos at the same time which would give the military an opportunity to make preparations for imminent air strikes against China.

The Laos crisis which reached a peak in April 1961 had the same elements for American air intervention (and ground intervention) as the Laos crisis of 1964, which led directly to the bombing of North Vietnam in early August 1964. But there was one important difference: Russia was centrally involved with the Pathet Lao in Laos in 1960–1961 whereas it was not in 1964. In the last two weeks of December 1960, Russian aircraft flew 184 missions to the Plaine des Jarres in support of neutralist and then pro–Pathet Lao Colonel Kong Le.[2] On January 8, 1961, Khrushchev gave a speech on Russian support for national liberation movements that sounded as if it had come directly out of the lexicon of Mao Tse-tung, Lin Piao, and Che Guevara. It soon became a guiding document for the counterinsurgency planners in the new Kennedy Administration. Since the airlift was mounted from Hanoi, the speech implied an intensified Russian involvement not just in Laos but in Indochina as a whole. Though the Joint Chiefs of Staff envisaged bombing China as a response to the Laos crisis, both the outgoing Eisenhower and the incoming Kennedy administrations saw the Laos crisis as directly involving Russia. Obviously, if Russia was directly involved in Laos, an attack against North Vietnam and China would immediately draw it in. While Washington was vigorously interested in the Sino-Soviet dispute, no one yet had the temerity to suggest that the Russian nuclear umbrella had become inoperative. The Chinese knew this too and must have found it somewhat reassuring, despite the split.

There is no evidence that during that terrible winter of 1960–1961 the Chinese feared an American attack or an American-supported attack coming from Taiwan. Ever since the Korean War, the Chinese knew that

[2] Donald S. Zagoria, *Vietnam Triangle*, p. 42.

some kind of "restraint" was operating in Washington. It had kept the tiger caged during the Korean War, the first Quemoy crisis of 1955, the second Quemoy crisis of 1958, and now during the Laos crisis of 1960–1961. If the Chinese leadership had really feared such an attack, they most likely would not have adopted the measures they did to cope with their internal troubles. In January 1961, they dramatically lifted controls and constraints on economic activity leading to a rapid return of quasi-market conditions. That decision bears some similarity to what the Yugoslavs did after their break with the Russians in 1948. Party cadres who had led the onslaughts on production the previous year were bitterly attacked, though the rectification campaign never achieved widespread publicity. In many regions, the army took over local administration—the army, one must note, was coming increasingly under the personal leadership of Mao Tse-tung. In a way, the Chinese introduced a kind of NEP policy. As in Russia during the early 1920s, the Peking leadership hoped that market incentives might coax the peasants to sell some of their food reserves. No one in the leadership, least of all Mao, was very happy over these policies, and there is little talk about that period in the Chinese press today, except that Liu Shao-ch'i is accused of openly advocating the "economism" of the time. To lift controls in the face of domestic crisis was risky enough, but to have done so in the face of a foreign threat would have been mad. I can only conclude that, despite the Alsop-type talk emanating from Washington and the gathering war clouds in Southeast Asia, the Chinese leaders did not feel that they were facing a clear and present external danger.

CURRENTS AND CHANGES IN CHINESE POLICIES

In the face of domestic crisis, the Chinese had to change their policies. The revolutionary surge of the Great Leap Forward was followed by a new call for solidarity, a united front with all elements, consolidation. The risks taken during the Great Leap Forward were replaced by caution. But on one policy the Chinese did not change: the policy of independence, which was expressed by their commitment to a nuclear capability. One can only guess at the incredible difficulties they faced in bringing the program to the point of detonating an atomic device, but obviously they persevered. To Khrushchev, and to many elsewhere, including China, the commitment to a nuclear capability must have seemed sheer madness or perversity. Had not the Russian nuclear umbrella proved once again during the Laos crisis that it could protect China? The Chinese nuclear program increasingly came to assume a dominant place in American foreign policy and national security thinking. If the Chinese were bent on fomenting revolution throughout the world and had nuclear weapons to back them up to boot, a danger was facing the free world even greater than that which emanated from the Russians in the post-1945 period. The combination of a Chinese nuclear madness with an American nuclear madness seemed to Khrushchev a sure path to disaster for all.

It is obvious from the bitter political struggles of the Cultural Revolution that deep differences over both foreign and domestic policy had riven the Chinese leadership for a long time. The great protagonists in the struggle emerging dramatically during the Cultural Revolution were Mao Tse-tung and Liu Shao-ch'i. Mao and Liu are depicted in Manichaean form as the personifications of good and evil, like characters in classical Peking operatic drama. Outsiders need not play a part in that drama and take one or the other side. The historical fact is that Mao won and Liu lost, and no one can quarrel with that. Each represented a deep-rooted current in China, and each played a major and necessary role in the Chinese Revolution. Mao was the thinker, the "teacher," as he would like to be called. Liu was the organizer, as he showed in almost all of his reflective writings. Mao had been attacked as a romantic, and Liu has recently been lauded as a pragmatist by some external observers of the Chinese scene. However one judges it, one has to admit that Mao had the vision and Liu Shao-ch'i, in good communist fashion, distrusted visions. One of the most popular portrayals of Mao during the Cultural Revolution showed him in scholar's gown with an umbrella walking on a high mountain ridge surrounded by distant peaks. Even during the period 1962–1966 when Liu was officially considered Mao's successor, he was always portrayed in the wooden, impersonal style common to Russian publications in Stalin's day. Mao deeply believed in his long-range goals for China and felt that any betrayal of them for short-range expediency (except for tactical retreats) would be disastrous. Liu felt that the only sure road to attaining the long-range goals was building, strengthening, and extending the one organizational structure and weapon he knew, the Communist party. Mao argued constantly that "one be divided into two," while Liu argued that all efforts should be made to keep divisiveness to a minimum: let the struggle be fought out within the closed walls of the party.

It was Liu Shao-ch'i's current that appeared to have won in the dark days of the early 1960s. In the summer of 1962, Liu's picture was featured alongside that of Mao with equal size and prominence. Not even during Lin Piao's period as Mao's officially sanctioned successor was he ever shown otherwise than in a subordinate, worshipful stance toward Mao. On August 1, 1962, China's army day, it was Liu's portrait that appeared on the front page of the *People's Daily*, implying his control over the army. That Liu's men had taken control of the country's official newspaper became apparent from the April 1966 prelude to the great explosion of the Cultural Revolution in May: one of Mao's first moves was to take over control of the *People's Daily* and all other media in the country. Liu's accession to prominence was marked by a strenuous effort to revive the party from the low point it had reached during the crisis period of the winter of 1960–1961. Provincial party machines began to develop throughout China, notably those of Li Ching-ch'üan in Szechwan and T'ao Chu in Kwangtung. The party began to play a greater and greater role in economic activities, for example, acting as middleman in the drawing up of procurement, production, and marketing contracts on which state economic planning was based. A pragmatic air did predominate as the sheer physical revival of the national economy was made the basic goal of economic planning. A "socialist education movement" was launched in the countryside which can be seen partly as an attempt to revive and strengthen party organization in the villages.

If Liu and his ally Teng Hsiao-p'ing dominated the party, Mao and his ally Lin Piao by and large dominated the army. The army became the main repository of Maoist thought, starting from a "communist education" campaign launched in 1961. But the army also began to move cautiously into the civilian sphere, assuming administrative roles in such key areas as banking and commerce. Key figures in the State Council, China's administrative bureaucracy, sided with the army and, thus, with Mao. Notable among them was the financial expert Li Hsien-nien, who had a prominent administrative role throughout the Cultural Revolution. Since the State Council has always been Chou En-lai's domain, it is not far-fetched to conclude that well before the Cultural Revolution he had sided with Mao and the army in their gradual entry into the sphere of civil administration. The Cultural Revolution has not made entirely clear what the basic domestic issues were between the Mao and Liu groups. The top priority given to agriculture and light industry does not seem to have been challenged by anyone. Nor does there appear to have been any serious challenge to the communes. Liu was later to be attacked for advocating a program of state-controlled and directed investment in agriculture. Mao advocated a more decentralized approach: allowing the peasants to keep their own food reserves and make their own investment decisions. Mao was more a decentralizer and Liu more a centralizer. But unlike in 1957, the Chinese economy was still in too fragile a state to allow for a grandiose new plan of development. Most of all, the boiling political disagreements at the top level of the leadership made the adoption of any unified developmental plan impossible. The 1961–1966 period was one of economic recovery. And, at least so far as the villages

were concerned, it remained so during the Cultural Revolution. Industry
was seriously disrupted but as a consequence of political strife, not of
divergent economic thrusts, as during the Great Leap Forward.

In the years following the January 1961 decisions, China's two main
concerns were foreign policy and internal politics, which were related.
Until those issues were resolved and a clearcut policy evolved supported
by a united leadership, it was difficult to formulate a new five-year plan.
China's practical approach to economic problems during the 1960s was
the result of circumstances, not of choice. But it worked, as is evident
now from the perspective of the early 1970s.

THE LIU SHAO-CH'I CURRENT

Was there a Liu Shao-ch'i line on foreign policy distinct from that of
Mao Tse-tung? The official attacks on Liu Shao-ch'i now pair him with
two of the arch-traitors of the Chinese Revolution, Ch'en Tu-hsiu and
Wang Ming. There is a wide range of arch-traitors with whom Liu Shao-
ch'i could have been paired, but the allegorical role of Ch'en and Wang
seemed best to fit him. They are regarded as "capitulationists." When the
Communist party was all but exterminated by Chiang Kai-shek in 1927,
Ch'en counseled the left forces in the Wuhan government not to resist.
And in 1937, when the Japanese invaded China, Wang Ming advised a
virtual merger with the Kuomintang, and after his expulsion from the
party fled to Moscow, where he still resides. While the historical truth is
obviously more complex than that, in Chinese eyes Ch'en Tu-hsiu and
Wang Ming symbolize men who counseled submission to an erstwhile
ally (the Kuomintang) who had turned on the Communist party in
vicious fashion, and justified such capitulation on the larger grounds of
the interests of the revolution and of China. The contemporary implication from these allegories is that Liu Shao-ch'i favored submission to
Russia in the Sino-Soviet dispute.

If that actually was the case, it was not apparent in the period leading
up to the Cultural Revolution. The Sino-Soviet dispute grew in intensity,
with all Chinese leaders, including those purged in the Cultural Revolution, making vigorous, public attacks against the Russians. In view of his
shabby treatment in the November 1960 meetings in Moscow, Liu had
no personal reason for feeling particularly friendly toward the Russians.
He had spent a few years in Russia during the 1920s where he learned
the practical organizational Leninism that became his main talent in the
Chinese Revolution. After the Liberation, he had no more and no fewer
contacts with the Russians than other top Chinese Communist leaders. In
the early 1960s, Liu and P'eng Chen, one of the first prominent public

victims of the Cultural Revolution, attacked "modern revisionism" more openly than even Mao, whose anti-Russian sentiments were usually expressed in private conversations with visiting foreign dignitaries. After the fall of P'eng Te-huai in the summer of 1959, there does not seem to have been any serious disagreement within the Chinese leadership that the dispute with the Russians had to be pursued resolutely and publicly.

Another issue on which all of the Chinese leadership (and the Russians and the Americans) were fully agreed was the growing importance of the Third World. The Chinese Communists had a natural affinity for other poor and backward countries, but in the 1950s, during the "Bandung" period, they concentrated on those closest to China. The Sino-Indian relationship, based on the *panj shila* or five principles of coexistence, symbolized Chinese foreign policy toward the Third World at the time. Like the Russians, the Chinese accepted neutralism as a valid stance and sought a range of agreements with countries willing to accept it. China evinced no particular practical concern with countries beyond Eastern, Southeastern, and Southern Asia. Thus, while relations with the Arab countries became more cordial and China refrained from reciprocating Israel's recognition, China's Middle East policies were not very important. But in the early 1960s, China rapidly developed a world-wide concern for revolutionary, progressive, and national liberation movements. Not only were ties to Cuba close, but the Chinese hailed every anti-American agitation in Latin America with great fanfare, notably Panama, where anti-American riots threatened the American hold on the Panama Canal. China began to play an active role in black Africa. And, of course, it became a vociferous champion of the Arabs and one of the most implacable foes of the Israelis.

China, Russia, and America seem to have simultaneously "discovered" the Third World. Whereas Eisenhower, despite his visits to India and later to East Asia, was temperamentally oriented toward Europe, Kennedy, reflecting the idealism of his party, developed a concern with Asia, Africa, and Latin America, as well as with Europe. He may have said, "*Ich bin ein Berliner,*" but he was enthusiastic about his Alianza para Progreso, excited by African politics, and engrossed by the problems of Asia. Khrushchev's January 1961 speech on national liberation movements dramatized Russia's intensifying concern with the Third World.

There are many reasons for this emergence of the Third World—Asia, Africa, and Latin America—into world consciousness during the early 1960s: American, Western European, and Japanese capitalism were again in an expansionist phase; orderly political independence seemed to be turning into social revolution in many Third World countries; both capitalist and socialist countries were pumping arms into the Third

World. "Problems of developing economies" became a prime academic and bureaucratic concern throughout the Western world and in the socialist countries as well; and prominent political figures of Third World countries and movements were warning the advanced countries of the growing dangers resulting from the widening gap between rich and poor in the world. Both the Russians and the Chinese believed that the Third World was the "soft underbelly" of imperialism—if national liberation movements swept Asia, Africa, and Latin America, then one of imperialism's main economic sources of power would be destroyed. Kennedy was in full agreement with that analysis and was determined that the Third World not be lost to communism. He was absolutely convinced that if Lumumbist power spread throughout the Congo and beyond, Fidelist power spread throughout Latin America, and the National Liberation Front took South Vietnam, the dominoes would indeed fall.

But within each of the three major countries' Third World policies were differing emphases, thrusts, and even conflicts. As in the 1950s, the Chinese cultivated state-to-state friendships with all possible countries in the eastern half of Asia, except for India with which they were embroiled on issues arising out of the Tibetan rebellion of 1959 and the Chinese military road in the disputed Aksai-Chin region. China developed close ties with North Korea, North Vietnam, Cambodia, Burma, Pakistan, and, above all, Indonesia. In Western Asia, it drew close to the progressive Arab countries, Egypt, Iraq, Syria, and Algeria. In black Africa, its closest friends were Ghana, Guinea, and Mali. But in addition to the state-to-state ties, the Chinese also developed notions of Third World revolutionary politics. These reached their most complete expression in Lin Piao's treatise "Long Live the Victory of the People's War," published on September 3, 1965. Lin sketched out a view of the world clearly based on the Chinese Revolution. The advanced countries were the "cities" of the world and the backward countries were the "villages." As in guerrilla warfare, revolutionary skirmishes, battles, and campaigns would erupt here, there, and everywhere, eventually leading to the surrounding and isolating of the "cities," which then would fall. McNamara quickly qualified Lin's treatise as China's *Mein Kampf*, a major ideological input into the American foreign policy process. Looked at more dispassionately now, it can be said that, aside from its colorful rhetoric, Lin's view of the world was not very different from that of the Russians and the Americans at the time. The Russians too saw national liberation movements sweeping over the Third World. The Americans, in their usual blander and more academic manner, put it in terms (Adlai Stevenson's) of "the revolution of rising expectations." All three agreed that the Third World was in turbulent movement, that Asians, Africans, and Latin Americans would no longer tolerate remaining hewers of wood and drawers of water for rich white men in America and Europe. Each naturally interpreted that movement in its own ways. The Americans, in Rostowian fashion, saw the basic drive as one for economic development. The Russians saw it as one for progressive governments which would at least be sympathetic to socialism. And the Chinese saw it as the people taking arms to rebel against exploitation and oppression. Neither Chinese, Americans, nor Russians in the early 1960s subscribed to benign neglect, which now, in the early 1970s, appears to be becoming the dominant policy of the advanced countries toward the Third World.

But within China's over-all Third World policies and in the context of the Sino-Soviet dispute, a particular line developed which can be ascribed to Liu Shao-ch'i, P'eng Chen, and other leaders who fell during the Cultural Revolution. Most likely Mao and Chou En-lai fully supported that line at the time, but, in late 1965, turned sharply against it. It was based on the conviction that within the world communist movement, the Chinese Communist party must seek to link itself as closely as possible with the communist parties of Third World countries, and beyond them, with all possible progressive parties in the Third World. Where communist parties opted for Moscow rather than Peking, it must encourage splits with a view toward either forcing that party back to a more neutral line or, if need be, establishing a rival communist party. By the mid-1950s, the international communist movement had become a powerful and awesome force, and by the early 1960s, it was even more powerful. By contrast, the international movement in the late 1940s, when the Americans were at the height of their anticommunist frenzy, was rather anemic. Stalin's Cominform was a pitiful collection of Eastern European communist parties, all satellites of Moscow, joined only by the French and Italian Communists. The only world-wide meetings of the left, such as those in Stockholm, were inchoate gatherings of progressives who were able to do little more than circulate appeals for peace.

In November 1957, only the communist and workers' parties of the socialist countries gathered to meet in Moscow. But in 1960, eighty-one Communist and workers' parties from throughout the world attended. Not even in the finest days of the Comintern had the left ever witnessed such a truly global gathering of its forces. Where the Cominform was exclusively European and the 1957 meeting was European-Asian but restricted to ruling parties, the November 1960 gathering included every communist party in the world. Powerful communist parties were emerging where only a few years before none had existed. Indonesia had an immense Communist party, the largest in the world outside of the socialist camp. India's Communist party was rapidly growing. Despite periodic repression, communist parties were making striking headway in the Arab countries. The old-line Cuban Communist party was playing a major role in the new revolutionary Cuba. Even more important than the existence of the communist parties themselves was the inclination of progressive governments in many countries, in the face of American opposition, to seek the support and cooperation of communists. Communists were not generally the leaders in the major national liberation movements. In Cuba, a middle-class lawyer named Castro led an amalgam of students, peasants, and revolutionaries to victory, which is also basically what happened in Algeria. Lumumba in the Congo certainly was no communist, nor was Gizenga. And regardless of what the Americans believed, neither was the National Liberation Front of South Vietnam or the Pathet Lao of Laos. But if communists were not the leaders of the revolution, they had the organizational force and discipline to create powerful political machines which the revolutionaries needed in order to gain and consolidate power. We are a force to be reckoned with everywhere—so went the thinking of Communists in the early 1960s. If the Communists had not had the power of the organized working class behind them in France and Italy in the post-1945 period, the reactionaries, aided and abetted by the Americans, would have destroyed them. In many Arab countries, Egypt for example, Communists periodically suffered repression, but again and again they popped up, and finally those progressive governments had to accept collaboration with them. Never did the Leninist teaching that the organized masses create power seem more true for the world as a whole than in the early 1960s.

If revolutionaries throughout the world needed the Communists, and if the Russians needed the revolutionaries, then the Russians, in their dispute with China, could be swayed "from below." At the turn of the decade, America, Russia, and China were agreed that whoever gained the support of the revolutionary Third World would have a decisive advantage in the game of world politics. It was, therefore, in America's interests to divert as many Third World regimes as possible into a pro-American path. This it did through a variety of devices (foreign aid, military assistance, technical advice, and just plain flag-showing and power politics). But it invariably involved the need to split the revolutionary regimes from the Communists. Acheson in 1949 had already foreshadowed the policies of the Kennedy period when he hinted to Mao that America would recognize the new People's Republic if it went Titoist and broke with the Russians. Therefore, anti-Americanism had to be the most fundamental policy of all communist parties, particularly in the Third World, unless they simply accepted a permanent status as a small ineffectual radical sect. Anti-Americanism also became a sign that the revolutionary regimes were willing to work with the Communists, and neutralism at least the absence of discouraging tendencies. The emerging Russian-American détente of the late 1950s was accepted by

many communist parties as necessary in order to banish the specter of
nuclear war, but it was also deeply distrusted by many of them. If the
Chinese were right and détente would simply lead to new American
aggression elsewhere in the world, then these parties would again find
themselves the victims of repression, with Russia unable to help or support them by virtue of its special relationship to America.

THE LIU CURRENT BECOMES DOMINANT

From 1962 to 1966, Liu Shao-ch'i shared with Mao the top leadership
of China. During that time, the Chinese Communist party rapidly revived
from the low point of the aftermath of the Great Leap Forward. But also
in that period, the Chinese Communists embarked on a world-wide effort
to gain the support of Third World communist parties (as well as noncommunist progressives) in their dispute with the Russians. The Chinese
were not unsuccessful in these efforts. In East Asia, the Japanese,
Koreans, Vietnamese, Laotians and Indonesians assumed a pro-Chinese
position, often equaling the Chinese in their denunciations of the Russians (this was particularly true of the Japanese Communists). In India,
a new "pro-Peking" Communist party arose which quickly outstripped
the old pro-Moscow party, and even gained state power in one Indian
state (Kerala) and, eventually, in another (West Bengal). The new
Communist party of Cuba, while generally friendly to Russia (more out
of necessity than inclination), made no secret of its preference for Chinese Communist revolutionary militance as against Russian Communist
caution. Even in Europe and America, splinter parties (like Progressive
Labor in the United States) emerged which attacked the revisionism of
the Russians. There was some speculation in both noncommunist and
communist circles that the Chinese might launch a new International,
but there is no evidence that they ever seriously considered doing so.

The Chinese position was consistently based upon the premise that the
socialist camp and the international communist movement were central
and integral elements of the world revolution. The Chinese vehemently
denied that it was they who were the "splitters." Their charges of "revisionism" accused the Russians of arbitrarily and unilaterally altering the
basic principles of the camp and the movement to suit their national egos
and interests, and then trying to force or cajole others in the camp and
the movement to accept those revisions so as to present a façade of unity
and solidarity. The polemics, marked mainly by an exchange of letters,
were conducted from party to party, implying that a fundamental tie
between the two remained, no matter how bitter and vicious the attacks.
The Russians, to this day, continue to assume that some sort of latent tie

still exists between the Communist Party USSR and a Chinese Communist party which they hope one day will rid itself of Mao or Maoism. On the Chinese side, the party-to-party polemics were broken off just before the Cultural Revolution. So far as the Chinese are concerned today, they only speak to the Russians on a state-to-state basis, as they speak to the Americans. They no longer recognize any party ties. But in the days of the polemics, the language of the letters, particularly on the Chinese side, was rigorously Marxist-Leninist. They understood each other perfectly since they both used the common "Latin" of doctrinal discourse. The Chinese would change their language radically with the onset of the Cultural Revolution.

It is not difficult to see that the way the Chinese conducted the dispute in the early 1960s, particularly by seeking alliances within the international communist movement, fitted the character and experience of Liu Shao-ch'i. Every communist party was an organized entity with a recognized leadership. One could deal, discuss, or argue with that leadership, and if agreement was reached, the organization would follow. As the pro-Chinese "caucus" grew within the movement, the Russians would no longer be able to sweep the disagreements under the rug. If the Indonesian Communists sided with the Chinese, this would influence Sukarno, who depended on the PKI (Indonesian Communist party) for his "Nasakom" policies. The Russians were heavily involved in Indonesia, so that Sukarno's swing in a Chinese direction could not but affect their interests. In this way, power in addition to ideology could be brought to bear against the Russians. Classical communist thinking always assumed that only power counted in the long run. Khrushchev used power against China, and the Chinese were quite prepared to use power against him.

Although the Chinese Communists developed far-flung contacts within the international communist movement, their main efforts concentrated on East Asia. If the communist parties of all countries from Northeast Asia through Southeast Asia to South Asia would take an antirevisionist (pro-Chinese) line, then the Chinese would have an extremely powerful caucus to back them in their dispute with the Russians. Moreover, if progressive leaders in those countries openly cultivated their ties with Peking, then the Chinese would have even greater force to bring to bear on the Russians. A test of this strategy came in the spring of 1963, as the Russians were preparing to take another step in their growing détente with the Americans, the concluding of a nuclear test ban. In April and May, Liu Shao-ch'i visited North Vietnam, Cambodia, and Indonesia. The North Vietnamese Lao Dong party was taking an antirevisionist line, as was the PKI of Indonesia. Sihanouk was drawing closer and closer to China. And Sukarno, despite some earlier difficulties with the Chinese, was likewise warming up to Peking. Burmese ties with China

had been close for some time. The Pathet Lao, which generally followed
the North Vietnamese line, could be counted on. The Thai Communist
party was particularly pro-Chinese since China was actively backing it.
Liu's visit to Southeast Asia served to dramatize the fact that on both a
party and a state basis, the Chinese had acquired considerable influence
in that part of the world. Kim Il Sung was sounding an antirevisionist
line and in Japan, the leading Communist, Kenji Miyamoto, appears to
have developed close ties to Liu Shao-ch'i, for which he would be severely attacked in the Chinese press during the Cultural Revolution. By
the summer of 1963, it could be said that the Chinese had succeeded in
creating a powerful Asian caucus within the international communist
movement. When the high-ranking party delegation of the Chinese
Communist party headed by Teng Hsiao-p'ing and P'eng Chen visited
Moscow in June 1963 to try to dissuade the Russians from signing the
Test Ban Treaty, they could confront Khrushchev not just as Chinese but
as leaders of a larger Asian caucus. Khrushchev would not be budged
from his determination to sign a test ban treaty, and during the period of
about a year and a half left to him as Russia's leader, more or less
washed his hands of Southeast Asia. Zagoria, focusing more narrowly on
time and place, says: "In 1964 Khrushchev sought to resolve the dilemma [of choosing between Washington and Hanoi] by disengaging the
Soviet Union from Indochina altogether."[3]

The Liu Shao-ch'i line on foreign policy (which was generally accepted at the time by all in the Chinese leadership) was a variant of a
typical Russian foreign policy line: unite with progressive national leaders, support local communist parties, and oppose American imperialism.
Indonesia was the most important country where it was practiced. Sukarno was the leader of Indonesia's liberation struggle against the Dutch
and appeared to have an unshakable charismatic hold on the people.
After some years of domestic confusion, he developed a clearcut operational strategy of rule based on the army and the Communist party. The
army was noncommunist and nationalistic, but was kept out of domestic
affairs. The Communists had superb organizational gifts by which they
managed to create a far-flung and deep-penetrating network of organization in a country spread out over thousands of islands and with no great
national tradition of unity. The army had no civilian cadres and the
Communists had no guns. Only Sukarno could hold them together. He
desperately needed foreign aid for his sickly economy, but the Americans
were constantly demanding that he break with his indispensable PKI.
Moreover, in the late fifties, the American CIA had backed a clumsy
revolt to topple Sukarno. The socialist countries were quite willing to

[3] Zagoria, *Vietnam Triangle*, p. 28.

pour aid into Indonesia, which increased the power of the PKI, but Sukarno had nothing to fear so long as the army remained an independent force. Sukarno's nationalism, like most other nationalisms in the world, was an ideology of power, and he sought to demonstrate his power by launching a campaign to crush the newly emerging Malaysia which, through Britain, was closely tied to the imperialist camp. Sukarno was the revolutionary leader, and an increasingly pro-Chinese PKI gave him his organizational base. That added up to a power that the American imperialists could not blithely ignore and that the Russians had to respect.

It was this specter of growing Chinese Communist influence throughout Southeast Asia that convinced the Americans of a "Chinese expansionism" which had to be stopped at all costs. From the Chinese viewpoint, the charge of "expansionism" seemed ludicrous. Expansionism implies policies of acquiring interests beyond national borders from which one can extract gain. As Ch'en Yi once put it, all China could ever hope to gain from Southeast Asia was a few million tons of extra rice, which it could get most easily by trade, without inheriting the hornet's nest of troubles that Southeast Asia has shown itself to be. The Chinese search for allies in Southeast Asia and elsewhere in the Third World during the 1960s must be seen in terms of their central preoccupation: the dispute with Russia. The alliance with Russia had been the foundation on which China's foreign policy and much of its domestic policy of economic development had been based. Either that alliance was restored on terms that the Chinese could accept or China was entering a dark forest with unimaginable uncertainties and dangers. Liu's foreign policy line, for all its vehement opposition to "Soviet revisionism," in the end could envisage no alternative to the Sino-Soviet alliance and the socialist camp. Like all policies that assume that goals can be achieved, Liu's line was convinced that it could marshal enough power to bring the Russians around. It seemed inconceivable that in the end the Russians would sacrifice China for the sake of an expedient agreement with the Americans, and even more inconceivable that they would shake off the entire Asian segment of the international communist movement and the progressive leaders and countries with whom this Asian segment was allied.

THE DEFEATS OF THE LIU CURRENT

The Liu Shao-ch'i foreign policy line received its first decisive defeat in the summer of 1963 when, despite the most intense high level talks between the two parties, the Russians went ahead and signed the Test Ban Treaty. That line received its second and most decisive defeat at the end of September 1965, when the great Indonesian Communist party was destroyed in the space of a few weeks. The destruction of the PKI was one of the most traumatic events that China experienced on the foreign scene. After an initial period of shock, Chinese newspapers poured out reams of material on the coup, trying, with considerable frankness and openness, to give readers in China a real sense of how and why it occurred. As in Hungary in October 1957, a great Communist party turned out to be a paper tiger. Where was the vaunted power of organization as hundreds of thousands of PKI cadres were hunted down and slaughtered? In September 1965, American ground combat troops were pouring into Indochina and American planes were ferociously pounding North Vietnam. The foreign policy line that China had pursued since the beginning of the 1960s had failed disastrously and completely. All the efforts to deflect the Russians from their growing détente with America had failed. The great bloc of Asian communist parties and progressives had crumbled into the dust as its leading communist party aside from the Chinese, the PKI of Indonesia, disappeared in bloody massacre. So for the rest of the Third World, where was the power that arose out of "Asian, African, Latin-American solidarity"? They had revealed themselves to be a bunch of squabbling states, and, even worse, were showing signs of swinging to the right, as was foreshadowed by the military coup that toppled Nkrumah of Ghana while he was visiting Peking. With Russia warmly colluding with America and Asian communism in disarray, a war with incalculable dangers for China had erupted on its southern doorstep.

I might be accused of unfairly placing the burden of blame on a leading figure of Chinese communism who already has been vilified to incredible lengths in China. Why should one say that the foreign policy line pursued during the first half of the 1960s was that of Liu Shao-ch'i, and not of Mao also? Is Mao to be given credit for all the successes, and all the blame for failures to be put on the shoulders of Liu Shao-ch'i? Did Mao Tse-tung have an alternative foreign policy line to the one that the entire Chinese leadership, himself included, seemed to be pursuing during this period? Mao did indeed have some alternative foreign policy notions, and in the spring of 1966, he would act on them with vigor and decisiveness. Mao has been described by Lin Piao, among others, as a leader firm in his principles but flexible in his actions. That he would have mulled over other possible foreign policies while the dominant one was being pursued with official unanimity and zealousness fits in with his character. It obviously makes sense to think of alternatives in case a particular line of action fails. Reading the conversations Mao had with foreign visitors during the first half of the 1960s, one gets some sense of these alternative notions. However, this does not imply that Mao was not in full agreement with the dominant foreign policy line of the time. Realistically, China had no alternative but to seek some sort of renewal of the Sino-Soviet alliance. There obviously were disagreements on how far China should go in making concessions to the Russians, but not on the central approach, that the only way to bring the Russians around was to struggle against them and build up as much power as possible to sway them back into a correct direction. If Chinese policy had succeeded, then Russian would have agreed not to sign the Test Ban Treaty, the PKI would still be in existence, and perhaps America would not have been so ready to launch a war in Indochina. If, in the process, the Chinese had persevered with their nuclear program as they actually did, then whoever was the architect of those policies would still be in power in China today. It is inconceivable that in the face of such policy successes, Mao would have been able to dispose of virtually the entire old leadership of the Chinese Communist party. In other words, Liu Shao-ch'i would still be around today as Mao's official successor.

In the spring of 1966, Liu Shao-ch'i and P'eng Chen made one desperate last effort to salvage the foreign policies they had been pursuing. Few people, least of all Mao, had suspected early in 1965 that the Americans would launch a full-scale war in Indochina. In the few months between Khrushchev's fall in October 1964 and the beginning of American air raids against North Vietnam on February 7, 1965, Sino-Soviet relations had warmed somewhat. Kosygin was in Hanoi the day the Americans began dropping bombs. His visit marked a sharp break with Khrushchev's policies of pulling out of Southeast Asia, and a re-commitment on the part of Russia to the North Vietnamese cause. Kosygin flew to Peking and saw Mao, who delivered himself of such anger against the Russians during that meeting that the mild thaw again froze over. However, early in 1966, when bombs were falling closer and closer to the Chinese border, certain Asian communist leaders began to propose something called "joint action." Kenji Miyamoto of the pro-Peking Japanese Communist party had traveled back and forth between Hanoi, Pyongyang, and Peking, working out a proposal through which China and Russia would put a moratorium on their dispute for the sake of expediting the sending of all military and economic aid possible to North Vietnam. Clearly, the Vietnamese favored such "joint action," and so did North Korea and, obviously, the Japanese Communist party. Late in March, Miyamoto met with P'eng Chen, which turned out to be the last public appearance in power of a man who was once rumored to be a possible successor to Mao. Only a few months later, P'eng Chen would be condemned as "a demon and a monster" and dragged out on a public stage with a placard around his neck to be denounced in the most violent terms by the Red Guards.

Nothing is known about the concrete details "joint action" (*lien-ho hsing-tung*) would have involved; what is known is that the Chinese press during the Cultural Revolution denounced it in the same terms as the demons and monsters, and then went on to rip Miyamoto to shreds. We also know that during the entire Cultural Revolution, Russian military equipment for North Vietnam continued to pass through China, with some occasional interruptions at the beginning. Therefore, one can presume that what Miyamoto and P'eng Chen had in mind was political rather than military in nature. But the only imaginable political result of "joint action" would have been a *public* declaration of solidarity in support of the Vietnamese by all members of the socialist camp and perhaps other communist parties. Mao had turned down a public declaration of solidarity in February 1965 during Kosygin's visit. In February 1966, the Russians had invited the Chinese to attend their Twenty-Third Party Congress, which was to begin at the end of March. The Chinese, publicly and with considerable vituperation, turned down the offer. The Vietnamese attended and were given great attention and respect. Early in April, Mao and the Chinese army started the moves that would lead to the May explosion. Readers of the Chinese press suddenly noticed that the *People's Daily* began to feature prominently editorials written by the *Liberation Daily* of the People's Liberation Army. One of the leading editors of the *People's Daily*, Teng T'o, came under attack. An attack began on the party apparatus of Peking which had been controlled by P'eng Chen, and by June, P'eng was being publicly attacked. Only one conclusion can be drawn from these events of the spring of 1966: Mao moved fast to prevent any move that would appear to heal the breach between China and Russia.

THE MAO TSE-TUNG CURRENT

The Russians have a simple answer to the question whether Mao Tse-tung had some alternative foreign policy notions during the early 1960s: of course he did, and they can be reduced to an implacable hatred of the Soviet Union which outweighed every other foreign policy consideration in his mind. Russian hatred of Mao personally has by now reached the levels of what they felt for Hitler, and their descriptions of him are increasingly put in Hitlerian terms. More abstractly, Mao's regime is described as a "military-bureaucratic dictatorship," based on a cult of personality, driven by chauvinism, nationalism, and "splitism" (*raskol'-nichestvo*), producing a Chinese expansionism which covets Siberia as well as much of the rest of Asia, and which is madly trying to incite a war between America and Russia so that the Chinese can pick up the pieces. Leaving aside the rhetoric, which says more about the Russian mentality than about the Chinese reality (just as American anticommunism says more about the American mentality or Chinese antirevisionism more about what bothers the Chinese themselves), there is truth in these Russian assertions. Mao began to develop a strain of thought on Russia quite different from that of his colleagues in the leadership, which most likely had its seed in the events of 1959 and 1960. To put it in terms of Mao's own Marxism-Leninism, he began to envisage the Soviet Union as an enemy of China, as a country with which China had to relate in terms of an antagonistic, not just a nonantagonistic, contradiction. During the entire dispute of the early 1960s, both the Chinese and the Russians still presumed that the struggle between them was nonantagonistic. The Russians presumed that so strongly that they repeatedly urged the Chinese not to make the polemics public, so that the disputes could be argued out in good communist fashion behind tightly sealed doors. The Chinese, undoubtedly on Mao's urgings, as vehemently insisted that the debate be kept open and defiantly published both their own and the Russian letters in the dispute. But public debate in and of itself did not imply an antagonistic relationship, and could be justified on the grounds that ever since the Stalin era, the shrouds of secrecy enfolding the international communist movement were being torn away. As long as the Chinese continued to subscribe to the notion of a socialist camp, the Sino-Soviet relationship could not be antagonistic. But Mao Tse-tung began to reflect on the possibility that the notion of a socialist camp was little more than a subterfuge for Russian control. If there was no camp and a dispute raged between the Chinese and the Russians, then the relationship had to be antagonistic, like the relationship between China and America.

In August 1964, Mao gave an interview to a group of leaders from the Japanese Socialist party in which he sounded out a theme that in a few years was to lead to official Chinese doctrines of "Soviet social imperialism." Mao first spoke in the usual way about how American imperialism, since the end of World War II, had "stretched its hands out" all over the world. But then he pointed out to his guests that the Russians had also been gobbling up territory since that time. He noted Russian acquisitions in Eastern Europe, surprisingly spoke of Russia's gaining control of Mongolia through the Yalta agreements, hinted that the Russians wanted to take over Sinkiang province, and called attention to Russian territorial acquisitions from Japan (the Kuril Islands). He also remarked on the fact that the Soviet Far East had really been Russian territory for only some hundred years. The Russians quickly interpreted the latter remarks as a sign of Mao's ambitions to annex Siberia. What Mao was actually pointing his finger to was the long-term Russian tendency toward expansionism. It must have been startling to the Kennanites in Washington to hear their own notions of Russian expansionism espoused by Mao Tse-tung, one of freedom's deadliest enemies.

The Chinese did have good grounds for being furious at Russian perfidy. In addition to the events of 1959 and 1960, there was Russian support for India during the Sino-Indian conflict of 1962. The year 1962 also witnessed the first overt clash between China and Russia along their borders when major troubles broke out in Sinkiang, particularly among the Kazakhs. The Kazakhs are a Turkic-speaking, tribal people, nomadic in their habits. Pastoralism forms the base of their economy. Chinese Kazakhs are indistinguishable from those in the Soviet Union where they have a republic, Kazakhstan, in which, incidentally, they are a minority of the population. Relations between the nomadic Kazakhs and the Chinese were traditionally always bad. During the period of Liberation, the Kazakhs led by Osman Bātur put up some of the fiercest resistance to the Chinese Communists in the entire province. Many fled to Pakistan and then to Turkey from where some migrated to America. The Chinese accused the Russians of stirring up the Kazakhs by inciteful broadcasts from across the border and, more directly, through the machinations of the Russian consulate in Ining. Tens of thousands of Kazakhs fled to the Soviet Union where they were warmly greeted by the Russians. The two vast far western provinces of China, Tibet and Sinkiang, have always been considered of high strategic importance by the Chinese. What made Sinkiang important, above all else, was that it was the location of China's nuclear test sites, its Oak Ridge and Los Alamos. Although the Lop Nor test site was far from the Russian border, the mobile, nomadic character of the Kazakhs, like that of the Tibetan Kham-bas, was cause for alarm. The CIA had dropped arms to the Kham-bas and incited them to harass Chinese military convoys moving between Hsikang province and Lhasa. The Chinese poured troops into the Lhasa region to fight the Kham-bas, and the Tibetans revolted in the spring of 1959. Similarly, when the Indians began threatening the Aksai-Chin road going from Sinkiang to Tibet, the Chinese struck back at them. When Mao accused the Russians of coveting Sinkiang, he was accusing them of posing a mortal threat to China's most sensitive national security program, its nuclear program.

One can espy a curious circular pattern here. If China's nuclear program was, indeed, under Mao's personal control (and was, therefore, a source of his power) and if the Russians regarded Mao rather than other Chinese leaders as their dire personal enemy, then weakening China's nuclear program would weaken Mao. Thus, if the Chinese had signed the Test Ban Treaty thereby ending China's nuclear program, this would have deprived Mao of one of his main material bases of power in China. Similarly, if the nuclear test sites could be physically destroyed or at least badly harassed, this would also serve to weaken and possibly do away with Mao's power. Even short of such overt aggression, a threat to the test sites through unruly Kazakh tribesmen would be a way of putting pressure on the Chinese to mend their ways, which could best be done by getting rid of Mao.

Mao was furious at Khrushchev in 1959 and 1960, but while Hunanese are reputed to be among the most temperamental of China's peoples, they also have a strong streak of common sense. Nothing could be more ludicrous than to see all that happened in China during the 1960s as the result of some volcanic temper tantrum that Mao spewed over his country and people, and to see whatever good came out of it as the result of constantly cooling down the angry old man. What Mao learned from the betrayals of 1959–1960 was that China had to go it alone, had to be absolutely and completely independent. In this commitment to self-reliance, he found much broader support among the Chinese people than his enemies in the Kremlin and the White House were willing to grant. Call it nationalism or national pride or the determination never again to be humiliated by foreigners, the Russian perfidy made a deep impression throughout the Chinese people, who only a short time before had been taught to look up to *Su-lien ko-ko,* our elder Soviet brother. Any leader who stood up to the Russians could count on widespread popular support. But in recent years, the Chinese have made even more serious allegations against the Russians, namely, that they have been engaged in constant and devious attempts to sway Chinese politics in their direction, particularly by agitating for the removal of Mao. As I shall demonstrate shortly, Russian and American determination to put an end to China's nuclear program became the keystones of their respective foreign policies. Russian and American motives and aims were not identical. One of the main differences was that the Americans tended to view the entire issue in purely military terms, whereas it was much more a political issue for the Russians (at least in the beginning, before the Chinese developed delivery capabilities which could seriously threaten Russia militarily). In short, as the sixties went on, the Russians became more and more determined to do whatever they could to get rid of Mao.

That Mao Tse-tung began to see Russian hostility toward him in terms of a larger vision of the trends of world history shows his greatness, without which he would now be little more than a longish paragraph in the history of Chinese communism. It also distinguishes him from such power-hungry figures as Chiang Kai-shek and similar fascist-feudal political types, whose vision is restricted by the limits of their actual and potential personal power. Since his adolescence, Mao has been a voracious reader, particularly of Western works in translation. That he likes to give this image to the great foreign leaders who now visit him is shown by the fact that he always receives them in a book-crammed study. Read,

read, read, he hints to these visitors, and stop relying on boiled-down briefings from bureaucratic advisers who think you too dimwitted to think on your own. Mao was in a kind of political eclipse in the early 1960s, so that he had time to reflect on broader issues. Interestingly, he confided many of his thoughts to foreign visitors, who became the only channel through which he could get these thoughts to the public. What he said to domestic visitors was either filed away in the archives or sanitized to suit whatever was the going party line. He obviously had sufficient power to force the authorities to issue invitations and visas to these visitors, even though some were rather unhappy over what he had to say. Rumors were rife that Mao had suffered a stroke and could barely walk, and at times, aides would come and suggest that, for his own health, Mao should *hsiu-hsi, hsiu-hsi,* "take a rest." Until the Cultural Revolution, few people knew what to make of these interviews. Obviously, it was not the Chinese government that was taking official positions through Mao. Moreover, so much of what Mao said seemed so rambling that it could just have been ascribed to idiosyncrasy. Yet, as we look back now from the perspective of the early 1960s, we see that those interviews expressed a line of thinking, a mode of analysis, a current which was to become dominant during and after the Cultural Revolution.

THE THEORY OF INTERMEDIATE ZONES

One of the elements of Mao's global vision which was to assume considerable prominence in Chinese foreign policy currents of the early 1970s was his "theory of the intermediate zone." In his August 1964 interview with the Japanese Socialists, he put it simply and bluntly: "At the present time, there exist two intermediate zones in the world. Asia, Africa, and Latin America constitute the first intermediate zone. Europe, North America, and Oceania constitute the second."[4] "Intermediate" implies something between two other things. In 1964, Mao presumably meant two intermediate zones between the socialist camp and the imperialist camp. Thus, the world is divided, politically, into four great zones. In 1964, Mao still saw China as part of the socialist camp. However, as the Cultural Revolution unfolded, the Chinese abandoned the notion of a socialist camp and came up with a new image of Russia as an imperialist nation along with America. In fact, there were only two imperialisms in the world, those of America and Russia. In Chinese eyes, not just China, but all other socialist countries, save revisionist, social-

[4] Franz Schurmann and Orville Schell, eds., *The China Reader*, vol. 3, p. 373.

imperialist Russia, were now part of the two intermediate zones. The definition of which countries belonged in which zones also changed somewhat, with the distinction being made increasingly in terms of developed and underdeveloped. Thus, Japan joined Western Europe, Canada, and Australia as part of the developed intermediate zone. But the developed countries of Eastern Europe also fell into this zone. The remainder of the world, largely Asia, Africa, and Latin America, fell into the other intermediate zone, in which China saw itself.

The Russians have generally been livid with rage at any Chinese assertion of theory, but the theory of intermediate zones has made them particularly angry. In a February 1972 article, they spoke of it in the following terms:

> In January 1964 the Maoists brought forth and renovated the so-called "theory of intermediate zones," which had been worked out as far back as 1946. According to the new interpretation, the second "intermediate zone" consisted of the industrially developed capitalist countries (except the U.S.A.) which allegedly had "something in common with the socialist countries and peoples of various other states." Similar "theoretical" findings were called upon to justify the policy of reorienting the ties of the People's Republic of China with the capitalist world, the policy of cooperation with the governing circles of the imperialist states, on the basis of the allegedly "anti-imperialist" position of the monopolistic bourgeoisie and also to interest the monopolistic bourgeoisie in the prospect of an anti-socialist alliance with Peking.[5]

It is not difficult to see why the Russians should be so angry. Not only were they revisionists, but imperialists as well. Moreover, the Chinese not only put them on a par with the Americans, but even indicate that they consider them the worse imperialists. And, the crowning insult, the Chinese regard all other countries of the world, including the capitalist ones, as victims of one or both of these imperialisms.

The official Russian theory of the basic divisions in the world has not changed appreciably over the last quarter-century. The world is divided into two great camps with neutrals floating in-between. The imperialist camp is still subject to the law of dialectical contradiction between different capitalist countries, so that rivalries between America, Western Europe, and Japan are real and can be exploited for the interests of socialism. No such contradictions operate within the socialist camp. Maoism is a degenerate, temporary deviation from which China will eventually recover and rejoin the socialist camp. The neutrals are, by

---

[5] *Evropa v planakh Pekina*, p. 26, in Franz Schurmann, David Milton, and Nancy Milton, eds., *The China Reader*, vol. 4 (forthcoming in 1974).

and large, in the Third World, where there is a tug of war between the progressive forces leaning toward socialism (Russia) and the reactionary forces leaning toward imperialism.

While the theory of intermediate zones may well go back to 1946, and while there were further hints of it in some Chinese articles of the post–Korean War period, one of the earliest major references to it was made by Mao himself in a speech to the Supreme Soviet on November 6, 1957:

> American imperialism stubbornly wants to interfere in the internal affairs of all countries, including the internal affairs of the Socialist countries—for example, in China's case interfering in its liberation of Taiwan, or in Hungary creating a counter-revolutionary rebellion. In particularly arbitrary fashion, it interferes in the internal affairs of the various countries of the intermediate zone situated between America and the Socialist Camp. America now still is plotting to use Turkey and Israel to aggress against independent Syria, still is plotting to overthrow the anti-colonialist government of Egypt. These insane aggressive policies of the United States not only create crisis in the Middle East but create the crisis of a new world war.[6]

At the time of this speech, neither Mao's Soviet listeners nor anyone else could have detected a strain in these remarks which in a little more than a decade would lead to a Chinese theory envisaging not one great imperialism in the world but two, the second being Russia. If one changes the geographical references and the words American imperialism to Soviet imperialism, Mao could have given the speech in the later 1960s or early 1970s. Interference in the internal affairs of other countries is the major accusation that the Chinese make against the Russians today.

The standard Russian vision of the world is a seemingly standard Marxist view of the neutral countries floating between the two camps. These are, by and large, countries just emerging from a feudalism destined to pass rapidly from the world scene. There are, therefore, only two powerful modes of production in the world, capitalist and socialist. The Russian Revolution demonstrated that backward countries could bypass the capitalist phase and enter socialism directly. Therefore, it is theoretically and practically possible for the countries of Asia, Africa, and Latin America to leap-frog over a capitalist phase, which would put them under American control, and enter a phase of socialism, which would make them natural allies of the socialist camp. The Third World, then, is basically little more than a passing phase. As for the advanced capitalist countries of Western Europe and Japan, they are part of the

---

[6] *Jen-min Shou-ts'e 1958* (*People's Handbook*, 1958), p. 295, translated by author.

international capitalist nexus whose imperialist head, at the time, was America.

Mao's notion of the intermediate zones, on the other hand, began to imply that the intermediate countries had more character than just a passing phase. One might have thought that the Chinese would have seized on the notions of a Third World which became popular in the early 1960s. But the term "Third World" is not often to be found in the Chinese literature. Rather, they preferred to use the bulky compound "Asia-Africa-Latin America." The simple fact is that the notion of a Third World excluded China, for originally the other two worlds implied were capitalism and socialism. Asia-Africa-Latin America (AALA), on the other hand, included China. When the Russians tried to have themselves accepted as an Asian power in various AALA conferences, the Chinese fought them bitterly, showing that they did not intend the notion to be understood in simple geographical terms. Obviously, Uzbekistan is in Asia, but how could the Soviet Union represent it in an AALA conference? While they might not have done so in the early 1960s, the Chinese now would probably fight a Russian attempt to gain AALA representation through Uzbekistan or some other non-European Russian republic on the same grounds that Mozambique or Angola should not be admitted. In spite of Chinese distaste for the term "Third World," the idea that there was a third "world" between imperialism and socialism appealed to them. The Chinese are one-worlders and think in terms of global political processes, so that the word "world" is unacceptable. But the connotation of some inherent unity in it appeals to them. In sum, therefore, by the early 1960s, Mao's notion of the intermediate zones led to the concept of Asia-Africa-Latin America, the Chinese functional equivalent of the better known notion of a Third World in the West.

In January 1964, in a *People's Daily* editorial, the Chinese expanded the notion of intermediate zones to include the countries of Western Europe. But, as Mao indicated in his interview with the Japanese Socialists, these constituted an intermediate zone of their own, distinct from Asia-Africa-Latin America. The inclusion of the capitalist countries of Western Europe made sense on only one theoretical ground: that they were striving for political and economic independence from American imperialism. Paired with China's own struggle to free itself from Russian control, Mao conjured up a vision of the two great camps in a process of dissolution. If nothing else, Mao is a practical, down-to-earth thinker (despite what his detractors say). When he makes a great abstract statement, he invariably has concrete and present reality in mind. In 1964, he happened to be exceedingly intrigued by France's struggle against America, not to mention de Gaulle's decision to develop his own nuclear *force de frappe*.

"COUNTRIES WANT INDEPENDENCE, NATIONS WANT LIBERATION, PEOPLES WANT REVOLUTION"

Unlike the Russians, the Chinese like to let their theories grow slowly and naturally, like plants responding to the environment. The theory of intermediate zones has grown slowly without the kind of "rigorous" academic analyses that Westerners are used to. In the early 1970s, the Chinese came up with a new notion that was designed to explain the dynamic processes in both intermediate zones. It is contained in a slogan which has become the leitmotiv of their foreign policy: "Countries want independence, nations want liberation, peoples want revolution." This slogan and the notion behind it undoubtedly come from Mao, who, since the Cultural Revolution, has been the guiding spirit behind Chinese foreign policy. That "independence" is now listed before "liberation" and "revolution" may or may not imply a priority in Chinese eyes. If it does, this has proved to be disappointing to those who see liberation or revolution as the key priorities in the world. By "independence" the Chinese mean loosening the shackles that bind any country to one or the other of the two imperialist superpowers, America and Russia. By "liberation" they mean the struggle of a foreign-dominated national entity, say, the Vietnamese or the Angolese, to cast off its foreign occupiers and oppressors and set up its own political state system. By "revolution" the Chinese now seem to mean class struggle in its strictest sense: the rising of one oppressed class against a dominant class in a particular society. Thus, they hailed the "events" of May–June 1968 in France as revolution. They regard the black movement in the United States as revolutionary. They saw the rising of Polish workers in Gdańsk as revolutionary. They see their own uprising against the capitalist-roaders as a revolution.

The Chinese now (in the early 1970s) apply the phrase "countries want independence" particularly, though not exclusively, to the actions, actual and potential, of countries in the second intermediate zone to secure autonomy from American or Russian control. They include the countries of Eastern Europe in that zone, so that, naturally, the Chinese warmly hailed Yugoslavia when it vowed to resist any Russian aggression against it in the aftermath of the occupation of Czechoslovakia. Despite a decade of tirades against Tito's revisionism, relations between Peking and Belgrade once again became cordial. The Chinese today are staunch supporters of the Common Market, seeing in it a new world power able to resist both America and Russia. While fearful of a possible Japanese militarism, they also are happy to see Japan loosen its ties to America, which became dramatically evident when Premier Kakuei

Tanaka visited Peking. They also support the efforts of the Middle Eastern oil-producing countries to free themselves from the domination of American and British oil companies. Thus, China's relations with Iran, a country considered to be in a reactionary state similar to that of the pre-1914 Stolypin period in Russia, have also become cordial, as shown by the visits of Iranian royalty to Peking and Chinese attendance at the great spectacle at Persepolis. In Latin America, they support Peru and Ecuador in their dispute with America over coastal waters, and naturally they supported Allende's Chile. The Chinese seem to conceive "countries wanting independence" in economic terms. The Common Market is declaring its independence of America by developing a free tariff zone and monetary arrangements that increasingly exclude the United States. The Middle Eastern countries seek independence by gaining full control over their oil resources. The lucrative fishing industry is the key issue of dispute between the Andean countries and America. And Chile is nationalizing foreign, chiefly American, corporations.

"Nations want liberation" is the oldest of the three concepts. This is the notion of national liberation movements in the lands of Asia, Africa, and Latin America which became so prominent in the thinking of China, America, and Russia in the 1960s. The Chinese regard the national liberation movements of the peoples of Indochina, the Palestinians in the Middle East, and the peoples of southern Africa as the chief ones at the present time. National liberation means casting off the vestiges of direct or indirect colonial rule. In Indochina, America is both an imperialist and a neocolonialist power. In the Middle East, the Chinese regard Zionism as no different from what French rule was in Algeria, and South Africa falls in the same category. Portugal is, of course, an out-and-out colonial power. Thus, if "countries want independence" characterizes the political dynamics of countries in the second intermediate zone and those in the first intermediate zone that already have secured national liberation, "nations want liberation" characterizes the dynamics of a number of major lands in Asia, Africa, and Latin America.

The phrase "peoples want revolution" appears to be a Chinese return to a narrow and orthodox Marxian notion of what revolution is. Revolution only occurs when a subordinate class rises against a dominant class, and is only successful when the subordinate class succeeds in overthrowing the dominant class. The Russian Revolution was a revolution, and so was the Chinese Revolution. So was the Cultural Revolution. A revolutionary process occurs everywhere that there is a rising class consciousness. Mao has long seen a revolutionary process within the United States. Sometimes it almost seems as if he thinks that that process was a factor in the rapprochement between America and China. The Chinese see a revolutionary process in Western Europe, of which they consider the

French "events" of May–June 1968 the most important manifestation. They also believe that there are revolutionary currents in Eastern Europe, which, they hope, will one day lead to the eruption of "cultural revolutions" to sweep the Liu Shao-ch'i or Brezhnev-type apparatchiki out of power. While they had nothing but disdain for the weak-kneed liberalism of Dubček, they nevertheless believed that there was a genuine revolutionary movement in Czechoslovakia aimed at exactly what Dubček kept insisting was not the target—Russian rule. It is easily understandable that the Russians and their allies in Eastern Europe see little difference between Chinese attempts to foment discontent in Eastern Europe and earlier attempts by American anticommunists.

The Chinese words for country, nation, and revolution are *kuo-chia*, *min-tsu*, and *ko-ming*. *Kuo-chia* means state power within defined territorial boundaries, in other words, a country. Its key characteristic is sovereignty, the rights and powers of the duly constituted government to exercise rule over its domains without foreign interference. The stubborn commitment of the Chinese to the notion of sovereignty (only briefly violated in passing support of Biafra) led them to take a principled and rather unpopular position on the Bangla Desh issue. They have negotiated boundary agreements with all countries on their borders save India and Russia. While they attack the unequal treaties concluded a few hundred years ago with Russia, they make no claims to Siberian territory, and except for disputed territory in the Aksai-Chin and North East Frontier Agency regions, they make no claim on Indian territory. The word *min-tsu* should really be translated as "race," in the sense in which it is understood in Europe rather than America. *Min-tsu* means a people with a language, culture, history, identity, distinct ethnicity. There are, of course, major races, like major languages, and then there are thousands of minor races throughout the world. The Chinese accept the notion of "minority," but they seem to make conventional differentiations between majority and minority: minorities are races of lesser number within any particular country. In theory, the Chinese grant the right of self-determination to all races. Obviously, there can be no self-determination under colonial, neocolonial, or crypto-colonial rule, so that the struggle for national liberation becomes the highest form for such races to achieve full self-determination. Since the Chinese do have sensitivities about their own numerous minorities, they prefer not to push the theoretical arguments about national liberation too far. A great deal has been written about *ko-ming*. It will do to repeat that in Chinese, the word has come to connote not just a larger abstract world historical process, but a real struggle in which thousands and millions of people participate actively as individuals.

Whether one likes or dislikes this new Chinese view of the world, one has to admit that it posits a world much more complex than that of the Russian view. In fact, the Chinese like to use the word *luan*, "trouble," to characterize the state of the world. They see the world as a volcanic terrain in which there constantly are small eruptions here and there, and consider it delusion or worse to pretend that this is not so. When Brezhnev began to speak of "limited sovereignty," the Chinese saw this as a reaffirmation of a Russian imperialism that just wanted to gobble up more territory under the guise of advancing the socialist camp in competition with the imperialist camp. But when Nixon, in his Kansas City speech of July 5, 1971, just before Kissinger went to Peking, spoke of a new world of five rather than two great powers, the Chinese read this as an American admission that bipolar supremacy by the two superpowers was no longer workable. It is not difficult to see why the Chinese with their guerrilla background should have such a world view, and why the Russians who won their civil war in almost classic military fashion by fanning out from Petrograd prefer to see a world of "camps."

THE MAO TSE-TUNG CURRENT IN PRACTICE

To return to the question of whether Mao Tse-tung, in the early 1960s, when he still apparently supported the dominant Chinese foreign policy line in the dispute with Russia, began to evolve an alternative line: he obviously did, as has become apparent in the years following the outbreak of the Cultural Revolution. But, for Mao, a key question always is, what are the practical consequences of a particular world view? What practical alternatives did China have to a Liu Shao-ch'i policy which, for all of its vehement attacks on the Soviet Union, still eventually envisaged a resurrection of the socialist camp? In the early 1960s, no practical and feasible alternative was available—either the socialist camp reunified itself or China faced a void in which, among other things, it would no longer have the protection of the Russian nuclear umbrella. But having no practical alternative did not mean that China should not try to see if such alternatives might not eventually develop. As in combat, the fact that one's main forces are involved in one crucial campaign does not mean that some spare regiments cannot be used to probe other areas to see whether a new front could be developed when and if the opportunity presents itself. A friend who met Mao once described his tactics as, "Let's jump in and then see what happens." During the early 1960s, Peking began to try out some new foreign policy feelers which at the time did not seem very important, and were not in conflict with the main struggle with Russia over the nature of the socialist camp. But as the dispute with Russia turned into enmity, it became gradually evident that these early feelers had begun to grow and came to constitute, by the late 1960s, the dominant current in Chinese foreign policy.

ALBANIA

From the early 1960s on, China began to single out a number of countries in the world with which it developed a special relationship or which were given an unusual amount of publicity in the press or sent an unusual number of delegations or high level visitors to Peking. The two countries highest in Chinese esteem were Albania and Vietnam. While Chinese ties with Vietnam appear to be readily understandable, those with Albania have been mystifying to most outsiders. Albania, like China itself, suffered a total break in economic relations with Russia and the remainder of Eastern Europe. The Chinese stepped in with a munificent aid program which enabled Albania to survive without turning to the West, as Yugoslavia did. Because of its small size, its distance from China, and its lack of resources, it is hard to argue that the Chinese had in mind developing concrete interests in Albania. Unlike Russia, the Chinese have no navy which could use bases on the Albanian coast. Albanian visitors have come to China in a never-ending stream, and many have talked personally with Mao. Being received by the Chairman is considered in China the ultimate sign of esteem for a foreign guest or at least a sign of the weight the Chinese attach to the meeting. Chinese support of Albania made sense in terms of a policy seeking a new solidarity of the socialist camp but based on the independence and integrity of each member. But it was also a way of indicating that someday the whole notion of a socialist camp might have to be abandoned. Not only Russia, but all Eastern European governments save Romania, broke diplomatic relations with Albania. Albania both withdrew and was excluded from the Warsaw Pact. Ideologically, the Albanians were far more radical than the Chinese in denouncing the Russians. Their ostentatious admiration of Stalin served to underline their rejection of all that the Soviet Union had become. Praise of Albania was already great before the Cultural Revolution, but after it began, Albania was virtually the only foreign country that continued to receive praise in the Chinese press. If it was Mao himself who spurred on the adulation of Albania to such heights, it could only have been for one overriding reason: he intended to serve notice on the Russians that China might someday too, like the Albanians, abandon the entire concept of a socialist camp and elect to deal with the Russians on a purely state-to-state basis, not the party-to-party basis that still was the case until the spring of 1966.

CAMBODIA

During the 1960s, the Chinese developed another symbolic relationship, with Cambodia. While China has important and sensitive interests in Vietnam and Laos, this has been much less the case with Cambodia, which is located hundreds of miles to the south of China. Since March 1970, when Prince Norodom Sihanouk went into exile in Peking, the Chinese press has been filled with publicity about him in a way as mystifying to foreigners as the earlier publicity about Albania was. Dozens of his rambling letters, written in good bourgeois style, have been published in the *People's Daily*. His every doing is recorded as if he were some great movie celebrity. Chinese-Cambodian relations have been good since 1954, and Cambodia's neutralist stance, maintained even under intense American pressure (until March 1970), naturally was pleasing to China. But while the Chinese did develop a *présence*, as the French would say, in Cambodia, their commitment to it has to be seen in ideological rather than interest terms. The effusive publicity given to Sihanouk was meant to symbolize something in foreign relations, and the slogan that seems to fit best is "countries want independence."

For all their remoteness from each other, what Albania and Cambodia have in common, in Chinese eyes, is that they are both small countries committed to their own independence in the face of overwhelmingly hostile surroundings. For Albania, the ultimate source of the threat is Russia. For Cambodia, it was and is America.

PAKISTAN

Another country in Asia with which China developed a special relationship in the 1960s was Pakistan—a relationship that has remained close through the traumatic events leading to the formation of Bangla Desh. China's ties with Pakistan warmed in direct relation to the cooling of its ties with India. Obviously, the common enmity of both China and Pakistan toward India was the main factor in their relationship, but there were other elements which went beyond common interests. Pakistan, unlike Albania and Cambodia, is a big country. Until Bangla Desh, its split territory was considered a part of both the Middle East and Southeast Asia, and as such, Pakistan became a member of both the CENTO and the SEATO alliances which Dulles formed. In the 1950s, conservative, Islamic Pakistan was a staunch ally of America, in contrast to neutralist India which, in American eyes, was dangerously friendly with China. Not only was India an enemy of Pakistan but, surprisingly, so was equally conservative and Islamic Afghanistan. Afghanistan was consistently neutral in the Russo-American cold war struggle. It feuded with Pakistan over the Pathan-inhabited territories of Pakistan. The Pathans not only formed a large part of Afghanistan's own population but were its dominant class and provided its official (if not popular) language, Pashtu. For Pakistan, however, the central problem always was India, symbolized by the dispute over Kashmir-Jammu. When China and India moved toward armed confrontation, Pakistan naturally gravitated toward China, a move that the Chinese welcomed despite the reactionary character of the Ayub Khan (and later Yahya Khan) regime.

While the Chinese have maintained good relations with the progressive Arab states, none can be regarded as the object of a special relationship. In the Middle East, the Chinese have given strong support to the Palestinian liberation movements without committing themselves to any particular one. Uncompromising opposition to Israel appears to be the foundation of Chinese policy in the Middle East, and whatever relations it develops with countries and movements derive from that.

ROMANIA

In Eastern Europe, there is one other country with which the Chinese have developed a special relationship, Romania. While it never had the adulation that Albania enjoyed, still, even during the Cultural Revolution, the Romanians were always granted special consideration in the press. There is no doubt whatsoever that the Sino-Romanian special relationship developed in direct relation with Romania's resistance against Russia. As the Russians tried to integrate Eastern Europe in response to Western European integration, the Romanians balked. From the mid-1960s on, a strong Romanian nationalism emerged which took openly anti-Russian forms. Ceausescu pursues orthodox communist policies within his country, but no Eastern European communist leader has come even close to voicing his anti-Russian sentiments. When the Russians occupied Czechoslovakia in August 1968, many Romanians were convinced that they were next on the list.

For all their remoteness from each other, Pakistan and Romania have something in common for the Chinese. If not superpowers, both are major countries. Both were once tightly imbedded in the American and Russian camps respectively, and both managed to free themselves, to some degree at least, from them.

TANZANIA

In Africa, the Chinese had a special relationship with Ghana in the early 1960s. But after Nkrumah's ouster, that relationship was switched to Tanzania, where they are now engaged in one of the biggest foreign aid projects in the world, the building of the Tanzania-Zambia railroad. For over a decade, the Chinese have had special concerns about Africa (curiously matched by Taiwan's far-flung efforts to spur rural development there). Nyerere's Tanzania is a socialist country with frugal, puritanical ways, which appeals to the Chinese. Chinese interest in Zanzibar, the more radical part of the Tanzanian union, has been even greater. Except for the period of turmoil in the Congo in the early 1960s, black Africa has, by and large, remained out of the orbit of great power politics. Mao Tse-tung appears to have a particular preoccupation with black peoples. Over the years, he has received scores of black African leaders, and hundreds of black African delegations have visited China. One of his few published statements about internal affairs within America was on the black liberation movement. I can see no other reason for this preoccupation than a revolutionary one, a belief that world revolution cannot be accomplished until the poorest of the poor have risen to a new human dignity. Nevertheless, the fact that black Africa has been generally neglected by both the Americans and the Russians may also account for China's presence there.

CANADA

There are two other countries with which China developed if not special then at least peculiar relationships—France and Canada. From late 1960 on, Canada became China's leading source of wheat to help overcome its food shortages. While Peking never officially announced the wheat purchases, the Chinese people became aware of Canada in another way, through the widespread popularization of the life story of Dr. Norman Bethune. Bethune was a Canadian doctor who served with the People's Liberation Army, and died from an infection received while operating on a wounded Communist soldier. As a result, there probably is no other foreign figure who has become so much a part of Chinese lore. While Americans were still rigidly excluded from China, fairly large numbers of Canadians traveled there, including the present Prime Minister Pierre Trudeau. Canada acquired an international role in East Asia when, in 1954, it agreed to serve on the Indochina International Control Commission (ICC). At that time, India was chosen as the neutral member, Poland as the member representing the socialist camp, and Canada as the member representing the free world (that is, America). When the Indochina war escalated in 1965, Canadians periodically served as emissaries to Hanoi for Washington. Whether they performed any similar function between Peking and Washington is not known. The Chinese were never under the illusion that Canada was straining to break loose from American domination, although Canadian nationalism often makes such demands. To the Chinese, Canadians were virtually indistinguishable from Americans, although some spoke French. Canada was indissolubly linked to America by geography, economic interests, language and culture, and mutual defense arrangements. It is hard to see Chinese interest in Canada as motivated by a conviction that Canada, like Romania and Pakistan, was a "country seeking independence." In concrete interest terms, Canada was a natural source of wheat for China. But if Washington had desired to prevent the sale of wheat, it probably could have done so, and forced China to look elsewhere. I see no other explanation for the symbolic aspect of the China-Canada relationship than that the Chinese considered Canada a kind of proxy for America. Their dealings with Canada were a way of testing their relationship to America and getting a sense of what a future direct relationship with America itself might be.

FRANCE

Although it did not seem so then and does not even now, the most fateful of China's special or peculiar relationships was with France. On January 27, 1964, France recognized the People's Republic of China, and a few days later de Gaulle gave a major speech on that recognition. On February 1, 1964, America began the secret operations known as the 34-A Op's (Operation Plan 34-A) against North Vietnam which a year later brought about the beginning of the bombing of North Vietnam. On January 30, 1964, the Saigon government of Duong Van Minh was overthrown and replaced by that of General Nguyen Khanh, who vowed a fight to the death against communism and neutralism. Those three events form integral parts of a drama, analyzed in Part III, which was played out in the last months of 1963 and the early months of 1964 and led to massive American involvement in the wars of Indochina.

There would have been no peculiar relationship between China and France had it not been for Mao Tse-tung and Charles de Gaulle. There were no great overriding historical ties between the two countries. The French did contribute the word *"Sinologie"* to the Western vocabulary and were the most ardent admirers of Chinese culture in Europe. They also had some interests in China prior to World War II. But all that counted for little after the Liberation in China. During the 1950s, the Chinese regarded France as a reactionary country, as wedded to American imperialism as Britain or any other Western European country. From 1962 on, however, Chinese attention toward France increased in direct relation with the strange policies that de Gaulle began to expound and pursue. In 1958, de Gaulle came to power on the shoulders of a right-wing coup sparked by elements favorable to the cause of *Algérie française*. In 1962, he extricated France from the Algerian war by coming to terms with the revolutionary leader Mohammed Ben Bella and crushing the French right wing, which had traditionally been imbedded in its armed forces. Like the Indochina war for the Americans, the Algerian war was like a terrible hemorrhage draining France's economic, political, and moral energies. If France could not extricate itself, it would decline as a European *and* a world power in the face of a resurgent Germany, an all-smothering ally America, and a Russia which, in the early 1960s, showed all the signs of rapid and sustained growth. By granting independence to all of its African colonies and finally by relinquishing Algeria, France was able to substitute its crumbling military power in Africa with a much more promising economic power. At the same time, by pursuing a nuclear policy that seemed designed to give France something it could never have, a credible nuclear capability, de Gaulle once again made it a power that had to be listened to. While the Americans and the Russians guffawed at the *force de frappe*, the result, as is now evident, was to make France the chief producer of high technology weaponry in Western Europe. Since Germany was debarred by international arrangements from producing such weaponry, France gained the only counterweight to Germany it could hope for. But in order to pursue his policies of *force de frappe*, de Gaulle had to turn against the American ally, who kept insisting that what the French were doing was redundant at best and dangerous at worst. To the French argument that they were developing their own nuclear capability because they could not rely on the American commitment, the Americans responded by offers to strengthen NATO, to form a true Atlantic Community, and by continuing insistence that they had no intention of withdrawing troops from Western Europe.

Like Mao, de Gaulle was one of the very few contemporary leaders with a vision, and, like Mao's, his vision was generally ridiculed by the more "pragmatic" British and Americans. De Gaulle believed deeply not only in France, but in Europe. He was originally linked to Adenauer and De Gasperi in a dream for a Western European Catholic union. In his later years, he spoke of a Europe reaching from the Atlantic to the Urals. Like all conservatives, he read history avidly and believed that the patterns it had created were still operative. For de Gaulle, the actors in Europe were its classic ones: France, Germany, Italy, the smaller states, Russia—and even Britain. He probably disliked the British and the Americans because of his personal experiences in London during World War II, but that was not a major factor in his vision. He believed that Britain had to choose whether to be a European power or an offshore island branch of the American empire. America's proper European role was that of friend, which it had been in the two world wars. The notion that Europe should be an American protectorate struck de Gaulle as ludicrous and noxious for Europe's own destiny. He looked at the world in classic historical terms and emerged with a vision that a cruder American terminology would call one of regional blocs. Western Europe was one such bloc (Britain could join if it met European conditions). He granted that Eastern Europe, with its Christian Orthodox traditions, was another such bloc. America had its own bloc in the Western Hemisphere. In East Asia, there was the great civilization of China which had spawned derivative civilizations all around it. In each of these blocs, certain nations were called upon by destiny to play the leading role. For de Gaulle, there never was any doubt that destiny had singled out France as a leader for Western Europe.

What de Gaulle wanted was France's independence and greatness, and to achieve those aims, the two great power blocs that had dominated the world since the end of World War II had to be dismantled. While France's aspirations for such a world-shaking goal could be laughed at as Gaullist romanticism, in conjunction with China seeking a similar goal, they could just barely have some teeth to them.

When de Gaulle died, Mao Tse-tung made the unusual gesture of sending his condolences to Mme. de Gaulle, which were prominently published in the Chinese press. But ever since former Premier Edgar Faure's first visit to China in 1957, Mao and other Chinese leaders had ample opportunity to express their admiration for de Gaulle, an admiration which grew strong after 1962. There can be no doubt that what attracted Mao Tse-tung to France was the evidence of a major country "seeking independence." But this country was seeking independence through the development of an operational nuclear capability, the same approach that China was taking. Mao Tse-tung is said to hold that everywhere and always there is a left, a right, and a center. Judging from his repeated disdain (in good Marxist-Leninist tradition) for "social democrats," liberals, revisionists, and so on, one can conclude that he would rather deal with the right than with the center. Mao has expressed a certain respect for even such a figure as Ngo Dinh Diem, and Chou En-lai has remarked that Chiang Kai-shek must not be criticized too harshly, for at least he retained his independence vis-à-vis the Americans. Thus, it is not surprising that Mao was not unduly bothered by de Gaulle's conservatism. De Gaulle was an open rightist, a reactionary (though not a fascist, in Chinese eyes). When he clashed with the revolutionaries in May–June 1968, the Chinese hailed the "French Revolution" as one of the great contemporary events of the world and devoted an immense amount of newsprint to it. But Chinese ideological support for the French revolutionaries of 1968 hardly caused a ripple in Sino-French state-to-state relations.

It might be noted that the various countries with which China developed a special relationship are also those with which de Gaulle's France developed similar relationships. Franco-Cambodian relations always remained close and were capped by de Gaulle's visit to Phnom Penh. France maintains an embassy in Tirana, and while neither side made any special propaganda about the relationship, Albania discreetly retained its ties to the two major Latin countries, Italy and France. De Gaulle visited Romania and particularly stressed that country's Latin background and traditional ties to France. He also visited Quebec, where his cry "Québec libre" aroused a storm of protest and was interpreted as a French effort to break Canadian unity and ties with the Anglo-American world.

Washington's fury at de Gaulle derived from a correct perception of his grand design to break up a Western alliance dominated by America. Naturally, Washington did not relish an upstart like de Gaulle brandishing about his grand design when mighty America was in the process of implementing its own grand design. In the same manner, Moscow was incensed at the pretensions of an Asiatic China to further its grand design in the face of mighty Russia, which was trying to build up the socialist camp for the security and prosperity of all its members.

After examining the peculiar relationship between China and France, one can say that the question of whether Mao Tse-tung had an alternative foreign policy line in the early 1960s is now answered. Like de Gaulle, who sought a break-up of the American-dominated Western alliance yet refrained from a frontal assault against it and repeatedly said he was not anti-American, Mao Tse-tung began to develop a subordinate foreign policy line, which, at the time, he felt did not endanger attempts of the dominant foreign policy line, that of Liu Shao-ch'i, to seek a restoration of the socialist camp on terms acceptable to the Chinese. Mao was throwing out feelers to see what kind of international relationships China might be able to develop in case the relationship with Russia finally collapsed.

If the line now called in China "countries want independence" was Mao Tse-tung's alternative, then subordinate foreign policy current in the early 1960s, what about the other two phrases, "nations want liberation" and "peoples want revolution"? Are these, too, Maoist alternatives to the then dominant foreign policy line? The answer is that "nations want liberation" is not particularly Maoist but "peoples want revolution" is.

NATIONAL LIBERATION MOVEMENTS–VIETNAM

While "nations want liberation" can mean Chinese support for all national liberation movements throughout the world, concretely it means Chinese support for the liberation struggle of the peoples of Indochina. Aside from the Indochina struggle, the Chinese lay greatest stress on the struggles of the Palestinians and of black Africa. References to other national liberation struggles become more general. It is not coincidental that in Indochina and the Middle East Chinese and Russian foreign policy lines still essentially coincide, for the policy of supporting national liberation movements arose at a time when the Sino-Russian relationship, though already endangered, was still essentially intact. The Chinese have applauded Egypt's ouster of Russian advisers and have accused the Russians of perfidy in undermining the Palestinian guerrilla movement. But on the basic issue of supporting the Arabs against the Israelis, there is little difference between China and Russia. Even more significant is the coincidence of policy on Indochina, with the exception of Cambodia. While the Chinese and the Russians have traded accusations over their Vietnam policies and Washington has tried frantically to manipulate and maneuver between, through, and against Peking and Moscow in order to achieve its aims in Vietnam, by and large both the Chinese and the Russians have had to acquiesce to the fact that it was and remains the Vietnamese who call the shots. While, for different reasons and at different times, the Chinese and the Russians may have wished to extricate themselves from the Indochina struggle, neither has been able or willing to do so. Both remain committed to the struggle of the Vietnamese against America.

In the West, the theory and practice of national liberation movements is considered eminently Maoist. But the honor of having waged the most extraordinary national liberation struggle in contemporary times, both in theory and in practice, must go to the Vietnamese, whose leaders Ho Chi Minh and Vo Nguyen Giap have taken people's war to a stage far higher than what was achieved during the Chinese Revolution. Still, it must be remembered that the revolutionary process that the Vietnamese revolution most closely resembles is the Chinese Revolution. The similarities were already evident in the first Indochina war, and even under the vastly changed circumstances of the present war, they remain. Mao has rarely commented in any detail on the Indochina war, the obvious reason being his prudent desire not to give advice from a distance to those actually involved in the struggle. But few Chinese who remember can help but see in the Vietnamese revolution a reincarnation of their own struggle against the Japanese and the Kuomintang. Mao Tse-tung, Lin Piao, Liu Shao-ch'i, Chou En-lai, or other Chinese leaders past or present may have taken different theoretical and practical approaches to the liberation struggle in Vietnam, but all were committed to it. Of course, the broader international context in which the Chinese placed their commitment to the Vietnamese has changed over the years. In the spring of 1961, Russian and Chinese support of the National Liberation Front's struggle was seen by both as part of a broader commitment by the socialist camp and the international communist movement to a fraternal party, an ally, and a national liberation movement. When "joint action" was proposed in the spring of 1966, Liu Shao-ch'i apparently was willing, still, to place the commitment to the Vietnamese in the context of the socialist camp. But while Mao vehemently rejected such a course, he has insisted that China's commitment remains what it always was. For years now, whenever the subject of Vietnam is dealt with in the *People's Daily*, the masthead invariably contains a slogan of Mao's: "The seven hundred million people of China are the firm rear shield of the Vietnamese people; the broad territory of China is the reliable rear area of the Vietnamese people."

"Nations want liberation" is part of a Chinese foreign policy current that has survived the Cultural Revolution intact. For the Vietnamese, it is the cornerstone of their own struggle, as well as of their view of the world revolution. They have a world view much like that which the Chinese expressed in the early 1960s. They believe that the socialist camp still exists and that Russia and China are its key members. They believe that the international communist movement still exists and maintain cordial relationships with all communist parties, seemingly oblivious to the wide chasms separating, for example, the Albanian and Bulgarian parties. They regard American imperialism as the most ferocious and dangerous enemy of mankind, and consider opposition to it the main criterion for determining who is friend, enemy, or neutral. The Vietnamese maintain a theoretical as well as, obviously, a practical link to China and Russia.

THE MAO TSE-TUNG CURRENT
AND REVOLUTION

"People want revolution" seems like a standard radical phrase, but it expresses a particular revolutionary approach of Mao's, exemplified by the Cultural Revolution. In the early 1960s, Mao Tse-tung began to consider the notion that true revolutions can occur independently of communist parties. Communist parties may and should arise out of these revolutions, but the party itself was not their *sine qua non*. In fact, as Mao implied several times during the Cultural Revolution, a communist party may actually serve to retard or distort the revolutionary process. If people "dare to rebel" against a class enemy and seize power from it, then that is a revolution, whether or not there was a vanguard communist party to guide it. If a communist party seeks to quash such an uprising or control it so as to make it safe, as happened in France in 1968, then the party is obviously counterrevolutionary, a characteristic arising out of its revisionist nature.

One of Mao's statements widely quoted today is:

> Stir up trouble, get defeated, stir up trouble again, get defeated again, up until they're destroyed—that is the logic of imperialism and all reactionary forces in the world in dealing with the people's affairs. They can never turn their backs on this logic. Struggle, get defeated, struggle again, get defeated again, struggle again until they win—that is the logic of the people. They too can never turn their back against this logic.

That statement conjures up a view of China widely held in America during the 1960s, and perhaps best symbolized in W. W. Rostow's notion of communists as "scavengers of the modernization process." Wherever there are tensions because human and social development cannot keep up with political and economic development, this notion held, communists will emerge to make trouble so that they can seize power for their own ends. Mao would agree perfectly. Exploitation, oppression, and reactionary domination are, in themselves, "trouble," and the people should rise and struggle against them. But, as Mao would continue, it is the revisionists who say, Do not rise and struggle but first organize a communist party, and let the party carry out the struggle, through its transcendent wisdom, for the people. In the 1960s, the Chinese were seen as the world's greatest troublemakers, as contrasted with the Russians, who had gained wisdom and insight from their *embourgeoisement*. American liberals at the time were furious that the Chinese were stirring up flames of revolt in Latin America where they had no interests whatsoever, not to mention the doings of Che Guevara. As the New Left began to emerge in the advanced countries, the very word "Maoism" came to mean a kind of anarchist, ultraleftist troublemaking-for-troublemaking's-sake. And when the New Left began to clash with the older communist parties, as in France, China was invoked as a new Marxist Rome sanctioning this path to revolution.

While this Maoist approach to revolution came to have major significance for the New Left, what did it mean practically for Chinese foreign policy? "Countries want independence" implied a tentative foreign policy line of seeking links with countries willing to break out of the two great blocs. "Nations want liberation" meant active support for the Indochinese and the Palestinians. The Liuist line of seeking links to antirevisionist communist parties, like Indonesia's, certainly did not put into practice what Mao had in mind by "peoples want revolution." Nor was the policy of supporting small anti-mainline communist parties, like some in Europe, particularly Belgium, one that Mao, who is basically very commonsensical, would greet with effusive enthusiasm. During the Cultural Revolution, the Chinese hailed, rhetorically anyway, a whole range of revolutionary upheavals throughout the world—not only the uprisings in France in May–June 1968, but the Naxalites in India, the black power movement in America, student movements in other Western European countries, Japan, and the United States, the struggles against Portuguese colonies in Africa. But hailing a revolutionary movement in the press and sending out tons of propaganda could hardly delude anyone in China into thinking that this was sufficient to ignite a great storm throughout the world. People in America and elsewhere should remember that much Chinese shouting and yelling is in the tradition of the Peking Opera, which while marvelously melodramatic is also incredibly loud. The Chinese people can distinguish perfectly well what goes on in the theater from the real world outside, but they often forget that outsiders may not be able to do so. While there were some moments of megalomaniacal self-delusion during the Cultural Revolution, it is highly doubtful that Mao ever seriously thought that a storm would sweep over the world as it did in Hunan and Kiangsi in 1927.

But "peoples want revolution" had the most profound effect on Chinese foreign policy because it was the principle on which Mao opted to unleash a cultural revolution of far-reaching scope within China at a time when American bombs were coming closer and closer to Chinese soil. Early in October 1965, the Liuist current on foreign policy had collapsed, the *coup de grâce* having been administered by the coup in Indonesia. At the same time, the Americans chose to unleash a major war on China's doorstep which had all the signs of eventually expanding into a war against China. To accept "joint action" in the spring of 1966 would have meant returning to the socialist camp with the admission of failure. At that time, China had few cards left to play against the Russians. The Vietnamese, who had earlier supported the Chinese in the campaign against revisionism, now swung back toward a more pro-Russian position. The Asian caucus that Liu had tried to build up was disintegrating. Moreover, China played no effective role on the international scene except as a conduit for matériel to Vietnam. Its influence in

Africa was at a nadir. It had alienated India. There is evidence to indicate that some Chinese leaders not only advocated acceptance of the
terms of "joint action" but were ready to intervene in the Indochina
conflict (or at least saw such intervention as inevitable). Whether the
Vietnamese at that time desired Chinese intervention is not clear but
doubtful. Still, in July 1966, North Vietnam decreed national mobilization, and in the event that its main force units went south, Chinese
troops might have become necessary to protect it against American invasion as well as to maintain support and logistical operations. If China
had intervened in 1966, it would have faced a new Korean War. At the
very least, this would have made the Cultural Revolution impossible, for
in times of war, people do not overthrow their leadership.

While the Cultural Revolution erupted dramatically in early May
1966, accompanied by a Chinese nuclear detonation on May 9, Mao had
taken his time preparing for it. In November 1965, Lo Jui-ch'ing, apparently more ready to intervene in Vietnam than other Chinese leaders,
was purged, and in the same month, Mao began to develop his Shanghai
base for an eventual "seizure of power" in Peking. "People want revolution" became the top and sole priority both domestically and internationally. China's foreign relations virtually ceased during the Cultural
Revolution, evident in the recall of all its ambassadors save Huang Hua
in Cairo. During the Cultural Revolution, the ultraleft, as they are now
called in China, did attempt to seize the Foreign Office and revolutionize
foreign affairs, but Mao clamped down sharply, thus protecting Chou En-
lai and Ch'en Yi from the fate of other leaders. Thus, whatever foreign
policy lines had been pursued were not to be destroyed but to be safely
kept in storage for a time when they could once again become prominent
or perhaps even dominant. *De facto* policy toward Vietnam did not
change, but at least in the early stages of the Cultural Revolution, Vietnam was hardly mentioned in the press, in contrast to the preceding
period. Liu's foreign policy may have collapsed, but Mao's alternatives
did not automatically take its place, save one: the final rupture with
Russia. Foreign policy as a whole went into limbo. Subsequent attacks
against foreign embassies in Peking (later attributed to ultraleft fanaticism) made some foreigners believe that China had reverted to the extreme xenophobia of the Boxer Rebellion. It seemed to be pursuing a
path of ultra-isolationism followed by only one other country in the
world, Albania.

Foreign and domestic policies are closely linked in all countries, including the United States. But by their nature, foreign policies can never
be pure extensions of domestic policies, as is evident in the case of
nuclear weapons. In the spring of 1966, however, despite all the external
dangers facing China, Mao decided that the coming revolution within

China had to take priority over all other matters. I believe that the horrifying events in Indonesia (like those in Hungary in 1956) had a much deeper effect on Mao than just in regard to foreign policy matters. What happened to the PKI could have been an augury of what might happen to China after his own passing. Suppose Communist China was another Ch'in Dynasty,[7] enormously innovative, powerful, and unified, but destined to last only some two score years. Then there would be a new Liu Pang, a peasant military commander who would sweep away a hated Communist party and restore (fu-pi) the old. The Han Dynasty two thousand years ago may be reckoned a glorious dynasty, but what would a post-Communist Han Dynasty be like? Most likely, the advanced "bourgeois" sectors would sweep farther and farther ahead of the backward inland areas, where a new ruling class would emerge on the heels of a Communist ruling class (the authoritarian power holders), and the fruits of the revolution would go to the few. To Mao, who represented the Yenan tradition of the Chinese Revolution, this was an intolerable future for China. In the declining years of his life, Mao Tse-tung was determined to make a decisive move to start the flames of revolution going again. The great Ch'in emperor had fastened a totalitarian control system on China so tight that virtually the whole nation was imprisoned. But as contradictions began to grow, he embarked on a foreign campaign to subdue Korea, where the energies of his army and his country were spent to exhaustion. Shortly after his natural death, his dynasty was overthrown and his name ever after execrated as a symbol of tyranny. Mao made the opposite choice. He loosened up the bonds of control in China ("dare to rebel") and vetoed intervention in Vietnam.

NEW DIRECTIONS IN CHINA'S TRADE

While it seemed for a while that China's foreign policies were little more than an extension of the struggles of the Cultural Revolution, this was not so. Just as the nuclear program was kept safely segregated from the revolution in China, so also foreign policy remained, by and large, segregated. It may have been in limbo, but the currents that had been developing were there, and emerged from their underground streambeds when the Cultural Revolution passed.

In practical, national interest terms, China, before the Cultural Revolution, pursued three major foreign policy directions. It was determined to acquire a nuclear capability; it carried on the dispute with Russia; and it began to reorient its trade away from the socialist countries to the

---

[7] Later in 1973, a vigorous campaign was launched in China to present the Ch'in emperor as a great leader and innovator who unified China. The implicit comparison with Mao was clear.

capitalist world. The first two I have already discussed, and the third I have touched briefly in terms of China's decision to import wheat from Canada during the food crisis of 1960–1961. That the nuclear question became the main determinant in China's state-to-state relations was evident in the situation surrounding the signing of the Test Ban Treaty in July 1963. China's policy of support for national liberation movements was not essentially different from that of Russia in the early 1960s, except that the Russians found that policy compatible with a détente with America and the Chinese did not. As we shall see, Khrushchev's eagerness for a decisive détente with America cooled his support for national liberation movements, particularly in Southeast Asia. Naturally, as this happened, China's support for those movements, particularly in Southeast Asia in the fateful years 1963–1964, became stronger. While all leaders in China, after the purge of P'eng Te-huai, probably supported the nuclear program, one has to see it as particularly advocated by Mao to give China "independence" and the great power status already reserved for it in the United Nations Security Council. Again, while the entire leadership subscribed to the directions the dispute with Russia took, its strategy and tactics were particularly characteristic of Liu Shao-ch'i. Thus, during the pre–Cultural Revolution period, the current of Mao Tse-tung and the current of Liu Shao-ch'i had core issues that were explosively contradictory, for the Russians insisted that China's independent nuclear capability was incompatible with a restoration of the unity of the socialist camp. But what of trade?

The decision of the Chinese leadership to reorient China's trade away from the socialist countries to the capitalist world cannot be seen as an inevitable outgrowth of the withdrawal of Russian technicians from China in July–August 1960. Sino-Soviet trade continued at a high level through 1961, and only began to drop sharply thereafter. Mikhail Suslov, in a February 1964 speech, put the blame on the Chinese for the drop in trade, and what evidence there is indicates that he probably was right.[8] The de-emphasis on heavy industry decreased Chinese need for Russian capital goods, but China still had to import a great deal in order to keep its economy moving. The Chinese were prevented, of course, from importing goods on the strategic embargo list from capitalist countries, but they began to cultivate active trading relationships with many countries regarded as satellites of America, notably Japan and West Germany. From Japan, they contracted for the delivery of whole plants to help to set up a chemical and fertilizer industry. A deal was apparently fully worked out for the West Germans to set up a steel plant somewhere in the interior of China (probably Szechwan), until the esca-

[8] John Gittings, *Survey of the Sino-Soviet Dispute*, pp. 140–42.

lation of the Vietnam war and the Cultural Revolution canceled it. The Chinese became active buyers and shoppers throughout Western Europe and Japan, and there was no sign that Washington was intervening with these countries to prevent trade with China.

In terms of the three currents sketched out earlier, one could say that in addition to those of Mao Tse-tung and Liu Shao-ch'i, the current I have ascribed to Ch'en Yün also played a role in Chinese foreign policy from late 1960 on. In a broader sense, one can say that the internal economic policy that the Chinese began to follow after the decisions of the January 1961 plenum was what Ch'en Yün had advocated in early 1957: slow but balanced development, emphasis on agriculture and consumer goods, and efforts to develop foreign trade. In 1957, Ch'en Yün's efforts to develop trade were destroyed by Dulles's dramatic closing of the slightly opened trade doors. But, as I have already indicated, by late 1960, Washington appears to have changed its policies on trade with China, not so much in regard to the United States as in regard to its allies and clients trading with China. While one could argue that there was always powerful pressure within Japan to trade with China, no such argument could be made for West Germany. West German trade with China was of only small importance to its economy, and if Washington had put pressure on Bonn to stop, it probably would have done so. The Erhard-Schroeder regime was solidly committed to the relationship with America and would not have hesitated to join a total quarantine of China if that was what Washington wanted. In the case of Britain in the late 1940s and early 1950s, one could argue that it resisted the embargo because it had major interests in China which were harmed by Washington's policies.

The Chinese leadership was able to break its trade ties with the socialist countries because an alternative elsewhere was available, which was not the case in the fall of 1949. The Canadian wheat deal must have been interpreted in Peking as a quiet sign from Washington that it was willing to start dropping the trade embargo against China.

CHOU EN-LAI AND POLICY CURRENTS

While I have attached the names of Mao and Liu to two of the three currents, that of Ch'en Yün no longer evokes much of a memory. Although he appeared on T'ien An Men Square in the early mass meetings of the Cultural Revolution, he is no longer referred to in the press. The most prominent figure who could be considered as the symbol of the Ch'en Yün current today is Chou En-lai. Chou En-lai has been premier of China since the People's Republic was established. But until February 1958, he also held the post of foreign minister. Administratively, the premier of China is the chairman of the State Council, which is the government of the country. The overwhelming bulk of the State Council's work consists of planning and managing China's economy. Thus, when Chou En-lai relinquished the foreign ministry in February 1958, his main duties, in effect, became the administration and management of China's economy. That new role was already evident in the spring of 1959 when Chou En-lai publicly pushed the policy of "all the country is a single chessboard," which attempted to bring some order to the tumultuous changes that had occurred the previous year. The Foreign Ministry passed into the hands of Ch'en Yi, a bluff and hearty general whose thoughts apparently closely coincided with those of Chou. Ch'en Yi was attacked during the Cultural Revolution for a short period of time, but Chairman Mao reportedly intervened to stop it. Known for his enjoyment of life, he was a natural target for ultraleft puritans, far more so than Liu Shao-ch'i, whose life style was much simpler. But the Foreign Ministry was kept essentially intact during the Cultural Revolution. Its turn for flowering came as China began to move out into the international diplomatic world. Chou En-lai has always been considered the "moderate," the "pragmatist" by Westerners (and apparently also by the Russians). His loyalty to Mao seems to be beyond question. Yet, unlike Liu Shao-ch'i or Lin Piao, he never has been considered a potential successor to Mao, although his name regularly appears in third or fourth place on official documents or celebrity rankings. While his military history is as glorious as that of all other leaders of the Chinese Revolution, during most of World War II he was in Chungking as the Communists' chief liaison with the Chiang regime and their chief negotiator with foreigners, mainly Americans. Since then, he has traveled widely throughout the world, in socialist as well as neutral countries, where he acquired the reputation of a brilliant, rational, and articulate representative of his country's interests. He has expressed such world views as were in force at any particular time but, unlike Liu Shao-ch'i or Lin Piao, he has not been an ideological spokesman. If there has been what I have called a Ch'en Yün current in China, then it seems appropriate to say that from the late 1960s on, Chou En-lai became its chief symbol and spokesman. This also makes it virtually impossible for Chou En-lai ever to succeed Mao, for the Ch'en Yün current played the least important role of the three in the Chinese Revolution.

In the past, when Chinese spoke of the national bourgeoisie, they invariably thought of Shanghai. But from the time of the January 1967 storm, Shanghai has been one of the most radical areas of China. Close allies of the Chairman, like Chang Ch'un-ch'iao and Yao Wen-yüan, come from Shanghai. Mao started the prelude to the Cultural Revolution in Shanghai, and the Chinese Communist party itself was founded there. If the successor to Mao should come out of the Shanghai experience,

then the context will be very different from the one that spawned the
Ch'en Yün current. In the early 1950s, the Chinese Communists justified
their retention of the national bourgeoisie on the grounds that these
businessmen had scarce managerial talents necessary to run the many
enterprises of the great coastal cities. Though today those bourgeois are a
truly vestigial class, the notion of a group of people with necessary
"expert" skills remains strong in China. Liu Shao-ch'i may have been
attacked for fetishizing expertise, but Mao himself has never attacked the
idea of expertise (meaning skills) as such. But if the experts are indispensable to China, they also can never become the fountainhead for its
ideology. During the antirightist movement of 1957, the bureaucracies of
the State Council, the country's main repository of expert talent, were
decimated. During the Cultural Revolution, however, those bureaucracies remained, by and large, intact, and the few attacks on them were
quickly halted and later denounced as ultraleft excesses. Again, like the
nuclear program or like Chou En-lai, the "expert" current has a kind of
enduring existence in China, without a chance of assuming power at the
top (nor wanting it), but always solidly entrenched in the wings.

In the summer of 1957, the Ch'en Yün current received a major
setback and was eliminated—temporarily—as a political force (its adherents were bitterly attacked during the antirightist movement). But in
January 1961, it made a comeback, and made its most spectacular
breakthrough in the area of trade with the capitalist world. During the
three years 1958–1960, the Great Leap Forward was the work of the
Mao and Liu currents, and many of the vagaries of that period were
obviously the result of clashes between them. But by the early 1960s, all
three currents were again operating on the Chinese political scene. If
Mao pressed forward with his nuclear program, Liu pressed forward
with his Asian caucus, and Chou En-lai and Ch'en Yi, let us say, pressed
forward with their new trade policies. Mao's major concern, naturally,
was the two great nuclear powers, America and Russia, who were bitterly opposed to his Chinese *force de frappe*. Liu was preoccupied with
gaining adherents among antirevisionist communist parties in the dispute
with the Russians, among whom not only the Indonesians but the Vietnamese Lao Dong party must be considered his most important allies.
Liu Shao-ch'i visited Hanoi in May 1963, indicating a particular Liuist
preoccupation with the issue of national liberaton movements. The main
preoccupation of the Ch'en Yün current, however, had to be the general
international situation as it affected trade and normal state-to-state relations. Because of the growing orientation of this current toward the
capitalist world and its more traditional concern with the Southeast
Asian trade, the country it had to think hardest about was the United
States. For this current, it was axiomatic (and proven by experience)
that the more hostile America was to China, the fewer the chances of

China's gaining a major international economic and political role. Thus, China had no chance of joining the United Nations so long as America maintained its opposition.

For the Liuist current, opposition to America in principle and in practice was the cornerstone of its world view. This was the only basis on which the unity and solidarity of the socialist camp could be restored. The struggle against revisionism had one overriding aim: to force the Soviet Union to halt its growing détente with America. The Liuist conception of America followed the classic Chinese perception of a rollback-minded American imperialism everywhere intent on expanding its own power and destroying socialist countries and communist movements. For the Ch'en Yün current, however, America was potentially a country with which China could peacefully coexist. If America evinced in Asia the same trade- and profit-motivated desire for peaceful coexistence it had shown in Europe, then China's national security interests would not only be secured but new possibilities for world-wide economic and political gain would open up. Obviously, the two currents had to be in direct opposition to each other, for how could America be a predatory power seeking China's destruction and at the same time make moves toward peaceful coexistence with China? This was precisely the paradox of the early 1960s. Two arms stretched from America toward China, one holding a sword and the other an olive branch, and both were real. Supposedly an active, conscious brain was in firm control of both arms. But that was not the case, as we shall see.

CHANGES IN MAO'S THINKING ON RUSSIA AND AMERICA AS ENEMIES

But what of the current of Mao Tse-tung? Since independence, symbolized by a nuclear capability, was its supreme foreign policy (or national security) goal, the unity and solidarity of the socialist camp fell to a lower priority. If P'eng Chen and Teng Hsiao-p'ing had succeeded, in the summer of 1963, in dissuading Moscow from signing the Test Ban Treaty, then the socialist camp would have been restored on a basis of equality between Russia and China. Russia would thereby have signified to China that it regarded their alliance as having greater importance than its desire for a détente with America or its fear of a Chinese nuclear capability. During the golden years of the Sino-Russian relationship (1954–1957), Russia and China were true equals, as were Khrushchev and Mao—each helped out the other in time of need and their foreign policies were virtually identical. But if Russia would not accept China's independence, then, as Mao saw it, the entire notion of a socialist camp might have to be sacrificed, for nothing was more sacred than the independence of his own nation and China's revolution. The same reasoning applied to America. If America was determined to destroy the independence of China, then it was an implacable enemy which had to be fought at all costs. But if America came around to accepting China's independence, accepting the fact that there was a People's Republic of China and that Taiwan was nothing more than an offshore island which would one day revert to China, then a new relationship with America might be possible. For the Mao current, political and military questions were the overriding ones, as befits the notion that "power grows out of the barrel of a gun."

From Camp David on (if not before, during the previous summer's Quemoy crisis), a train of thought began to develop in Mao's mind that increasingly convinced him that Russia would never truly accept China's independence, that the Russians regarded themselves as the sole rulers of all socialist countries and as the best equipped to negotiate with the Americans on the interests of all the members of what they regarded as their camp. In his November 1957 speech before the Supreme Soviet, Mao accused American imperialism of stubbornly wanting to interfere in the internal affairs of the socialist countries. From 1959 on, he came to believe that Russia was a worse offender than even America in this respect. Eventually this would lead to the conception of a "Soviet social imperialism" more dangerous than the "waning" imperialism of America. Obviously, if America was joined with Russia in a Holy Alliance to rule the world, then both had to be implacable enemies of China. If America showed itself to be less and less an enemy, however, then only one principal enemy remained, Russia.

As I have already written, Mao makes a distinction between "principal enemy" and "secondary enemy." From the fall of 1949 on, Mao (and all other Chinese leaders) made the decision that America was China's principal enemy. When the *People's Daily* on August 17, 1971, during the height of the Lin Piao crisis, published the editorial "A Mighty Weapon for Unifying the People in Victorious Struggle Against the Enemy," it was clear that Russia had assumed the position of principal enemy. That status became even more explicit in the editorial published on October 1, 1972. If Camp David marked the Sino-Soviet split, then at some point between 1959 and 1971, a transition was made in the definition of principal enemy. That point can be specified with convincing accuracy. It came in the spring of 1966 when Mao rejected "joint action" and launched the Cultural Revolution. At that time, party-to-party relations were broken off and Russia became a hostile power which could be dealt with only on a state-to-state basis. But if Russia had become an enemy, then Mao's thinking would demand a further definition of whether it was a principal or a secondary enemy. Obviously,

during the Cultural Revolution, which coincided with the most dangerous period of the Vietnam war, the Chinese left that definition in limbo,
with most of their foreign policy. But, by the fall of 1968, just after the
American election, the first signs, weak as they were, began to come
from China that the definition had been made. The border war of the
following months with the Russians made it clear to all Chinese that
Russia was a deadly enemy. While in Peking, in late November 1972,
Joseph Alsop wrote that the Russians in 1969 "vainly asked for U.S.
support" for an attack on China.[9] If that was the case, then obviously
Russia was the principal enemy and America had signified its demotion
to "secondary enemy" status by refusing to condone such an attack.

In terms of currents, one can say that in those circumstances where
America was clearly the principal enemy, as in late 1949 and in 1957,
Mao leaned decisively and openly toward the Liu current. But as Russia
began to assume the status of former friend, then hostile neighbor, and
finally principal enemy, Mao began to gravitate toward the Ch'en Yün
current, which we can now safely say was symbolized, from the beginning of the Cultural Revolution, by Chou En-lai. That current continued
throughout the Cultural Revolution. During the great mass meetings of
mid-August 1966, three principal figures appeared on the podium on
T'ien An Men Square, Mao Tse-tung, Lin Piao, and Chou En-lai. Lin
and the People's Liberation Army were substituted for Liu and his party.
When the army once again receded into the background, Lin himself was
purged, and a new party leadership and structure began to come to the
fore early in the 1970s (Yao Wen-yüan and Chang Ch'un-ch'iao); Chou
En-lai remained as always.

The picture of Mao's vision is now essentially complete. It probably
has its roots long before the Liberation, but it was not until the early
1960s that Mao began to cultivate it as an alternative to the policies
dominant at the time. His vision involved China becoming part of the
intermediate zones between America and Russia. In its developed aspects, it shared characteristics with the developed countries of the second
intermediate zone (chiefly Japan and Western Europe). As a still poor
and backward country, it was obviously a part of the first intermediate
zone or what the West calls the Third World. His vision is a national one
in that it regards countries with sovereignty, independence, and national
power as the essential units of the world, not camps or alliances or blocs.
He believes that the dynamics pushing political men are the desires for
independence, liberation, and revolution. Since these are not particularly
economic conceptions, Mao could be accused of taking a non-Marxist
approach to politics. Yet for Mao, struggle, not theories of monopoly

[9] *San Francisco Chronicle*, December 1, 1972.

capitalism, has always been the essential teaching of Marxism. He has a vision of the oppressed everywhere constantly rising up to seize destiny in their own hands, again not an exclusively Marxist notion. De Tocqueville, on the basis of his American experience, saw this as an inevitable process in the world. In that struggle, all of mankind has one over-all enemy which must be rooted out to the core—imperialism. For Mao, imperialism is the system of domination by superpowers which try to bend all the world to their will, and the two great contemporary imperialisms are the American empire and the Russian empire. Until imperialism is destroyed, independence, liberation, and revolution cannot achieve their final triumph, but the drive for those goals can hasten the destruction of imperialism and the prevention of a third world war.

Like it or not, Mao's vision is the only powerful competitor to the dominant visions that have guided world politics until now, symbolized by the words "free world" and "socialist camp." In some ways, it is radical, favoring trouble and more trouble throughout the world as the only way man can achieve his aspirations. In other ways, it is old-fashioned, with its stress on national sovereignties and a relish for competitive pluralism in the world. Even San Marino has its honored place in Peking. Mao's vision is in direct contradiction to both the Russian and American world views which hold that nuclear weapons have made the world so dangerous that only if the responsible powers hold it in check will mankind be prevented from destroying itself. For the Russians, Mao is no different from those petits bourgeois student revolutionaries whom they detest—radical at times to the point of adventurism, they quickly revert to conservatism and reaction. They are not of the working class, for they are hostile to *organization*, which even the monopoly capitalist managers of American imperialism have learned to appreciate. Organize the whole world and there will be peace and plenty for all, so goes the Russian notion. The American view is little different, though having a greater, more powerful, efficient, pervasive, and productive organizational structure, the Americans take organization for granted and do not make a fetish of it as the Russians do. Both are betting, however, that Mao's vision is destined to pass, for organization will once again triumph in China, the bureaucrats will return, chains of command will reassert themselves, and new elites will come to power. Time alone will tell.

THE LOGIC OF A BIPOLAR WORLD

As the decade of the 1960s began, the iron logic of a bipolar world seemed irrefutable. America and Russia so obviously were the world's superpowers and their status as such was assured for some decades at least. Other countries like China, India, or Brazil had vast land areas, but their industrial capabilities would take decades to achieve even what some of the smaller European powers already had. Germany and Japan were economically powerful, but military midgets. Britain was increasingly a memory rather than a political force, and de Gaulle's France was little more than an irritant. The two giant economies, the American and the Russian, would dominate the world for decades to come. Their nuclear capabilities had so far outstripped competitors that no other credible nuclear power seemed to be in sight. The American and Russian educational systems were the most advanced in the world, and even America was willing to "learn from Ivan." Naturally, each of the superpowers had a host of interests and commitments and unruly allies which made agreement difficult. And, of course, they distrusted each other ideologically. Yet both had one avdantage—stable political systems with powerful leaderships at the top. Naturally, as a democracy, America was not as capable of one-man decision making as the Soviet dictatorship, but still, as Kennedy tried to demonstrate in his three years in office, there was an enormous power in the Presidency which his predecessor was disinclined to utilize. Eisenhower had begun summitry, which became something of a tradition. Kennedy had failed in his first face-to-face meeting with Khrushchev in Vienna, but summitry need not always involve face-to-face meetings. Summitry means using the vast political power at the apexes of both systems in order to hammer out agreements between the two countries. The Washington-Moscow "hot line," installed after the Cuban missile crisis, symbolized this new form of summitry politics.

From the moment of his electoral victory, Kennedy was determined to use the latent power of the Presidency to achieve the idealistic goals to which the Democrats, at least their liberal wing, had always been committed. The logic of the Russian-American relationship dictated that sooner or later the two countries would have to reach some concrete understanding on the nuclear question. If the will and intent were present on both sides, then, at least on the American side, the power of the Presidency could be used to bring it about sooner rather than later. What was called the Soviet-American détente did begin under Eisenhower, but it was Kennedy who made it into the cornerstone of his foreign policy. Johnson not only inherited the policy but pursued it with even greater vigor than Kennedy throughout his administration. The *sine qua non* of that policy had to be an agreement with the Russians stabilizing the nuclear relationship between the two countries.

In the light of American genocide in Vietnam, it may seem cynical to say anything mild about Kennedy's counterinsurgency, but from the perspective of 1961, it had in it none of the horrifying potentialities finally realized in Vietnam. In January 1961, Khrushchev had boasted that Russia would support national liberation movements throughout the world. In American eyes, such movements taken to their extreme could only result in communist dictatorships. Why should America not play at the same game, involving itself in the political ferment of the Third World countries by backing moderate, middle-of-the-road elements who would create democratic rather than communist regimes? If central nuclear war was henceforth excluded from the political scene, then why should America not do exactly what Khrushchev had challenged it to do—compete? The Kennedyites were convinced that right-wing regimes constituted a one-way road to eventual communist revolution, as China had made clear. But revolution could be avoided if the right-wing regimes were replaced by governments like that of Rómulo Betancourt in Venezuela. If American involvement necessitated counterinsurgency against communists, as in Vietnam, this was justified on the grounds that it gave an opportunity to the moderate elements to assume power and start the process of nation-building which would create the political and economic stability adequate to meet any communist threat from a position of internal strength. Counterinsurgency coupled with economic aid and Peace Corps volunteers was America's revolutionary answer to the subversive machinations of the Sino-Soviet bloc.

An atmosphere of idealism pervaded the Kennedy camp after the election victory. America could finally emerge from the strait jacket of Dullesian anticommunism and once again play its historically progressive role in the world. There would no longer be any question of unleashing World War III. While Russia was still an unacceptable dictatorship and China a repulsive ultrarevolutionary monster, neither had to fear American attack. India would become a far more shining example of progress under freedom than China under dictatorship, and men like John Kenneth Galbraith and Chester Bowles symbolized liberal America's generous commitment to backward India. True, America was fighting to put down a Communist insurgency in South Vietnam, but it was a small, restricted, and not very costly effort. Had not the British put down the Communists in Malaya and so set the stage for the prosperous Malaya of the early 1960s? Had not Ramón Magsaysay finally eliminated the Huks by introducing land reform and turned the Philippines into a sturdy and progressing nation? No idealist could quarrel with the imperative to be tough in the larger interests of peace and progress for the world as a whole.

The grand designs of Kennedy and Khrushchev were a kind of mirror image of each other. Both believed that the economic competition between America and Russia would decide the fate of the world as a whole. Khrushchev believed that a mighty Soviet economy would not only outdistance America, but pull much of the rest of the world along.

Kennedy was determined to give the lie to Russian Marxist notions about the inevitable collapse of capitalist economies. America would have not only a speeded-up growth rate but a surplus far greater than that of Russia with which it, not Russia, could rescue the Third World for Freedom. The early Kennedy period was a heyday for the economists, and a kind of fetishism of economics reigned in Washington. Both Kennedy and Khrushchev were determined to rid their respective countries of the military and defense-spending burden they were carrying. Kennedy, of course, hiked defense spending, which alarmed Khrushchev, but his ultimate aim was to bring America's vast military machine under control and then cut back on defense spending. Both believed that the main source of domestic stability lay in consumer affluence and greater civil rights. Kennedy began the programs of reform that eventually became Johnson's Great Society, including civil rights for blacks. Khrushchev remained committed to freeing the Russian people from the repressiveness of Stalinism. Each was also convinced that his country's foreign interests were best served by moving boldly and widely everywhere possible, handing out money, distributing machines and weapons, gathering in clients and allies.

It all still sounds quite good if one erases recent memories and dredges up thoughts and sentiments from the early 1960s. That there were fatal flaws is evident. That the grand designs did not work still puzzles many of those who were centrally involved at the time. The word "sincere" is bandied about again and again to describe men such as John Kennedy, Robert McNamara, John McNaughton, and others involved in the Vietnam story. "Sincere" can only mean that these men thought that what they were doing would work. It did not work for one simple and central reason: they did not have the power to make it work. Kennedy made the most gigantic misjudgment of all. He vastly overestimated the power of the Presidency of America, and of the chosen few to bend the doings of the multitudes to their will. Kennedy correctly sensed the ideological power inherent in the Presidency and used it fully. But he believed operational power followed automatically from the fact that he and his men held the supreme command posts of the American, and therefore much of the world's, political structure. Strangely enough, his successor Johnson, who seemed to epitomize the arrogant American, had a much keener sense of the limitations of presidential power, but unlike Truman who managed to control the political process, Johnson was overwhelmed by it. Khrushchev made the same mistake as Kennedy. Having grown up under Stalin, he thought that he too was the great leader, the *vozhd*, simply because he occupied that position. He had fought down enemies right and left and emerged triumphant. How else could it be explained except through the power of presiding over the Presidium?

HOW CHIEF EXECUTIVES HAVE
POWER IN COMMON

The emerging logic of the American-Russian nuclear relationship indicated that, even under conditions of arms control and mutual deterrence, their relationship could be used to generate new and different "inputs" into their respective political processes. The real form that relationship took was one between the two executives, the President of the United States and the Chairman of the Presidium of the USSR. The President and the Chairman faced comparable problems, despite the differences in "social systems." Each had to deal with a broad array of contending bureaucracies which, by necessity, had to oppose the will of the executive from time to time. The executives had to make painful decisions in a never-ending zero-sum situation which eventually antagonized even those who might have been temporarily benefited by a particular decision. Each had to deal with a broad array of client countries, situations, and conflicts in which the interests and commitments of his country were deeply imbedded. Furthermore, each had one supreme goal for himself: to expand, strengthen, and consolidate executive power, either for himself as leader or for his own tight collective of top leaders.

This began to suggest a new form that the nuclear relationship between the two superpowers could take. Why should not the two executives help each other to generate unique inputs into their own political processes? If Kennedy could deliver a hard-and-fast concession from Khrushchev on a matter of major importance to certain American bureaucracies, for instance military, then his over-all power vis-à-vis those bureaucracies would be enhanced. They might have to threaten Khrushchev to gain comparable concessions or make vast new claims on scarce budgetary resources to generate new deterrent capabilities, but Kennedy could achieve that same goal just by "talking" with Khrushchev.

America was the leader of the free world and Russia was the leader of the socialist camp. Many if not most of their external interests and commitments were in areas of conflict between the two blocs. The bureaucracies had their own reasons for wishing a continuation of those conflicts, for they were (and remain) a source of their own power. But all conflicts are waged, ostensibly anyway, for certain goals, and it is, therefore, very hard for a bureaucracy to insist that a conflict continue just for the sake of its own vested power interests. If those goals can be achieved in an extrabureaucratic manner, through great power agreement, then the bureaucracies involved will lose a major reason and source of their own power. It is always in the interest of the executive to reduce the powers of his bureaucracies so that he can have more latitude to make and implement his decisions. In this way, a triangular process began to suggest itself whereby the chief executives of the two super-powers could use their own power to make concessions to each other in areas of conflict between them, which, in turn, would weaken the vested interests of their own bureaucracies in those areas and, thus, result in expanded executive power for both.

Nothing so dramatically illustrates this aspect of the nuclear relation-ship between America and Russia as their attempts to settle the Vietnam war through each other. Johnson and Rusk demanded of Kosygin that he put pressure on Hanoi for concessions. With such concessions, Johnson would have had greater power to oppose his own hawks and get them to make reciprocal concessions. But, of course, Kosygin was not able to deliver those concessions, and Johnson's power vis-à-vis his military-bureaucratic hawks was further reduced. The irony is that Kosygin was in a similar position of dubious power. He was asking Johnson for concessions so that *he* could demonstrate his power, to his own bureau-crats and to his Vietnamese allies.

CHINA: THE FLAW IN THE BIPOLAR LOGIC

But there was a flaw in the logic which quickly came to preoccupy both Russians and Americans—China. The Sino-Soviet dispute began to dis-rupt that iron logic of great power relationships between America and Russia which, in the early 1960s, had just started to take on exciting new operational forms. It is not coincidental that the chief issue of the dis-pute, the developing Chinese nuclear capability, was one of supreme importance not just to the American and Russian executives, but to the Chinese executive as well. For the new American-Russian relationship to work, it was absolutely essential that other powers not acquire a credible nuclear capability. Not only would an ordered world be impossible if a whole range of nations started detonating their own atomic bombs, but it seemed self-evident at the time that this was a one-way highway toward a third world war. The only two nations that seriously threatened the American-Russian nuclear monopoly were China and France, and the most dangerous of the two, in both American and Russian eyes, was China.

The national security thinkers of the Kennedy Administration did not know what to make of the Sino-Soviet dispute. Arthur Schlesinger, Jr., has ridiculed those in the State Department (presumably Dean Rusk) who woodenly held to the notion of a Sino-Soviet bloc when that bloc was disintegrating for all to see. Yet neither Rusk in the State Department nor the Joint Chiefs of Staff can be blamed for not wishing to relinquish a world view that had shaped their goals, strategies, and tactics since 1950. Nor was the dispute definitive in the early 1960s. There was always the possibility that it could suddenly be resolved, perhaps by a change of leadership in one of the countries. Nor was it ever convincingly clear that the Russian nuclear umbrella had been withdrawn from China, despite the vehemence of Chinese attacks against Russia. Yet one hard and cold fact was clear to all involved: the Chinese were moving fast to develop a nuclear capability which, while it did not seem to threaten Russia militarily, certainly threatened it politically. Both Rusk and the Joint Chiefs of Staff were absolutely aware of what the Chinese were doing in their remote Lop Nor region of Sinkiang.

Since the Sino-Soviet dispute did not fit any of the parameters that had been worked into the bureaucratic world view, it naturally was left to the intellectuals to argue it out. The operational thrust of the liberal view, which held that the Sino-Soviet dispute was real, was that America should make use of the golden opportunities offered for a new kind of "flexible response" to the chief challenges in the world. In the early 1960s, those challenges were seen as the rising of the Third World and its desire for political independence, economic development, and social justice. If America could guide the revolutionary processes of the Third World into truly progressive and reformist paths, then Chinese expansionism would be blocked. Once blocked from access to the world revolution, China would have no choice but to occupy itself with its own internal problems. If it did so in a rational manner, eventually its own development would produce the same kind of *embourgeoisement* that had arisen in Russia. At that point, moderates would come to power as they had in Russia, in the form of Khrushchev. But the dispute offered a new and exciting way of achieving this goal, for now America could use its erstwhile principal enemy, Russia, to put pressure on China to desist from its expansionist, ultrarevolutionary course. If both Russians and Americans agreed on the supreme need for world peace, then this could constitute powerful leverage on a mad Chinese leadership, which seemed to relish the thought of a nuclear holocaust so that communism could triumph on the ashes of what was left of the civilized world.

But while this new vision of a Russian-American alliance to put the Chinese in their proper place excited the intellectuals, it posed grave dangers for the logics on which the bureaucratic politics of Washington functioned. If the dispute was real, then Moscow had lost its control over China. The disappearance of a Russian nuclear umbrella over China might please the hawks, who would see this as further decreasing the likelihood of dangerous consequences if America decided to deal forcefully with China. Yet it also meant a dramatic decline in the power of the

Russian executive, for one of the essential attributes of that power was the capability to "deliver" countries within its orbit. Thus, Moscow was always able to "deliver" Ulbricht on any issue regarding Berlin because it kept a firm hand over East Germany, not least through its occupation troops. China, of course, was a vast geographical fact in a region where the dangers of war had been the greatest in the world since the end of World War II. If China should slip out of Russian control, America would have to deal with it. But until the Sino-Soviet dispute became so real and self-evident, let us say, as it was in the spring of 1969 when Russian and Chinese troops fought on the Ussuri, any American attempt to resolve the China problem could just lead to a repetition of the same kind of dangerous confrontations with Russia that had occurred in the past over Korea, Quemoy, and Laos. Few in Washington in the early 1960s hungered for a major new war in East Asia. The military had bitter memories of the Korean War and desired no repetition. Moreover, it soon became embroiled in a major domestic war against a man it increasingly came to see as an archenemy of the independence of the services, Robert McNamara. The military saw the Kennedyites brandishing about all sorts of new ideas and programs which seemed to spell only one thing so far as the military was concerned: reducing and containing its power. It naturally remained deeply suspicious of all the talk about a Sino-Soviet dispute and clung to the conservative view that the Sino-Soviet bloc remained a military and political reality. The Kennedyites certainly wanted no major war in East Asia, for their global idealism again and again stressed peace, as Kennedy indicated by organizing his Peace Corps. Officially and bureaucratically, therefore, the conservative view prevailed. All the polemics within American defense intellectual circles about the Sino-Soviet dispute did not bring about a change in the predominant world view in Washington. It continued to be that of containment, which presumed the existence of a Sino-Soviet bloc and a free world, headed respectively by Russia and America.

CHINA'S A-BOMB: KENNEDY'S NIGHTMARE

If all the great events of the world seemed to be going Kennedy's way, one phenomenon began to loom more and more as a threat that could shatter everything. That was the specter of China armed with deliverable nuclear weapons. If China managed to break the Russian-American nuclear monopoly (intelligence estimates indicated it would detonate its first atomic device by the summer of 1964), then the entire world could be plunged in a chasm of uncertainty so deep that even the worst contingencies were thinkable. The national security planners well remem-

bered how fast the balance of forces in the world changed after the
Russian atomic breakthrough in September 1949. China need not have
sophisticated delivery systems in order to be a threat. One atomic device
hidden aboard a junk could be smuggled into a harbor and readied for
detonation. However laughable such a scenario may seem, it was seriously discussed by defense intellectuals in the early 1960s. The moment
the Chinese detonated their first atomic device, the Russians would lose
their power to control events in East Asia. Then America would have to
deal with China directly, as it had dealt with Russia in the late 1940s
and early 1950s. Russia was then at the height of its expansionism, or so
the Kennanites proclaimed, and in the early 1960s, China seemed to be
entering its own expansionist phase. How often the West had come to
the brink of nuclear war in dealing with the Russians during those earlier
years! Would America now have to face a succession of similar crises
until the Chinese reached a more responsible posture or decided to renounce their nuclear program?

No one in the Kennedy Administration had any sympathy for Chinese
efforts to acquire nuclear weapons, and some felt so strongly that they
advocated using long-range bombers to destroy the sites and plants before the Chinese achieved a breakthrough. Averell Harriman is reported
to have asked Khrushchev in 1964 what Russia would do if Washington
decided to take out the Chinese nuclear sites. While few believed that the
Chinese would blow up the world, most Kennedyites were convinced that
nuclear capability meant expansionism. Was that not the case with Russia in the late 1940s? Naturally, no one even dreamed of suggesting that
nuclear capability as an instrument for expansionism and imperialism
applied primarily to America. But all knew or sensed that nuclear power
meant world power for the country concerned, and China was just not
regarded as a fit and safe member of the world community.

The Kennedy Administration, with its array of brilliant intellectuals,
radiated the power of logic and reason. McNamara symbolized the new
rationalism as he tried to use reason to impose new organizational and
budgetary forms on the reluctant and intellectually far less brilliant military. Kennedy's grand design was rational, logical, and unsentimental,
befitting the image of the Kennedyites as intellectual tough guys. But
China remained a gaping hole in that logic. Ever since 1949, China did
not exist for Washington, even though it was massively real for the right
wing. The only kind of existence Washington seemed timidly ready to
substitute for that of the right wing was what emerged from a "two-
China policy." But for China to agree to a two-China policy meant, in
effect, to accept its status as defined by containment policy, which, paradoxically, demanded that it remain a good and obedient member of the
socialist camp doing Moscow's bidding. If now China was pulling away

from the camp, as Albania did in 1961, then what kind of existence could be granted to it? To accept China as a great power was unthinkable, not just because it would have infuriated the American right wing, but because it would call for so radical a redefinition of the forces of world politics that Kennedy's grand design would crumble.

Kennedy himself was reportedly fascinated with China and undoubtedly had all kinds of thoughts on the subject that did not enter the normal bureaucratic process. He must have discussed it many times with various French leaders, de Gaulle and others, with whom he had amicable relations despite Franco-American differences. Did he begin to toy with the idea of a new relationship with China, perhaps mediated through de Gaulle? It is, after all, one of the prerogatives of the supreme executive to consider alternative policy lines while remaining loyal to the dominant ones. Mao began to evolve his notions of the two intermediate zones while remaining committed to the dominant policy line of seeking to re-establish the unity of the socialist camp on terms acceptable to China. But dominant currents and policy lines are not broken by the simple musing of even so august a figure as the chief executive of a state.

Concretely, what was American policy toward China in 1963? The formal policy was not just nonrecognition, but recognition of the Republic of China as the sole legitimate government of all of China. That policy had been adopted by the Truman Administration as a concession to the nationalist right wing and has, formally anyway, remained in force until the present day. Recognition of the Taipei regime implied tacit acceptance of the principle of rollback and the goal of reconquering the Mainland. In fact, however, Washington had begun to develop some alternative policy lines toward China which reflected the other currents determining American foreign policy in general, containment and internationalism. In 1957, Dulles had denied any concessions to internationalism by flatly ruling out trade or other forms of normal intercourse with China. But by late 1960, Washington began to soften its line on trade. Roger Hilsman's December 13, 1963, speech on China in San Francisco must be regarded as a further concession to the internationalist current. That it was given in San Francisco, the place in America that had symbolically become associated with the trade question, made that clear. Whether Kennedy, had he lived, would have intended that speech to imply more than just an acceptance of the notion of trade and cultural contacts cannot be known. The fact that it came only a little more than a month before France's recognition of China would certainly have suggested to observers that Washington was throwing out some feelers, particularly in view of the personal relationship between Kennedy and de Gaulle. Even as the Vietnam conflict escalated, Washington continued to soften its policy on contacts with China. It validated the passports of numerous scholars and scientists for visits to China, going far beyond Dulles's reluctant consent to a few journalists. In fact, Washington began to argue in the mid and late 1960s that it was China that was keeping out Americans rather than the reverse.

While Washington was making concessions on trade and cultural contacts to the internationalists, still its main concern was to evolve a containment-type policy toward China. From the mid-1950s, that policy came to be known as the "two-China policy." Its overt aims were to replicate for China what had been achieved, more or less, with Germany and Korea and what Washington also wanted to achieve in Vietnam. The People's Republic of China and the Republic of China were both to be accepted as sovereign independent states. In the case of Germany, both West and East Germany have now accepted and recognized each other as separate states while professing a common nationhood. Washington's containment officials would have been delighted if Peking and Taipei had accepted a similar solution to the "China problem." But no policy has been more castigated, more reviled, more opposed by Peking (and Taipei) than the two-China policy. For Chiang Kai-shek, accepting it would have not only extinguished what faint hope he had of getting back to the Mainland but undercut the legitimacy of his Mainlander rule over the Taiwanese. For Mao Tse-tung to have accepted a two-China policy would have meant abandoning the most sacred principle of China's independence, sovereignty, and territorial integrity. In other words, it would have put China on a par, at best, with a nation like Germany; at worst, with small nations like Korea. There were, of course, far more important reasons than the desire to be accepted as a great nation which motivated Peking's hostility to a two-China policy. But the fact that historically China has been a great nation and not an appendage of a foreign monarchy located thousands of miles away cannot be dismissed out of hand. To accept equality with a quasi-artificial midget like the Republic of China is a humiliation no Chinese leader could swallow.

Washington, however, added a further precondition for its own acceptance of its two-China policy: that China renounce the use of force in the Taiwan Straits. Because China would not promise not to use force to retake Taiwan, the Seventh Fleet had to remain in the Taiwan Straits. As the world learned from the two Quemoy crises, the confrontation of the armed forces of the People's Republic and the Seventh Fleet was a constant source of global crisis. Washington, of course, could not remove the Seventh Fleet without some "help" from Peking, meaning a commitment not to commit "aggression" against Taiwan. What that precondition did, however, was to make the military question predominant in the Taiwan Straits, at least in Washington's view. In other words,

China's military power was in and of itself a constant threat to its neighbors. It justified the immense accumulation of bases, weaponry, and deployments in East Asia with a potential for crisis of which Washington was well aware. If Peking, therefore, would do something to remove its substantial forces from the Fukien coast, Washington would be satisfied that it had no intention to invade and could withdraw the Seventh Fleet. Only early in 1969, when Chinese forces were massing on the Sino-Soviet frontier to deal with the Russian threat, did Washington finally succeed in removing the Seventh Fleet from the Taiwan Straits. But the Chinese had no intention of making such a military gesture in return for an American policy of two Chinas, which they never had the slightest intention of accepting. Peking might have responded if Washington had offered to recognize it as the legitimate government of China, a move totally out of the question so far as Washington was concerned. Refusing to recognize Peking was not just a lingering concession to the right, but an essential part of containment policy. Washington would not recognize Peking until Peking recognized Taipei.

As the Chinese nuclear program came closer to the testing stage, cries for a preventive strike against China began to surface in America. Until well into the late 1960s, these cries were periodically voiced in the right-wing *New York Daily News*, which suggested that Chiang be given some B-52s so that he could take out the Chinese nuclear installations in Sinkiang. For the containment liberals to have acquiesced to such a strike would have signified a cave-in to the right wing with all their policies shattered, not to mention the risk of a third world war. But something had to be done to prevent the Chinese from achieving a nuclear capability. The best solution would be if the Chinese signed the Test Ban Treaty along with other nations, but by August 1963 it was crystal clear that they would not, and, indeed, regarded the Russians' signing as an act of supreme, irreparable betrayal. Roger Hilsman has written that "it was perfectly clear from our intelligence that Communist China was working furiously on an atomic bomb and that she would probably succeed in exploding one by mid-1964."[10] Only the slightest memory of the paranoia that gripped Washington in 1949 when the Russians exploded their first atomic bomb or in 1957 when they launched their first ICBM suffices to conjure up the atmosphere of Washington in those last months of the Kennedy Administration. Kennedy had just signed the momentous Test Ban Treaty with the Russians in the face of bitter opposition from his own military, yet the entire global political structure that that treaty promised to generate could crumble in the face of a Chinese atomic bomb. Moderates like Hilsman suggested

[10] Roger Hilsman, *To Move a Nation*, p. 349.

bringing China into disarmament talks, but nothing indicated that it had the slightest intention of "disarming" except on conditions that Washington considered completely unacceptable. Chou En-lai had offered his own version of an Asian Rapacki plan—a nuclear-free zone throughout the Pacific. But no one in Washington could even afford to suggest that it be considered. The Joint Chiefs of Staff would never have accepted any further limitation on weaponry, certainly not to please the Chinese. So far as Washington was concerned, the paramount urgent problem was to prevent the Chinese from acquiring a nuclear capability.

Whatever private musings about China Kennedy may have had, the currents determining foreign policy in Washington left him with only three alternatives: 1) unleash the United States military (or its Taiwan clients) to take out the nuclear sites and plants with air power; 2) attempt to develop a joint Russian-American effort to force the Chinese to go along with the Test Ban Treaty; or 3) make independent concilia-tory moves toward Peking to try to elicit some reciprocal response. Hilsman claims that he himself suggested that Washington invite China to the Geneva disarmament conference and modify the trade restrictions against it.[11] But like the arguments of the more conciliatory interna-tionalists of the post-1945 period about Russia, these proposals could hardly carry much weight in the face of the awesome prospect of a nuclear China. While it was dismissed as namby-pamby, the internation-alist current, like the tortoise in the race, did manage to gain some concessions during the following years. The internationalist current played only a minor role in the Sino-American breakthrough which oc-curred during the Nixon Administration. But the fact that Washington kept on making concessions to it indicates that Washington hoped to offset the massiveness of the response which it was contemplat-ing against China and eventually implemented against Vietnam. From the perspective of late 1972, after the huge Russian-American trade deals and the smaller ones between China and America, the tortoise may well yet win the race. But in the context of 1963 and the following years, trade with China (or cultural contacts) was so inconsequential an issue that even the most rabid of the hawks acquiesced to it.

But it would be wrong to leave this third namby-pamby alternative at this inconsequential point. As I have indicated, Mao Tse-tung took due note of changes in American policy on trade in late 1960. As he himself was musing on alternatives to dominant Chinese foreign policy, these seemingly small moves on trade portended something more important. It is significant, in this respect, to note a variant on the definition of the "second intermediate zone" in the major editorial of the *People's*

11 Hilsman, *To Move a Nation*, p. 349.

Daily of January 21, 1964, just before France's recognition of Peking. Whereas in August, Mao had spoken broadly of the second intermediate zone as including "Europe, North America, and Oceania;" in January, the editorial defined it as "all of Western Europe, Oceania, and Canada." Canada meant trade to the Chinese, but it also was a bellwether for eventual American policy toward China. The *People's Daily*, while criticizing the Hilsman speech the previous December, did take note of it.

But so far as Kennedy himself was concerned in those few months left to him after the signing of the Test Ban Treaty, there were only two feasible alternatives to dealing with the looming Chinese nuclear threat: either take them out militarily or work with the Russians to somehow contain China. All Kennedy had to work with were the classic alternative parameters of rollback and containment which had dominated American policy in the Far East since 1950. Using force to take out the nuclear installations meant to cave in to a Far Eastern rollback policy that he had consistently opposed since his TV debates with Nixon, in which he vehemently attacked Eisenhower's policies on Quemoy. There were even weightier reasons for not resorting to the military alternative. Kennedy had undertaken an ambitious attempt to bring the military under control, and nothing would so endanger it as a major shooting war in Asia. Lastly, the same consideration that made Eisenhower veto bombing China during the two Quemoy crises, namely, the fear of a nuclear confrontation with Russia, still carried weight in the summer of 1963 and would continue to do so. Kennedy had taken containment policy to its highest point, and central to that policy was the avoidance of World War III.

But the only alternative left to him, working with the Russians to contain China, was mortally threatened by the Sino-Soviet dispute. If a deal had been possible in 1959 between Eisenhower and Khrushchev, no such deal was possible in 1963. Khrushchev had withdrawn his technical assistance from China, but the Chinese still had managed to develop a nuclear program promising its first payoff in 1964. If the Russians "lost" China, then Khrushchev's power would be dealt a terrible blow, comparable to America's loss in power if Japan or Britain or Germany suddenly became communist or neutralist. For Khrushchev, the Russian executive, to lose power just at a time when both the American and Russian chief executives were moving toward a glorious new stage for settling the world's problems would automatically mean a loss of power for Kennedy. The Joint Chiefs of Staff would interpret China's nuclear program as an insidious Russian attempt to circumvent the test ban restrictions imposed by the treaty. While the White House and the Atomic Energy Commission had solemnly promised that underground testing would achieve all that aboveground testing could, the military remained skeptical. That Washington was not able to force France to sign the treaty was not surprising, for the free world was free. But how could there be a monolithic Sino-Soviet bloc without Moscow being able to dictate Peking's actions? If the Chinese persisted in setting off detonations in the atmosphere, then it must be by perfidious Russian design. Once again, the Russians had managed to put one over on the Americans.

Or—and military ears began to prick up—all the blather about a Sino-Soviet dispute was true, and the Russians truly had lost control over China. In that case, the Russian nuclear umbrella was no longer in force, and B-52s could take out the nuclear sites without any fear of Russian retaliation. The military, or at least its most hawkish elements, played down the danger of Russian intervention in the case of a "limited" strike against China or Cuba or Vietnam anyway, but the existence of a Sino-Soviet dispute would remove even the slightest possibility that the Russians might feel impelled to honor their commitments.

As China began to weave in and out of the great logics that had been developing, it began to dawn on the Kennedyites how destructive China was to those logics. If one were to accept the liberal and even ultraliberal thesis that the split between Russia and China was definitive, then the only obvious way of dealing with an ultrarevolutionary nuclear China was to strike at it militarily. But that was a rollback action which every American administration had consistently opposed since Truman vetoed MacArthur's dreams of liberating the Chinese from communism. But if one were to go along with the still dominant conservative view of a Sino-Soviet bloc, then any Chinese nuclear effort or Chinese or seemingly Chinese forward move would be an example of Russian treachery and, thus, invalidate all the understandings on which the Test Ban Treaty was based. It was not just a matter of sentiment, therefore, that so many of the Kennedyites came to hate China with passion. Rusk's hatred was the most visceral, probably reflecting his experiences in the China-Burma-India theater during World War II. The coolly rational McNamara finally showed his anger when he castigated Lin Piao's treatise on people's war as China's *Mein Kampf* and became enraged at scholars who pointed out that he was wrong. John McCone's hatred was less public but was reflected in the policies he and his CIA were advocating. Maxwell Taylor's feelings about China can only be inferred from his words and actions concerning the Viet Cong.

One thing seems clear—John F. Kennedy knew that China was going to be America's main problem in 1964 and perhaps for his entire second term. It is highly unlikely that he would have condoned any rash move to deal with the China problem once and for all, but he must have known that, as the fatal moment for the first Chinese atomic detonation approached, the pressures on him to "do something" would mount, just as with the Cuban missile crisis. That detonation came on October 16, 1964, the same day that Khrushchev fell from power in Moscow. The circumstances under which it came, with the gathering war clouds in Vietnam, were far different from those of the last months of Kennedy's life. Just as during the Cuban missile crisis, he would have been faced with demands from the military that they be allowed to go in and take out the nuclear sites. But unlike Cuba, there was no one in Peking he could talk to to arrange a deal. If Kennedy had lived, he would have been deeply alarmed by Khrushchev's fall, seeing in it a blow to the kind of world he and the Russian had tried to construct together.

SURGICAL STRIKE AT CHINA'S NUCLEAR TEST SITES

Since the Kennedy Administration was rich in intellectual talent, hundreds of brains were put to work to figure out some way to get the Chinese to end their nuclear program or, as it was put, to sign the Test Ban Treaty. One of the ideas that emerged was that it might be possible to force the Chinese to sign the treaty by exerting pressure on them at escalating levels of severity. At some point, the Chinese might face the choice of either signing the treaty or seeing some of their prize developmental projects go up in smoke. This approach was called "graduated escalation." In a conference at Airlie House just before the Tonkin Gulf incidents of August 1964, ostensibly to discuss Chinese attitudes toward disarmament, I heard one learned Harvard defense economist propose "graduated escalation" as a way of getting the Chinese to knuckle under. When an Australian member of the conference asked in horror, "Would you do all that without a declaration of war?" the learned economist responded, "We can arrange for that too." At the same time, I was approached by some similarly learned members of the RAND Corporation to join them in working out some of the game problems involved in such an approach. What was exciting about this notion to the mathematically minded defense intellectuals of the time was that it fitted beautifully into game theory. But if the game theory fascinated the defense intellectuals, the politics of the idea fascinated others in Washington.

A preventive strike at China to take out the nuclear installations was clearly and simply an act of war. Despite the Harvard economist's comment about declarations of war, the central notion of all the policies dominant in Washington was that there could no longer be war in the modern world. War is all-out combat between two parties where each seeks the complete submission or annihilation of the other. But if Washington announced that it was prepared to take limited and well-defined action for some similarly limited and well-defined goal, an enemy could not construe that as all-out war. The threat to carry out such an action would really be a call to negotiate. If the enemy responded, then the threat would have paid off. If he refused to negotiate, then the strike would be carried out, followed by another call for negotiations. If he responded to the first threat or the first strike by some other form of aggressive action, then this not only would invite further strikes but would lead to a much more massive response on America's part. He would then have the choice of doing nothing, risking war, or negotiating. While Washington had abandoned Dulles's habits of brinkmanship, it remained cardinal doctrine that war had to be risked to avoid war. With central nuclear war increasingly excluded as a possibility, risking war in the 1960s meant risking limited war (massive retaliation, one might remember, risked central nuclear war). In game theory, an enemy is presumed to have full knowledge and consciousness of the consequences of all moves. If he does not, these are spelled out for him. Graduated escalation is a way the game can be spelled out for an enemy so that consequences come clear to him long before the damage inflicted reaches crippling magnitudes.

As in chess, game theory assumes that both players are in firm control of their pieces. It would be laughable to think that pawns or bishops or rooks could walk from one square to another by themselves. Russia, China, and North Vietnam are communist nations run by tightly knit little collectives called Politburos. The United States is a free nation in which the President carries out foreign policy with the advice and consent of the Senate. If Washington decided to carry out a policy of graduated escalation against China, the President and he alone would orchestrate every single military and diplomatic move. In conventional wartime situations, the President hands over operational responsibilities for prosecuting the war to the military. But in graduated escalation, the President both sets policy and determines operations. He thereby becomes his own general staff.

The idea of graduated escalation appealed to the Kennedyites. As a tactic, it could only be carried out by and through the concentrated power of the Presidency. In theory, therefore, the more it were practiced, the greater that power should become as the President points to this, that, and other targets and his generals humbly obey. In the context of the China problem facing Kennedy (and then Johnson), graduated escalation offered the only acceptable though risky way of getting China to stop its nuclear program without risking a third world war. Graduated escalation would send signals to the Russians that Washington had no aims other than ending China's nuclear program. It did not intend to bomb its cities or allow Chiang Kai-shek to return to the Mainland or harass China diplomatically anywhere in the world. In fact, Washington might even be willing to drop its trade barriers against China and allow American scholars to apply for scholarships at Chinese universities. No aggression against the sovereign territory of China was contemplated other than those "surgical strikes" necessary to excise the offending member from the body of China.

Though graduated escalation was to be touted later as the policy that guided American air attacks against North Vietnam, some residue of nonacademic common sense that remained in the Kennedy and Johnson administrations finally convinced policy makers that what worked in the equations of the game theorists might not work in practice. For other reasons that I have yet to explain, Washington decided consistently that any strike against China was too much of a risk to take. The propaganda about graduated escalation against North Vietnam, however, has to be seen as a frantic attempt by the White House to make the world, the American public, and, above all, the leaders of the enemy camp believe that it was the White House, not the military or someone else, that was in full policy and operational control of the war.

The flowering of the idea of graduated escalation in 1963 and 1964 was a gimmicky but characteristic response of the Kennedyites to the looming threat that the Sino-Soviet split posed for the new world order which had been evolving, an order based on the cooperation and competition within increasingly agreed upon rules of the game between America and Russia. The entire thrust of the Kennedy Administration was to expand and enhance the power of the Presidency. John F. Kennedy and his brother Robert considered themselves masters of the game of power. They made a man Secretary of Defense who was determined finally to bring the military establishment under the kind of presidential control that had been promised ever since the passage of the National Security Act of 1947. While Robert Kennedy could only barely budge J. Edgar Hoover, he put teeth into the Attorney General's office. Had Kennedy lived, there is no doubt that he would have continued to pursue the ends and use the means of power to solve the problems he faced, China included. In the very last days of his life, he seemed intent on withdrawing from Vietnam. Yet it is equally possible that even with such a withdrawal he would have ordered graduated strikes against China to resolve the nuclear dilemma once and for all. Withdrawal from Vietnam could only be justified in larger power terms if Kennedy had succeeded in making the proud Chinese bend to his will.

Kennedy's death created a momentary power vacuum at the pinnacle of the American political system into which certain bureaucratic forces rushed in the pursuit of their own ends. Had it not been for China, historians could point with wonderment to the incredible things that Kennedy achieved in the thousand days of his reign. If China was an issue that played a role in Khrushchev's ouster, it also threatened Kennedy's presidential power at a time when it had never seemed so supreme. His bureaucratic enemies and seeming allies were gathering their forces in the wings preparing to challenge him. Vietnam and Southeast Asia in general were where the challenge would come.

PART III

VIETNAM

CHAPTER 1

Ideological and Bureaucratic
Sources of the Vietnam War

Until the last months of the Eisenhower Administration when another
Laos crisis brought a Russian air lift onto the Indochina scene, Washington did not regard American involvement there as centrally related to its
global politics vis-à-vis Russia. In the wake of the Geneva Accords of
1954, America had been developing special interests in South Vietnam
and Laos. These arose less through deliberate presidential policy than as
the result of the thrusts of right-wing American forces that were expanding the empire they had built up in East Asia since World War II.
Eisenhower, in effect, granted East Asia to the right wing as its domain.
So long as their actions did not threaten larger global politics, they could
do what they wished and would be generously backed by presidential
policies.

The public form those policies took was munificent support for right-
wing regimes in several East Asian countries. In the latter part of the
1950s, the model regimes were those of Chiang Kai-shek in Taiwan,
Syngman Rhee in South Korea, and Ngo Dinh Diem in South Vietnam.
Chiang, Rhee, and Diem had all come to power through American
doing. Chiang would have receded into oblivion in 1949 had the American right wing and the United States Navy not rescued him and permitted him to establish his regime on Taiwan. Rhee had spent years of exile
in Honolulu and Washington until American arms carried him back to
Korea in 1945. Diem was found in a Maryknoll monastery in the United
States and brought back to set up a regime in South Vietnam which
would oust what remained of French power and influence and replace it
with American power and influence. Taiwan, South Korea, and South
Vietnam, while populous by the standards of many members of the
United Nations, nevertheless were small, economically fragile countries.
There was no way for them to survive except by massive infusions of
American aid. Moreover, all three were seemingly threatened by com-
munist aggression. Thus, as dollars began to pour into those countries,
so did a wide assortment of American political, military, and economic

figures. The American presence soon became evident in the growth of American-style communities around the capitals and other key cities. Military bases and other installations soon led to the flowering of those accouterments of luxury that the American military establishment increasingly requires in order to carry out its missions. Like the *coloniae* of Roman legionnaires, those of the Americans stimulated the formation of large native spin-off communities consisting of bars, shops, whore houses, and sundry other enterprises catering to or feeding off the Americans.

Admirals, generals, ambassadors, foreign aid administrators, CIA "chief spooks," rough-and-ready businessmen, and various other powerful Americans freely consorted with their counterparts in the regimes of Taiwan, South Korea, South Vietnam, and other countries as well. Despite the gaping differences in formal salary levels, the extra sources of income available to the native chieftains made it possible for them to associate with the Americans on a basis of equality. In fact, they could often do for the Americans what the Americans could not do for themselves. They were able to furnish types of entertainment from their limitless pool of native resources which quickly enchanted the Americans with the romance and charms of the Orient. Right down to the lowest status level of the American presence, the same relationships prevailed between Americans and natives. Even the lowliest GI had a woman to do his laundry, a *mama-san* to procure him pleasure, and swarms of urchins to do the sundry menial tasks which he was disinclined to do. As Americans, white, black, brown, or yellow, they were a superior race among the natives. No member of the empire, no matter how lowly, had ever to dream of performing the back-breaking labor or living in the austere poverty of the natives. Eventually, the American legionary had to fight and die, but this was honorable, and a price that had to be paid at times for the glory of living in that empire.

The only part of the world where the Americans ever tasted empire the way the Romans did in their frontier regions or the British did in India was East Asia. Before World War II, virtually no Americans lived and worked abroad under conditions of empire. Guantánamo, the Canal Zone, and Hawaii were minor points and barely tolerated by a country that still boasted of its anti-imperial tradition. World War II brought swarms of Americans to Europe and East Asia, where many remained. But while some Americans occasionally looked upon Europeans as natives, Europe was no place for setting up an American empire. Europeans were white, accustomed to some level of affluence, certain of their own destiny. Not too long after the end of World War II, Americans in Europe became just another army, another set of tourists, another set of businessmen, looked up to by most of the people there but not so much as to make them feel like sahibs. East Asia was different. While the leaders appeared to be civilized, vast masses of them lived in squalor that no self-respecting white man would ever live in. The Japanese seemed to show the most promise of becoming like the white man, but the rest of them seemed hopeless. Their moral level was so low as to be virtually nonexistent—they stole, lied, cheated, intrigued in their wierd languages. Like the French *pied-noir* in Algeria, most ordinary Americans who served that empire in the postwar period were convinced that their very presence was a boon and blessing. America was maintaining law and order for them, or helping them to do so. America was protecting them against communism. America was pumping dollars into their rickety economies. America was not killing their people, as the Japanese had done and the communists were doing, and not seizing their lands, as the French did in parts of Indochina to pay off their World War II veterans. Above all, America was giving them the most generous and selfless assistance to help them to rise out of their squalor and achieve some semblance of human dignity.

One has to have had some experience among Americans in East Asia, in the soldiers' and sailors' bars, not just in an antiseptic embassy office, to understand how deep-rooted these sentiments were. The great majority of white Americans who went to Asia as members of the empire were of ordinary backgrounds. They were racist in the way most white Americans were racist then and are still now. Deep down they believed in the natural superiority of the white man but, at the same time, they felt that it was the white man's moral duty to help the colored to uplift themselves. Hate-filled Southern racists were generally unpopular and only occasionally set the tone for everyday American policies. The legacy of Rooseveltian idealism dominated the thinking of many if not most Americans, but a part of that thinking involved a notion of the "little man." Maybe these Americans were "little men" at home, but in East Asia, surrounded by millions of people who literally were "little men," they were the "big brothers."

The attitudes and sentiments of expansionism and imperialism met in East Asia. If East Asia and Latin America were the traditional areas of American frontier expansionism, World War II brought American imperialism to East Asia where it remains to this day. The two meshed neatly in World War II and in the following quarter-century until the trauma of Vietnam. Roosevelt himself symbolized this wedlock of expansionism and imperialism in Asia. As a pro-Navy man, he naturally believed that America's frontier extended well into the Western Pacific. As an imperialist, he felt that America must play its God-given role to uplift the Asian masses. In later years, no matter how great the scandals and horrors the Americans might commit for their own interests, they were always outweighed by the imperial ideology of idealism which could point to hundreds of generous aid programs. Only when the New Left began to destroy the ideology of imperialism in the latter 1960s did the scandals and horrors begin to stand forth without the protective covering of ideology. That they have persisted despite this nakedness shows how deeply entrenched those interests are.

TAIWAN, SOUTH KOREA, SOUTH VIETNAM

The three countries Taiwan, South Korea, and South Vietnam were ideal areas for American interests to expand into precisely because they really were not countries. All three were artificial constructs which then sought to become real countries by gaining international diplomatic recognition. South Korea and South Vietnam were both zones of a divided country, and Taiwan was an offshore island. Prior to 1945, all three had been colonies, two of Japan and one of France. All were involved in major wars with revolutionary compatriots who were communist which they regarded as still going on. No other regimes in the world, therefore, were as anticommunist as these. The artificiality of the three countries provided certain real advantages for American expansionism, for it meant that they were not as hamstrung by traditional vested interests as more natural countries. Before 1945, the Japanese in Korea did not rule "indirectly" through native elites, as the British and the French did in so many of their colonies. They imposed a purely Japanese administration, Japanized those Koreans who chose to collaborate with them, and proclaimed a policy of eventual Japanization of the entire peninsula. When Japan was defeated, the entire administration crumbled and had to be resurrected from scratch.

Although Japanese rule was milder in Taiwan than in Korea, the principles were the same: a Japanese administration ran the entire island. When China resumed sovereignty in 1945, Nanking was too busy fighting Communists to spend much time integrating Taiwan into the Mainland administrative system. As a result, a repressive and corrupt carpetbagger regime sprouted up, against which the people rose in bloody rebellion in 1947. When two million Mainlanders fled to Taiwan in 1949–1950, they set up an entirely new administrative system which they kept firmly in their own hands. An extensive and successful land reform program appeased some of the deepest grievances of the Taiwanese, helped to spur economic development, and also got rid of many entrenched Taiwanese interests that remained from the Japanese period.

There were far more entrenched interests in South Vietnam when Diem took over the government than in South Korea or Taiwan. South

Vietnam was a land of sects, some religious, some political, some professional, some criminal. The French had generally practiced a kind of indirect rule in Indochina, and when they lost the war in 1954, they felt that they could continue to maintain a presence by exploiting their links with these sects. Particularly notorious was the criminal sect of the Binh Xuyen, which was linked to criminal counterparts in France. Diem was determined to crush not just this sect but all the others also in order to have untrammeled power. In a way, the Communists were just another sect to him, though more dangerous because of their ties with North Vietnam. The Americans supported Diem in his war against the sects because it was a way of getting both the French and the North Vietnamese out of South Vietnam and clearing the way for their own presence. If Bao Dai had remained as Emperor of Annam and Cochin China, he would have ruled as a thin overarching umbrella over the myriads of interests in his realm. Diem had no intention of doing that. While a mandarin in his bearing, he also saw himself as a revolutionary figure who would regenerate his people, rid them of their many political malignancies, and unify Vietnam around his personal rule.

All three of these countries had certain mini-Napoleonic qualities: they were dominated by a leader and his army. Syngman Rhee was too old and too much a civilian to play this role, but his successor Park Chung Hee has shown himself to be just that—a leader with an army. Chiang, of course, always was a soldier, and his rule on Taiwan was based on his immense army numbering some 600,000 men. Diem had no army when he set foot on South Vietnam's shores, but with the help of the Americans (and by throwing out the French), he created a big army which also became the basis of his power. Napoleonic in words but obviously not in actions, they constantly talked about "attacking the North," "returning to the Mainland," fighting communism. Chiang sincerely believed that he was fulfilling the revolutionary testament of Sun Yat-sen, which had been temporarily interrupted by alien Russian conquest of his country. Even after the armistice of 1953, Rhee spoke constantly about marching northward to liberate North Korea. Diem was more moderate in his calls for *bắc tien*, march northward, but he never hid his determination to achieve unification someday.

Each of the three regimes influenced American policies and actions as much as they were influenced by the Americans. Rhee and Park in Korea, Chiang Kai-shek and his son Ching-kuo in Taiwan, and Ngo Dinh Diem and his brother Nhu could never seriously be considered puppets.

The Chiang regime on Taiwan, after December 1949, became a kind of prototype for the others. It has been far different from his disastrous rule in China itself, where he held unstable control over a vast and motley array of interests on which his power was based but whose selfishness and intrigues sapped whatever vitality there had been in the Nanking government. Defeat on the Mainland had one salutary effect for Chiang—it swept all those interests away and allowed him to build an entirely new political structure. That structure was formed by a trinity of army, party, and secret police. With generous American help, Chiang rebuilt his shattered military remnants into a fine army of 600,000 men, virtually entirely officered by Mainland Chinese. He developed small but powerful air and naval forces. The Kuomintang party, which on the Mainland had been an empty shell, became a much more useful instrument on Taiwan. It had originally been structured on the model of the Russian communist party in the early 1920s, but had never been able to develop real political force on the Mainland. But in Taiwan, the Kuomintang tried to copy its Communist enemies on the Mainland. Anyone who held political office on the island had to be a member of the Kuomintang. It spread its arms far and wide among Overseas Chinese and became an important instrument for Chiang Kai-shek to sink his roots into the Overseas Chinese community. On the Mainland, Chiang had had a secret police headed by a man named Tai Li, whom General Joseph Stilwell described as the Himmler of China. But on Taiwan, a new secret police arose headed by Chiang's son Ching-kuo, which became a formidable force on the island and abroad.

In Taiwan (as in Rhee's South Korea and Diem's South Vietnam), the ruling political structure kept a tight dictatorial grip on the country. But the compensation for political dictatorship was a policy of general economic development for the population as a whole. The land reform on Taiwan did away with a landlord class which was never as powerful as it had been in China itself. This created incentives for the peasants to produce, and they found a ready-made capitalistic market in the swollen cities of the island. With American aid, capital goods began to flow into the island which through both public and private means were used to invest in agriculture. As agriculture began to flourish, light industry began to develop in the cities. This created an export industry which enabled Taiwan to earn foreign exchange and gradually free itself from abject dependence on American aid. As the economy began to develop, foreign investment, overwhelmingly Japanese and American, came into the country. Standards of living began to rise so that at least the economic causes of social discontent were removed. What Chiang Kai-shek achieved on Taiwan can also be considered a prototype of many other military dictatorships that since then have arisen in different parts of the world. Brazil and Greece are examples of military dictatorships that have spurred economic development. Even the "leftish" military dictatorships of Peru and Ecuador fit this model.

Syngman Rhee's South Korea was far less successful than Chiang's

Taiwan in this respect, but Park Chung Hee's South Korea has caught up with a vengeance. Park's rule, like that of Chiang, is based on a trinity of army, party, and secret police, although, at least until 1972, opposition parties were able to operate publicly. Ngo Dinh Diem in South Vietnam obviously did not do as well as Chiang Kai-shek but he did better than Rhee during the 1950s. Once the sects were smashed, he built up an army, organized a secret police under the control of his brother Nhu, and organized a party called the Can Lao which, like the Kuomintang, was modeled on the Communist party. It is hardly now remembered that in the late 1950s, South Vietnam was hailed by the Americans as a fine example of nation building. Guided by the roving American land reform expert Wolf Ladejinsky (who had laid out the lines of Japanese land reform after 1945), a large-scale land reform program was instituted in South Vietnam. While it was not particularly successful, at the end of the 1950s South Vietnam could still boast convincing signs of economic development. It was a major rice exporter and had a net surplus in its balance of payments. Rural conditions were bad but not as bad as those in South Korea, which were just about disastrous. South Vietnam with its lush environment was a naturally rich region, like Indonesia. Aside from economic and technical assistance, the Americans provided Diem major help in training a new police force and a new corps of officials and administrators.

While the character of these three regimes offended the democratic sensibilities of some Americans, they all maintained that there was no other way for them to be "effective" than by rule through army, party, and secret police. The alternative was not democracy but chaos or, worse, communism. The American right wing, particularly the military and the CIA, needed no convincing on this score. For Eisenhower, whether or not these were democratic regimes was a matter of indifference. But the fact was that each of them had elements of such instability that the trinitarian dictatorships were constantly threatened from within. In Korea, the Rhee regime was finally overthrown by a student-led uprising in 1960. In November of that same year, Ngo Dinh Diem came within a hair's breadth of being overthrown by a coup. Taiwan appeared to be the most stable of the three countries, but in the late 1950s and early 1960s, the rising resentment of the native Taiwanese coupled with hostility against Chiang's son Ching-kuo of elements within the Kuomintang political structure threatened to provoke instability there. But Taiwan had one advantage over South Korea and South Vietnam: it had far fewer ancient entrenched interests. Diem seemed to have conquered the sects, but myriads of political, religious, and economic interests remained intact. A powerful Chinese community held sway over much of the commercial economy, as it did elsewhere in Southeast Asia.

There were all kinds of old political "parties" sending tentacles deep into the Diem administration. Landlord interests were particularly powerful and determinedly opposed to any kind of land reform. As the vigor of Diem's fight against the sects and his various reform programs began to wane, he found that he had no recourse but to do what other politicians did, compromise with the interests.

But compromising, like fighting, usually created more conflict than it resolved. Impatient with these squabbles, Diem resorted more and more to "personal" rule, *personalisme* as he called it in French. That meant simply that he attempted to put his own agents into the command posts of the army and the administration and into the villages. But *personalisme* became an increasingly tenuous instrument for rule. Like Rhee and Chiang, Diem soon discovered that there was only one common ideological denominator that had a hope of holding these contending interests together and preventing a centrifugal collapse of the whole structure—anticommunism. The North Korean occupation of South Korea had been brutal, and Syngman Rhee and Park Chung Hee always knew, as did Chiang and Diem, that they could get a response from all their enemies inside the country if they invoked the cry of communist danger. Naturally, anticommunism was the one ideological stance tailor-made to please the American right wing, so that it had the double effect of helping to unify the country and gaining more American dollars and guns.

ROLLBACK REGIMES

All three regimes were rollback regimes, publicly, ideologically, and to some extent operationally committed to winning back the parts of their countries that had been lost to the Communists. While Washington often nervously pooh-poohed the rollback pronunciamentos from Seoul, Taipei, and Saigon as just rhetoric, there were hard and cold reasons why they were committed to rollback. All three countries had experienced influxes of refugees from the Communist areas. Two million Koreans fled southward during the Korean War. Two million Chinese fled to Taiwan after 1949. Somewhat under a million North Vietnamese fled to the South after 1954. Just like their European counterparts (Germans, Hungarians, Poles, Ukrainians), these refugees were ferociously and blood-thirstily anticommunist. But unlike the European refugees who finally melted into one or another Western population, the Korean, Chinese, and Vietnamese refugees were the source for many of the cadres of the rump regimes that had been set up. The Taiwan administration and army were exclusively Mainlander. In Korea, the refugees crowded into the cities where they also found employment in the government and the military (Park himself is a Northerner). The Vietnamese refugees were overwhelmingly Catholic and Diem, himself a staunch Catholic, naturally found them to be his most reliable cadres. The refugees were resented by the local populations and often responded with an arrogance which exacerbated the resentment. The northern parts of many countries seem to have a prestige advantage over the southern parts, so that people from Pyongyang looked down on those in Taegu and Pusan. Those from Peking and Shanghai looked down on the crude rustics of Taiwan who spoke a barbarous Amoy dialect. Those from dignified Hanoi disdained the so patently Southeast Asian Saigonese. Like refugees anywhere, most wanted to return home someday, and the only way for them to do so was through reconquest by war.

Short of a third world war, none of these three regimes had any realistic hopes of ever getting back their lost territories. The Korean War and subsequent crises like Quemoy made it clear that America was not about to risk a world war. However, like anticommunist refugees throughout the world, they all felt that there was a chance, slim perhaps but still a chance, that their Communist enemies could "collapse." They were all convinced that these regimes were brittle totalitarian shells barely managing to hold down a seething population. In their eyes, the Communists had so violated every tenet of traditional culture in their countries that their only support came from their own agents buttressed by Russian power. If a rebellion of some magnitude were to occur, then it could spread like wildfire engulfing the entire regime. The Cuban mercenaries who carried out the Bay of Pigs operation were convinced that as soon as they landed, Cubans all over the island would rise against the Castro regime. The Hungarian rebellion was hailed by anticommunists throughout the world as proof of what could easily happen in any communist country. Chiang Kai-shek constantly talked about uprisings in China, and merely asked the Americans to allow him to land his troops on the Mainland if this occurred. When peasant uprisings did take place in North Vietnam in 1956, Diem was so busy fighting his own sects that he made no great noises about wishing to liberate the North. Still, he shared the same sentiments as other anticommunists about the brittleness of communist rule.

All three regimes were convinced that their Communist enemies were constantly conspiring to overthrow them. They regarded communism as a vast international conspiracy with no other aim than to soften up the free world for the final kill. In their own countries, they smelled communism in every act of opposition against their rule. Looking at flabby, democratic America, they were convinced that communistic influence lurked behind every rejection of their demands. They saw Washington as riven by the same kind of factional strife that they themselves had to face. And just as they knew that many of their opponents who pretended to be moderates or middle-of-the-roaders were either communist dupes or agents, they saw the same phenomenon in Washington. Chiang Kai-shek had hated the China experts in the State Department ever since the days of Stilwell. When Joseph McCarthy decided to launch his anti-communist crusade, Chiang's agents fed him with the names and information he needed. When McCarthy himself collapsed, the Asian anticommunists learned that it was unwise to interfere so blatantly in American politics and began to resort to subtler, less offensive methods. But within their own countries, they had no compunctions against stamping out (or trying to) every shred of opposition.

Chiang Kai-shek, the most prototypical and ideologically fanatic of the three leaders, was also the most frank about what he regarded as his regime's true relationship to the Communists. For Chiang (as for the Communists), the civil war had never ended. He was at war with the Communists and only the constraints of the battlefield situation prevented him from going all-out. Although a full-scale military onslaught against the Chinese Mainland was impossible, this did not preclude attacks, harassments, disruptions, sabotage, and other kinds of pressure against the Communists. If there was indeed a boiling and seething within China, then such pressure could only hasten the day when the people would rise up. While the prevailing image is that Chiang has been sitting still on Taiwan since 1949 with his 600,000-men army, in fact, in collaboration with the Americans and other anticommunist forces in Asia, he has waged a relentless and far-flung covert war against his Chinese Communist enemies. Only the barest fragments of this war are known, for it depended on secrecy. If Chiang's saboteurs managed to blow up a bridge within China, it had to seem to be a spontaneous act, the beginning of a chain reaction of revolt within China. Secrecy was also necessary because Chiang's main ally in this war was the American CIA.

THE CIA, ROLLBACK, AND COVERT WAR

While the "analysis" sector of the CIA was concerned with conventional intelligence activities, its "operations" sector, from the late 1940s on, became a political force whose main purpose was advancing the interests of America by seeking to affect the governments of other countries. The most extreme form this took was the overthrow of governments, like those of Arbenz in Guatemala and Mossadegh in Iran. A more normal form of action was the cementing of operational alliances with friendly governments (or segments thereof) or friendly political forces within a country. The CIA's closest link to a government in East Asia was with the Chiang regime, specifically with Chiang Ching-kuo's secret police apparatus. In Vietnam, until October 1963 when Kennedy summarily broke the link, the CIA maintained a similar relationship with Ngo Dinh Nhu, who ruled a secret police apparatus much like that of Chiang Ching-kuo. In Laos, the CIA allied itself with a political force that was based on the great Laotian families of the southern part of the country and whose chief political actor, until 1964, was Phoumi Nosavan. In Laos, the CIA also undertook the formation of an Armée Clandestine, as it is called in French, recruited from Meo tribesmen. In one sense, the American CIA had just inherited the old French (and British) practice of making alliances with rustic mountain highlanders as a counterweight to the politically more powerful lowlanders. But the Meos (known as Miao in China) were part of a widely scattered group of nomadic mountain peoples who inhabited southern China as well as the mountain regions of Vietnam, Laos, Thailand, and Burma. Even after the Liberation of China, the Meos crossed back and forth with considerable freedom into China.

There is no evidence that the CIA as a whole was governed by some grand design for the rollback of communism. Many of its agents, particularly in Washington, fancied themselves as liberals. Others, especially out in the field, were ferocious anticommunists. But the CIA, like all other bureaucracies of the United States government, acted on the principle that America was engaged in a war, admittedly "cold" but still a war, with communism. If all governments could be classified on a scale running from full communism to full anticommunism, then the more anticommunist a government, assuming it was viable, the better for the United States. The CIA, of course, had limited means for influencing the governments of big countries like India. It might acquire a few channels of influence into them, but the major work of influencing had to be done back at the summit in Washington. Small countries were a different matter, particularly where the central governments were unstable. In Laos, there was little chance for government-to-government relations to influence a regime like that of Souvanna Phouma, which could barely control its capital cities. But one could influence him by building up the right wing to such a powerful force that he would either be swept aside or forced to compromise with it rather than with the Pathet Lao. In the case of Taiwan, Chiang Kai-shek distrusted the officials in Washington and preferred to work directly with the American military and political structures that were sympathetic to his cause. The regimes in South Korea and South Vietnam had built up powerful police and intelligence bodies, which made it easy for the CIA to work with them.

The close relationships the CIA developed with the rollback regimes of Taiwan, South Korea, and South Vietnam made it inevitable that it would come to share their rollback ideology. While Allen Dulles could be accounted a conservative like his brother, and not a right-wing reactionary, nevertheless, he was the director of the CIA during the 1950s, when it developed a far-reaching covert war in East Asia. American anticommunism and Asian rollback began to interact with each other in such a way that the *de facto* stance of the CIA in that part of the world was rollback, just as it proved to be in the case of the Bay of Pigs invasion.

While much of the training of Nationalist Chinese guerrillas went on in Taiwan, much also took place in more remote areas. Taiwan, for all its security, was a hard place to keep things hidden. Just like Camp Retulheu in Nicaragua, there have been CIA training bases for Nationalist and other anticommunist guerrillas on some of the remoter islands of the Marianas and Carolines. Anticommunist Asian special forces have been trained in various parts of the United States, Okinawa, Thailand, northern Malaya. What became apparent to the CIA in the 1950s was the existence in East Asia of a large pool of men willing to become soldiers of fortune in the cause of anticommunism. Nationalist Chinese were available not just to make a commando raid on the Fukien coast, but as pilots, technicians, and doctors for service throughout Southeast Asia. So were many Filipinos, who have a tradition of serving the Americans and had the advantage of speaking American English. Then there were peoples like the Chinese-speaking Nungs, who served as bodyguards for American forces, and the Vietnamese Khmers, who had a reputation for pugnaciousness. There were Koreans willing to serve the Americans as their parents had served the Japanese in order to get a chance to leave their cold country. There were, of course, the Meos. While some may have been convinced anticommunists, most were probably dazzled by the sight of a new empire in the making in East Asia and wanted to get on the bandwagon.

If the appetite comes in the eating, there certainly was an immense feast awaiting the CIA in East Asia. Often Langley (CIA headquarters) probably had only the vaguest idea what its operatives were doing in the field, not because they falsified reports but because they were as often the instruments of the forces they were supposed to manipulate as the reverse. Americans, for all their democratic heritage, have the curious conviction that power and influence always go from the top down. Thus, because the President is at the top, he must have perfect knowledge and control over what his underlings do. Power and influence go both ways, and people in East Asia, with long and complex political traditions of their own, understand that better than Americans. The dual process of disruption and development had created large anticommunist populations of skilled and displaced peoples in East Asia. What chances did they have in overcrowded Taipei, Seoul, Saigon, or other hugely swollen cities of that part of the world? Working for the Americans gave them a chance for money, adventure, training, education, and satisfaction of their hatreds. For the regimes in Taipei, Seoul, and Saigon, this was a not unwelcome phenomenon, for it cemented the ties between the Americans and themselves. By surrounding impressionable Americans with anticommunist Chinese or Koreans or Vietnamese these regimes could transmit their ideologies and concerns into the innards of the American empire. These people, except for a chosen few who were granted American citizenship, remained citizens of their own countries and subject to the discipline of their own governments.

While it might appear that the single-minded obsession of these CIA and Asian covert warriors was to overthrow communism in Peking, Pyongyang, and Hanoi, in fact, a much different kind of reality began to emerge. The CIA gradually found itself enveloped in all the intricacies of East Asian business, politics, and crime. One need not believe that the CIA had some grand design for flooding the world with dope to believe that it got entrapped in the dope business. If Meos raised opium as their main cash crop, then one would have to put aside one's puritanical beliefs about opium in order to gain their support for more important causes. If Chinese businessmen in Bangkok and Hong Kong helped to process and smuggle the opium to various parts of the world, it was exceedingly deplorable. But since they formed an invaluable intelligence network linked to the CIA's friend and ally Chiang Ching-kuo in Taipei, that too had to be overlooked. If Air America was supposed to help the anticommunist covert war in Laos, who could prevent its Asian and American operatives from making some money on the side? It is quite possible that during the late 1940s and early 1950s, the CIA was determined to gain access to the intricate world of Overseas Chinese communities for political reasons. But the business of that community is business, and much of it is shady in a manner typical of all up and coming entrepreneurial capitalisms. As the 1950s and 1960s passed on, despite the Indochina war, the scope for covert war began to narrow more and more. It had always been difficult to send raiding parties into Communist territory, but by the mid-1960s, it was virtually impossible. But the whole swollen structure of CIA-Asian covert war remained, with thousands of agents, mercenaries, and operatives supported by a huge "infrastructure."

How much damage this covert war inflicted on China, North Korea, and North Vietnam is impossible to say. Obviously, it did not prevent them from doing what they wanted to do. There were periodic reports in the Chinese, North Korean, and North Vietnamese press of commandos and saboteurs who were captured and severely punished after trial. There are undoubtedly some spectacular acts of sabotage recorded in the CIA's files. But since even the French Resistance, under far more favorable circumstances, had little effect on the German occupiers, it is not difficult to conclude that the entire covert war was ineffective. Not only did the supposedly oppressed peoples of the communist countries not rise up in rebellion, but, as at the Bay of Pigs invasion or at Valmy in 1792, they sprang to the defense of their countries against external invasion. There is no more shining example than North Vietnam of a country unified by war waged against it in all its aspects, including covert. So confident were the leaders of North Vietnam in their people during the dark days of 1965 that they distributed arms to them for defense against just those acts of sabotage envisioned by covert war.

THE NAVY, ROLLBACK, AND AIR POWER

Covert war was only a part of the rollback notions held by Chiang Kai-shek. Ever since his first association with General Claire Chennault, Chiang was a devout believer in air power. During the difficult days of World War II, he, more than Stilwell could have suspected, was perfectly aware of the incredible corruption that afflicted his ground forces. His army was a motley amalgam of all the military-political vested interests that came out of China's warlord period. For Chiang to have accepted Stilwell's reform proposals would have been tantamount to risking a political revolution within his own ranks. If Sun Li-jen, the progressive Kuomintang general who fought with Stilwell in Burma, was to be the model for a reformed army, then better no reform at all, for Sun was an ambitious man who would just use the Americans to vault himself into power at Chiang's expense. Chennault was a different matter. He offered to organize an air force for Chiang alone. Foreigners might command and staff it, but so long as they were not Chinese, they would never become a part of the byzantine maze that was Kuomintang politics. Through his own air force, Chiang could vastly increase his power vis-à-vis his internal enemies. As the air power craze began to mount in America, Chiang naturally came to see its usefulness in the Chinese civil war, and when, despite the urgings of Chennault and the right wing, America would not provide him with the planes he wanted, he joined the general chorus that ascribed the loss of China to the unavailability of air power (plus treason in the State Department). On Taiwan, Chiang began to nurture further notions about the role of air power in the reconquest of the Mainland.

Chinese Communist forces were basically ground combat forces with virtually no air and naval power. During the Korean War, they had some air power, but mainly because of the proximity of Russia and the fact that Russian pilots flew some of the Migs in combat. Deeper down in China, it would be just about impossible for the Russians to move in any sizable tactical air power capabilities. In the 1950s, Chiang probably granted the fact that the Communists had considerable popular support during the civil war which turned out to be militarily useful. But in his thinking, by the 1950s, the Chinese people had finally learned the true cruelty of communism. Therefore, if he reinvaded the Mainland then, they would no longer have the advantage of popular support. It would be one army against another, just like his successful campaigns in Kiangsi in the early 1930s, and again Chiang would have absolute technological superiority. If troops were to land on the China coast, air power could form a protective shield so tight that the troops could consolidate their positions and ready themselves for a further thrust inland. What was the difference between holding an impregnable Quemoy and holding a sizable beachhead somewhere along the China coast? Even if the hoped-for uprising did not materialize, the points occupied could be held against all attacks until the opportunity for another move presented itself.

During much of the 1950s and early 1960s, Washington was fearful that Chaing might just decide to do that. It kept Chiang's air force on such short gasoline rations that it could only operate for a few days if the Americans decided to withhold further gasoline. When Eisenhower "unleashed" Chiang after his inauguration, Washington's containment liberals feared that the way was open for Chiang to provoke a new incident which would draw America into his scheme for reconquering the Mainland. During the first Quemoy crisis of early 1955, it seemed that this might happen. But while it happened neither then nor afterward, the doctrine that air power was the one vital ingredient in any offensive action against an Asian communist enemy began to take shape.

In the postwar period, the Navy was convinced that carriers were more than ever the secret to success in any war against a major Eurasian power. While it was willing to grant that Russia posed special problems perhaps better handled by the Air Force and the Army, China was an ideal enemy for the Navy. Most of its main cities were within easy reach of carrier-based bombers. China had a long coastline on which amphibious landings (of the Inchon type) were possible. And although its supply lines were land rather than sea based, as in the case of Imperial Japan, it still had to depend on road and rail traffic, which was vulnerable to bombing. China had no navy that could threaten the Seventh Fleet which, anyway, flaunted its invulnerability by sailing up and down the Taiwan Straits. China's air force was puny and could easily be knocked out by bombing its airfields.

In short, the two major American actors in East Asia, aside from the more rarefied role of the United States government as such, were the Navy and the CIA. The Navy, first through the Seventh Fleet and, since mid-1957, through its theater command in Honolulu, where CINCPAC presided, pursued its "traditional role in diplomacy" by cultivating relationships with governmental and military figures throughout the region. CINCPAC personnel periodically would go on grand state visits to the capitals of the countries in the region to discuss defense problems. CINCPAC had the responsibility for drawing up the general defense plans for the entire Western Pacific, which he preferred to do by himself and only shared in a limited way with SEATO. The Navy's main role was to make plans and deployments to bring as much power to bear as rapidly as possible and as close as possible to a crisis point. If an enemy threat was pinpointed by higher authorities somewhere in the region, CINCPAC's duties were to ready his forces for instant intervention, which primarily meant air power. In fact, it meant bringing in carriers as close as possible to the crisis point and readying the planes for attack so that all that was needed was the "execute" order from Washington. The rules of engagement were clear, and nothing prevented CINCPAC from carrying out his duties to the outermost limits of those rules.

For all the shenanigans the CIA was engaged in, its primary role remained intelligence, and particularly intelligence on the intentions, capabilities, and general conditions of the communist countries. The National Security Agency (NSA) might gather technological intelligence, the Defense Intelligence Agency (DIA) might gather complex military intelligence, the State Department might prepare exhaustive reports from its political officers, but in the end it was the CIA that was presumed to have the most most dependable estimations of the enemy. Others might have excellent knowledge of the enemy's capabilities and general conditions, but whose intelligence was to be trusted when it came to gauging the enemy's intentions? This was particularly crucial in crisis situations where incidents might appear to be trivial in themselves but more intensive analysis might show them to be of gravest moment. In the Cuban missile crisis, questions of Russian intent seemed immaterial in the face of the obvious fact that Russian missiles based in Cuba were capable of reaching deep into the continental United States. But the enemy's intentions were of great importance in crises like Quemoy, Laos, Tonkin, or the *Pueblo*. In this context, the CIA could boast not only some of the finest analytical talent in America but also, through its own "diplomatic" role, contacts with all kinds of governmental elements in all kinds of countries, including communist ones. What Washington national security bureaucracy, therefore, had better claim to being able to make reliable judgments on enemy intentions than the CIA?

CRISES

The history of East Asia since 1950 has been one of crisis following upon crisis. In 1950, North Korea, so it seemed to the free world, attacked South Korea. America promptly responded by unleashing a war against North Korea. Dienbienphu was a crisis, as Washington saw it, but could hardly be seen as a Pearl Harbor sneak attack. It was the expected culmination of a long war between the Vietnamese and the French. Still, Washington saw it as another communist thrust into the free world and came close to intervening with air power, and possibly even with nuclear weapons. The first Quemoy crisis came in the spring of 1955 when the Chinese Communists were on the point of seizing the small islands of Quemoy and Matsu off the Fukien coast, and again, Washington seemed to be about to intervene with air power. The same crisis repeated itself with Quemoy II in 1958, though this time Chiang's provocative actions in stuffing Quemoy with some 100,000 troops were seen as equally guilty of provoking the crisis as Communist intent to commit aggression. In the late winter of 1960–1961, the Seventh Fleet was again ready to intervene with air power as the Plaine des Jarres "fell" to the Communists, albeit mainly by the defection of Kong Le's neutralists. In May 1962, as Communist forces threatened Nam Tha, a town in Laos close to the Chinese border, the Seventh Fleet was on the point of steaming into the Gulf of Siam. When the Plaine des Jarres "fell" once more to the Communists in May 1964, American air power finally got its chance to intervene. In August 1964, as "South Vietnamese" commandos were raiding North Vietnamese shoreline positions, the Seventh Fleet "clashed" with North Vietnamese patrol boats and retaliated by attacking North Vietnam for the first time.

There were, of course, repeated crises in other parts of the world, notably Berlin and Cuba. But in those, it was easier to see a direct threat to American interests or America itself and easier to understand that Washington was ready to respond as if America were faced with another Pearl Harbor. American troops were stationed in West Berlin and Russian rockets were only ninety miles from American shores in Cuba. But the East Asian crises were in locations distant from both America and American interests. The incredulity that arose when it seemed as if World War III might erupt from the 1958 Quemoy crisis helped to strengthen Eisenhower's resolve to keep the Seventh Fleet out of the fray. Even more incredible was the notion that World War III might erupt over a crisis about some obscure town in the already obscure kingdom of Laos. Yet it was the many crises that erupted over Laos that finally led to the escalated war in Indochina.

Typical of the Laotian crises was that over the small town of Nam

Tha in May 1962. Like Chiang on Quemoy, Phoumi Nosavan, the CIA backed right-wing Laotian leader, stuffed thousands of troops into the town only a few miles from the Chinese border. In early May, according to the Americans, North Vietnamese troops attacked and captured the town. That meant external aggression and a domino-type threat to all of Southeast Asia. As in the earlier Laotian crises, demands surged up in Washington to bomb North Vietnam and China, deploy the Seventh Fleet to the Gulf of Siam, and send troops to Thailand and Laos. Because the Geneva Accords on Laos were signed only a few weeks later, the Nam Tha crisis was forgotten. However, Nam Tha signified one of the most serious defeats the forces of rollback suffered in Southeast Asia.

Nam Tha, like other mountain towns in Laos, was a staging area for covert operations against North Vietnam and China.[1] These were carried out by nomadic tribes, like the Meo, which traditionally went back and forth across the frontiers. Small airstrips in mountain valleys were used by Air America to supply the clandestine forces, and the small towns like Nam Tha were headquarters for these operations. Aside from American operatives, there were numerous others from the Asian rollback regimes. Pathet Lao sources claim that in 1961–1962, in the upper Laos region, there were 3,500 Thai troops, 3,000 Nationalist Chinese and "specialized units and commando groups" from South Vietnam.[2] For the security of these operations it was imperative that the Laotian right wing, though based in southern Laos, maintain control over all the mountain towns, particularly those like Nam Tha and Sam Neua close to China and North Vietnam.

In Washington, the liberals met the right wing's demand for carrier-based air strikes with counterproposals to send troops to Thailand and Laos. But the real intention of sending troops was not to retake Nam Tha or to protect the other endangered mountain outposts, but to secure the Mekong Valley strip. Because this meant abandoning the high mountain regions to the Communists, the troop proposals were rejected by the right wing. Since the Korean War, the right wing had been against using American troops to fight ground wars in Asia. It saw the troop proposals as a diversion from the main task—to use American air power and native Asian troops to mount a counteroffensive in retaliation for the loss of Nam Tha, one that might just possibly go into Communist territory itself.

---

[1] In September 1970, Michael Morrow of Dispatch News Service reported on CIA spy teams going into China from the town of Ban Houei Sai. As one of his sources put it, "There always is a team in China" (*San Francisco Chronicle*, September 4, 1970).

[2] *Douze années d'intervention et d'agression des impérialistes américains au Laos* (July 1966).

The spring of 1962 was one of growing crisis in all of East Asia as the forces of rollback, watching China's economic difficulties, began to think of finally operationalizing their dreams. So serious was the situation that the Chinese that spring approached the Americans directly during the ambassadorial talks at Warsaw to inquire whether Washington would condone or support a Nationalist Chinese attack against Mainland China.[3] The growth of the general crisis was heralded by those mysterious "SecDef" (Secretary of Defense) conferences in Honolulu that were to play so important a role in the Vietnam crises of two years hence. These conferences saw the strange spectacle of virtually the entire national security leadership of the American government, save the President, flying out to Honolulu to meet with CINCPAC. The first conference was held in December 1961; the second on March 21, 1962; and the third on July 24, just a day after the signing of the Geneva Accords.

Not just the loss of Nam Tha but Washington's decision to go for neutralization of Laos rather than to launch war against North Vietnam and China marked a major defeat for the trinity of right-wing forces that was pressing for rollback in East Asia: the CIA, the Navy, and the native rollback regimes, notably Chiang's on Taiwan. That there was a crisis was evident from the newspapers and the statements of government officials whose credibility was still absolute. But what was not understood—nor would be during the entire subsequent Indochina war —was that the epicenter of the crisis was in Washington where the various political currents were in bitter conflict. Nam Tha and the numerous other crises that finally led to the escalated war were the outer ripples where an enemy provocation could always be cited to justify the presentation of the situation as a crisis.

THE STRATEGIC THINKING OF
THE KENNEDYITES

President John F. Kennedy came to power with a grand design to do what Roosevelt had dreamed of: spread a Pax Americana over the entire world which would guarantee security from war, stability for all, and development for the poor. Kennedy's progressivism and his imperialism were inseparable. The progressivism which gave rise to the Peace Corps reawakened an American idealism that had lain dormant since Roosevelt's death, and is still remembered in America's ghettos, where Kennedy's picture hangs in many poor homes. The imperialism, however, was manifest in a kind of hard, unsentimental rationality common to those who regard power as a technical instrument for achieving goals

[3] *New York Times*, June 27, 1962.

superior to all other instruments in society. In foreign affairs, this led to a flowering of officially condoned strategic thinking which was to shape the dominant political currents and antagonize the subordinate currents within the American government.

As in the late 1940s, the national security planners of the Kennedy Administration assumed that the Soviet Union was and would remain America's chief adversary in the world. While China was granted the chance of becoming a major military power (in hardware terms) in the future, that future was so remote that it could not be fitted into current planning. Aside from the United States, the Soviet Union was the world's only nuclear power worthy of consideration. Since the doctrines of Russian expansionism were still sacrosanct, it was automatically assumed that any shift in the balance of military power toward Russia would lead to an extension of Russian power and influence throughout the world. As Senator Henry Jackson put it in September 1972 in words that could have been spoken a decade and more earlier:

> The tendency has been to treat strategic arms as an action-reaction type of thing, particularly in terms of a nuclear war. Too many people overlook the fact that it is the diplomatic and foreign policy implications of this power in the hands of the Soviet Union that we have to be thinking about, and how they will be using that power to achieve their foreign policy objectives without fighting a war, so to speak.[4]

While avoidance of central nuclear war was and remains a central concern in the Russian-American nuclear relationship, what really mattered, as Jackson said at the same time, was "nuclear blackmail" practiced by the Russians to achieve basic foreign policy objectives. Naturally, Jackson would never dream of implying that America itself practiced "nuclear blackmail."

The core of the strategic thinking of the Kennedy Administration was that America and Russia were caught in a global competition in which the chief prize was the Third World. Containment had succeeded in bringing about tacit agreement between the two superpowers that certain regions on both sides (the socialist countries and the allies of the United States in Western Europe and East Asia) could not be attacked or subverted without risking the danger of central nuclear war. But there remained the vast regions of Asia, Africa, and Latin America which had not yet been worked into those agreements. Both sides understood that the competition for these regions could not risk the danger of central nuclear war. If that should happen, as it did over Laos and Cuba, talks

---

[4] U.S., Congress, Senate, *Congressional Record*, 92d Cong., 2d Sess., September 6, 1972, S 14181.

at the superpower level were immediately necessary so that the conflict could be limited, or better still an arrangement arrived at to settle it by some kind of consensus.

It was from this operational view of the world that the Kennedyites evolved what they thought would be the optimum strategic posture of the United States: a powerful strategic deterrent and capabilities for fighting "brush-fire" wars in the gray regions of the Third World. While there was much talk about "limited war" during the Kennedy Administration, few believed that such a war could ever again erupt. The Korean War had been a true limited war, but it had risked central nuclear war so often that it was felt that if such a war ever threatened again, it would quickly either lead to an open confrontation between the Americans and the Russians or be settled. Both Laos and Cuba in 1962 appeared to confirm the correctness of this estimation. Laos didn't lead to a Russian-American confrontation in 1962 but was settled (or so it seemed at the time). Cuba led to a nerve-rattling confrontation in October 1962, but it, too, was settled as the result of direct contact between the two chief executives.

Ancillary to this operational view of the world was another conviction of the Kennedyites that defense spending had to be brought under control. No term was more beloved by McNamara than "cost effective." While it sounded like a fine technical term coming out of an advanced business administration course, it was essentially no different from the cruder earlier version, "a bigger bang for a buck." McNamara himself had moved into the Ford Motor Company after World War II and helped to turn an ailing corporate giant falling farther and farther behind General Motors into a prosperous and competitive producer. Despite his failures with the Edsel, it seemed to have been the new methods of cost effectiveness and program budgeting that secured this success for Ford. For all the complicated verbiage, the basic idea behind McNamara's cost effectiveness policies was very simple. The nation's defense establishment was like a gigantic corporation. What counted, as in any corporation, was output, sales, and profits. But since every giant corporation faced stiff competition, efficiency was the only assurance that its output, sales, and profits would surpass those of its competitors. America's defense establishment was involved in a gigantic competition with Russia. Its output was military hardware. Its sales were the capabilities it could emplace and develop throughout the world. Its profits were the advantages it reaped for America's foreign policy and national security goals. The shareholders of this corporation were the entire American people who, if they were satisfied with the performance, would show it by voting confidence in the administration.

For the Kennedyites, the notion of the military as a force in and of itself made no sense. The military was an instrument of foreign policy just like every other agency of the government concerned with foreign matters. The policy for all was to be worked out at the highest levels of leadership and the broad operational outlines orchestrated there. Only the details of the operations themselves were to be worked out within the particular bureaucracies, the military included. In this scheme of presidential power and mission, service interests were a dangerous impediment even when they might on occasion be in accord with grander policy. Even more dangerous was the fact that the services might have national security and foreign policy doctrines of their own. The fact that the Navy would continue to enjoy its "traditional role in diplomacy" was intolerable at a time when tight policy centralization had to be maintained. Centralization was necessary because circumstances changed so fast that only some form of absolute control at the top could give the policy and decision makers flexibility.

McNAMARA'S HOSTILITY TO CARRIERS AND BOMBERS

No Secretary of Defense was more hated by the military in the quarter-century history of the Department of Defense than Robert McNamara. Nathan Twining likened him to Hitler for his dictatorial manner. McNamara was determined to crack the hitherto impenetrable walls of service autonomy and to finally implement the unification of the armed services and defense establishment for which Congress had given the executive a mandate back in 1947. Nothing illustrates that policy so much as the TFX affair. McNamara insisted on the development of a fighter-bomber that both the Navy and the Air Force would use. It was to be a multipurpose aircraft which could be used for nuclear delivery as well as for tactical battlefield purposes. It could take off from the deck of a carrier as well as from land bases. And McNamara insisted that it be designed and produced by General Dynamics, in spite of immense pressure from segments of Congress and the military that the award go to Boeing. The unbelievable failures of the TFX final product, the F-111, dramatically symbolize the utter bankruptcy of McNamara's policies, but in the early 1960s, it must be reckoned the supreme effort of the Kennedy Administration to use presidential power to crack the autonomy of the military.

McNamara was openly hostile to both carriers and manned bombers. He argued again and again that missiles had made manned bombers redundant. The original purpose of the Strategic Air Command was to deliver nuclear bombs deep into the Russian heartland. But with the development of solid-fueled rockets, America had acquired a delivery capability which, barring some spectacular Russian leap forward in anti-ballistics capabilities, was invulnerable. Bombers were, by comparison, lumbering giants ever more vulnerable to surface-to-air missiles. Before his forced retirement in November 1967, McNamara had several times predicted the final phasing out of the Strategic Air Command by 1970, another of his predictions that did not materialize. The Air Force coun-terargument, vehemently advanced by the Strategic Air Command's most enthusiastic advocate, Curtis LeMay, that bombers could get through what remained of Russian air defenses after initial strikes on both sides seemed increasingly ludicrous, particularly after the development of missile-carrying submarines, which seemed to be invulnerable to any conceivable form of Russian targeting. If manned bombers were redun-dant, they were also frightfully expensive, too expensive to be granted to the military as a trade-off.

The argument against carriers was somewhat more difficult to ad-vance. James Roherty points out how McNamara constantly justified his opposition to a new nuclear-powered carrier (and implicitly to carriers as such) by arguing that it would not strengthen the United States vis-à-vis the Soviets. He notes that the scenarios drawn up by the Navy were "much broader in scope, and, in fact, concentrate[d] on contingencies arising in the Pacific and Far East as the result of Communist Chinese action."[5] The chief argument against carriers was that in the event of major hostilities with Russia, they were sitting ducks. Like the capital ships of an earlier day, they were vulnerable to air attack and, even more, to attack by ever more effective ground-to-ground missiles.

The classic Navy argument for carriers had always been that they could quickly bring tactical air power to bear in any conflict situation within range of carrier-based aircraft. Within a few days' time, carriers could be moved into areas where there might be no American air bases. This could be for the purpose of "showing the flag" to deter an adversary from committing aggression or, more importantly, would serve a purpose in limited war situations. But even in limited war, the Navy argument met difficulties. While great power understandings might preserve the carriers from hostile missile attack, limited war would rapidly see the development of base facilities in sanctuary regions or in the rear areas of combat zones. From these bases, tactical aircraft could be launched to play combat-support or supply-interdiction roles. The Navy again coun-tered with the flexibility argument that whereas land bases were fixed, carriers could move toward new areas of danger.

As the Vietnam war escalated, McNamara's opposition to carriers began to melt away (as did most of the rest of his policies), and he came

[5] James M. Roherty, *Decisions of Robert S. McNamara*, p. 162.

around to the Navy view advocating a force of fifteen attack carriers. But even then, he tried to introduce notions of his own that would whittle down some of the mushrooming operational power of the Navy. He advanced a "forward floating air base" concept whereby the carriers would operate with less than their maximum complement of aircraft and "additional aircraft would be flown to the carriers as needed."[6] Needless to say, the Navy was vehemently opposed and the concept withered on the vine.

The concept of "flexible response," so beloved by the Kennedyites, provides the main clue to McNamara's hostility to carriers. A carrier was a capital ship, as battleships once had been. With its crew of some 5,000 men and a host of smaller ships making up the task force, it was like a small feudal domain ruled over by a lord admiral who in turn was subject to his king, the theater commander. Pomp and ceremony have always played a large role in the Navy and tradition is considered hallowed. Nothing was less designed to be fitted into the computer programming McNamara envisaged for the defense establishment than the notion of a capital ship and its traditions. That notion implied an inflexible commitment, which was intolerable in a world that demanded flexibility of action for success. A carrier task force assigned to a certain region of the world implied a commitment of men and resources, which soon became an unassailable line item that had always to be honored. Nothing was as irksome to McNamara as the dirty politics of line items in budgets that had to be satisfied for reasons of convenience rather than rationality. Setting up a carrier task force was like setting up a new bureaucracy whose budgetary appetite would become enormous.

But there may also have been other, deeper considerations for McNamara. Carriers, above all else, meant an augmentation of naval forces in the Pacific and, therefore, a bolstering of the commitments the United States already had there. McNamara was well aware of what Morris Janowitz calls "absolute" military doctrines, particularly of the Navy. The Navy had been concerned with China for a quarter-century and made no secret of the fact that it considered China the most terrible threat facing America. Its main intellectual weapon was a geopolitical world view which saw Eurasian communism expanding into the World Island's soft underbelly, Southeast Asia ("World Island" being their geopolitical term for the Euro-Afro-Asian land mass that America faced as a distant offshore island).

The Navy's geopolitical views were contemptuously disregarded by the civilian defense intellectuals. Geopolitics was out of fashion and game theory was in. Moreover, they smacked of right-wing fanaticism. Navy men could expound their views in Navy League meetings, in de-

[6] Roherty, *Decisions of McNamara*, p. 171.

fense seminars, publish in service-related journals, but the dominant tone was set by the defense intellectuals with prestigious Ph.D.s who clustered around the office of the Secretary of Defense. During the Kennedy Administration, such views were silently tolerated, but they could not be taken seriously by those who were making the building blocks of a rational and effective foreign policy.

But there was one infallible way the Navy, and the military in general, could advance its views on foreign policy—through the issue of weaponry. The military fires the weapons and, thus, has a right to be heard on any and all weapons questions. The Navy and the Air Force ranked weapons systems differently in terms of political importance. For the Navy, the carriers, their capital ships, were the core and essence of their entire being. For the Air Force, it was manned bombers. It is highly significant for the internal struggles within the Navy and the Air Force that, from the mid-1950s on, new types of capital weapons systems began to emerge which competed with the older ones for top political importance. In the case of the Navy, it was the missile-firing, nuclear-powered submarine. In the case of the Air Force, it was land-based missiles. It does not strain the imagination to see why McNamara would much prefer submarines and missiles to carriers and bombers. Submarines, and missiles even more, were pure weapons systems and, as strategic weapons, came within the control of the highest levels of policy making. The controversy in the late 1950s over Admiral Hyman Rickover arose not because of his Jewish origin but because he became the leading advocate of a high technology weapons policy which, in the end, would have doomed carriers. Rickover, like Maxwell Taylor or Alexander Haig or Elmo Zumwalt, was a maverick, not a comfortable member of the team. Advocating submarines meant furthering the foreign policy views of presidential policy makers, but sticking up for carriers meant being loyal not only to the Navy but to the global views current in the Navy, in particular, the central role of Pacific affairs.

There is an Aesopian quality to all the lengthy discussions on weapons systems that go on during hearings over appropriations. Few members of Congress even hint at the possibility that advocacy by the military of a particular weapons system is, in fact, advocacy of a certain foreign policy current. The ideology of civilian control of the military is so sacrosanct that military men always testify only in their role as military professionals, cleverly referring all policy questions to their civilian superiors. There is a lot of play acting that goes on in those hearings, not unusual for highly ideologized bureaucracies. But like the lengthy and stylized perorations of communist party congresses, there are always ways of getting a sense of what the stylized terminology means. Publics are not supposed to know about bureaucratic struggles, for they may

disturb public tranquillity and inspire doubts about government's legitimacy and effectiveness. But these struggles have to be waged semipub-
licly (e.g., through congressional hearings), for each agency needs allies
and support in its struggle with others. Thus, they have to communicate
what they advocate, but must do it in such a way that the coded signals
are understood by the actors and not by the viewing public. Aesopian
language is bureaucratic jargon, but it is indispensable in the jungle of
bureaucratic politics.

THE BOMBER ISSUE

If the issue of carriers had strong undercurrents of a Pacific policy with
China as the principal enemy, the issue of manned bombers, which
reached explosive proportions in the controversy between McNamara
and LeMay, had similar undercurrents. The Strategic Air Command had
risen, phoenixlike, in the aftermath of Hiroshima and Nagasaki as the
chief instrument of American policy toward Russia. The Air Force, since
the late 1940s, not only was the elite service in terms of budgets and
respect but enjoyed great renown among intellectuals. It was the Air
Force that set up the great defense university known as the RAND
Corporation on the beaches of Santa Monica. The most prestigious
defense-related research was done through Air Force contracts (other
than nuclear research contracted for by the Atomic Energy Commission). The Navy ran a poor second in intellectual prestige and the Army
was pitiful. In fact, one of the feeble attempts the Army made to get into
sophisticated social science research was Project Camelot, which exploded in its face. RAND was started to do highly sophisticated research
on potential targets for Air Force strikes in Russia. Although it branched
out into all kinds of new fields (such as a massive project on Vietnam
and Southeast Asia in general in the early 1960s), target research on the
Soviet Union reflected the major policy thrust of the Air Force. The
Strategic Air Command was the cream and pinnacle of the Air Force,
and its main enemy always was Russia, the only power in the world
technologically comparable to America. The mission of the Air Force
was and remains primarily the neutralization of the Russian threat.

The Air Force was always technologically more flexible than the tra-
dition-encrusted Navy, and eagerly jumped into any line of research and
development that could come up with a new weapons system. But by the
early 1960s, Air Force generals began to show that same sort of conservative devotion to existing systems that had characterized the Navy.
The manned bomber became as sacrosanct to the Air Force as the
carrier was to the Navy. While, particularly after sputnik, the Russians

were granted technological capabilities on a par with those of America, the Air Force argued that they never would be able to develop manned air power comparable to America's. Thus, the Russians might eventually match every item in America's missile capability, but the Americans could always hold a decisive edge in long-range manned aircraft. All American defense planning presumed that after the worst imaginable Russian first strike, America would still retain enough of a second-strike capability to administer the *coup de grâce* to the Russians. Strategic Air Command planes, one-third of which were in the air at all times, would zoom straight toward Russia and, as LeMay vehemently argued, would be able to penetrate Russian air defenses with enough punch to make the deciding difference.

But what the Air Force could not fight was the growing conviction about mutual deterrence which began to grow up in both Russian and American policy circles. If the Russians had been developing a first-strike capability, that was easily ascertainable. Satellite photography made it possible not only to pinpoint Russian missile silos but to determine their capabilities with considerable accuracy. Moreover, considerable lead time was necessary if the Russians had such intentions and this could be learned through a variety of intelligence sources. In the first years of the Kennedy Administration, the news from Russia was discouraging. Despite their ICBM breakthrough in 1957, there was no evidence (until the mid-1960s) that the Russians were pushing a massive ICBM program. Moreover, in view of the immense missile program the Americans had launched, it became gradually evident that the real first-strike capability lay on the American side. The Strategic Air Command generals now found themselves trapped by their own unlimited enthusiasm for technology. If it, indeed, was the Americans who had a first-strike capability, they would obviously not need manned bombers to finish the task of wiping out targets, for no target worthy of the name would exist after such a strike. And if the Russians were not developing a first-strike capability, then there was nothing manned bombers could do that missiles could not do hundreds of times better. Thus, the Air Force was left with arguments about the worst possible contingency, that the Russians would lurch forward and try to achieve parity or superiority over American missile systems, that long lead times were necessary to develop new manned bombers, and that failure to do so would be interpreted as weakness by the enemy and further encourage him in his aggressive appetites.

The military (and conservative members of Congress) generally was unhappy about the Test Ban Treaty, but none was as hostile as the Air Force. Though the specifics of the treaty related only to aboveground testing of nuclear devices, its real implication was that it was the first arms control agreement concluded between the two enemies. One of its understandings was that both superpowers would undertake not to allow the proliferation to other countries of nuclear knowledge and capabilities, which, as was pointed out, was the chief reason for China's opposition. But arms control had domestic implications as well. It meant that the executives of both superpowers would agree to impose such a high degree of control over their own weaponry programs that a true game theory situation would emerge between the two. The obvious assumption taken for granted in any chess game is that each player moves firmly according to the rules and does not suddenly become subject to epileptic fits which overturn the entire board. Game theories only work if the actors are in firm control of themselves and abide by the rules. For the Air Force (as for the Navy) nothing was more intolerable than an even more "highly centralized defense establishment" with its "fear of escalation and proliferation," as General Twining put it.[7] The Air Force (and the Navy) feared centralized control as much as any giant corporation. They were convinced that America's security was best guaranteed by a lively competitive scene between America and Russia as well as among the military services. In that free competition, they were convinced that America would win. But lurking not far from their surface remarks was the conviction that the Kennedy dictatorship was consigning the manned bomber to the oblivion of the horse-drawn chariot.

THE NAVY–AIR FORCE ALLIANCE

During the late 1940s and the 1950s, the Navy and the Air Force had been bitter competitors over whose weapons systems would play the prime role in America's national security posture, but both became aware of a rapidly growing new enemy whose power flowed directly out of the White House into the office of the Secretary of Defense. Neither of these two services was a monolithic entity. Battles raged within the Navy between the technological innovators and the conservative fleet admirals. In the Air Force, the Strategic Air Command generals found themselves in the same position as the fleet admirals, facing a threat from a host of zealots who would turn the Air Force into an automated system based on missile-firing capabilities. But the political power of the Air Force and the Navy rested in the hands of the Strategic Air Command generals and the fleet admirals, while what power the innovators had came surreptitiously from the White House through the Pentagon. Quickly the generals and admirals came to see McNamara as their mortal enemy, for if they could break him, they could break the chain that went from the

[7] Nathan F. Twining, *Neither Liberty Nor Safety*, p. 290.

White House to their own dissidents, radicals, and nonconformists. Neither the Air Force nor the Navy really minded the dissidents as such, but they were furious at any usurpation of power reaching down from the top, passing over them, and going into the ranks.

In the early 1960s, the Navy and the Air Force formed an alliance against McNamara (and, therefore, really against the President) for the preservation of their capital weapons systems, carriers and manned bombers respectively. That alliance also meant resolute Navy–Air Force commitment to the foreign policy lines implied by carriers and manned bombers which can be succinctly stated as absolute opposition to the Sino-Soviet bloc. Neither in terms of doctrine nor in terms of reality was there any contradiction between the Navy's obsession with China and the Air Force's obsession with Russia. The contradiction came with the foreign policy of the White House.

Under Kennedy, the foreign policy current that had been evolving since the days of Truman took a major leap forward. The Kennedyites took the doctrine of massive retaliation, divided it into two parts, and forged a positive and vigorous foreign policy based on them. Massive retaliation had threatened the Russians with nuclear war if they did not forthwith cease from making trouble in some distant part of the world. Realizing the increasing vacuousness of the nuclear threat, the Kennedyites decided on a policy of actively seeking arms control agreements with the Russians, mainly to exorcise the danger of central nuclear war. At the same time, they undertook far-reaching programs to make certain that potential trouble spots would be immune in and of themselves to any possible Sino-Soviet threat save outright invasion. Arms control at the national level and counterinsurgency at the local level were the two main arms of the Kennedyites' foreign policy. If this policy had succeeded, limited war of the Korean type would have become less and less likely, and in place of it would be, in Maxwell Taylor's words, "brush-fire wars." Those were best fought with the complex political, economic, military, psychological, and diplomatic means for which counterinsurgency was a conceptual umbrella. On the military side, curious formations, known as Special Forces, became increasingly beloved by the Kennedyites. While military in character, they were conceived as playing a role similar to that of communist cadres, who might fight on occasion but whose main work was organizing populations for political purposes. The Special Forces were loathsome to all the military services and by the late 1960s, had disappeared into oblivion. But in the early 1960s, a foreign policy of arms control with counterinsurgency was a dire threat to the Navy and the Air Force. (Eventually the Army joined the grand alliance as well, although, as befits its tradition, it always remained more amenable to presidential control.)

DOCTRINE AND AUTHORITY IN THE MILITARY

All three military services operate with something they call doctrine. This starts from a view of the world as a whole and goes down to detailed rules of engagement. The Joint Chiefs of Staff publish a handbook of operational terms which are said to be the practical guidelines with which the military operates. The military services are the closest thing we have in America to the communist parties of the socialist countries. Like communist parties, the military consists of elite cadres, operates with a kind of democratic centralism (chain of command), and has no other function than to carry out the highest social purpose of the nation. The analogy should not be shocking, for Lenin envisaged the ideal party as modeled on the army, not on those bureaucratic congeries that the social democratic parties turned into early in this century. As in communist parties, ideology plays a central role in the armed services (in contrast to civil corporations where ideology generally plays only a small role). As one goes up the ladder of military career, the ideological atmosphere becomes denser. Generals and admirals talk far more ideologically than young officers. This is partly because they sense themselves closer to the seat of power and develop the kind of talk requisite to that position. But ideology also is a major source of action, and successful action is what counts in the game of personal and collective advancement. Hunger for power is always intense at the top of an organizational structure. While in civil organizations, power can be achieved in a variety of ways, in a communist party or in the military, the surest means of advancement is successful action. And if that action is the result of a particular doctrine for which one is advocate or zealot, then the advancement could be spectacular.

During the 1960s, the world became aware of the depth and fury of doctrinal struggles within the once seemingly harmonious and monolithic communist world. Less spectacular and less noticed have been the doctrinal controversies between the United States services and within each one of them. To McNamara, weapons controversies seemed like clearcut matters which could be rationally decided after all the systems had been analyzed. But for the military, in addition to the technical aspects of a weapons system, there was the doctrinal aspect, which so baffled and infuriated McNamara. If the Kennedyites loathed the strident ideology of Asian communists, they equally loathed the ideological mouthings of the American military. But if they suspected, correctly much of the time, that doctrine was merely a cover for power advancement and power struggle, they never understood how vital it was for any military service. What they saw was that the governing doctrines of the services differed sharply from each other, and within each of those doctrines were even further splits. Why could not this entire bafflegab be replaced by hard and cold systems analysis, which would substitute the true face of reality for the distorted images produced by doctrine? But, for all its inanities, doctrine was to triumph over systems analysis.

For the military, doctrine begins with the definition of the nature of the enemy. During the Kennedy and Johnson administrations, the Pentagon was said to have had plans to wage "two and one-half wars" simultaneously. The "two" referred to Russia and China; the "one-half" was a major limited war which, in practice, turned out to be Vietnam. For the Air Force, there never was any question that the principal enemy was Russia. Air Force planning was based on the assumption that the chief threat came from Russia and that United States response had to consist of delivering a knockout punch to the enemy's heartland. For the Navy, the chief enemy was the heartland of the "World Island," the Sino-Soviet bloc. But practically, the Navy's principal enemy was China. Blocked in Europe by NATO and in the Middle East by CENTO nations, uninterested in South Asia, Sino-Soviet expansionism flowed through the open door of Southeast Asia. That naturally made China the immediate source of the threat. Admiral Rickover's submarine zealotry was a dangerous challenge to traditional Navy doctrine, for it began to substitute Russia for China as the Navy's principal enemy. The Army, a more democratic institution than either the Navy or the Air Force, has traditionally been less wedded to doctrine than the other services. But in the late 1950s, Maxwell Taylor tried to remedy that by propounding his new doctrines of fighting brush-fire wars.

Doctrine, as any student of the Catholic Church or of communist parties knows, is vital to any large-scale organization fighting for higher purposes, in contrast to an industrial corporation producing for profit. Doctrine is as vital to the United States armed services as it is to Catholics and communists. But it is one of the historical peculiarities of doctrine that it requires a fountainhead. Nonorganizational religions like Islam, Judaism, Protestantism, and Buddhism do not have doctrine, only their holy books. But the Catholic Church needs a Pope as the living voice of authority, for when disputes arise, his line, correct or not, at least serves (or should serve) to restore unity. To the surprise of urbane Western European Marxists, Stalin had become the pope of a vast international movement that saw itself in the forefront of the struggle for rationality and science. Without him, the international communist movement would have exploded into small fragments in that seemingly inevitable process of fission which, again and again, afflicts the left. It is not hard to derive a working proposition on the subject of doctrine, organization, and pope, namely, that when organizations that are held

together mainly by ideology or doctrine undergo major ideological or
doctrinal change, then the conditions are given for a pope to arise in the
form of the leader at the apex. There may have been peculiarly Russian
reasons for Stalin's transformation into a new Tsar, but the international
communist movement needed him as doctrinal fountainhead as much as
Russia did. In fact, one could argue that Stalin was rescued as a Marxist
largely because of his international role in the movement.

The simple fact is that since doctrine is vital to the armed services,
they require a fountainhead of doctrine that can only be the President or,
in more organizational terms, presidential policy. The civil order in
America is also based on doctrine, law, which has its fountainhead in the
Constitution. But the Constitution, like a holy book, is a document,
whereas the President is a living being. The civil order is supposed to
change slowly and generally does, but the military order deals with war,
which is constant, rapid change. All military systems are unstable by
nature, for they are oriented to deal with extraordinary situations, like
sudden attack, rather than with the routine problems of society. Thus,
there is no way a Constitution could ever be the ultimate source of
authority for the military. The military needs a living commander in
whom the trappings of sovereignty are invested.

The more the military is involved in disputes, doctrinal and operational, the more it needs the President as source and agent of authority.
While some military commanders in the United States have undoubtedly
dreamed at times of carrying out a military *coup d'état* in the fashion of
the film *Seven Days in May*, it would only create chaos by bringing to
power an illegitimate and fragile alliance of hostile military groups. A
Presidency exercised by the Joint Chiefs of Staff would simply mean the
continuation of the bitter battles between the services that had been
going on before, but at the cost of civil order. The dominant pattern
would still be one of rival militaries needing the Presidency as source of
legitimacy and agency of power.

The ferocity of the United States military, particularly vis-à-vis
Asians, is still hard to comprehend. It is even harder to speak about
these military men in the bland terms required of an approach to politics
that assumes that logics, not just passions, govern matters of war and
peace. But from an organizational point of view, the ferocity of the
United States military can be explained by its instability: the incessant
interservice rivalries, the constant attempts by the executive to control
and re-form, unrest among officers and men, the contempt in which the
military was still held by civilians, the pervasiveness of right-wing ideologies with their pained sense of inferiority and persecution. Every Air
Force and Navy chieftain was desperately anxious to prove that with one
swift blow and at small cost he could achieve for America's grandeur

and security abroad what all the maneuverings of the civilians with their fear of war could not. With swaggering *machismo*, the air-minded brass yearned to prove itself and was convinced that once free men stood up to communists, the communists would wilt.

That virtually the entire top echelon of the United States military wanted a war of sorts has to be seen as a major factor in the origins of the Vietnam war. Whatever the crisis in East Asia, the Navy and the Air Force were always ready to launch air attacks, confident that no larger war would ensue, and presumably ready to handle it if it should. The wonder is not that the Vietnam war escalated in 1964 and 1965, but that the air strikes did not come years before, during the Quemoy or Laotian crises.

The key question about why the 1964 and 1965 escalations took place is why presidential power was able to contain the Navy in earlier crises but failed to do so then. Why did President Johnson give an "execute" order to Admiral Sharp's planes in August 1964 but President Kennedy veto similar orders on the Laotian crisis of 1962? Some may seek an explanation in the personalities of the two Presidents, but more persuasive explanations can be found in the changed logics of presidential policy, logics produced by the real world, not by the particular personalities of the men involved.

TWO KINDS OF WAR IN EAST ASIA

While it is evident that some of the air-minded United States military were anxious for a whack at China (and pretended no fear of Russia), there was one kind of Asian war they seemed strongly disinclined to engage in—a ground combat war. In fact, whenever proposals were raised to send ground combat troops into Laos or Thailand and South Vietnam, the military was generally opposed. Roger Hilsman has described in some detail the inevitable opposition of the Joint Chiefs of Staff to any plan of the President's to commit ground combat forces to Southeast Asia lest it get the United States involved in a new Korea-type limited war. The "never again school" argued that America should never again get involved in an Asian ground war unless nuclear weapons were used. But who would nuclear weapons be used against? Obviously, Russia and China or perhaps North Vietnam, but hardly against infiltrating guerrillas on the Ho Chi Minh Trail. The rebuttal against the "never again" position was that nuclear weapons meant World War III, an unacceptable risk to take.

The paradox of the United States military seeking one kind of war but

strongly opposed to a different kind is revealed in a short sentence from
the Pentagon Papers from November 1964:

> The JCS, for their own reasons, sought to avoid a commitment of
> ground forces to Vietnam and argued instead for punitive air and
> naval actions.[8]

But W. W. Rostow, as White House counselor,

> felt that by forceful and meaningful demonstrations of national
> resolve, including the commitment of ground forces to South Viet-
> nam, direct use of force against the Communist nations need be
> minimal.[9]

The contrast in the views of the Joint Chiefs and Rostow reflecting
White House trends of thought could be seen in various Southeast Asian
crises before November 1964. In Laos in 1962, when Harriman and
Hilsman proposed sending both the Seventh Fleet to the Gulf of Siam
and some thousand troops up to the Thai-Lao border on the Mekong,
this "was met by exactly the opposition from the Pentagon that had been
expected: moving the fleet was all right, but not the troops."[10] The key
difference in points of view was between those on the Joint Chiefs of
Staff who wanted massive air strikes against the communist enemy but
opposed the commitment of ground troops and the others who, whatever
their position on air strikes, wanted to commit troops to one or more
countries in Southeast Asia.

On the surface, the reasons why the "never again school" was opposed to the commitment of ground troops in Southeast Asia seem obvious. The Korean War seemed to be a final convincing lesson that
Western ground troops unable to use nuclear weapons could do little
more than hold their own against Asian communist forces. But to deduce
from this that the American military was reluctant to get involved in
Vietnam is false. Just the contrary was the case. The Navy, of course,
had deep commitments to virtually every part of Southeast Asia that was
not under communist control. With Taylor's appointment as chairman of
the Joint Chiefs of Staff, the Army began to envision a new role in the
world other than that of constabulary force in Germany, Japan, and
Korea. China has always been an attractive target for Air Force planning, and the possibility of new air bases in Thailand and South Vietnam
offered exciting new prospects. At the turn of the decade of the 1950s,
the American military found itself in a period of transition. Where it had
been predominately a Europe-oriented force, it began to become an
Asian-oriented force. Vietnam was not the cause but only a consequence

[8] U.S., Department of Defense, *United States-Vietnam Relations*, IV.C.A.(c), p. 37.
[9] *Ibid.*
[10] Roger Hilsman, *To Move a Nation* (New York: Doubleday & Co., 1967), p. 143.

of this shift in orientation. Global strategic defense depended almost entirely on missiles. In Europe, the Europeans provided more and more of the bulk of conventional power against the Russians, with American forces playing a symbolic role signifying commitment. But in East Asia, the bulk of the conventional power came to be provided by the three American military services. The Joint Chiefs of Staff never had any doubts about the importance of the American commitment to Vietnam.

To speak of the thinking of the Joint Chiefs' on the subject is an oversimplification. The "never again school" was formed mainly by a composite of Navy and Air Force views. Those views on Vietnam held that the war *within* South Vietnam could never be won unless one got at the *source* of aggression in North Vietnam and China and cut off the tentacles through which the lifeblood of the insurgency flowed from the center to the limbs. As the spectacular success of the war against Japan showed, once the head was crushed and the limbs severed, the entire structure of the Japanese empire crumbled. Why could not that feat be repated against the Sino-Soviet enemy?

As CINCPAC admirals made their innumerable ceremonial calls on anticommunist Asian potentates (like Admiral Felt on the day of Diem's overthrow), they expressed a definite Navy foreign policy current involving the question of ground troops. In Asia, ground combat functions were to be performed by Asian troops commanded by anticommunist governments. The Navy believed in strong traditional leadership, and men like Chiang Kai-shek and Ngo Dinh Diem seemed more than admirable in this respect. Strong leaders can create and command loyal military forces, and the proper role for America is to support such forces to the hilt. With over half a million men each in South Korea and Taiwan and with a mushrooming ARVN (Army of the Republic of Vietnam) in South Vietnam, why should America have to commit its own ground troops? Advisers, of course, and technicians to handle equipment the natives cannot handle, but not infantrymen. How could American troops, ignorant of the ways and languages of the Far East, do any better than even the worst native troops?

Traditional Navy doctrine on ground combat troops is much like that expressed under the Nixon Doctrine, symbolically first enunciated on Guam, a Navy redoubt: the United States will supply the air and naval power, but ground forces are to be supplied by Asian regimes. Indeed, the Nixon Doctrine had been Navy doctrine for years in East Asia. The only way the United States could achieve its purposes against the Sino-Soviet enemy was by maintaining massive air and naval power and at the same time giving full support to the anticommunist regimes solidly in power, which would in turn provide the ground combat forces necessary to counterbalance those of the communist countries.

THE FUNCTION OF DISPATCHING
AMERICAN GROUND COMBAT TROOPS

If one looks at the history of American ground combat involvement in South Vietnam from the summer of 1965 until the announcement of troop withdrawals by Nixon after his 1968 election victory, one political fact emerges: the South Vietnamese lost virtual political control of their country to the Americans. When Nixon began to withdraw troops, he also reverted to a policy of trying to build up a solid South Vietnamese regime under Thieu, a regime that would be like that of Diem in its best days or of Chiang Kai-shek or Park Chung Hee. Paradoxically, while the Nixon Doctrine was a conservative reaction to the liberal Kennedy-Johnson policies on South Vietnam, it also granted greater recognition, in principle anyway, to the independence of the Saigon regime (though that was difficult to do in practice). During the arduous negotiations in Paris, the priority item for the North Vietnamese and the National Liberation Front (NLF) always was the presence of American troops in South Vietnam: they had to leave. That was more important to them than stopping the bombing. What the Vietnamese revolutionaries and the United States Navy both recognized was that the presence of American troops in South Vietnam was as much a political as a military fact: it signified American control over the Saigon regime. So long as those troops remained, whatever government was in power in Saigon would be little more than an American puppet. But a puppet of whom? For CINCPAC, it made a difference whether a proud leader like Diem could deal with the Honolulu admirals on a basis of equality or his successors would beg for handouts at MAC/V (Military Assistance Command, Vietnam) or at the doors of the United States Embassy in Saigon. By withdrawing troops from South Vietnam and instituting Vietnamization, Nixon was taking a right-wing position which happened also to coincide superficially with the left liberal cry for withdrawal from Vietnam. Yet at the same time, that position implied greater commitment to the air war against the "sources of aggression."

Looking at another organizational fact of the American ground involvement in South Vietnam, one sees that placing MAC/V under direct Washington command in March 1964 (bypassing the theater command in Honolulu) turned South Vietnam into an adjunct of White House politics. In August 1964, Maxwell Taylor, the former chairman of the Joint Chiefs of Staff and a man traditionally close to the White House, became Washington's proconsul in Saigon. Putting American troops into South Vietnam not only eventually weakened the native regimes, but turned South Vietnam into a presidential satrapy. Since March 1964, the war within the borders of South Vietnam ceased being a responsibility of the theater commander, CINCPAC. Even the Seventh Air Force was under dual command: one, for operations outside of South Vietnam, going to Honolulu, and the other, for operations within South Vietnam, going to MAC/V. One thing that McNamara did achieve was to take the war away from CINCPAC and make it his own, "McNamara's war."

In the years 1965–1968, American ground troops were to fight a series of bloody and unsuccessful campaigns against the Vietnamese revolutionaries. Naturally, the United States Army was as anxious to prove itself in combat as the Navy and the Air Force. But this should not make us overlook the fact that sending in United States ground troops had from the beginning a basic political purpose: to assume control over the country in question and make it responsive to presidential power in Washington. If that took the war away from the South Vietnamese, it also took it away from CINCPAC, the CIA, and sundry other agencies of the American national security labyrinth. Since sending ground troops into a country implied changes in command and control relationships, one can see why the Joint Chiefs would be opposed, especially why the Navy and the Air Force would be vigorously opposed and convince the collective Joint Chiefs of Staff to go along with their position in the interests of harmony. The Joint Chiefs of Staff were political conservatives. They wanted no change in the political balance of power within Washington and no radical political changes in foreign regimes with which they had to deal, certainly no changes of the kind induced by the Americans, like the overthrow of Diem.

In addition to the political implications of ground troops, there was another, diplomatic one which highly displeased the military. The proposals offered during the various Laos crises to send in ground troops were designed as much to limit the potential conflict as to defend positions. No one, least of all Kennedy, proposed to parachute troops into Nam Tha. What the Kennedyites wanted to do was to lay claim on the Mekong Valley, but with the clear signal to the Communists that they were ready to abandon Nam Tha—which they did. As during the Quemoy crises, the liberals laid claim to Taiwan but were willing to let the Communists have Quemoy and Matsu. During the many Berlin crises, Western troops served not so much the purpose of defending West Berlin as of telling the Russians that West Berlin was within the West's domain. Ground troops were America's instruments in Europe for realizing a containment policy—forces-in-being, as they were called. Whether they would, realistically, ever have any conceivable function in defending against hypothetical Russian attack is hard to say, but their presence in Germany is vital for diplomatic reasons. Those troops tell the Russians that a containment policy that vows not to attack Eastern Europe

but asserts American influence if not control over Western Europe remains in force.

If ground troops were to serve the same containment purposes in East
Asia as in Western Europe, then one can understand the Navy's hostility
to the commitment of United States ground troops. It was a way of
signaling to the enemy not just that America was laying claim to some
territory but also that it had no intention of allowing the war to spread to
enemy territory. The proposal to send troops to Thailand during the
Laos crisis in 1962 (and others like it) was not just part of a larger
military scenario including air strikes by the Seventh Fleet but was, the
Navy suspected, a substitute for such air strikes. This was the reverse of
their notion that air strikes were all right but not the sending of troops:
air strikes against enemy territory could precipitate a clash with the
Russians, risking World War III, but troops would render them unnecessary.

What made ground troops even more attractive for containment policy
was the fact that, like nuclear weapons, they were primarily instruments
of presidential policy and not in the domain of jealously autonomous
services. The Army was much more manipulable by the Presidency than
the Navy or the Air Force. The violent opposition to Universal Military
Training (UMT) in the late 1940s was motivated by the conviction of
conservatives that it would just strengthen presidential dictatorship. The
Democrats traditionally have been more partial to the Army than the
Republicans, and generally this is ascribed to the popular democratic
character of the Army as contrasted with the other two elite services. But
the Army is also much more compatible with a powerful Presidency,
which the Democrats have always advocated. It was no surprise that the
Kennedyites were enamored of missiles and of a counterinsurgency to be
fought by the Army. McNamara wanted to transform American strategic
defenses into a system relying entirely on missiles. Taylor, who along
with McNamara symbolized Kennedy's military policy, expounded strategies to control distant regions and keep them within the empire. Mc-
Namara's missile policy and Taylor's counterinsurgency policy both
served to strengthen presidential power, a key aim of the Kennedyites.

CONTAINMENT POLICY—TROOPS;
ROLLBACK POLICY—AIR STRIKES

The policy line of troops but no air strikes was advocated by the containment liberals. The line of no troops but air strikes was advocated by
the rollback conservatives. This leads me to the proposition that when
sending ground troops and air strikes became a massive reality in 1965,

there came into being *not one* but *two* wars in Vietnam. One was a presidential war fought with ground troops to keep South Vietnam under American control. The second was a presidentially sanctioned war designed to get at "the source of the aggression." That source was officially presumed to be North Vietnam, but, as was obvious from reading the military conservatives' literature, even more it meant China. Militarily, there appeared to be no contradiction between sending in United States ground troops to clear and hold territory and using air power to destroy enemy supply lines. But politically, there was an irreconcilable contradiction because the presidential war was essentially political whereas the presidentially sanctioned air war was thought to be mainly military (by the conservatives if not the containment liberals). The presidential war presumed that while killing the enemy one also was talking to him (at first indirectly through Moscow and then more directly in Paris). The other war could not comprehend that restraints were imposed to prevent the full might of United States air power from raining down on North Vietnam or being extended into China.

The ground war in South Vietnam was the war of the containment liberals. The air war against North Vietnam was the war of the rollback right-wingers. The official presidential pretense was that the air war was being carefully modulated to bring the North Vietnamese to the conference table. In fact, it was waged by the conservative military (notably the Navy) as they saw fit, except for the restraints that Johnson frantically sought to impose and keep imposed. The pretense was that air strikes served purposes of "interdiction" of supplies. The reality was that they strained to get at North Vietnamese industrial plants, airfields, dikes, power sources, and rail lines leading to China, where even juicier targets were available.

The contradiction came from the most fundamental doctrinal difference between advocates of containment and rollback. Containment held that negotiations among the great powers were essential to preventing World War III, so that even while a limited war might be fought, talk among the enemies had to go on. For the rollback conservatives, this assumption seemed utterly incomprehensible. Wars had laws of their own and talk came into the picture only when one side was willing to call it quits. Victory and defeat were the only categories the rollbackers recognized, and short of that, war would go on subject only to the normal constraints of capabilities and caution.

Although Eisenhower reportedly favored sending troops to Thailand and Laos during his last Laotian crisis in the fall of 1960, by and large he tried to keep containment-type troop commitments to a minimum in East Asia. It was Kennedy who sent United States advisers to South Vietnam and built them up to a force of some 16,000 men by the time of his assassination. Containment and rollback thus came into conflict in East Asia, as they had not under Eisenhower. Eisenhower used his presidential powers at critical junctures to veto offensive action by the rollbackers, but he did not try to substitute a particular presidential policy for policies that were in effect in East Asia. It was Kennedy who generated a distinctive presidential policy through which to secure South Vietnam and other threatened lands for the free world. There was nothing accidental or miscalculated about it. The Kennedyites wanted global peace, but they also were determined to advance the Pax Americana against the communist threat because they believed that democracy could do more for the progress of the poor than communism. Rostow's arrogance and fawning advocacy of the bombing viewpoint should not make one forget that his writings truly expressed the spirit of the Kennedyites and that, through the eyes of the early 1960s, they were by no means ridiculous.

If Eisenhower's approach to the Presidency was minimalist and Kennedy's was maximalist, if Eisenhower was cautious and Kennedy experimentally daring, the fact still remains that the Presidency was the source and agent of containment policy. And that containment policy, which had begun in Europe, would sooner or later make itself felt in East Asia as well. All American Presidents, including Nixon during his first term, have been advocates of containment for the simple reason that the office of the Presidency and containment policy had become inextricable. The office shaped the man more than the man shaped the office. As an agency of government, the White House strove for greater power just as any other agency, and the policy line that helped it most in that quest was containment, the building of an American empire abroad.

Until the disenchantment over Vietnam set in, the liberals supported a strong Presidency as the instrument of justice at home and abroad. The right railed against it as the road straight to socialist dictatorship. The Navy had always been opposed to a powerful Presidency and the Air Force, which grew out of such a Presidency, came to oppose it in the early 1960s. The left began to oppose the strong Presidency on grounds that dictatorship was leading to more criminality abroad and more repression at home. The right opposed it on the traditional grounds that strong government was bad for the interests. Right-wing defense of the military invariably involved attacks on the office of the Secretary of Defense.

But the hostility of the right and the left against the center can also be understood in policy and issue terms. The center was the creator and maintainer of American imperialism, and no centrists tried as vigorously and daringly to carry American imperialism throughout the world as the Kennedyites. The right was, strange as it may sound, anti-imperialist.

They wanted no mass of American commitments to distant parts of the world that would cost immense amounts of money and effort. They called for unflinching support of effective anticommunist regimes and hitting the communists with everything America had. They were convinced that World War III never would arise out of such a policy. The communists would crawl back in their holes, lick their wounds, and prepare for a future day. They held that American interests were best served by anticommunist regimes which would allow American private enterprise to come in and make a profit. As befits conservatives, they felt that the poor should fend for themselves and, in any case, would gain more from a new American plant than from all the socialist welfare schemes that communists or liberals might impose. The left, of course, also came to oppose imperialism and, interestingly, on grounds that were new for it, namely, that big centralized government was bad, and has shown itself in Vietnam to be regressive and repressive rather than progressive.

CHAPTER 2

The Indochina War

On July 23, 1962, the same day that the fourteen-nation declaration on the neutrality of Laos was adopted in Geneva, a SecDef Conference was held in Honolulu, where it was decided to initiate planning for a "phased withdrawal of United States forces" by 1965. This curious episode of phased withdrawal, which was formally terminated in March 1964, constitutes one of the more interesting revelations of the Pentagon Papers. It has been construed by some as evidence of Kennedy's attempts to end American involvement in Vietnam, which were thwarted by Johnson's accession to the power. Others have interpreted it more literally as a withdrawal prompted by an optimism which was destroyed by events late in 1963 and in 1964. In any case, it demands more analysis than it has received and was clearly prompted by broader trends of events, as the date July 23 indicates. Since events in Laos have always been intimately connected with those in Vietnam, we shall have to begin by considering the Geneva Accords on Laos.

It was hardly coincidental that the events surrounding Nam Tha were followed in short order by the formation of a coalition government in Laos and the adoption of the fourteen-nation accords. Nam Tha fell on May 6. The Seventh Fleet was ordered to the Gulf of Siam on May 12, and American troops were dispatched to Thailand on May 16. On June 11, Souvanna Phouma announced that agreement had been reached on a coalition government.[1] The key to the agreement clearly was the will and intent of the great powers involved (America, Russia, and China) that there be an agreement.

The containment liberals have always considered their policies in Laos a basic success. They maintain that the July 1962 accords were followed by a break between the Pathet Lao and Kong Le's neutralists, thus confuting the conservatives' argument that the neutralists were merely communist dupes. But more importantly, the Soviet-American understandings on Laos persisted well into the period of the escalated Vietnam war. Even when Souvanna had so patently become a creature of the

[1] Roger Hilsman, *To Move a Nation*, pp. 141, 150–51.

American Embassy, the Russians continued to support him. In fact, all parties in Laos, including the left, still subscribe in theory to a tripartite coalition government headed by Souvanna or the neutralists. The sad fact is that while the liberals' policies succeeded brilliantly, reality went its own way, which, by 1968, was to bring about genocidal American bombing.

What the Geneva Accords on Laos signified was that the two super-powers, America and Russia, had agreed to shift principal support for their respective right and left clients in Laos to a common centrist, neutralist figure. For the accords to work, both superpowers would have to show that they could maintain effective control over their Laotian clients.

PHASED WITHDRAWAL OF AMERICAN TROOPS FROM SOUTH VIETNAM (1962–1964)

If Nam Tha and the Geneva Accords were a defeat for the American right wing and their rollback-minded Asian allies, then, under the rules of the game of American bureaucratic politics, one would expect a trade-off; the losers would be compensated in some other area. The fact that the same day the Geneva Accords were signed, planning for phased withdrawal began in Honolulu, the headquarters of the right-wing Pacific military, suggests that phased withdrawal was meant as a compensation for the right-wing losers. This is a startling notion to those who inter-preted it as a first step in an eventual Kennedy program to extricate the United States from South Vietnam. But looking at phased withdrawal and comparing it with its younger sibling, Nixon's Vietnamization pol-icy, one can see that it got America more rather than less involved in South Vietnam and, particularly, in a manner favored by the right wing.

The Pentagon Papers describe the planning for phased withdrawal as follows:

> On 26 July, the JCS formally directed CINCPAC to develop a Comprehensive Plan for South Vietnam (CPSVN) in accordance with the Secretary's directives. Thus began an intricate, involved and sometimes arbitrary bargaining process, involving mainly MACV, the Joint Staff, and ISA [International Security Agency]. There were two main pegs that persisted throughout this process: MAP planning for the support and build-up of RVNAF [Republic of Vietnam Armed Forces], and draw-downs on U.S. advisory and training personnel.[2]

---

[2] U.S., Department of Defense, *United States-Vietnam Relations*, IV.B.4, p. iv.

What phased withdrawal (like Nixon's Vietnamization) intended was to build up Diem's armed forces, but at the same time to pull out the military personnel Kennedy had introduced in 1961. That it accorded with CINCPAC's desires is evident from a recommendation communicated to General Taylor by Admiral Felt as the former was on his way to Saigon in 1961. Having gone through the pros and cons of sending troops, Felt concluded by saying, "A summary of the above appears to me to add up in favor of our not introducing U.S. combat forces until we have exhausted other means for helping Diem."[3] CINCPAC's preferences, which reflected Navy and generally right-wing views, were against United States troop commitments but for maximal aid to Diem. One can find variations of the same "military" viewpoint expressed time and again throughout the Pentagon Papers. Thus, to the "no troops but air strikes" advocacy of the right wing, we must add another: "no troops but support of Diem." In 1961, then Vice President Lyndon Johnson singled out Diem of South Vietnam, Chiang of Taiwan, Sarit of Thailand, and Ayub of Pakistan, who were concerned about the Laotian crisis.[4] These were the leaders of the anticommunist regimes with whom the right wing military generally felt particular closeness. But they also, as I have already pointed out in the case of Chiang, were themselves ardent zealots not just for their own air power but for America's as well.

During the entire cold war, the right-wing point of view has been clear and consistent: America should support anticommunist ground forces with air and naval power in their endless fight with the communists, *but* without committing American troops. Even in the shrill cries of the right wing to aid Chiang's China before it collapsed, none of them advocated sending in troops. What they advocated were fleets of American planes bombing and strafing Communist positions. The Bay of Pigs invasion could have become a perfect right-wing scenario if Kennedy had not vetoed air strikes from the carrier *Essex*, which was sitting off Cuban shores.

It was not just the right wing that opposed United States troop commitments, but Diem (and Chiang) also. The Pentagon Papers make clear that Diem had no wish to see American ground troops brought into South Vietnam and would only accept them if there was an "open invasion."[5] There is evidence, however, that Diem wanted a bilateral defense treaty with America. He apparently made that desire known in a meeting with Admiral Felt and Ambassador Nolting, both advocates of right-wing policies in Vietnam. Whether it was Diem or Felt or Nolting who

[3] DOD, *U.S.-Vietnam Relations*, IV.B.1, pp. 88–90.
[4] *Ibid.*, p. 53.
[5] *Ibid.*, p. 52.

fathered that suggestion is not possible to say. But there already existed a model for a bilateral treaty which spoke to CINCPAC's and the right wing's heart: the 1954 treaty with Chiang's Taiwan. That treaty produced a fine working relationship between Chiang, CINCPAC, and the American ambassador, who was invariably a right-winger (like Karl Rankin). It enabled Chiang to create a 600,000-man army with only a minimum of American military personnel on Taiwan. Diem, Felt, and Nolting wanted to repeat that feat for South Vietnam.[6]

Why were both the Asian and the American right wings so opposed to commitments of United States ground troops? Reading the involved maneuverings that finally led to Kennedy's decision to commit American advisers in 1961, one sees that it was not simply the making of a military commitment that prompted it, but even more the desire to put pressure on Diem to carry out internal reforms. Taylor, who was not only a strong advocate of sending in advisers but also an advocate of reform, had several conversations with Big Minh during his October 1961 visit who, naturally, pointed out all of Diem's shortcomings. From the very beginnings of his administration, Kennedy believed that Diem would collapse unless he introduced reforms. Kennedy knew about the Stilwell episode in China and concluded, like most liberals in the 1960s, that if Stilwell had only had the chance to introduce reforms into the corrupt structure of the Nationalist Chinese armies, then, quite possibly, the Communists would not have taken over China. The key to victory in South Vietnam, as the Kennedyites saw it, was to bring about a regime that had the support of the people. That could be accomplished only by doing away with excessive privilege and corruption, by military reform, and by stimulating healthy economic growth. If Diem was unwilling to reform on his own, then he had to be pressured into doing so, and what better way was there than to send in American military "advisers."

Barbara Tuchman's account of Stilwell in China again makes Vinegar Joe's commitments to Kuomintang reform seem so progressive and Chiang, backed by American right-wingers, so reactionary. Only a few reviewers, such as James Peck, saw the striking similarities between what Stilwell advocated for Chiang and what the Kennedyites advocated for Diem (and the Johnsonites advocated for the various Saigon regimes they dealt with). Maxwell Taylor was straight in the Stilwell tradition, and while in the 1970s he has assumed that reactionary character common among many cold war liberals, in the 1960s he was hailed as a progressive addition to the Joint Chiefs of Staff. Whether Stilwell's program for China would have prevented a Communist victory is impossible to say. Certainly, the commitment of half a million American ground

[6] *Ibid.*

troops to South Vietnam contributed immensely to the vast slaughter and destruction it generated. But sending in those troops gave Washington *control* over South Vietnam, which is what the old New Dealer Johnson wanted as much as the New Frontiersman Kennedy. Kennedy was dead-set against a bilateral treaty with Diem because that would have meant an open-ended American commitment to a regime that the Kennedyites distrusted. But he had no intention of surrendering South Vietnam to the Communists. The only alternative was to introduce American presidential power in the form of troops and to use that power to bring about the reforms (military, political, and economic) that the Kennedyites were convinced would lead to drying up the insurgency.

The same thing that motivated Claire Chennault and the World War II admirals to look with disfavor upon Stilwell's program for China motivated them to regard with deep suspicion the troops plus reform proposals of the Kennedyites for South Vietnam. Troops not only undercut Diem but also threatened to undercut CINCPAC's empire in East Asia, modestly called a "theater of operations." Thus, the phased withdrawal plan initiated on July 23, 1962, spoke strongly to Admiral Felt's notions that the right way to fight communism in Vietnam was to back Diem to the hilt and stop trying to pressure him to carry out reforms by introducing American advisers, particularly advisers that were under White House rather than theater control.

If phased withdrawal was essentially a right-wing policy, one would expect to find a build-up of the air power component as part of it. And, indeed, this was the case, although it does not become apparent in the Pentagon Papers until the spring of 1963. In the section on "phased withdrawal," one of the authors speaks of a "counter-current" to phased withdrawal evident early in 1963, by which he meant an increase in United States commitments to South Vietnam. In one paragraph, he notes:

> This current, this counter-current dynamic can be illustrated well by Mr. McNamara's decisions of late March. As part of the Secretary's policy of demanding strict accounting and tight control on authorized U.S. in-country strength ceilings, he asked for the latest readings on projected U.S. military strength to be reached in Vietnam. He was re-assured by the Chairman, JCS [Taylor], that the estimated peak would not exceed 15,640 personnel. Yet, on this very same day, the Secretary approved a substantial force augmentation, requested earlier, for FARMGATE and airlift support, involving 111 additional aircraft and a total of approximately 1475 additional personnel.[7]

[7] DOD, *U.S.-Vietnam Relations*, IV.B.4, p. 11.

FARMGATE was a clandestine United States air program designed to provide tactical air support for the ARVN troops as well as to carry out reconnaissance and other actions against North Vietnam. That these requests for greater air capabilities were a "counter-current" to phased withdrawal is simply the opinion of the author of that section of the Pentagon Papers. In fact, they were very much a part of phased withdrawal, which assumed a vigorous offensive against the Communists so that the war could be won by 1965.

"OPTIMISTS" VERSUS "PESSIMISTS"

The story is well known how General Victor Krulak of the Marines and Joseph Mendenhall of the State Department both came back from South Vietnam with diametrically opposed appraisals of the situation, and then were asked by Kennedy, Did you both visit the same country? But the significance of the story is obscured if Krulak and Mendenhall are understood simply as sincere men forming their own opinions. Both were active members of bureaucracies deeply involved in Vietnam, and their "opinions" carried major bureaucratic weight. The question of how Krulak's "optimism" and Mendenhall's "pessimism" related to Vietnamese reality is less important than how these opinions related to the bureaucratic struggle in Washington.

Krulak's optimism was in complete accord with the spirit that dominated phased withdrawal and with virtually the entire United States military, CINCPAC as well as the Joint Chiefs of Staff. That optimism held that if the ARVNs led by Diem made a big push with certain critical inputs of American military support (like FARMGATE), then the war could be won by 1965. "Optimism" is a favorite military stance designed to justify more rather than fewer inputs, for it argues that with just one more small effort final victory can be achieved. What additional inputs the military was pressing for were to become evident (at least within the highest councils of government) a few days after Kennedy's assassination. What the Pentagon Papers call the "counter-current" was actually part of phased withdrawal, and involved covert war against North Vietnam and air strikes against Laos, North Vietnam, and possibly China. Krulak has remained one of the bitterest anticommunists among the retired generals and has continued to fulminate against China even after Nixon's visit. His "optimism" in those autumn days of 1963 was identical with CINCPAC's. Both implied that the war could be won if America gave full support to Diem and provided certain critical inputs to win the war, notably air power.

Mendenhall's "pessimism" was part of the Kennedyite current which advocated Stilwellian reforms in South Vietnam and which, by late 1963, was plotting the removal of Diem from power. Kennedy, like other strong chief executives, had discovered that he could not always exercise his presidential will through existing bureaucracies. Thus, he began to make use of a variety of newer and lesser agencies, as well as individuals within entrenched agencies, to do what he wanted done. Anthony Downs has noted that it is the American habit to set up new agencies rather than to change old ones if a new policy is to be implemented. Notable among these presidential instruments were the Special Forces, INR (Intelligence Research) in the State Department, and his own agents within the CIA. Most important for Kennedy's purposes was the fact that Henry Cabot Lodge, the American ambassador to South Vietnam, swung into an anti-Diem position. How these Kennedyite agents intrigued with South Vietnamese generals to bring about the overthrow of Diem is still not clear. What is clear is that the plots were vehemently opposed by the United States military, though some, notably Taylor, were willing to put pressure on Diem to get rid of Nhu. For CINCPAC, the idea of removing Diem was a heinous mortal sin. Mendenhall's "pessimism" was a bureaucratic rivulet, part of the larger current of containment liberalism.

If one looks more closely at these bureaucratic rivulets of "optimism" and "pessimism," then some conclusions emerge different from the "war is going well or badly" implications of the words. The optimists, largely the military, held that the war could be won if America wanted to. The only means for guaranteeing victory was the use of air power. It is difficult to believe that the military actually thought that the Saigon army could, on its own, eradicate the insurgency on the ground. The battle of Ap Bac in January 1963 had demonstrated the capability of the liberation forces to defeat ARVN units many times their own size and far better equipped with United States weaponry. The military, however, was convinced that a strong, well-organized ARVN force could prevent the Viet Cong from taking major towns or cities. Strategic hamlets could then start emptying the most dangerous rural areas of population and, thus, deny "the ocean to the fish." Subsequently, the United States military discovered that bombing could have the same result as strategic hamlets and was more effective and less clumsy. Free-fire zones helped to empty Viet Cong villages and drive the population into the cities, where they could be controlled by the Saigon government. But Navy doctrine, which the Air Force was quick to adopt as well (suitably fortified with massive RAND studies), had been proclaiming that communist insurgencies could never be eradicated unless one got at the source, which meant, at least, North Vietnam. Optimism was not so much an opinion about how the war was going as about how it could go if one kept on with existing programs. Those programs centered on phased withdrawal, essential to which were covert warfare and eventual clandestine or open bombing of North Vietnam. The Geneva Accords on Vietnam prohibited the introduction of foreign air power, but FARM-GATE was a convenient way of circumventing that.

The "pessimists" feared that a crisis might ensue if South Vietnam was lost like China. Demands would immediately billow up from military and right-wing circles for a massive blow at China or Russia to compensate for the loss. They loathed Diem as a figure who might do anything from attacking North Vietnam to making a deal with the North Vietnamese. They suspected him of being capable of fomenting a crisis in order to get America more deeply involved. They were more aware of and more concerned about Viet Cong successes in the rural areas. The pessimists were in the current that favored sending troops to South Vietnam, favored counterinsurgency programs seeking to win "the hearts and minds of the people," wanted United States advisers at all echelons of the ARVN forces, and, above all, wanted to remake the Saigon government to be more amenable to Washington. The pessimists had no intention of getting out of South Vietnam, and were not keen on phased withdrawal. As containment liberals, they were prepared to go to great lengths to keep South Vietnam under American domination. But unlike the optimists, who saw the key to victory in covert warfare and air strikes, the pessimists saw it in major political changes within the Saigon government. Diem's overthrow and assassination dealt the optimists a severe blow. They had suffered an earlier blow when, early in October, CIA station chief John Richardson was forced out of Saigon (over McCone's objections). The traditional alliance of Asian potentate, the CIA, and the Navy had been shattered. The way seemed to have been cleared for new policies. Only a few weeks later, however, President Kennedy was assassinated, and NSAM 273, the first major policy document of the new Johnson Administration adopted on the Tuesday following the Friday of Kennedy's death, launched the escalated Vietnam war.

THE COMING CHINESE A-BOMB DETONATION

The Navy and the CIA got in NSAM 273 what they lost or did not get at the time of the Laotian Geneva agreement. While it tempts some advocates of the Kennedy legend to put the blame for unleashing the war on Johnson, there was another far more impersonal factor that made the situation of November 1963 radically different from that of May 1962. Put in simplest terms, China was known to be less than a year away from its first nuclear detonation and the Chinese had vehemently refused to sign the Test Ban Treaty. Not only were the Russians solidly behind the treaty and its détente implications, but their dispute with the Chinese began to assume the proportions of a chasm. The Test Ban Treaty infuriated the Air Force because of the détente with Russia but offered it some enticing new possibilities. The Air Force and Navy had always argued, in justification of proposed air strikes, that the Russians would not intervene. And always, until the Sino-Soviet dispute, they had been refuted by liberals or presidential officials who did not want to take the chance of unleashing nuclear war. The dispute now seemed to give substantive affirmation to the view that if United States bombers struck China, the Russians would not intervene, particularly if the objective was specified as solely the destruction of the nuclear test sites and not an overthrow of the Communist government. At the time of the Nam Tha crisis, the Russian nuclear umbrella still reached across China. After July 1963, it had been withdrawn—or so it seemed. There then ensued a period of a few years until the time when the Chinese developed a deliverable nuclear capability and became a nuclear power in a class with the Americans and the Russians. During that interim, China was vulnerable to air attack, but also in no position, either on its own or through Russia, to menace American air actions against North Vietnam or itself. China had no air defenses capable of shooting down B-52s.

Except for Europeanists like George Ball, all national security officials in Washington were convinced that a nuclear China would undermine America's entire position in Asia and force it to move its defense perimeter all the way back to Hawaii. A nuclear China would make it too risky to attack North Vietnam and would act as an umbrella for North Vietnamese forces infiltrating into South Vietnam. A nuclear China would terrify Thailand and force it back to its traditional neutrality. It would force Japan to accommodate to China and weaken its pro-American stance. For the rollbackers, it was imperative that China be weakened as much as possible through covert warfare, air strikes, and any other kind of harassment that Chiang could mount without posing unacceptable risks for America. The availability of a target, the absence of air defenses, and the over-all safety created by a strike seemed ample justification for any kind of hostile action against China. For the containment people, what mattered most was that America secure its empire along the demarcation lines: that South Vietnam, Souvanna's Laos, and Thailand be made safe for the free world, which would have a deterrent effect on Indonesia's Sukarno, who was playing dangerous games with China. South Vietnam had to be secured before China's nuclear power made that impossible.

Thus, containing China meant two things: doing something about China's nuclear capability and consolidating America's position in Asia, particularly in South Vietnam. In his September 12, 1963 speech, Kennedy made explicit his intention of staying in Vietnam: "We have a very simple policy in that area . . . we want the war to be won, the Communists to be contained, and the Americans to go home."[8] If the war in South Vietnam were won, then a Chinese nuclear capability would be less of a threat. As in Europe, a solid phalanx of pro-American states would ring the fringes of China and its communist allies. China could then gain advantage only by outright attack, which would bring immediate retaliation. Doing something about China must have been a concern for Kennedy even greater than that of Vietnam. Every option was exceedingly risky.

America had experienced crises before, but they were momentary storms which passed. The Chinese nuclear program induced a permanent crisis atmosphere in the national security establishment, and as every new option seemed even more risky than the old ones, nerves got frayed. Even without the Diem and Kennedy assassinations, Washington would have been in a state of high tension during those critical years. But there was one certain course of action which virtually all agreed on: America could not afford to lose South Vietnam. To lose South Vietnam would be a victory for "Chinese expansionism," a refrain Dean Rusk was to sound again and again. Whatever personal thoughts on Vietnam Kennedy may have revealed to his closest associates, the parameters of bureaucratic power within which he was caught allowed no policy toward Vietnam that was not some mix of containment and rollback. And it was precisely China's nuclear program that made it imperative for America to take an active, aggressive stance which would shake the fist of American power in China's face.

OPLAN 34-A

The sustained bombing of North Vietnam which began in March 1965 had its origins in the tit-for-tat reprisal bombings of February 7, 1965, for Pleiku and August 4, 1964, for Tonkin. Those bombings had their origins in American-led and American-initiated bombing of Laos which began on May 17, 1964. That bombing as well as Operation Rolling Thunder had their origins in a new program of covert warfare against North Vietnam which went into effect on February 1, 1964, and was known as Operation Plan 34-A (OPLAN 34-A or 34-A Op's). Plans for OPLAN 34-A were originally reported to President Johnson by Marine Corps General Victor H. Krulak on January 2, 1964. On December 21, 1963, President Johnson had asked Krulak to chair a committee to

[8] Hilsman, *To Move a Nation*, p. 506.

devise a "least risk" plan for covert warfare against North Vietnam. It was this plan that was implemented as OPLAN 34-A. But sometime in February 1964, Krulak was relieved from command over the operations and it was placed in the hands of Major Rollen H. Anthis of the Air Force. The Joint Chiefs of Staff themselves undertook to evaluate the operations for Secretary of Defense McNamara.[9] Putting an Air Force general in charge of covert operations revealed the thinking behind what was being planned. Hindsight certainly is persuasive in seeing a thread leading from Anthis's appointment to the bombing of Laos, the terrain par excellence for covert operations directed against North Vietnam, and then finally to Tonkin and to the full-scale air war.

In analyzing the origins of OPLAN 34-A, which the authors of the Pentagon Papers correctly see as the root of the air war, they cite public evidence from Roger Hilsman's book *To Move a Nation* to show that in mid-December 1963, W. W. Rostow urged President Johnson to consider bombing North Vietnam.[10] In the words of the study:

> According to the then Assistant Secretary of State, Roger Hilsman, it was just a few days before the military-CIA submission [of OPLAN 34-A on December 19, 1963] that the State Department Counselor, Walt Rostow, passed to the President "a well-reasoned case for a gradual escalation." Rostow was well-known as an advocate of taking direct measures against the external sources of guerrilla support, having hammered away at this theme since he first presented it at Fort Bragg in April 1961.[11]

Before December 21, 1963, the history of OPLAN 34-A is murky and sketchy. According to the Pentagon Papers, the program was "spawned" in May 1963, when the Joint Chiefs of Staff directed CINCPAC in Honolulu, then in command of all operations in South Vietnam, to prepare a plan for South Vietnamese forces to carry out hit-and-run operations against North Vietnam. They approved it as CINCPAC OPLAN 34-63 on September 9. At this point, we come to the murkiest part of the history. According to the Pentagon Papers,

> the plan was discussed during the Vietnam policy conference at Honolulu, 20 November 1963. Here a decision was made to develop a combined COMUSVAC-CAS, Saigon plan for a 12-month program of covert operations.

The very next lines read:

[9] DOD, *U.S.-Vietnam Relations*, III.C.A.A.; Gerald Gold, Allan M. Siegal, and Samuel Abt, eds., *The Pentagon Papers* (*New York Times* edition), pp. 235, 238.
[10] Hilsman, *To Move a Nation*, pp. 422, 534.
[11] DOD, *U.S.-Vietnam Relations*, IV.C.2.2.

Instructions forwarded by the J.C.S. on 26 November specifically requested provision for: "(1) harassment; (2) diversion; (3) political pressure; (4) capture of prisoners; (5) physical destruction; (6) acquisition of intelligence; (7) generation of intelligence; and (8) diversion of DRV [Democratic Republic of (North) Vietnam] resources." Further, that the plan provide for "selected actions of graduated scope and intensity to include commando type coastal raids." To this guidance was added that given by President Johnson to the effect that "planning should include . . . estimates of such factors as: (1) resulting damage to NVN; (2) the plausibility of denial; (3) possible NVN retaliation; and (4) other international reaction." The MACV-CAS [CIA] plan, designated as OPLAN 34-A, and providing for "a spectrum of capabilities for RVNAF [Republic of (South) Vietnam Armed Forces] execute against NVN," was forwarded by CINCPAC on 19 December 1963."[12]

The reason for breaking the quotation is that between the two dates of November 20, 1963 (the Honolulu Conference), and November 26, 1963 (when the Joint Chiefs of Staff requested CINCPAC to arrange for the combined MACV-CAS plan), President Kennedy was assassinated. What is most significant about the quotation is that President Johnson already took an active hand in the formulation of OPLAN 34-A as early as November 26, 1963, when he had been barely four days in office.

The date November 26, 1963, is significant for another reason. On that day, NSAM 273 was adopted by the National Security Council as basic policy guidelines for Vietnam. According to one of the anonymous authors of the Pentagon Papers:

NSAM 273 was an interim, don't rock-the-boat document. Its central significance was that although the two assassinations had changed many things, U.S. policy proposed to remain substantially the same.[13]

But according to another anonymous author:

And in conclusion [of NSAM 273], plans were requested for clandestine operations by GVN [Government of (South) Vietnam] against the North and also for operations up to 50 kilometers into Laos; and, as a justification for such measures, State was directed to develop a strong, documented case "to demonstrate to the world the degree to which the Viet Cong is controlled, sustained and supplied from Hanoi, through Laos and other channels."[14]

12 DOD, *U.S.-Vietnam Relations*, IV.C.2., p. 2.
13 *Ibid.*, IV.C.1, p. 1.
14 *Ibid.*, IV.B.5, p. 66; the excerpts from NSAM 273 are brought together in *New York Times, Pentagon Papers*, pp. 232–33.

These National Security Action Memoranda ("Neesams," in bureau-cratic parlance) were basic policy documents containing presidential decisions and, thus, formed the pieces of legitimate paper various bu-reaucracies needed to launch new actions. They were the key documents on the basis of which the Joint Chiefs of Staff constructed their rules of engagement. More perhaps than for any other governmental bureauc-racy, it was vital for the military to have its point of view legitimated in a NSAM before it could act.

The Pentagon Papers, as already mentioned, place the origins of OPLAN 34-A in May 1963, when McNamara approved substantial force augmentations for FARMGATE. FARMGATE was a clandestine United States Air Force unit operating in South Vietnam, flying planes with South Vietnamese markings. While FARMGATE aircraft probably were used for some actions within South Vietnam, their main purpose was to be ready for air actions against Laos and North Vietnam involv-ing landings of commando units from air and sea. FARMGATE, as an ostensibly South Vietnamese force, would have played a major role in these operations, and to the extent that such operations were carried out, it actually did. What these few fragments of information on OPLAN 34-A indicate is that as CINCPAC was making his moves to get such a plan inserted into the policy documents, his Air Force allies were mak-ing deployments (notably FARMGATE) to get ready to move once the policy go-ahead was given.

There is an earlier history to convert war against North Vietnam going back far into the Eisenhower years. But there also is an earlier history for the Kennedy Administration. On May 11, 1961, two days after Vice President Johnson left for his visit to Saigon, President Kennedy issued specific and secret instructions for covert warfare. This involved sending agents and sabotage teams into North Vietnam and Laos, and conduct-ing leaflet-dropping and reconnaissance flights over North Vietnam. Kennedy also approved using civilian American air crews over North Vietnam and Laos. There is no doubt that the covert warfare was vig-orously put into practice, as Hedrick Smith's analysis in the *New York Times* indicates. North Vietnam shot down an American spy plane and repeatedly protested to the International Control Commission about acts of sabotage and violation of its sovereignty. However, as Smith notes, "The study [*Pentagon Papers*] does not report on the actual operations of the units during the Kennedy years."[15]

Obviously, if a new plan for covert war had to be initiated in May 1963, the old covert war authorized by Kennedy must have lapsed. In October 1961, the Kennedy Administration finally made the decision to

[15] *New York Times, Pentagon Papers*, pp. 91–92.

commit troops to South Vietnam, an act we can now see as a containment move, certainly designed to keep South Vietnam under American control but also designed as a substitute for the far riskier rollback actions of covert war and the ever-present danger of United States air strikes being unleashed. Until the Geneva Accords on Laos were signed, covert war always involved Laos. Commandos were exfiltrated into North Vietnam *up* the Ho Chi Minh Trail, and operations were launched from numerous advance CIA outposts on the Meo or Tai inhabited mountain highlands of northeastern Laos. As I have already argued, the Geneva Accords dealt a serious blow to covert war in that they constituted a tacit understanding between Washington and Hanoi which, on the American side, involved halting such operations. It took Kennedy a little over one year to repulse the rollback thrust of NSAM 52, and one year after that, the rollbackers were marshaling their forces for a counterattack.

PERIOD BEFORE AND AFTER THE KENNEDY ASSASSINATION

The Pentagon Papers are exceedingly murky about the period just before and after the Kennedy assassination. Its various authors all take the accepted line that the assassination made no difference and that the new President just carried on policies developed earlier. This book argues that the assassination did make a difference. No final judgment can be made, however, until the political events that transpired only two days before the assassination are taken out of the obscurity that the Pentagon Papers alone of the available material have shed slim rays of light on. On November 20, 1963, a major meeting of top Washington policy makers with CINCPAC officers and top officials from the United States country team in South Vietnam was held in Honolulu. A total of sixty United States officials participated: Rusk, Bundy, McNamara, Taylor, and Lodge (there is some question whether or not McCone was there, but *Pentagon Papers* Book 3, B.4.25 indicates the presence of the "Director of the CIA"). Another of the authors of the Pentagon Papers devotes a little over two pages to the conference, but neither his description nor his conclusion gives any suggestion whatsoever that anything new, any new "counter-current," had been decided on. He notes that the conference "ended inconclusively with respect to the military situation." What that meant is easy to surmise. The struggle between the "optimists" (like Krulak) and the "pessimists" (like Mendenhall) was still raging, and the participants could not agree on an estimation. The author then continues, "[The conference] did, however, underscore U.S. support for the

new regime and focus official U.S. concern on the urgency and gravity of
the economic problem confronting the new government." That too is
quite clear. Before Diem's overthrow, Washington had alternately
threatened (or made as if to threaten) to cut off aid to Saigon unless
Saigon pulled itself together politically and made fresh efforts to fight the
Viet Cong. Honolulu presumably decided that Washington should give
full economic support to the new regime. Lastly, the author notes:

> An uninformative press release after the conference took note of
> U.S. support for the new government in facing difficult political
> and economic problems in South Vietnam, and pointedly re-iterated
> the plan to withdraw 1,000 U.S. troops by the end of the year with
> 300 to leave on December 3.[16]

That is essentially all this author has to say about the Honolulu Conference. But since he is the same author who supplied the excerpts from
NSAM 273 of November 1963, which requested plans for clandestine
operations against North Vietnam and border operations into Laos, it is
strange that he would not have picked up any indication that such operations had been discussed or decided upon at Honolulu.

Peter Dale Scott is one of the few scholars of the Vietnam war who
has identified the sequence of events surrounding the Honolulu Conference, the Kennedy assassination, and NSAM 273 as crucial to the escalation of the war.[17] Scott, to whose work I owe much of my own
understanding of the war, has tended to take the phased withdrawal
policy as a sign of Kennedy's desire to pull back from Vietnam and its
reversal under Johnson as an indication of a newer and more dangerous
commitment. But my own thinking on the subject has led me to the
opposite conclusion, that phased withdrawal was essentially a right-wing
policy linked more to rollback-type escalation than to a true liquidation
of American involvement. This approach suggests that OPLAN 34–63
was discussed at the Honolulu Conference, and that the only formal
announcement made afterward, that 1,000 United States troops would
be withdrawn before the end of the year, implied that a new rollback
thrust was in the works.

The various Honolulu conferences never focused on Vietnam alone.
Since CINCPAC's theater command extended over all of East Asia,
Asian problems in general were discussed. If OPLAN 34–63 was discussed on November 20, then that included so-called "border control"
operations vis-à-vis Laos and Cambodia. The day before the Honolulu

---

16 DOD, *U.S.-Vietnam Relations*, IV.B.5, pp. 65–67.
17 Peter Dale Scott, "Vietnamization and the Drama of the Pentagon Papers," in
*The Pentagon Papers: The Defense Department History of United States Decision-
making in Vietnam*, the Senator Gravel Edition, vol. 5; Noam Chomsky and Howard Zinn, eds., *The Pentagon Papers: Critical Essays*, pp. 211 ff.

Conference, Prince Sihanouk abruptly broke off all economic and military ties with the United States. The following day, Chinese Foreign Minister Ch'en Yi accused the United States of trying to overthrow Prince Sihanouk.[18] In his memoirs, Sihanouk describes the November 1963 break with America as the ouster of the CIA and its network of Asian operatives in Cambodia who were plotting his overthrow and using ethnic Cambodians from South Vietnam (the Khmer Serei) to do so. National Liberation Front forces had just shortly before overrun an American-run Khmer Serei training camp in South Vietnam, capturing incriminating documents. In any case, Sihanouk's moves, whatever their ultimate motivation, boded ill for the projected "border control" operations.

The Honolulu conferences were always crisis conferences, but it is not credible that South Vietnam's "going down the drain" in the wake of Diem's assassination constituted the crisis. It is also not likely, given Prince Sihanouk's mercurial behavior, that his sudden breaking of ties with America constituted the crisis. The bureaucratic expression of the crisis was framed in terms of the issue of troop withdrawals from South Vietnam. As Scott has shown, even before Diem's assassination, that issue epitomized basic American policy conflicts over Indochina.[19] According to my reasoning, the formal announcement of troop withdrawals implied that the chief matters discussed at Honolulu were offensive-type operations, namely OPLAN 34-63. If CINCPAC was demanding authorization to launch a far-reaching new covert war in Cambodia, Laos, and North Vietnam, a major new crisis was in the works similar to the Laos crisis of the first months of the Kennedy Administration. OPLAN 34-63 could easily lead to mushrooming war at a time when Kennedy, in his tours of military bases, was constantly talking of peace.

No one will ever be able to show with conviction what Kennedy might have done had he lived for the simple reason that Kennedy himself probably did not know. My own speculation is that Kennedy, when faced with open crisis, would have done just what he did during the Cuban missile crisis: as virtually all his top officials came in with proposals for air strikes and invasion, he played for time until he got a break at the summit-to-summit level. Failing that, he would have sent more troops to Vietnam, just as Johnson did.

*   *   *

In terms of the broader historical forces, it seems hard to see how the Vietnam war could have been averted. Little has been said so far about the Vietnamese realities underlying the war, not because of an elitist preference for global as opposed to people's politics, but because the

---

[18] *Jen-min jih-pao* (*People's Daily*), November 21–22, 1963.
[19] Scott, "Vietnamization and Drama of Pentagon Papers," p. 223.

Vietnam war, on the American side, was mainly an episode in the global struggle for which Vietnam happened to be the arena. Much has been said about the "idealism" that prompted the American involvement in Vietnam, and there is a grain of truth to it. The Kennedy years were years of imperialistic idealism, and what was done in that spirit was not all bad. There were many Americans in Vietnam, military and civil, who were dedicated to the Vietnamese and tried to serve them in one fashion or another. But as one went up the military and civil ranks into the bureaucratic corridors, what counted was the larger game. The Vietnamese hardly mattered. This bureaucratic indifference coupled with the perfectly acceptable bureaucratic notion of "body counts" (the greater the measurable performance, the better the chance of advancement) impelled nonidealistic aspects of the American character, professionalism ("I've got a job to do") and racism ("they're all gooks"), to come to the fore and produce genocide. There were good Americans, bad Americans, and professional Americans in Vietnam, but none really determined the war. Its nerve center was always in Washington, with a main branch in Honolulu and Saigon. The war was a bureaucratic war from beginning to end.

The main reality of Vietnam since 1945 has been civil war. Only when Kissinger finally announced the ceasefire did he admit for the first time, in his bureaucratic capacity, that there was an element of civil war involved. For years, Dean Rusk had adamantly insisted that it was "aggression from the North." Few men so well fit the bureaucratic image as the quiet, subservient Rusk. His woodenness was perfect for his role, for he was giving the only bureaucratic definition of the war adequate for the struggles over it within the American bureaucracies. When the war was over, the bureaucrats could afford to speak about realities because the bureaucratic war also was over. Kissinger could state blithely what he may have believed privately but could not say publicly.

The bureaucratic lenses required that the Viet Cong be seen as tools of North Vietnam which, in turn, was a tool of the Sino-Soviet bloc or variants thereof. In 1963, the containment and rollback currents were still in bitter contention over the way to defeat or check communism and assure American supremacy. No one in Washington who counted dreamed that America might indeed be a paper tiger, whose armies and dollars would soon degenerate. It is hard to see how Kennedy could have bucked both of these currents for the sake of peace, and at the same time created a regime at the Pentagon that would muzzle the military. If the popular mood was peaceful, the bureaucratic mood was militant. Historically, it seems almost inevitable that Kennedy was assassinated.

NSAM 273—THE WAR IS LAUNCHED

NSAM 273 was a hastily drawn up document; in the Pentagon Papers, it is described as "not comprehensive."[20] Presumably the basic decisions had been made the previous Sunday, the morning of November 24, when Johnson conferred with Rusk, McNamara, Lodge, Taylor, and McCone on the subject of Vietnam. That meeting, two days after the assassination, was noted with great interest by the North Vietnamese and the Chinese. Xuan Thuy, the North Vietnamese foreign minister, pointed out in a letter to the two cochairmen of the Geneva Conference, Russia and Britain, that President Johnson, two days after assuming office, said, "We are going to win in Vietnam."[21] A major editorial in the Chinese *People's Daily* signed Commentator, on December 2, 1963, noted the same thing:

> The very first thing that Johnson who succeeded Kennedy to the American presidency did in the area of foreign policy when he assumed office was to issue a directive to military personnel carrying out aggression in Vietnam that "they were to carry out plans already set by Kennedy," and that "we are going to win" the fight.

The Pentagon Papers suggest that the shift may have come even earlier than Sunday, November 24:

> The only hint that something might be different from on-going plans came in a Secretary of Defense memo for the President three days prior to the NSC meeting [of November 26]. In that memo, Mr. McNamara said that the new South Vietnamese government was confronted by serious financial problems, and that the U.S. must be prepared to raise planned MAP [Military Assistance Program] levels.[22]

However, only three days earlier, at the Honolulu Conference of November 20, McNamara had taken a different line:

> The Secretary of Defense made it clear that he felt the proposed CINCPAC MAP could be cut back and directed that the program be reviewed to refine it and cut costs to stay as close as possible to the OSD [Office of the Secretary of Defense] ceiling of $175.5 million. He was equally emphatic, however, that while he could not tolerate fat or inefficiency in the program, he was prepared to provide whatever funds might be required under MAP to support the GVN.[23]

[20] DOD, *U.S.-Vietnam Relations*, IV.C.1, p. 2.
[21] *People's Daily*, December 8, 1963.
[22] DOD, *U.S.-Vietnam Relations*, IV.B.4, p. 26.
[23] *Ibid.*, p. 25.

Here we have the remarkable spectacle of McNamara telling the gathered dignitaries on November 20 that they must keep military assistance costs to Saigon down, even though they might eventually have to go up, and three days later telling the new President that these same military assistance costs must be raised!

There is little mystery as to why and how NSAM 273 suddenly arose. From the moment he was sworn in, Johnson was President of the United States. His views on Vietnam were communicated bluntly to Henry Cabot Lodge that Sunday: "I am not going to lose Vietnam. . . . I am not going to be the President who saw Southeast Asia go the way China went."[24] Like Truman in his first days in office, Johnson assumed the tough stance of a nationalist, anticommunist right-winger. That was just enough for the full recommendations of the Honolulu Conference of November 20 to be given policy force in NSAM 273.

WASHINGTON'S FEAR OF NEUTRALIZATION

The new political wind blowing in Washington created a climate ever more favorable to the policy intent of NSAM 273 during the subsequent weeks. While President Johnson produced a thick book of memoirs, he did not have much to say on the foreign policy events following his rise to the Presidency. He notes that the situation in Vietnam was "considerably more serious than earlier reports had indicated," thereby implying a gradual conversion from "optimist" to "pessimist." The one utterance of McNamara's that he quotes is: "Current trends, unless reversed in the next two or three months, will lead to neutralization at best and more likely to a Communist-controlled state." Then he castigates de Gaulle's August 1963 Vietnam unification and Indochina neutralization proposals as a sure road toward "the swift communization of all of Vietnam," and quotes (at length, in view of the briefness of the section) a rather ambiguous Kennedy response to the neutralization proposals.[25]

A deleted section of the Pentagon Papers carried in the Senator Gravel version suggests that some kind of neutralization maneuvering was going on. The comments made by the Italian ambassador to Saigon D'Orlandi on January 20, 1964, made a considerable impression on the Americans:

> In discussing the current French initiative on Asia (recognition of Communist China and advocacy of neutralization of Southeast

[24]Tom Wicker, *JFK and LBJ: The Influence of Personality Upon Politics* (New York: William Morrow, 1968), pp. 205–206, quoted in Scott, "Vietnamization and Drama of Pentagon Papers," p. 218.
[25]Lyndon B. Johnson, *The Vantage Point*, pp. 62–63.

Asia), the Italian ambassador had said that the greatest danger to the U.S. position in Southeast Asia lay in the effect it might have upon certain pro-French and politically neutralist members of the MRC [the post-Diem Saigon Military Revolutionary Committee].[26]

When General Nguyen Khanh overthrew the Minh regime on January 30, 1964, he accused members of the previous regime of adopting "a servile attitude, paving the way for neutralism and thus selling out the country."[27]

General Khanh, who in the early 1970s was operating a restaurant in Paris, was a ferocious-sounding rollbacker. In early May 1964 he "specifically asked if the U.S. would be prepared to undertake tit-for-tat bombing each time there was such interference [in South Vietnam's internal affairs]." He talked "somewhat wildly, of defying Cambodia and breaking diplomatic relations with France. . . . He conveyed the impression of a desperate desire for an early military decision by outright war with the DRV." He seemed not to be too worried about Chinese intervention and talked of "interdicting [the Chinese Army's] supply lines." "He could not envision the U.S. putting into Asia an Army the size of the U.S. Army in Europe in World War II. . . . 10,000 could do in Asia as much as any Army group had done in Europe."[28] The words could have come directly out of CINCPAC, the Navy, the Air Force, or the American right wing.

Washington was alarmed by Khanh's views and "reactions had to be developed with great care," considering that Khanh's umbilical cord went to Honolulu and thence to other bureaucracies in Washington. The response was to tell him that the United States "did not intend to provide military support nor undertake the military objective of rolling back Communist control in North Vietnam."[29]

Khanh came to power on January 30, and on February 1, the 34-A Op's were launched. In theory and in practice, such covert war could not be launched without the active cooperation of the Saigon government. Duong Van Minh was an indecisive chief presiding over a junta with deep internal divisions. Even if he had not been involved in some maneuvering with the French (likely because of his close ties to them), his dithering would have been distasteful to Air Force General Anthis, who was ready to move fast with his exciting new program. How the United States has brought about coups is difficult to detail, but if the coup leaders of satellite nations such as South Vietnam did not have advance

---

[26] *Pentagon Papers*, Senator Gravel Edition, vol. 3, p. 37.
[27] Franz Schurmann, Peter Dale Scott, and Reginald Zelnik, *The Politics of Escalation in Vietnam*, p. 26, *also* pp. 26–34.
[28] DOD, *U.S.-Vietnam Relations*, IV.C.9, p. 68.
[29] *Ibid.*, p. 69.

assurance of American support after the seizure of power, they would not move. That some United States operatives were dickering with Khanh before the coup is possible; other operatives had dickered with other generals before the anti-Diem coup. Khanh came into power when the spirit of NSAM 273 reigned in Washington. But the May 1964 response to his rollback proposals took place in the context of NSAM 288, which was a different kind of policy document.

That there was a real "danger of neutralization" is indicated by an appeal issued by the National Liberation Front on November 8, 1963, calling for the "opening of negotiations between various interest groups in South Vietnam, in order to arrive at a cease-fire and a solution to the great problems of the country."[30] To the surprise of the Americans, the National Liberation Front appeared to be unwilling to take advantage of the crisis produced by the coup against Diem. The Pentagon Papers quote Douglas Pike, a Vietnam expert hewing the Washington line:

> Had the N.L.F. leadership wished to do so, it could have used its impressive struggle machine to launch in the name of the Buddha a nation-wide struggle movement that conceivably could have ended with its long-pursued General Uprising. . . . In truth, the N.L.F. posture during this period remains something of a mystery.[31]

There is no mystery if one can conceive of the possibility that the National Liberation Front, too, saw a neutralist solution in the offing. If it attacked the new Minh regime, it would have provoked resistance. If it restrained its military and political forces, the new regime would be more willing and likely to negotiate with it.

In late November and December 1963, there was not the slightest possibility that Viet Cong armies would soon be marching down Tu Do Street in Saigon. In early October, the National Liberation Front had scored an important victory at Loc Ninh, in the Camau peninsula. But they themselves, in historical retrospect, simply say, "Locninh showed new tactical progress by the L.A.F. now able to cope successfully with heliborne units in open country, far from their bases."[32] In other words, the National Liberation Front felt that Ap Bac and Loc Ninh demonstrated that Saigon was incapable of militarily eradicating the Viet Cong (a lesson General Westmoreland would have to learn with his United States troops a few years later). But there was nothing comparable in South Vietnam to Chinese Communist troops taking one city after another. There was even no Dienbienphu. The "optimists" were right in the sense that they did not consider the Viet Cong a mortal danger to the survival of the Saigon regime and were convinced that the war could

[30] Schurmann, Scott, and Zelnik, *Politics of Escalation*, p. 28.
[31] DOD, *U.S.-Vietnam Relations*, IV.B.5, p. 65.
[32] *The Failure of "Special War," 1961–65*, Vietnamese Studies, no. 11, p. 82.

easily be won with a few well-placed air strikes against North Vietnam and maybe China, with the insurgency then "withering on the vine."

Tons of documents and articles have been written by Americans on the goals, strategies, and tactics of the Vietnamese liberation forces, yet, in retrospect, their policies and actions, like those of the Americans, have been simple and consistent until turning points came. They, too, have policy currents. The one overriding political-military goal of the National Liberation Front has been to take the South Vietnamese countryside, and all Saigon regimes since 1954 have tried, by various means, all unsuccessful, to deny them the countryside. North Vietnamese main force units came into the picture to battle with United States ground troops, then remained to battle with Vietnamized ARVN units. Except for Tết in 1968, whose aim was to provoke a "general uprising" in the cities, there is no firm indication of how the liberation forces practically aimed to gain power in the cities. "General uprisings" play a major part in Vietnamese revolutionary history—a general uprising in August 1945 led to independence. But others have failed, and there have been even more failures of general uprisings in Chinese revolutionary history. What does emerge from Vietnamese writings is a persistent current holding that power in the cities can ultimately be obtained only through political means, through some form of united front or accommodation or understanding with urban political forces. Tết succeeded in turning American policy around, but did not gain much for the liberation forces in the cities.

If Ap Bac and Loc Ninh convinced the National Liberation Front (if not the Americans) that its forces could eventually take and hold the countryside, and if it had no practical way of getting directly into the cities, then it would have nothing to lose by grasping at any political opportunity offered to it. The NLF certainly could not have known what course "neutralization" would take, and had no reason whatsoever to trust the French. The Vietnamese had no trust in Kennedy, which *Nhan Dan*'s remarks on his death showed:

> Kennedy thought out all sorts of ways to combine the most adventuristic of methods with the cleverest of strategems, with the result that people were terrified of his threats yet intoxicated by his magic potions.[33]

But with all the pitfalls neutralization presented, it was an opportunity. Confident of their own discipline and organization, they felt that something could happen within the flabby, corrupt, and immobile structure of the Saigon regime to give them power. They also knew that neutralization was not just an emanation from Saigon but came from larger global politics. If not the nationalists, the communists within the National Lib-

[33] Quoted in *People's Daily*, November 27, 1963.

eration Front had that larger world view and were able to project from it to their own particular situation.

On December 17, the National Security Council met to review the situation in Vietnam. It heard a report by General Krulak, hitherto the chief "optimist" on Vietnam. This report continued in the earlier vein of optimism. He noted that "the new GVN shows a desire to respond to U.S. advice and improve its military effectiveness and has the capability to do so."[34] But President Johnson was not satisfied, and immediately ordered McNamara and McCone to proceed to Saigon. McNamara had been scheduled to attend a NATO meeting, and made a "quick visit" to Saigon afterward. His report, submitted on December 21, "was gloomy and expressed fear that the situation had been deteriorating long before any deterioration had been suspected (officially)."[35]

It might seem that McNamara had become a convert to Henry Cabot Lodge's pessimism, expressed in a December 7 memorandum detailing the failure of the strategic hamlet program in one South Vietnamese province. There must have been hundreds of similar memos in the file, including others written by Lodge himself, but this one was picked up at the presidential level. Johnson refers to it in his memoirs, and it is given prominent space in the Pentagon Papers. Lodge's general theme was the insufficiency of troops to protect the hamlets and the ineffectiveness of the Saigon government. But it strains credulity to believe that McNamara and McCone went to Saigon to check on the hamlet situation in Long An province. Much more likely, McNamara was given a leisurely briefing by McCone during the long plane flights. McCone was a hard-line anticommunist whom Hilsman describes as "an 'alley-fighter' who will stop at nothing."[36] While he probably gave McNamara straight dope on the hamlet situation, in the vein of Lodge's memo, he also filled him in on the dangerous machinations covered by the innocuous word "neutralization," in effect, a Franco-Chinese conspiracy to weaken the United States in Asia operating through a variety of neutralists, first and foremost among whom was Sihanouk, but who also could be found in alarming numbers in Saigon.

THE URGENCY TO DO SOMETHING ABOUT CHINA

If it was the dread specter of neutralization that caused McNamara to perceive the "deterioration" of the Vietnam situation, then China was in the picture. There is evidence from the Chinese side that covert war

[34] DOD, *U.S.-Vietnam Relations*, IV.C.1, p. 17.
[35] *Ibid.*, p. 19.
[36] Hilsman, *To Move a Nation*, pp. 46–47.

against China was being stepped up in the fall of 1963. On November 2, 1963, the Chinese announced that the previous day a U-2 had been shot down over their east coast. During the following days, the Chinese press was filled with accounts about the U-2. It also reported the capture of "U.S.-KMT agents" both in China and in North Vietnam. A few days later, Chiang Kai-shek called an emergency meeting in Taipei, presumably to discuss the U-2 incident. The first U-2 taking off from Taiwan to be downed by the Chinese was shot down on September 9, 1962, just as the Cuban crisis was developing.[37] In September 1963, Chiang Ching-kuo, the Generalissimo's son and heir apparent, made his first visit to the United States, presumably to ask for aid to overthrow the Mainland government and most certainly to push the U-2 program and the landing of agents within China. From the long history of the American military's insistence on maintaining overflights of enemy territory, it is not difficult to conclude that the shooting down of the second U-2 alarmed the Joint Chiefs of Staff. It implied that the Chinese might have air defenses more advanced than they suspected, and intensified the sense of urgency to do something about China before it was no longer possible.

In the early 1970s, when the Sino-American relationship is moving in warmer directions, it is well to recall what dominant American military thinking on China was a decade ago. Thus, General Twining, whose opinions were shared throughout the Air Force and the Navy:

> If we give the Hitler-type mentality which now dominates Red China a little more time, we will have a real problem. Up to this writing [1965], the current Administration has done nothing about this clearly developing threat. In short, the Johnson Administration has thus far given no assurance that it will face up to the Red Chinese leadership at places and times which are most favorable to the destiny of free men.

Then, writing in contingency plan fashion, Twining implies some particular recommendations:

> U.S. military forces could neutralize sufficient military targets in Red China overnight and set that nation back to an industrial and technical base more consistent with its medieval concept of government, law, and order. If ever there was a "paper tiger" in fact, it was not the United States of America. It was Red China—and still is.[38]

The rhetoric recalls Curtis LeMay's "bomb them back to the Stone Age" prescriptions for the bombing of North Vietnam. But the crudity should not make one disdain the reasoning behind the words. The air power

[37] Hilsman, *To Move a Nation*, p. 174.
[38] Nathan F. Twining, *Neither Liberty Nor Safety*, p. 293.

advocates believed that bombing China's and North Vietnam's "industrial and technical base" would cripple them economically. Rostow abetted them in these convictions by arguing that Hanoi would concede much before risking its newly built industrial plants, particularly the steel mill at Thai Nguyen. In fact, some military leaders advocated an American version of periodic cultural revolutions: bomb the Chinese every ten or twenty years to set them back to their starting point, like a rat knocked off the rungs of a treadmill. The obsession of the air power zealots about denying that they were a "paper tiger" may imply some defect of virility covered over by *machismo*, but much more importantly, it reflected a fury that cherished operational ideologies like "victory through air power" were being challenged by white-collared missile civilians like McNamara. The litany that the war could be won if only the wraps were taken off the military would be heard incessantly from the right wing in subsequent years. But in the early 1960s, it meant victory over not just North Vietnam, but China.

Twining was probably correct in his estimation that the Chinese did not have air defenses adequate to prevent American B-52s from roaming their air space virtually at will. In August 1966, Harrison Salisbury, presumably after briefings by competent Washington officials, wrote the following:

> The [Chinese] air component is relatively weak, comprising 3,500 planes of all types, largely Soviet prototypes. The Chinese build their own MIG-19's. They have only a handful of MiG-21's, and are not believed to have the capacity to make them. Their anti-aircraft defenses are not strong, but they do have an improving radar system and some surface-to-air missiles acquired from the Russians before the Peking-Moscow rift. As late as 1963, they had only eight air-defense missile sites.[39]

If that was the case, the temptation in Air Force and Navy circles to take a crack at China must have been overwhelming. And, indeed, certain events indicated mounting pressure in that direction. In early November 1963, a military-bureaucratic move was made in Washington which was duly noted by the Chinese and disturbed them. The United States Strike Command, which had been organized in 1961 and programmed to strike simultaneously at both Russia and China, was reorganized into two separate forces at this time. The European Strike Command had jurisdiction over the Middle East, Africa, and South Asia (India and Pakistan). The Asian Strike Command had jurisdiction over the remainder of Asia. This was the first indication that the Sino-Soviet split had generated concrete plans for separate strategic wars against

[39] *New York Times*, August 15, 1966.

Russia and China.[40] This entire Strike Command was abolished in July 1971, when Nixon, through Kissinger, was making his momentous breakthrough in Peking.[41]

In late 1963, the military trends were favorable for the Vietnamese liberation forces in South Vietnam but far from decisive. Throughout Southeast Asia, however, the political trends were becoming more and more favorable to the communist forces. Nowhere did this seem more the case than in Indonesia, the biggest and by far most populous and richest country of Southeast Asia. Sukarno ruled through two pillars, the Army and the Communist party—he needed the Army to exercise power, the Communist party to organize the country, and both to counterbalance each other, leaving him in the middle and on top. His seemingly unstoppable swing leftward ensured him massive foreign aid from Russia and China, the loyalty of the young and the poor, and a developing great power position in Southeast Asia. Malaya was torn by interethnic strife. Thailand, already then America's anchor in Southeast Asia, was fearful of being squeezed between a hostile Burma and Cambodia and a fuzzily neutralist Laos; threatened by a China it suspected of fomenting insurgencies in its northern regions; unhelped by a Malaya deprived of British support; unprotected by a weak SEATO; and, worst of all, perhaps eventually to be abandoned by a faltering America, lacking "in will," to use a favorite Washington term.

It was not difficult for right-wingers and centrists alike to conjure up the domino images of one country falling after another. In fact, both analyses of the troubles in Asia converged as they rarely had during the cold war. The leftward trend came from neutralists like Sukarno or Sihanouk who, terrified of communists and insurgencies, moved leftward to placate them and saw China, not America, as the great power to be reckoned with. If the pink tide overwhelmed Indonesia, Burma, and all three Indochina countries, what was left for an Asian containment policy? Nothing, for America would have lost control. Japan might slip out of the American orbit. Whatever differences McNamara, McCone, LeMay, Felt, Rusk, and other top officials may have had, in December 1963 they could all agree on an analysis of the situation that pointed its finger at China as the greatest threat facing America.

If the specter of a China expanding through a combination of wars of national liberation and neutralism haunted Washington, the imminence of a first Chinese atomic detonation, much more than the military deterioration in South Vietnam, fired the sense of urgency. Hilsman wrote: "It was perfectly clear from our intelligence that Communist China was

---

[40] See *People's Daily*, November 9, 1963; and Donald S. Zagoria, *Vietnam Triangle*, pp. 26–27.
[41] *San Francisco Chronicle*, July 9, 1971.

working furiously on an atomic bomb and that she would probably succeed in exploding one by mid-1964."[42] However remote it might have seemed from 1963 and 1964, the September 1949 Russian nuclear breakthrough was sufficiently remembered as an event that altered the global military balance of power, a matter of particular concern to the Joint Chiefs of Staff.

VIOLENT DEBATE ON BOMBERS VERSUS MISSiLES

A third factor poured fuel on the flames of urgency during the winter of 1963–1964 and the following spring—a violent debate on the issue of manned aircraft versus missiles. In March, Roswell Gilpatric, who had been ousted as Deputy Secretary of Defense in January, published an article in *Foreign Affairs* which argued for a 25 percent cut in defense spending by 1970, particularly through the elimination of strategic bombers, meaning the Strategic Air Command. McNamara himself was to sound the theme from time to time of abolishing the Strategic Air Command by 1970. The functions of the office of Deputy Secretary of Defense, judging from Gilpatric's own record and those of his successors (Cyrus Vance, David Packard, William Clements), relate to dealings with the "military-industrial complex"—in other words, he handles military contracts. Gilpatric played a prominent role in the awarding of the TFX contract for the F-111 to General Dynamics, an award bitterly opposed by the Air Force and the Navy. Only a few days before Kennedy's assassination, it came to light that Gilpatric was still associated with General Dynamics's New York law firm. Like McNamara after his dismissal, Gilpatric took the opportunity to make public views that he had advocated while in the department, which McNamara clearly shared. To the Air Force, it must have seemed that a general attack on the credibility of air power was being mounted. In Vietnam, American pilots complained about the quality of their planes. The new helicopter program was under the command of the Army, causing some Air Force critics to worry aloud that the Army was attempting to take over the function of their Tactical Air Command by giving air support for ground operations.[43] McNamara's fiscal 1965 budget message allowed existing B-52 and B-58 wings to be retained, but provided for no new manned aircraft programs.

U.S. News & World Report usually reflected military views, both right-wing and hard-line liberal. On May 4, 1964, it chose to print a

[42] Hilsman, *To Move a Nation*, p. 349.
[43] *See* U.S. News & World Report, April 20, 1964.

letter from a pilot subsequently killed in Vietnam which reflected the fierce hostility to McNamara that pervaded the Air Force and the Navy:

> McNamara was here, spent his usual time, and has gone back home to run the war with his screwed-up bunch of people. We call them "McNamara's Band." I hope and pray that somehow this man does something right pretty soon. . . . A brilliant man. He's lucky to be alive. Some of the guys honestly had to be held back from beating this idiot up. This man McNamara and his whole idiot band will cause me not to vote for Johnson no matter how much I like his policies.

It would be hard to judge which of the many fights within the defense establishment since the end of World War II was the most violent, but the 1963–1964 one which pitted the combined Navy and Air Force against McNamara and his civilian "whiz kids" was probably the most bitter. Kennedy had tried to soften the controversy; thus, as Clark Mollenhoff notes, "from the start, the McNamara Pentagon was stacked with Johnson men."[44] Johnson men, like his "protégé"[45] Cyrus Vance, who replaced Gilpatric, were presumably more acceptable to the military than the systems analysts. But the issues formed the office, which in turn formed the men. A strategic doctrine had been in the making for a long time that America must have the technologically finest possible deterrent against Russia. In the early 1960s, that meant missiles, not bombers. It also meant submarines rather than carriers. In addition, PPBS (Planned Program Budgeting System) threatened to make a shambles of the tradition-proud services.

McNAMARA TAKES OVER THE WAR

In March 1964, McNamara, clearly with Johnson's support, seemed to be taking over singlehanded control over the entire Vietnam war. The journalists said it was "McNamara's War," and so it was—for a brief while—politically, bureaucratically, and organizationally.

In March 1964, a number of major bureaucratic events occurred all designed to bring the entire Vietnam operation under White House control. Johnson announced the formation of a special White House committee to coordinate Vietnam policy, headed by William Sullivan, formerly of Averell Harriman's staff. Sullivan later became ambassador to Laos, and in 1972 played a "technical" role in the Paris peace negotiations. For all his early hostility to Russian communism, Harriman had

---

[44] Clark Mollenhoff, ed., *The Pentagon*, p. 244.
[45] *Ibid.*

become an advocate of Russian-American collaboration. Since Russian-American cooperation in Laos continued on well into the late 1960s, it was not accidental that Sullivan moved on from Washington to Vientiane. Dean Rusk's basic policy thrust was to seek the "help" of the Russians in putting pressure on Hanoi to stop its aggression against the South. While Sullivan was too junior a figure to head so major a body as the Vietnam group (later to be superseded by the "Tuesday lunch"), this signified that, for the first time, the White House intended to assume direct control and supervision over the Vietnam war.

Between March 8 and 12, McNamara made his fourth trip to South Vietnam (the second having been in October 1963 and the third in December 1963). As *Aviation Week and Space Technology* (March 23, 1964) put it:

> Defense Secretary Robert S. McNamara increased the impact of his recent visit to South Vietnam by making several major military and policy decisions on-the-spot, rather than sending them through the usual time-consuming channels back home. This was done with the full backing of President Johnson. McNamara is expected to continue bringing a full complement of governmental policy makers with him on South Vietnam visits so this streamlined decision-making can be continued.

Nothing could be more out of line with military chain of command procedures than for the Secretary of Defense to make decisions "on-the-spot" without going through the line down to the Joint Chiefs of Staff, then to CINCPAC, and finally to MAC/V. McNamara, in effect, was giving orders directly to MAC/V. While the Pentagon Papers carefully skirt any discussion of internal American chain of command issues, press reports at the time make it possible to deduce what actually happened: the chain of command was detached from Honolulu and ran directly from Saigon to Washington. If this deep, dark secret was not openly talked about even in the secret Pentagon Papers, the North Vietnamese were well aware of what had transpired. As they wrote in 1967:

> In March, McNamara came back to Saigon. The Johnson-McNamara plan adopted on the 17th [NSAM 288] included the following points:
>
> 1) The U.S.A. would set up an "inter-ministerial Commission" entrusted with the direction of the war. Depending no longer on the Pacific Command, the U.S. Command in South Vietnam would be placed directly under the Pentagon. A joint U.S.-puppet command would be established. "U.S. advisers" would be present in each company. The puppet army would receive

more equipment, increase its air force, fluvial fleet and mobile forces. . . .[46]

While the translation is awkward (perhaps going from Vietnamese to French and then English), the meaning is quite clear.

Until 1971, the jurisdiction of MAC/V was restricted to South Vietnam alone. Operations over the remainder of Indochina remained within the jurisdiction of CINCPAC. The invasion of Cambodia in 1970 was a limited and temporary extension of MAC/V's jurisdiction. Air strikes over Cambodia, however, remained under the Pacific command. In the spring of 1971, MAC/V was given extended jurisdiction over portions of the Ho Chi Minh Trail adjacent to South Vietnam. But from March 1964 until the abolition of MAC/V in 1972, it was an operational command separate from the over-all Pacific command based in Honolulu.

Also in March, Johnson named Admiral Ulysses Grant Sharp to succeed Admiral Harry Felt as CINCPAC. Sharp was a conservative hardliner like Felt and, in the fine tradition of the Pacific Navy, was an ardent advocate of the air war against North Vietnam. While this change of Pacific command was routine, cutting out all of South Vietnam from its jurisdiction was certainly not. From Honolulu's perspective, McNamara must have appeared more than ever as an arrogant dictator aspiring to total power.

NSAM 288—THE MOMENTUM SLOWS DOWN

Out of this welter of events, which largely sprang out of the cauldron of American bureaucratic struggles, came the most important policy document in the genesis of the greater Vietnam war—NSAM 288 of March 17, 1964. Since the authors of the Pentagon Papers did not or could not include the entire document in their study, it has to be pieced together, as the *New York Times* did.[47] The author of this section of the Papers recognized NSAM 288's importance:

> Whereas, in NSAM 273, the objectives were expressly limited to helping the government of South Vietnam win its contest against an externally directed Communist conspiracy, NSAM 288 escalated the objectives into a defense of all of Southeast Asia and the West Pacific and redefined American foreign policy and American security generally. . . .[48] A struggle so defined came close to calling for war *à outrance* [all-out war, in plain English]—not the cen-

---

[46] *The Failure of "Special War,"* p. 86.
[47] *New York Times, Pentagon Papers,* pp. 283–85.
[48] DOD, *U.S.-Vietnam Relations,* IV.C.1, p. 46.

trally political war, with severe restrictions upon violent means, following counter-guerrilla warfare theory.[49]

NSAM 288 lays forth the notion of falling dominoes, indicating that what officials were saying publicly they also were willing to put into major policy documents. Since the domino notion has been basic to American foreign policy thinking since 1945, I shall quote the section in its entirety:

> Unless we can achieve this objective in South Vietnam, almost all of Southeast Asia will probably fall under Communist dominance (all of Vietnam, Laos, and Cambodia), accommodate to Communism so as to remove effective U.S. and anti-Communist influence (Burma), or fall under the domination of forces not now explicitly Communist but likely then to become so (Indonesia taking over Malaysia). Thailand might hold for a period without help, but would be under grave pressure. Even the Philippines would become shaky, and the threat to India on the West, Australia and New Zealand to the South, and Taiwan, Korea, and Japan to the North and East would be greatly increased.[50]

The domino notion naturally appealed to the geopolitical minds in the Navy, and even Admiral Sharp could have had little to cavil at in such a ringing declaration of America's determination not to be pushed out of Southeast Asia.

Yet, as one reads the fragments of NSAM 288, it becomes clear that, for all its high-flown verbiage, it was a strong assertion of containment doctrine with a lot of double-talk designed to pacify the rollback advocates of air strikes against the northern enemy or enemies. The Joint Chiefs of Staff, anticipating on March 14 that Johnson would accept McNamara's recommendations (which he did and made into NSAM 288), were opposed. As the Pentagon Papers put it, "One major dissent had been registered by the JCS. . . . who believed that the source of VC strength in the North must be neutralized."[51]

Recommendation number 12 of NSAM 288 involved:

> 1) preparation for "retaliatory actions," defined to include "overt high and/or low level reconnaissance flights" . . . over North Vietnam, as well as "tit-for-tat" bombing strikes and commando-type raids; and [2] planning and preparations "to be in a position on 30 days notice to initiate the [sic] program of "Graduated Overt Military Pressure" against North Vietnam.[52]

[49] Ibid., p. 48.
[50] Ibid., p. 47.
[51] Ibid., p. 54.
[52] DOD, U.S.-Vietnam Relations, IV.C.2.(a), p. 9.

Indeed, the *New York Times*'s piecing together of NSAM 288 put these sentences at the very beginning.[53] Yet, on the very same page in which McNamara's recommendation number 12 is reported, is the statement: "When he returned from his visit to South Vietnam, Secretary McNamara recommended against either the United States or the GVN undertaking overt actions against North Vietnam 'at this time.' " McNamara regarded such actions as "extremely delicate," citing three reasons: difficulties of justification, chances of "communist escalation," and pressures for premature negotiations.

The authors of the Pentagon Papers sensed that, despite the ringing assertion of the domino notion and the insertion of recommendation number 12, NSAM 288 was not exactly a call for all-out attack against North Vietnam:

> Despite the encompassing nature of the definition of the objectives, and although NSAM 288 proposed a marked increase in U.S. involvement, our implementing programs remained comparatively limited as if we did not fully believe these strong words. We even expressed agreement with the older idea of helping the Vietnamese to help themselves.[54]

But, aside from the declaration of commitments, what was the form of this "marked increase in U.S. involvement"? NSAM 288 not only finally halted the old policy of phased withdrawal, but initiated an increase in American personnel assigned to Vietnam. As the Pentagon Papers say:

> Along with this increase in Vietnamese administrative personnel there was to be an increase in U.S. advisory personnel to assist them. . . . On April 30. . . . Lodge said Khanh was willing to accept U.S. administrators in pacified areas provided the U.S. felt willing to accept casualties.[55]

The North Vietnamese and the National Liberation Front were well aware of these operational implications of NSAM 288, noting that " 'U.S. advisers' would be present in each company." The actual personnel commitments to South Vietnam were minor and muddled. The real importance of NSAM 288 was that it laid the policy groundwork for sending, eventually, over a half-million American troops to South Vietnam.

While NSAM 288 did not mention China by name (at least in the fragments known), the implication was clear that if firm action was not taken to save South Vietnam, the Communists (Chinese) would soon dominate all of Southeast Asia, directly or through "accommodations."

---

[53] *New York Times, Pentagon Papers*, p. 283.
[54] DOD, *U.S.-Vietnam Relations*, C.1, p. 48.
[55] *Ibid.*, p. 61.

But there were only two policy currents suggesting how this could be prevented: either strike at the source of the aggression in North Vietnam and China or take over South Vietnam, put down the insurgency, and turn the 17th parallel into the same iron curtain as the 38th parallel in Korea or the original Iron Curtain in Europe. NSAM 288 could be read as a compromise between these two currents, for the advocates of air strikes and covert war ("border control operations") had their original breakthrough in NSAM 273 reconfirmed. But NSAM 52 of May 1961 also had built-in air strike and covert war recommendations, which had come to nought with the Geneva Accords of 1962. Moreover, unless there was deliberate falsification in a document supposed to be secret anyway, NSAM 288 did not seem to attach great importance to OPLAN 34-A:

> We are not acting against North Vietnam except by a modest "covert" program operated by South Vietnamese (and a few Chinese Nationalists)—a program so limited that it is unlikely to have any significant effect.[56]

But was Oplan 34-A really so "limited"?

TAKING THE WAR NORTH

From the early testimony of McNamara and particularly the later one on the Tonkin incident, it was clear that "South Vietnamese" commandos were raiding North Vietnamese coastal positions as a part of the 34-A Op's program. Chinese Nationalists were most likely involved, since Hainan Island lies just on the eastern side of the Gulf of Tonkin. But an item in the April 6, 1964, edition of *Aviation Week and Space Technology* revealed that the scope of the 34-A Op's was large enough to make the word "limited" inappropriate:

> . . . with U.S. backing in aircraft, weapons, and money, an estimated 50,000 élite South Vietnamese special forces troops are being trained to take the offensive in over-the-border strikes at Communist supply centers and communications routes. . . . Objective of these operations is to stop the southward flow of weapons and trained Viet Cong troops along the routes in Laos and Cambodia as well as inside North Vietnam.

Coincidentally or not, 50,000 happened to be just the number of troops NSAM 288 recommended be added to the South Vietnamese army.[57] There need be no mystery about the scope and scale of covert war,

[56] *Ibid.*, p. 48.
[57] *Ibid.*, p. 51.

which had a two decades old tradition in East Asia. Ever since May 1963, when CINCPAC began drafting what was to become OPLAN 34-A, covert war had been on the upswing in East Asia. It was given a powerful boost by NSAM 273, and the formal launching of OPLAN 34-A on February 1, 1964, was a go-ahead for bigger and better operations.

What is significant is that a presidential policy document made a deliberate effort to play down covert war and to leave preparations for air strikes against North Vietnam on the same contingency burner where they had always been. It is idle to talk of deception. McNamara, with his famous mind for cramming facts and figures, knew perfectly well what was going on. But both publicly and privately, he indicated no great enthusiasm for bombing the North, and repeatedly invoked the great dangers it might entail. The effect of NSAM 288 was to move the policy machinery away from NSAM 273 and back to the containment channels appropriate to the Presidency.

In 1962, the move away from NSAM 52 involved an American-Russian agreement to settle the affairs of Laos, with the Pathet Lao conceding the Mekong Valley to the free world. But in March 1964, no great power diplomacy was possible. Russian leverage over North Vietnam was limited, evident in North Vietnam's open siding with the Chinese in the Sino-Soviet dispute. And diplomatic contacts with China were out of the question because of China's refusal to bargain on its nuclear program. In 1962, Kennedy threatened to send troops into Laos but did not have to do so because the Geneva Accords came into being. But in March 1964, Washington was totally opposed to any "premature negotiations." If policy was to avoid the great risks of rollback and stay on the containment track, there was only one bureaucratically feasible solution—to send in United States troops. That would happen some sixteen months later, but NSAM 288, adopted over the opposition of the Joint Chiefs of Staff and most particularly the Navy–Air Force alliance, laid the groundwork.

The Pentagon Papers, one must remember, were commissioned by McNamara as a history of the war from his perspective. That perspective, by and large shared by the authors, was that of the office of the Secretary of Defense, civilian staffs assisting the President's chosen instrument in the Defense Department. The Papers basically try to explain the presidential policy of securing South Vietnam through American ground combat troops. But in telling the story, they adhere to the bureaucratic constraints that came naturally to them anyway. Little is said about China in the Pentagon Papers and, except for references to positions of the Joint Chiefs of Staff on this or that question, not much more on the military side. But China and the United States military just happened to be the key elements in the situation, far more important than suppressing a Communist insurgency in the South Vietnamese jungles. NSAM 288 was designed not only to contain China (and its Vietnamese arms), but also to contain the hawks seeking to unleash air strikes and full-scale covert war against the Communists to the north. McNamara's entire policy within the Defense Department was designed to contain the military, and centralizing control in his own hands was his means of doing that. For McNamara, Vietnam was a test case of his policies. He had to win in order to show that his methods could achieve agreed-upon goals with less risk, more effectiveness, and possibly fewer costs than the old-fashioned attack tactics preferred by the military. McNamara was exceedingly deficient in political sense, else he might have seen the traps he was being dragged into as soon as the issue of advisers and troops was posed. But he could not escape the forcing logic of his bureaucratic position. The Pentagon Papers are his story, with the exuberant period of "McNamara's War" played down and the later periods of disenchantment highlighted.

The logic of NSAM 288 flowing out of the containment current was not the only one operating. With OPLAN 34-A launched, another logic was gathering powerful strength and swept past NSAM 288 to achieve, on May 17, 1964, what it had been hungering for for years—the first air strike against the communist enemy.

THE AIR WAR BEGINS IN LAOS—MAY 1964

The Pentagon Papers duly and blandly note the Laos crisis of mid-May 1964:

> On May 17, pro-Communist forces in Laos began an offensive which led to their control of a significant portion of the Plaine des Jarres. On the 21st, the United States obtained Souvanna Phouma's permission to conduct low-level reconnaissance operations over the occupied areas. For several weeks the offensive threatened to destroy the security of the neutralist-rightist position—and with it the political underpinning of U.S.–Laotian policy. These developments lent a greater sense of urgency to the arguments of those advisers favoring prompt measures to strengthen the U.S. position in Southeast Asia.[58]

The account of the offensive is amusing because, like much else in Laos, it was a phantom. But until the bombs came, the phantoms were the reality out of which great policies were fashioned in Washington.

[58] DOD, U.S.-Vietnam Relations, IV.C.2.(a), p. 20.

While one can disregard the substance of the above paragraph, the Pentagon Papers accurately pinpoint the time and place of the crisis, and then add: "The most avid of those urging prompt action were the JCS."[59] A few pages later, discussing the Honolulu Conference of June 1–2, 1964, the Papers note that the spokesman for the Joint Chiefs of Staff did not share their views.[60] Since that spokesman obviously was the chairman, Maxwell Taylor, who as an Army man and an arm of the White House reflected presidential policy currents, we are back to our old Navy–Air Force alliance avidly pushing for air strikes.

It is hard to get from the Pentagon Papers any sense that war had broken out. *Aviation Week and Space Technology*, in its June 15, 1964, issue, was direct and frank:

> Now we have the incredible spectacle of eight USAF F-100 fighter-bombers making a strike on foreign soil—the first U.S. offensive military action since Korea—and the government trying to suppress this news and keep it from the American people.

Unlike *U.S. News & World Report*, whose political slant is thinly disguised, *Aviation Week* seems to be a technical trade journal. But it does reflect current opinions and attitudes within the air power community, notably the Air Force. In 1964, the air power community was gung ho for taking a crack at communists in East Asia. What *Aviation Week* could not understand was why Washington had to cover it up. The authors of the Pentagon Papers perpetuated the cover-up because of habit, even in their turgid bureaucratic memos.

On May 17, the horrifying news spread throughout the world that *Tha Thom had Fallen*. United States planes roared off the decks of the carriers *Kitty Hawk* and *Constellation* to "reconnoiter" Laos. American T-28s, "given" to what was officially called the "Royal Lao Air Force," began bombing and strafing Pathet Lao positions. On June 6, 1964, the first American jet was shot down over the Plaine des Jarres. On June 11, American bombs fell on the Chinese economic-cultural delegation office in neutralist-held Khang Khay (an office set up by official agreement with the Vientiane regime). From May 17, 1964, until February 1973, Laos was bombed in one of the most brutal, repulsive campaigns in the history of warfare—"milk runs" over Laos were safe, unlike the more dangerous targets in North Vietnam. But May 17 was just the first step to juicier targets far beyond Laos.

During the brief period between the Vietnam and Laotian ceasefires in January–February 1973, the Honolulu Pacific Command at last came into the open as the operational source of the bombing of Laos. Every

---

[59] *Ibid.*
[60] *Ibid.*, p. 29.

time a bombing raid was announced, the laconic phrase "at the request of the Royal Laotian government" would be added. To our knowledge, there never was a specific presidential decision authorizing the bombing of Laos, nor does the Pentagon Papers' account of the Honolulu Conference suggest anything more than that America might consider supporting Laotian Air Force T-28 operations.[61] The State Department, after the fact on May 21, did announce agreement with Souvanna for reconnaissance flights. But as we know from the bombing of North Vietnam during Nixon's first term, reconnaissance has a way of turning into protective reaction flights with hundreds of sorties. Protective reaction was born in Laos, for the reconnaissance planes were accompanied by armed jets which, naturally, bombed to protect the reconnaissance. But in protocol terms, the Navy got what it wanted: the Royal Government of Laos could, at its own discretion, request armed reconnaissance flights.

Laos has always been a mixture of tragedy, comedy, and especially mystery, and no people has less deserved their fate than the gentle, life-respecting Laotians. Judging from the disciplined character of the Pathet Lao, America may have succeeded in turning them into a martial race. Probably no government has had less relationship to its own social reality than that collection of ministers and generals which is collectively called the Royal Lao government. Naïve, weak, and greedy enough to be manipulated, it truly deserves the name puppet. But whose puppet? The American Embassy's or the CIA's or Bangkok's? There were many more string pullers than marionettes. The only Laotian figure the world at large knows is Souvanna Phouma, an urbane, French-educated Royal Lao prince. Coming in as a neutral in the spirit of the 1950s, he became a neutralist in the spirit of 1962, and from mid-May 1964, became a pliant tool of the American Embassy. By 1973, in a ceasefire that recognized only two (not three) sides in Laos, he finally was shoved into the right wing. The prelude to the escalation of May 17 was the reconstruction of the Vientiane government through a coup that took place one month before (much as would be the case in Cambodia in 1970).

THE APRIL 1964 COUP IN LAOS

After the signing of the Geneva Accords on Laos, the internal situation there remained volatile. As Kong Le's neutralists moved further to the right, the Pathet Lao became increasingly nervous. And every time the Pathet Lao made a move, the right wing had to make a countermove.

---

[61] DOD, U.S.-Vietnam Relations, IV.C.2.(a), p. 33.

Each time a brick in the wobbly Laotian political structure slipped out, Souvanna Phouma rushed abroad to get international help to put his house in order. In the spring of 1964, the house wobbled again, and in March, Souvanna flew to Hanoi and Peking to persuade the North Vietnamese and the Chinese to use their influence to keep the Pathet Lao in check. By mid-April, things appeared to be settling down again. On April 18, the leaders of the three factions—Souvanna for the neutralists, Souphanouvong for the left, and Phoumi for the right—met in the Plaine des Jarres and reportedly achieved a new agreement.

But on April 19, a right-wing coup erupted in Vientiane which shattered the agreement. The coup was led by Kouprasith Abhay, commander of the troops in the Vientiane region, and Siho Lamphoutacoul, chief of the national gendarmery. Although the left forces accused Phoumi of being behind the coup, it is not clear that this was the case. In earlier years, Phoumi was the CIA's man. But the CIA had suffered a bad defeat at Nam Tha. In March, Souvanna's government expelled Air America from Laos[62]—an act obviously revoked shortly thereafter, but at the time a blow to the CIA. Phoumi's subsequent disappearance from the Laotian political scene suggests that he was part of an old, discredited right wing, which was replaced by a rising new right wing with close ties to the American and Thai military headed by Kouprasith (Siho was subsequently murdered under mysterious circumstances and never played a major role).

The coup was denounced not only by the socialist countries, but also by the United States. Washington called for an immediate return to the tripartite government ratified by the 1962 agreements. Particularly significant is that Washington consulted with the Russians, both in their respective capitals and on the spot in Vientiane. In few other parts of the world did Washington and Moscow "collude" (as the Chinese would say) so amicably as they did in Laos that year. The warmer the Russian-American collaboration became, the more violent the Sino-Soviet rift. The Chinese accused the Russians of organizing anti-China meetings throughout the country and carrying the dispute to the mass level.

Souvanna immediately returned to Vientiane to try to undo the coup. On May 5, he released a declaration stating that Phoumi had handed all powers over to him and that he had unified the right-wing and neutralist forces. Thereupon he went to Khang Khay, where the neutralists had their headquarters, to persuade the Pathet Lao who had gone there from Vientiane to return to the government. Souphanouvong retorted that Souvanna was deluding himself, that actually he had fallen under control of the coup leaders Kouprasith and Siho. That charge is borne out by the

[62] *Aviation Week and Space Technology*, March 23, 1964.

fact that Kouprasith named himself minister of defense and Siho minister for internal affairs—in other words, the army and the police were in the hands of the coup leaders. The Pathet Lao charged that the right wing was using Souvanna to "swallow up" the 8,000-man force of neutralists into their own 50,000-man force.[63]

A few days after Souvanna's declaration, a group of neutralists split from Kong Le's pro-Souvanna command and proclaimed themselves the "true neutralists," and, like the Pathet Lao, refused to return to Vientiane. The defection of the "true neutralists," as officials in Vientiane saw it, upset the balance of power. On May 15, it was reported that Pathet Lao forces captured the town of Tha Thom astride a road leading to the Thai frontier. Tha Thom had once been held by the Pathet Lao, but was taken by right-wing forces in 1962. As the *Bangkok Post* made clear at the time, Tha Thom had been a staging area for right-wing forces to strike into Pathet Lao territory. The fighting actually erupted when a group of "true neutralists" revolted and some Pathet Lao forces moved into the town.

Trivial as this incident appears in retrospect, at the time, it created a crisis of world-wide dimensions. The Thais shouted that Paksane, on the Thai-Laotian frontier, was threatened by a major new Communist offensive. Thai troops were rushed into northeast Thailand and some reportedly crossed into Laos. Within Washington's bureaucracies the incident seemed momentous. If the Communists were aiming at Paksane, that meant a strike into the Mekong Valley, which containment had committed itself to defend. Again, as in mid-December 1963 and often thereafter when containment's and rollback's stars were in line, great troubles were to ensue.

A few days after that, the Pathet Lao protested that, on May 17, three AD-6 Skyraiders had attacked "true neutralist" forces in the Plaine des Jarres. The AD-6 is a Navy fighter-bomber. Where did it come from? Two weeks later, *U.S. News & World Report* revealed:

> One reconnaissance jet, a Navy plane on a low-level photographic mission, was hit by ground fire. The plane was only slightly damaged and the pilot, uninjured, flew back safely to the carrier *Kitty Hawk* in the South China Sea.[64]

On May 21, State Department spokesman Robert McCloskey admitted that American planes were flying reconnaissance over the Plaine des Jarres, and that they were taking off and landing from points outside of Laos.

In subsequent days, the Pathet Lao continued to report American raids over neutralist and Pathet Lao territory, although largely by T-28

[63] *People's Daily*, May 6, 1964.
[64] *U.S. News & World Report*, June 1, 1964.

trainers, which Washington officially admitted having given to the Vientiane government. In its June 15 issue, *Aviation Week and Space Technology* reported:

> President Johnson has decided upon a punch-for-punch military policy for Southeast Asia with the built-in safety valve of not admitting to such strikes as the bombing last week of the Red Pathet Lao headquarters and flak concentration in the Plaine des Jarres by eight USAF-North American F-100's from Clark Field in the Philippines. The strike came after Communist ground fire downed two U.S. aircraft over the same area.[65]

Thus, by June 15, the readers of *Aviation Week*, though neither the general public nor, apparently, the authors of the Pentagon Papers, knew that there was a war going on.

Considering the issues that were building up in Laos, it is not difficult to figure out a reason for the coup. If OPLAN 34-A was to go into effect as planned, as many as 50,000 South Vietnamese would start moving up the Ho Chi Minh Trail and "South Vietnamese" planes would bomb targets in North Vietnam. Both operations would require the kind of forward mountain top outposts that were done away with by the 1962 Laos accords. While hard to document, it appears that the CIA began to train and arm Vang Pao's Armée Clandestine in 1964 to move out from their base at Long Cheng at the southern end of the Plaine des Jarres deep into the highlands of northeastern Laos, which was the natural habitat of the Meo anyway. With the Plaine des Jarres in enemy hands, it would be very hard to mount a covert war against North Vietnam or China. While Souvanna was genuinely fearful of a North Vietnamese presence, until the April 19 coup, his neutralist politics precluded any return to covert war. Phoumi, the old right-winger, apparently also was not interested in a return to covert war. But Kouprasith and the Thais and Americans in Bangkok and Honolulu were another matter. Oplan 34-A required a more amenable government in Vientiane, which came about, but with Souvanna remaining as a fig leaf implying that neutralism (Russian-American cooperation) was still the government's true policy.

CONFLICTS AND CRISIS IN
WASHINGTON—MAY 1964

The general political atmosphere in Washington in mid-May 1964 was tense, not just because of the primary campaigns but because the old right-wing alliance of Southern Democrats and Republicans was once

[65] *Aviation Week and Space Technology*, June 15, 1964.

again zeroing in on McNamara. On May 16, the House Armed Services Committee, under the chairmanship of the Georgian Carl Vinson, announced that it was going to hold hearings on the allegedly substandard planes furnished to American fighting men in South Vietnam[66]—this even before America was officially involved in the war. The House and Senate military committees, traditionally chaired by hard-liners, have always been forums where intrabureaucratic conflicts could be brought out in the open in a manner that seemed compatible with democratic procedures. The Southern relationship to the American military is one of the most important, though least explored, aspects of American politics. Vinson's announcement was in effect a low key declaration of war against McNamara by a member of Johnson's own party. That Barry Goldwater was the spokesman of the Navy–Air Force alliance was troublesome to Johnson, but the defection of Southern Democrats to the right-wing hawk line was most dangerous of all in an election year.

Both the press at the time and the Pentagon Papers make clear that in mid-May, crisis erupted in Washington. As the Papers put it; "In mid-May 1964, a new factor entered the policy-shaping process—a factor which cast a shadow of crisis management over the entire decision-making environment."[67] The source of that crisis was an announcement on May 16 by the Laotian Defense Minister controlled by Kouprasith Abhay, the author of the April 19 coup, that the fall of Tha Thom marked a general Pathet Lao offensive aimed at Paksane. The Defense Ministry also revealed that Chinese troops had been participating in military actions in northern Laos.[68] On May 17, Souvanna entered the act with a warning that Pathet Lao troops were only twenty miles from Paksane, and agreed with Kouprasith that the Pathet Lao had started a general offensive. The Thai press (judging from the English-language Bangkok Post) took up the cry of a mortal threat to the northeastern region. While Souvanna began to hedge quickly on his claim of a Pathet Lao general offensive, the Laotian Defense Ministry kept on churning out reports on it.

The offensive was a phantom, and on May 29, the New York Times reported that fighting in Laos was tapering off. But since phantoms were the reality in Laos, they served the purpose in Washington. On May 21, Dean Rusk gave one of the toughest speeches of his career before the American Law Institute. He warned that America might be forced to widen the war or withdraw completely from Southeast Asia. He directly accused China and North Vietnam of fomenting aggression in Laos as well as in South Vietnam.

[66] New York Times, May 17, 1964.
[67] DOD, U.S.-Vietnam Relations, IV.C.2.(a), p. 20.
[68] New York Times, May 16, 1964.

The Pentagon Papers chronology quoted above gives us a clear idea of what happened during those days:

17 MAY 64: The Pathet Lao seized a significant portion of the Plaine des Jarres in Laos—a major setback for RLG (Royal Laotian Government) forces

19 MAY 64: Clearly indicating the crisis management aspects of the scene created by the Pathet Lao gains, the JCS now called for new, more intensive covert operations during the second [*sic!*] phase of OPLAN 34-A.

On May 16, the Joint Chiefs of Staff were criticizing McNamara's recommendations as too lax; on May 17, the horrifying news of the Pathet Lao offensive swept over the world; and on May 19, in the crisis management atmosphere created by the offensive, the Joint Chiefs demanded full implementation of OPLAN 34-A. But the first American air attacks had come on May 17—directed against Muong Phanh on the Plaine des Jarres, as reported by the Pathet Lao.[69]

Since there is nothing in the Pentagon Papers that indicates what *Aviation Week and Space Technology* knew and published on the outbreak of war in May–June 1964, there obviously is no information on how this came about. The Pentagon Papers deal with Laos only indirectly, so that we have no information on a NSAM specifically related to Laos. But there obviously must have been one, and it must have contained recommendations for aerial reconnaissance and possible air strikes, just as NSAM 288 did for North Vietnam. Judging from the Tonkin situation when Admiral Sharp incessantly implored President Johnson for the "execute" order to start bombing, one can infer that the same thing happened in May 1964 (Felt still being CINCPAC at the time). As soon as news of the offensive broke, CINCPAC, as theater commander, requested permission from the Joint Chiefs of Staff for air strikes, and when told it would require presidential decision, went directly to the White House.

THE SEEDS OF WAR SPROUT IN WASHINGTON AND HONOLULU

On May 28, when the Pathet Lao general offensive was already publicly known to have wafted away, President Johnson ordered the convening of a top level Honolulu Conference to review the entire situation in Southeast Asia.[70] That there was a sense of urgency to the meeting was ob-

---

[69] *People's Daily*, May 21, 1964.
[70] *New York Times*, May 29, 1964.

vious from the press. On May 30, the *New York Times* reported in a dispatch from Okinawa that military units there were ready on hours' notice to be sent anywhere in Southeast Asia. Those units included seventy-five warships and two bomber squadrons based on aircraft carriers. In the short space of six and one-half hours, transport planes could move Marines to Thailand or South Vietnam. The Chinese and North Vietnamese knew in detail about these American deployments and they were reported in their press. That President Johnson attached great importance to the meeting is evident from the fact that almost the entire top layer of the foreign policy establishment was sent to Honolulu: Rusk (coming in from Nehru's funeral), McNamara, McCone, William Bundy, Harlan Cleveland, Robert Manning, Arthur Sylvester, and Ambassadors Lodge and Martin, joined by Westmoreland, Carl Rowan, and McNaughton. Somewhat surprising, in view of the virtual news blackout on the conference, was the addition of public information officials (Sylvester and Rowan). Putting Rusk in charge undoubtedly was meant to avoid having McNamara grate even more on military sensitivities.

It is hard to get much of a sense of the Honolulu Conference from the two sections of the Pentagon Papers where it is discussed.[71] The chronology of the latter section says " 'Operational'—not policy—aspects of air operations against NVN were the main points of discussion with attention centered on the effect of pressures in Laos, preparatory steps necessary for a Laotian contingency and probably repercussions." To translate from bureaucratese, that means that the air strikes in Laos and their implications for an eventual Operation Rolling Thunder against North Vietnam were the main items of discussion. Naturally, the theater command in Honolulu would be just the place for discussions on operations to go on. But again, the press tells us more than the Pentagon Papers about the results of the conference. Max Frankel of the *New York Times* was there and, noting that the mood of crisis had dissipated, wrote that "no direct intervention in Laos is now planned."[72]

Yet on June 7, United States jets from Clark Field in the Philippines bombed Pathet Lao headquarters at Khanh Khay on the Plaine des Jarres—what Robert Hotz of *Aviation Week* called the first offensive American action since the Korean War.

The Pathet Lao did shoot down a United States jet on June 6 and announced it.[73] During the previous days, they reported repeated incursions of American planes for "reconnaissance, trouble-making, and disruptive activities." They did not specifically accuse the Americans of

---

[71] DOD, *U.S.-Vietnam Relations*, IV.C.1, pp. 76 ff; IV.C.2.(a), pp. 28ff. (The first section erroneously dates the conference as May 30.)
[72] *New York Times*, June 3, 1964.
[73] *People's Daily*, June 8, 1964.

bombing, which may imply that CINCPAC did moderate its hawks in the aftermath of Honolulu. But it hardly matters, except for protocol sticklers, whether bombing preceded shooting down or the reverse. The fact was that United States planes were roaming the skies over the Plaine des Jarres and the Pathet Lao obviously had anti-aircraft weapons supplied by the bigger communist powers. That alone was enough to irritate CINCPAC. Once the first jet had been shot down, the punch-for-punch or, as Johnson liked to call it, tit-for-tat "retaliation" could go into effect. It would only be at Tonkin two months later that the public would hear of this reprisal policy.

Although in retrospect May 17 marked the outbreak of war, it still was not completely clear at the time. But June 7 left no doubt any longer that war had begun—no doubt, that is, in the minds of the bureaucracies. For, as the Pentagon Papers indicate, "the week of June 8 saw the planning for a Congressional resolution being brought to a head."[74] The impulse for that resolution came directly from the President and "most agencies" were for it. The final planning was done in a "crucial inter-agency meeting" held at the State Department on June 15. William Bundy circulated a memorandum at the meeting that expressed what was to become intended presidential policy in subsequent months and years: limited military action against North Vietnam, coupled with certain diplomatic thrusts and intensified American involvement in South Vietnam.

The Bundy memorandum mentioned "reconnaissance-strike" operations in Laos and "small-scale" ones against North Vietnam (carried out by South Vietnamese aircraft). But it is clear that there was no great enthusiasm from this quarter for such operations, not out of moral considerations but out of fear that they might provoke larger Chinese or Russian reactions. Instead, Bundy pushed for "our diplomatic track in Laos," meaning collaboration with the Russians, and advocated a "shift of U.S. role from advice to direction." The latter recommendation was another small step toward the eventual commitment of over a half-million troops.

But CINCPAC (as well as MAC/V commander Westmoreland) indicated at the Honolulu Conference that he was opposed to "this extension of advisers to company level."[75] One of the major reasons was fear of "the inevitable increase in U.S. casualties."

Again, as so often before and afterward, we meet the troops versus air strikes issue in Bundy's memorandum. While stressing the limited nature of the proposed strikes against the North, he proposed an augmentation of the American ground role in South Vietnam. On June 23, Washington appointed Maxwell Taylor to succeed Lodge as ambassador to Saigon.

[74] DOD, *U.S.-Vietnam Relations,* IV.C.a.(a), p. 38.
[75] *Ibid.,* IV.C.1, pp. 80–81.

Here was America's then most prominent Army man, advocate of conventional ground forces to fight brush-fire wars, at some degree of odds with the Navy and the Air Force over bombing of the North (and beyond), going as the President's personal representative to Saigon. What could that mean as a harbinger of policy other than a reversion to Kennedy's 1961 policy of committing American ground forces to South Vietnam? Of course, we know all this in retrospect, but then, Johnson need not have appointed Taylor as ambassador.

The congressional resolution of August 7, 1964, became a controversial issue in the late 1960s leading to congressional attempts to limit the war-making powers of the Presidency. But judging from that controversy and from the sudden, overwhelming vote in favor at the time, few congressmen knew what Lyndon Johnson was trying to do. Most thought it was a vote of confidence in his conduct of a very delicate foreign policy, in the spirit of bipartisanship. In fact, what Johnson wanted was popular support to prop up his crumbling control of the military situation in Southeast Asia. If in March, McNamara was the commander handing out orders right and left, by early August, as his Tonkin testimony shows, he was frantically trying to counsel restraint as events moved beyond him. The new chairman of the Joint Chiefs of Staff, Earle Wheeler, was a colorless administrator who would hardly be Johnson's hammer and anvil. Unless events could be brought under presidential control, America might be swept into World War III, a fear that became one of Johnson's favorite rationales: we are fighting in Vietnam to avoid World War III. The Tonkin resolution was designed ultimately to reinforce and assert Johnson's role as commander-in-chief.

But there was another major reason for the resolution. It was intended as a substitute for a formal declaration of war, an act that seems no longer to be possible under contemporary conditions. To have declared war against North Vietnam would have implied and most probably signified a declaration of belligerency against Russia, with all the dangers of unleashing central nuclear war. A formal declaration of war would have pleased the right wing, which had deep suspicions of the "diplomatic tracks" going on with the Russians, but it would have meant the death of containment policy—then and there, rather than later by natural causes. But declarations of war have another major function which the Tonkin resolution was supposed to provide. They signify widespread popular backing for an actual or impending war. And a war that involves sending hundreds of thousands of troops abroad, as earlier wars did, needs popular support. The issue of troops was delicate, for the right-wingers opposed them on the grounds that the whole war against communism could be won in less costly (to Americans) and better ways. Johnson sensed the peace mood in the 1964 election campaign ("I seek no wider war"), and probably he truly did not expect such a massive bloodletting as Vietnam was to become. He and his containment liberal advisers were convinced that if American troops could secure and hold South Vietnam, then a single- or double-track diplomatic approach could finally bring Hanoi around to accept the 17th parallel. But any ground troop role absolutely required popular support, in contrast to Nixon's policy, which, based on American aircraft and Vietnamese bodies, needed it far less.

The events from May 17 to June 15, 1964, set a pattern which was to be repeated again and again until March 31, 1968, when Johnson announced the bombing halt over North Vietnam and quit the presidential race: in response to crisis, the hawks lunged with air strikes, followed by desperate presidential efforts to bring the escalation under control, until a new crisis erupted and the pattern repeated itself. Tonkin on August 4–5 and Pleiku on February 7 the following year were major crises which sparked the massive escalations. But even crisis decision making became routinized, as one can see in the Pentagon Papers. Invariably the President would be presented with three "options" (a hawk one, a dove one, and a middling dawk one, to use a term from the times). The middling option was invariably chosen, the dove option generally functioning as a straw man with which to counterbalance the hawk one.

PATTERNS OF PRESIDENTIAL DECISION MAKING

One of the most detailed accounts in the Pentagon Papers of this decision-making process relates to November 1964. On November 1, National Liberation Front forces attacked the United States air base at Bien Hoa. Normally, Washington would have retaliated, but since the elections were only days away, virtue overcame temptation. A day later, the "NSC Working Group on South Vietnam/Southeast Asia" was formed to hammer out options. Options can be defined as possible actions recommended by the various bureaucracies involved, from which the President was to choose one. In fact, the options were often worked out so as to suggest the proper decision to the President, which invariably was the one he was going to make anyway. The technical sounding flimflam of the systems analysts should not be allowed to obscure the simple, direct politics behind the options. The members of this option-manufacturing Working Group were mostly second echelon officials from the Joint Chiefs of Staff, the CIA, the State Department, and ISA (International Security Affairs, the liberal whiz kid bastion in the Department of Defense). In the course of their deliberations, the Working Group hammered out three options, labeled A, B, and C. These more or less set the decision-making parameters for the subsequent years.

Option A was regarded as minimal: no new military strikes with continued resistance to negotiation. Option B was regarded as maximal: "progressively heavy military pressures against North Vietnam" with resistance to negotiation. Option C was seen as middling: some new but milder strikes at North Vietnam with a declared willingness to negotiate.[76] All members of the Working Group favored some variant of Option C, "other than the JCS member."[77] In fact, the Joint Chiefs of Staff were angry at the way the Working Group had drawn up the options and, later in November, submitted five alternative options, of which they naturally favored the strongest. One called for an "advanced decision to continue military pressures, if necessary, to the full limits of what military pressures can contribute toward U.S. national objectives," and another called for "intense military pressures. . . . designed to have major military and psychological impact from the outset."[78] While not easy to translate into ordinary language, the first option seems to imply an air war which might eventually reach into China, whereas the second implied a massive sudden strike at North Vietnam designed to wipe it off the map. These options did not become the working options, but the Navy–Air Force combine had no difficulty in making its case known to the President. Interestingly, the Working Group member from the Joint Chiefs of Staff was angry at the inference of other members that the intensive actions favored by the Joint Chiefs were "not controllable."[79]

While the Pentagon Papers make it appear as if the options of the Joint Chiefs of Staff were some among many from which the President chose, in fact, the policy current that propelled America forward in Indochina since NSAM 273 came out of the Navy, the Air Force, and the CIA. The policy current that emanated from the White House and was personified by McNamara strove desperately to regain control of what it feared was an uncontrollable progression of events. In May 1964, McNamara told General Nguyen Khanh that while the United States commitment did not "rule out the use of force against North Vietnam, such actions must be supplementary to and not a substitute for successful counter-insurgency in the South," and that "we do not intend to provide support nor undertake the military objective of 'rolling back' communist control in North Vietnam."[80] But the Joint Chiefs' view was precisely that military action against the North was primary, not supple-

[76] DOD, *U.S.-Vietnam Relations,* IV.C.2.(c), p. 18.
[77] *Ibid.,* p. 21.
[78] *Ibid.,* p. 34.
[79] *Ibid.,* p. 35.
[80] DOD, *U.S.-Vietnam Relations,* IV.C.2.(a), p. 19.

mental, for the achievement of United States objectives in South Vietnam and Southeast Asia in general. The policy current that surged ahead at this time, despite pious denials from the President's men, was *rollback*.

Rollback held sway until April 1, 1965, when President Johnson, to the bureaucracies' surprise, made the sudden and unexpected decision to commit American ground combat forces to South Vietnam.

There probably never will be any way to discover how the Navy and the Air Force conceived of "victory" in practical terms. After the Vietnam ceasefire was signed, Admiral Thomas Moorer revealed that the Joint Chiefs had advocated an invasion of North Vietnam.[81] The only precedent for that was MacArthur's Inchon landing, which began to roll back communist power in North Korea. But an invasion of North Vietnam would almost certainly have triggered Chinese intervention, something the Joint Chiefs were well aware of. Naturally, there would be no "Manchurian sanctuaries" in China this time. OPLAN 34-A had two seedlings which could easily have sprouted into a full-scale rollback attempt against North Vietnam: one was the bombing that turned into Rolling Thunder, the other was exfiltration of commandos, which could have been the forerunner of actual invasion by South Vietnamese and other Asian ground forces with American naval and air support. Even if there was no precise scenario *à la* Inchon, the military most likely saw no harm in escalating actions since so little risk to America was involved (to their way of thinking). Moreover, increasing the quotient of pain might just produce some surprising results.

The professional East Asian rollbackers in Taiwan and South Vietnam had some concrete ideas as to what would happen. They were convinced that uprisings would occur and, even if artificially generated by counterrevolutionary incitements, they would spread among a disaffected population. While the containment liberals constantly played down these rollback notions as the ravings of excitable anticommunists, in one important respect they accorded with certain key notions of the military. The military was convinced that both China and North Vietnam were militarily weak and politically unstable. While impressed with Maoist guerrilla tactics, it was unimpressed with seemingly lagging economic performance and constant internal bickering in those countries. Johnson's characterization of North Vietnam as a "raggedy ass third-rate nation" was an echo of the general military view of the primitiveness and brittleness of the Democratic Republic of Vietnam.

From the purely military point of view, there could be only one credible reason for the United States to refrain from an all-out onslaught

[81] *New York Times*, February 27, 1973.

(with United States air and sea power and Asian troops) against North Vietnam and possibly China. That was the risk of Russian intervention and the threat of nuclear war, or that Russia might create trouble in other parts of the world. In a memorandum of late March 1965, made famous by the release of the Pentagon Papers, John McNaughton listed the successive rungs of the escalatory ladder ending with a "Chinese/Soviet" confrontation with the United States. McNaughton's fifth "red flash point" (coming right after United States strikes against Red River Delta industrial and population targets) was strikes against Chinese railroads, followed by clashes with Chinese Migs and hot pursuit of Migs into China. His ninth flash point mentioned Soviet-manned SAMs (surface-to-air missiles), presumably in China.[82] But the Chinese had no SAMs of their own, and the Soviet presence had been completely eliminated from China.

During the 1964 election campaign, the issue of rollback, which the Republicans openly called for in 1952, had a new incarnation in the form of a demand to bomb North Vietnam. In May 1964, in the midst of the Laos crisis, Barry Goldwater publicly called for the bombing of targets in North Vietnam and China. Nelson Rockefeller from the Republican party's liberal wing took a hawkish line on Vietnam.[83] On May 21, Max Frankel wrote in the New York Times: "[Some officials] say the use of American force in some direct fashion is inevitable and the sooner the better if the doubters are to be held." The "doubters" were mounting a three-pronged attack against the administration: from the Navy and Air Force; from the Republicans as a whole; and from powerful Southern-dominated congressional military committees. While the electorate was expecting peace as the boom of the 1960s gained momentum, the Washington power structure took a sharp turn toward bellicosity. Johnson may have been confident of an ultimate election victory, but he could not ignore the fact that Goldwater voiced the sentiments of many of the most powerful political and military leaders in Washington, with whom he would have to live bureaucratically for the succeeding four years.

No one in Washington wanted a repetition of the Korean War with thousands of American soldiers sent into combat. But the mood for taking a heavy whack at the Asian communists was widespread. Yet, as I have already noted, in the late 1940s the aggressive mood was strongest among the losers in the game of power. From the perspective of the 1970s, when the United States Navy is the dominant service, it is hard to remember that until the Vietnam war, the Navy saw itself in a loser role. In the early 1960s, the Air Force, once mighty and proud, saw itself

[82] DOD, U.S. Vietnam Relations, IV.C.3, pp. 85–90.
[83] Interview in U.S. News & World Report, March 16, 1964.

likewise threatened by McNamaraism. The Republicans in 1964 were almost convinced that they were doomed to permanent minority status. And the Southerners, for all their committee power, knew that they were old men representing a way of life that was fast passing from the scene. This trinity of what Frankel so politely called "doubters" can truly be called reactionary. They saw a tide of forces abroad and at home, communist and liberal, which was sweeping aside all that they considered sacred, not to mention, of course, very concrete material interests. They could not react against the domestic enemy because they disagreed too sharply over who he was. But all agreed that foreign communism was an enemy, and worst of all was Asian communism. They suspected that many liberals covertly sympathized with the Chinese. A devastating, paralyzing blow at China and its tentacles would be a safe object lesson for the liberals: safe in not involving nuclear war and in being directed against an external enemy (unlike McCarthyism).

There was nothing secret about the reactionaries' warlike mood in 1964. Nor was there anything secret about the liberals' commitment to keeping South Vietnam under an American aegis. What was not known was that war had already begun on May 17, 1964. And when Tonkin flared up, it was quickly forgotten as an isolated incident. What virtually no one suspected in 1964 was that, in the spring of 1965, Johnson would see no way out of the dilemma he was thrust into than to launch a ground war which no one wanted except for a few none-too-bright Army generals.

JOHNSON'S DECISION TO COMMIT TROOPS

On April 1, 1965, President Johnson made the move that finally committed America to ground combat in South Vietnam. That decision was embodied in NSAM 328, adopted on April 6. As the Pentagon Papers say: "NSAM 328 is a pivotal document. It marks the acceptance by the President of the United States of the concept that U.S. troops would engage in offensive ground actions against Asian insurgents."[84] President Johnson arrived at that decision in haste, in secrecy, and in great privacy. There was no overwhelming bureaucratic pressure to send in troops. In fact, Maxwell Taylor, whose military theories would normally have predisposed him toward a direct American combat role, underwent a notable shift to the right after his arrival as ambassador in Saigon. He became a forceful advocate of will-breaking bombing of North Vietnam and opposed the introduction of United States ground combat troops. In

[84] *Ibid.*, IV.C.5, p. 59.

fact, Johnson's April 1 decision infuriated Taylor. As the Pentagon
Papers note:

> By the middle of April [1965], communications between Washing-
> ton and Saigon were becoming increasingly strained, as it began to
> dawn upon Ambassador Taylor that Washington was determined,
> with the President's sanction, to go far beyond the agreement to
> which Taylor had been a party at the beginning of April and that has
> been formalized in NSAM 328. From April 8 onward, Taylor had
> been bombarded with messages and instructions from Washington
> testifying to an eagerness to speed up the introduction to Vietnam
> of U.S. and Third Country ground forces and to employ them in a
> combat role, all far beyond anything that had been authorized in
> the April 2 NSC decisions. Ambassador Taylor's ill-concealed an-
> noyance at these mounting pressures and progressively more radical
> proposals changed to outright anger and open protest when, on
> April 18, he received another instruction, allegedly with the sanc-
> tion of "highest authority," proposing seven additional complicated
> measures having to do with combat force deployment and employ-
> ment, on the justification that "something new must be added in
> the South to achieve victory."[85]

On March 29, terrorists, allegedly Viet Cong, exploded a bomb outside the United States Embassy in Saigon killing and wounding many
Americans and Vietnamese. Admiral Sharp immediately urged "an out-
of-turn spectacular bombing attack upon a significant target in the DRV
outside of the framework of Rolling Thunder." Then comes the sentence: "At this point, the President preferred to maneuver quietly to help
the nation get used to living with the Vietnam crisis." And a few para-
graphs beyond:

> But the President was being less than candid. The proposals that
> were at that moment being promulgated, and on which he reached
> significant decisions the following day, did involve far-reaching
> strategy change: acceptance of the concept of U.S. troops engaged
> in offensive ground operations against Asian insurgents. That issue
> greatly overshadowed all other Vietnam questions then being re-
> considered.[86]

By the end of March, Rolling Thunder had almost gotten out of
control. Sustained Rolling Thunder bombing had just begun on March
19. On April 4, according to the North Vietnamese, American planes
bombed a major dam near Thanh Hoa, an act obviously outside the
carefully modulated framework of Rolling Thunder. Bombing a dam was

85 *Ibid.*, IV.C.3, p. 99.
86 *Ibid.*, pp. 84–85.

designed to "break the will" of the enemy, not for "interdiction" of enemy supply lines (thereafter the official McNamaraesque justification for the bombing). Pressure was already mounting from CINCPAC, the Joint Chiefs of Staff, and other military sources to bomb North Vietnamese airfields, particularly Phuc Yen near Hanoi. If the airfields were bombed, then North Vietnamese Migs would have to use Chinese bases, which would then provide excellent grounds for hot pursuit. McNaughton's memo of March 24 laid out the escalatory ladder quite clearly, undoubtedly impressing Johnson with how fast escalation could lead to a great power confrontation.

Like the shooting down of the first American plane over Laos on June 6, 1964, like Tonkin, like Bien Hoa, like Pleiku, the bomb blast at the United States Embassy in Pavlovian fashion got CINCPAC screaming for massive reprisals. It made little difference whether it was the Viet Cong who planted the bomb or some other anti-American group or, as is quite likely, South Vietnamese government agents who had learned that Viet Cong outrages elicited the desired American response. The simple fact is that Rolling Thunder was moving fast up the escalatory ladder and was just looking for excuses to move faster.

President Johnson's decision to commit American troops to offensive action in South Vietnam came out of the blue. It had not even been recommended by Army Chief of Staff Harold Johnson in early March, who merely proposed that an American division replace ARVN "security missions" so that the latter could be freed to fight the Viet Cong.[87] The Navy and the Air Force were against it. Taylor in Saigon was against it. One of the most famous oppositions to the sending of ground troops was from CIA director John McCone, whose memo is extensively quoted in the Pentagon Papers and by Johnson in his memoirs (obviously because it was already public knowledge). McCone declared that he could only agree with President Johnson's decision "if our air strikes against the North are sufficiently heavy and damaging really to hurt the North Vietnamese."[88] McCone soon thereafter quit (or was ousted) and was replaced by a Navy technician, Admiral William Raborn, whose stance seemed less extreme. On April 1, McGeorge Bundy prepared a memo advocating a modest bombing campaign with the removal of combat restrictions on the Marines, which Johnson used as the basis for his decision the following day.

What emerges from the material is what other writers on the war have long suspected: the key decisions were made in presidential secrecy and privacy. Lyndon Johnson moved fast on April 1–2 to make a germinal policy decision which would lead to a massive ground war. NSAM 328

[87] *Ibid.*, IV.C.5, p. 66.
[88] *Ibid.*, IV.C.4, pp. 90–93.

was like NSAM 273 in that both had germinal policy decisions thrust into them in a sudden almost couplike fashion.

But like NSAM 288, NSAM 328 was also designed to slow down the escalatory tempo. On April 20, a Honolulu conference was held, and as the Pentagon Papers report:

> . . . it seems apparent that Honolulu marked the relative down-grading of pressures against the North. . . . attention had shifted from the air war to the subject of U.S. combat force deployments. . . . interdiction was now a major objective of the [air] strikes.[89]

In his suddenly announced Baltimore speech of April 7, Johnson opened a negotiating track, coupled with offers of postwar aid to North Vietnam. In May came the first five-day bombing halt.

ONE-MAN PRESIDENTIAL DECISION MAKING

The notion of Stalin-like, one-man decision making is both baffling and repugnant to Americans who are professionally or academically involved with politics. Dictators, of course, are one-man decision makers, but an American President consults, weighs options, and makes his decision. Even if the final decision is arbitrary or accidental or personal, still the bureaucratically prepared options make certain that it is never quixotic. But where were the range of options on April 1? The memo prepared by McGeorge Bundy hardly passes the test of an option. It is generally known that Johnson's decision not to seek re-election, tacked on to the end of his March 31, 1968, bombing halt speech, was sudden and unexpected and very personal. That 1968 decision was the crucial political act which convinced the North Vietnamese that Johnson's bombing halt was serious (as I know from what they said to me in Hanoi a few hours after the speech). But the Pentagon Papers now indicate the same for the April 1, 1965, decision.

Beyond being baffling and repugnant, the notion of one-man decision making is frightening, for people know that the President can, at any time, press the nuclear trigger. Films have been made and hundreds of scenarios written about madmen pressing that trigger. For a while, it was assumed that if the Chinese got nuclear bombs, an insane Mao would just blow up the entire world. What seemed reassuring in the American case was the consultative character of the presidential role. But from the perspective of the early 1970s, when the notion of presidential dictatorship is being openly discussed, it is no longer so difficult to conceive of a one-man presidential decision maker deciding the fate of millions in the

[89] *Ibid.*, IV.C.3, p. 101.

lonely privacy of his own mind and feelings. There are some simple political facts that explain the phenomenon of one-man presidential decision making.

Every politician is above all else concerned with maintaining his power, his ability to get others to work for the achievement of his goals and to mobilize resources to that end. Lesser politicians may covet influence or wealth in addition to power. But at the presidential level, power and power alone counts. The goals of the Presidency are not fortuitous or responses to particular urgencies. There is a tradition of presidential policy which each President assumes and carries on to some extent. During the four years in office, his main obsession is his own power. But the only way he can assert that power is by asserting the presidential policies he has inherited. If he does not assert presidential power, he runs the risk of the domino effects·of runaway bureaucracies, producing a jungle of uncontrollable interbureaucratic conflict. Presidents are predisposed by character toward huge appetites for power, else they wouldn't be Presidents. But the exercise of their power is invariably directed, under normal circumstances, against their bureaucracies. The only real test of a President's power is whether he can tame the tigers of his bureaucracies, particularly the military. National leaders have often engaged in foreign adventures as a way out of internal conflict (Napoleon, for example). To see the Vietnam adventure as a way out of bitter conflict in Washington is part of the truth. A President cannot assert his power by becoming the instrument of his bureaucracies because he has to choose which one. Siding with one will always provoke the fury of the others. He can try to impose his will, as Kennedy tried to do, resulting in defeat (as evident from McNamara's fate).

The most effective way for a President to exercise or restore his power is by asserting policies that have been sanctioned by previous decisions or precedents. Deciding to send ground combat troops to South Vietnam was a decision guaranteed to have virtually no popular support, and was kept secret until June. But ever since Truman, every President had used the mechanism of sending in troops, with or without war, to assert presidential control over a dangerous developing situation. Johnson mentions in his memoirs that he consulted with Eisenhower on troops in mid-February 1965 and Eisenhower indicated "merit in the idea suggested by General Wheeler of putting an American division into Vietnam just south of the demilitarized zone."[90]

When a President invokes a previous moribund policy, it often mobilizes lesser bureaucracies to his side, who see in the new policy a chance for a return to glory. In the spring of 1965, the Army was the least of the

---

[90] Lyndon B. Johnson, *The Vantage Point*, p. 131.

three services. Since what counted in interservice rivalry was sophisticated hardware, the Navy and the Air Force had a virtual monopoly, hopelessly eclipsing the Army. Vietnam gave the Army a chance to show that it would be able to do the kind of effective counterinsurgency everyone was talking about. That swarms of helicopter gunships, massive search and destroy operations, offensive sweeps against the Viet Cong could bring victory was a not completely improbable idea in the spring of 1965. If the Viet Cong, supported by North Vietnamese regulars, were to move to a higher level of operations, they would have to fight in main force units, thereby making themselves vulnerable to air power. And what better way of delivering air power than through helicopters, the Army version of air power (all three services were preoccupied with air power). Johnson later had General William Westmoreland honored as the hero of the Vietnam war, despite the stench of barbarism that his campaigns spread about. Johnson thereby thanked Westmoreland for having come to his aid in the spring of 1965 for a cause far more glorious than just killing Viet Cong—avoiding World War III. Westmoreland became Johnson's instrument in Vietnam. What McNamara tried to do in March 1964, make the war Washington's not Honolulu's special preserve, now became a reality based on a personal tie between Johnson and Westmoreland as well as direct MAC/V-Washington chain of command links. Taylor was ousted in July 1965 and replaced by the old anti-Diemist Henry Cabot Lodge and, eventually, in the spring of 1967, by Ellsworth Bunker, an old Johnson troubleshooter (for example, in the Dominican Republic).

For all their service to Johnson, it is unlikely that any of the Army generals (Wheeler, Harold Johnson, Westmoreland) played a major role in persuading him to commit troops. Nor did McGeorge Bundy have much to do with it. Johnson's most probable confidant on the April 1 decision was Dean Rusk. Rusk remains an enigmatic figure for both the Kennedy and the Johnson administrations. His known hard line on China (expressed during his service to Truman) most likely played a role in his original nomination as Secretary of State (Kennedy would be his own foreign minister on everything but East Asia, where he had to make concessions to the right). But Rusk's general thinking on foreign policy under Johnson is known. He was convinced that China was the greatest threat to America's national security. He also believed in collaboration between Moscow and Washington to settle the affairs of the world, along the lines of the Laos accords. He consulted frequently with Dobrynin. Rusk had served in the China-Burma-India theater during World War II and was militarily inclined, like most Southerners. He was not a service partisan, like Goldwater, for example, and certainly was open to Army arguments that it might be able to do the job. What makes it likely that Rusk was Johnson's main confidant on the decision is the April 7 Baltimore speech in which Johnson invoked the negotiating track and proposed a vast new foreign aid program for all of Indochina including North Vietnam. That speech marked Johnson's real entry onto the stage of foreign affairs. During the 1964 campaign he concentrated mainly on domestic issues, pushing for his Great Society programs. The Baltimore speech was in the finest tradition of the containment current. The assumption was that Moscow could or should put pressure on Hanoi to accept American terms, a line espoused by Rusk. The carrot held out a little over a month later was the bombing halt, and the corollary of that was an intensive ground effort to secure South Vietnam.

Even if we are left with the conclusion that it was primarily Rusk who advised Johnson in his lonely decision, as such decisions are customarily described, it is hard to argue that Rusk represented any particular bureaucratic faction. He was isolated and disliked in the State Department. As president of the Rockefeller Foundation, he certainly consorted with the corporate establishment, and there can be little doubt that carried ideological if not bureaucratic or interest group weight. Ideologically (as well as in background) he had much in common with Lyndon Johnson, and the very fact that he had no troops made him an ideal confidant. But then we are still left with the phenomenon of one man making a momentous decision affecting a large part of the world and its history.

Kings, emperors, and popes have been with civilized mankind for a long time, but as modernization, so to speak, has progressed, it had been assumed that this kind of governance would give way to more impersonal, more systematized forms. After World War II, it was believed that totalitarian dictatorship was a communist phenomenon and one-man rule (as in Paraguay) a manifestation of more primitive states. Since Vietnam, Americans are beginning to wonder whether one-man rule may not be arising in America. I can offer some theoretical explanations of why this is the case. During rapid change or perpetual crises, power always flows toward the top. Under conditions of routinization, power tends to settle down in the middle, where skeins of interest are most powerful. Power has generally shifted upward in America since the end of World War II. But there has been a bifurcation between foreign and domestic political spheres. Until Nixon's second term, conditions of routinization generally prevailed on the domestic front, so that interest group power conditions still generally prevailed. But in the foreign sphere, the situation was much different. American foreign policy has actually been national security policy, as the *U.S. News & World Report* candidly indicated in its review of the line-up in the second Nixon Administration. That has meant extreme crisis abroad (war) and intense intrabureaucracy conflicts within the Washington power structure. Thus, the military rationale for one commander-in-chief has been extended to cover the nature of the Presidency as a whole. Power not only has flowed to the top, but has flowed into one and only one position—the Presidency.

A President can lose his power in two ways. He can become an instrument of one of his powerful interest groups and degenerate into the dummy public relations president of the corporation. Or he can fly off into the ideological stratosphere far beyond where the thoughts and sentiments of his broad constituents are, in which case he turns into an adventurer. The middle course, which guarantees him most power, is an ideological consistency above and beyond that of his bureaucracies but close enough to that of his constituents for the bureaucracies to know it. Napoleon and Hitler were adventurers who pushed certain ideological tendencies to extremes and, during their successful periods, managed to carry their quarreling bureaucracies with them. Kennedy and his Russian counterpart Khrushchev were both adventurers who went too far. Johnson, with his parliamentary experience, was more cautious. But in those last days of March 1965, he sensed that his ideological consistency (or image, as Americans like to say) was being ripped to shreds.

Johnson was elected as a peace President who vowed to lead America onto the paths of a Great Society. For him to follow the Goldwaterite path of the Air Force and the Navy into a war with China would destroy his power. In fact, Vietnam *did* destroy his power, because he could not be the war President abroad and the Great Society President at home. But in late March 1965, he thought he saw a way out. If the war could be won in the South, then he could achieve two political objectives at the same time. By giving the military and the right wing a war, he began to run with their ideological football. But by restricting the war essentially to South Vietnam, he could preserve the general aura of peace with the expectation that once the war was over (or won or whatever else), people would rapidly forget it.

JOHNSON OPTS BUREAUCRATICALLY FOR THE GROUND WAR

The key lay in the policy machinery that he himself helped to build since NSAM 273. His first act as President was to move the country toward war, and on April 1, he made an *operational* choice of what kind of war it should be. If he had decided to end the war once and for all, the right-wing trinity would have risen up in violent opposition to him. Opting for the ground combat war disarmed his opposition long enough for the operations to take form and generate interests powerful enough to counterbalance the single-minded Navy–Air Force push toward war with China. He was able to make that operational choice because sending in troops was a well-sanctioned presidential policy option.

While the world saw America rushing into war, the perspective from within the bureaucracies was different. The April 1 decision (and its public announcement on June 8) actually slowed down that rush. Washington officials were astounded that people did not believe the incredibly restrained and temperate actions they were taking in the face of horrendous Communist provocations. The State Department even produced a White Paper to show a flood of men and matériel coming down the Ho Chi Minh Trail. The "information" presented in the White Paper was demolished early in the escalatory period, but when North Vietnamese army units did come down the trail in force, the argument became moot. The fact is that presidential actions were restrained, not so much in regard to Communist actions, which went on in their usual slow, steady, and long-term-oriented manner, but in regard to the intense pressure from military quarters for a massive and quick knockout blow against the enemy or enemies. Naturally, Washington could not tell the public that however aggressive the President's actions were, they were by far more moderate than those proposed by the service chiefs.

The Pentagon Papers divide the year from May 1, 1965, to May 1, 1966, into two phases: the first, until November 1965, marked by troop build-ups; the second from November 1965 until May 1, 1966, when large-scale ground combat began.[91] Naturally, some time was necessary before United States troops could begin large-scale combat. But it also happened to be a period, appearances to the contrary, of relatively restrained Rolling Thunder bombing. In early November, the Joint Chiefs of Staff again voiced their dissatisfaction with "the measured pace of the bombing program" and pressed for a "sharp intensification."[92] The military knew that a flurry of negotiational activity was going on through intermediaries of various nationalities. Whether some in the military consciously wished to sabotage those negotiations or were simply pressing for massive strikes before the specter of peace should erupt made no difference in terms of bureaucratic politics. Military pressure meant political pressure to continue the war and raise the level of American negotiational goals far above what the other side could accept. On December 15, 1965, Navy planes bombed the Uong Bi power plant in Haiphong, hitting for the first time one of the sanctuary targets that risked Chinese and/or Russian intervention. Coincidentally or not, mid-November was also when the first large-scale ground action between American and National Liberation Front forces took place, the battle of

91 DOD, *U.S.-Vietnam Relations*, IV.C.6.(a), p. 46.
92 *Ibid.*, IV.C.7.(a), p. 74.

the Ia Drang Valley. On December 24, the thirty-seven-day bombing halt began. But from the moment it ended on January 31, 1966, Rolling Thunder resumed with an escalating fury, reaching a climax on June 29, 1966, when American planes struck at POL (Petroleum-Oil-Lubricant) facilities in Haiphong, and Lyndon Johnson told his daughter in a small Catholic chapel that her daddy might have started World War III.

Restrained Rolling Thunder bombing (if one may so call it without gagging) during the period May–November 1965 was a consequence of the two-track policy approach that Johnson had opened up with his April 1 decision. The first track consisted of trying to clear and hold South Vietnam with United States troops; the second consisted of invoking the larger global relationship with Russia to try to get Moscow to put pressure on Hanoi to accede to American demands. This approach accepted the hawks' goals, but rejected their means for others that would be equally efficacious. Westmoreland was confident that he could clear and hold South Vietnam. Rusk was confident that he could get the Russians to put unbearable pressure on Hanoi to cease its aggression in the South.

The history of United States combat operations in South Vietnam is fairly well known, at least in terms of news coverage. Not only does it constitute one of the most inglorious, cruel, and stupid chapters in American military history, but it led to the demoralization of the United States Army and one of the most important changes in the American defense structure since World War II. The Army's failure in South Vietnam was, in the end, containment's failure, and played a major role in its demise as a key current in American foreign policy.

Much has been written and much still will be on why the United States Army failed in South Vietnam. The simplest explanation is that the Americans intruded into a revolutionary civil war that had been going on ever since 1945, if not before, that all their bombs, napalm, and dollars managed to kill and corrupt lots of people but, in the end, were not able to affect the nature of the real war. The Americans came in arrogantly confident that with superior know-how and superior fire power fueled with floods of dollars they could turn the situation in their favor. But one must realize that technological fetishism is an essential element of American society. America has no choice but to use technology to the hilt in its attempt to win the war.

Westmoreland himself eventually succumbed to technological fetishism. As it became apparent that American infantrymen would not or could not go deep into the jungles to tangle with the enemy, he devised a new tactic. Troops would be used to make contact with enemy main force units, then suddenly pulled back, and massive helicopter gunship strikes called in to wipe out the enemy. According to the laws of guerrilla warfare, the Viet Cong had to move toward some form of regular warfare if they wanted to win (and when they could not, North Vietnamese army troops, regulars rather than guerrillas, came in.) If they stood and fought, they would be decimated by helicopters and other forms of air power; if they did not, they would be pressed farther and farther back until they were pushed entirely out of South Vietnam. Pacification would then take care of the local Viet Cong. What failed so miserably and drastically was the helicopter, so much so that the United States Army has quietly abandoned its once vaunted helicopter-based battle tactics. For all the disparities in weaponry capabilities, the fighters of the National Liberation Front managed to shoot down thousands. In the latter years of the war, particularly after the great helicopter defeat of the Laos invasion of spring 1971, safer forms of air power were used, culminating in the use of milk-run B-52 missions to carpet bomb the enemy in rice paddies. What an ending for the mighty B-52, designed to give America supreme security with its capability to take out Russian cities and missile sites!

In 1965, it was hard for anyone to foresee the magnitude of the quagmire that United States troops would be drawn into. Most of the military, including some segments of the Army, had doubts about fighting a land war in South Vietnam, but there had been so much talk about new methods of fighting insurgencies that one could not rule out success. The ARVNs were losing battles because they were ineffective. Why should not fresh, munificently equipped, well-led American troops be able to prevail against the Viet Cong and North Vietnamese army who, after all, were Vietnamese like the ARVNs?

"NEGOTIATIONS" AND "DISCUSSIONS"

While American troops were pouring into South Vietnam, and Rusk and McNamara were desperately trying to entice Third Country forces there, Washington was actively pursuing the negotiation track. Although Johnson is far less than candid in his memoirs on most Vietnam matters, he spends some pages discussing his Baltimore speech, in which he proposed "unconditional discussions" to Hanoi. In fact, he goes to great trouble to show that as far back as June 1964 he was greatly interested in the Canadian diplomat Blair Seaborn's mission to Hanoi. From then on right to the end of the war early in 1973, one saw the curious spectacle of a small but steady stream of intermediaries going to Hanoi. Eventually Americans would go as well, some as antiwar activists, others as more conscious intermediaries (like the Ashmore-Baggs trip in March–April 1968, which Johnson mentions in his memoirs). In retrospect, it appears that all the Americans, including those of extreme anti-imperialist persuasion, served the cause of building a pipeline between the White House and the governing groups of North Vietnam. While some of the intermediaries thought that they were transmitting real signals which were then rejected, in fact, what counted was the process of pipeline building, not any specific act in and of itself. Rusk would periodically hold his hand to his ear waiting for a "signal" from Hanoi, but the first public signal only came on April 4, 1968, when North Vietnam agreed to enter into negotiations with Washington. At that time, Washington reluctantly accepted North Vietnam as an equal negotiating partner independent from all other powers. But in 1965, such an idea seemed ludicrous in Washington. It could "discuss" with Hanoi, but "negotiations," such as those at Geneva, could only come when the great powers, particularly Russia, were present. After all, North Vietnam was just a satellite of one or both of the big communist powers. The Hanoi Politburo was, of course, split between pro-Russian (Le Duan) and pro-Chinese (Truong Chinh) members, so that there was a dual chain of command, one leading to Moscow and the other to Peking. But the idea that Ho Chi Minh and his colleagues made their own decisions seemed laughable to the Washington national security bureaucrats. Even if they believed it, such thinking was not possible within the then given bureaucratic parameters. An official may think what he wishes privately, but bureaucratically he must think woodenly, lest he lose his power and influence.

The story of the missions of the intermediaries was the subject of the "missing" four volumes of the Pentagon Papers, but much of it was already known, even before the Papers were revealed. That Washington did more than quietly tolerate these missions and subsequent trips by Americans to Hanoi is indicated by the fact that a number of Americans who went there (like myself) had State Department permission and others who went without permission were scarcely even reprimanded. By contrast, when the journalist William Worthy went to China in the mid-1950s, he was subsequently indicted. A few feeble attempts were made by right-wingers (like Richard Ichord of the Un-American Activities Committee), but they petered out for the simple reason that part of the accommodation between the rollback rightists and the containment liberals was acceptance by the former of the negotiating track. If the White House had not wanted it, there would have been few intermediaries in Hanoi and even fewer Americans (except for prisoners of war).

In 1965, the track leading to Hanoi could involve "discussions," but the real negotiating track went from Washington to Moscow and from there, presumably, down to and back from Hanoi. So far as Peking was concerned, neither discussions nor negotiations were possible, from the

American or the Chinese side. Although in 1964, China still advocated a
reconvening of the Geneva Conference, from the first days of the American bombing of North Vietnam, it adopted a stance of extreme hostility
toward any talks on Vietnam. The reason for the opposition is readily
understandable: the Chinese were convinced that any conference on
Vietnam would be dominated by the two superpowers and would intensify the isolation of China. In his first press conference of January 27,
1969, Nixon expressed a new concept of "linkage" in the conduct of
American foreign policy—for example, offering the Russians arms or
trade agreements in return for "help" on Vietnam or the Middle East.
But that same "linkage" between Washington-Moscow relations and the
two major conflict areas was the basis of the Johnson-Rusk policy. If the
North Vietnamese had accepted Johnson's April 7, 1965, offer of "unconditional discussions," this would have indicated to Washington's
policy analysts that Hanoi was leaning in a pro-Soviet direction and,
therefore, was amenable to Russian leverage which could bring about a
settlement satisfactory to Washington.

THE RUSSIAN-AMERICAN
WEAPONRY RELATIONSHIP

Under the Johnson Administration, as under Kennedy's, the Washington-
Moscow relationship was the cornerstone of virtually all American foreign
policies. While Vietnam grabbed the headlines in February 1965, Johnson, Rusk, and McNamara hoped for a quick end to the war so that they
could get on with the larger business of arranging a peaceful and stable
world with Russian cooperation. In 1965, McNamara still believed that
the war would be over by the end of 1967. Then, except for the vexing
problem of China, the decks would be clear for implementing a policy
that would bring about the coexistence of a Pax Americana and a Pax
Sovietica in their respective camps.

The key to the Russian-American relationship, as McNamara saw it,
was a parity in strategic weaponry which would create an absolute deterrent on both sides. On the American side, capabilities had to be sufficient
to destroy the Soviet Union as a viable society and to take out its missile-
launching sites even after absorbing a Russian "first strike." That was
called an "assured destruction" capability. Naturally, no one in Washington could call upon the Russians to match that American capability
and so create a true "balance of terror." But the same net effect was
achieved by opposing any kind of "damage limitation" systems, namely,
antiballistic missiles (ABMs) and fallout shelter programs. That meant
that Russia could launch a surprise first strike against America and

inflict heavy damage, but not sufficient to prevent America from retaliating with such force that it would literally wipe out the entire Soviet Union, people, property, and nature. Since it has to be assumed that every society's primal goal is its own survival, the Russians would have no incentive, barring madness, to inflict a surprise attack against America.

Thus, if America and Russia maintained a stable weaponry relationship, then that would be a political indication that their respective leaderships would not make any qualitatively different or quantitatively threatening moves on the global scene. Both countries, of course, constantly did things that upset the other, but no move was as threatening as a change in the weaponry relationship, for the simple reason that strategic weaponry had implications for long-term behavior. If either side added a new weapon to its arsenal or enormously increased its existing capabilities, the other would interpret that as a signal of a more aggressive foreign policy in general over the succeeding years. The strategic weaponry relationship, for all its sophisticated technology, was ideological. It was an expression of fundamental foreign policy.

In 1965, McNamara had no cause to be worried about the strategic weaponry relationship with Russia. While America carried out a virtual crash program to deploy ICBMs (intercontinental ballistic missiles) upon Kennedy's coming into office, the Russians did not respond in kind, despite the fact that they had developed an ICBM capability earlier than the Americans. There was a modest increase in Russian ICBM deployments in 1964, but in 1965, the increase slowed down. Most important of all, the American missile program reached a plateau of sorts in 1965. America undoubtedly had a *de facto* first-strike "counterforce" capability in the early 1960s, that is, it could take out all of Russia's ICBM sites. But Russian deterrence was not based on their ability to destroy the United States as a viable society. Russian rockets were zeroed in on Western Europe and huge Russian armies were in a position to overrun the entire European continent. Thus, Russian deterrence rested on a capability to destroy Western Europe and Japan, and militarily to occupy much of the Eurasian land mass, even under conditions of nuclear holocaust. The Americans, of course, constantly reiterated that they would never be the first to strike. But whatever the technical realities of the weaponry relationship, in 1965, both America and Russia accepted the fact of mutual deterrence or the "balance of terror." And, except for Southeast Asia, there did not appear to be a third country region of conflict sufficiently serious to risk a confrontation between the two superpowers.

In 1966, however, the situation began to change, alarming the Americans. Every chart on Russian and American missile capabilities shows a steep acceleration in Russian ICBM deployments beginning in the sum-

THE RUSSIAN-AMERICAN ARMS RACE

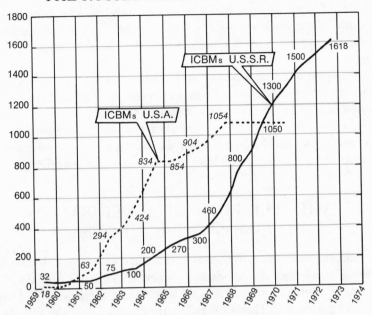

From *Le Monde*   (November 22, 1972)

mer of 1966. From the beginning of 1964 to mid-1966, Russian ICBMs rose from 200 to 270. But from mid-1966 to the beginning of 1969, they rose to about 1,000 and kept on rising. The American response, in action-reaction fashion, was a modest rise in both ICBMs and submarine-launched missiles, but they could not mount a new missile race and fight a war in Vietnam at the same time. The Americans came to believe that the Russians were installing an ABM system around Moscow. It was not farfetched to presume that the Russians could achieve ICBM parity with America and with a workable ABM system could threaten it with a true first-strike capability. That thought gave nightmares to McNamara and Johnson.

Anti-ballistic missiles were dangerous in another respect. To research, develop, and deploy an ABM system would require enormous budgetary outlays. Senator Symington once estimated the final cost of an ABM system at 400 billion dollars. For the Russians to start building an ABM meant that they had radically changed their budgetary policies since the days of Khrushchev. Khrushchev had fought hard to cut the defense budget and divert resources into agriculture and consumer goods industries. He was convinced that Russian foreign policy objectives could best be met by economic competition with America. Until mid-1966, there was no indication, publicly anyway, that the Russians were deviating from that policy line. But in 1966, the Russian moves on ICBM and ABM implied that the "steel-eaters" had won out again in the resource allocation debates in the Kremlin. If America had to respond with an ABM of its own, havoc would be wreaked with Lyndon Johnson's own Great Society program, not to mention the immense burden for the taxpayer to carry Vietnam, ABM, the Great Society, and much else.

When Johnson met Kosygin at Glassboro in late June 1967, their main subject of conversation was not Vietnam but the missile race. Johnson tells in his memoirs how he raised that subject, particularly the ABM, again and again, but Kosygin always brought the discussion back to Vietnam and the Middle East or demanded that both offensive and defensive strategic weapons be discussed.[93] Glassboro was a failure.

WHY THE RUSSIANS ACCELERATED THE MISSILE RACE IN 1966

Why did the Russians in 1966 make what they knew would be the most alarming move they could vis-à-vis America? Did Moscow decide to pressure Washington on Vietnam by accelerating the arms race? Despite Kosygin's presence in Hanoi on February 7, 1965, when the first American bombs fell on North Vietnam, Russian interest in Indochina could hardly be called massive. Donald Zagoria has written that "in 1964 Khrushchev sought to resolve the dilemma by disengaging the Soviet Union from Indochina altogether."[94] The Russians have never regarded Southeast Asia as a vital national security interest comparable to the Middle East or Europe. In Laos, confrontation with the Americans eventually led to what they wanted most of all: a working bipolar relationship with the United States. Nothing would have pleased Moscow more than to see a Vietnam version of the 1962 Geneva conference on Laos. But deploying vast numbers of new ICBMs was designed to wreck a relationship which peace in Vietnam should have built up.

There is a clue to the Russian decision (which the Americans knew or suspected) in an event in July 1966. At a meeting of Warsaw Pact nations in Bucharest that month, the Russians reissued a call for an all-European conference on security and cooperation. The proposal had a history going back to 1954, but it had lain dormant for some time. From July 1966 on, the Russians continued pressing for the idea until, in late 1972, such a conference actually began in Helsinki. In the early 1970s, it was crystal clear why the Russians wanted the conference. With a quarter of their armed forces concentrated on the Chinese border, they had to stabilize the European military situation—peace in Europe would

[93] Johnson, Vantage Point, pp. 483–85.
[94] Donald S. Zagoria, Vietnam Triangle: Moscow, Peking, Hanoi, p. 28.

free their hands for dealing with China. By July 1966, the rupture between China and Russia was final—the failure of "joint action" in late March finally cut the last link between the two erstwhile allies. Mao's dramatic return to the political scene in July must finally have convinced the Russians that their archenemy was firmly in power. The Russians are accustomed to making long-range decisions—*perspektivnoe planirovanie*, perspective planning, as they call it. It is possible that at that time, in the wake of Brezhnev's rise to number one position at the March Twenty-third Party Congress, the Russians may have made a "perspective" decision that China along with America would have to be considered a mortal enemy.

In that case, all Russian military planning would be turned upside down. Until then, it had been assumed that China, a fraternal ally, would provide the conventional capabilities for fighting in Asia, as Russia itself was doing for Europe. Russian troops, therefore, were concentrated entirely in the West, where they constituted a major deterrent force against America and NATO. But if substantial forces were moved to the eastern frontier, then Russia's deterrent capability vis-à-vis America would be gravely weakened unless compensated for. And there was only one means of doing this: to develop a long-range missile capability that could match that of the Americans.

It has been reported that the Joint Chiefs of Staff accepted the reality of the Sino-Soviet dispute only when Chinese and Russian forces clashed on the Ussuri early in 1969. But the Russian missile build-up was an indisputable reality since mid-1966. In the military's conservative doctrinal terms ("Sino-Soviet bloc"), that build-up could only mean that the communists were threatening America at a time of deepening involvement in Vietnam. But if there was indeed a Sino-Soviet rupture, then the uncontested desirability of striking at China might no longer be so uncontested. If America got itself embroiled in a full-scale war in Asia, the Russians could reap its benefits everywhere else in the world.

Military doctrine, like foreign policy currents or bureaucratic modes of thought, evolves very slowly. By the early 1970s, major changes had taken place in American military doctrine. Not only was the Sino-Soviet split recognized, but war between the two gigantic Eurasian powers was accepted as a real ("fifty-fifty") possibility. Russia was seen as stronger than China, so that, naturally, the notion of some Sino-American line-up, be it ever so tacit, was possible. In 1966, however, military doctrine was still where it had been since 1950, with the existence of the Sino-Soviet bloc as America's principal enemy. While the military conservatives mistrusted much of what the CIA liberal analysts were spreading regarding the Sino-Soviet conflict, the facts eventually prevailed. While it is always hard to date the beginnings of a change in mode of thinking, it is reasonable to presume that just when the United States Navy and Air Force were eagerly pressing forward with their air war in East Asia, the doctrinal bases of that war were starting to crumble.

CHINA AND AMERICA ON A COLLISION COURSE

For the White House, which advanced its two-track approach (troops and negotiations) and counted on "linkage" bringing favorable results, the Russian missile build-up and the Sino-Soviet split created great problems. If linkage could not be invoked, then it made no sense to get deeper embroiled in South Vietnam with troops. Therefore, to achieve agreed on goals, no alternative would remain but to give a full red light to the air war and let it go where it wanted to, which happened to be China.

In early 1973, Joseph Alsop, freshly back from China, said what had been rumored and reported before: "President Kennedy, who took an exceedingly dark view of the Chinese nuclear program, had ordered exploration of the idea of destroying that program in some sort of collaboration with the Soviets."[95] As a Kennedy confidant and friend of the Pentagon generals, Alsop knew about and supported the idea at the time. It takes only the slightest effort to remember the fulminations about "Chinese expansionism" that administration spokesmen used to justify the United States effort in Vietnam. McNamara labeled Lin Piao's "Long Live the Victory of People's War" as China's *Mein Kampf*. McNamara's signals on China were mixed, but the anti-China drumbeat from the Johnson Administration was unmistakable.

If Washington's negotiating track in 1965 led through Moscow, and if Washington was convinced that China was the ultimate source of aggression in Indochina (both through support of the insurgencies and by developing an uncontrolled nuclear capability), then why not propose to Moscow a double-barreled solution: 1) a surgical B-52 strike at China's nuclear sites and plants; and 2) a compromise Vietnam settlement based on Johnson's April 7 proposals? The Russians could feign outrage and even make gestures to aid the Chinese, but they undoubtedly would hope that with China's nuclear program destroyed, Mao would be ousted and a regime more willing to accept its proper role in the socialist camp come to power. Russia and America could work together throughout Southeast Asia to secure stability and development with much greater promise of success than in the Middle East, where both had complex commitments.

In the spring of 1966, China and America seemed to be on a collision course. The air war against North Vietnam resumed with a fury that by

95 Joseph Alsop, *New York Times Magazine*, March 11, 1973, p. 31.

April was creeping closer and closer to the Chinese borders. On April 12, B-52 bombers were sent over North Vietnam to bomb the Mu Ghia Pass. Some political personages outside the bureaucracies, like Senator Mansfield, were well aware of what the use of B-52s meant. The Strategic Air Command was designed for strategic not tactical bombing and, with its nuclear bomb delivery capabilities, was primarily designed to strike at Russian and Chinese strategic targets. On April 27, James Reston wrote in the *New York Times* that "the official policy of the United States is that our bombers are now free to attack the base of any planes that intercept our fliers in North Vietnam, even if those bases are inside Communist China." On May 8, American planes bombed a vital rail bridge linking Vietnam with China. On the following day, all four rail links with Hanoi were cut. What Reston reported was, in fact, a policy of no sanctuary in China, a reversal from the policy during the Korean War. During the entire course of the air war, there were veiled references in the press about the sensitivity of attacking airfields in North Vietnam. The "Lavelle affair" actually began with an "unauthorized" attack against Quang Lan airfield on November 7, 1971. But earlier, the most sensitive issue was that of Phuc Yen military airfield near Hanoi. The McNaughton scenario of late March 1965 listed an attack against Phuc Yen airfield as one of the red flash points that could lead to confrontation with China (or Russia). The airfield was finally bombed on October 25, 1967 (another extremely dangerous confrontational period after that of the spring of 1966), but not before then. While no hard and fast information is available, there are grounds for believing that according to agreements between China and North Vietnam, North Vietnamese Migs were allowed to use Chinese air bases. The kind of "hot pursuit" authorized in April 1966, according to Reston, could only have meant pursuit of Migs into Chinese territory.[96]

While it is understandable that from a "military" viewpoint every target had its attractions, hitting the airfields had a particular purpose. Since both China and North Vietnam were still deficient in SAM capabilities, the Migs posed the main threat to high-flying B-52s. If all the airfields well north of the China-Vietnam border could be taken out and the LOCs (lines of communication) bombed deep into China (so that rail shipments of war matériel would be impeded), with Haiphong port destroyed, all of North Vietnam would be exposed to B-52 saturation bombing at little risk to the Americans. The recommendations from the

[96] A *New York Times* editorial (March 28, 1967) evidently believed just that: "Destruction of those [air]fields would very likely lead Communist China to make its airfields available to the North Vietnamese air force. The result would be to restore ground sanctuary or, if American planes were then to attack Chinese bases, virtually to assure an air war—if not a ground war—with Communist China." *See also* George Ball's memo of January 1966 in the Pentagon Papers (DOD, *U.S.-Vietnam Relations*, IV.C.7.(a).48).

military for bombing the airfields naturally were couched in strictly military terms so that nobody could suspect them of smuggling rollback notions into the policy-making process. But successful Strategic Air Command bombing of North Vietnam raised the possibility that it could be repeated all the way to Peking.

Much of the discussion in the Pentagon Papers on this period deals with the evolution of the decision to bomb the POL sites in Haiphong. When they were bombed, Johnson feared that he might have set the spark launching World War III. But the Navy and Air Force pressed hard for the bombing not only of Haiphong but of the airfields and the supply lines going to the Chinese border. On June 29, 1966, Haiphong was bombed, but the airfields were not. CINCPAC Admiral Sharp demanded heatedly that Phuc Yen and all other airfields be bombed, but "the attack on North Vietnam's POL system was the last major escalation of the air war recommended by Secretary McNamara."[97] As McNamara became "disenchanted" with the air war, Sharp's enthusiasm for it rose higher and higher. What can easily be deduced is that an attack on Haiphong essentially risked a confrontation with Russia, whereas attacks on the airfields and rail lines risked a confrontation with China. Except for military matériel, Russian oil and other economic supplies came in by ship through Haiphong. Chinese matériel came in by rail and road directly across the border. In May 1972, Nixon was careful to bomb both Haiphong and the rail lines, thereby showing Moscow and Peking that he was treating them equally. In June 1966, Washington decided to bomb Haiphong but not to bomb the airfields.

Whether bombing Haiphong risked a Cuban-type Russian-American confrontation is hard to say (but unlikely), but allowing the pattern of the air war of that spring to continue would surely soon have led to a spill-over across the China border. Congress was aware of the danger, and both the House and the Senate held hearings on China. Fulbright warned that "China and America may be heading toward war with each other and it is essential that we do all that can be done to prevent that calamity."[98] Dean Rusk hardly reassured the public in mid-April 1966 when he told the House, "There are, of course, risks of war with China."[99] American public opinion took the darkest view of China, the fruit of two decades of propaganda, and a safe, costless strike against it would hardly be opposed. If one adds to all those pressures the one for doing away with China's nuclear capabilities, then the surprise is that it did not happen.

[97] DOD, U.S.-Vietnam Relations, IV.C.7.(a), p. 138.
[98] See Franz Schurmann and Orville Schell, eds., The China Reader, vol. 3, frontispiece.
[99] Ibid., p. 513.

NEW WASHINGTON SIGNALS TO
CHINA—MAY 1966

Not only did the air war not spill over into China, but new signals began to emanate from Washington, feebly at first, but with an unmistakable message: an assurance to the Chinese that America did not seek war with them. The most prominent of these signals was a speech McNamara gave in Montreal on May 18, 1966:

> There is nothing to be gained from our seeking an ideological rapprochement [with China]; but breaching the isolation of great nations like Red China, even when that isolation is largely of its own making, reduces the danger of potentially catastrophic misunderstandings and increases the incentive on both sides to resolve disputes by reason rather than by force.[100]

McNamara reiterated the same theme in an interview with a Japanese journalist on July 15, 1966, stressing the need to avoid "a serious miscalculation with China."[101] Canada was a favorite place for sending signals to China (for the same reason as San Francisco—trade), and the choice of Montreal for McNamara's speech is not coincidental in the play acting world of global diplomacy.

Although rhetoric would seem to be cheap, the broken momentum of the air war and the worried statements of the Russians indicate that something major had transpired in Washington and/or between Washington and Peking. In early September, the Russian press published reports of a Sino-American "get-together" in their Warsaw talks, provoking an unprecedented denial by the Chinese ambassador to Poland.[102] The Russians later claimed that the Chinese and the Americans had made some sort of deal over Vietnam. As one anti-Chinese publication put it in early 1967:

> Chinese and American leaders have exchanged a series of public declarations about the "undesirability" of a direct armed clash between the two countries over Vietnam. . . . Deepening their antisovietism, rejecting proposals for joint action, and carrying out splitting and deviationist policies within the socialist camp, the Mao Tse-tung group is in fact aiding American imperialism to carry out its escalation of the war in Southeast Asia.[103]

From late 1966, one would see the curious spectacle of the Chinese attacking Russian-American collusion, while the Russians spoke darkly

---

[100] U.S., Department of State, *State Department Bulletin*, May 18, 1966.
[101] U.S., Department of State, *State Department Bulletin*, August 29, 1966.
[102] *New York Times*, September 8, 1966.
[103] *K sobytiiam v Kitae* (*On the Events in China*) (Moscow: June 1967), p. 62.

of shady deals between the Chinese and the Americans aimed at Russia. Each accused the other of selling out the Vietnamese.

Readers need hardly be reminded that the months April through July 1966 were pivotal for all three great powers. The struggle over the air war (the POL debate) reached a decisive point within the Washington power structure late in June. The Russians at that time began to implement their fateful decision to match the American ICBM capability. And in China, the Cultural Revolution erupted. This same period also was pivotal for Vietnam. Beginning in March, popular agitation erupted against the Thieu-Ky regime which, by May, had reached such proportions that Danang and Hué had fallen out of Saigon's control and had to be reconquered by Ky's troops. There obviously was intense popular antagonism against the Thieu-Ky regime. However, the key factor in the repression of the uprising was not Ky's power, but an American decision to support his effort to put it down. Until May 15, Ky's troops, which had been transported to Danang in American helicopters, had been confined to the United States base there, while the city itself was in rebel hands. But on May 15, Ky got the go-ahead signal from the Americans, took Danang and shortly afterward rebel-held Hué as well. Since that signal came out of Washington, one can presume some link to the larger skein of global politics.

CHINA IN MID-1966

On May 9, the Chinese exploded a 200-kiloton thermonuclear device, by far the biggest until then. It was their third detonation; the first was on October 14, 1964, and the second on May 14, 1965. There are good grounds for believing that the Chinese have always tried to detonate their nuclear explosions at politically important periods—after all, if the bomb is set to go, why not wait for a suitable moment to transmit a political message? The second detonation occurred during the May 13–18, 1965, five-day bombing pause which had been announced on May 11. The May 9 explosion occurred the same day that the first "demons and monsters" article appeared in the *People's Daily*,[104] launching the first stage in the Cultural Revolution, which culminated, publicly, with the ouster of P'eng Chen, Peking Party First Secretary, at the beginning of June. At that time, Premier Chou En-lai issued a four-point statement on China's policy toward America.[105] In essence, the statement said: China wants to avoid a war with America over Vietnam; China will maintain its aid and support commitments to North Vietnam

[104] See Schurmann and Schell, eds., *China Reader*, vol. 3, pp. 615–18.
[105] The statement had originally been made on April 10 in an interview with a correspondent of the Pakistani newspaper *Dawn*, but was rereleased by the Chinese on May 9 (*New York Times*, May 10, 1966).

and the National Liberation Front; if America attacks China on the ground or with nuclear weapons, it will be sucked into an endless war; if America decides to attack China just with air and naval weapons, the Chinese will counterattack on the ground ("If you can come from the sky, why can't we fight back on the ground?").[106] On May 12, American planes shot down a Chinese fighter over Chinese territory, which made the prospect of an American air war against China just a hair's breadth away from reality. The obvious question is, Why should Mao Tse-tung have plunged China into a political convulsion just as the flames of war were burning fiercer and fiercer along its southern border?

Obviously, the great issues of the Cultural Revolution had been fermenting for a long time. Unlike the Soviet Communist party, which came straight out of the Bolshevik tradition, the Chinese Communist party, from 1927 on, had a rural and an urban wing which diverged more often than they converged. Mao was the leader of the Yenan tradition and Liu Shao-ch'i, as head of the party underground apparatus, led and symbolized the other tradition. Under the seemingly harmonious façade of the Chinese leadership, there had been intense conflicts. But in May 1966, Mao decided to let the conflict explode openly. It had started in a mild and moderate way (discussions on incorrect literary products) and gained momentum in April, but until the "demons and monsters" articles appeared, there was no hint of the explosiveness the conflict would assume. An overriding sense of urgency impelled Mao to launch the decisive struggle. Part of that urgency may have come from a sense of impending death ("I shall soon see God, he told Edgar Snow in January 1965). But another part, if not most, came from the specter of China on the verge of being involved in another Korean War, fighting an enemy that Mao was convinced was fated to withdraw eventually from Asia. Mao then and now considers America a "reactionary" power, like Chiang Kai-shek's China. As he said in his paper tiger theses, reactionaries are very dangerous in the short term, but in the long term (not too long, in fact), they are doomed to decline. The revisionist Soviet Union always was a more lasting and dangerous enemy. Therefore, why should China exhaust itself in a meaningless struggle with America? If the Americans made China's renunciation of support to the Vietnamese a condition for not attacking, China would refuse. But short of that, a repetition of the Korean War would be worthless and even dangerous for China. For at the end of such a war, socialism might still be in power in China but under an authoritarian Soviet-style regime, which Mao was convinced would last little longer than the Ch'in Dynasty of two thousand years before.

But if Mao and other Chinese leaders did not want war with America,

---

[106] Schurmann and Schell, eds., *China Reader*, vol. 3, pp. 521–22.

America was fast thrusting war upon China. In May 1965, then Chief of Staff Lo Jui-ch'ing had suggested a strategy of "active defense" vis-à-vis Vietnam, which implied that China might as well intervene at the moment most favorable to it since a confrontation with the Americans was inevitable anyway. But Lo Jui-ch'ing was purged in November, the month the seeds of the Cultural Revolution began to sprout. It is doubtful that even the "capitalist-roaders" favored taking such a risk. The question in April–May 1966, however, was no longer one of active defense but of pure defense: What should China do if United States planes start bombing Chinese targets? Chou En-lai's statement indicated that the Chinese would have no alternative but, sooner or later, to move on the ground, which would have meant a move not toward South Vietnam but into Laos and especially Thailand. We know from the Pentagon Papers that it was established politico-military doctrine that if Chinese forces should enter Southeast Asia en masse, America would respond with (tactical) nuclear weapons, as it was prepared to do in Europe against Russian ground forces. Naturally, the Chinese would not lightly send troops pouring into Thailand, nor would the Americans lightly take recourse to nuclear weapons. But the air war was an opening wedge to just such a conflict. In that November 1964 sketching out of A, B, and C options, the Working Group recognized clearly that "the course of military events vis-à-vis Communist China *might* give us a defensible case to destroy the Chinese Communist nuclear production capability."[107] It was conceivable that the Chinese might practice restraint if just a few of their airfields were hit, but what could they do but accept the challenge of full-scale war if United States planes decided to destroy China's nuclear facilities?

McNamara's May 18 Montreal speech turned out to be the beginning of a small rivulet of new policy thinking about China which was publicly voiced by Johnson in a press conference on September 8, 1966.[108] Johnson said that he was encouraged by China's apparent shift toward the view that it did not face a military confrontation with the United States. Shortly before, the press reported that Washington was seriously considering a change of tactics on the question of admitting Peking to the United Nations.[109] In his State of the Union message in January 1967, Johnson took the most conciliatory tone toward the People's Republic of China that any President had yet dared to take. Dean Rusk remained clearly tougher and harder toward China than Johnson. He

---

[107] DOD, *U.S.-Vietnam Relations*, IV.C.2.(c), p. 28.
[108] *New York Times*, September 9, 1966. In his "nervous nellies" speech of May 17, 1966, Johnson specifically noted that Ambassador John Gronouski was returning with news from Warsaw where, obviously, he had been talking with the Chinese (*New York Times*, May 18, 1966).
[109] *Christian Science Monitor*, August 25, 1966.

was not a rollbacker, despite some private inclinations in that direction, but he acted as a kind of middleman with the military whom he greatly admired, so that while his policy approach was still essentially containment, he would have shown little hesitation to accepting a policy that led to war with China. Nonetheless, something had changed and some new decision or non-decision had been made.

The May 9 blast was massive—200 kilotons. The next one, on October 27, was more ominous—a 20-kiloton bomb fired from a 400-mile-range missile.[110] Thus, by October 27, it was known that the Chinese had an operational nuclear delivery capability. Obviously, American intelligence must have known that the Chinese were working on it, and in view of their amazing success with the over-all nuclear program, it was the better part of wisdom to bet that they would succeed. In their successive communiqués on their nuclear detonations, the Chinese invariably referred to the need to counter American (and Soviet) "nuclear blackmail." In the communiqué on their eighth detonation of December 28, 1968, they expressly linked the detonations with the Vietnam war. But no verbalization from the Chinese was needed to transmit a signal to Washington that China's nuclear program was designed to have a deterrent effect on America. No one in Washington that May 1966 could have argued that the Chinese nuclear program was really directed against the Russians. Since it was so obviously directed against America and clearly developing so rapidly toward an operational capability, Washington was faced with an urgent go/no-go decision. The pressures for a go decision were intense, and even if some vocal elements in Congress were fearful of a larger war, the prowar bloc still predominated. If a no-go decision was made, then the cost of a strike at a later date might involve fearsome prospects of nuclear war which would automatically dictate a no-go decision.

Early in 1967, the French journalist René Dabernat, foreign editor of *Paris-Match* with close ties to the Quai d'Orsay, reported that in the spring of 1966 Peking had transmitted three conditions to Washington for remaining out of the Vietnam war: that America not attack China, that it not invade North Vietnam, and that it not bomb the Red River dike system. These had been transmitted through the French foreign ministry, and a short time later, President Johnson and other top level American officials "gave the necessary signals to Peking in various public speeches to show that they agreed to these conditions."[111] If Dabernat was correct, then the Chinese must have made the approach to the

[110] Jonathan D. Pollack, "Chinese Attitudes Toward Nuclear Weapons, 1964–1969," p. 271.
[111] *New York Times*, January 16, 1967.

Americans before May 18, probably around the time of the nuclear explosion (perhaps even before).

The purge of Lo Jui-ch'ing in November 1965 eliminated the most prominent advocate of "active defense." The purge of P'eng Chen, presumably some time in April (publicly announced at the beginning of June), eliminated the most prominent advocate of "joint action." (Despite his vehement attacks on revisionism, which earned him opprobrium among the Russians, he was amenable to Kenji Miyamoto's proposals for burying the hatchet for the sake of aiding Vietnam.) Had it not been for the deeper underlying issues of the Cultural Revolution, the purges might have stopped there. But Liu Shao-ch'i knew that a storm was brewing and moved to put the lid on, as he had managed to do in June 1957. While Mao was in control in that crucial mid-May period, by the end of the month, Liu moved again into a commanding position for about fifty days.

It might be well here to jump ahead a bit to relate some subsequent anticlimactic events involving Liu Shao-ch'i. After America decided to attack the POL facilities in Haiphong on June 29, North Vietnam decreed national mobilization on July 17. Immense demonstrations were held in China. But the key move was made by Liu Shao-ch'i, who, in his last public act, on July 22, signed a decree in the name of the Chinese government declaring that China was the "rear area" for North Vietnam. Three days later, the Chinese press featured the news of Mao's epoch-making swim of the Yangtze. Mao returned to Peking and managed to delay the meeting of the Central Committee until he felt assured of a commanding voice. The Central Committee met during the first part of August and a triumphant Mao and a rapidly declining Liu emerged. In late 1967, when American planes were again bombing close to China, the Chinese would openly refer to themselves as the "rear area" of Vietnam. That designation eventually came to be featured on the masthead of the *People's Daily* as a Mao quotation every time the subject of Vietnam came up, right down to the signing of the ceasefire early in 1973. But between July 22 and July 25, Mao decided that China was not yet fully ready to become North Vietnam's "rear area."

China was committed to support Vietnam, but the "rear area" designation implied that North Vietnamese Migs might use Chinese air bases. It seems hardly coincidental that CINCPAC, who prided himself on his headquarters' Sinological knowledge, again recommended on July 24 that Phuc Yen and Kep airfields be struck.[112] By late 1967, China clearly felt secure enough to raise its commitments to North Vietnam several notches, but in the summer of 1966, Mao wanted to avoid a

[112] DOD, *U.S.-Vietnam Relations*, IV.C.7.(a), pp. 140–41.

military confrontation with America at all costs short of betrayal of North Vietnam. Why Liu decided to make this move is not clear, but it is possible he hoped to provoke a national emergency and thereby put a lid on the boiling political struggles. Wars have a way of doing that. CINCPAC's interests were clear and consistent. Admiral Sharp was a right-winger who saw great opportunities in the Vietnam war and considered China the devil incarnate. Liu Shao-ch'i's declaration was a clear provocation to which America should respond in kind. CINCPAC would gather its strength and in August of the following year seek allies in Congress to unleash a full-scale bombing war against North Vietnam (and, it hoped, beyond). But by mid-July, the no-go decision against China had already been firmed up—the POL facilities but not the airfields were attacked.

If the Chinese message on conditions for entry into the Vietnam war got to Washington sometime in early May (as Chou En-lai's public statement would imply), then Mao was still in full command in Peking. Whatever images the national estimators sketched of Mao to the policy makers, one thing was certain: Mao hated the Russians. It would not have been difficult to argue that his hatred was so deep that he rejected joint action just on that account. Whatever the nature of the analysis operating in Washington, the evidence was overwhelming (even for the conservative "Sino-Soviet bloc" holdouts) that a decisive split had occurred between China and Russia. A year later, it would become clear that the split did not interrupt the flow of military matériel (particularly missiles) from Russia over Chinese rail lines to North Vietnam. However they did it, those extraordinary leaders in Hanoi managed to get China and Russia to agree to unrestricted transport of Russian supplies across China. But in May 1966, that was by no means certain. In fact, it seemed most probable that a decisive Sino-Soviet schism would end up by putting North Vietnam into a hopeless squeeze. Either Hanoi opted for Russia against China, in which case "linkage" could force a settlement, or Hanoi opted for China, which would mean the loss of sophisticated anti-aircraft weaponry as well as other forms of conventional weaponry—North Vietnam, and for that matter China, could be pounded unrestrainedly from the air.

BOMBING OF HAIPHONG (JUNE 1966) AND THE AMERICA-RUSSIA-CHINA TRIANGLE

It is clear from the Pentagon Papers that Johnson delayed a decision on the POL bombings as long as possible, but, according to the Papers, he "apparently some time late in May" finally decided to authorize them.[113] Then he delayed some more, on Rusk's urgings, to see whether the mission to Hanoi by the Canadian diplomat Chester Ronning might produce something. Rusk wanted a signal from Hanoi indicating that it was leaning in a pro-Soviet, therefore moderate, direction. The strikes finally came on June 29. Lyndon Johnson is virtually mute in his memoirs on the subject of the POL bombings, so that we have only the testimony of the Pentagon Papers to pinpoint the decision as having been made toward the end of May. Johnson also took the unusual step of briefing British Prime Minister Harold Wilson on June 2. Though unusual, the reason was obvious: Wilson was shortly to meet with Kosygin, and the POL bombings were bound to have a major impact on American-Russian relations.

Militarily, the way to strangle North Vietnam was to destroy all port facilities, all rail lines, bomb all roads, wreck all plants and depots, burn the cities to the ground, and keep this up until they called it quits. For the right-wing military, larger global implications were relevant only in terms of the well-known struggle between the free world and the Sino-Soviet bloc. If it was militarily safe to destroy North Vietnam, there was no reason it should not be done. Moreover, since the military constantly took the position that the bloc would not and could not retaliate without running the risk of total destruction, there seemed only the flimsiest of objections to doing it. But for the containment liberals, the political implications of the bombing were crucial. Bombing Haiphong was, above all, a challenge to the Russians. Bombing the airfields was a challenge to China. To have bombed both at the same time, as CINC-PAC was vehemently demanding, would have meant tacit acceptance of CINCPAC's traditional view of the world ("Sino-Soviet bloc"). To have vetoed the POL bombings but authorized bombing Kep and Phuc Yen airfields would almost certainly have led to war between China and America. As it was, Johnson did authorize the bombing of Kep's radar, but no airfields were bombed until the following April 24 (and Phuc Yen not until October 25). But the authorization to strike at Haiphong was politically a challenge directed at Russia and implicitly not at China. In the weird and involuted world of global politics, the bombing of Haiphong was a concrete recognition of the Sino-Soviet split, but in a way that alarmed the Russians, who had grown accustomed to a Russian-American détente.

The action-reaction pattern of decisions seems, thus far, to have involved a Chinese act which internationally signified a decisive break with the Russians followed by an American decision to commit an act of war which would challenge the Russians. Why should Johnson have made such a decision, again as previously in a private and secretive manner?

---

[113] *Ibid.*, IV.C.7.(a), p. 120.

The issue of Russian intent and policy comes into the picture and finally the power of the Presidency.

By the fall of 1966, the Russian-American détente was threatened with a new arms race. As an article in the *Washington Post* put it on November 21: "The world's arms race has reached a critical new phase in which man's weapons have far outdistanced his policies for controlling them." The article listed three major new strategic weapons threats: the new MIRVed Poseidon missile, the Russian ABM, and the rapidly developing Chinese nuclear capability. In a speech delivered on August 26, Johnson made an "unusually strong and eloquent appeal" to the Russians to work with Washington for world peace and arms control. That fall, he asked for a special study of Soviet penetration of the Middle East, speaking darkly of the threat of "an expanding Soviet presence in this strategic region."[114] Similarly in September, McNamara announced that the United States now had 7,000 nuclear warheads in Western Europe, "a fantastically high inventory," in his words.[115] One year later it had become clear that America was embarked on a full-scale program to develop, test, and deploy MIRVs.[116] Thus, by the late summer of 1966, a new Russian-American arms race was in full swing, a phenomenon that the spirit of the 1963 Test Ban Treaty was supposed to prevent.

The seeds of that arms race lie in decisions taken earlier by both Americans and Russians. Late in April 1966, the Senate Armed Services Committee chaired by Senator Richard Russell of Georgia authorized some 167.9 million dollars in funds for the deployment of an ABM system. The committee rejected McNamara's objections and sided with the "unanimous" recommendation of the Joint Chiefs of Staff. The full Congress later voted a higher appropriation of 195 million dollars. On July 20, James Reston sounded the alarms of this new program: "Great political and military events have a way of starting in quiet ways with small commitments that are scarcely noticed in the beginning . . . we may be on the verge of slipping into another commitment—this time against the will and intention of the Administration."[117]

McNamara was resolutely opposed to ABM until, in September 1967, he announced his "anti-China ABM," a halfhearted concession to the ABM advocates. As an ardent proponent of the Test Ban Treaty's letter and spirit, McNamara was convinced that the superpowers could and should reach a plateau of parity on which they could both live. He could fight down the pressure from the military and congressional hawks so long as the Russians reciprocated, but if they didn't, he was in trouble.

[114] Johnson, *Vantage Point*, p. 288.
[115] *Herald Tribune* (Paris), September 25, 1966.
[116] *San Francisco Chronicle*, September 30, 1967.
[117] *New York Times*, July 20, 1966.

McNamara's fall from power may have been mainly related to his strategic weaponry policies more than to the Vietnam war. It is significant that Clark Clifford, while a dove on Vietnam, advocated "superiority" vis-à-vis the Russians in his testimony before Congress on his appointment to succeed McNamara. In the late spring of 1966, McNamara's parity was under attack from the ever-present advocates of superiority in the military and in Congress, but unlike 1963 when Russian political good will seemed demonstrable, in 1966 they were moving unilaterally toward a resumption of the arms race. They were also deepening their commitments in the Middle East. All this at a time when the Americans were being dragged deeper and deeper into an Asian war.

That entire spring, the pressure on Johnson from the military, the right wing, and even Ambassador Lodge to bomb Haiphong was intense. In mid-March, James Reston wrote that "the pressure seems to be building up in the Senate for a policy of bombing, mining, or blockading the North Vietnamese harbor of Haiphong." The scenario he sketched out was that of a Soviet ship carrying munitions to North Vietnam possibly being blown out of the water by an American destroyer.[118] Of course, lurking behind the Haiphong rhetoric was pressure for bombing all targets in North Vietnam, including airfields. Premier Ky, speaking more candidly than his American military friends, put it bluntly in April: "I have told the Americans that some day soon they will have to have a face-to-face confrontation with Red China, and to solve the war in Vietnam they will have to attack Red China."[119] So with the entire Joint Chiefs of Staff, a substantial segment of the Senate led by the influential Richard Russell, Ambassador Lodge, Premier Ky, and a "near consensus among his top advisers" favoring the bombing of Haiphong,[120] Johnson had to make some sort of move. It testifies to the unique, nonbureaucratic nature of the Presidency that he was able to delay the decision for so long. What he did was to maneuver and delay until a time when he could salvage as much as possible from this dangerous situation for the power of the Presidency.

For Lyndon Johnson to have given in to the pressures for bombing Haiphong, striking toward and into China, and resuming the arms race with the Russians (ABM) might have started World War III. But in a less dramatic way, it would have meant the President's abdication of power to his contending bureaucracies. Domino theorizing was popular in Washington, and it was easy to foresee a cataclysmic chain of events arising as the American President lost control of his bureaucracies (and perhaps Mao of his and Brezhnev of his). Henry Kissinger later was said

[118] New York Times, March 23, 1966.
[119] Quoted in James Reston's column, New York Times, April 13, 1966.
[120] DOD, U.S.-Vietnam Relations, IV.C.7(a), p. 118.

to be deeply disturbed by the precarious structure of power among the Russian leadership. While true of Russia, perhaps, it certainly was eminently true of America in 1966. To salvage the power of a Presidency that Lyndon Johnson thought would be used to make America into a Great Society and to uplift the entire Third World to peace and progress, he had to assert his own will and power even when it went against just about all his advisers. He did finally give in to the pressure, but in such a way that the bombing was largely a one-shot affair meant to convey a strong message to the Russians, and broke for a year or so the onrushing danger of a direct confrontation with China.

There are those who say that Mao went ahead with the Cultural Revolution when the Americans assured him that they would not attack China.[121] Certainly a major push was given to the Cultural Revolution by the May 16 circular that gave the go-ahead to the agitation that erupted on the campuses of Peking's universities later that month. Whatever the circumstances and timing of the signals exchanged between Peking and Washington, the receding of the American threat strengthened Mao's hand as a chief executive. For one thing, it made it fairly certain that the army could be used as a shield and a political framework during the internal struggles and not sent south to fight the Americans. Obviously the verbal assurances and reassurances that traveled between Peking and Washington carried little weight in themselves. But neither Mao nor Johnson, for their own reasons, wanted a war with each other, and both had much to lose as chief executives if war broke out.

The conditions were as favorable as they could ever be for a strike to achieve the "nuclear castration" of China, to use Alsop's words. But the risks were too great and Johnson made a decision which, in effect, made China the third nuclear power in the world (though it would take a little time before that became apparent), and, thus, the third great power in the world. The bipolar world ended in May 1966.

Decisions (or non-decisions) are pivotal only in retrospect, which makes historians useful. Currents are currents only when they have flowed for some time, not when they gush out of a spring. Johnson's decision not to let the air war spill over into China is pivotal only when seen in the light of the remarkable Sino-American rapprochement that became visible on July 15, 1971, when President Nixon accepted an invitation to visit China. By the early 1970s, the notion of an American-Russia-China triangle was widely accepted. In the mid-1960s, it was permissible to speak of a Moscow-Peking-Hanoi triangle, but not of one including America. But clearly the triangle was there in 1966 and had been there before. The notion of a triangular relationship not only im-

---

[121] Mao made a dramatic reappearance after months of rumors about his illness on May 10 in company with the Albanians (symbolic meaning: anti-Russian).

plied that what the three great countries do affects each other, but also has a concrete content in the special relationship between their chief executives. "Summitry," developed in the mid-1950s, is a manifestation of a curious political phenomenon that sometimes makes it seem as if the chief executives of all the great countries have more in common with each other than with their own bureaucracies. That phenomenon is not new, having been common in Europe for centuries until the French Revolution ended it. In 1966, the Sino-American ambassadorial talks in Warsaw became serious and started a process which finally led to true summit relations inaugurated by Nixon in 1971.

The Russian-American détente began to flower in 1959 at Camp David and, despite some difficult moments, continued to develop until 1966. A concomitant of that détente, as I have already discussed, was a more aggressive American policy toward China culminating in the Vietnam war and in a narrowly averted air war against China. In 1966, the pendulum began to swing in the opposite direction again. Russian-American rivalry resumed, not in Europe nor over Cuba but in the Middle East, the Mediterranean, and, eventually, on the Indian subcontinent. By early 1973, the alarms had grown loud about Soviet penetration of the Middle East, Soviet challenge to American naval power, and the dangers from Soviet missile build-ups. East Asia had simmered down to a shaky but promising ceasefire in Vietnam and Laos. The triangular notion implies a zero-sum condition: what two do together is at the expense of the third; if two fight each other, the third will be spared. In any case, 1966 saw the beginning of a period of slowly growing Russian-American rivalry accompanied by an even more slowly developing American-Chinese détente.

JOHNSON'S NO ALTERNATIVE BUT TO POUR IN TROOPS

Containment policy had always meant forces-in-being or troops, so that while Johnson had reined in the air war in May, he had no alternative but to pour "troops, more troops" into South Vietnam. In June, Mc-Namara approved Westmoreland's requests for 391,000 American soldiers in South Vietnam by the end of 1966, and 431,000 by June 1967. Wars have their own logics, and once one starts, it keeps going and going until something drastic stops it. Bureaucratically, this is because once the bureaucracy is set in motion with men, budgets, and resources, it consumes more and more, way beyond the limits of rationality. But while civilian bureaucracies can to some extent be held in check, the mystique of combat helps the military bureaucracy to keep up its acceleration.

Westmoreland's demands for more men kept coming in faster and faster until the breaking point was reached in early 1968. With over a half-million American soldiers in South Vietnam (not including non-Army personnel offshore and elsewhere in Southeast Asia), Westmoreland wanted another quarter-million. What with troops from other countries, notably the 50,000 soldiers from the South Korean army, the number of non-Vietnamese troops in South Vietnam would soon reach the million mark.

Westmoreland's great challenge came in 1967. He was convinced that with the ARVNs doing pacification and United States troops "searching and destroying, clearing and holding," the Viet Cong and the North Vietnamese Army (NVA) could be crushed or pushed entirely out of South Vietnam. The North Vietnamese and the National Liberation Front believe that Operation Junction City in the spring of 1967 was the turning point of the war. Junction City was a campaign to clear all Viet Cong and NVA out of Tay Ninh province, adjoining Cambodia west of Saigon. Their most important sanctuaries in Cambodia were just across the border past Parrot's Beak and Fish Hook in the great rubber plantations. If clear-and-hold had worked in Tay Ninh, it could have worked anywhere in South Vietnam. What would then have been left was pacification or, more likely, without main force support, the insurgency would simply have withered away.

Whether Junction City was a turning point or not, it is a fact that the air war began to heat up dramatically in the spring. That summer, Admiral Sharp appeared before the Senate Armed Services Committee to demand that all restraints on the bombing be lifted. It had been commonplace in peacetime for generals and admirals to go to their congressional friends to put pressure on the White House. But this was during wartime and also at a time of extremely sensitive and delicate global politics. In a way, it seemed as if Admiral Sharp had been willing to let General Westmoreland have a try. After all, in May and June 1966, it was still not certain that the United States Army could not bring back the coonskin, as Lyndon Johnson so ardently hoped. But a year later, the auguries were poor, and Admiral Sharp lost no time trying to get the air war moving at full throttle. The airfields were bombed, and so were Hanoi and Haiphong. As United States failure on the ground was becoming more and more evident, Sharp and his Navy–Air Force colleagues needed only to point out that they held the key to "victory through air power."

Then came the *Pueblo* and then Têt. The Johnson Administration was simultaneously faced with a global and a Vietnam crisis. The air war that fall had escalated to such a point that the Chinese, judging from the intense press coverage of the bombing, seemed fearful that the war might finally come to China after all. With Phuc Yen bombed, North Vietnamese Migs had no airfields in North Vietnam and were dependent on Chinese fields. In South Vietnam, it was evident that the NVA and Viet Cong were massing forces for an offensive push after having blunted the Americans' push earlier in 1967. In the case of the *Pueblo* affair, both sides seemed to be looking for an incident. The electronic snooping of the *Pueblo* could not but alarm the North Koreans, but the decision to seize it must have been made in the awareness of the larger political-military picture of the time. North Korea was at that time cool toward both China and Russia but avidly supported North Vietnam—a fact not unrelated to South Korea's role in South Vietnam. In 1950, the North Koreans committed acts that quickly turned out to have grave implications for global politics. They did the same in January 1968. The fact that in 1968 they did so without consulting either of the two great communist powers suggests that they may have acted on their own in 1950 as well. In any case, Kim Il Sung and Admiral Sharp seemed equally ready to commit acts with grave implications for global politics. As the nuclear-powered aircraft carrier *Enterprise* began to steam into the Yellow Sea, the specter of air strikes against North Korea or "Son Tay"-type raids to free the *Pueblo* quickly loomed up.

Days later, Têt exploded. NVA and Viet Cong forces quickly smashed through the ARVN-held defense perimeters around the cities, stormed into Saigon and Hué, and invaded the American Embassy. The United States Army's explanation that it was a military defeat for the NVA and Viet Cong but a "psychological victory" missed the entire point of what Westmoreland's war was supposed to be about. United States Army policy from 1965 had been offensive, to seek out the enemy, destroy or push him out of South Vietnam. For that same enemy now to take the offensive with main force units as well as guerrillas testified unmistakably to the defeat of Westmoreland's "concept." It is likely that the National Liberation Front expected much more of a "general uprising" than actually took place. But Têt marked the beginning of a new NVA/Viet Cong offensive phase which continued until the 1973 ceasefire.

Considering the magnitude of these Communist provocations in January–February 1968 compared to the puny nature of the famous incidents of 1964 and 1965, Johnson's restraint was indeed remarkable. But seen in terms of the available policy options his restraint appears more as paralysis in the face of choices all of which were bad.

JOHNSON'S DECISION TO HALT THE BOMBING OF THE NORTH

Much has already been written on Johnson's momentous March 31 speech announcing a bombing halt for most of North Vietnam and his own decision not to stand for re-election. He himself has written about that speech and the decisions it represented, but unfortunately with the same degree of murky candor that marks most of the sensitive subjects in his memoirs. From the pattern of previous decisions (and from some internal evidence as well), one can conclude that Johnson made the bombing halt and abdication decisions in privacy, secrecy, and alone. What many people have written on the loneliness of chief executives can be explained, as I have tried to do, in organizational terms. That does not mean that these decisions are idiosyncratic, for they arise out of the confluence of currents which at times can produce key breakthroughs over river banks.[122]

I was in Hanoi when Johnson made his speech, at the same time as the Ashmore-Baggs mission which he writes about in his memoirs. About an hour later, some Vietnamese officials gave me a quick initial analysis which turned out to be the operative one on subsequent days. For them, the key element in the speech was just the last lines. It was Johnson's abdication from power that convinced them that he was serious, that the offer to negotiate and to halt the bombing of the North signified a real change of policy. When policies fail, officials are purged, they said. But this time, as they put it in French, Johnson *"s'est limogé lui-même"* (Johnson purged himself). They considered the offer to negotiate of somewhat lesser importance and least important of all, the bombing halt (much to the surprise of the Americans there).

Communist movements and nations attach great importance to policy. A policy is a direction in which an organization moves. It will continue moving in that direction until the policy is changed, and only the supreme leadership of the organization can change policy. The offer to negotiate indicated a policy shift from the days when Johnson only proposed to "discuss," but was still too insubstantial to be accepted at face value. Most discredited of all were the bombing halts with which the North Vietnamese were already acquainted. Bombing halts had a way of stopping and starting, as they discovered. But for the chief executive of the United States to abdicate from power could only imply that a major decision to change policy had been made. A day or so later, another

---

[122]Townsend Hoopes quotes Clark Clifford on the March 31 decision as saying, "Presidents have difficult decisions to make and go about making them in mysterious ways" (*The Limits of Intervention*, p. 224).

Vietnamese official, expressing confidence that the negotiations would succeed, said, *"Un mécanisme s'est engagé"* (A mechanism has been set in motion), implying that the March 31 speech did form a turning point.

Although from the Vietnamese point of view the bombing halt was third in priority of importance, it was the central decision so far as Johnson was concerned. In his memoirs, he takes pains to explain something which we in Hanoi knew of but which was overlooked or quickly forgotten in America. In his speech, Johnson clearly said that all bombing of North Vietnam would halt except just north of the demilitarized zone.[123] In Hanoi, that was the morning of April 1. That evening, around five o'clock Hanoi time, we heard the news that Navy planes had attacked targets near Thanh Hoa, on the 20th parallel. Then a few days later, it was announced that all bombing was to be halted north of the 19th parallel—that seemed to be a compromise between the White House and Admiral Sharp. Whether or not Sharp committed a Lavelle-type "unauthorized" raid is immaterial. The decision to halt the air war was just about the gravest blow that could have been aimed at CINCPAC, short of depriving him of his carriers. In the storm that ensued, the compromise at the 19th parallel was worked out.

In the past, Johnson was able to finesse pressure for a step-up in the air war by sending more troops into South Vietnam. But by early 1968, when the *New York Times* revealed Westmoreland's latest requests for another quarter-million men, that option became increasingly untenable. It was on the troop issue that much of the antiwar sentiment was aroused. In organizational terms, the United States Army became the main casualty of the Vietnam war. In America (as in other societies), the land army was always the democratic institution within the military contrasted with the Navy's traditionalism and the Air Force's elitism. The discontents of American society were reflected much more in the Army than in the other services. In Vietnam, it also was the Army that did most of the fighting, bleeding, and dying. But giving Westmoreland more cannon fodder required calling up the reserves, which would have needed some kind of congressional declaration of national emergency or even a declaration of war. Even if Johnson could have rammed it through Congress, the effect in a presidential election year would have been disastrous. What had been Johnson's favorite moderate option for maintaining America's commitment to South Vietnam only a short time before had turned into a tunnel of horror.

If the one track of troops fell away, the other track of negotiations seemed as bleak. The Chinese were as vehemently opposed to negotiations as they had been in the past, and for the same reasons: negotiations could mean a revival of Russian-American collusion to settle the affairs

[123]Quoted in Johnson, *Vantage Point*, pp. 493–94.

of Southeast Asia. They were also convinced that negotiations would quickly lead to a sellout of the National Liberation Front, comparable to what happened to the Viet Minh in South Vietnam in 1954. While the Russians were more interested in negotiations, they still had not recovered from their indirect defeat in Egypt the previous June, were busily furnishing SAMs to North Vietnam, and enjoyed less influence in Hanoi than they hoped for. For both the DRV and the NLF, the key issue was American troops in South Vietnam. So long as they remained, they could hold on to the cities and surrounding areas forever. American troops were immune to Vietnamese political processes, but Saigon troops were not. In early 1973, the oft-reported PRG (Provisional Revolutionary Government) confidence that they had won a "great victory" expressed just that: with the Americans gone and despite the frantic efforts of a swollen Saigon military force to score gains against the Viet Cong, the political process would finally see a crumbling of Saigon forces from within (just as happened to the Kuomintang armies in China). But before March 31, 1968, the Vietnamese had no explicit indication that the Americans were prepared to begin to withdraw. Nor for that matter did they until after Nixon was elected. Johnson reports that Nguyen Van Thieu in their July meeting "urged that we put an announcement of [troop withdrawals] in our communiqué," but Johnson demurred.[124] The Vietnamese left and right both wanted United States troop withdrawals for their own reasons, but the American center was not yet willing to grant them that.

WHY DID NORTH VIETNAM
AGREE TO NEGOTIATE?

If the Americans did not offer the DRV and NLF troop withdrawals in March 1968, why should the North Vietnamese accept the offer to negotiate? Did they fear total destruction from the air? Surprising as this may sound, a visitor to North Vietnam early in 1968 found them digging all over Hanoi but with an air of confidence that they could and would take the worst the Americans could deliver. Regardless of what United States Air Force manuals said about destroying the "psycho-social infrastructure" of the enemy, the people of North Vietnam seemed to be accomplishing stupendous feats under the bombing. When I raised the question of nuclear weapons, they shrugged back an unconcerned answer: others have them too (meaning the Russians and Chinese).

If the North Vietnamese did not greatly fear a further intensification of the air war (at least not enough to agree to negotiate), then why

[124] Johnson, *Vantage Point*, p. 512.

would they finally agree to negotiate in the absence of any clearcut American concession on the troop withdrawal issue? It appears that they did believe that Johnson had made a major gesture on the troop issue, which was the announcement on March 22 that Westmoreland was being relieved of command. In Hanoi, they spoke of the purging (*"limogeage"* in French) of Westmoreland and likened it to the "purging" of General De Saussure after the failure of Operation Junction City in 1967. In his March 31 speech, Johnson indicated that a small increment of men would continue to be sent to South Vietnam. His words, therefore, implied nothing so far as troop withdrawals were concerned. But Westmoreland was the architect of the American ground effort in South Vietnam and his departure signaled to the North Vietnamese and National Liberation Front South Vietnamese that a major change in policy was in the works.

In this book, I have written little about the Vietnamese side of the conflict and, thus, can say little about the detailed context that finally impelled the Hanoi leadership to enter into negotiations on April 3. The numerous conversations I had with Vietnamese from March 18, when I arrived in Hanoi, until the April 3 acceptance all radiated a basic confidence. They particularly singled out three currents of events which indicated that the balance of forces was shifting in their favor. In South Vietnam, the Americans had abandoned the offensive and were going back to the defensive and a *de facto* enclaves policy. While they never referred to the Sino-Soviet rupture, they indicated their belief that the general balance of forces in the world favored the socialist camp more and more. Naturally, the looming American balance of payments crisis contributed to those changes. Lastly, they felt that world public opinion and popular pressure was on their side. Of course, no one spoke to me about the costs of the war, the bloodletting of Têt, the ferocious air bombardments at Khe Sanh, the vast swath of destruction in North Vietnam. There was no visible sign of war weariness among the population, so far as a guided observer could tell.

It has been written, mainly by American analysts, that the North Vietnamese have a Dienbienphu mentality. While it certainly is true that they take great pride in Dienbienphu and have a remarkable mock-up of that battle with skillfully emplaced lights showing its progression, Dienbienphu was for them mainly a political phenomenon. What myriads of American military thinkers with their weapons fetishes never understood was that for the Vietnamese revolutionaries the political juxtaposition of forces always was the main issue in the struggle. "Political" means whoever holds power in the institutions of governance from the hamlet to the presidential palace in Saigon. But until all foreigners quit Vietnam, power within Vietnam was inextricably emmeshed with world politics. What Dienbienphu produced was not just a spectacular military victory, but a dramatic shift in power in Paris. When the Laniel cabinet collapsed and Mendès-France became premier, Paris sent a signal to the Viet Minh that France was ready to end the war. That was the key crack in the façade that the Viet Minh had been waiting for. Without that change in policy, even the spectacular surrender of the French at the fallen outpost would have simply been a propaganda victory.

The Americans noted the similarities between Khe Sanh and Dienbienphu, claiming with satisfaction that Khe Sanh was no Dienbienphu, for had not American air power scored a spectacular victory?[125] Perhaps, and maybe it was sufficient justification for another four years of effort to achieve victory through air power. But it is entirely out of keeping with Vietnamese thinking to assume that Dienbienphu required a march-out of defeated Americans from conquered Khe Sanh. Khe Sanh was a Dienbienphu because it led to a dramatic shift in power in Washington, just as happened in 1954. The North Vietnamese were later shown to be wrong in their belief that the mechanism of negotiations would quickly lead to an end to the war. On April 1, North Vietnamese army forces began withdrawing from Khe Sanh. Whether that move took place because of victory through air power or because a political decision had been made in Hanoi is impossible to say. But on that day, the leaders in Hanoi can hardly be faulted for seeing an analogy between what happened in 1954 and Lyndon Johnson's abdication.

JOHNSON PURGES HIMSELF FROM POWER

Alexis de Tocqueville wrote in the early 1830s that all an American President thought about was getting re-elected. Until March 31, there was no sign whatsoever that Lyndon Johnson had abandoned an iron-clad determination to continue as President from 1968 to 1972. There is sufficient evidence from the period after March 31 to indicate that sly old LBJ had not entirely deep down in his heart abandoned all hope of being President until 1972. But to win in 1968 as he had in 1964, he would have to appear as a peace President, assuming just the mantle that Nixon donned and Humphrey fumbled with. But he could not be a peace President unless he ended the war and made some dramatic break with his record as the war President. To abdicate on March 31 but to resume the throne, say, in early August would permit him to return with a new image. Apparently Johnson was ready just before the convention to fly to Moscow and negotiate some sort of arms control understanding and while there, naturally, could have invoked his old negotiating track

[125] Hoopes, *Limits of Intervention*, pp. 211–14.

(Hanoi via Moscow). Johnson's name was put in nomination and a triumphant breakthrough in Moscow could have induced the party regulars to drop Humphrey and flock back to him. The Russian occupation of Czechoslovakia dashed that hope.

Johnson, popular thinking to the contrary, could not just issue an order to de-escalate the war. The March 31 decisions, which recognized North Vietnam as an equal negotiating partner with the United States as well as depriving Honolulu of its beloved air war, were momentous and partisan. They were partisan in that they came down on the side of the doves and, therefore, against the hawks. Earlier, Johnson was able to balance off gifts to the doves with others to the hawks. Thus, for every travel restriction to China or North Vietnam lifted, the Navy and Air Force got some new targets to bomb. Or he was able to deflect the demands of the dangerous hawks like Sharp by giving more to the less dangerous ones like Westmoreland. But March 31 was a clearcut anti-hawk decision, the first one Johnson had made. It meant taking sides with Clifford, for example, against the Joint Chiefs of Staff. Presidential decisions that are factional, particularly in the area of foreign affairs, invariably arouse counterattack. Despite growing antiwar sentiment in Congress, the old right-wing–military alliance was still intact and could be set in motion again, as happened in August 1967, to nullify the decision. Without the abdication, the hawks would have regarded the de-escalation as betrayal and capitulation to cowards, traitors, and opportunists for the sake of re-election.

In terms of policy currents, Johnson's March 31 decision was in consonance with the May 1966 decision to veto an extension of the air war into China. If the ground war could not produce victory, as most of the military had long been arguing, then no other route to victory was open than what had been pursued in earlier years: build up the South Vietnamese ground forces, carry out devastating air attacks against the source of the aggression (North Vietnam and China), and plan an Inchon-type landing in North Vietnam. The March 31 speech did call for a strengthening of Saigon's ground forces, and so foreshadowed Nixon's Vietnamization. The Vietnam war policy of the first Nixon Administration actually marked a return to this right-wing policy, even though troop withdrawals seemed to imply a desire to end the war. But after the October 30 total bombing halt (over North Vietnam alone), it was much safer for Nixon to do than for Johnson to have done on March 31. The bureaucratic fact is that without the troops-negotiations option, Johnson had only one option left, that which the military had been pressing for for years: victory through air power against all the sources of aggression (save Russia, perhaps). De-escalating the war was not a bureaucratic option unless it occurred as the result of achievement of goals. Certainly, in March 1968, no one could argue that victory was in sight. The only way for Johnson to create and invoke this new policy option was to announce it to the entire world and then cancel out his power. Thus, there was no way the hawks could counterattack, for they had to ready themselves for a new President.

It is ironic but yet in line with the necessities imposed by history that Johnson came to power as the result of assassination and left by committing political suicide. And that his first stroke of power was to plunge the country deep into the Vietnam war and his last act of power, the final total bombing halt of October 30, pulled the country out of the internationally most dangerous aspects of that war. Johnson, like Truman, grew up and thrived in domestic politics. Both were frontier nationalists who relished the idea of American victories, but they were also practical politicians. Roosevelt the aristocrat relished foreign affairs, as did Kennedy and as does Nixon. But Johnson dreamed of his war on poverty, of eradicating discrimination, of beautifying America. What Johnson never fully understood (or maybe he finally did) was that the politics of the realm of ideology were far different from those of the realm of interests. In Congress, he could wheel and deal, give and take, jawbone here, cajole there, threaten every once in a while. As Vice President, he may have had some sense of what the presidential political world was about, but most likely not very much. But as President, he found himself in a different world, one of bureaucracies and armies and diplomacies governed by doctrines and formalisms that made the practical give and take of the realm of interests impossible. Johnson, like many other Democrats who came out of machine politics, thought that bureaucratic politics were just another variant of congressional politics. In domestic affairs, it was still possible to politick for programs. But in foreign affairs, Johnson had to be an imperial figure commanding, coordinating, and radiating some kind of vision. Johnson did try to project a vision—the Great Society—but unfortunately the only images of his Vietnam policies that stuck in the public mind were those of the coonskin and the nervous nellies. Nixon seems to feel much more at home in the realm of foreign affairs. Unlike Johnson, he has no interest or experience in domestic affairs. But also unlike Johnson, Nixon's career was ideological and not practical. His anticommunism, curiously enough, probably enabled him to slip into the presidential role better than Johnson.

It is true that popular pressure toppled Johnson. The Democratic party, as the ideological one of the two parties, was being torn by Vietnam and by black revolt. Black anger was at a fever pitch during just the years when Johnson's momentous civil rights and welfare legislation seemed to be inaugurating a new era for the country's non-white minorities. Blacks and students (the activists in the antiwar movement) were crucial to the Democratic party's ideology, for they were what reform and hope was supposed to be all about. Johnson was an Old Reformer who believed that the discontent of the black and young was not very different from the discontents of workers and farmers in his Texan youth during the 1930s. He had rallied them in 1964 and knew that he had to rally them again in 1968 to get re-elected. Johnson was bothered by the fact that he could no longer appear in public because of the danger of hostile demonstrations. Like other supreme rulers, he yearned for that direct contact with the people that seemed to infuse some sort of mana into the ruler's body. The Wisconsin primary told Johnson that one of the most progressive states in the Union was going to repudiate him because of the war. If he wanted to get re-elected in November, he would first have to abdicate and break the people's image of him as the war President. If re-election proved to be impossible, better to abdicate under honorable conditions than to be turned out of office by the people.

The Vietnamese Dienbienphu analysis, so to speak, had three components, as I have already indicated: 1) the military and political balance of forces in South Vietnam; 2) the balance of forces in the world as a whole; and 3) world and American public opinion. In early 1968, the leaders in Hanoi felt that the auguries for them on all three of these components were favorable. Whatever the fearful toll in lives and effort Têt may have cost, they were convinced that they had definitively passed from the defensive to the offensive stage (a conviction that turned out to be true in the long run, but not in the short, for Nixon's Vietnamization was to involve a new offensive effort). On the world scene, with which, as Marxists, they were intimately acquainted, they were equally convinced that America's position was being threatened everywhere. China's nuclear capability, Russian strength in the Middle East (despite the 1967 Egyptian defeat), and, above all, the rapidly declining stock of United States gold reserves indicated that Washington could no longer afford the luxury of a distant war not vital to its national interests. And throughout the world, popular forces were rising against America, whose only defenders were government officials or occasional cold war academics. France, though hardly a world power in 1954, was in a comparable situation: it was losing in Indochina, its position was being threatened by a rapidly recovering Germany, and the people surged into the streets protesting "*la sale guerre*" (the dirty war).

If Johnson's reasons for abdicating were different from those of the Vietnamese analysis, the end result was the same. For a small country to defeat a big one, a decisive change in policy had to be brought about in the big country, the only credible sign of which was a change in government. This was easier in France than in America, where it could happen only once every four years. But Johnson's abdication in March served the purpose.

ANTIWAR CURRENT AND THE END OF DEMOCRATIC IMPERIALISM

Social currents also enter the bureaucracies from the bottom, through their lowliest recruits. The United States Army found itself the chief victim of this subversion from below. Too often for the comfort of crewcut lifer officers and non-commissioned officers, the typical draftee grunt was a long-haired, beaded recalcitrant or a militant Afro-styled black. The same was true of the other services and of the civilian bureaucracies back in Washington. The antiwar movement began to reach deep into the bureaucracies, even into the Pentagon. With their technological fetishism, the military brass finally conceded their soldiers and employees some rights to free speech and life style but expected that they "do their jobs." "I'm doing a job" was the most common response a journalist got from a pilot asked about B-52 milk-runs or similar exploits. The response is not new, going back into Korean War and World War II days and maybe even earlier. It is a good American organizational notion that opinion and performance can be separated. But even the brass must have had some dim memories of something called "morale" as a key factor in war and combat, though the technologization of the war was designed to expunge human morale and volition as a factor in war-making. But whatever the brass did, in the end, they could not prevent these currents from rising up closer and closer to them.

The Chinese hold that America now has become a "waning" imperialism, like England earlier in this century. I believe that Johnson's March 31 speech symbolized the end of an era of democratic imperialism which began in Roosevelt's New Deal. Johnson's grandiose plans, announced in his April 7, 1965, Baltimore speech, for a TVA-type Mekong Valley project were in this tradition. America overextended itself and the Rooseveltian Pax Americana had to give way to a Nixonian balance of power. But democratic imperialism also presumed the support of the people for America's efforts to build a Pax Americana. Since the end of World War II, the Americans actually operated internationally in much the same way that they presumed the Communists did. Hundreds of thousands of Americans acted as cadres for a variety of American governmental purposes ranging from foreign assistance to subversion. The vast majority worked for the government, a lesser number worked for United States corporations. American troops were stationed throughout the world. Scholarships sent United States students into all kinds of exotic countries. The Peace Corps, influenced by the communists' success at the village level, tried to get the American cadres into the villages of the underdeveloped countries. That vast effort depended on a popu-

lar mandate, for nongovernmental interests were upset over the huge
sums going for foreign aid and the commitments arising with no demonstrable utilitarian purpose.

The outpouring of Americans over the world after World War II was
an outpouring of youth. But in 1968, a theme was sounded that alarmed
the Old Reformers: that of isolationism, a withdrawing inward. While
Dean Rusk may have believed some of his talk about the threat of
United States power washing back to its continental shores, the real
content of those themes was not so much foreign policy as the attitudes
of people, particularly the young. A substantial part of American youth
has turned inward, and nothing illustrates it as well as the drug culture
and the new religious currents. The generation of World War II, by
contrast, turned outward and abroad. Democratic imperialism would
have been impossible without young cadres, as the Peace Corps exemplified. The Peace Corps today wants technical operatives, who are increasingly the type of Americans working abroad, whether for the government
or corporations or making war.

No United States commitment more exemplifies democratic imperialism than that to Israel. For Americans, Israel is a product of World War
II, where America fought a progressive, democratic war against a totalitarian dictator to help the oppressed, foremost among whom were the
Jews of Europe against whom the most heinous of crimes had been
committed—genocide. Israel was a democratic experiment in a feudal
backwater which would someday spread light and progress to the entire
Middle East. Moreover, its opponents included some of the biggest
United States corporations, notably the oil companies, with their interests in the Arab countries. The commitment to Israel was clearly ideological because it equally clearly went against United States material
interests in the region. In the 1950s, progressives journeyed to Israel
much as later they would go to Cuba—to see a new society in action.
That Jews were numerous, wealthy, and powerful in America was an
obvious reason for the commitment to Israel, but not the only one. Nor
was Gentile guilt over Hitler's genocide the reason, as seems to be the
case with West Germany. Israel exemplified what the Democratic party's
ideology had been preaching since the beginning of the cold war: that a
progressive, socialistic, pro-American and noncommunist state could
arise. In spite of Israel's special circumstances, it seemed that the same
could eventually happen throughout the Third World. In the early
1970s, that special United States–Israel ideological relationship was
transformed into a simple political-military tie. Israel's tough armed
forces play a crucial role in the anti-Soviet balance of forces in the
Middle East. Gone are the rapturous days of the kibbutzim or United
States labor leaders planting trees in the Judaean hills. The United States

–Israel relationship actually says much about the new kind of presidential ideology now operating in Washington, one that does not require the same kind of popular support that the ideology of democratic imperialism did.

It is a commonplace in history that great leaders have often gone to the people for support. But for that support to be granted requires that the leader have a sense of the thoughts, aspirations, discontents, beliefs, angers of the people. The greatest man of vision of the twentieth century who is also an effective leader and unifier is Mao. His vision had power because it was finely attuned to China's social forces, which Mao's extraordinary hearing enabled him to perceive. Johnson had a vision even though history passed it by and Nixon then dismantled its remnants. As a visionary, he felt that he had to have a sense of the people. That fact alone distinguished him from all the various political or bureaucratic elitists around him. Whether it was narrow thinking about the up-coming Wisconsin primary or broader mulling over the changing social forces that were destroying his popular mandate, Johnson knew that Vietnam expressed some deep change within the United States.

CHAPTER 3

An Ending and a Beginning

Johnson made one more major decision on Vietnam before leaving office. On October 30, he decreed a total bombing halt for all of North Vietnam. But little noticed at the time was the item in his statement that indicated that bombing would continue in Laos. In fact, the entire air campaign was shifted to Laos, which was subjected to one of the most massive and murderous bombardments in history. That decision was a remarkably clear example of a trade-off of policy for power. In return for accepting the policy of no more bombing of North Vietnam and, by implication, no prospect of bombing China, the Joint Chiefs of Staff and particularly the new CINCPAC Admiral John McCain were able to retain the real power inherent in waging an air war from carriers and land bases. For the Air Force, strategic and tactical air power retained an active role as the usual menacing budgetary and planning debates over follow-up manned aircraft were going on. For the Navy, an ongoing air war assured the need for a continuing carrier role.

But that kind of policy-for-power trade-off also suited the military as a whole. While McCain and other Pacific admirals still stuck to the traditional notion of a dual menace from China and Russia, some rethinking of doctrine, evident in military publications, was going on. The changes in Russian military policy from 1966 on and the Sino-Soviet rupture were the major elements forcing a reshaping of military geopolitics. The resistance to change naturally came from the hugeness of the structure of the military bureaucracy. Caught in its own fierce rivalries, there was nothing it less desired than a change in the nature of the enemy. If the Russians suddenly started building a lot of submarines, this would be a low blow at the American carrier admirals and highly suspicious support for the submarine zealots. Whatever its elements of electoral opportunism, Johnson's October 30 decision satisfied both the bureaucratic pressures for no change in the air war and the changing doctrinal mood of the military that began to question the wisdom of a strike against China.

VIETNAMIZATION: NIXON'S POLICY
OF PHASED WITHDRAWAL

Nixon's official policy on Vietnam seemed to be that two-track approach outlined by Kissinger in his famous *Foreign Affairs* article: either peace would be achieved at Paris through negotiations or it would be achieved through "Vietnamization." Vietnamization meant that American troops would be withdrawn and that ARVN forces would replace them in all ground combat functions, with American air and logistical support to the hilt. Johnson's March 31 decisions were the real source of his troop withdrawal policy. The ARVNs were the only available manpower pool and their numbers could be vastly increased by drafting more men in South Vietnam. Then the presence of such large numbers of American troops loses its significance. Westmoreland's tactics of using infantry to make contact with the enemy but moving back fast so that air power could go in for the kill seemed to make the morale factor of the infantry-man less important. Unmotivated South Vietnamese could carry rifles as well as unmotivated Americans.

Nixon's Vietnamization policy was, in effect, a return to the "phased withdrawal" program of the Kennedy Administration. That involved a crash program to build up the military capabilities of the Diem regime to carry the war to the Communists. At that time, it also involved reliance on covert war to weaken the enemy on his home ground, and implied the eventual use of air power against the enemy's capabilities. Vietnamization was, indeed, a crash program to turn Thieu's army into a formidable fighting force. Within South Vietnam, covert war took the form of a vigorous pacification. It reached its highest expression in the Phoenix program, which, among other things, carried out the murder of suspected Viet Cong cadres (as similar assassination teams had earlier been dispatched into North Vietnam). Outside of South Vietnam, Vang Pao's Armée Clandestine began to play an increasingly active role penetrating Pathet Lao–held regions. Air power was certainly liberally applied in South Vietnam in tonnages that were staggering by comparison with World War II. But the most dangerous thrust of Vietnamization, as with phased withdrawal, was the pressure to use air power to the hilt to get at the source of the aggression. That meant not only resuming the bombing of North Vietnam, but obliterating it, and perhaps also moving on into China, though such a step had become much riskier than it was in 1963.

In looking back at the four years of the first Nixon Administration, it is clear (and was already then) that little stock was put in the Paris negotiations. Johnson had agreed to "negotiate" with the North Vietnamese, but the idea that a superpower could negotiate with a small country was not acceptable in principle to the foreign policy thinking of the new Nixon Administration. Somehow it had to go through another superpower. Hanoi's annoying independence made "serious" negotiations impossible. In reality, the negotiating track was a holdover from the Johnson Administration, and, in that Ruskian spirit, Washington would periodically look to Moscow to see whether the Russians could help out in Vietnam. When the ceasefire was signed in 1973, it was Washington and Hanoi alone (without benefit of Moscow or Peking) who concluded it. But in 1969 and 1970, the negotiating track still went via Moscow, and for that reason Washington was not very optimistic that results would ensue.

Vietnamization was pleasing to the right wing, particularly if the doors were opened again to victory through air power. Thus, when Nixon announced troop withdrawals, he made moves designed to please both hawks and doves, right and left. But if he acted as an Old Rightist in his Vietnam policies, the appointment of Henry Kissinger as his presidential adviser on foreign affairs—an appointment hailed by the liberals— implied something else. Kissinger had been associated with the Rocke- feller or "liberal" wing of the Republican party. In fact and in symbol, he was a Europe-firster. He was born in Germany, taught at Harvard, admired Metternich and Bismarck, distrusted the Russians, and was blank on Asia. The previous Republican President Eisenhower had an internationalist as foreign minister, John Foster Dulles. And now Nixon, who greatly admired Eisenhower, picked another internationalist as his foreign adviser. For all of Dulles's anticommunist fulminations and his role in the Japanese peace treaty, the Dulles epoch was a Europe-first one, which was Eisenhower's predilection as well. The appointment of Kissinger can be seen in the same light, implying a shift back from a preoccupation with East Asia to a general concern with America's prob- lems elsewhere, particularly in the West. Whatever Nixon's reasons for appointing Kissinger (appeasing the Rockefeller wing of the party, carry- ing on the Eisenhower tradition, seeking a return to consensus on foreign policy), it showed that he hoped to get far beyond Vietnam in his first term.

Aside from his political and academic credentials, Kissinger had the additional advantage of having dabbled in Vietnam negotiations, like so many other private citizens (with the tacit support of the government). Neither he nor Nixon could have foreseen the extraordinary negotiating role that he would play with the Vietnamese, the Chinese, and others. But negotiating was the one contribution that he could make to the new Nixon Administration. Vietnamization was in Laird's domain, and the air war and other forms of military action belonged to the Joint Chiefs of

Staff. Secretary of State Rogers handled other foreign affairs, especially the Middle East where he and Joseph Sisco were particularly active during Nixon's first term.

A "NEGOTIATING TRACK" THROUGH PEKING?

Nixon and Kissinger have to be credited with a brilliant innovation of the negotiating track. Ever since the beginnings of Russian-American summitry, it was assumed in Washington that any negotiating track would have to go through Moscow. Like Columbus and the egg, they hit upon the afterward self-evident notion that a negotiating track might just possibly go through Peking. Kissinger had heard much about China from his Harvard colleagues and, probably, from friends in French foreign affairs circles who had good relations with China—had heard enough to make China at least seem "complex." Nixon was desperately anxious to end the Vietnam affair so that he could get on to the true greatness of America. If Kissinger admired Metternich and Bismarck, Nixon admired de Gaulle. De Gaulle had ended France's second dirty war in Algeria, but, in the process, gave conservative government a firm foundation, renewed France's power throughout much of its former empire, and won it a major military and economic role in Europe. Nixon could hope to be an American de Gaulle only if he could end America's own *sale guerre* in Vietnam. But unlike de Gaulle, who hurled the gauntlet down to the military rightists and then smashed them, Nixon would have to placate them. "Peace with honor" was the only feasible solution, but how to get it was the trickiest of questions. Vietnamization was part of the answer but not all, for it carried with it the threat of a wider war. Why could not the other part be a new negotiating track going through Peking?

The most compelling reason (even to the military) for thinking that a negotiating track might go over Peking was the Sino-Soviet conflict, which erupted into open warfare in March 1969. If Russia was so worried about China's nuclear build-up that it approached the Nixon Administration on a possible preventive strike and deployed a substantial part of its armed forces on the China border, then China might have reason, for all its ideological peculiarities, to seek a respite in the conflict raging to the south. China would have little to gain from a Vietnamese victory, but much to lose in case of Russian attack. The Chinese were world revolutionaries as the United States military firmly believed, but the Harvard and Paris schools of Sinology held that deep down in their hearts they were nationalists, that Mao was a reincarnation of the Son of Heaven, and that communism was an organizational veneer covering an unchanging Chinese reality. Political Science taught Kissinger that national interest ultimately was (or should be) the only basis of a nation's foreign policy. Nixon learned the same thing by going through a political process that seemed ideological on the surface but cloaked the most extraordinary kinds of material interests beneath. Both Nixon and Kissinger loathe and fear ideology as disruptive to balances of power. It obviously was in China's national interest not to be attacked. Aiding the world revolution in Vietnam had to be of second priority (interest comes before ideology). Therefore, if China came to its senses after the idiocy of the Cultural Revolution, it would begin more to perceive its national interests and be less preoccupied with ideology. Ideologically, America was China's archenemy, but not from the viewpoint of national interest. Therefore, if China made an approach to America, it could be construed not as propaganda or subterfuge, but as a long-awaited return to rationality and moderation on China's part. Even the Joint Chiefs of Staff could understand that China would not want to wage a two-front war. Fortunately for Nixon and Kissinger, it was in early 1969 that they finally came to accept the Sino-Soviet split.

The Chinese made their first approach in late November, only a few weeks after Nixon's election. The February issue of *Red Flag* carried the full text of Nixon's inaugural address, implying to its readers that the leaders of China thought that the change in administrations in Washington had more than routine significance. This approach to America aroused bitter conflict within the Chinese leadership, which became clear later with the Lin Piao affair. It is not difficult to surmise the arguments that were raised in Peking against making the November overture to Nixon. The Chinese were well aware of the fact, evident in Russian publications, that the Russians were haunted by the specter of a Sino-American alliance directed against them. And if they felt that such an alliance might be in the making with a President who had been bitterly hostile to Russia, then they might be tempted to launch a preventive strike against China. But the offer was made, publicly to give it credence, and was taken very seriously among the emerging policy makers of the new Nixon Administration.

The only China policy the Nixon Administration inherited from its predecessors was that of an emerging "containment without isolation." But since the core of that policy was China's acceptance of two China's, the chances of China reacting positively to it were nil. Moreover, in view of America's decision not to attack China's nuclear sites and an apparent decision not to let the air war against North Vietnam spread into China, Washington could no longer offer Peking security against attack in return for its accepting a two-China policy. The Nixon Administration did, in fact, pursue a containment without isolation policy, but it was Rogers and his State Department who did so, not Nixon and Kissinger. That policy died a final death during the United Nations debates of the fall of 1971 over China's admission. While Rogers fought hard for a two-China solution with the full backing of Satō's Japan, Kissinger was in Peking weaving the threads of a new and different China policy. Japan's active involvement in the two-China policy reflected a cardinal principle of containment: the maintenance of United States alliances with Japan and Western Europe. Obviously, when Nixon and Kissinger sprung a totally new China policy onto the world, shock waves hit Japan (the "Nixon shock"). Satō fought hard with Rogers to salvage containment, but when it failed, he (and his faction) lost the premiership and a new era in Japanese foreign policy arose with the premiership of Kakuei Tanaka.

Johnson was committed to the alliance system of containment policy, though the alliances were harmed by the obsession with Vietnam. Nixon, however, seemed not overly concerned about the alliance systems, particularly in the case of Japan, and all the old ones have been eroded during his administration. It seems safe to say that the Nixon Administration came to power with a philosophy that held that America's national interests should be the sole determinants of foreign policy, and that the ideological obsessions that had trapped all administrations since the end of World War II had to be rooted out. If Nixon and Kissinger were generally disenchanted with containment policy at the beginning of the first Nixon term and were thinking of a new China policy, it would make no sense to maintain an old and bankrupt two-China policy. That they did shows how long it takes for unreplenished currents finally to dry up.

On July 15, 1971, it became clear what the new China policy was to be: direct summit contact between the chief executives of both countries. The Russian-American détente had arisen out of an earlier tradition of summitry. Now Nixon might do with China what his Republican predecessor and family relative Eisenhower did with Russia. In July 1969, Nixon made a surprise visit to Bucharest, journeying there via the Far East. Premier Ceausescu was then and has remained since a warm friend of China. In retrospect, the Bucharest trip can be seen as a prelude to the China trip in February 1972.[1] Thus, it must have been quite early in the Nixon Administration that the idea surfaced for a dramatic summitry-type breakthrough to China.

On his way to Bucharest, Nixon stopped in Guam and enunciated the Nixon Doctrine, which was Vietnamization generalized to the rest of East Asia and to the world as a whole. While it spelled a withdrawal of American ground forces from Asia, it also vouchsafed a major role to American naval and air power, which would support native regimes

[1] *See* Rowland Evans, Jr., and Robert D. Novak, *Nixon in the White House*, pp. 97–101.

resisting communist aggression. That summer of 1969, one could not have suspected the magnitude of the American bombing campaign in the years to come. On Guam, Nixon delivered some tough words on the subject of China (understandable considering where he was), but in Bucharest his tone was very probably different as he discussed China with Ceausescu. But the tough words on China had an ominous ring due to the fact that the Nixon Doctrine in general and Vietnamization in particular opened the gates to a vastly extended air war. Naturally, China was the country most threatened, aside from those in Indochina.

The new Nixon Administration found itself pursuing two completely contradictory policy currents. Vietnamization was a reversion to an older right-wing policy that always saw China as the main enemy. But the new emerging summit relationship with China recognized it as a nuclear power and, therefore, ruled out war. The Vietnamese and the Chinese have old policies of "fight, fight—talk, talk," and the Americans adopted them with the initiation of the Paris talks. But it was beyond credence that the air war could creep back up to China's borders as Nixon was planning a trip to Peking. Yet that is exactly what happened from November 7, 1971, when General Lavelle launched his first "unauthorized" raid against North Vietnam until the great Christmas raids of 1972.

The Nixon Doctrine, misunderstood as a doctrine for American withdrawal from East Asia, was actually a doctrine only for the withdrawal of American ground forces. It constituted final presidential acceptance of the old "never again" military beliefs that America could not fight a land war on the Asian mainland. But it by no means indicated any abandonment of America's Asian allies to the communists. The old combination of native Asian armies, American air and naval power, and American-directed covert war would be put back into operation, as it had been during the Eisenhower period. What was new in the doctrine was largely the increased role assigned to air power.

But Bucharest symbolized something new, and not just in regard to China. A new policy current began to become evident during the first Nixon Administration which superseded containment as presidential policy. The key to it was a changing perspective on the Russian-American relationship. The détente had cooled considerably, beginning in 1966, but Dean Rusk never gave up hope that it could be warmed up again. Nixon himself never entirely gave up hope that the old negotiating track through Moscow might yet work. His visit to Moscow in May 1972 was crowned with the signing of a SALT agreement of a sort that Johnson and Rusk had always yearned for. But even before the agreement was submitted for ratification, the Jackson amendment, covertly supported by the White House, began to remove some of its spirit and intent. While it was easy to see that Johnson and Rusk wanted such arms agreements, it is not so easy to discern a similar desire within the Nixon Administration. There was virtually no one in the Pentagon who really wanted a SALT agreement. Melvin Laird constantly warned of the Russian threat. When Nixon's visit to Moscow was announced, the *New York Times* commented editorially: "Secretary Laird's alarmist reports on the Soviet strategic missile buildup at sea and on land contrasts curiously with President Nixon's optimism about stabilization of the nuclear arms race."[2] The new policy current is most evident in military publications, particularly of the Navy. It holds that American interests are being globally threatened in the 1970s by a rapidly growing Russian strategic capability, by Russian military expansion into far-flung corners of the world, and by America's declining ability to maintain the security systems to which it has been committed. Some of the most outspoken proponents of the new doctrine have attacked the Vietnam war as a drainage of American will and resources, which only served to leave other fields wide open for Russian penetration. With the Joint Chiefs of Staff traditionally hostile to any arms control agreement, with the Arms Control and Disarmament Agency weaker than ever, with Kissinger's reputed anti-Russian sentiments, who within the bureaucracy wanted a SALT agreement? Quite possibly Nixon's trip to Moscow and the hurriedly arranged SALT agreement were devised in October 1971 partly in anticipation of a year of fierce fighting in Indochina during 1972 which could jeopardize the trip to China and partly to allay Russian fears that a Sino-American alliance was too rapidly in the making.

THE "ONE-AND-ONE-HALF WAR" CONCEPT

The new policy current became evident in 1969 in the form of what was called a "long-range military policy." William Beecher, the *New York Times* Pentagon correspondent, summarized it on October 24, 1969:

> Nine months into its term, the Nixon Administration is beginning to shape a long-range military policy that is, at once, riskier and more cautious than that of its Democratic predecessors.
>
> The new Administration is determined to cut back sharply on non-nuclear forces—the planes, tanks, ships and battalions that provide the traditional military power—accepting the risks implicit in supporting undiminished global commitments with diminished forces. . . .
>
> Commitments, as of now, are not being reduced. But rather than planning forces for simultaneous wars in both Europe and Asia,

[2] *New York Times*, October 26, 1971.

the forces will be tailored to fight on a large scale in either place, *but not in both at once* [my italics]. . . .

Previous administrations felt it prudent to plan to fight on two distant fronts at once, primarily because the United States has specific commitments in both Europe and Asia, and in World War II was forced to fight in both places at once. *If major crises should happen to develop on both fronts in the future, the nation's leaders will simply have to make a choice* [my italics].

But in the realm of nuclear weapons—missiles, anti-missiles, and bombers—the opposite appears to be the case. While willing, even eager, some contend, to seek an arms control agreement with the Soviet Union, the Administration has made a policy decision to prevent the Russians from being in a position to do more damage to the United States than the country could do in return.

What Beecher, of course, reported was presidential thinking on military policy; the Navy and the Air Force were hardly in a mood for cutbacks in ships and planes. But that thinking signified a move away from the forces-in-being concepts that had governed Democratic administrations and toward a new version of massive retaliation, the military policy of the Eisenhower era. Translated into foreign policy terms, the new Nixon military policy saw Russia as a major competitor and, therefore, stressed the strategic weapons build-up. But the most significant thing Beecher reported was the abandonment of the old two-and-one-half war concept for a new one-and-one-half war concept. In terms of military planning, the concept had little meaning (some ridiculed it as a zero war concept), but in terms of foreign policy, it had considerable meaning. Since America could not afford to have both Russia and China as principal enemies (to use the Maoist term), it had to make a probability choice in its long-range estimations: Which of the two would more probably be a long-range enemy or competitor?

If the Nixon Administration in 1969 decided on a policy of cutting back on conventional weapons and building up its strategic weapons, then consciously or unconsciously it was assuming that the probable long-range enemy was more likely to be Russia than China.

The two-and-one-half war concept implied that America could fight Russia and China simultaneously regardless of the relations between them. The one-and-one-half war concept made a triangular relationship between the three great powers inevitable. In zero-sum terms, it meant two against one or some variant thereof.

But practically, the one-and-one-half war concept faced the Nixon Administration with some dilemmas. If a "crisis" (so defined by Washington) did erupt, say in Southeast Asia and the Middle East at the same time, it could not react simultaneously on both fronts—not so much in terms of actual military capabilities, but in terms of the deepening commitments every act of political or military intervention represents. As we shall see, that was the dilemma Nixon faced at the time of the invasion of Cambodia, which is why I have selected that crisis as the last to be analyzed in this book.

The "half" in both concepts meant, in practice, Indochina. Under both concepts, therefore, America could go on fighting a war in Indochina. But while such a notion was credible in raw military terms, politically it was not. What the war was all about was stopping communist aggression that originated in North Vietnam but also, and more importantly, farther up, in Peking or Moscow or both. There was no way that "one-half war" could be detached from global politics.

Bureaucratically that "one-half war" dominated the foreign policy of the entire first Nixon Administration. But the war had been conceived at a time and in a context in which China was the principal enemy. The interests that had built up around it were oriented toward fighting China directly or indirectly. Naturally, they had no desire for a redefinition of the situation which could reduce their roles. CINCPAC Admiral John McCain continued to emphasize China as America's principal enemy in the Pacific even after the announcement of Nixon's visit to Peking. In a speech in December 1971, he reiterated: "Certainly, the major potential source of danger in the Western Pacific is Communist China."[3] By contrast, other Navy publications were stressing China's weakness and the growing Russian naval threat.

That "one-half war" prevented the Nixon Administration from achieving the "one-and-one-half war" policy that Beecher described in late 1969. It was a war of conventional weapons (ships, planes, and still some troops) and, thus, retarded the cutback on conventional forces. It was implicitly aimed at China, counteracting the emerging policy of rapprochement with China. And as a war sustained primarily by military-bureaucratic interests, it worked against the larger aims and power of presidential policy.

THE INVASION OF CAMBODIA— AIR WAR PRELUDE IN LAOS

The invasion of Cambodia announced by Nixon on April 30, 1970, marked a watershed of his first administration. Until then, it seemed as if Vietnamization might proceed without a return to full-scale air war. After April 30, the air war intensified until it reached a climax in May

[3] U.S., Congress, *Congressional Record*, 91st Cong., 2d Sess., December 6, 1971, E13032–37.

1972. The "one-half war" that Nixon and Kissinger had hoped could be settled in the interests of larger global politics came back onto the scene and would remain there—dangerously—until the end of the first Nixon Administration.

Although the Joint Chiefs of Staff had been eager to take out the Cambodian sanctuaries for years, the evidence does not indicate that the invasion of Cambodia had been planned or decided on long before. The best evidence are the two Nixon speeches of April 20 and April 30. The difference in tone alone showed that different circumstances prevailed for each. On April 20, a calm Richard Nixon announced that 150,000 American soldiers would be withdrawn from South Vietnam over the coming year. He evinced full faith in his Vietnamization policy and appeared to be on the same track that he had been on since assuming office. Ten days later, he seemed in near panic, vowing that the United States would never be defeated and sending American ground combat troops into Cambodia in an operation that stunned the world, including the highest officials of his own government. The tone as much as the content of the speech communicated itself to millions of protestors and played a major part in the immediate explosion of demonstrations. As Max Frankel of the *New York Times* asked on May 2, What happened to jolt Nixon?

The invasion, since touted by the Nixonites as a great victory, was a military farce. Ostensibly, it was supposed to root out Viet Cong sanctuaries and, in particular, the operational command center called COSVN (Chief of Station, CIA, Vietnam) in the American literature. The invasion succeeded in destroying virtually all the Cambodian border towns and further decimated the rubber plantations on the Cambodian side of the border. But there was not much contact with the enemy, nor was any trace of COSVN found. By June 30, all the Americans were out of Cambodia and the sanctuaries resumed their former shape. Nothing had changed militarily, as was so often the case in Vietnam when the Americans or the ARVNs launched an operation.

Covert war's sibling, the air war, got a big boost with the invasion of Cambodia. On May 1, four massive air strikes were mounted against North Vietnam, constituting the first sizable violation of Johnson's October 30, 1968, bombing halt, though there had been bombing of North Vietnam before then.

The resumption of the air war against North Vietnam also went by way of Laos, as in 1964. And as always in Laos, air strikes and covert war went hand in hand. In 1969, the Vientiane forces had managed to retake the Plaine des Jarres from the Pathet Lao. But early in 1970, the Pathet Lao (or North Vietnamese, as Vientiane always alleged) retook it, leaving only Long Cheng, the CIA/Vang Pao central headquarters, in government hands. Immediately, Vientiane ground out the familiar domino cries of crisis as NVA forces were readying to take Luang Prabang and Vientiane and sweep down into Thailand, etc. Suddenly, 400 American Navy and Air Force planes swept over Laos, both the Ho Chi Minh Trail and the Plaine des Jarres, and carried out one of the heaviest raids in Southeast Asian history. The shock at that attack was only slightly less than at the decision to invade Cambodia. The congressional doves, notably Senator Mansfield, vehemently protested and demanded categorically that there be no more. What alarmed Senator Mansfield most was that B-52s designed for strategic bombing had taken part in the raids against the Plaine des Jarres. The crisis was so serious that President Nixon, on March 6, issued the first official American statement of American policy in Laos, which supposedly cooled the crisis.

What was politically significant about the massive Laos raids of February 1970 was that they were overt, undisguised American actions against the Plaine des Jarres, a part of Laos that was not directly linked to the war in South Vietnam. In early March, Washington indicated that the Ho Chi Minh Trail in eastern Laos was considered part of that war by giving General Abrams command of all air operations over it, thus taking it away from Honolulu.[4] But operations over the Plaine des Jarres remained in CINCPAC's jurisdiction. The story of the great CIA base at Long Cheng became known in 1971. The Americans had created a "clandestine army" made up of Meos, some of whom were hardly adolescents, which was described as the Royal Lao government's most effective fighting force. The Vang Pao Meos were not just main force units that were supposed to hold territory, but counterguerrillas who, as in the past, ranged deep into Pathet Lao, North Vietnamese, and Chinese territory.

The taking, retaking, losing, and gaining of the Plaine des Jarres by one side or the other was seasonal. Whether the Pathet Lao and the NVA were determined to wipe out Vang Pao's forces in early 1970 as they finally did in late 1971 is difficult to say. But committing massive American air power in support of Vang Pao was in the old 1950s roll-back tradition. At that time, the Chinese had several thousand soldiers in northern Laos, where they were building a road toward the Mekong. The American military had strict orders to stay away from them.[5] But the anti-China as well as anti–North Vietnam thrust of the February raids was obvious, despite Nixon's attempt in early March to play it down.[5a]

[4] *San Francisco Chronicle*, March 2, 1970.
[5] *New York Times*, March 3, 1970.
[5a] New light on the air war was revealed later in 1973 by congressional hearings into "unauthorized" bombings of Cambodia. Significantly, these raids began in March 1969, the same month Nixon was sending signals to Peking through de Gaulle.

The mounting of massive raids against the Plaine des Jarres, including B-52s, could have no meaning other than a Washington policy decision to revert to the fateful policies of 1964. Nixon's March 6 statement on Laos appealed to Russia to help restore the status quo ante, but made no mention of China.

The bombing of Laos was as ferocious as ever, but the raids against the Plaine des Jarres had ominous implications so far as Washington policy was concerned—the dagger was being pointed again toward North Vietnam and China.

There was nothing much happening in South Vietnam to justify the escalation in Laos. In early March, all reports from South Vietnam indicated that the fighting was tapering off. NVA units remained stationary along the Cambodian border and in two base camps in the Mekong Delta. The month of February recorded one of the lowest figures of "enemy initiated incidents" within memory. Even American commanders were practicing restraint, no longer engaging the enemy so long as he remained in his jungle and mountain camps. James Sterba of the *New York Times* reported on March 10 that there were three sets of opinions on this phenomenon. Some military commanders felt that the enemy had been decisively weakened. Others felt that he was just waiting until April, when the next round of troop withdrawals would be announced, to launch attacks. Others, largely civilian analysts in Saigon, apparently felt that the enemy was reverting to protracted warfare. Thus, there was no military crisis on the ground that spring of 1970 (unlike 1972, when there was a large-scale NLF/NVA offensive). In fact, after the overthrow of Sihanouk, American commanders and some reporters (notably Joseph Alsop) began to speak of the "golden opportunity" the new situation in Cambodia presented finally to take out the sanctuaries. The sense of crisis in Nixon's April 30 speech could hardly have come from the military situation in South Vietnam itself, which, on the surface, seemed to be better for the Thieu regime than before.

MARCH 1970 COUP IN CAMBODIA

If the bombing of the Plaine des Jarres seemed to presage a return to the 1964 policies, the overthrow of Sihanouk on March 18 did even more so. Even though Souvanna remained and Sihanouk went, the similarities between the April 1964 coup in Laos and the March 1970 coup in Cambodia were evident. In Laos, Russian-American cooperation continued going through the figure of Souvanna. In Cambodia, something analogous happened. While Sihanouk sought refuge in Peking, the Russians stayed in Phnom Penh and recognized the Lon Nol regime (though they claimed to be giving support to the Cambodian liberation movement, the NUFK). While Sihanouk was still in power, he had no particular antagonism to the Russians, such as he developed after Russian refusal to recognize the new government in Peking. Sihanouk has been credited with having executed extraordinary feats of juggling and balancing among all the hostile powers, great and small, that surrounded Cambodia, for the one purpose of keeping the war distant and his country independent. While he was at times antagonistic to the Americans, he was clever enough to realize that he had to come to terms with them. In fact, early in 1970, he seemed to be veering back toward a more friendly stance vis-à-vis the Americans. In February 1970, he said it was "American imperialism" that assured Cambodia's independence and territorial integrity and was an essential ingredient for the respect, friendship, and aid of "our socialist friends."[6] Translated into clearer terms: Cambodia needs the Americans to keep the Vietnamese at bay and both Russia and China understand that.

Whatever the actual circumstances of the coup, it was welcome to Washington and to the American military, evident in the frequent references to "golden opportunities." The new ruler Lon Nol, naturally, began requesting American aid. His puny army was almost immediately beefed up by American-trained Khmer Serei ethnic Cambodians from South Vietnam. His second-in-command, Sirik Matak, was hailed by the Americans as an able administrator, unusual in Cambodia. If the Joint Chiefs of Staff were seriously thinking that spring of finally fully implementing NSAM 273, it meant carrying out Laos-Cambodia border control operations. Souvanna could be relied on to go along with anything the Americans proposed, but Sihanouk was tricky and hostile. Those border control operations involved much more than clearing out sanctuaries. For example, they required denying the port of Sihanoukville to the National Liberation Front operating in the Mekong Delta. Throughout the Pentagon Papers and in many newspaper columns of the time are expressions of right-wing and/or military opinions calling for the closing of the port of Sihanoukville (and, of course, Haiphong as well). The military was convinced that supplies were all that sustained the insurgencies and that they originated in Russia and China. Sihanoukville was frequented by Chinese ships, which the military was convinced were carrying weapons and matériel. If the port could be closed, then it would take a long time before alternative supply lines could be set up from the Ho Chi Minh Trail. Moreover, Sihanoukville symbolized a vast commercial operation with arms reaching into the Saigon black market, the NVA base camps in the U Minh forest, and the officials of the Sihanouk government.

Like the Indonesian coup in September 1965, the coup against Si-

---

[6] *New York Times*, February 7, 1970.

hanouk got considerable support from the citizenry of Phnom Penh
(though the peasants remained staunchly in support of Sihanouk). He
was portrayed as a reactionary, corrupt, feudal ruler who was being
replaced by a progressive republican government. Corruption was rife in
the government and it was not difficult to arouse popular antagonism to
Sihanouk's officials. It was also a simple matter to arouse popular antagonism against the large Vietnamese minority living in the country.
Thousands were slaughtered by Lon Nol's soldiers. As everywhere in
Southeast Asia, there is popular resentment against the harder-working
Chinese and Vietnamese. Lon Nol, thus, found it easy to mount a cause
that was at once anti-Sihanouk, anticorruption, and anti-Vietnamese. To
be anti-Vietnamese cleared the way for an alliance with Washington and
Saigon. To be anticorruption cleared the way for smashing the commercial nexus on the Vietnam-Cambodian border that so bothered the
Americans. But the anti-Sihanouk aspect of Lon Nol's cause was to have
much broader and deeper implications than he realized. With Cambodia
having become more than ever China's special concern, an anti-Sihanouk
stance was automatically an anti-China stance, as the Russians made
clear by recognizing Lon Nol. But Lon Nol, like Chiang Kai-shek and
Diem and so many other reactionaries, underestimated the latent power
of the Cambodian peasantry and the ability of a revolutionary movement
to gain power in the countryside. In 1970, the Americans considered the
NUFK a joke or a fig leaf masking Vietnamese guerrillas. News reports
invariably only spoke of battles between Cambodians and Viet Cong. In
early 1973, the NUFK had liberated virtually the entire countryside and
captured a number of major towns, and the American press no longer
felt it possible or useful to deny that the war in Cambodia was one
between Cambodians.

WHAT PANICKED NIXON?

Thus, on April 20, 1970, when Nixon announced the withdrawal of
another 150,000 troops within the year, the military situation in South
Vietnam and the political situation in Cambodia seemed definitely to be
going in a direction favorable to the Americans. Whatever the Americans wanted to do about the sanctuaries they could do with Vietnamese
and Cambodian forces, and what they couldn't do they could also not
possibly do with American troops—the chances of clearing and holding
the sanctuaries were beyond anyone's capabilities. What happened, then,
to plunge Nixon into panic and make him throw his entire Vietnamization policy into reverse gear?

There were some startling events, but they occurred outside of Indo-

china. They had to do with the global politics that are the special preserve of the Presidency. But no President could get up and publicly say
that a military move in Cambodia was a pawn pushed in a vastly larger
chess game of world politics. The notion of that chess game, which is
what this book is about, had little acceptance either among the general
public or in Congress. Most citizens still held that war is waged for the
purpose of defense or resisting aggression (like resisting Communist
aggression in Vietnam). And Congress still felt that wars should be
waged only with the advice and consent of the Senate. But the nuclear
chess game was not compatible with either popular sovereignty or parliamentary rule. As it was, the President preferred to appeal to the
bottom over the middle. He spoke to what he felt was the majority's
opposition to any American defeat, appealing to their nationalism. He
could not tell them what kind of defeat was impending, but he hoped
that mentioning the possibility of defeat would rally support behind him.
Like any President, he had to go to his constituencies when he faced a
great crisis within his bureaucratic ranks and ask for their support.

A number of news reports at the time indicated that the night of
Monday, April 27, was when Nixon made his decision to send American
ground troops into Cambodia.[7] Max Frankel spoke of it as "the fateful
night of April 27." A regular National Security Council meeting had
been scheduled for April 24 but was postponed until April 28.[8] What
happened to influence the decision must have occurred before April 27.

On April 24, China launched its first earth-orbiting satellite, thereby
announcing to the world a delivery capability equivalent to what would
be needed to shoot an ICBM. The April 27 issue of the *People's Daily*
listed all of the cities over which the satellite flew—one was Washington,
another was Moscow. Satellites meant guidance systems, which could
also be used to drop a nuclear payload anywhere they might want to. It
took the Russians eight years to get from atomic explosion to satellite/
ICBM; it took the Chinese less than six years. While there was relatively
little scare publicity about the Chinese feat, it was comparable to the
Russian 1957 breakthrough, which aroused a furious missile gap controversy in America.

On April 24 and 25, the leaders of North Vietnam, the National
Liberation Front, the Pathet Lao, and the NUFK met in southern China
near Canton to announce the formation of a united Indochinese front to
resist American imperialism. On April 25, Premier Chou En-lai went to
the meeting to guarantee Chinese support and to announce to them
officially China's new space feat.

---

[7] Max Frankel, *New York Times*, May 2, 1970; Flora Lewis, *Newsday*, May 2, 1970;
    San Francisco Chronicle, May 2, 1970.
[8] Tad Szulc, *New York Times*, April 27, 1970.

One can be certain, judging from earlier examples, that the Chinese timed their satellite shot (presumably in all confidence that it would work) to coincide with the Indochina summit conference. Thus, as in communiqués announcing earlier nuclear detonations, the Chinese made explicit that they considered their newly augmented nuclear power a deterrent against the United States and a warning not to go too far in Indochina.

The political significance of the Indochina summit conference was considerable. It signaled that henceforth the wars in North Vietnam, South Vietnam, Laos, and Cambodia (to come) were a single Indochina-wide war. The official American position and that of the Russians was that these various wars were separate affairs in principle even if they overlapped in practice. The notion of many different wars in Indochina was also rejected by the American military, which took the common-sensical position that it was just a war of communists against anticom-munists. NSAM 273 already gave expression to that view. Washington was desperately committed to the notion of many wars because it was essential to any hope of leverage or linkage through great power politics. Thus, several times in his April 30 speech, Nixon reiterated that the invasion of Cambodia was not launched in response to Lon Nol's request for aid but for the narrow military purposes of clearing out the sanctu-aries. The Russians took the same position because one single Indochina war could only mean loss of the leverage and influence that many wars gave them. The fact that the April 24–25 Indochina summit conference was held in China and attended at the end by Chou En-lai could only have been seen by the Russians as a gain for the Chinese.

The participants of the summit conference must have known that the proclamation of a single Indochina-wide war would just lead to the Americans taking the same line. Most likely, they had concluded that the Americans already were taking and implementing that line. Around April 17, South Vietnamese forces launched an invasion of Cambodia in the Parrot's Beak sector. The invasion was fully backed by the Ameri-cans and, except for the presence of American ground combat soldiers on Cambodian soil, was essentially similar to the one the ARVNs would launch against the Ho Chi Minh Trail the following spring. With the huge bombings in Laos and the steadily escalating air strikes against North Vietnam, the leaders of the Indochina forces and the Chinese leaders could hardly be faulted for concluding that Nixon was finally going to try to win the war in the way his military had been recommend-ing for years: hit them hard all over Indochina and maybe China as well. The Cambodian coup, which they were convinced was instigated by the Americans, sent the same political message: Washington was ready to overturn the political rules of the game that had existed until March 18 and move directly toward some kind of out-and-out victory.

That the invasion of Cambodia was a fearsome crisis was evident not just from the immense protest within America and elsewhere, but from the Chinese reaction. On May 20, Mao Tse-tung issued one of his rare statements on foreign policy in which he warned that the danger of a new world war still existed. For all their ideological shrillness, the Chinese are basically commonsensical about important matters. Mao's May 20 statement said, in effect, that the extension of the Indochina war to China, which had been avoided for so long, might yet occur.

While Nixon's decision to order American ground units into Cambodia through the Fishhook sector satisfied General Abrams and Ambassador Bunker, it must have appeared ludicrously weak to the rest of the military. Flora Lewis reported that United States military chiefs, notably Admiral Moorer, proposed an amphibious landing with 30,000 American soldiers to seize the port of Sihanoukville.[9] This was to supplement operations planned for the Cambodia-Vietnam border region. Attorney General Mitchell was described as enthusiastic, but Laird and Rogers were opposed. The second of the three options placed before Nixon, "massive military assistance to Cambodia itself," was discarded fairly early in the planning stage. The third option, to invade at the Fishhook sector, was finally adopted. Laird supported this option, although Rogers was opposed. Thus, as so often in the past among hawk-dawk-dove options, the President chose the dawk one. Rogers's "dove" option was hopeless, for it was predicated on the already discredited notion that the United States could get its Asian allies (like Indonesia) involved in Cambodia.

The most interesting option, of course, was the one to take Sihanoukville with 30,000 troops. Because of the puny nature of the Cambodian army and because the Viet Cong forces were mainly guerrilla forces (all the alleged NVA forces were positioned in relation to military action in the Mekong Delta), 30,000 seems an excessively large number to take the port. But since Admiral Moorer finally revealed that the Joint Chiefs of Staff favored an invasion of North Vietnam,[10] the Sihanoukville operation was most likely conceived as a training exercise for that real invasion to come later.

Until April 24, Nixon and Kissinger thought that they could proceed at a leisurely pace to increase the pressure in Indochina (say, through a South Vietnamese invasion of Cambodia and some more bombing of Laos and, in bits and pieces, of North Vietnam), and at the same time continue making their negotiating track overtures to the Chinese. Thus, in the process of fight, fight—talk, talk, the Chinese would realize that America was determined to be tough but also willing to be reasonable. But then came the Chinese satellite on April 24 and the Indochina

[9] *Newsday*, May 5, 1970.
[10] *New York Times*, February 24, 1973.

summit conference. Nixon and Kissinger found themselves suddenly with the same crisis that had afflicted their White House predecessors. Seizing the opportunity, the military came rushing in with proposals to get the war going again in a way that would be winnable.

The Chinese space shot and the Indochina summit conference were not the only significant events of that week. Immediately following the Chinese space shot, the Russians launched a new space marvel of their own—a satellite that spewed forth eight smaller satellites. Whatever that meant in precise technical terms, there can be no doubt that in the minds of American strategic planners it conjured up the possibility that the Russians had also finally mastered the technology of MIRV.

There was an event in the Middle East, widely reported in the press, that also impinged on American interests. American and Israeli intelligence revealed that Russian pilots were flying combat aircraft in Egypt. For the Israelis, this was a bitter blow because it destroyed their uncontested air supremacy in Egyptian skies. They had mounted a number of bombing raids on Cairo to show what they could do if the Egyptians wanted to start hostilities again along the Suez Canal. There were also rumors that the Israelis hoped to provoke a change of regime in Cairo to one that might be willing to make peace with Israel. For the Americans, the Russian combat presence in the Middle East was alarming because it threatened a balance of power that had been emerging since the Six Day War of 1967. By September 1970, the worst Middle East crisis since 1967 erupted in Jordan. King Hussein decided to annihilate the Palestinian guerrillas, and in response, Syrian tanks began moving into Jordan. Washington threatened intervention, the tanks withdrew, and Hussein succeeded in destroying the Palestinians. The Israelis also apparently threatened to intervene if Hussein was overthrown. Whatever the causal sequence from the introduction of Russian pilots into Egypt in April to the September crisis, it seemed to bear out the conviction of policy makers that sudden changes in the balance of power between countries produce crises.

There could be little doubt in the mind of anyone who saw Nixon on television on April 30 that he felt that America was in crisis. His reference to its being threatened with defeat like a "pitiful, helpless giant" was similar to one he made two days earlier to a group of right-wing, promilitary people (from the Navy League, the American Security Council, etc.). In fact, he confided to them the morning of April 28, just after the decision-making evening of April 27, the "imperative action he was going to take in Cambodia if we were to escape the probability of total and humiliating defeat."[11] That Nixon felt he had to placate the right wing is evident from his constant reiteration of the theme "peace

[11] *Christian Science Monitor*, May 27, 1970.

with honor." Robert Semple of the *New York Times* wrote in July that behind Nixon's policy on the war was fear not of the left but of the right. There was only one man who could bring peace in Vietnam, Nixon indicated, and that was he, the President. If confidence in him was destroyed, the outcome would be "Caesarism."[12] Nixon appears to have voiced fears of a right-wing reaction a number of times to journalists. The British journalist Henry Brandon reported in the London Sunday *Times* in December 1972 that Nixon feared Caesarism if there was an evident defeat in Vietnam. The Nixon line seems to be that if confidence in the institutions of government, in particular the Presidency, is destroyed, then it will become a "physical test of strength"[13] between left and right, which will lead to right-wing Caesarism.

There was a real crisis that week in April and Nixon felt that it was important, on the morning after the decision making, to announce his tough new moves to the right-wing, promilitary delegations that visited him in the White House. But the crisis did not directly involve Indochina even though the people of Indochina would have to pay in blood for its resolution. The four events I have described suddenly appeared to shift the balance of power at both a global and a regional level to America's disadvantage. While Kent State and the massive antiwar demonstrations focused public attention on Indochina, others understood the real crisis behind the public one. On May 23, 1970 General Thomas ("Tough Tommy") Power, former Strategic Air Command commander, wrote in an "Op Ed" page article in the *New York Times*:

> We can face all of the problems facing us today, i.e., inflation, pollution, poverty, racial unrest, the war in Vietnam, drug addiction, law and order, etc., and still lose everything if we fail to prevent nuclear war or nuclear blackmail.

A Chinese ICBM and a Russian MIRV would give those two powers the ability to press their own goals in their respective areas of commitment, Indochina and the Middle East. In General Power's eyes, both seemed to be doing just that, with the Indochina summit conference and with Russian combat pilots in Egypt.

Exactly what General Power thought that America should do about this "nuclear blackmail" he did not see fit to publish in the *Times*. But the Joint Chiefs of Staff were eager to resume the air war against all of Indochina and plan for an invasion of North Vietnam (which General Maxwell Taylor in March 1973 implied that he favored).[14] In terms of the choice of principal enemies that the 1969 military policy review laid

12 *New York Times,* July 6, 1970.
13 Robert Semple, *New York Times,* July 6, 1970.
14 *Washington Post,* March 29, 1973.

out, that would have meant automatically selecting China as the principal enemy—a return to an older policy masking itself under the cover-name of "military viewpoint," but in reality rollback.

Nixon, for all of his right-wing origins, acted the way his presidential predecessors did: he opted against the extreme "options" proposed by the military and decided to send troops into Cambodia, as Johnson had done earlier. In fact, rumors began to circulate that Nixon might halt entirely the troop withdrawal program. This was in spite of the advice of Secretary of State William Rogers and Secretary of Defense Melvin Laird. Rogers had told Congress just on April 23: "If United States troops go into Cambodia, our whole [Vietnamization] program is defeated."[15] And in November 1969, Laird, testifying behind closed doors in Congress, said: "If Vietnamization fails in South Vietnam, the 'Nixon Doctrine' for all Asia goes down the drain."[16] But faced by a mushrooming crisis that could quickly get out of control, Nixon suddenly abandoned his own basic policies and reached back to the discredited policies of his predecessors.

TOWARD THE CHINESE-AMERICAN BREAKTHROUGH

The crisis passed and Nixon withdrew American troops from Cambodia on June 30 as scheduled. As in May 1966, the fact of a "Russian" as well as a "Chinese" crisis undoubtedly strengthened Nixon's hand in vetoing the extreme measures proposed by the Joint Chiefs of Staff. But the newly emerging "Russian" problem was reflected in a growing doctrinal split within the military that would not become apparent for another year or two. That doctrinal split also strengthened Nixon's hand against the Joint Chiefs. In 1972, it was surprising to see once bitterly anti-China Navy publications lauding Nixon's visit to China. Not sentiment but a new geopolitics was the source of that praise. Russia, the Russian navy, and varied threats to America's energy sources (chiefly oil) were perceived as the most serious threats to American national interests. China was seen as weak and mortally imperiled by the threat of Russian nuclear attack. The proponents of this new Navy geopolitics also were the military most disenchanted with the Indochina war, despite the unrelenting enthusiasm the carrier admirals still showed for it. Nixon's top military appointments, like Admiral Zumwalt or General Haig, reflected a presidential predilection for the rising new currents, though his original appointment of Admiral Moorer as chairman of the Joint

15 Murray Marder, *Washington Post*, May 6, 1970.
16 *Ibid.*, December 11, 1969.

Chiefs of Staff was a concession to the Pacific interests. While the Joint Chiefs, like the praesidium of a communist government, prefer to make unanimous recommendations to the President, not much military-bureaucratic wisdom is necessary to know where the cleavages are. The invasion of Cambodia was a low risk gamble. If it worked, the sanctuaries would be destroyed; if it did not, not much was risked and little was lost. It was a stalling device which would allow the fever heat of the crisis to pass.

Nixon and Kissinger must have known that another Cambodia-type crisis was bound to erupt. Unless they allowed themselves to slide into the only policy groove that seemed to promise victory in Indochina (all-out war against North Vietnam and its Chinese rear area), they had only one alternative action to prevent that and channel American foreign policies into the new directions they hoped to follow: to seek some direct and dramatic breakthrough to China. The creeping State Department policy of "containment without isolation" could not even be seriously considered. Nixon apparently had been sending presidential signals to Peking ever since his early 1969 visit to Paris. But without a come-on signal from the Chinese, nothing could be attempted. On December 25, 1970, the readers of the *People's Daily* saw a photograph of Chairman Mao and Edgar Snow cover the entire top half of the paper. In an interview with Snow, which *Life* magazine published on April 30, 1971, Chairman Mao extended an invitation to President Nixon to visit China. Nixon himself had intimated publicly that he might like to visit China someday. The public signals from both sides indicated that something was in the wind, though nothing was guaranteed to come off.

There is evidence from the Chinese side that they considered the crisis engendered by the Laos invasion early in 1971 as the turning point in their attitudes toward America. Unlike the Cambodian invasion, which could only strike at the terminus of the supply lines, the invasion of Laos aimed to do what the military had constantly yearned for: to cut all the lines going down the trail and starve the insurgency to death. The invasion was a classic test of Vietnamization. American fixed wing and helicopter aircraft did most of the fighting, with ARVNs being ferried in largely to hold areas on both sides of Route 9, set up fire bases, and leap frog farther and farther inland. The victory of Route 9 was a glorious one for the liberation forces. Not only were large numbers of helicopters shot down, but the concept of heliborne battle tactics, so beloved by the Army, was shattered beyond repair. The fire bases that the ARVNs thought invulnerable to attack were taken one after the other. The ARVNs, whom the proponents of Vietnamization once hoped could become an offensive force, were reduced to the only role in which they were able to perform, defense.

As the defeat (and it was a total and humiliating defeat) became more evident, rumors flew that Washington might take more drastic action. Early in February, the Chinese openly accused America of planning to use nuclear weapons in Laos. Chou En-lai, accompanied by a large political-military delegation, came to Hanoi early in March and concluded agreement for coordinated action in the war. Nixon had given Admiral Moorer considerable scope to try out his ideas for winning the war, including renewed bombing in North Vietnam. But there was no crisis in Washington, and, thus, Nixon did nothing.

This impressed the Chinese. In late March, they issued their invitation to an American Ping-Pong team to visit China. That began a growing inpouring of Americans, with a number of prestigious journalists already going in April and May. On July 15, 1971, Nixon announced acceptance of an invitation to visit China.

The July 15 announcement was a momentous achievement. In effect, Nixon recognized China as a nuclear power and, therefore, one to be dealt with on terms comparable to those on which America dealt with Russia. That finally ruled out an extension of the war in Indochina to China.

In bureaucratic-political terms, what Nixon succeeded in doing was gaining a trade-off of policy for power. While he and Kissinger may have seen the visit to China as a decisive move on the new negotiating track, in effect, Nixon guaranteed the conservative military that in return for acquiescence to the new China policy, they could have their war in Indochina and all the power trappings it represented (carrier missions, for instance). For Nixon, that Faustian bargain was a good one. Whatever happened in Indochina, the White House was shielded against a crisis that could lead to a major widening of the war. North Vietnam might be reduced to ashes, but the grass would remain green on the Chinese side of the border. He managed to detach that annoying one-half war from the issue of central war.

In late October 1971, when Nixon announced a visit to Moscow as well in May 1972, his not yet scheduled visit to Peking was not entirely certain. The war was heating up in Laos and Cambodia with strong indications that the NLF/NVA forces were preparing for a big push in the year 1972. Without the threat of Chinese intervention, Nixon could have no valid objections to military plans to reduce North Vietnam to ashes, or to mud puddles, as Goldwater proposed. But obviously, the Chinese had powerful commitments to North Vietnam, which they said again and again they would honor if pressed by the Americans. Thus, the military could yet outfox Nixon and Kissinger by intensifying the war, provoking the Chinese to cancel the visit, and bringing policy right back to where it was going so nicely in 1964. If that happened, it might be just as well to have an insurance policy in the older relationship with Moscow, which the Russians were eager to restore. Kissinger might have suggested the Moscow visit as a way of playing the triangle or even in order to discourage the Russians from launching an attack against China. But for Nixon, Vietnam remained the crushing burden he had to rid himself of completely before he could think of more ambitious foreign policies.

The DRV and PRG Vietnamese had no intention of entrusting their cause to the new global politics going through Peking, just as they never trusted the old global politics going through Moscow. The Chinese could well think in terms of broad currents of history, which taught that the Americans were getting out of Indochina, but the Vietnamese had a real war on their hands whose fate they were not going to allow others to determine for them. For the Vietnamese, 1968 had been a Dienbienphu year, though, alas, not decisive. For four long years, they prepared for another Dienbienphu year in 1972 when an election signaled the chance for another change in regime and/or a change in policy within the superpower they were battling. At the very end of March 1972, after Nixon's visit to Peking, the Vietnamese liberation forces mounted a powerful and far-ranging offensive against the ARVNs. In response, Washington unleashed the most ferocious air bombardment in human history. That bombing alone enabled the ARVNs to hold out defensively in places like An Loc and to recapture Quang Tri City. But as the American election neared, it seemed as if Nixon was willing to end the war—and then, early in 1973, a ceasefire was signed.

As the ceasefire went into effect, the clouds of Watergate gathered in Washington. In mid-April 1973, when it seemed as if the air war might again be unleashed against North Vietnam, the storm broke. As government in Washington became paralyzed, only the ferocious bombing of Cambodia continued. The men whom Watergate swept out of office were right-wingers like Mitchell, Kleindienst, and Agnew. Whatever was to happen, it was apparent, even at the time of writing (late May 1973), that Watergate marked a turning point in the political currents of Washington. The Vietnam ceasefire was also a turning point. For all the obvious differences between the conspiratorial cabals of Watergate and the riotous street politics (as well as factional in-fighting) of the Cultural Revolution, there seem to be some similarities. In both cases, a "small handful" of power wielders at the pinnacle of power were ousted, launching currents of change whose direction did not become apparent until years afterward. American imperialism and expansionism are not dead, but the forms, both centrist and rightist, which they took since 1945 are. America can no longer impose a Pax Americana on the world. And with the decline of the dollar, defeats on the battlefields, and the erosion of morale within America, the expansionist drives have slackened. But America remains the world's most formidable military and economic power and with that power comes the temptation to control world events and bend them to its will. In so doing, contradictions will again arise within America to be exported abroad and to be fought out until imperialism finally vanishes as a system of governance.

Epilogue

I began writing this book in March 1972 and finished in June 1973. While I had for some time given thought to splicing together some long un-published analyses of the Indochina war, it was a particular incident which made me decide to discard those essays and write a book from scratch. The publication of the Pentagon Papers prompted much writing by critics of the war based on the new revelations. I was asked to write an essay on the Pentagon Papers, did so, was reasonably satisfied with it, and was then surprised when the essay was rejected. On rereading it, I concluded that the rejection was justified. Because of the necessary brevity of an essay, I could not spell out the many ideas on which the analysis was based. These ideas arose during seven years' participation in the antiwar movement in which I and my colleagues, notably Peter Dale Scott, considered it imperative to examine the national security apparatus of the American government. They also relate to an intellectual career in which thinking about the nature of the state in a number of countries and historical periods has formed a major part of my work. I decided to pull ideas and analyses together and construct a book.

There are other political and scholarly reasons for this book. I believe that the central political fact in the world is the American government, yet few political phenomena are treated with such banal interpretations and mystification as that government. America, despite some loss of power, wealth, and prestige, remains the prime mover in the world. But, strange as it may seem, contrasted to the minute academic and intelligence dissections of Russian and Chinese politics, there are few convincing analyses of the contemporary political processes that govern the executive branch of the American government. Nothing illustrates the intellectual failure of Americanology so well as the open-mouthed bafflement which the events arising out of the Watergate incident have aroused among political scholars. It is understandable that members, advisers, and hangers-on of the establishment, being on the "team," would not wish to analyze their own side too deeply. In many countries that would be an offense punishable by death. But it is harder to understand why critics in this country, whose right to write freely is still protected by the First Amendment, have not had the intellectual creativity to develop some convincing new understandings of the American state. Too much critical writing has remained in liberal and radical doctrinal ruts, and while often sharp, has preferred the club to the scalpel.

But the deepest reason for writing this book was political and moral. Joining the antiwar movement meant a choice for politics as against nonpolitical professionalism or against remaining somehow within a "team" that was associated with a government practicing barbarism against Asians. As long as the war raged, I did not consider it necessary to define my political attitudes with any great precision. The movement was a broad amalgam of old and new leftists with all kinds of beliefs, causes, and special concerns thrown together. The main purpose was to gather enough people and interests together to force the government to get out of Indochina. But when the war ebbed, as an issue anyway, I began to sense the need to think out a political position.

I never shared the view of some radicals who considered America a mistake from the moment the Pilgrims landed. For all the viler motives behind its actions in the immediate postwar years, I felt that America played a progressive role at the time. I also felt that the antiwar movement showed that a revolutionary spirit still lived in America as a current, there since the American Revolution. I have been strongly influenced by Marxist ideas and believe that class struggle is a major political phenomenon. But in America I see class struggle not as one between a few power holders at the top and the vast majority below, rather as a split between the majority middle class and the minority poor. I believe that the tenacity of the middle classes in holding onto their property is ultimately related to the ferocity with which Americans waged war in Indochina. I am not an anarchist and believe that no society can function without a state. But I do not believe that simply substituting the power of the people for the power of the interests will bring about the good society—the history of Russia should disabuse people of that notion. What I came to understand about the American state is that it has a Jekyll and Hyde quality which professional bureaucratic management has not been able to erase. The same idealism that created a welfare imperialism gave rise to a war imperialism. I have also come to believe that these Jekyll and Hyde qualities are true of all state powers that come out of revolutionary traditions. To the possible question of why not let nations be governed by technical managers who are beyond ideology and seek only the "steady state" of the system, the answer is given by the Indochina war, which showed that when the managers could not manage themselves, they exported their contradictions abroad so that others died to maintain the steady state at home. However crude these political and moral positions may be, they at least became clearer to me in the process of writing this book.

This book is shaped by certain ideas. It will not suffice to document their origins in mammoth footnotes or imply their legitimacy or professional standing by fattened bibliographies. They are my ideas which I have been mulling over for a long time, and I take sole responsibility for them. But since all ideas come from somewhere, I shall give a brief intellectual autobiography.

Nothing has influenced my political thinking so much as years of immersion in the writings of the Chinese Communists, both formal, like the canonical works of Mao Tse-tung, and the hundreds of mundane pieces in the daily newspapers. Their notions of class struggle, of ideology, and of contradictions have fed into my thinking. Unlike much Western political thinking that is becoming increasingly techno-bureaucratic, that of the Chinese remains absolutely democratic—people shape politics, not the other way round. If not always explicit, their understanding of class is far more elastic than that of doctrinal Marxism. Above all, they regard struggle and conflict as inherent in all political structures, especially the state. It was reading the Chinese on world affairs that showed me how ideology serves as a kind of systems analysis for fitting the complex facts of world politics into empirically meaningful patterns. The Chinese notion of contradictions is diametrically opposed to the more comfortable American pluralism and has been considered theological by pluralists in the positivist tradition. But the Chinese understanding of contradictions is partly of military origin, for in battle there are always two sides with a vaguer third side of neutrals or friends.

I have often asked myself if I am a Marxist, and usually begin by answering that I am not a Leninist. Leninism's brilliant but single-minded pursuit of power strikes me as a kind of Nietzschean triumph of the will mentality common around the turn of the century. I grant that Leninism was indispensible for both the Chinese and the Vietnamese revolutions, inasmuch as they were made in societies where the concept of political organization was alien. Huey P. Newton has spoken of revolution as "a process, not a conclusion." I believe that both the Chinese and the Vietnamese see their revolutions as long-enduring processes in contrast to the Germano-Russian approach which produced a thunderclap seizure of power in 1917. One cannot be a Marxist without believing in the inevitability and desirability of popular revolution. And it is only self-delusion to think that revolution is anything but bloody civil war, which no sane person would wish upon his own people. But Marx argued —as have Lenin and Mao Tse-tung—that ruling classes will devour themselves in violent competition, destroying what they themselves have built. Thus, revolution occurs only when the people finish the process of destruction and begin building a new society.

For all the vast multilingual literature of Marxism, I have not found Marx's specific ideas on the economy or on politics operationally useful for understanding contemporary political economy. Yet I find myself again and again drawn to the Marxian vision which still captures the minds of millions of people. Marx predicts that industrial capitalism will unify the world, that even the poorest of the poor will enter modern society through work in the productive system, and that revolutionary democracy will supplant class rule on a world-wide scale. If one believes that ideologies just stir mass passions, and that government can only be technical management of political and economic "problems," then Marx's vision is little more than religion for primitives. But visions have ebbs and flows, and Marx's vision always returns to life when a social system, particularly in an advanced capitalist country, begins to crack. The secret of Marxism's resilience is what Marx thought it was: a vision or theory grounded on human reason and not divine revelation that teaches there is moral purpose and inevitability to history.

On matters of political economy, I have been much influenced by the Austrian economist Joseph Schumpeter, particularly his essay on imperialism. My own distinctions between imperialism and expansionism are Schumpetrian, as is my view that state and society, therefore state and economy, are much more separate entities than the Marxist tradition would grant. This is a notion common to classical economics which Marx shared but which became obscured in the writings on imperialism coming from the Lenin-Hobson school. They took the approach that imperialist states were the instruments for organizing the export of capital for their own bourgeoisies. While good for propaganda purposes, I have not found such writing useful for analyzing the nature of the contemporary capitalist state. Karl Polanyi's *The Great Transformation* argued that the world market system flowing out of Britain was as much if not more of an achievement than the invention of power-driven machinery during the Industrial Revolution. One can say that Polanyi stood Marx upside down: rather than production being the independent and exchange the dependent variable, Polanyi argues the opposite. Polanyi also pointed out the threat posed to this emerging international system by the rise of militarily competing great powers, a phenomenon caused in part by the growing power of the working classes. It is to Polanyi that I owe my notions on internationalism and nationalism. I also find myself close to the view that an economic system whose government is committed to the centrality of production will tend in nationalist directions, whereas one committed to the centrality of exchange will move toward internationalism. There is, I believe, a serious defect in Marx's thinking that socialism will have the same world-unifying effects as capitalism.

On the matter of organization, the Chinese influence is clear, including that of the now discredited Liu Shao-ch'i. What the Chinese thinkers have achieved is a sophisticated and operationally useful version of Leninist organizational theory. But I have also been influenced by other writers. The French scholar on administration Henri Fayol wrote many decades ago on the functions of the executive not as decision maker but as leader. My own three functions of the executive are derived from his five: foresee (*prévoir*), organize, command, coordinate, and control. Max Weber has always provided insights, but in particular a little-known schema of government of his analyzed by Wilhelm Mommsen—the trinitarian notion of a "personal-plebiscitarian leader," a technical-legal bureaucracy, and an interest-representing parliament. A writer little known in America, possibly because of his associations with the Hitler regime, is Carl Schmitt, whose scholarly study *Die Diktatur* has explored the peculiar nature of executive governmental power arising out of crisis situations (*ausnahme-zustände*), a phenomenon relevant to the subject matter of this book. I have also learned much from Anthony Downs's many insights into bureaucratic situations, and Aaron Wildavsky's work on budgets. And I owe much to Moyibi Amoda's treatment of "cosmology, group, and authority."

In this book I have presented a conception of state executive power which diverges from predominant currents in political and organizational thinking. While dictatorship is granted for nondemocratic societies, in democratic societies the executive is seen as decision maker, one who gathers all the facts, weighs them against the pressures of contending interests, and then makes an "optimal" or "satisfactory" decision. My own thinking on the subject has been shaped by examining the "loneliness" of Presidents, often commented on since World War II, and by my own interpretations of how the key presidential decisions on the Vietnam war were made. But my view of the American Presidency which, conceptually anyway, I regard the same way I do the executives of China and Russia, has also been influenced by study of societies in which personal executive power has been historically important. While much of my work has focused on East Asia, I have also read on absolutism in post-Renaissance Europe in conjunction with the rise of urban middle classes, the formation of large governmental bureaucracies, and expansive and ambitious foreign policies.

I have not done what academics call original research for this book, and even if I had a chance to delve into the secret archives of the Americans, Russians, and Chinese, I am not sure I would do so confident that startling new insights would emerge. In my readings of the histories of various countries, I cannot remember any examples where the revelations of secret archives in themselves made clear what was obscure. Understanding still requires analysis, which requires reasoning to offer convincing theories, hypotheses, and generalizations. All good analysis should spark response even if it produces a counteranalysis that refutes the original.

My reinterpretation of the Marshall Plan and what I call the internationalist current is based to a considerable extent on the attitudes of the American business class toward world trade and its ideological generalizations of "universalism," as discussed by Gabriel Kolko. After the book was written, toward the latter part of 1973, the great Washington debate on détente broke out, in which the American business community became the most vigorous proponent of East-West détente.* I have never felt comfortable with notions of the business origins of the cold war, even though I do not question the profit greed and expansionist rapaciousness of international business. While the attitudes of business toward defense spending have changed over the quarter-century since 1945, as the researches of Clarence Lo of the University of California, Berkeley, indicate, I believe that the attitudes shown in 1973 on détente are not fundamentally different from those manifested in the immediate postwar period. I consider business's political thinking on détente in 1973 the expression of a current that can be traced back at least two decades. While many will disagree with that analysis, I believe that if the concept of political currents has merit, then it is possible to use data from a later period to reinterpret comparable events of an earlier one.

My interpretation of containment owes much to Dean Rusk. It was examining Rusk's stubborn insistence on restoring the inviolability of the 17th parallel in Vietnam that made clear a long history of demarcation line drawing that began with the occupation zones of various countries arising out of World War II. The revisionist historical literature, particularly that of David Horowitz and Gabriel Kolko, has sparked a general re-examination of containment, as one can see in many articles appearing in the journal *Foreign Policy*, one of whose editors is Samuel P. Huntington.

My reinterpretation of the much-debated China question of the late 1940s is mainly due to looking at the role of the United States Navy at the time. This convinced me that the Navy was a major if silent force in the foreign policy struggles in Washington that led to America's recommitment to the cause of Chiang Kai-shek. For all the revisionist thinking that has gone on, least has been done on the subject of the American military's influence on foreign policy. I learned a lot about the Navy from Peter Karsten's excellently researched and thought out study *The*

* *See*, for example, Laurence Stern, "Détente Blurring Political Frontiers," *Washington Post*, October 6, 1973.

Naval Aristocracy, though it barely touched the period I was interested in. But reading *Seapower* and the *Proceedings of U.S. Naval Institute* made the Navy viewpoint quite clear, even more so when it was put across in *U.S. News & World Report* at some key juncture in the course of foreign policy formation.

My analysis of the relations between Russia, China, and America is a by-product of my earlier work on China which, in published form, dealt mainly with China's internal problems. There is a great amount of material on the Sino-Soviet split, most of it academic and journalistic, informed by United States intelligence views. By and large, it is of little value because the writers could not or would not examine the American role in the split. By the late 1960s, some of these writers were prepared to admit that there was a "triangular" relationship between the three great powers, but that has not led to any significant reinterpretation. Understanding of that triangular relationship is greatly hampered by the fact that all the writing on the subject from all sides is in an esoteric Aesopian vein that hints at issues but never spells them out. It has long been accepted that to study contemporary China and Russia, one has to learn their particular coded languages. But for understanding of world politics to be complete, one has similarly to learn how to decode the coded language of the American government, as, for example, in the documents of the Pentagon Papers.

There are few subjects I consider more important for the understanding of what *U.S. News & World Report* now calls national security rather than foreign policy than the weaponry controversies which have gone on since World War II. They involve not only budgets of importance to the military-industrial complex, but balances of power between various contending military-bureaucratic forces within the government, and are, above all, tangible expressions of the objectives, strategies, and tactics of national security policy. There is a vast literature on the subject, most of it buried in transcripts of congressional hearings. I have found the writings of Samuel P. Huntington and Paul Y. Hammond to be particularly instructive, full of veiled insights that can easily be pursued farther if one does not fear offending the bureaucracies.

Regarding the Indochina war, my intellectual debts are more personal and experiential than scholarly. One of my tasks in the antiwar movement was to apply the analytical scalpel to the national security apparatus of the American government to determine, wherever possible, what Washington's political and military moves meant. It is to Peter Dale Scott of the University of California and to Richard J. Barnet of the Institute for Policy Studies (Washington) that I owe hundreds of hours of animated discussion on the war, on America, on world politics. I consider their works, Scott's *The War Conspiracy* and Barnet's *Roots of War*, the best analytical books to date on the Indochina war. Scott has analyzed crisis points in minute detail to show how contending forces within the bureaucracy used (or sometimes fabricated) the crises to advance their own power positions. Barnet identified the national security bureaucracy as an apparatus, not just a number of decision makers and their staffs. Linked to the corporate establishment by social and career origins, the apparatus also works peculiarly on its own to foster American power in the world. While some of my general and particular views differ from theirs, the important fact is that they have done analysis in contrast to the great bulk of the literature on the Indochina war.

I also owe my understandings of the Indochina war to large clipping files that I began in 1966. In my opinion, the newspapers—those like the *New York Times* and the *Washington Post* or those of Hanoi, Peking, Paris, Saigon—remain the most important sources of data on the war and even on the conflicts within the American national security bureaucracies. Journalists have to write fast, and speed always assures a modicum of honesty contrasted to the tortuous distortions that so often appear in bureaucractic documents. While he seems old-fashioned now, it was D. F. Fleming who showed that it was possible to write a history of the cold war from files of newspaper clippings.

Here follows a list of the books and articles I used in this book. The occasional comments are meant to point out how an item was useful for my own writing.

Berding, Andrew H. *Dulles on Diplomacy*. New York: D. Van Nostrand, 1965.

Bernstein, Barton J., and Matusow, Allen J. *The Truman Administration*. New York: Harper & Row, Colophon Books, 1968. A reader.

Brodine, Virginia, and Selden, Mark. *Open Street: The Kissinger-Nixon Doctrine in Asia*. Harper & Row, Perennial Books, 1972.

Burns, James MacGregor. *Roosevelt: The Soldier of Freedom*. New York: Harcourt Brace Jovanovich, 1970. Roosevelt as leader and politician as contrasted with Willard Range's analysis of Roosevelt as visionary (q.v.).

Butow, Robert C. *Tojo and the Coming of the War*. Stanford: Stanford University Press, 1961. Suggestive for comparative purposes to the role of the military in American foreign policy.

Cho, N. Y. "Drei Elemente der Aussenpolitik der Volksrepublik China." *Europa Archiv, Folge* 21 (1972): 745–50. A brief analysis of Chinese policies on independence, liberation, and revolution.

Chomsky, Noam, and Zinn, Howard, eds. *The Pentagon Papers: Critical Essays*. Boston: Beacon Press, 1972.

Christian, George. *The President Steps Down*. New York: Macmillan, 1970. Many insights into the events leading to the March 1968 decisions by LBJ's former press secretary.

Clemens, Walter C., Jr. *The Arms Race and Sino-Soviet Relations*. Stanford: The Hoover Institution on War, Peace, and Revolution, 1968.

Donovan, James A. *Militarism U.S.A.* New York: Charles Scribner's Sons, 1970.

Downs, Anthony. *Inside Bureaucracy*. Boston: Little Brown and Co., 1967. A wide-range analysis of the kind of bureaucracy constituted by the Department of Defense. I found Chapter XIX on bureaucratic ideologies particularly useful.

Evans, Rowland, Jr., and Novak, Robert. *Lyndon B. Johnson: The Exercise of Power*. New York: New American Library, Signet Books, 1966.

————. *Nixon in the White House*. New York: Random House, 1971.

Fayol, Henri. *Administration industrielle et générale*. Paris: Dunod, 1941. (*General and Industrial Management*. London: Pitman, 1949.)

Fitch, Robert, and Oppenheimer, Mary. "Who Rules the Corporations?" *Socialist Revolution* 4, 5, 6 (1970). Important article for the new "finance capital" polemic on the left.

Fleming, D. F. *The Cold War and Its Origins*. 2 vols. New York: Doubleday & Co., 1961.

Fontaine, André. *The Cold War*. Vol. I, *From the October Revolution to the Korean War 1917–1950*. New York: Pantheon Books, 1968. Vol. II, *From the Korean War to the Present*. New York: Random House, 1970.

Gilpin, Robert. *American Scientists and Nuclear Weapons Policy*. Princeton: Princeton University Press, 1962.

Gittings, John. *Survey of the Sino-Soviet Dispute*. New York: Oxford University Press, 1968.

Goulden, Joseph C. *Truth is the First Casualty*. Skokie, Ill.: Rand McNally & Co., 1969. On covert war and Tonkin.

Griffith, William E. *Sino-Soviet Relations 1964–1965*. Cambridge, Mass.: M.I.T. Press, 1967.

————. *The Sino-Soviet Rift*. Cambridge, Mass.: M.I.T. Press, 1964.

Hahn, Walter F., and Neff, John C. *American Strategy for the Nuclear Age*. New York: Doubleday & Co., 1960.

Halle, Louis J. *The Cold War As History*. New York: Harper & Row, Colophon Books, 1967.

Halperin, A. M. *Policies Toward China*. New York: McGraw-Hill Book Co., 1965.

Halperin, Morton H. "Chinese Attitudes Toward the Use and Control of Nuclear Weapons." In *China in Crisis*, edited by Tang Tsou, vol. II, pp. 135–60. Chicago: University of Chicago Press, 1968.

Hammond, Paul Y. "Directives for the Occupation of Germany: The Washington Controversy." In Stein, ed., q.v., pp. 311–464.

————. "Super Carriers and B-36 Bombers: Appropriations Strategy and Politics." In Stein, ed., q.v., pp. 465–568. An important analysis of the "admirals' revolt" of 1949.

Harvey, Frank. *Air War Vietnam*. New York: Bantam Books, 1967.

Hilsman, Roger. *To Move a Nation*. New York: Doubleday & Co., 1967. An early but still valuable analysis of the road to war in Indochina by one of the makers of those policies dismissed by Johnson in January 1964.

Hitch, Charles J. *Decision-making for Defense*. Berkeley: University of California Press, 1965. By one of the leaders in McNamara's abortive efforts to practice centralization through PPBS in the Defense Department.

Hitch, Charles J., and McKean, Roland N. *The Economics of the Nuclear Age*. New York: Atheneum, 1966.

Hoopes, Townsend. *The Limits of Intervention*. New York: David McKay Co., 1969. Analysis by a former undersecretary of the Air Force explaining the events leading to the March 1968 decisions.

Hsiao, Gene T., ed. *The Role of the External Powers in the Indochina Crisis*. Carbondale: Southern Illinois University Press, 1973.

Hsieh, Alice Langley. *Communist China's Strategy in the Nuclear Era*. Englewood Cliffs, N.J.: Prentice-Hall, 1962. Still a fine analysis of Chinese military thinking.

Hudson, Michael. "Epitaph for Bretton Woods." *Journal of International Affairs* 23, no. 2 (Spring 1969): 166–301.

Huntington, Samuel P. *The Common Defense*. New York: Columbia University Press, 1961. One of the best analyses of national security matters. Limited by the author's disinclination to go too far into proscribed territory.

Jackson, Senator Henry. *The National Security Council—Jackson Sub-committee Papers on Policy-making at the Presidential Level*. New York: Praeger, 1965.

Janowitz, Morris. *The Professional Soldier*. New York: Free Press, 1960.

Johnson, Lyndon Baines. *The Vantage Point: Perspectives of the Presidency 1963–1969*. New York: Popular Library, 1971. Like too many memoirs, disappointing but with numerous nuggets.

Kahin, George McTurnan, and Lewis, John W. *The United States in Vietnam*. 2nd edition. New York: Dell Publishing Co., Delta Books, 1969.

Kalb, Marvin, and Abel, Elie. *Roots of Involvement: The U.S. in Asia 1784–1971*. New York: W. W. Norton & Co., 1971.

Karsten, Peter. *The Naval Aristocracy*. New York: Free Press, 1972. See particularly the last dozen pages.

Kennan, George F. *Memoirs: 1925–1950*. New York: Bantam Books, 1967.

Kissinger, Henry A. "Reflections on American Diplomacy." *Foreign Affairs* (October, 1956): 36–56. A remarkable little paragraph on page 39 on creative executive as contrasted with routine decision-making by experts and bureaucrats.

Klare, Michael T. *War Without End*. New York: Vintage Books, 1972. An excellent account of American military and political stratagems for pursuing imperial policies abroad.

Kolko, Gabriel. *The Politics of War*. New York: Vintage Books, 1968.

Kolko, Joyce, and Kolko, Gabriel. *The Limits of Power*. New York: Harper & Row, 1972. Takes the analysis of *The Politics of War* into the 1950s.

Langer, William L. *Our Vichy Gamble*. New York: W. W. Norton and Co., 1947. World War II Vichy policy elucidates internationalist peace-mindedness and anticommunism.

Lapp, Ralph. *The Weapons Culture*. Baltimore: Penguin Books, 1968.

Littauer, Raphael, and Uphoff, Norman. *The Air War in Indochina*. Boston: Beacon Press, 1972.

McNamara, Robert S. *The Essence of Security*. New York: Harper & Row, 1968. In effect, McNamara's memoirs as Secretary of Defense.

Mao Tse-tung. *Selected Works*, vol. IV. Peking, 1960. I have used Chinese originals throughout, but the corresponding English versions are easy to locate from the citations in the book.

Martin, Laurence W. "The American Decision to Rearm Germany." In Stein, ed., q.v., pp. 643–66.

Melman, Seymour. *Pentagon Capitalism*. New York: McGraw-Hill, 1970. Melman's thesis of the Pentagon as "state management" constitutes a major theoretical advance in thinking about the American state.

Milton, David, Milton, Nancy, and Schurmann, Franz. *The China Reader*, vol. IV. New York: Random House, 1974.

Mollenhoff, Clark R. *The Pentagon*. New York: G. P. Putnam's Sons, 1969.

Mommsen, Wilhelm. *Max Weber und die Deutsche Politik*. Tübingen: Mohr, 1959.

Moody, Peter R. *The Politics of the Eighth Central Committee of the Communist Party of China*. Hamden, Conn.: Shoe String Press, 1973. Useful analysis of various currents within China.

Navasky, Victor S. *Kennedy Justice*. New York: Atheneum, 1971. Analysis of the relationship between the Justice Department and the FBI, analagous, I believe, to that of the Presidency and the military.

Newhouse, John. "Annals of Diplomacy SALT." *New Yorker*, in five installments, May 5–June 2, 1973.

Oberdorfer, Don. *Têt: The Story of a Battle and Its Historic Aftermath*. New York: Doubleday & Co., 1971.

O'Connor, Richard. *Pacific Destiny*. Boston: Little, Brown and Co., 1969. A narrative account of American expansion into the Pacific.

Pavlov, V. "Europe in the Plans of Peking." In Milton, q.v., pp. 583–95.

Peck, James. "America and the Chinese Revolution, 1942–1946: An Interpretation." In *American–East Asian Relations: A Survey*, edited by Ernest R. May and James C. Thomson, Jr. Cambridge: Harvard University Press, 1972.

Perlo, Victor. *Militarism and Industry*. New York: International Publishers Co., 1963. A good presentation of the communist thesis of a basic split in the American ruling classes.

Peeters, Paul, *Massive Retaliation: The Policy and Its Critics*. Chicago: Henry Regnery Co., 1958. A right-wing view at the time of the great strategic debates of the late 1950s.

Phillips, Cabell. *The Truman Presidency*. Baltimore: Penguin Books, 1966.

Polanyi, Karl. *The Great Transformation*. Boston: Beacon Press, 1944. A great book, in my estimation.

Pollack, Jonathan D. "Chinese Attitudes Toward Nuclear Weapons 1964–1969." *China Quarterly* 50 (April–June, 1972): 244–71.

Range, Willard. *Franklin D. Roosevelt's World Order*. Athens, Ga.: University of Georgia Press, 1959. By an author who seriously analyzes Roosevelt's global vision.

Ransom, Harry Howe. *Can American Democracy Survive the Cold War?* New York: Doubleday & Co., 1964. An inquiry into the politics of defense and national security.

Rappaport, Armin. *The Navy League of the United States*. Detroit: Wayne State University Press, 1962.

Raymond, Jack. *Power in the Pentagon*. New York: Harper & Row, 1964.

Roherty, James M. *Decisions of Robert S. McNamara*. Coral Gables, Fla.: University of Miami Press, 1970.

Sapolsky, Harvey M. *The Polaris System Development*. Cambridge, Mass.: Harvard University Press, 1972.

Schmitt, Carl. *Die Diktatur*. Reprint of second edition published in 1928. Berlin: Duncker & Humblot, 1963.

Schumpeter, Joseph. *Imperialsim/Social Classes*. New York: World Publishing Co., 1955.

Schurmann, Franz, and Schell, Orville. *The China Reader*, vol. III. New York: Random House, 1967. *See also* Milton.

Schurmann, Franz. *Ideology and Organization in Communist China*. 2nd edition. Berkeley: University of California Press, 1967.

Schurmann, Franz, Scott, Peter, and Zelnik, Reginald. *The Politics of Escalation*. New York: Fawcett World Library, 1966.

Schwarz, Urs. *American Strategy*. New York: Doubleday & Co., 1966.

Scott, Peter Dale. "Vietnamization and the Drama of the Pentagon Papers." In Chomsky and Zinn, eds. q.v., pp. 211–47. Incisive analysis of the transition from Kennedy to Johnson relating to Vietnam escalation.

Scott, Peter Dale. *The War Conspiracy*. Indianapolis: Bobbs-Merrill Co., 1972.

Sheehan, Neil. *The Arnheiter Affair*. New York: Random House, 1971. Valuable for insights into how the Navy operates internally.

Shonfield, Andrew. *Modern Capitalism*. New York: Oxford University Press, 1965. Excellent chapter on Germany.

Shoup, David. "New American Militarism." *Atlantic Monthly*, April 1969. Explains the Vietnam war in terms of interservice rivalry, an explanation closer to reality than most others by one who knew from experience as former commandant of the Marine Corps.

Sihanouk, Norodom. *My War With the CIA: The Memoirs of Prince Sihanouk*. New York: Pantheon Books, 1973.

Simpich, Fredrick, Jr. *Anatomy of Hawaii*. New York: Avon Books, 1972.

Snow, Edgar. *The Long Revolution*. New York: Random House, 1972.

Spanier, John W. *The Truman-MacArthur Controversy and the Korean War*. New York: W. W. Norton & Co., 1965.

Stavins, Ralph, Barnet, Richard J., and Raskin, Marcus G. *Washington Plans an Aggressive War*. New York: Vintage Books, 1971. Stavins's essay discusses conflicts between Kennedy and the Joint Chiefs.

Stein, Harold, ed. *American Civil-Military Decisions*. University of Alabama Press, 1963.

Swomley, John M., Jr. *The Military Establishment*. Boston: Beacon Press, 1964.

Tatu, Michel. *Power in the Kremlin from Khrushchev to Kosygin*. New York: Viking, 1969.

Thee, Marek. *Notes of a Witness*. New York: Vintage Books, 1973. Memoirs of a Polish member of the International Control Commission in Laos.

Tsou, Tang. *America's Failure in China*. Chicago: University of Chicago Press, 1963. Still a basic book on U.S.-China relations of the 1940s.

Turner, Gordon B., and Challener, Richard D. *National Security in the Nuclear Age*. New York: Praeger, 1960.

Twining, Nathan F. *Neither Liberty Nor Safety*. New York: Holt, Rinehart and Winston, 1966. Excellent source for Air Force thinking on foreign policy.

Ulam, Adam. *Expansionism and Co-existence: The History of Soviet Foreign Policy 1917–1967*. New York: Praeger, 1968.

Warner, Dennis. *The Last Confucian*. Baltimore: Penguin Books, 1964. Perceptive book on Indochina despite the author's anticommunism.

Whiting, Allen. "What Nixon Must Do to Make Friends in Peking." *New York Review of Books*, October 7, 1971.

Wildavsky, Aaron. *The Politics of the Budgetary Process*. Boston: Little, Brown and Co., 1964.

Yahuda, Michael. "Kremlinology and the Chinese Strategic Debate 1965–1966." *China Quarterly* 49 (January–March 1972): 32–75.

Yarmolinsky, Adam. *The Military Establishment*. New York: Harper & Row, 1971.

Zagoria, Donald. *The Sino-Soviet Conflict 1956–1961* New York: Atheneum, 1964.

――――. *Vietnam Triangle*. Indianapolis: Pegasus, 1967.

Zanegin, B., Mironov, A., and Mikhailov, Ia. *K sobytiiam v Kitae (On the Events in China)*. Moscow, 1967. An early version of the Russian view of China after the beginning of the Cultural Revolution.

Jen-min Shou-ts'e 1958 (People's Handbook, 1958). Peking, 1958. A collection of major documents regarding 1957.

People of the World Unite for the Complete, Thorough, Total and Resolute Prohibition and Destruction of Nuclear Weapons. Peking: Foreign Languages Press, 1963. The most important collection of documents, including Russian, ever issued by the Chinese on the nuclear question, appearing just after the signing of the Partial Nuclear Test Ban Treaty.

The Failure of "Special War" 1961–1965, Vietnamese Studies, No. 11. Hanoi, n.d.

In Face of American Aggression 1965–1967, Vietnamese Studies, No. 16. Hanoi, n.d.

Indochina 1971–1972, Vietnamese Studies, No. 33. Hanoi, 1972.

Douze années d'intervention et d'agression des impérialistes américains au Laos. Neo Lao Haksat, July 1966. This and the three preceding items are only a minute fraction of the literature available on Indochina seen from the perspective of the liberation forces available in English and French. While disdained at the time as "communist propaganda," they contain much information which can be matched against Western reports.

U.S., Department of Defense, *United States-Vietnam Relations 1945–1967*. Washington, D.C.: U.S. Government Printing Office, March 1969. 12 volumes. This is the version of the Pentagon Papers released by the House Committee on Armed Services with deletions. The full texts can be found in the Senator Gravel edition, though the government edition has items not included in the former. For a comparison of the two texts, see Chomsky, ed., q.v., pp. 314–19. I have generally used the government edition in this book.

The Pentagon Papers: The Defense Department History of United States Decision-making on Vietnam (The Senator Gravel Edition). 5 vols. Boston: Beacon Press, 1971–1972.

Gold, Gerald, Siegal, Allan M., and Abt, Samuel, eds., *The Pentagon Papers*. New York: Bantam Books, for the *New York Times*, 1971. Contains the original analyses done at the time of the revelation of the Pentagon Papers. The pieces by Neil Sheehan and Hedrick Smith were particularly useful.

The Pentagon's Secrets and Half-secrets. Hanoi, 1971. The Vietnamese analysis of the Pentagon Papers.

SIPRI (Stockholm International Peace Research Institute) *Yearbook of World Armament and Disarmament 1968–1969*. Stockholm, 1969; *1970–1971*. Stockholm, 1972.

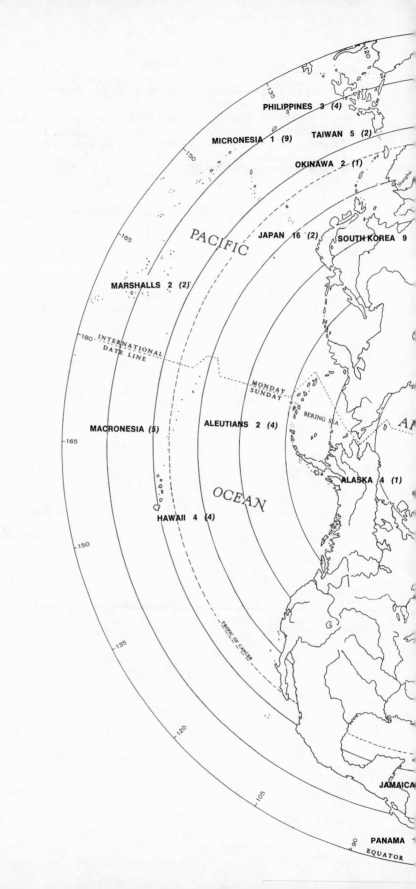

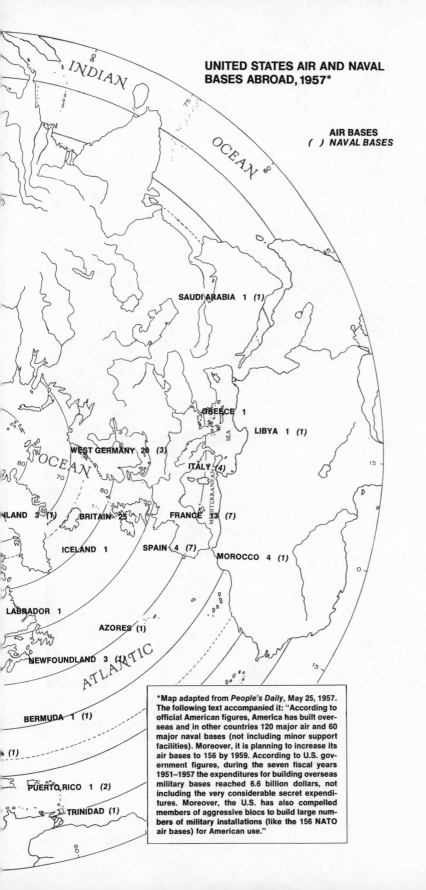

UNITED STATES AIR AND NAVAL BASES ABROAD, 1957*

AIR BASES
( ) NAVAL BASES

SAUDI ARABIA 1 *(1)*

GREECE 1

LIBYA 1 *(1)*

WEST GERMANY 20 *(3)*

ITALY *(4)*

ICELAND 1

SPAIN 4 *(7)*

MOROCCO 4 *(1)*

FRANCE 13 *(7)*

BRITAIN 25

LAND 3 *(1)*

LABRADOR 1

AZORES *(1)*

NEWFOUNDLAND 3 *(1)*

BERMUDA 1 *(1)*

(1)

PUERTO RICO 1 *(2)*

TRINIDAD *(1)*

*Map adapted from *People's Daily*, May 25, 1957. The following text accompanied it: "According to official American figures, America has built overseas and in other countries 120 major air and 60 major naval bases (not including minor support facilities). Moreover, it is planning to increase its air bases to 156 by 1959. According to U.S. government figures, during the seven fiscal years 1951–1957 the expenditures for building overseas military bases reached 6.6 billion dollars, not including the very considerable secret expenditures. Moreover, the U.S. has also compelled members of aggressive blocs to build large numbers of military installations (like the 156 NATO air bases) for American use."

LAOS—1962

Zone under the control of the Neo Lao Haksat and the Neutralist forces at the time of the signing of the 1962 Geneva Accords. (Ceasefire lines are drawn from *Twelve Years of American Intervention and Aggression in Laos*, Neo Lao Haksat Publications, 1966).

Unshaded area of Laos was under the control of the Right Wing party.

HOW U.S. POWER DOMINATES MOST OF THE WORLD

As U.S. Military Officials Now Assess the Balance—

U.S. IN AIR

- 750 long-range nuclear ICBM's, based in U.S.
- 540 intercontinental atomic bombers on constant alert, hundreds of others in reserve.

  This force alone could annihilate Communist triangle.

  RUSSIA'S strategic air and missile force, still developing, is now only about one third as strong as America's.

COMMUNIST MILITARY POWER IS SUPERIOR INSIDE THIS TRIANGLE.

CHINA

Red China's 2.5 million troops control the East.

Russia's 2.5 million troops control the heartland.

U.S.S.R.

EUROPE

Eastern Europe's 2 million troops face the West.

U. S. A.

U.S. AT SEA

- 836-ship Navy in four fleets, by far mightiest in world.
- 1,000 nuclear planes aboard 15 roving attack carriers.
- 192 "city busting" Polaris missiles aboard nuclear subs.

  This force alone could badly cripple Communist triangle.

  RUSSIA'S naval force is fraction of this and, except for submarines, severely limited in range.

U.S. ON LAND

- 5 Army divisions in Europe, total of 240,000 men as spearhead of a 2-million-man Allied European force.
- 8 Army divisions in U.S.-based strike force, ready for quick movement anywhere.
- 3 Army divisions on guard in Far East.
- 3 Marine Corps divisions, ready to fight anywhere.

  RUSSIA'S land force is superior in numbers, but lacks air and sea lift to carry it to trouble spots outside the triangle.

DESPITE Communist superiority inside the triangle, U. S. officials do not consider the disadvantage in conventional forces "intolerable." With clear superiority in strategic forces, U. S. is confident it could win if a showdown came.

ADDED TOGETHER, these factors enable President Johnson to take a new, confident approach to decision making in the White House.

INDEX

ABOUT THE AUTHOR

Franz Schurmann is Professor of Sociology and History at the University of California, Berkeley, and is internationally known as one of the foremost observers of both American and Chinese society. His widely acclaimed *Ideology and Organization in Communist China* is already recognized as a classic; he is coeditor of the *China Reader* and author of numerous other books.